Working with Families

SEVENTH EDITION

RENA SHIMONI

Bow Valley College

JOANNE BAXTER

Mount Royal University

 **Pearson**

Toronto

VICE PRESIDENT, EDITORIAL: Anne Williams
PORTFOLIO MANAGER: Keriann McGoogan
MARKETING MANAGER: Euan White
CONTENT MANAGER: Madhu Ranadive
PROJECT MANAGER: Ainsley Somerville
CONTENT DEVELOPER: Christine Langone

PRODUCTION SERVICES: iEnergizer Aptara®, Ltd.
PERMISSIONS PROJECT MANAGER: Shruti Jamadagni
PHOTO PERMISSIONS RESEARCH: Integra Publishing Services, Inc.
TEXT PERMISSIONS RESEARCH: Integra Publishing Services, Inc.
COVER DESIGNER: Anthony Leung
COVER IMAGE: franzidraws/123RF

Pearson Canada Inc., 26 Prince Andrew Place, North York, Ontario M3C 2H4.

ISBN 978-0-13-451321-8

2   18

Library and Archives Canada Cataloguing in Publication
Shimoni, Rena, 1948-, author
   Working with families / Rena Shimoni, Joanne Baxter. — Seventh edition.

ISBN 978-0-13-451321-8 (softcover)

   1. Family social work—Textbooks.   2. Social work with children—Textbooks.   3. Families—Textbooks.   4. Textbooks.   I. Baxter, Joanne Marlena, 1955-, author   II. Title.

LB1139.23.S55 2018   362.82   C2017-906864-4

Contents

About This Book

More often than not, people entering the early childhood field see children as the prime focus of their work. As they learn about their profession and begin to practise, they realize that to understand children, they need to understand the families of the children they work with. Moreover, they learn that the well-being of children and the well-being of families are inextricably connected, and that early childhood professionals have an ethical responsibility to support families and promote their involvement in the care and education of their children. That being so, most educational programs for early childhood professionals and child and youth workers include at least one course on families. Scholars from many disciplines write about families—sociologists, psychologists, and anthropologists, to name but a few—and each discipline enriches the knowledge base with its own particular perspective. This book synthesizes the relevant knowledge from the broad range of disciplines into a practical book for early childhood professionals.

We are pleased to be able to work with children and families. While we both spent many years of our professional life in early childhood education, both of us have come into the early childhood profession with a background in other "helping professions"—psychology and social work. We have practical experience working with families from a range of orientations and have continued to be involved in the field as well as in the classroom. During the years we have taught courses on the family, we have collected stories and anecdotes about the families of our students, who have repeatedly shared rich and unique perspectives that illustrate how they are different from "textbook" families. In this book, we have combined our theoretical knowledge with our professional experience, and added to these the wisdom gained from listening to our students.

Over the years that we have developed, revised, and redeveloped our thoughts and practices around engaging with families, we have witnessed many changes in early learning. The first five years of life have been recognized as critical to lifelong health and mental health, and the body of knowledge in this area has been expanding. This lens has led to discussions about the potential for "learning" in the early years and the need for educated professionals to be engaged with young children. Many jurisdictions across Canada have added or increased educational requirements for the early years, while some (e.g., Ontario) have mandated minimum educational requirements. Along with targeted education in early learning and child care, many provinces have created and developed curriculum frameworks specifically for the early years in child-care settings. These curriculum frameworks have been drawn from fundamental principles specific to early learning. With the essence of foundational knowledge in place, educators are beginning to develop and pursue practices that they, as professionals, deem most appropriate.

Although programs with outlined and structured foundations continue to exist and some jurisdictions are driven by school readiness or developmental gains, many early learning professionals are learning to critically reflect on and scrutinize their practice with the children and families in their communities and embed practices most fitting with their philosophical foundations. This seventh edition has captured the spirit of this evolving professional; it provides a range of relevant approaches, theoretical perspectives, and practical strategies so that educators can make choices among the best current practices to determine what is most suitable to their children, families, programs, and communities. At the same time, we hope that the approaches and ideas presented will resonate with all early learning professionals working in all types of program models searching for new perspectives on working with families.

This book is divided into three parts.

- Part 1, "Understanding Families," provides the conceptual framework for understanding families. We have attempted to use the most inclusive definition of families in this section, and have provided examples of nontraditional as well as traditional families.

- Part 2, "Engaging Families," offers a framework for early childhood professionals to apply their understanding of family in their efforts to engage families in the care and education of the children in meaningful ways.

- Part 3, "Family Diversity," consists of 13 chapters devoted to the diversity that exists in Canadian families. Early childhood professionals are very likely, in the course of their careers, to work with children who have dealt with a death in the family or a divorce. Many children are from single-parent families, families who live in poverty, or families in which one of the members has special needs. Understanding these families' challenges will help early childhood professionals offer support in a nonjudgmental and empathic manner.

We hope that our readers will share our interest in and respect for the diversity among us that is rooted in the various cultures, backgrounds, and perspectives from which we come. We have attempted to portray diversity by including excerpts from interviews with students, colleagues, and educators. There is a wide range in age, social class, culture, ethnicity, and religion represented in these stories. Keep in mind, however, that the students featured in this book are telling their own personal stories and speaking of their own personal beliefs and attitudes. Although they all recognize that their heritage has affected their beliefs, they don't necessarily represent a particular group or culture.

NEW TO THIS EDITION

Key points of revision in the seventh edition include the following:

- The book has been reorganized. The first part will provide a foundation for understanding families. The second part will outline how to engage with families as part of early childhood practice. The third part will examine the diversity that exists in Canadian families and how this diversity may affect the child or the family.

- In keeping with the recommendations of the Truth and Reconciliation Commission of Canada, it's important that all professionals dealing with children and families gain an understanding of the history of the Indigenous peoples of Canada as well as an initial understanding of key elements of their culture. We have therefore included the chapter "Indigenous Families of Canada" (Chapter 8), which was written in close collaboration with Indigenous colleagues.

- A new chapter called "Gender Diverse Families" (Chapter 18) provides insight into the issues and challenges of LGBTQ families, from both an individual and a societal perspective. The role of the early childhood educator in providing inclusive child care is emphasized.

- The first part of the book has been expanded to include perspectives that help explain some of the key challenges facing families today (e.g., change, transitions, and trauma) and concepts that explain the interrelationships between families, their communities, and broader society.

- The second part of the book has been expanded to include the many approaches that early childhood educators may take in engaging families. Research has shown that family engagement is beneficial for the child, the family, and, ultimately, the program.

Educated professionals in early learning understand the importance of different approaches that may enhance their practice with families.

- Resources have been updated to provide Internet links to current and relevant topics for further reading and enrichment.
- The entire book has been updated with new references and research, reflecting current research and academic literature.

Features

Each chapter begins with a list of objectives that clearly state the expected learning outcomes for the reader. It is followed by a vignette taken from real-life experiences relevant to the chapter topic. Scattered throughout the chapter are Scenario boxes, which contain real-life perspectives on particular issues, and Perspectives boxes, which allows for another's person's point of view. The Examine Your Attitudes box provides questions for educators to reflect upon their own attitudes and perspectives. Each chapter ends with a Chapter Summary, a list of further Resources, and a set of Exercises.

Acknowledgments

Our thanks are due to many people who have contributed to our understanding of family. First and foremost, our own families—our mothers and fathers, siblings, and grandparents; our husbands, Dave Baxter and Yakhim Shimoni; and our daughters, Orit, Galit, and Tammy Shimoni, and Chelsea and Carissa Baxter; and more recently our grandchildren, who have provided us with a very different perspective on families. Our colleagues at Mount Royal University College and Bow Valley College have, as always, offered support and ideas. In addition, early childhood colleagues who have used the book have provided ideas and input—Cathy Smey Carston, Brenda Sauve, Becky Kelley, and Cheryl Kinzel. Most of all, our students over the years have given us a window into the lives of many different kinds of families, so that we could enrich our understanding and sensitivity. To all, a warm thank-you.

In this edition, we are especially grateful to two Indigenous friends and colleagues who shared their ideas along with their critique of the chapter "Indigenous Families of Canada." Lori Pritchard provided guidance and her expertise as an Indigenous educator. Lori lives in Calgary, Alberta, and is a Métis learner, teacher, and leader. Angela Dawne Knockwood is a graduate student at the University of Prince Edward Island. She is a Mi'kmaq woman and mother of three wonderful boys and hails from the unceded territory of Mi'kmak'i. Brett Bergie, M.A., Chief of Staff at Bow Valley College, has shared some of his story in the chapter "Gender Diverse Families" and has generously given us much guidance on the writing of this chapter. Your contributions have provided significant perspectives.

A well-deserved thank-you is also extended to the crew at Pearson Canada for their encouragement and not-so-subtle prodding, but mostly for their faith in our ability. We have been delighted with the very positive feedback we have received about the book from students and instructors, and hope that the additions and changes we have made will meet the expectations of our readers. Our special thanks to Christine Langone, who provided us with thoughtful and insightful late-night comments that enhanced the book in a multitude of ways. Her deep understanding of the perspective of the textbook made our collaborations a pleasure.

Lastly, though perhaps unconventionally, we want to thank each other. This is the second book we have co-authored. We have gone through many stages of work together and have experienced the excitement, disappointments, stresses, and ultimate satisfaction at arriving at a worthwhile final product. We have now been collaborating for many years, including the updates, revisions, and enhancements to each of the six editions of this book. We attempted to make more thoughtful changes to this edition, which provided the forum for in-depth dialogue and sharing. We have worked as co-teachers, co-authors, and friends, and hope that we will continue to do so for many years to come.

Authentic writing requires, in our view, that writers have direct experience with the subjects about which they write. In addition to our main roles at our respective colleges, Joanne has been actively involved in programs with children and families in the Calgary region; in developing and implementing accreditation guidelines for child care, family child care, and school-age care in Alberta; in developing a website resource for aides, family, and educational staff working with children with behavioural challenges; and most recently, in exploring approaches to putting a provincial curriculum framework for early childhood educators into practice in the province of Alberta. This work has brought her in contact with many of the issues in this book as she works closely with a broad range of children's services in the community. Rena taught early childhood education for many years, and has been a program developer and evaluator for a range of programs for new Canadian families, in addition to her work as the Dean of Health and Human Services and the Dean of Applied Research at a college that is known for its commitment to diversity and serving students from every corner of the world. We hope that our experience in these realms brings life to the issues discussed in this book. It is our students from whom we learn the most. As we continue to teach about families, we learn more and more about families from the stories our students tell us about their own lives, and about the lives of the families with whom they work.

PART ONE

Understanding Families

Most people understand families based on their own experiences. They sometimes see differences as undesirable or somehow wrong. However, everyone has different family experiences and expectations about how families should function. It is our intention that early childhood educators read through the first three chapters in this section, reflect on their own family experiences, and become aware of how these have affected their lives as adults. We also hope that educators will reflect on the diversity that exists within and among families. In the end, early childhood educators should come away with an enhanced understanding of and appreciation for the children and families with whom they work.

Chapter 1 provides the context for this book. It explains why working with families is a critical component of the role of the early childhood educator and provides a brief overview of the evolution of the role of the early childhood educator as it relates to working with and engaging families.

Chapter 2 asks the question "What is a family?" and attempts to answer that question in a manner that captures the diversity of Canadian families.

continues ▶

► *continues* Chapter 3 describes conceptual frameworks or theories that can help students gain an understanding of dynamics within family units and various interconnections between families and the society in which they live.

Chapter 4 discusses the concept of resilience that today is understood to be of vital importance to the healthy development of children, families, and communities. It explains how early childhood educators can integrate resilience building skills into their practice.

CHAPTER 1

Engaging with Parents as Early Childhood Educators

OBJECTIVES

- To discuss the centrality of engaging with parents in early childhood education

- To introduce the concept of parent involvement and family-centred practice

- To consider the socio-cultural perspective as a basis for engagement with families

- To emphasize the importance of self-awareness in working with families

Ever since I was a teenager, I knew that I wanted to be a preschool teacher and looked forward to studying for my diploma in ELCC [early learning and child care]. I didn't know that we would be learning about families as a requirement for the diploma. I thought the course on families was interesting—it made me think a lot about my own family and challenged some of the ideas I had about family. But I didn't really realize how this understanding would be relevant to my day-to-day work as a preschool teacher, that is, until my first day at work. I watched parents bring their children in the morning. Some parents looked stressed and hurried as they dropped off their children; others looked sad, as if they didn't want to part; and still others just dropped off their children with confidence and a smile, as if they simply knew that everything would work out fine. I know we can't generalize, but what I learned about families really made me think about what might be behind those different ways of bringing children to preschool, and how I might be able to make the morning drop-off a pleasant time for both the children and their parents.

WHY EARLY CHILDHOOD PROFESSIONALS STUDY FAMILY

Most people who enter the field of early childhood care and education see children as the primary focus of their work. As they learn about their profession and begin to practise, they realize that to understand children, they need to understand the families of these children, and that working with children involves working with their families, either directly or indirectly. Over half a century of scientific research has demonstrated the strong connection between the well-being of children and the well-being of their families, and much of this research points to the importance of the relationship between the family and the early

Courtesy of Davin B.

Davin, Age 5

childhood setting in which children spend many hours every day (Center for the Study of Social Policy, 2015; Harvard Family Research Project, 2006; Lopez, 2010). When good relationships exist between the families of the children in early childhood settings and the educators who work directly with those children, there is increased satisfaction both at home and at the centre. The children also benefit from positive relationships between staff and parents. As we will learn in this book, the early childhood professional can, through an understanding of and support for the family, have an immeasurable positive impact on the child. The more we learn about families, the more effective we will be at developing and maintaining positive, supportive relationships with them.

THE EVOLUTION OF THE CONCEPT OF WORKING WITH FAMILIES

Over the past decade, there has been a noticeable shift in the thinking about working with families. In the past, the thought of working with families evoked a sense of fear and trepidation in many educators. It was something that was on the "to-do list," but it was also avoided as much as possible. One reason that early childhood educators were hesitant about working with families was that they often felt that families perceived them as caregivers or babysitters and not as experts whom they could learn from. Perhaps another reason for this hesitancy was the fact that experts espoused many different models of working with parents and/or involving parents in child care that somehow didn't fit the realities of child care. For example, parent education was proposed as a key component of early childhood programs (Couchenour & Christman, 2008; Powell, 1989; Shimoni, 1992a), and staff were expected to provide both ongoing education and educational programs for parents.

Most early childhood professionals working in child care today feel that it's not feasible to hold formal parent education sessions—both in terms of the time commitment and the desire and/or ability of parents to participate. Today much early childhood information is readily available to parents on the Internet and in community settings. Moreover, early childhood professionals have moved away from assuming the role of "expert" with parents to "working with" parents. In the past, family involvement consisted of keeping parents happy and informed. The literature espoused many approaches required for family involvement or partnership with families. They included approaches to parent education and building partnerships with parents, and models for bridging home and child care (continuity of care).

Today the focus is on working with or alongside families. For example, parents and educators often seek to have an open dialogue as equals who are both invested in the best interests of the child. Many parents have come to understand and respect educators and early learning programs in their own right and are less apt to view educators as "babysitters" or learning programs as "services that I pay for." Similarly, many educators see parents as the child's first teachers and focused on the child's best interests. The relationship between educators and families is ever-evolving, and a growing body of knowledge about the importance of the early years, and of the kinds of interactions a child experiences with caring adults at home and in child care, has contributed to this change.

RECENT DEVELOPMENTS IN EARLY CHILDHOOD EDUCATION

The field of early childhood education is a profession with a core body of knowledge, professional standards, and professional recognition (Curtis & Carter, 2013), and, like all professions, has evolved as new knowledge became available. The importance of the early years on brain development and future mental and physical health has been actively researched (e.g., at the Center on the Developing Child at Harvard University). Many jurisdictions have created child-centred, emergent early learning frameworks built on a foundation of core values around children. At the same time, many jurisdictions have moved toward outcomes-driven and assessment-driven programs based on goals associated with school readiness (Curtis & Carter, 2013).

Dramatic findings in neuroscience (study of the brain) research unequivocally support the fact that brain development in the first five years has significant lifelong impact on the child in all aspects of development (Center on the Developing Child at Harvard University, 2017b; Shonkoff et al., 2012). Young children require adults who provide stimulating environments with a lot of contact and interactions involving physical, verbal, and emotional spheres. Simply put, adults need to create safe and engaging environments for young children and interact with them in ways that provide stimulation, security, and support. This need has long been known by early childhood educators, but brain science has proven it as well. Research has also shown that adults who work with young children require a fundamental understanding of child development and the related needs of children to ensure that children have the best start in life. This research created the situation where educators could demonstrate their knowledge and expertise, and there is now a growing respect for early childhood educators. Today, there is a more general understanding that those who are responsible for the care of children (in many cases, early childhood professionals and parents) are working together toward the same goals (National Scientific Council on the Developing Child, 2004).

One of the most significant changes to early childhood education in Canada has been the development of early learning frameworks, which began in 2007 in Ontario (Government of Ontario, 2007). In Canada, early learning frameworks have emerged in Ontario, New Brunswick, Prince Edward Island, Manitoba, Saskatchewan, British Columbia, and Alberta. Other jurisdictions are studying these curriculum frameworks and have frameworks in various stages of development. These frameworks have been built on universal values, beliefs, and understandings that lead to practices based on children's developmental needs. When educators seek to understand their image of the child and value children for who they are as individuals, they attempt to make childhood visible and the learning that occurs during childhood visible (Curtis & Carter, 2013). This shift includes creating curriculum collaboratively with children and families. By involving children and families in the creation of curriculum, families and educators can gain a deeper understanding of how the children learn and how they feel about their learning. Curriculum comes from an understanding of the child as capable and from a place of curiosity. Many of these early learning frameworks have been built upon universal foundations from Reggio Emilia Aotearoa New Zealand and Te Whāriki (the national curriculum for children in New Zealand), and other approaches where the child is the centre of practice.

Early learning frameworks begin with values, beliefs, and principles that guide practice. Foundational to implementation is educators' deep understanding of these factors and how to put them into practice. As educators make their "teaching" visible, they are in essence making the children's "learning" visible. This process forces educators to start with what they believe, what they value, and what they know. It is important for educators to examine and critically reflect on their practice. This self-reflexive process has created a dynamic between educators and parents in which parents begin to see the knowledge and expertise educators bring to their practice. It has also led educators to understand the knowledge and practice they bring to their own practice and, accordingly, what they need to do to improve their practice. As educators and administrators implement early learning frameworks, they begin to challenge their values, beliefs, and practices with children and with the environment, both physical and social. Just as educators reflect on their image of the child in relation to their practice, they are also challenged to reflect on their image of the family. A starting point in many early learning frameworks is to have educators reflect on their image of the child (Makovichuk, Hewes, Lirette, & Thomas, 2014). This reflection often reveals underlying values and beliefs that educators hold (knowingly or not), which form the foundation of their practice. For example, if your image of the child is based on the belief that a child needs protection, your environment and activities will look very different than if you believe that a child can, with support, learn to protect him or herself. Beliefs about the family also underlie your practice with families.

SCENARIO

PARENT INVOLVEMENT

At a recent child-care conference presentation focusing on engaging families, I asked the audience of educators what their image of the parent was. The first responses to be shared were "crazy," "busy," and "crazy busy." When asked to elaborate, most educators felt that parents were largely disinterested in any attempts they made to involve them, except for the select few who were always interested. When they were asked to consider what impact this made on their practice, most were eager to state that they need not spend time on parent involvement because their efforts were unnoticed and underappreciated.

This value base may be shared by many educators. There were, however, many educators who spoke positively of their parent involvement and the multiple ways that they attempt to keep parents updated. The essential element here is understanding practice based on the values and beliefs that each educator brings to his or her practice and the ability to reflect on this practice in light of these perspectives.

Another significant influence on early childhood practice has been the adaptation and development of approaches to working with children and families that are prevalent in other helping professions, such as nursing, psychology, and social work. For example, an approach called "family-centred practice" is based on the understanding that while one specific member of the family may be the focus of treatment, the professional takes into account the family context, and often works with some or all members of the family. Another concept that has become central to many professions is "resilience," which will be discussed in Chapter 4. An understanding of resilience has led many professionals to consider how they may help their patient or client develop the skills required to cope with stressful situations. Knowledge related to resilience has become integrated into early learning curricula, and this knowledge relates both to working with children and working with families (Reaching IN . . . Reaching OUT, 2017). Many Canadian early childhood educators today are expanding their practice based on resources from the American Center on the Social and Emotional Foundations for Early Learning (2017), which provides resources to educators for their practice with young children, especially children with challenging behaviour, as well as strategies and resources for parents. The Center developed a model to guide practice referred to as "the pyramid model," which begins with the concept of a safe and supportive environment as a foundation for interactions and interventions. The pyramid model was developed originally as a resource for Head Start programs for early childhood in the United States, and is now used broadly in Canada and the United States by professionals from different disciplines who work with young children and families.

The profession of early childhood education has also been influenced by new approaches to strengthening families, and now there is a wealth of information available on this topic (Center for the Study of Social Policy, 2005). Developments in this area have provided tangible strategies that can and should be integrated into the role of the early childhood professional. At their essence, these new approaches are based on the belief that educators can engage and support parents and families in meaningful ways. Further, they are based on the belief that doing so will result in mutually supportive relationships for the parent, educator, and, ultimately, the child.

THE SOCIO-CULTURAL PERSPECTIVE

Early childhood professionals today, along with professionals in health and psychology, are aware of the importance of a child's circumstances and how a child's behaviour is affected by surrounding social and cultural factors. The socio-cultural perspective "emphasizes the influence of the society that we live in on our learning process. According to the sociocultural approach, cultural factors such as language, art, social norms and social structures can play a significant role in the development of our cognitive abilities." ("Sociocultural Approach," n.d.). Socio-cultural perspective theory helps us understand how we communicate with, understand, relate to, and cope with one another. The socio-cultural perspective can shed light on how many aspects of the culture we are raised in impacts our spiritual, mental, physical, emotional, and physiological being.

However we work with families, it is essential to understand and appreciate families in all their diversity. Variations exist in areas that include the organization of the family unit, the roles that individual members play, cultural background, and religious background. Moreover, all families face challenges—some of these challenges are quite typical or universal, and others very specific. It is important for professionals working with children to understand how these challenges affect the child, the parents, and the family unit.

A first step in developing a rapport with families is awareness and understanding. We need to know what the family may be experiencing and be able to understand the multiple layers of that experience. This knowledge helps us empathize—to imagine what it feels like to be in another person's situation. Although we can never completely understand what another person thinks and feels, we can try to imagine what it is like to "walk in their shoes." Only with this understanding and empathy can early childhood educators support children and their families.

THE IMPORTANCE OF SELF-AWARENESS

One of the hallmarks of an effective early childhood educator is self-awareness. Over and over, we learn that before we can be effective in helping others, we must have a good understanding of our personal beliefs, our values, and our attitudes (Portrie & Hill, 2005). At the root of understanding ourselves is understanding the families we came from. Therefore, any study of the family must involve some reflection on the way that this new knowledge "fits" with our own experience of family. We should gain a deeper understanding of what affected our own families as we were growing up, and this understanding should help clarify our own values regarding family. It is hoped that this process will contribute to personal and professional development.

CONCLUSION

Working with families has been an essential component of early childhood education since its inception as a profession. However, the expectations of the early childhood educator in terms of working with families have undergone many developments. These are discussed in more detail in Part 2. Today, largely due to the dramatic developments in brain research, the role of the early childhood educator and guidelines for practice are based on new knowledge and research findings. Developments in brain research have confirmed the vital importance of a safe, secure, and stimulating environment for children in the early years, and sociocultural perspective theory has emphasized the importance of understanding the child in the context of the environment in which he or she grows up. Similarly, research and practice guidelines related to resilience have influenced early childhood education. As leaders in early childhood education develop curriculum frameworks for the preparation of early childhood professionals, many new developments are integrated to ensure the centrality of values, beliefs, and principles to practice (e.g., concepts such as the image of the child, parent, or educator). By being aware of how our own values and beliefs along with our experience have affected our views, and by learning more about the major influences on families today, we will become more competent as professionals who work with children and families.

Chapter Summary

- Working with families is integral to the work of early childhood educators.
- The nature of the role of the early childhood professionals in relation to families has changed over the years.
- Today the role of the early childhood professional with families is informed by recent developments in child brain research.

- Practices in early childhood education have been impacted by a deeper understanding of the importance of developing resilience in children and families.

- A socio-cultural approach refers to the importance of the circumstances surrounding individuals and how their behaviours are affected specifically by their surrounding social and cultural factors.

- Working with families requires empathy. An understanding of how one's own family history and circumstances affect one's behaviour and attitudes helps one become more empathic toward others.

RESOURCES

The Canadian Council on Social Development (CCSD) is one of Canada's most authoritative voices in promoting better social and economic security for Canadians:
http://www.ccsd.ca

The Canadian Child Care Federation relates to working with families:
http://www.cccf-fcsge.ca

The National Association for the Education of Young Children is a rich resource on working with families for early childhood professionals:
https://www.naeyc.org

The Child Care Advocacy Association of Canada is a resource for parents that emphasizes the key role of child care in family and child well-being:
https://ccaac.ca/about-child-care-advocacy-association-of-canada/

EXERCISES

1. Reflect on your "image of the family" and your "image of the parent." Think of the assumptions that you make about parents (or a specific parent) and about families. How might these assumptions impact your relationship with families?

2. Reflect on your work from a socio-cultural perspective. When you are observing the development of children, what aspects of the child's culture might weigh in on your views (e.g., diet, physical activity)?

3. Describe in a paragraph or two how you see yourself working with parents. How comfortable are you with this role? What strengths do you see in yourself that might help you be supportive to families? What challenges do you think you might face? When you have finished this book (or the course on families), come back to this paragraph and see what, if anything, has changed in how you see yourself in this role.

CHAPTER 2
Defining and Describing Families

OBJECTIVES

- To clarify the concept of family

- To highlight the diversity in today's families

- To review some of the key roles of family members

- To examine the impact of social trends on family life

- To discuss the relevance of the study of family for professionals who work with children

At a grade 12 graduation ceremony, a five-member rock group provided musical entertainment. After an enthusiastic round of applause, the leader of the group bowed and said to the audience, "Now I'd like to introduce you to my family." His parents, who were in the audience, were about to stand up proudly, but the young man proceeded to introduce his fellow band members as his family. Proud as they were of their son, his parents still looked a trifle disappointed.

WHAT IS A FAMILY?

Each of us comes from a family of some sort, and many of us have or will go on to create our own families. Because of our experiences, the word *family* brings forth certain mental pictures and associations, some that we share with many other people and some that are unique to us. Families are being defined and redefined continually, both by those who study people and society (such as psychologists and sociologists) and by those who influence laws and policies that affect families (such as lawmakers who determine spousal and child benefits and maternity and paternity leave policies). Some kinds of families are so new that research and policies have not kept pace. As societies evolve, they continually challenge more traditional notions of the concept of family as they try new kinds of emotional, financial, and living arrangements. Social scientists, policy makers, and legal experts are being called upon to expand definitions of *the family* (Holtzman, 2006). At the same time, some entities (e.g., Cardus, formerly the Institute of Marriage and Family Canada) seek to return to more traditional definitions.

We live in a multicultural society. Each cultural group has its own traditions, beliefs, and values regarding child-rearing and, either consciously or unconsciously, its own definition of the family. We can learn much from other cultures and thereby add to our understanding of children (and ourselves). Awareness of the cultural norms and rules of various cultures will help us be sensitive to the fact that some children's experiences at the child-care centre or in nursery school are very different from those they have with their families. It's vital that we, as professionals, avoid stereotyping cultural groups and recognize the diversity that exists among families within the same cultural group. Culture and religion are often interpreted and reflected differently by each family and by each family member. One way to avoid making stereotypical assumptions is to ask people directly about their beliefs, customs, and traditions. We have done so, and throughout the book we provide examples describing the perspectives of people from different countries and cultures and with different religious orientations. They speak not as representatives of their ethnic group or culture, but rather as individuals whose ideas about families have been strongly (but not exclusively) influenced by their cultural heritage.

Canada's families are diverse in many ways. For example, there are many kinds of family structures, including single-parent families, two-parent families, and extended family units. As well, families differ significantly in the roles of individual members; mothers and fathers may have traditional or nontraditional roles in a family, and extended family members may be integral members of a family unit. Moreover, the socio-economic status of families across the country ranges from those struggling to make ends meet to the very wealthy. All of these differences and others may affect children, and enhancing our knowledge of this diversity will help us better relate to and work with the families of the children in our care.

Perspectives

Alemu Ayallel is a 40-year-old man from Ethiopia who describes himself as an Orthodox Christian.

"I arrived in Canada from Ethiopia in 1988. I am married and have one daughter, aged 7. I was unable to return to my country due to the political climate there. I had nowhere else to go; I either had to stay in a refugee camp in Sudan or come to a place where I could be accepted on a humanitarian basis. Fortunately, I had a cousin in Canada who could sponsor me. Because of the civil war in Ethiopia, my extended family was dispersed, and I don't even know where many of them are today, or if they are alive.

"I came from an old country with old traditions. In that culture, the mother's role is to nurture her children and stay at home. The father is the breadwinner; he is the guardian of the family, and the brother is socialized to become the father figure later on. He is given responsibility in the family.

"Grandparents are treated with a great deal of respect. If someone rejects or disrespects their grandparents, they are considered an outsider by their community. Grandparents have the power and control in family decisions. The paternal grandparents have more influence than the maternal grandparents. While many marriages are arranged, not all are. However, the wife needs to be accepted by the husband's parents and extended family. Marriage in our country is not only a relationship between husband and wife, but a relationship between two sets of extended families. These relationships have a great influence on the married couple. Therefore, it's extremely important that the extended families accept each other.

"The traditional family life that I have described does not relate to all parts of my country. In many urban areas, the lifestyle is very different.

"The roles in my family here have changed somewhat. I now contribute to household chores, and my wife works outside the home, so there are two breadwinners. Decision making is mutual. I don't have a son, but if I did, I would try to treat him more on an equal basis than what has been traditional.

"I am quite comfortable with these changing values. I would expect more discipline and respect for parents than is common today. I am uncomfortable with violence and open sexuality in the media. I feel that these things are disrespectful to the family. I believe that we are still far away from full acceptance and integration of people of colour in Canadian society, and I want to instill in my daughter a sense of pride in her roots and her heritage."

This book takes an approach to the diversity of Canadian families that was well described by the Governor General of Canada in 2016, when he said that "families, no matter what their background or makeup, bring new and special patterns to our diverse Canadian tapestry" (Vanier Institute of the Family, 2016).

PERCEPTIONS OF FAMILY

Our definition of *family* is usually rooted in our own experience and is affected less by the latest sociological, psychological, and legal definitions. As early childhood professionals, however, it's important that we be aware of current definitions and debates about what constitutes a family. There are many approaches to studying families—sociologists, psychologists, anthropologists, and those in the health disciplines have all contributed to the immense body of knowledge on families. Early childhood professionals are fortunate to be able to draw on knowledge from several disciplines to help shape their understanding of families. This knowledge, combined with an awareness of our own beliefs and feelings about family, will enhance our ability to understand and work with families.

Definitions of Family

While probably few people in North America would disagree that a married couple living together with their biological children is a family, there is less consensus about other family constellations. For example, consider the following situations:

- If a couple has cohabited, had a child together, and then separated, are the parents and child still considered a family?
- Is a cohabiting but unmarried heterosexual couple a family?
- Is a gay couple who lives with the biological child of one of the partners a family?
- Is a child who was never formally adopted but has grown up with a couple and their biological children a member of that family?

The answer to some of these questions will be "It depends." It depends on whether one looks at the concept of family as it relates to the emotional bonds between members (e.g., the rock group who considered its members a family) or its legal aspects (e.g., benefits and parental leave policies). The answer to these questions will in turn depend on the time and place they are asked. For example, since 2010 gay couples can be legally married across Canada (the capacity to marry is under the jurisdiction of the federal government) (Woodford, 2010). Although gay couples are gradually becoming more accepted in North American society, they still meet with much opposition, especially in the political-legal sphere in parts of the United States and in religious communities, but throughout much of Canada as well. Cohabiting couples were not legally accepted as families until 2000, when the Canadian parliament extended benefits and obligations to common-law couples, be they of opposite or the same sex (CBC News, 2015).

Government Definition of Family

Government definitions of *family* typically differ from people's general understanding or from sociological definitions, since the purpose of these definitions varies. Governments require strict definitions for the purposes of collecting census data and of planning and determining benefits. Government definitions tend to see families as small groups based on an affiliation or legal bonds, not on feelings, roles, or responsibilities. As of 2006, Statistics Canada has provided a plain language definition of "census family" "as a married couple and the children, if any, of either and/or both spouses; a couple living common law and the children, if any, of either and/or both partners; or a lone parent of any marital status with at least one child living in the same dwelling and that child or those children" (Statistics Canada, 2016d).

An Inclusive Definition of Family

While similarities do exist in the way the concept of the family has been described, it's clear that there is no one "right" way of defining families and little probability that scholars will ever come to a consensus on the topic (Holtzman, 2006). However, it's important to have a working definition of the family that reflects the realities of life in North America rather than one particular group's ideal. More importantly, it's essential as professionals to understand the complexities of family life to better understand children in a socio-cultural context.

The Vanier Institute of the Family's Definition of Family

The Vanier Institute of the Family defines families by their function, that is, by what they actually do, rather than focusing on the identity of the members of the family. The Institute defines a *family* as "any combination of two or more persons who are bound together over time by ties of mutual consent, birth and/or adoption or placement, and who together assume responsibilities for variant combinations of some of the following:

- Physical maintenance and care of group members
- Addition of new members through procreation or adoption
- Socialization of children
- Social control of members
- Production, consumption, distribution of goods and services
- Affective nurturance—love"

Source: Used with permission from The Vanier Institute of the Family, 2017

Early childhood educators strive to be accepting, respectful, and understanding of the challenges faced by the wide variety of families. It may be interesting to compare your views on families with those of other Canadians. According to a 2006 national study (Bibby, 2006), almost all Canadians see a married man and woman with at least one child as a family. Six out of 10 Canadians see a single parent with a child as a family, and 5 out of 10 Canadians see same-sex parents with a child as a family. Only 3 out of 10 Canadians see cohabiting couples with no children as a family, and only 2 out of 5 Canadians see gay couples as a family. However, there are very significant differences in these opinions among different age groups. For example, 68% of Canadians between the ages of 18 and 34 see two people of the same sex with at least one child as a family, whereas only 24% of Canadians over the age of 55 share that view. The trend seems to be that the younger generation, many of whom have grown up in nontraditional families, are setting the stage for a more inclusive definition of family. Are attitudes different today?

A recent CBC News article suggests that people's perceptions of family may have changed (CBC News, 2012). According to the article, data from the 2011 census made it clear "that in this country, 'family' can mean almost anything at all." That is, there "is no such thing as a generic Canadian family." The 2011 census included at least eight different "family" categories, some so complex that census officials had to develop a flow chart just to explain their meaning. According to the article:

> At its most basic level, Statistics Canada defines a family as a couple—with or without children, married or common-law—or a lone parent with at least one child in the same house.

In other words, it takes at least two people to make a family. Beyond that, almost anything goes.

There are skip-generation families, intact families, simple stepfamilies, complex stepfamilies, opposite-sex families and same-sex families.

CHARACTERISTICS OF HEALTHY FAMILIES

So far, we have addressed the question "What is a family?" from different perspectives. We have avoided making value judgments about what a "good family" is because this is a tricky question and because the answer we give is greatly influenced by our own beliefs and values, and is certainly affected by our cultural background. As early childhood educators, working within a socio-cultural context, understanding the complexities around family is relevant to our work with children. However, as tricky as the question may be, all professionals who work with families must ask themselves what they believe the components of a healthy family are, and they must combine their personal knowledge and beliefs with their professional knowledge about this subject. Below, we consider some characteristics of a "healthy family," as derived from Western psychology and sociology. We must consider these ideas in light of ideas about healthy families in other cultures. Note that healthy families are described in terms of what happens within the family rather than in terms of the structure of the family. That is, regardless of whether the family has a traditional structure (a married couple with children) or a nontraditional one (the rock-group family described earlier), these characteristics could apply.

Characteristics of Healthy Families

1. *Commitment.* Family members are committed to promoting each other's welfare and to investing time and energy in the family group.

2. *Appreciation.* Family members appreciate, support, and encourage each other.

3. *Effective communication patterns.* Family members spend time talking with each other and listening to each other. They solve problems effectively, and feel free to express ideas and emotions with each other.

4. *Spending time together.* Efforts are made to ensure that joint family times happen (meals, recreation, chores). Time together is spent in "active interaction" (rather than in passive activities, such as watching television).

5. *Shared value system.* Family members share and base their actions on the same value system. This system could be based on religion, but that is not always the case.

6. *Coping with stress.* Families have to cope with stress, which includes being aware of stressors and working together to cope with those stressors.

7. *Balancing of needs.* A healthy family finds ways to balance the needs of the family as a group with the individual needs of its members. For example, while parents spend much time meeting the needs of their children, they also realize that they need to spend time together as a couple and to find time to develop their own interests as individuals. Also, parents understand that developing children need to spend time with their peers to make and have friends beyond the family.

This list is not definitive; we provide it simply as a framework for discussion. Questions you may want to ask include the following:

- Does this list, or parts of it, relate to "real" or "ideal" families?
- Does this list, or parts of it, relate to all families, or is it culture biased?
- What would you add to this list, and why?
- What would you remove from this list, and why?
- Think of two or three families you know. Does the list apply to them?

DIVERSITY IN NORTH AMERICAN FAMILIES

As you work out your own definition of family, consider the following scenario, in which a 22-year-old social work student tries to come to grips with what the word *family* has meant in her life.

SCENARIO

WHO IS FAMILY?

"When I was a little girl, my parents took in two foster children for three years. The children then returned to their biological parents, but we remained very close. When we finished high school, we got together again, and we've been sharing an apartment now for four years. We truly are a family.

"Last month I got engaged. My fiancé immigrated to Canada a few years ago, and most of his extended family still live in Greece. At our engagement party, I looked around the room at his wonderful family, with whom I couldn't communicate because I don't speak their language, and whose way of life seems so different from mine. These people, after the marriage, would become my family. Then I looked at my former foster sisters who have shared so much of my life and so many of my most intimate thoughts. It's amazing that these people are not really considered family."

This is a touching example of how formal definitions of family often don't capture the feelings and relationships that are connected with the concept of family.

The following scenario is a remarkable example of the diversity in structures that we see today.

SCENARIO

EXPECT THE UNEXPECTED

A 4-year-old at a child-care centre was enthusiastically telling his early childhood educator that he was going to Vancouver with his parents to visit his uncle. The educator asked the child what they were going to do when they got there. "Oh," said the child, "I'm going to take him for a walk in his stroller." The educator smiled and said, "You mean you're going to take your *cousin* for a walk in the stroller?" "No, he's my uncle," said the child as he strutted off to play. When the mother arrived to pick up her son, the educator related the conversation to her and said that perhaps the child was confused about the meaning of the words *uncle* and *cousin*. The mother laughed and told her an enlightening story. "My mother died four years ago, and my 75-year-old father soon after remarried a woman much younger than him, and they had a baby." This $1\frac{1}{2}$-year-old baby was indeed the uncle of her 4-year-old son!

Clearly, in the preceding scenario, the early childhood educator's perception of family had led her to assume that uncles are adults and cousins are children.

At the conclusion of this chapter, there are exercises that will help you reflect on how your own family has affected your perception of how families are defined. As early childhood educators, however, we must understand families not only from our personal perspectives, but also from a more theoretical point of view. We need to become educated about different kinds of families as a means of ensuring that our relationships with families are not hindered by stigmatization or prejudice.

Family Statistics in Canada

Of the 9.9 million families in Canada:

- Over 464 000 are step-parent families.
- 65 000 are same-sex couple families.
- 1.5 million are lone-parent families.
- 6.3 million families have at least one member who belongs to a visible minority group.

Sources: Statistics Canada, 2012; Vézina, 2012.

FAMILY MEMBERS AND FAMILY ROLES

After completing the exercise on your "image of the family" in Chapter 1, you probably realized that opinions regarding who is (and is not) considered a family member are quite diverse. A parent's partner, an aunt, uncle, cousin, friend, nanny, or caregiver may well be included in many families. As professionals working with young children, you may have the opportunity to interact with many people who are considered family, whether or not they conform to biological or legal definitions of family. Therefore, although the discussion in this chapter focuses on mothers, fathers, siblings, and grandparents, it's important to be aware of the significance and role that other members of the child's extended family may have.

Our society is undergoing a dramatic change in the traditional roles of parents and grandparents. Many fathers have been taking on much of the caring and nurturing roles traditionally associated with mothers, and many mothers have become breadwinners (Vanier Institute of the Family, 2010). For example, statistics from 2007 indicate that 85% of Canadian families have two or more earners (Vanier Institute of the Family, 2010). Societal changes such as the prevalence of single-parent and dual-income families have resulted in a rediscovering of the potential of grandparents as nurturers and providers of care and support to the family (e! Science News, 2012; Lever & Wilson, 2005).

Parents

The basic traditional role of parent is generally understood to include nurturing, educating, and disciplining children, managing the home, and financially supporting the family. The parenting role was once clearly divided between mothers and fathers. As noted earlier, today many fathers actively participate in nurturing and caring for children and in household activities, and many mothers contribute to the financial stability of the family. In fact, some would argue that a discussion of the roles of mothers and fathers separately might be an outdated concept, as the lines between these roles have blurred and are sometimes reversed. Parents of young children who are in the process of sorting out these roles in their families often find these role changes confusing and stressful.

SCENARIO

BATTLING TRADITIONAL ROLES

When Pam and Tony were expecting their first child, they talked about how things would be different from the way it was in their own more traditional families. After their two children were born and they were trying to cope with two full-time jobs (one was shift work), they were surprised at how deeply rooted those roles were. The expectation of who cuddled the kids at night or who did more of the housework or whose job was more important often became the focus of contentious battles. Integrating their new ideas into the concepts instilled by their own family experience proved to be more difficult than they had predicted.

Research tells us that even with societal trends that blur the boundaries between mother and father roles, some issues and challenges are fairly unique to each role. Therefore, the roles of mothers and fathers are discussed separately below. Further, it's important to recognize that there are many single-parent families today in which one parent assumes the range of roles that were traditionally met by two parents. We have devoted a separate chapter to single parents later in the book (Chapter 11).

Mothers

Although many people consider mothering to be "instinctual and natural," the roles mothers play have changed over time and differ across cultures. The most central issue today concerning the role of mothers relates to employment. There have been significant changes in women's participation in the labour force, from 22% in the 1940s to 57% in the 1990s (Cleveland & Krashinsky, 1998). In 2009, almost 75% of mothers of children were working mothers (Statistics Canada, 2009).

Taylor, Age 5

Mothers Who Stay Home and Mothers Who Work

The emotional debates about whether it's better for women to stay home with children or to go to work have been ongoing for over 40 years, with vocal advocates both for mothers staying home and for mothers working. Both sides can find research to back up their claim that they have happier families (Baydar & Brooks-Gunn, 1995; McDaniel, 2010; McDaniel & Tepperman, 2007). In fact, researchers have not been able to provide definitive evidence to support the claim that one way is superior to the other. Definitive evidence may be lacking because too many factors come into play—such as the availability of quality child care, the existence of support networks, and the role the father plays in child-rearing and household tasks—all of which affect how a working or nonworking mother influences family life (McDaniel, 2010; McDaniel & Tepperman, 2014; Nayyar, 2006). Although strong feelings may exist on both sides of the divide between mothers who stay home and mothers who work, most families in Canada do depend on the mother's income to make ends meet. The focus should now move away from whether mothers should work to how working mothers can be supported by their employers in providing flexible work schedules and return-to-work options (Goodman, Crouter, Lanza, & Cox, 2008; Nayyar, 2006), and by access to flexible, high-quality child care (European Commission, 2014; McDaniel, 2010). A popular book recently published in the United States called *The Fifth Trimester* (Smith-Brody, 2017) presents a vivid picture of the emotional turmoil and practical difficulties of a new mother as she returns to work, echoing the research findings on the need for supportive employers and child care.

Supermothers

A brief online search of "motherhood" will result in an overwhelming number of posts about "what mothers should do," "what mothers are doing wrong," "helicopter mothers," "mothers who don't spend enough time with their children," and "mothers who spend too much time with their children." According to the Internet, some "mothers go back to work instead of staying home with their children, [which] leads to delinquents . . . ," and "Staying home with your kids leads to maladjusted, antisocial children who rely on their mothers for everything . . ." (Giles, 2017).

For many women, the task of nurturing and rearing their children is the most fulfilling and rewarding experience they will ever have. Yet mothering in our society is not always easy, and the stressors faced by mothers today affect the entire family. One of these stressors seems to be the high expectation that many women perceive as needing to be "the best" in all aspects of their life: the perfect employee, the perfect partner, and the perfect mother. The following scenario presents one mother's point of view on mothering.

SCENARIO

THE PRESSURE TO BE SUPERMOM

"When I read some of the magazines, I get the impression that mothers are supposed to be these 'superbeings' who rise at dawn to exercise, jump into the shower, and run downstairs to prepare hot breakfasts for their families. Then they put on their business suits, successfully finalize two or three business deals at work, and pick up their children from child care and school. On the way home, they lead singalongs of 'The Wheels on the Bus' as they battle the traffic. After serving nutritious meals, engaging in quality time with their children, and then bathing and putting them to bed, these women miraculously transform themselves into loving and sexy wives before the evening ends."

Mothers as Project Managers

For better or for worse, mothers are often now being referred to as "project managers" (Malvik, 2013). One of the key stressors facing all family members, but mothers in particular, is the lack of time required to fulfill all their tasks and meet expectations. Terms like *time crunch*, *juggling*, and *second shift* reflect the growing sense of guilt and frustration many mothers feel about needing to "get it all done" and never having enough time for families and children (Milkie, Raley, & Bianchi, 2009).

Kerry Daly (2000) accurately describes the woes of a hurried society:

> The demands of time are so paramount in families now that it is almost pure folly to think of families living without sophisticated scheduling tools. The family calendar usually maintained by mothers serves a critical and essential function in the family, ensuring a carefully orchestrated set of picks ups and drop offs. In the early morning hours, clock radios chime in unison throughout the household, calling both adults and children to their individual temporal routines outside of the home. Where once families were more likely to live and work together in the household, their daily routine is now more akin to a ritual of dispersion, with babies being called to the drop off time for day care, children to the schedules of school, and virtually all parents to the demands of their paid work. At the end of the day, families re-converge on the household only to face additional responsibilities that include meal preparation, homework, lessons, shopping, and scheduling for the next day. The cumulative impact of these bloated schedules is that time has become a more urgent preoccupation in managing the many demands of contemporary work and family life. (p. 123)

It's important to note that the strain of the "second shift" or the time crunch mothers face is increasingly being faced by fathers as well (Harrington, Van Deusen, & Humberd, 2011).

In her book *The Burnout Cure: An Emotional Survival Guide for Overwhelmed Women*, Julie de Azevedo Hanks (2013) wrote that our fast-paced, hectic society is making parenting more challenging. She cited new technology, changing family dynamics, and the 24/7 news cycle as a few of the underlying causes.

Attitudes Toward Mothers

A simple word-association exercise can be helpful in beginning to understand the vast range of society's attitudes (both positive and some negative) of mothers. When our classes of early childhood students have been asked to quickly write down the first associations that come to mind when the word *mother* is mentioned, the whiteboard fills up with a wide range of adjectives: *loving, caring, nurturing, steadfast, nagging, cranky, always there*, and *never there* are but a few examples. Some students have considered their mothers their closest friends, while others would not even think of having an intimate conversation with their mothers. Understanding that the assumptions we make about family are often based on our own experiences can help us avoid being judgmental of others.

►► Examine Your Attitudes

What do you think of mothers?

1. Complete the following sentences:
   a. Mothers are _____.
   b. Mothers should _____.
   c. Mothers could _____.
2. Write the word *Mother* at the top of a blank sheet of paper, and then fill the page with other words this term suggests to you.

Consider the results of both exercises. Are your feelings about mothers predominantly positive? Are they negative? Or are they mixed? How strongly do you think your attitudes toward other mothers have been determined by your relationship with your own mother? How could your attitudes about mothers impact your practice with mothers? With children in your care?

Preparation for Motherhood

In previous times and in many other cultures today, by the time a woman becomes a mother she has participated in the care and nurturing of either younger siblings or babies of neighbours or extended family members. For many women in North America, however, their own experience of childbirth is often the first time they have had contact with babies. This remains true even though childbirth is occurring at a later age for many women. Furthermore, there is a value conflict inherent in motherhood. Over 40 years ago, Sheila Kitzinger (1978) wrote a classic study on mothers that still rings true today. According to Kitzinger, the school system prepares young women to be successful members of society, which entails training them, from a very young age, to be task-oriented—to establish timelines and schedules, to be precise, and to work hard toward a successful finished product. These skills are not necessarily the same ones required of mothers. Today, ironically, these scheduling skills seem to be an absolute requirement for managing a household, and yet they do not meet the requirements of the essence of parenthood, which is about being open and responsive to children's ever-changing needs.

THE BEST-LAID PLANS . . .

A 40-year-old woman who held a managerial position at a large institution had the first year of motherhood all planned out from two weeks after the baby was conceived. According to her plan, she would take a two-month maternity leave, after which the nanny (who had already been interviewed and hired) would begin. She had all her appointments scheduled for the next year based on her well-thought-out plan. Eight months after the birth of the baby, she met her friend in a park. "I thought you were going back to work!" the friend commented with surprise. The mother laughed and said, "I had everything all figured out, but I didn't consider for a moment that the baby wouldn't endorse my plans."

Motherhood doesn't neatly fit into a system of values that promotes high productivity and a fast pace. Mothers can't learn "perfect procedures" for child-rearing because the child is constantly changing and developing. In motherhood, there is no "finished product" by which mothers can measure their success as there is in academic or business settings.

MIXED MESSAGES

"I stayed home with my first baby until she was 4 years old. Wherever I went, people would ask me what I did. 'I'm at home with my baby' was my reply. In so many words, the usual response was, 'Is that all you're doing?'

"When my second child was born, I went back to work after a six-month maternity leave and placed my child in a child-care centre. Now when people ask me what I do, I get a variety of responses that range from accusations of child neglect to pity for my child and me. Talk about mixed messages."

Early childhood educators can sometimes inadvertently add to the stress and guilt that mothers feel. A study of the relationship between early childhood educators and parents (Shimoni, 1992b) indicated that some educators felt quite strongly that mothers should be at home with their children unless they absolutely had to work. Early childhood educators grew especially angry when mothers left their children at the centre at times when they weren't actually at work (to do shopping or simply to rest at home). Mothers very well might perceive these feelings. One mother (Shimoni, 1992b) reported that when she tried to discuss her son's problem behaviour, the early childhood educator stated outright that perhaps the solution would be to spend more time with her son. These negative attitudes toward working mothers have definitely decreased over the past 40 years (Pearson, 2015), although remnants of these attitudes remain. Moreover, attitudes that "blame" working mothers have decreased, while supportive attitudes toward working mothers have increased, particularly in the millennial generation.

Early childhood educators can be instrumental in providing support and understanding to mothers. The first step in this direction is to understand the complexities of mothering and then developing the ability to empathize with the problems and challenges that mothers face as they raise their children in a rapidly changing society.

Mothers and Experts

WHO KNOWS BEST?

"Before the birth of my first baby, I spent many hours talking with my grandmother, who had nursed her children until they could walk. The expression on her face as she talked about her babies said more than any advice book could. Two months after my baby was born, I was visited by the community health nurse, who told me that I should begin the baby on solid foods. Reluctantly, I did as she said, and shortly after that my baby didn't want to nurse anymore. Two and a half years later, my second child was born. The same community health nurse visited, sat in the same chair as she had two years before, and with the same expert manner proceeded to tell me that solid food should not be introduced for several months, and that breastfeeding was by far the preferable method."

Historians of childhood have studied the extraordinary amount of advice from experts (Schaub, 2010). The difficulty is that experts don't seem to agree on many topics, and sorting out the contradictory messages can be confusing. Often mothers are unsure of what is the "best" advice to follow (this is commonly referred to as "analysis paralysis"). Consider how many different opinions there are today for how children should be treated at bedtime. Should they be allowed to cry to learn to cope with going to sleep alone? Or should they be comforted until they fall asleep? The answer will depend on which expert opinion you're reading. In addition, parents today are bombarded with advertisements for books, toys, computer programs, and foods that will make their babies smarter and more successful. Parents who are on limited budgets and can't afford many of these items are also at risk of feeling guilty and inadequate. More importantly, these contradictory messages leave mothers and parents feeling confused.

As educators in early childhood development, we have come to appreciate the scientific knowledge available to help guide our interactions with children. But the preceding examples should make us humble. Every few years, as research and theories develop, new ideas emerge on the subject of what is best for children. Some of the practices that seemed unquestionably right are re-examined and reconsidered in light of new knowledge. At the same time, misleading information, supposedly based on scientific study, can grasp public attention and be very convincing. For example, the highly exaggerated notion, popularized by celebrities, of the danger of vaccinations, which has been proven false time and time again, has led to many parents' decision not to vaccinate their children. This has led to significant concerns in the health care community as the rates of communicable and preventable diseases (e.g., measles and mumps) continue to rise. Regardless of the factual and correct information presented, parents still believe these inaccurate messages provided by so-called experts.

"Expert advice," whether it be in the form of books, magazine articles, websites, or parenting classes, can sometimes undermine a mother's confidence and make her feel that she can never learn how to do things right. Expert advice can be highly important and helpful, of course. Professionals in a variety of fields, including medicine, psychology, social work, and education, have provided parents with an abundance of knowledge concerning health and development matters. At the same time, many authorities on parent education acknowledge the importance of parents' expertise and of working with parents in a way that is collaborative and empowering (Shimoni, 1992). The Center for the Study of Social Policy developed the "Strengthening Families" program to help early educators better support families. "Strengthening Families" focuses on supporting parents' ability to parent effectively and engaging parents in mutually supportive relationships that build protective factors (Center for the Study of Social Policy, 2017). Providing support to families is especially important in a culturally diverse society, where there are many different ways of interacting with children, and no one "right" way. We hope that the understanding gained from reading this book will help early childhood educators find ways to share this knowledge with parents in a manner that is respectful and empowering.

Many mothers (fathers too, but less so according to the research [Duggan, Lenhart, Lampe, & Ellison, 2015]) find social media to be both a valued source of information and support. Sometimes, knowing that other mothers face the same challenges or learning from other mothers what worked for them can be very helpful. As with the information that comes from "experts," the multitude of posts with advice on social media can be overwhelming, and are often contradictory. It's helpful to remember that the advice givers usually aren't familiar with the individual child or mother. Thus, early childhood professionals can play an important role in helping mothers determine whether advice found on social media aligns with the needs and abilities of their child. This kind of discussion is an opportunity for early childhood professionals to apply their knowledge about children and families along with their knowledge of a particular child to address the family's wants or needs.

Fathers

The roles of and expectations for fathers have been changing drastically in our society (Harrington et al., 2011). Many of today's fathers are moving closer to the current ideal of being equal partners with mothers in child-rearing (Battams, 2016). However, the transition from the traditional image of the father as provider and disciplinarian to the new image as equal partner in child-rearing has by no means been smooth. The changing role of fathers evokes strong emotions, as summarized by Diane Dubeau (2002) in the following box.

▶▶ Examine Your Attitudes

Examine your attitudes by reflecting on how many of the following statements you could see yourself saying or agreeing with:

"Given the current economic situation, wanting to offer more services to fathers means we'll have to cut services we offer to mothers" (*a social service professional*).

"It's true that fathers play an important role and now, whenever I phone (a student's) home to discuss a problem, I'm careful not to ask to speak to the mother. But often it is the father himself who says, 'Just a minute, I'll put my wife on the phone'" (*a school psychologist*).

"I did everything around the house. Now that we're divorced, I'm told he does the wash, the cooking, and when he has the children, he reads them their bedtime story, gives them their baths, etc. Why didn't he do that when we were together? It isn't because I didn't ask him to, believe me" (*a divorced mother*).

"I'd like to do my share of the work, really. But according to her, it was never done right. It wasn't just a case of doing things—they had to be done as she liked. In the end, I gave up" (*the father of a four-year-old boy*).

"People keep saying that nowadays fathers are more involved than the fathers of the generation before. OK, but can we maybe agree that mothers often still do most of the work when it comes to the child's daily care and education?" (*a female university researcher*).

Source: Used with permission from The Vanier Institute of Family, Dubeau, D. Portraits of Fathers. *Contemporary Family Trends*, 2002.

Historians have noted that before the Industrial Revolution, fathers played an important role in their children's lives (Couchman, 1994). Although mothers fed and cared for their infants and toddlers, fathers assumed responsibility for children's moral education while they were still quite young. Children (particularly sons) would work alongside their fathers in childhood and adolescence to learn their means of livelihood. As industrialization drew men out of the home and into the marketplace, father involvement with and influence on their children declined. While many men remained the disciplinarians, the hours spent away from the family resulted in emotional distance, and child-rearing became the almost exclusive domain of women.

For many years, the literature on fathers focused on the impact of the absence of fathers (e.g., due to death or divorce). More recently, it has focused on the role of fathers (Pruett & Pruett, 2009). In their book *Partnership Parenting*, Kyle and Marsha Pruett note that most parenting books offer advice to mothers and largely ignore the ever-changing role of fathers. Further, they contend that the literature on co-parenting typically focuses on couples who are divorced rather than parents who are together and learning to work as a team to parent their children. The Pruetts' book provides theoretical and practical approaches to parenting together. They make the case that fathers and mothers parent differently but that the role of the father is just as important as the role of the mother in the child's overall development. Understanding fathers from this perspective provides a refreshing and important perspective to educators and fathers alike.

With the rapid social changes that have occurred in the past four decades, the role of father as the "provider" for children has changed. Perhaps the most noticeable change is the number of fathers who don't live with their children. The concept of fathering is all the more complex in light of the statistics on divorce and remarriage. While most men begin their parenting career with their own biological child, today it's not unusual for some men to begin fathering as a stepfather. In his lifetime, a man might be the father of children who no longer live with him while being a stepfather to his new wife's children. Then, with his new wife, he might once again become a new father (Dubeau, 2002). A teacher from the ProsPère community program in Quebec, which promotes father involvement, gave a good example of the complexity of studying fathers. When she asked children about activities with fathers, she was surprised by their responses: "What father exactly? My real father or my new father?" and "I don't have a father." As well, the teacher noted one mother's response to her son's drawing of his father playing hockey with him: "He's never played hockey—he never sees him" (Dubeau, 2002, p. 6).

While there is a high number of fathers who don't live with their children, there has also been a significant increase in the percentage of fathers who are the primary caregivers of their children (Marshall, 2008). This increase may be due to single parenting, as there has been a 57.5% increase in single-father single-parent households. There has been a notable increase in the number of lone-parent families with children—from 289 000 in 1976 to 698 000 in 2014 (Statistics Canada, 2015a). A study on Canadian fathers based on census and national surveys suggests that the gap in how much caregiving men and women participate in is lessening (Ravena & Hoffman, 2012).

In addition, the number of stay-at-home fathers has grown (Statistics Canada, 2015a). The proportion of fathers taking time off and receiving paid parental leave benefits has increased sharply as well, due at least partly to changes in the Government of Canada's Parental Benefit Leave program, which allows fathers to take optional time off when their child is born (MacNaull, 2016).

There is still much to be learned about stay-at-home fathers. A recent Australian study (Baxter, 2017) found that stay-at-home dads spend only a little more time in child care than working mothers. The study also highlighted the fact that the majority of fathers who stay at home do so for economic reasons; that is, perhaps they are looking for work, or their spouse is in a high-paying job that makes it efficient for the father to stay at home. However, they noted that the population of stay-at-home fathers is diverse.

Many fathers are involved in child-rearing right from the beginning; they accompany their partners to childbirth preparation classes and participate in the birth experience. Psychologists have observed this trend of newly involved fathers, and have concluded that men indeed can, and do, engage in many of the activities of child-rearing with as much success as women. They can, for instance, soothe babies as capably as mothers can, and they react to babies' signals as appropriately as mothers do. Yet, psychological studies of father–child interaction point out that the way in which many fathers respond to and interact with their children is different from that of mothers (Pruett & Pruett, 2009). Play with fathers seems more intense and "rough and tumble" than mother–child play (Flanders, Leo, Paquette, Pihl, & Séguin, 2009). Fathers tend to read and play less quietly with their tots than mothers do; as well, fathers are less likely to sing and talk to their children quietly, or to play at routine care times such as during diapering and bathing. Fathers tend to interact verbally with their children less than mothers do. More recent writings have pointed out that conclusions drawn from such studies need to emphasize that these differences do not indicate parenting that is better or worse—just different.

Expectations of men have changed in recent years. As discussed, their participation in child-rearing has increased significantly (Lamb, 2010; Marshall, 2006). Their participation in housework has increased as well. The Vanier Institute of the Family has reported (Luxton, 2011) modest changes in participation rates in child-rearing and domestic tasks as well. An American study noted that fathers have more than doubled the time spent doing household chores, and nearly tripled the time spent with children since 1965 (Parker & Livingston, 2016). As well, a European study found an increase in the contribution of younger, more educated fathers to child care and household work. However, the study authors noted that this situation occurred more in countries that had a very low birthrate (Sullivan, Billari, & Altintas, 2014). There is still a significant gap between fathers and mothers in relation to their contribution to housework and child-rearing (Sullivan et al., 2014).

Researchers of fatherhood have been criticized for being "mother-centric" (Ball, 2013); that is, understanding fatherhood through the lens of what mothers do. However, over the past decade, researchers have begun to study fatherhood independently of motherhood (Blewett & Lamb, 2008; Lamb, 2010; Waller, 2009). Pruett and Pruett (2009) discuss the role of fathers—not in relation to lack of involvement but in relation to what they contribute to their children's development. Fathers bring different perspectives and dimensions to the lives of children that are just as important as what mothers bring. Fathers have their own way of holding children, responding to children, and playing and communicating with children (Pruett & Pruett, 2009). The point is that fathers are not "substitute mothers" (Pruett & Pruett, 2009, p. 28). Instead, they have a distinct and valuable role in the development of the whole child.

Since there are no "recipes" for good fathering, families develop their own patterns and norms. In some senses, society has had a hand in influencing the image of the good father, especially through the portraits conveyed by television, newspaper and magazine articles, and advertising. Some fathers complain that the image of a good dad really means that dad is a good "mom."

Many fathers claim that caring for their children is the most rewarding and enriching experience of their lives. Relating to their children on a deeply emotional level "liberates" men from the restraining stereotype of males. Indeed, many men who derive great pleasure from the cuddles, kisses, and diaper changing have no memories of physical contact with their own fathers other than a handshake.

MEN'S CHANGING ROLES

One day Timothy, who was 5 years old, came home from his preschool with tears in his eyes. Brian, his father, paused in his lunch preparation to find out what was wrong with his son.

"They called me a sissy today," Timothy explained.

"Why do you think they did that?" asked Brian.

"Because I was pretend cooking."

"Who called you a sissy?" Brian continued to probe.

"Petey and Mark."

"Well," said Brian thoughtfully, "I cook. Am I a sissy?"

"No, of course not, Daddy."

"And we're friends with both Mark's and Petey's parents, and both of their dads cook sometimes. Are they sissies?"

"Daddy! Of course not!"

"So, do you think cooking makes you a sissy?"

"No—I guess not."

"So then, what will you say to them the next time they call you that?"

"I'll say that my daddy cooks and he's not a sissy and he's bigger than your daddy and can beat him up."

Well, thought Brian to himself, *this is the 21st century and men's roles are changing. We're allowed to be in the kitchen as long as we can still beat other people up!*

Growing evidence tells us that when fathers are directly involved in caring for their children, there are many benefits to both the children and to the relationship between the parents (American Psychological Association, 2017c). Yet many fathers feel that they are disadvantaged because their workplaces are not tolerant of adjusting schedules to accommodate fathers' roles at home. A recent large Australian study found that when fathers struggle with the conflict between work and parenting, stress levels increase and the quality of parenting declines (Cooklin, Westrupp, Strazdins, Giallo, Martin, & Nicholson, 2014). Therefore, outside the immediate family, fathers can be supported by more public acknowledgment of their child-rearing role, and this could be reflected in paternal leave policies and informal support at the workplace. Many fathers have admitted that they're ashamed to tell anyone that they're missing work for reasons associated with their children, as the following scenario indicates. There is a need to ensure that current national and provincial legislation and employment-related policies reflect the changing nature of fathers' involvement in child-rearing (Lamb, 2010; Lero, Ashbourne, & Whitehead, 2006).

WHITE LIES

"When my two children were young, I helped out quite a bit. I would chauffeur them to their ballet lessons, take them to the doctor, dentist, and orthodontist, and often stay home with them when they were sick. Looking back on that time now, I realize how many times I told 'white lies' to my boss and my co-workers. Any excuse for absence was better than actually admitting that I was busy with my kids."

PARENTAL LEAVE

"When our daughter was born, I worked for a company with a strong 'family-first' ethic. New dads splitting maternity leave benefits was hugely popular and almost expected. So, when our daughter was born, my wife took the first eight months and I took the last four months. Those four months were amazing and gave me such a different perspective about our daughter and my role as her dad. My relationship with my daughter, based on that early experience, is strong (even though she is only five). Three years later, when we were expecting our second child, the company had shifted its policies significantly. The previous family-first ethic and policies were no longer in place with the new management. I didn't even consider taking a leave, and would never have even suggested doing so to my superiors (the same management team) in the new climate."

As the preceding scenario suggests, workplace and society have an impact on the roles that fathers want to and can play. This father would have loved to have taken parental leave with his second child, but the workplace had changed its parental leave policy significantly. The expectations of men as fathers providing for their families and their involvement continue to be a factor in decisions families make. Canadians can sometimes look to other countries for leadership regarding family-friendly policies. Swedish parents are entitled to 480 days of paid parental leave, and of those, 90 days are reserved for the father. In 2014, 25% of total parental leave was taken by fathers in Sweden (Swedish Institute, 2017).

Supporting Fathers

In spite of the increasing number of manuals, advice books, and television shows about fathering, many men still feel that they are relatively unsupported. Some complain of "the mothering double standard"—although women complain that men don't participate enough in child-rearing, women are hesitant to "let go" and allow men to take part. This is referred to as "gatekeeping" (Schoppe-Sullivan, Brown, Cannon, Mangelsdorf, & Sokolowski, 2008). Mothers learn at an early age that child-rearing is their domain and feel obligated to train their partners to do it the "right" way. While we must be careful not to generalize and blame mothers for the lack of father involvement, gatekeeping may be a factor in some families. In cases where this is so, mothers can be encouraged to give fathers more opportunities alone with the children, to acknowledge the differences in parenting styles, and to build fathers' confidence by repressing the urge to "check up on" or "correct" them.

Early childhood educators can help by ensuring that they are addressing fathers as well as mothers in their efforts to work with parents. Many programs are adding events and activities for fathers. A number of parent resource centres, libraries, and child-care centres offer programs directed at fathers. Some programs focus on developing parenting skills in fathers, others promote conversation between dads, and still others provide the opportunity for fathers and their young children to enjoy each other in play. Experience has shown that programs that support father involvement can positively impact a child's self-esteem and emotional well-being, lead to increased success at school, and result in fewer behavioural challenges (Best Start Resource Centre, 2012a).

Society's attitudes toward fathering are both inconsistent and changing (Lewis & Lamb, 2010). We all have different ideas concerning the role (real and ideal) of fathers, and we must not let our personal views interfere with our acceptance of the diverse nature of fathering styles that we come in contact with. Our own acceptance of the diversity in fathering styles and roles may help family members be more accepting of each other, if that is appropriate, or support each other as they try to alter their roles and lifestyles. There are many excellent resources for supporting fathers, and for engaging fathers in early childhood programs. For example, the Best Start Resource Centre in Ontario is one of many resources that provides information and support for fathers.

Siblings

Most of the children in the world have at least one sibling, although in Western countries today the number of families with one child only is increasing. Nina Howe and Holly Recchia (2014) point out that the relationship between siblings is likely the most long-lasting relationship in one's life, though the nature of sibling relationships in adulthood can vary from a total lack of contact to a deep and intimate relationship. Howe and Recchia (2014) summarize the research-based knowledge on siblings as follows: "In the early years, the sibling relationship may become a training ground for learning to get along in the world, cooperating and sharing joyous experiences, expressing one's desires, . . . [and] overcoming conflict" (p. 155). Due to the large amount of time that siblings spend together, the relationship often forms the basis for providing much emotional support. Through their play and their conflicts, they can learn to understand one another's points of view. Further, Howe and Recchia (2008) have suggested that conflict-resolution skills are learned most often in sibling interactions. This view is consistent with earlier research that suggests that sibling relationships may have as much influence on the development of children as the parent–child relationship, or more (Kluger, 2006; Tucker & Updegraff, 2009). During childhood, it's likely that siblings spend more time together than with their parents or with friends. Although conflicts are inevitable among siblings, sometimes the relationship is characterized by warmth, affection, and mutual support, while in other families, jealousy and rivalry extend into the adult years (Stefanac, 2015). Sibling rivalry exists in different ways for different family members, as the following scenario shows.

someone would always say they got more because Dad liked him or her best. I always knew that this was a standard family joke, but my parents were offended when this joking got out of hand and would step in to declare that we were all treated the same."

Parents can play a vital role in fostering healthy sibling relationships. Sometimes, however, we tend to simplistically blame the parents when siblings don't get along. In reality, many factors affect how siblings relate to one another. The gender of the siblings, the spacing between them, the temperament and personalities of both parents and children, and external factors all come into play. Although sibling relationships have been the focus of a number of studies in recent years (Kowal, Krull, & Kramer, 2006; Lawson & Mace, 2010; Tucker & Updegraff, 2009), there is still much that needs to be learned.

Older siblings have been shown to be both negative and positive role models (Stefanac, 2015), and their influence is becoming an important area of study. Some researchers have found that older sibling delinquency has a significant effect on younger sibling delinquency (Craine, Tanaka, Nishina, & Conger, 2009). Others have found that siblings can have a positive effect on one another (Kramer & Conger, 2009).

How do the structure and dynamics of the family affect sibling relationships? Researchers (Dunn, O'Connor, & Cheng, 2005; Strow & Strow, 2008) studied differences in sibling relationships in different family types (nonstep, stepfather, stepmother, and single mother) as well as sibling type (full siblings and half-siblings). Dunn et al. (2005) and Deater-Deckard, Dunn, & Lussier (2002) suggested that negative relationships between siblings, such as more conflict and aggression, were more prevalent in single-mother homes. Strow and Strow (2008) found that children in families with half-siblings (i.e., biological children and stepchildren living together) had more behavioural problems and scored worse on reading achievement lists. These examples may suggest how complexities in family and family structure impact the relationships of the people within those families.

Not surprisingly, family dynamics have been shown to impact sibling relationships (Updegraff, Thayer, Whiteman, Denning, & McHale, 2005). When older and younger siblings experienced more warmth and involvement from parents, aggression among siblings was decreased, compared with conditions in which less warmth and involvement were provided. Less positive relationship experiences with mothers and fathers contribute to aggression between siblings. Conversely, the quality of sibling relationships can affect the outcome of family risk factors (Conger, Stocker, & McGuire, 2009; East & Siek, 2005).

Parents' Role in Facilitating Healthy Sibling Relations

Unfortunately, there are no simple formulas to help parents foster good relations among siblings, despite the number of advice books or parent courses available on the topic. Certainly, it's thought important to help older siblings adjust to the birth of a new baby in the family by ensuring that they feel important (e.g., by giving them tasks, or preparing a snack for the older child to eat when the mother is breastfeeding the baby). While these strategies can be significant, they are only a small factor in ongoing sibling relations.

Parents sometimes feel that they must treat all their children in the same way, but this is probably impossible to do when the children have sharply different personalities. One sibling, for example, might need a lot of support and coaching in school work, while another manages independently. Yet the latter may feel jealous of the attention received by the former. These problems may be exacerbated when one of the siblings has special needs.

Rather than attempting to treat each child in the same way, it might be more helpful to focus on family communication. Children who grow up in families in which they feel free to discuss their emotions, including the common feeling of being treated unfairly, may be less likely to suffer from the jealousy and rivalry that plague the relations of so many brothers and sisters. Although we still have much to learn about the ways brothers and sisters influence each other's lives, it's clear that the impact of growing up in a family with other children is very potent indeed, and that the family's sibling subsystem can be one of the few constants in a rapidly changing society.

Handling Sibling Rivalry

1. Keep in mind that most siblings fight a good deal of the time. It's quite normal behaviour.
2. Consider how you may use these conflicts to teach children problem-solving skills. Rather than simply taking the toy away or separating children when there is a conflict, support the children to find a way to play together or compromise.
3. Make a rule that they can't call each other names or hurt each other physically. If you sense that they are about to do so, step in.
4. Don't become their judge and jury; help them work it out. Try to keep in mind all the times that they play together nicely.
5. Try not to pay too much attention to fighting siblings, since this may result in even more fighting.
6. Recognize that as a parent, perhaps your best and surest recipe for peace of mind is to expect considerable conflict between your children, appreciate its normalcy, and do what you can to manage it. However, keep in mind that fighting and squabbling are a way of life for many children. They may "enjoy" it. Even the very young child tends to have a strong sense of self-preservation. Most could avoid a major part of their fighting if they wanted to.

The advice to parents in the preceding box reflects ideas and expectations regarding conflict, sibling relations, and parent–child relations. Early childhood educators need to view this advice with caution and sensitivity. For example, are parents able to follow through with some of these ideas? Does the advice take cultural differences into consideration? Early childhood educators are aware of the vital role played by adults in modelling desired behaviour for children and in mediating conflict situations when children don't have the skills required to do this on their own. The preceding suggestions don't reflect this aspect of adult–child relations. For example, parents may feel that it's their responsibility to stop conflict rather than teach negotiation skills. Finally, it's important to ask whether conflict and squabbling are normal or whether this idea is peculiar to our culture. Some parents may want to raise their children with values that encourage mutual respect, sharing, and compromise, and conflict may be considered "normal" only because it's deemed so by the predominant culture.

Birth Order, Family Size, and the "Only Child Syndrome"
It has often been said that the order in which children are born has a strong influence on their development. This belief is so strong among both psychologists and lay people that one often hears children being described as a "typical first-born" or of having a "middle-child syndrome." The first-born child is often thought of as a perfectionist and an ambitious high achiever (Booth & Kee, 2009). Since first-born children have no siblings acting as models, they have to look up to and learn from their parents. Parents have more time for their first child, so their influence on him or her is thought to be stronger than on subsequent children. Only children often have more and longer interactions with adults than with children, and so learn to interact with adults in different ways. The middle children are thought to be secretive and rebellious but more social than the first-born. They are considered to be more socially competent with peers than first-born children, and their success with peers is somehow connected to their need to make up for the lack of parental

attention through companionship with other children. The last-born is often thought to be a charmer. By the time the third child is born, parents are thought to have relaxed their expectations and to prefer to pamper rather than discipline (Harrigan, 1992).

Studies have pointed to some of the differences in children based on birth order (Howe, 2014). First-borns tend to engage more in leadership, teaching, and helping roles; second-borns are more likely to imitate and follow; and third-born and subsequent children often imitate the older siblings' actions.

The problem with birth-order theory is that children's development is influenced by so many different factors: gender, age spacing, peer and school experiences, accidents, illnesses, random events, and economic factors (Booth & Kee, 2009). The research on birth order is not at all conclusive and is sometimes contradictory. While some studies do show that first-borns seem to have higher IQs and achieve more in school and in careers (Booth & Kee, 2009; Haan, 2009), these statistical differences are quite small. Studies have shown that differences commonly attributed to birth order have more to do with the parents having less time for caregiving and decreased financial resources (due to the increase in family size) than with personality or genetic differences (Gugl & Welling, 2010). In addition, there is a greater recognition that child temperament can explain differences in child development (Popkin, 2007; Turecki, 2000).

On a similar note, a much-studied topic in child development is the effect of family size on children. Studies have shown that children from large families tend to be less successful in school and careers than children from smaller families, which is usually attributed to the "dilution of parental resources" (Ambert, 2006b; Gugl & Welling, 2010). As mentioned earlier, with each additional child, parents have less time and financial resources. However, these studies failed to look at the possible benefits of growing up in large families. Zajonc and Mullally (1997) suggest that children from large families are more affectionate, good leaders, and less prone to depression, and may be less individualistic and more cooperative. Siblings act as role models and encourage and support each other (Åslund & Grönqvist, 2010).

On the other hand, the only child has earned a negative reputation in our folklore, and is often considered to be spoiled and inconsiderate, lacking in self-control, more dependent on parents, and more self-centred than are children with siblings. However, the research seems to indicate that, although only children may be like first-borns in IQ and achievement, in reality the negative traits mentioned are not necessarily associated with being an only child (Milevsky, 2015).

One small study suggests that only children are less autonomous than first-born children. The authors suggest that this finding may be because the process of separating from parents involves aggression toward them. When there are no sibling relationships for "backup," children may fear this individuation process (Byrd, DeRosa, & Craig, 1995). Another study contradicts this idea, however, and concludes that only children tend to be more autonomous than children who have siblings (Mellor, 1995). Since family size is decreasing and more parents are having only one child, researchers will have ample opportunity to devote more study to the nature of parent–child relationships in single-child families.

Early childhood educators who view the world from a socio-cultural perspective are aware that birth order is only one of a multitude of factors that impact children and families. While all this research is fascinating and, at times, seems to explain behaviour, it must be considered in context.

Grandparents

For many people, the word *grandparent* evokes idyllic pictures of a little old lady with grey hair fixed in a bun and an apron, retrieving a baking tin full of cookies from the oven while her kindly husband works in the garden. For others, it evokes a picture of frail and elderly people dependent on a young family for assistance and support. The fact is, though, that fairy tale images rarely reflect the realities of our society, and these are no exception. There are many different meanings associated with grandparenting, and grandparents can take on many roles (Thiel & Whelan, 2006). Increased life expectancy, women's increased participation in the labour force, and the fact that Canadians are working longer mean that many grandparents fulfill work-related and other family roles (Kemp, 2003). Nevertheless, stereotyping of grandparents is still quite prevalent (Helmes, 2009). Consider one grandparent's view about grandparent stereotypes in the media, described in the following scenario.

SCENARIO

CAILLOU'S GRANDPARENTS

"There's a popular children's cartoon in Canada called *Caillou*. Caillou's grandparents are elderly with grey hair, stooped over, and often seen sitting in rocking chairs. My grandson loves Caillou, and we had the chance to chat about an episode in which the grandmother was central. In his view, Caillou's grandmother was not like me but more like his 'Oma,' who is his great-grandmother."

As the preceding scenario indicates, the depiction of grandparents on popular television shows doesn't align with the grandparents many children know. For example, the child viewed his grandmother as "younger" and not like the grandmother he saw in *Caillou*. However, it's important to note that some children's grandparents are indeed elderly, so it's important that we not stereotype grandparents.

Canada's aging population and increase in life experience have brought more attention to the roles of grandparents. There are now more than 7.1 million grandparents in Canada, and nearly 600 000 grandparents live in the same households as their grandchildren (Battams, 2016). Grandparents can be as young as in their thirties or as elderly as in their nineties, and they can be totally committed to raising their grandchildren or have totally separate lives. As older adults' health and life expectancy have increased, grandparents are gradually becoming recognized as a vital force in the family system—a force that warrants much more consideration than it has received to date.

In one early childhood class about families, students were asked to identify the most constant relationship in their life. Many students named their grandparents and talked about their appreciation of the love and support their parents' parents showed them (often in much more positive terms than they used when discussing their own parents).

Cheriline, a First Nations social work student, had the following to say about her grandmother.

SCENARIO

THE CONTRIBUTION OF ELDERS

"On my reserve, the grandmothers raise the children. I never would have been able to look after my kids without my mother's help. She didn't only look after my children, she brought up her sister's children, too. But, you know, life on the reserve is changing as well. Some of our elders are beginning to realize that they want their freedom too. Our traditions are changing, just like the rest of the world."

In the United States, researchers have highlighted the fact that during times of tremendous familial difficulties, grandmothers who themselves have low income and may have impaired physical health, are assuming responsibility for their grandchildren (Bachman & Chase-Lansdale, 2005). In some cases, taking on the care of grandchildren is related to increased stress and depression (Edwards, 2003), health problems, and fatigue (Rosenthal & Gladstone, 2007), while in others it's associated with heightened well-being (Szinovacz & Davey, 2006). For example, some grandparents reported high satisfaction from the role related to the joys of children, the tasks of child-rearing, participating in the grandchildren's activities, and watching the child's accomplishments (Dunne & Kettler, 2008). Many grandparents show amazing strength and resilience as they overcome stressors and difficulties to provide loving and committed care to their grandchildren.

Researchers have described some of the roles that grandparents play, which seem to be fairly universal. Grandparents are the family's historians. They can provide the grandchildren with a sense of "where they have come from" and often have a treasure chest full of family stories, sometimes going back several generations. In many cultures, grandparents are a source of spiritual guidance. Often they are the caretakers of family members; also, they can be role models, playmates, and supporters of families (Arpino & Bordone, 2014; Bernal & Anucibay, 2008; Gauthier, 2002). The role of grandparents, like all family roles, is affected by cultural norms and expectations. While grandparents in many parts of the world may share common attributes, differences can be seen based on factors such as culture, religion, personality, gender, age, and geographical distance (Roer-Strier, Kosner, & Shimoni, 2017).

» Perspectives

Jan is a 29-year-old college student and the mother of a 2-year-old daughter. She comes from St. Lucia, which she left at the age of 8. Jan's mother moved from St. Lucia to Toronto in 1968 with the hope of getting settled in Canada and then sending for her two daughters so that they could have a better life and education in their new home. From the age of 2 until the age of 8, Jan lived with her grandmother and sister in St. Lucia.

"My grandmother was very strict. We were brought up with the expectation of proper behaviour at all times, and especially that we would show respect to our elders. Because my sister was four years older than me, I was expected to respect her as well and do what she said. My older sister, as in many West Indian families, was expected to look after me when Gramma was busy. And I was expected to do as my sister said. Gramma was from the old school, a devout Catholic who stressed the importance of self-discipline and study.

"I don't remember my grandmother expressing affection readily. She seemed more concerned about raising us as proper young ladies. When I was 8, we moved to Canada to join my mother. The pattern of interaction between me and my sister stayed the same throughout my childhood. My mother was a single working mother who relied on my sister's help in raising me and maintaining the household. Even today, all these years later, when I talk about my parents I am really referring to my sister and my mother. Having lived in Canada for most of my life, I think that if I have two children, I will want their relationship to be different. I would not want my older child to have the responsibility of raising her younger sibling, and I would want a more equal relationship between the siblings than I had with my sister.

"I've obviously been influenced by Canadian culture in terms of what I want for my children. However, when I look back on my childhood and think of the adult I am today, I see how valuable it was for me to have respect for older family members. That seems to be lacking in North America today, and in my view this is a loss of a valuable aspect of family life."

While culture seems to play an important role in determining the role of grandparents, there is likely almost as much diversity within each ethnic group as there is across ethnic groups. This diversity is even apparent within families, as a Jewish student relates in the following scenario.

DIFFERENCES WITHIN FAMILIES

"My grandmother on my father's side came to Canada from Poland. She spoke Yiddish, was the best cook in the entire world, and fit practically all the stereotyped notions of the typical Jewish grandmother, or 'Bubby.' I loved going to her house for Sabbath and holiday meals; she and my grandfather kept Jewish tradition alive in my family. My mother's mother was a professional woman. She hardly ever cooked, and in her free time she played bridge, golfed, and read. She would take us out for dinner and even sometimes on trips. But there was nothing 'traditional' about this grandmother—she was a very modern woman."

Grandparents can affect the family in a number of positive ways. Many factors will influence the relationship between grandparents and grandchildren: geography, personalities, and the nature of the relationship between the parents and the grandparents. Although grandparents can be heroes to their grandchildren, it's not uncommon for conflicts to arise between parents and grandparents. These conflicts may sometimes be related to the fact that child-rearing norms have changed considerably over the years, and what is now accepted as positive parenting may seem like "spoiling" to grandparents. On the other hand, grandparents often glean so much enjoyment from being with their grandchildren without having to worry about discipline that parents claim they're spoiling the children. Often, when grandparents are involved in the rearing of their grandchildren, roles and family boundaries may be confused. This confusion might be especially problematic in single-parent families where the grandmother lives with her daughter and grandchildren, and where the mother has to balance the responsibilities of being a daughter and a mother at the same time.

It's clear that grandparents play a vital role in the lives of many families, and for many this role provides positive experiences. Early childhood educators may find that grandparents who play a key role in the lives and development of their grandchildren can benefit from advice and support. Grandparents may require information about child-rearing because much has changed since they were parents or they may need current information related to play. They may need information about their right of access to their grandchildren when separation or divorce occurs. This issue has become important as grandparents have fought for the right to maintain contact with their grandchildren after divorce (Henderson, 2005). As well, grandparents may need some encouragement and support in working out old conflicts with their own children so that they will be welcome to share in the joys and challenges of raising their children's children. Successful programs, as well as policies, have demonstrated that with appropriate support grandchildren fared better as educators became more informed about issues facing grandparents (Cox, 2010).

CONCLUSION

In this chapter, we have provided a brief overview of some of the key family roles. North American society encompasses a considerable degree of diversity in the way mothers, fathers, siblings, and grandparents perform their roles. Some of this diversity is related to culture and ethnicity. Social, economic, and geographical factors also influence the way in which family members relate to one another, and their expectations of one another. Understanding and appreciating this diversity will help early childhood educators in their work with families. Considering families from a socio-cultural perspective will highlight each of these dimensions and relationships. While other extended family members (e.g., siblings, aunts, uncles, cousins, and grandparents) play a pivotal role in family life in many cultures, there is little research that can inform us of the impact of these roles on children. However, extended family members may be integral members of the family unit. Thus, early childhood educators should be open to inviting key extended family members to activities where possible, and be mindful of these relationships in day-to-day interactions with the children and parents.

Chapter Summary

- Understanding the roles of key players within the child's family broadens an understanding and ability to provide a supportive environment.
- Attitudes toward mothers have historically been complex and have contributed to feelings of guilt. Expert advice can be confusing and can also inadvertently add to stress and guilt. One of the biggest challenges facing mothers today is the "time crunch."
- Canadian fathers are becoming more actively involved in domestic life and child-rearing.
- The influence of siblings on a child's development is profound and can affect social behaviour in both positive and negative ways.
- An increasing number of grandparents are caring for children. The role of grandparents is influenced by cultural norms and expectations, as well as by economic circumstances.

RESOURCES

Voices of Canadians: Seeking Work–Life Balance:
http://publications.gc.ca/collections/Collection/RH54-12-2003E.pdf

The University of Guelph's Centre for Families, Work & Well-Being:
www.worklifecanada.ca

FRIENDS National Center for Community-Based Child Abuse Prevention:
https://friendsnrc.org

Public Health Agency of Canada, "The Father Toolkit":
www.phac-aspc.gc.ca/hp-ps/dca-dea/prog-ini/funding-financement/npf-fpn/father-papa/index-eng.php

Dad Central Canada:
www.dadcentral.ca

Fatherhood Institute:
www.fatherhoodinstitute.org

Canadian Council on Social Development:
www.ccsd.ca

Public Health Agency of Canada:
www.canada.ca/en/public-health.html

Canadian Child Care Federation:
www.cccf-fcsge.ca

Global Family Research Project:
https://globalfrp.org

Vanier Institute of the Family:
http://vanierinstitute.ca

Father Involvement Research Alliance (FIRA), "Canadian Dads @Home":
www.fira.ca/article.php?id=140

EXERCISES

1. In this exercise, you will draw a family map. This will bring to light many factors that have had an impact on your own family, and will help you in identifying the range of factors that have influenced your concept of family.

   For this exercise, you will need a large sheet of paper and markers. Use symbols or pictures rather than words to illustrate some of the most influential factors in shaping who you are today. You may include family members, friends, places of worship (church, synagogue, mosque, temple), activities, interests, travel, and any other factors that occur to you. Try to draw the symbols in order of importance or in chronological order.

   After you have completed your family map, compare it with others' maps or reflect upon what you've drawn. Which factors were most prominent in your development?

   How are the factors in your diagram interrelated? For example, some students recall that happy family memories are associated with holidays, leisure activities, or religious festivities. Unhappy memories may be associated with events such as a divorce or a death in the family. A consideration of the family map leads to an awareness of how factors outside the home, such as the nature of the community, influence the family.

2. One simple but effective method for evoking thoughts about the family is simply to draw a picture of a festive family dinner. Include in the drawing empty chairs for family members who are not present. Notice the seating arrangements around the table. Who is sitting next to whom, and why? Who is not present, and why? Who is actively engaged in food preparation and distribution? A description of a family meal can sometimes tell us a great deal about a family's relationships and norms.

3. On a sheet of paper, make columns listing the following relationships in your life: parents, siblings, extended family, friends, classmates or co-workers, and strangers. Then ask the question, Whom would you tell about . . . ?

   The list of situations that complete this question should range from very personal (e.g., trouble in an intimate relationship) to quite superficial (e.g., a good book I've read). Compare your "whom would I tell about" chart with those of your fellow students, and note similarities and differences. What does this tell you about your own family?

4. Think of some "expert advice" you have been given, or ask a new mother about any advice she has been given from professional sources. Discuss whether you (or the mother) took the advice, whether or not it was helpful, and how you or the mother would change the advice based on your/her experience.

5. Interview some mothers and fathers and ask them about the challenges and problems they face as parents raising children in today's society.

6. Compare the problems, joys, and challenges of parenting today with parenting a generation ago.

7. Discuss what you think you'll be like as a grandparent, and how similar or different you think you'll be from your grandparents.

CHAPTER 3

Perspectives That Enhance the Understanding of Families

OBJECTIVES

- To consider the family as a system within a system

- To understand the potential impact of social and economic barriers on families

- To consider the impact of change, loss, and trauma on children and families

- To appreciate the importance of a family-centred approach in early childhood education

A young teacher recounted her daughter's first morning at school. "Tammy and I were so excited about her first day. I was enthusiastic about the new possibilities for her learning, and for me, it represented a new stage in our relationship and in my parenting abilities. I could now help her to explore, to learn, and to interpret the new parts of her world just waiting to be discovered. We arrived to find many other parents and children, all suitably attired for their first day. Some children looked excited, others looked apprehensive, and some looked scared. After the introductions were complete and the children made their way to their new classrooms and new teachers, all the parents left. I was amazed at the number of parents outside in tears because the first day of school signified that their 'babies' had grown up and didn't need them anymore. They certainly weren't feeling the enthusiasm and excitement that my daughter and I had felt on that morning."

PERSPECTIVES FOR UNDERSTANDING FAMILIES

Models and perspectives for understanding families have been gleaned from many disciplines and fill many textbooks. Most professions today would claim that they have a unique body of knowledge and theory on which their practice is based. Early childhood educators have often stated that they felt awkward about not being able to "claim" a specific theory but are expected to work from the perspectives of the many professionals who interact with families (e.g., social workers, psychologists, health care professionals). Our intention is to provide early learning educators with the knowledge most relevant to their unique practice with families. The previous chapters have related to the socio-cultural perspective, which has become integral to every aspect of the profession. In this chapter, we describe six additional perspectives that are highly relevant to the understanding of families and, thus, to the work of early childhood professionals. These perspectives are family systems theory, the ecological model, the family development approach, intersectionality, the theory of loss, and the strengths-based perspective. The concept of resilience, an understanding of which is essential for professionals working with children, is described in Chapter 4. Each perspective has practical considerations that will be discussed briefly. Some perspectives seek to explain the dynamics within the family and between family members, while others focus more on how different aspects of society impact families.

FAMILY: A SYSTEM WITHIN A SYSTEM

A family is a system that lives within a larger system, and all the components of these systems interact with one another. Most would agree that when a group of people are connected by family ties, what happens to one member of the family usually affects other members. Parents often bring home stresses from their work environment, and children pick up and often act out that tension. A situation as common as a child with a cold or an ear infection often affects the entire family dynamic. If parents are up with a sick child several nights in a row, their exhaustion may well influence their relations with each other and with other children in the family, as well as the siblings' relations with each other. Because family members function as a unit composed of interacting members, psychologists think of families as "systems."

Family systems theory provides us with a way of looking at individuals, families, and groups to get a better understanding of how each of these units functions both separately and as a whole. While family systems theory is used mostly in family counselling and therapy, it's highly relevant to early childhood settings (Garris-Christian, 2006). The main concept in family systems theory is that the family includes interconnected members, each member influencing the others in predictable and recurring ways (Van Velsor & Cox, 2000). This theory focuses on family behaviour, and it considers communication patterns, separateness, connectedness, loyalty, and dependence, as well as how families adapt to stress (Garris-Christian, 2006). A major contribution of this theory is the ability to see the family both as a whole and as a series of interconnected parts. Just as people who are concerned about the environment talk about an ecosystem, in which what happens to one part (e.g., using chemicals for weed control) eventually affects other parts (the water supply), professionals who advocate a systems approach to family therapy see the members of a family as forming an interconnected whole.

While this interconnectedness seems obvious, considering the family as a system has not traditionally been part of the work of early childhood professionals and other professionals who work with families. It's still quite common for a child with behavioural problems to be seen by a therapist who has little or no contact with the parents. Teachers will sometimes have a conference with parents and expect them to carry out certain tasks with their children (such as homework) without attempting to gain an understanding of the bigger picture of how that family functions as a system. On the other hand, professionals such as social workers may seek to gather information on all family members to provide service for one.

SCENARIO

NOT AS EASY AS IT SEEMS

The mother of a 5-year-old developmentally delayed boy was asked to carry out a "simple" behavioural program at home. The mother was to make sure that her son always made an attempt to communicate verbally before being given what he wanted. This task seemed simple enough, and the early childhood educator wondered why the mother seemed reluctant to do it. She was unaware that the mother had two younger children, that she helped with her husband's business, and that she was caring for her aged, chronically ill mother, all in addition to working part-time. This simple request was not as simple as it had seemed.

One concept from the family systems approach suggests that families, like all other systems, can be open or closed. An open family system is thought to be more flexible and adaptable to change, and a family system that is closed is considered less adaptable to change. Open family systems can react to and cope with changes—both positive and negative—more readily than closed family systems.

Understanding this concept can make early childhood educators' interactions with different families a little easier. For example, closed families may be less likely to discuss their problems or concerns or to look for outside sources of support. Families that are more open tend to discuss their concerns and to use outside supports. The degree to which a family is open or closed will often be a prime consideration in determining how the early childhood educator will interact with the family.

Moreover, the degree to which a family is open or closed may be affected by factors outside the family, such as prejudice or preconceived ideas, as well as by internal factors. Culture also plays a role. Garris-Christian (2006) observed that educators in the past may have worked from the assumption that openness is equated with "better" parenting; however, differences in openness do not equate with differences in quality of parenting.

Family Balance

All systems strive to maintain some kind of a balance. For example, if we think of the human body as a system, we see that there are many mechanisms in place to protect a state of balance. For example, when the weather is very hot and the body heats up, there are systems in place that activate the sweat glands to cool body temperature so that it remains around 37°C. Likewise, a family system finds ways to maintain its balance. One analogy to the preceding example is the way various families "let off steam" to maintain balance when tension arises. Taking a vacation, with or without the children, could be seen as an attempt to maintain balance. Similarly, many families develop ways of discussing and solving problems as a method of maintaining balance. However, sometimes less positive measures are employed to maintain family balance, and many of these are not even conscious. Family therapists often relate anecdotes of how children become ill when tension develops between parents.

SCENARIO

A SYSTEM OUT OF KILTER

One therapist tells of a family in which the youngest son had a severe stutter. The parents had been experiencing serious marital problems but decided to put their own problems aside in an effort to help their son. Due to the parents' efforts, the child received treatment and support and soon his symptoms almost disappeared. However, it seemed that as the son got better, the tension and conflict between the parents worsened. As the stress in the home increased, the boy's stuttering returned.

The preceding scenario is not atypical. In some families, a child may function as a "stress barometer." As the stress rises, so too does the incidence of behaviours such as stuttering, bedwetting, and nail biting. Professionals working with adolescents using a residential placement approach have found that treating the child removed from the family may have benefits but often see the old behaviours return as soon as the child is returned to the family home. A family approach to treatment has become much more common.

Balance and consistency in families are important for providing children with a secure environment. Rituals and customs help keep families together during times of change and stress. Early childhood educators can assist families in establishing and maintaining equilibrium through providing as much consistency as possible when the family is undergoing change and stress, and providing families with information about routines and rituals that can give children a sense of balance while the family is going through change (Garris-Christian, 2006).

Family Rules

Rules govern all systems, including the family. Some of these rules are clear and some are not so clear. Some families, for example, may clearly state that the family will eat supper together or that the children are to tidy their rooms before watching television. Other rules may not be as clear, though they may be evident to an astute observer of families. A discussion that took place among early childhood students yielded some interesting examples of family rules:

- Boys play hockey; girls play quietly.
- Daughters clear the table after meals; sons do their homework.
- We don't want to know if you had a bad day.
- Complaining gets you nowhere.
- Crying helps you get your way.

Nobody talks about these informal rules in the family, but everyone seems to know them. Children's behaviour is certainly influenced by these rules. The first indication of this is often when the 4- or 5-year-old begins to play with other children in their homes and sees different things happening. Young children will often bring these examples home and make comparisons with their own family. For example, they might remark, "At Lindsay's house, her dad cooks," or "Jill and her brother take baths together." When families experience conflict, a family counsellor or therapist might try to help the family understand how these "unstated rules" are affecting relationships.

Early childhood educators working with families need to be sensitive to family rules, even though some may not be congruent with the professional's ideas about raising children. For example, in some families there is a clear division of sibling roles based on gender, and boys do not participate in activities such as housekeeping and playing with dolls. Child-care centres can and should distinguish between home and centre rules, being sensitive and respectful to the home environment. Early childhood educators can watch for unspoken rules, and ask for families' input and assistance when there is a discrepancy between home and centre rules (Garris-Christian, 2006).

SCENARIO

NOT IN OUR FAMILY

A father came to pick up his 4-year-old son from child care. When he arrived, Jonathan was in the housekeeping corner dressed in a long yellow gown, a floppy hat, and high heels. The staff explained that Jonathan loved to pretend that he was a princess. Jonathan's father was extremely embarrassed. He reprimanded his son and the staff openly, saying that in his family men didn't dress like women and he did not want his son playing there again.

This type of situation has caused grief for many early childhood educators. However, an effort must be made to respect the beliefs and values of the family. The family systems approach is broad and complex, and our purpose has been to familiarize early childhood educators with some key concepts, especially as they relate to professionals' work with children and families. Although early childhood educators don't engage in family therapy, understanding some of these concepts will heighten their awareness of how they may inadvertently or purposefully affect the family as a whole (Garris-Christian, 2006).

THE WIDER SYSTEM: AN ECOLOGICAL APPROACH TO THE FAMILY

Just as a child is affected by the entire family system, so too are families affected by other systems with which they interact. These include the neighbourhood in which they live, the parents' workplace, and the nature and scope of available support services. These aspects of family life are affected, in turn, by the social policies and ideologies prevalent in our society. An ecological approach recognizes that interrelated factors ultimately affect the way in which each child develops. An understanding of the ecological model can help early childhood educators empathize with families and better understand their role in supporting and helping families.

The conceptual foundation of the ecological model stems from the work of Urie Bronfenbrenner (1979, 1990), who outlined four basic structures—microsystem, mesosystem, exosystem, and macrosystem—in which relationships and interactions that affect human development take place. A later development in ecological theory added a fifth structure, the chronosystem. Today, more than 30 years after Bronfenbrenner developed ecological theory, it remains a foundational concept in early childhood education.

The first of the four basic structures within the ecological approach is the microsystem. The microsystem consists of settings or environments with which the individual has direct, ongoing contact. The family, the school, and the peer group are examples of microsystems with which the child interacts to significantly affect development. The workplace, place of worship, bowling club, golf course, or community centre are examples of microsystems with which adults in the family may interact. Another aspect of the microsystem today is the virtual microsystem. Family life has been altered significantly by technology—television, the Internet, and cellphones (Little, Sillence, Taylor, & Sellen, 2009). We will likely learn more in future years about the influence of the virtual microsystem on families and children.

The second structure is the mesosystem. The mesosystem consists of links and relationships between two or more of the microsystems with which the individual interacts. Examples include the relationship between a family and the child-care centre or a workplace and the child-care centre. These connections between microsystems can be weak or strong, positive or negative.

The third structure in the ecological approach is the exosystem. The exosystem consists of the many structures in a society that affect people's lives even though they may have no direct contact with them. These include institutional and government decisions and policies, societal norms, and laws.

The fourth component of the ecological approach is the macrosystem. The macrosystem encompasses the beliefs and values (i.e., the ideology) and lifestyles of the dominant culture and the subcultures within a society. Macrosystems are viewed as patterns or frameworks for exosystems, mesosystems, and microsystems (Berk, 2000). For example, policies made at the exosystem level (such as universal access to school) are based on shared assumptions and beliefs about the value of education in our society.

The fifth component of the ecological approach is the chronosystem. The chronosystem refers to changes over time, at both the individual level and the societal level.

The ecological model describes the influence of different systems on each other as dynamic and reciprocal. This means that individuals or families can influence policies just as much as they are influenced by them. Consider the following example: a government decision (an exosystem) to reduce funding for services to children with special needs can affect many of the microsystems with which family members are involved. The schools (a microsystem) may have fewer resource teachers to help children with special needs, which may result in policies (an exosystem) that discourage the integration of children with special needs into the school system. These children will be in need of much family (microsystem) support. However, if the families of these children join forces with the schools (forming a mesosystem), they may be able to advocate effectively enough to force the government (the exosystem) to rethink its policy. In addition, if policies and services change over time (the chronosystem), we can trace how these changes have affected or could affect families and their children.

Applying the Ecological Model

By providing high-quality child care and support to families, most early childhood professionals are working within the microsystem and mesosystem of the ecological model. However, many early childhood educators don't see themselves as having the knowledge and expertise to engage in efforts beyond those systems, such as trying to influence issues on a broader community and policy area. Joan Lombardi (2017), a well-known expert in early childhood education, has been a long-standing leader in the movement to create healthy child development and healthy families. She also emphasizes the importance of the ecological approach because it acknowledges that children's families are influenced by their communities, which in turn are influenced by government policies at all levels (municipal, provincial, and federal). Lombardi (2017) suggests that the best way to promote policies and actions that can make a difference in the lives of children is to "jump in—call a meeting, and demonstrate leadership, and begin to envision how the community can be more supportive." Some early childhood professionals may find getting involved in making a difference beyond the broader community to be a unique and rewarding experience.

FAMILY DEVELOPMENT

Early childhood educators have a broad understanding of children's stages of development. Families change and grow over time, just as each individual member changes and grows. Some of these changes are predictable. Family life will change drastically, for instance, with the arrival of a new baby, and it will change again when children grow up and leave home. Other transitions are more subtle and are recognized only in retrospect or upon reflection.

The following scenario illustrates quite normal developmental changes in the child, along with the required adaptation in parenting abilities and the resulting changes in the marital subsystem and in the entire family unit.

SCENARIO

IT'S HARD TO KEEP UP

The mother of a teenage boy was having some difficulties with his behaviour. There was a growing feeling of tension in the family, and the parents noticed that they were quarrelling much more often, both with each other and with their son. As a result, they decided to attend a series of parenting seminars. After listening to hours of advice and reading volumes of material, the mother commented that parenting was hard work. "We just got the knack of being parents to a new baby and turned into a toddler. By the time we figured out how to deal with the 'terrible 2s,' and he turned into a sweet and loveable 3-year-old. Things changed again when he started school, and my husband and I actually managed to remember that we had a relationship with each other!!! It seems as if we just figured out what we should be doing, and he changed again."

Over the years, scholars have identified various stages of family life—from the formation of the marital or couple bond to parenting infants, toddlers, preschoolers, school-aged children, teenagers, and young adults—that have been used to understand the typical challenges families face. Family development theory also includes the stages where middle-aged parents launch their children and start retirement as well as the aging couple in retirement to the end of life. Family development theory was very widely used as a basis for understanding families and appeared in most textbooks. However, it has fallen into disfavour in recent years because of the many changes in modern society (Office of Family Science, Education, Research and Policy, 2017). It has been criticized for its lack of ability to account for different family forms, genders, ethnic and cultural differences, and alternative lifestyle choices. For example, in many families today, a marriage may occur years after the birth of a child. Instead of "empty nests," we hear of "revolving doors" as young adults live with parents much longer than previously, or leave and then come back.

The Benefits of Family Development Theory

Family development theory suggests to us that many of the problems faced by families as they enter and emerge from transitional periods are normal. Many families derive comfort from this realization. If family members are aware of the potential stressors associated with impending transitions, they can prepare for them. For example, couples expecting a baby may discuss how they will share the responsibility, or how they may try to reserve some time to share together alone. A mother who has stayed home to rear her children can begin to think about and plan for the changes that will occur when her children grow up. She may consider retraining for employment or furthering her education, for example.

Every family passes through life's transitions in its own unique way. A stressful transition for one family can be a joyous one for another. The age and developmental stages of each family member, their inner and outer resources, and economic and cultural factors all play a role in family development. Family members often learn about transitions from older family members or from friends, and sharing these experiences can be extremely helpful. The theoretical knowledge available about family development is an additional source of information that can be useful to families and to professionals who work with them.

Transitions in Parenting

Parenting involves transition and changes in every aspect of life: money, sex, sleep, meals, social life, and finances. These changes may occur easily and be welcomed by parents or may cause stress and conflict. The adjustment to parenthood will vary from family to family, and will be influenced by family structure (a new blended family or a first-time family; single or couple parenting), and also by factors such as economic situation and culture. The adjustment to parenthood is impacted by social, economic, and cultural factors, as well as individual differences and the degree and kind of support available. All of these factors play a role in the way parenthood is experienced. What is important for the early childhood professional to keep in mind is that parenting is a developmental process, and for new parents the processes are sometimes challenging. Some of the transitions that new parents experience may be anticipated and subtle, and others may cause tension for the family members involved. An awareness and an understanding of the changes that accompany the transition to parenthood will be helpful to professionals whose work involves supporting families.

INTERSECTIONALITY

Intersectionality is defined as a complex mix of identities that influences the way an individual participates in all or any level of society. Specifically, it focuses on how the different social identities of a person or group (e.g., gender, ethnicity, socio-economic status) often overlap and are linked to systems of exclusion, oppression, and domination (Crenshaw, 2016). The concept of intersectionality was first developed by feminist sociologists to illustrate how multiple factors interact to influence individuals or communities. It has also been used in the health care field (epigenetics) to understand the impact that many factors have on an individual and his or her health. In human services, it has been referred to as a cross-sectorial approach. At its basic level, this approach asks us to consider all of the factors that might impact a family together rather than consider each in isolation. For example, a single parent may be impacted by economic change, change of relationships within the family and with friends, a change of residence, and a change of roles with his or her children. There are many layers to understanding the complexities of this type of family. While the concept of intersectionality is fairly complex, learning its basic tenets will help early childhood professionals gain insight into families that face multiple barriers.

As you will see in the following chapters, many of the challenges that families face are discussed and understood separately. For example, we discuss the challenges faced by families such as those where a child or parent has an illness or disability; immigrant families; lesbian, gay, bisexual, and transgender (LGBT) families; and families who live in poverty. Yet, as we know, most people don't fit into neat and tidy categories. A person who is a visible minority may face some prejudice in his daily life. However, if this person has a disability, belongs to an LGBT community, and has an income below the poverty line, he or she faces multiple threats of discrimination. Researchers of intersectionality attempt to explore and describe how these various factors interact with one another, and the impact they may have on all families. More importantly, an intersectional approach can "help us ensure that we don't continue to overlook the challenges that exist for people belonging to multiple marginalized groups because it allows contextualization of each group membership and the relationships between them" (Bell, 2016).

Some of the key tenets of intersectionality include the notion that human lives can't be explained by taking into account single categories such as gender, race, or economic status. Thus, when attempting to understand a social problem, we can't focus on one factor or structure at a time, but rather, must seek to understand how the factors are linked or layered.

As you go through this book, you will see how factors such as prejudice, economic status, and access to resources are often linked or layered in a way that makes it imperative to look at the "whole picture." As researchers Hancock (2007) and Hankivisky (2014) have explained, while inequality between people is very often the basis of many of the social problems we face, it's rarely the result of a single, distinct factor. Rather, it's the result of intersections between many different factors, such as social class, experiences, and the relative power of different groups in society.

Intersectionality is a relatively new approach that, although fairly complex, is gaining recognition by scholars and policy analysts who see it as a way to better understand the origins, root causes, and characteristics of social issues. In our work with families, it helps guide us to think about the many layers of complex challenges that families can face. This may give us some insight about engaging families and how we can facilitate the development of resilience in families. While intersectionality may seem highly theoretical and removed from the daily work of early childhood professionals, its main lesson is important to our practice (as you will see in the following sections, which outline some layers that affect families).

CHANGE, LOSS, AND TRAUMA

The well-known proverb "One can never stand in the same river more than once" reflects the notion that change is a constant factor in our lives. Very little stays the same. While many instances of change in our lives are positive, change often comes with varying degrees of stress. A number of changes can affect a family, including a change in geographical location or child-care centre; a new sibling in the family; an illness or death in the family; and separation, divorce, or blending of families. Children are better supported in coping with all of these changes and other life events if there is an understanding of how the change might affect both the adults and the children.

Much of the literature on responses to change was based on the theory of loss first described by Elisabeth Kübler-Ross (1969, 2017), which included five stages: denial, anger, bargaining, depression, and acceptance. The theory is helpful in understanding the key elements of loss and/or change, but it's important to note that not everyone goes through these stages in the same way, or even in the same order, and the time it takes to move from stage to stage varies significantly. Although Kübler-Ross's model for understanding loss and change was developed in the context of death, it has been adapted to innumerable contexts and is commonly used in organizations to support employees during management changes, job changes, location changes, or job losses. Kelley and Conner (1979) revisited Kübler-Ross's model and sought to highlight the difference in response to change when the change was a choice, rather than one that befell people. They found that even when people make a change for what they consider the better, they will undergo a predictable emotional cycle. They labelled the five stages as follows: uninformed optimism (an excitement about the change); informed pessimism (where one begins to feel problems arising and experiences feelings of letdown); hopeful realism (where one becomes more familiar with the new situation); informed optimism (where one comes to terms with the choice and feels less anxious about it); and completion (where one has worked through most of the problems and feels that the change is complete).

Children's reactions to change and loss depend on many factors, including their developmental stage. However, it's common to see children react with sadness, anger, difficulty sleeping, loss of appetite, physical complaints (such as stomach aches), loss of interest in play, regression, and fear (Dyer, 2002). Specific suggestions adults can use to help children cope with change will be discussed in subsequent chapters, but they include the following:

- Give the child advance warning of the change, and involve the child as much as possible in the change. For example, if the family is going to move, a child (depending on the age) may be able to be involved in choosing which toys will be packed to move and which may be given away.

- Try to keep routines as much the same as possible around the time of the change. For example, if a new baby is expected, this is not an ideal time to move his or her older sibling from a crib to a bed!

- Understand that preschoolers may have a lot of questions about the upcoming change, from small ones such as "Will I still be able to have cocoa every morning?" to big ones, such as "Will Daddy still love us after you divorce?" Children may ask the same questions over and over much to the annoyance of their parent(s). But as an adult, it's important to remember that this may be the child's way of developing an understanding of the change.

- Be prepared for some regression in children after a major change. For example, children may return to stuttering, bedwetting, or temper tantrums. While regressions are normal, if they persist for too long, it may be time to seek professional consultation.

- Understand that some children may not say anything or act differently during a change. This does not mean that the child is trying to cope with the issue on their own.

- Be aware that children may act out the change during play. Parents are sometimes taken aback when their child is acting out a funeral they just attended. However, play may be the way the child comes to cope with the change.

- Allow the child to be sad and to grieve when a change occurs. Parents and educators may want to label these feelings for children (e.g., "You look sad. Are you sad about not having your friends next door?") (Bright Horizons Family Solutions, 2017).

Regardless of the situation or the magnitude of the change or loss, it's important to remember that change and loss impact adults and children and need attention. A child who loses his or her favourite blanket must be responded to with similar empathy as when the child loses a pet.

It's important for early childhood professionals to keep one final point in mind when dealing with children who are experiencing change or loss. The most important people whom the child usually depends on for support are often going through their own processes of reaction and may find it very difficult to provide their children with the extra support and consideration required. This means that parents may be absorbed in their own emotional turmoil and not be able to listen to or help the child cope with the change or loss. Think about parents during a divorce. Their personal lives may be shattered and they may be overwhelmed by the change and loss, leaving them unable to cope with what their children may be experiencing.

Trauma

Children and families can experience significant trauma in a number of circumstances. In 2013, the province of Alberta experienced a natural disaster of major proportions. There was a terrible flood that destroyed houses, businesses, and farmland. The destruction was devastating. Three people died and over 100 000 people were displaced (Ogrodnik, 2013). Thousands of families were forced to evacuate their homes, many lost all their possessions, and today whole communities, families, and individuals are still in the process of rebuilding their lives. In 2016, Fort McMurray experienced devastating fires that required families to evacuate with hours' notice. These families relocated across the province and country, and for many weeks had no idea whether their homes were still standing. Today, as in the past, Canada has opened its doors to refugees from countries that are ravaged by war and/or terrorist activities, where children have been victims of violence or witnessed unspeakable brutality toward loved ones, and who have lived in conditions of uncertainty and fear that many would find hard to imagine. In some seemingly "normal" Canadian communities and homes, incidences of violence or abuse occur that are simply unthinkable.

Trauma is defined as a physical or psychological threat or assault to a child's sense of self, safety, or survival or to the safety of another person significant to the child (Schwartz, 2011). Trauma can stem from many sources, including abuse, neglect, serious illness, accidents, natural disaster, and war. We don't have an accurate way of knowing how many Canadian children are suffering from trauma. However, a 2008 national study found that 85 440 children experienced physical abuse, sexual abuse, neglect, emotional maltreatment, or exposure to intimate partner violence (Schwartz, 2011). Further, this study illuminated the implications of intersectionality; for example, children living in disadvantaged circumstances (e.g., living in poverty or with a parent who has a mental illness or criminal record) had a fourfold risk of being exposed to trauma. It also highlighted that trauma must be considered from different perspectives—health, mental health, security, and its effect on different areas of a child's life.

The experience of trauma can have long-term effects on children; it can increase their risk for post-traumatic stress disorder, depression, substance abuse, and mood or anxiety disorders. Children who suffered from multiple traumas "were found to experience significantly more impairments, including relationship, school and physical health difficulties" (Schwartz, 2011, p. 4). Educators and teachers in High River, Alberta, one of the communities most affected by the 2013 flood, will attest to the fact that children struggled with the floods years later. It appeared in their play, their artwork, and their activities.

Children's response to trauma will differ, depending on many factors such as the type of trauma, the duration of the traumatic situation, their life circumstances, and their personality and temperament. Young children might show regression, signs of separation anxiety, become more clingy, cry, scream, or tremble when separating from parents. They may engage in self-soothing behaviours (e.g., thumb-sucking) or repetitive actions (e.g., rocking) as attempts to manage their anxiety. They could very well be having nightmares or flashbacks, but often can't articulate that they are. School-age children may also regress, show difficulties in social activities and school work, or become withdrawn or disruptive (Lingley, 2016). Developmental level and the child's cultural background affect how the child perceives the trauma, as well as resources for coping and family interactions.

The severity and long-term effects of trauma experienced by children will depend to a large extent on the support they receive. For this reason, it's vital for early childhood educators to be able to recognize the signs of trauma and to encourage families to access the help that they require. Today, many educational and social service organizations use the term *trauma informed*, which infers that they are aware of the impact of trauma and apply this knowledge in a way that will meet the developmental needs of the children in their care. Early childhood educators, like other professionals involved with the family, can help children and families understand expected and normal trauma reactions, and identify and use their existing coping skills. As well, and importantly, they know when to encourage families to seek additional help.

The American Psychological Association (APA) provides tips about children and trauma for mental health professionals (American Psychological Association, 2017a). The APA emphasizes the fact that many children will suffer from a traumatic event in childhood, after which almost all will suffer from acute distress. It also notes that the reaction of family members who are also affected by the trauma impacts the children and that while many children do recover, many others require professional help. Early childhood professionals can help children and their families who experience trauma by

- identifying signs of trauma in children and providing culturally appropriate support;
- helping families and children make connections for professional support and intervention;
- providing education and hope;
- gradually re-establishing normal roles and routines;
- allowing children to express their feelings and listening carefully to the child and family; and
- asking about and respecting cultural and spiritual perspectives on trauma, reactions, and interventions.

At the same time, the APA (2017a) recommends taking care not to assume that all children will respond to trauma in the same way, or to assume that all trauma results in long-term psychological damage. Moreover, while early childhood professionals need to listen carefully to a child who wants to talk about a trauma he or she experienced, they should never force a child to do so.

It's important to recognize that often in communities where children have experienced trauma, so too have the adults in the same community, including the early childhood educators. So it's vital for early childhood educators to take care of themselves, and to seek professional or spiritual guidance as needed.

A STRENGTHS-BASED PERSPECTIVE FOR WORKING WITH FAMILIES

Most professionals who work with families today recognize how important it is to focus on "what works for the child (or his family)" rather than "what is wrong with the child (or her family)." In the past, when professionals were consulted about a problem, they would first identify "deficits" or "needs" that needed to be addressed or fixed. A 1989 quote by Ron Kral states a well-known truth that professionals sometimes forget: "If we ask people to look for deficits, they will usually find them, and their view of the situation will be colored by this. If we ask people to look for successes, they will usually find it, and their view of the situation will be colored by this" (as cited in Resiliency Initiatives, 2011).

The strengths-based approach stems from positive psychology, which is a perspective that emphasizes the strengths, capabilities, and resources of children, youth, and families. Rather than emphasizing problems or deficits, it looks at internal strengths and resources that can help meet life's challenges. As noted by experts in the field, "it is important to understand the strength-based perspective is not about denying that [there are] . . . problems and challenges and that these issues need to be addressed" (Resiliency Initiatives,

2011, p. 2). Instead, it is about believing that most children and families hold the key to the positive changes that are required for addressing problems.

As you learn more about different kinds of families, the challenges they face, and strategies to provide them with support, it's important to consider what you learn through a lens that recognizes families' strengths. The main components of strengths-based practice include the following:

- Every member of the family has strengths that can be developed, built on, and channelled in a direction that is positive for the family.
- Everyone has the potential for growth and change within a supportive environment.
- Most parents want to be good parents.
- Hardships can be challenging for families, but those hardships can also be an opportunity for growth and positive change.

CONCLUSION

This chapter has outlined some of the theoretical definitions and concepts of families to provide a framework for the information contained in the rest of this book. These perspectives may help us gain a deeper understanding of the families we engage in. At even the most basic level, for example, understanding that families are systems and that what happens to one member can impact the entire family may both increase our empathy and our ability to support families who are experiencing stress. The ecological model shows us the importance of engagement in community and policy issues connected to the well-being of children. Intersectionality illustrates the complexities confronting families who face multiple barriers. As well, an understanding of children's and adults' responses to change, loss, and trauma has become essential for early childhood professionals. One of the most important perspectives for engaging with families relates to resilience. This topic is of such major importance to early childhood educators that we have devoted an entire chapter to it (Chapter 4).

Chapter Summary

- A systems approach to families sees the family as a system distinct from its environment, with a boundary that separates it from the environment, and with each part influenced by other parts.
- An ecological approach considers families in the context of microsystem, mesosystem, exosystem, macrosystem, and chronosystem.
- The experiences of families and children must be considered from the perspective of multiple layers. Intersectionality is an approach that helps us to better understand the many layers of complex challenges that families can face.
- Though loss and change are a part of life, understanding the processes involved and the impact on children and families can help early childhood professionals in providing appropriate support.
- Many Canadian children and families have experienced trauma. *Trauma* is defined as a physical or psychological threat or assault to a child's sense of self, safety, or survival or to the safety of another person significant to the child.

- The strengths-based approach stems from positive psychology, a perspective that emphasizes the strengths, capabilities, and resources of children, youth, and families. Rather than emphasizing problems or deficits, it looks at internal strengths and resources that can help meet life's challenges.
- Early childhood programs that work in mutually supportive relationships with families provide better support to children. Effective work with families requires an understanding and appreciation of families in all their diversity.

RESOURCES

The Canadian Council on Social Development (CCSD) is one of Canada's most authoritative voices promoting better social and economic security for all Canadians:
www.ccsd.ca/factsheets

Canadian Association of Family Resource Programs, "The Guiding Principles of Family Support":
www.frp.ca/_data/global/images/resources/guiding-e.pdf

Canadian Child Care Foundation:
www.cccf-fcsge.ca

National Association for the Education of Young Children:
www.naeyc.org

Statistics Canada:
www.statcan.gc.ca/eng/start

Vanier Institute of the Family:
http://vanierinstitute.ca

American Psychological Association, "Children and Trauma: Tips for Mental Health Professionals":
www.apa.org/pi/families/resources/children-trauma-tips.aspx

EXERCISES

1. What were the spoken and unspoken rules in your family? How did you learn about the unspoken rules?

2. How do you think your views and experiences affect your work with families?

3. Describe a possible role of the early childhood educator that relates to the microsystem, mesosystem, exosystem, and macrosystem.

4. Identify the many layers that a child may experience with the birth of a new sibling or addition of a step sibling into the family. How might each of these affect the child? The parent? The relationship between the child and the parent?

5. Loss is a very personal experience, and everyone responds to it in a unique way. However, Kübler-Ross identified five stages in the response to loss that seem to be quite universal. Do you think that these stages are congruent with losses that you might have experienced? How can knowing about these stages help? Or can it?

6. What resources are you aware of in your community that support children and families who have experienced trauma?

7. What would be the difference between a strengths-based approach and a deficit-based approach to a problem such as "Tommy comes to preschool late almost every day and misses the morning activity"?

CHAPTER 4

Resilience

OBJECTIVES

- To gain an understanding of the crucial role of resilience in children and families

- To gain an understanding of the role of educators in promoting resilience in children

- To gain an understanding of the role educators play in helping families develop strategies for resilience

- To understand how educators can provide support to strengthen families

Jorge grew up in a family with two siblings and his parents. His father was an alcoholic until all three children were in their teens. They dealt with periods of poverty, unemployment, fighting, and arguing as they grew up. Jorge reflected on these experiences as an adult and talked about how they helped to make him stronger: he learned to be more independent, to know whom to approach to get his needs met, and where he could go to escape the chaos in his house. Yet, he said, his older brother never seemed to be able to cope. "He was always having trouble at school, which caused more fighting and arguing at home. He has had trouble in relationships, and his marriage is falling apart. His last counsellor told him it was partly because of his mother and parenting when he was little," Jorge said. However, Jorge thought, "I had the same mother and father and lived in the same house with the same issues and I'm okay." He ended by saying, "I think this is what resilience is and what resilience looks like."

WHAT RESILIENCE MEANS

The concept of resilience provides a useful starting point for understanding the educator's role in helping children cope with difficult situations. Resilience has existed as a concept in education for many years, and there have been many programs to promote resilience in children. Understanding resilience and the characteristics associated with it may help educators support the children in their care, especially when the child or family is dealing with challenges. However, it should be noted that promoting resilience is not reserved only for times when children are experiencing challenges; promoting resilience in everyday practice can help children cope with difficult situations better, whatever those situations may be.

The term *resilience* has been defined as the ability to bounce back or cope in the face of adversity. Although it varies in different contexts, it's marked by the ability to persevere and adapt when things don't go as expected (Hall & Pearson, 2007). Resilience includes the capacity to cope with adversity or risk. Resilience helps people deal with stress and challenges in their daily lives. We cannot prevent challenges or stress for the children we work with, but we can help them deal with it in more positive ways. Research suggests that resilient people are healthier, more successful at school and work, and generally happier and less prone to depression (Hall & Pearson, 2007; Pearson & Kordich Hall, 2006). Thinking plays a large part in resilience. How we think about the daily challenges and stress in our lives can make a difference in how we cope with them. Although we may not be able to control challenges (e.g., bills, hours of child care), we can control how we think about them. If we feel helpless, we may just give up. However, if we feel that we can overcome the situation, we will find ways to cope. These skills of resilience can be learned.

Continuing research serves to further clarify what resilience is and how it may be developed. For the purposes of this text, we have focused on the definition and concepts currently used by the Reaching IN . . . Reaching OUT (RIRO) program (www.reachinginreachingout.com/aboutresilience.htm). This organization provides an abundance of information specific to young children and their educators.

UNDERSTANDING THE MEANING OF RESILIENCE

Resilience is often conceptualized as a balance of risk factors and protective factors. *Protective factors* are those qualities or situations that help to deal with expected negative outcomes. Resilience can be promoted by providing and nurturing these qualities or by providing these types of situations. *Risk factors* are those that have the potential to cause difficulty, either short term or long term. These can be cultural, economic, disabling, or health conditions that limit opportunities for optimal development. These factors can be thought of from the perspective of the child, the family, or the community.

Protective Factors

Protective factors can be *intrinsic* (i.e., existing within the child) or *extrinsic* (i.e., existing in the child's environment). Intrinsic factors tend to include personality, temperamental traits, and abilities. While it is possible to change and develop abilities (e.g., communication skills, problem-solving skills), changing one's temperament and personality may be more difficult, although individuals can come to understand them better and so better cope.

SCENARIO

GETTING TO KNOW YOURSELF

When learning about temperament in class, one student provided this example. She was always "shy," and new situations caused her much anxiety. However, she knew she wanted to work with children and families and that she had to develop strategies to overcome her tendency to withdraw from social situations. She practised ways to engage with others by setting goals for herself (e.g., I will start a conversation with a new parent, I will speak with a parent that I experienced challenges with, and I will ask my supervisor for a change of shift). These small goals and practice helped her change her temperament and her view of herself. She now says she used to be shy.

Protective factors may exist within the child, the family, and the community, and include the following:

Child

- Sense of being loved
- Sense of belonging
- Self-esteem
- Empathy
- Sense of control
- Cognitive and reasoning skills
- Social skills
- Good communication skills

Family

- Trusting relationships
- Supportive relationships
- Parental monitoring
- Financial security

Community

- Access to supportive caring communities—child care and schools
- Positive child-care and school experiences
- Educators as caring role models
- Availability of social activities with caring adults
- Positive peer influences

Resilience research indicates that during the early childhood years, it's important for children to have good-quality care—including opportunities for learning, adequate nutrition, and

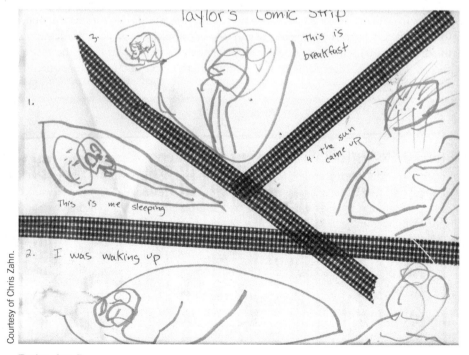

Courtesy of Chris Zahn.

Taylor, Age 5

community support for families—to facilitate positive development of cognitive, social, and self-regulation skills. The foundation of the Strengthening Families approach (Center for the Study of Social Policy, 2017) focuses on building resilience in parents and families. In early childhood, it is particularly important that children have the protections afforded by attachment bonds with competent and loving caregivers, the stimulation and nutrition required for healthy brain development, opportunities to learn and experience the pleasure of mastering new skills, and the limit-setting or structure needed to develop self-control (Masten & Gewirtz, 2006).

Risk Factors

Risk factors are those that may cause difficulties or put the child at higher risk. Risk factors may exist within the child, the family, and the community, and include the following:

Child

- Poor nutrition
- Poor physical health
- Low self-esteem
- Developmental delays
- Delayed communication

Family

- Unstable family relationships
- Poor attachment
- Lack of support from mothers or fathers
- Poverty
- Mental health issues

Community

- Lack of access to health care
- Social isolation
- Lack of access to resources
- Lack of available green spaces

SCENARIO

THE IMPACT OF THE ENVIRONMENT

Maria had a friend, Rose, who lived in California. They were roommates at school and kept in close contact after they graduated and had families. Rose came to visit in the middle of winter. The weather was extremely cold and miserable, and Maria told Rose that her children were grumpy and restless because it had been too cold to go outside all week. Rose asked if there were higher rates of child abuse here. Maria was surprised by the question and asked Rose why she would think this. Rose replied, "Well, at home, if the children are getting overly rambunctious or grouchy, they just go outside and blow off some steam and I have a bit of break. How do you or the children get that kind of break here?" Maria realized that the environment may impact how we interact with children.

Resilience involves the balancing of stressful life events or risk factors with protective factors (Gonzalez-Mena, 2002). To reduce risk factors, early childhood educators need to first understand the risks that exist with a particular child or family and then to try, as much as possible, to help alleviate those risks. Reducing risk factors may be as simple as helping parents find child care after hours, or it may involve accessing community support services for parents and families. Early childhood educators may not be able to solve some of the difficulties or resolve all of the risks, of course, but they may be able to provide parents with resources so that they can better cope with the stresses they may be experiencing. Sometimes, it may be sufficient for educators to simply understand the situation and provide a little support or understanding (e.g., if a parent forgets something or a child is late). Early childhood educators can also play a role by knowing the community resources that are available and advocating for community supports for children and families.

Educators play a significant role in supporting children to develop resilience in their thinking through modelling. Educators who intentionally model resilient thinking when they interact with children can promote the development of this type of thinking in children. In fact, researchers point to just how crucial adult modelling is. Children 2 and 3 years old are able to mimic the thinking styles of primary caregivers around them. By 8 years of age, most children have already developed a thinking style, or habitual way of responding to stressors (Hall & Pearson, 2007, p. 12).

Creating an environment of resilience will support resilience in children and families.

SCENARIO

BEING FLEXIBLE

The children in Martha's playroom had planned an outing, which included a picnic, to a local park. Everyone was excited about the outing and had enthusiastically engaged in the planning. On the morning of the outing, Martha called in sick due to the sudden onset of the stomach flu. The other educator and relief person felt unprepared to take on the outing, and the program director would not allow the trip to the local park without Martha. However, rather than cancel the outing altogether, the program director and educators decided to plan an outing and picnic in the office tower in which the child-care program was located. The educators and children explored different floors and displays in different parts of the building. They also had a picnic in a small atrium on one of the floors. The educators took pictures to document the outing, and when the children returned to the playroom, they drew pictures about their adventures. Rather than forgo the outing, the director and educators adapted and created an opportunity for the plans to proceed within their limitations. By doing so, they demonstrated flexible thinking and how to make changes when things happen that are out of your control.

The other factor in resilience is enhancing protective factors (Drummond, Kysela, McDonald, Alexander, & Fleming, 1998; National Child Traumatic Stress Network, 2017). As stated earlier, protective factors may be developed within the individual (e.g., by promoting health, self-esteem, self-efficacy, a feeling of control, social competence), within families (e.g., by developing communication and effective parenting, providing supports or coping strategies), and within communities (e.g., by developing a sense of community, increasing access to services). Resilience can be enhanced by helping to develop protective factors while attempting to control or decrease existing risk factors.

Early childhood educators (like educators for older children) have a crucial role in facilitating the development of protective factors in children. Using modelling and resilient thinking skills in daily interactions with children has been shown to promote the development of resilient thinking in children (Hall & Pearson, 2003; Masten & Coatsworth, 1998). Research suggests that the skills associated with resilient thinking can be learned at an early age. "It is thinking style that determines resilience—more than genetics, more than intelligence, more than any other single factor" (Hall & Pearson, 2003, p. 3). Educators can assist children in identifying their feelings, communicating their feelings, calming themselves, and putting challenges into perspective.

SCENARIO

BEING RESILIENT

In a preschool program for vulnerable children, the educators taught the young children a variety of different ways to deal with their emotions. Many of the techniques were relaxation-type exercises suited to young children. When a child was frustrated or angry, they taught the child to blow up a pretend balloon. After the technique was taught, the educators made themselves available in the playroom to practise this relaxation exercise in the moment. Practice started with the educator handing the child a pretend balloon, asking the child to slowly blow it up and then slowly release the air. The balloon would be put back in the educator's or child's pocket for the next time it was needed.

Four-year-old Cyrus had learned to use this technique on his own and only needed occasional prompts from the educator to remind him to use the balloon. One day his mom came to pick him up at the end of the day. She had had a very bad day at work, got caught in traffic, and was frazzled. She was short with Cyrus in getting ready and finally snapped at him. Cyrus looked up at her and said, "Here, Mom," handing her the pretend balloon. "I think you need this," he said, and proceeded to show her how to blow up the balloon.

Next we will review the characteristics associated with resilience in more detail so that educators can feel more comfortable in developing and promoting these protective factors.

CHARACTERISTICS OF RESILIENCE

Researchers have identified several key factors associated with resilience:

- Availability of someone special in a trusting relationship
- Temperamental or personality characteristics of the child
- Ability of the child to seek out someone to help
- Children who tend to view experiences positively and constructively
- Children who have been needed by others
- Warm, secure family relationships
- Supportive, predictable environments
- Development of coping strategies
- Individuals who listen
- Children who have a sense of control over their own lives and are provided some degree of control

As you can see, a number of factors are associated with resilience. Some are personality or temperamental characteristics, and some are abilities or skills that educators can help to develop, which will be our focus. However, it's important to remember that one key factor discussed over and over is the availability of someone who has a special relationship with the child. This person may be a parent, a sibling, an extended family member, a teacher, a coach, or an educator. You may be the special person in a child's life who provides the foundation for resilience—what a privilege and what a responsibility! In your everyday interaction with children, this point is important to remember so that you'll always be mindful of what children need and will be prepared to provide it to them.

The key abilities associated with resilience that can be enhanced or promoted include the following:

- *Emotional regulation* is the ability to manage children's emotions so that they can remain calm and in control. The expression of emotions, both positive and negative, is important. Emotional regulation does not mean that children keep negative emotions bottled up. It means that they learn how to express emotions, especially negative ones, in an appropriate and responsible way. Children can learn to be in charge of their emotions. Children begin to learn to calm and soothe themselves at an early age by sucking their thumb or by seeking out their blanket. As children grow and develop, they begin to understand more about their feelings and begin to express themselves in more ways (e.g., more than just crying). They need to learn that some ways of expressing themselves are not acceptable even though the feeling may be very real. Children need to understand the feelings they experience (e.g., anger), but they also need to know the limits for expressing those feelings (e.g., it's not okay to throw the toy or hit someone). Educators and parents play a huge role in helping children develop emotional control. Educators can help children identify their emotions and name them and can teach strategies to deal with stress (e.g., blowing up a balloon or blowing out candles).

  Impulse control is related to emotional regulation (when a child doesn't get what he or she wants, strong emotions often follow). It consists of being able to manage our urges and make a choice about the next step. Impulse control helps us learn to delay gratification. Children need to learn to wait for something that they want or see. Young children will see an object or food item and want it immediately (e.g., a candy bar in a grocery store), but they must learn to wait. Teaching children to control their impulses can be very difficult—just ask the parent of a toddler! Educators can help children control their impulses and desires and choose a better way to express themselves. They can also show restraint in their own behaviour and help children divert their attention while waiting (Hall & Pearson, 2007).

- *Problem solving* is the way in which children work through the challenges in their lives. It includes a number of skills and takes a long time to develop. Research suggests that our thoughts about what caused a problem will determine how we respond to it. Children can learn to analyze problems and determine what the cause is so that they can take action. Children will need to learn a wide range of social and communication skills to solve problems effectively. Educators and parents can help children first understand the dimensions of a problem, acknowledge the associated emotions that the child experiences, offer different ways of looking at the problem, and ultimately find reasonable ways to solve the problem. This includes acknowledging the child's feelings, accepting the feelings but putting limits on actions, defining the problem clearly for the child, and helping the child determine possible solutions and then try them out. Educators are often quick to stop behaviours from escalating by taking a toy away or by separating children when they are in conflict. Sometimes, stepping in and using the opportunity to teach problem solving can be very beneficial. However, educators will likely agree that there aren't enough hours in the day to do so every time a problem or difficulty arises. While this may be true, it's still important for educators and parents to capitalize on these moments as often as possible.

- *Self-confidence* involves children having a strong but realistic belief in themselves and their abilities. It includes feeling valued and loved, having a sense of belonging and acceptance, and having self-efficacy, or the belief that what one does matters (Hall & Pearson, 2006). This self-confidence begins early when we give children choices so that they learn they have control over what they do. When children succeed at making good choices, their confidence grows. As a result, they develop the belief that they are capable of solving problems. Educators and parents can foster a sense of self-confidence in multiple ways throughout the child's life. Self-confidence is important because it facilitates coping with challenges and maintaining a positive view of the world.

- *A sense of optimism* has also been associated with resilience (Hall & Pearson, 2007). Optimism is the ability to maintain a positive outlook and believing that you can make the best out of a situation. It develops when children have self-confidence and believe that they can make choices, control their behaviour, and solve problems effectively.

- *Empathy* involves understanding the feelings or needs of others. Adults often think that children are not capable of empathy since they are egocentric and think they are the centre of the universe. While it is true that young children are egocentric, they do learn to see other perspectives and are better able to understand that others have feelings and needs that may be different from their own. Adults can promote the development of empathy by helping children identify and express emotions in themselves and others and by modelling empathy. When children see adults responding to and comforting other children, they are learning empathy.

- *Seeking support.* One last characteristic associated with resilience is the child's ability to seek support when he or she needs it. Children need to learn to reach out for new opportunities and to take risks. They need to learn that making mistakes is inevitable and part of learning. Educators can demonstrate how they cope and fix their own mistakes and can normalize mistakes with children (e.g., Everyone spills their milk once in a while. What can we do about it?) When children are able to seize these opportunities, it will become easier for them to seek support and guidance when they are struggling. The ability to seek out and ask for help when it is needed is a key feature of resilience. Educators and parents can model this skill and support it in children. In addition, children need to learn to ask in appropriate ways. For example, adults often have a low tolerance for children who whine, but these children may have real concerns and difficulties, and may need to learn how to express their needs to better access support.

THE ROLE OF THE EARLY CHILDHOOD EDUCATOR

The role of good-quality child care has been consistently discussed as one potential solution to serving children at risk. This trend involving the role of child care in healthy development must be taken seriously by educators, since good-quality child care can bring long-lasting benefits to children and families.

Your role as an educator in regard to resilience is embedded in your practice and is complex. Educators intentionally create opportunities to build resilience in children and parents and seize moments as they happen. The following two scenarios will illustrate these complex roles.

SCENARIO

CREATING OPPORTUNITIES TO DEVELOP RESILIENCE IN CHILDREN

Aziza had been an art teacher for several years, and then moved into the role of educator in an early learning setting. At the beginning of the school year, she spent a lot of time planning creative activities for the children. After reflecting on her environment through the lens of an early learning framework, she decided to create an open art centre for the children that would be fully available for the morning and afternoon programs. At the end of the school year, Aziza reflected on the significant effect the art centre had had on the children. One example stood out. Four-year-old Sabine had been adopted early in the school year. Sabine spent a lot of time at the open art centre, where she drew a number of pictures about her adoption. Over the year, she had drawn pictures of her old foster family, the move, and her new family. Her feelings were part of the pictures (from dark, nondescript images to colourful pictures with flowers and sunshine). Her adoptive parents and

continues ▶

► *continues*

social worker had commented on the ease of the transition, and Aziza wondered what role the open access art centre had played. Although the change to the early learning environment was not made for this child specifically, the impact on her major life transition was significant.

SCENARIO

SUPPORTING PARENTS IN BUILDING RESILIENCE

As the director of a diverse child-care and preschool program, Madeline had spent considerable time working with a team to support children with special needs, from early identification to implementing learning supports. Very often, she was frustrated by parents who blocked any involvement with the support team, as parent consent was a prerequisite to any support. Madeline worked closely with the team coordinator to develop a parent workshop on children who display challenging behaviours as a forum to discuss development. All parents with children in preschool and child care were invited to the workshop. Madeline also extended a personal invitation to the parents of children whose behaviour had raised concerns. These special invitations could only be made based on the trusting relationship she had created with parents.

The preceding two scenarios illustrate the multifaceted role of the educator. In the first, a review of time, space, and materials led a preschool teacher to provide a space for children to work through events in their lives through art, creating opportunities for them to build resilience. In the second, a director worked intentionally to create an opportunity to help build parents' resilience.

Educators are in a key position to support the development of resilience, not only in children but also in families. Of course, educators aren't limited to the ideas in the preceding scenarios. It is hoped that this chapter will help you think about your role in building resilience in children and families so that as you progress through the chapters, you may focus on developing resilience in your practice. In addition, it should be noted that resilience is part of the development of many other skills you support every day, including communication skills, social skills (e.g., working through problems in friendships), and building attachments.

Perspectives

Educators are in a unique position to promote resilience. Since children's relationships are key to their developing a range of social skills (e.g., interpersonal communication, regulating emotions, empathy), your relationship may serve as a protective factor for a child experiencing adverse conditions (e.g., poverty, neglect). The following guidelines may be helpful in fostering resilience (Hall & Pearson, 2007):

■ **Learn to identify risk factors and protective factors.** Educators can become aware of and try to alleviate risk factors in children or families and promote protective factors. For example, they can focus on enhancing children's social competence by noticing and listening to children, by acknowledging children's feelings, and by structuring activities for cooperation rather than competition.

■ **Model coping behaviours.** Remember the impact of modelling: children develop resilience and associated skills by watching how adults in their world cope with problems and adversity. Adults can talk about their thoughts and feelings (e.g., "OW! I shut my finger in the cupboard door and it hurts! I'm angry!"). Then adults can model how to calm themselves down (e.g., taking a deep breath, taking care of the problem, finding a way to settle down).

■ **Teach social skills to make connections and gain support.** Helping children express their feelings and emotions begins with children understanding their own emotions and putting labels to them. It continues when children learn to understand how those feelings feel and then learn ways to cope with them (hopefully, appropriate ways).

- **Help children differentiate between reality and fantasy as they become developmentally ready to understand.** Use short but accurate explanations. Art, stories and books, and dramatic play can be used to promote discussion with children about complex and emotionally laden issues.

- **Become a special, caring person in the life of a young child.** Nonfamily members, such as teachers, coaches, and counsellors, can often cushion a child from the adverse effects of a disturbing family situation. The presence of an adult who provides sensitive caregiving has been linked with adaptive functioning later in life.

- **Practise responsive caregiving.** Provide opportunities for children to develop confidence in the support others provide, to develop confidence in themselves, to view themselves as worthy, and to experience a sense of mastery of their world. You can enhance the development of self-esteem by encouraging children to try and reinforcing their accomplishments (e.g., "I see that you shared the sand toys with Billie, and you both played so well together!"). The importance of this position cannot be overstated.

- **Give children responsibilities.** Give children chores or have them help care for younger children, plants, or animals (Gonzalez-Mena, 2002).

  Children need to experience mastery in their world. You can facilitate this experience by giving them choices, guiding them to make their own appropriate choices, and highlighting successes.

- **Help children develop problem-solving skills in daily interactions.** For example, use everyday situations to teach children to solve interpersonal problems when they come up. Although it's very tempting to take the toy away or separate children when they're not getting along, these are perfect occasions to teach children how to solve the problem themselves. It does take time

(which educators don't always have), but being aware of the opportunities and capturing these teachable moments will have far-reaching benefits.

- **Be a good source of information for the child.** Educators may be in a unique situation to provide information (e.g., why some mommies give their children up for adoption) in a clear and less emotional way, and to provide the child with support (e.g., suggesting a better way of dealing with the hurt than hitting or acting out).

  Use stories, songs, and puppets to help children understand and develop some of these concepts. Providing different ways of experiencing and understanding these complex concepts will enhance learning.

- **Support parents.** Educators can be instrumental in helping parents understand the child's view and providing support at home (e.g., helping the parent understand that the preschooler will ask over and over in an attempt to comprehend something, not because the child doesn't grasp it or because he or she is trying to drive the parent crazy, but because that's the stage the child is at). Educators will need to work together with parents as situations arise to ensure that the child comes to understand and learns to cope. Educators can provide parents with explanations that may be easy for the child to understand, supportive books, and activities they can try at home.

- **Engage in professional development.** Be prepared to deal with difficult situations, such as substance abuse in the family or your possible discomfort with homosexual parents.

- **Get support from friends, family, and professionals.** Dealing with difficult situations that may be encountered or witnessing children in distress takes an emotional toll on educators. You must protect yourself from overinvolvement and/or burnout by getting support for yourself.

Research (Hall & Pearson, 2006) has demonstrated that when early childhood educators understand resilience and plan their program around its concepts, they too derive benefits. A pilot study in which early childhood educators learned evidence-based resilience skills to use with young children found that these educators felt their approach and language changed after the training. Educators first focused on asking children about their feelings, and later asked them about their thinking; these educators were able to help children change their thinking about situations and find workable solutions. RIRO has developed strategies for working with young children and is an excellent resource for educators to use to enhance their own skill development. Other programs have been developed for use with older children and youth by the Resilience Research Centre at Dalhousie University (Resilience Research Centre, 2017).

FOSTERING RESILIENCE IN FAMILIES

As early childhood educators, understanding resilience can be of assistance in helping parents foster this quality in their children. Educators can promote resilience by supporting attachment between the parent and the child on a daily basis. For example, educators may find ways to ensure that families are represented in the program or to promote ways of communicating during the day or afterward. Parents too will learn by modelling the ways educators interact with children. For example, respectful approaches to encouraging children to cooperate will help support attachment between the parent and the child (especially on those days when everything has gone wrong).

Early childhood educators can also provide parents with resources to develop resilience. The RIRO website has an extensive list of children's books focused on resilience. These books could be used in the child-care program or referred to parents for use in particular situations, such as a new sibling, moving, separation, or divorce. Educators need to know when it's appropriate to use these books in the child-care centre as part of a group story-time, when to use them one on one, and when to suggest that the parent read the book to the child. Sometimes starting a difficult conversation with a storybook can work very well.

The RIRO program also has developed resources specifically geared to parents. In addition, there are many local and national parenting programs and online resources on resilience. For example, the Alberta Mental Health Board developed a series of resources for parents called *The Bounce Back Book: Building Resiliency Skills*. One book was developed for parents of infants and toddlers, one for preschoolers, and one for the early school years. The books provide readily understandable information about resilience and a series of ideas that parents can use in their daily interactions with children, primarily in the home environment. Parents and educators have found many excellent ideas in these books.

Early childhood educators can also play a role in reducing risk factors. This may be accomplished by knowing what community resources and supports are offered and by making this information available to parents. Many of the ideas discussed in Chapter 5, which focuses on parent engagement, will also provide opportunities for families to develop the skills associated with resilience.

THE STRENGTHENING FAMILIES APPROACH

The "Strengthening Families" approach (Center for the Study of Social Policy, 2017) is currently being used by many early childhood programs across Canada. It has a strengths-based focus and is but one of many programs of this nature.

Strengthening Families is founded on building protective and promotive factors; using an approach instead of a model, program, or curriculum; changing the relationship with parents; and aligning practice with developmental science (Center for the Study of Social Policy, 2015). This approach is meant to be integrated in practice with young children and their families. Fundamental to the approach is the idea of engaging families through mutually supportive relationships and through the program (Center for the Study of Social Policy, 2017).

The Strengthening Families approach focuses on engaging programs and families in building five key protective factors:

- Parental resilience
- Social connections
- Knowledge of parenting and child development
- Concrete support in times of need
- Social and emotional competence of children (Center for the Study of Social Policy, 2017)

Parental resilience is fostered when educators honour and value parents in daily interactions. It is further fostered when educators support parents, especially in times of stress. *Social connections* are built on positive relationships that provide support to parents and families. These positive relationships may become the catalyst for developing skills parents need for parenting. *Knowledge of parenting and child development* may be nurtured when parents witness positive practice or when they gain specific knowledge. When educators provide support to families in times of stress or crisis, they are providing *concrete support in times of need*. This support may include providing an extra bit of child care or information on community-based supports. The *social and emotional competence of children* is built through modelling and positive program practices that help children develop skills.

In our relationship-based practice, it's easy to see where multiple opportunities to work with and alongside parents can emerge. We can also see where our interactions with children can provide a way to support parents. Although many of these interactions happen naturally in our everyday practice, as professionals we may need to be intentional about creating these opportunities, especially when children or families are experiencing times of stress.

CONCLUSION

Resilience, as a concept in education, has been around for quite some time. More recently, educators have considered how resilience can be incorporated into programs for young children, since research has shown that resilience can be fostered in the early years. This has led to the development of strength-based approaches in working with children and families and has provided further ideas for working with families.

Chapter Summary

- Resilience is the ability to cope or bounce back.
- Resilience involves the balancing of protective factors and risk factors.
- Protective factors may be intrinsic (e.g., personality, abilities) or extrinsic (e.g., in the environment, the community).
- Many of the skills associated with resilience can be fostered in children or individuals, families, and communities.
- As part of good child-care practices, educators may intentionally help promote a number of key capabilities associated with resilience in young children. Educators may help foster resilience in times of stress as well.
- Early childhood educators may also foster resilience in families and parents by supporting them in minimizing risk factors (e.g., by providing a stable environment) or increasing protective factors (e.g., by modelling good child-care practices).

RESOURCES

Resilience Research Centre:
www.resilienceproject.org

Encyclopedia on Early Childhood Development, "Resilience":
www.child-encyclopedia.com/en-ca/child-resilience/perspectives.html?RId=CA

Reaching IN . . . Reaching OUT (RIRO):
www.reachinginreachingout.com

Reaching IN . . . Reaching OUT (RIRO), "Skills Videos":
www.reachinginreachingout.com/resources-skillsvideo.htm

American Psychological Association, "The Road to Resilience":
www.apa.org/helpcenter/road-resilience.aspx

National Child Traumatic Stress Network, "Protective Factors: Enhancing Resilience in Young Children and Families":
www.nctsn.org/content/protective-factors-enhancing-resilience-young-children-and-families

Center for the Study of Social Policy, "Strengthening Families":
www.cssp.org/reform/strengtheningfamilies

Devereux Center for Resilient Children, "Promoting Resilience in Infants and Toddlers—Webinar":
www.youtube.com/watch?v=FfBe68C7s8Q

EXERCISES

1. Check the RIRO website for checklists focused on resilience. Complete one of the checklists to better understand your coping skills. Share the results with a classmate or colleague.

2. Consider all the ways in which you promote resilience during a typical day. How do you foster protective factors? How do you decrease risk factors for the children in your care?

3. Develop a list of ways that you can promote resilience in children. For example, how can you teach emotional regulation, sharing, and cooperation? How can you teach children to communicate their needs and desires appropriately? How can promoting resilience be part of your intentional practice with children?

4. Develop a list of ways that you can support parents in promoting resilience in their children. For example, what resilient behaviours can you model? What skills can you support parents with? What useful information can you provide to parents?

5. Check community resources that might help families to (a) reduce risk factors (e.g., clothing or toy swaps, babysitting co-ops), and (b) improve protective factors (e.g., free recreational activities so that families can spend time together; equipment swaps so that children can be involved in sports).

PART TWO

Engaging with Families

CHAPTER 5
Understanding Parent Engagement

CHAPTER 6
Enhancing Parent–Educator Engagement

CHAPTER 7
Resolving Conflicts and Tensions

Early childhood educators have long recognized the importance and relevance of working with parents. The need to maintain positive parent–early childhood educator relationships has been studied and well documented in the literature. Engaging with parents and families in meaningful ways is critical to strengthening families and providing support critical to the child's development in the early years. Collaborating with parents provides one way of promoting resilience—by helping minimize risks (e.g., through observations and documentation, modelling techniques and approaches) and by strengthening protective factors (e.g., accessing community supports for families). This section provides theoretical and practical knowledge focused specifically on collaborating with parents.

Chapter 5 examines different perspectives on parent engagement. This examination provides a conceptual framework that will help early childhood educators reflect on their own beliefs and develop practices aligned with their beliefs.

Chapter 6 provides a range of practical suggestions for collaborating with parents and families. This information will be helpful when educators want to determine the activities that may be most meaningful to a particular group of parents.

Chapter 7 examines the potential sources of conflict and tension that can exist between parents and early childhood educators. Guidelines for preventing and resolving conflicts are presented. However, educators need to remember that building meaningful relationships is the foundation to healthy relationships and that recognizing tension and its sources can be the first step toward resolution. The chapter ends with ideas focused on caring for the educator, as it is recognized that teaching can be demanding.

CHAPTER 5
Understanding Parent Engagement

OBJECTIVES

- To understand the importance and meaning of parent engagement

- To discuss the concept of parent education

- To discuss the issues related to parental influence and control

- To examine the importance of continuity of care

- To consider the importance of supporting and empowering parents

- To consider the family-centred approach as part of practice

- To view parent engagement in the context of relevant theoretical perspectives

"I was an early childhood educator and a director in a child-care centre for several years and thought that I was quite an expert on parent engagement. Then I had my first baby and joined the ranks of all the struggling parents who juggle work, child care, and family. Parent engagement took on a very different meaning for me after I became a parent and experienced the world from a different perspective."

THE IMPORTANCE OF PARENT ENGAGEMENT

Working with families, especially with parents, has always been widely accepted among early childhood educators as "an integral aspect of the early childhood teacher's job" (Galinsky, 1990, p. 2). The National Association for the Education of Young Children (NAEYC) continues to support the notion that working with families is the cornerstone of practice. In addition, the Canadian Child Care Federation (CCCF) (2008) continues to cite the critical importance of partnerships with parents in practice. Most education programs for early childhood educators, and most early childhood textbooks, contain at least one unit on working with parents. As well, close relationships between early childhood educators and parents improve the quality of care (Baker & Manfredi-Petitt, 2004) and are important in the prevention of problems (Wilson, 2010). Research continues to tell us that family involvement is a crucial component in children's healthy development and the prevention of developmental or educational delays (Wilson, 2014). Yet many early childhood educators admit that working with parents is frequently the most frustrating part of their job and the aspect they feel most unprepared for (Ebbeck & Waniganayake, 2003; Eldridge, 2001; Wilson, 2010).

Family-centred practice, strengths-based or relationship-based practice, partnership with parents, collaboration with parents, and *parent involvement* are but a few of the terms we see repeatedly in the professional literature. The term *parent involvement* has tended to be associated with one-way approaches to working with parents (e.g., educators providing parents with information or parents controlling the centre). Approaches that use family-centred, partnership, and collaborative terms tend to focus on sharing information and to recognize the strengths that parents and educators bring to their relationship. "Joint responsibility between parents and educators is an important difference maker when it comes to the developmental progress of children. Outreach to parents can be informal, but some parents will need to be brought into the process through flexible program models that support a two-way relationship" (Pascal, 2009, p. 29).

Before we accept that we should work with parents, we should be able to answer three basic questions:

- What specifically are we attempting to achieve in our work with parents?
- What is the purpose to work toward these particular goals?
- What strategies can we use to achieve these goals?

A historical perspective can reveal to us where many of today's assumptions come from. Sometimes we accept models that worked in the past but that may not be appropriate under today's social conditions. For example, a common strategy for working with parents in the 1960s was to make home visits. Many well-researched programs (Bromwich, 1981; Lombard, 1994) demonstrated the effectiveness of early childhood educators who provided education and support to parents through regular home visits. Most of these programs, though, were designed to serve families whose children were at risk of school failure because of environmental factors or handicapping conditions. Although past and present interest in home-visiting programs indicates that they can be successful in some circumstances, they may be more difficult for staff or parents in many child-care centres. Most parents with children in child care work during the day, and it can be difficult for educators to be available for home visits in the evening.

In the same way, many model early childhood programs that were begun in the 1970s included a parent-involvement component in which parents would regularly participate in a preschool setting as volunteers or as paid aides (Katz, 1994). Although this strategy has many potential benefits, it may not be feasible for many working parents to attend a child-care setting regularly unless their work schedules are extremely flexible. Many preschool programs have abandoned the requirement that parents volunteer on a regular basis due to changes in the family.

As responsible early childhood educators, then, we need to understand the approaches and strategies that have been used in the past and then carefully evaluate both the appropriateness and the effectiveness of different ways of working with families. To do this properly, we have to examine the usefulness of each proposed strategy from the perspective of staff, children, and parents.

DEFINING PARENT ENGAGEMENT

In this edition, we have chosen to focus on *parent engagement* rather than *parent involvement*. *Parent engagement* is a broad-based term that encompasses the many ways that educators interact with the families of children they work with. It is based on a reciprocal relationship with families built on a foundation of respect and sharing. It is meant to be more open ended in an attempt to meet the diverse needs of children and families in our care. It provides permission to use a multifaceted rather than a single approach to addressing the needs of children and families within the context of the program and its parameters. Some educators advocate for the use of technology to promote communication between "busy" parents and program staff. Others believe that face-to-face contact with parents is paramount in developing and maintaining relationships. Both approaches—and others—are useful in educator–parent relations.

This chapter will focus on the many ways that educators can interact with and support families. Although many approaches have particular roots, educators can adopt and adapt approaches to fit the needs of their children and families. For example, home visits have roots in the Project Head Start movement, but they are used in programs in intentional ways to engage children and families of a variety of socio-economic backgrounds.

Educators work within a practice of relationships. Within this practice, "the educator demonstrates care, respect, honour, sharing and thoughtful listening to gain knowledge and appreciation of family, social, and cultural practices and traditions" (Makovichuk, Hewes, Lirette, & Thomas, 2014, p. 29). As a result, it's imperative that educators consider approaches to engage families and children in meaningful ways.

The socio-cultural perspective, embedded in the curriculum framework of early childhood education, has guided the evolution of concepts and practices related to working with parents from early practices to what is considered current quality practice today. The socio-cultural perspective has become prevalent in current early learning frameworks (Makovichuk et al., 2014). This perspective is built upon the theories of Lev Vygotsky, who proposed that social and cultural processes shape all aspects of development. Vygotsky's perspective "sees learning as a context-dependent, socially mediated process that results in development" (p. 273). In addition to theories of individual growth and development as the foundation of practice, early learning educators understand the influence of social context. Hence, the child in the context of the family provides powerful learning opportunities and increases the value of engaging families. Reggio Emilia Aotearoa New Zealand provides a framework for working with families based on these philosophical ideas, as does the te whāriki national early childhood curriculum in New Zealand. The question "What is your image of the family?" is relevant to educators, as is "What is your image of the child?" Although specific practices may vary, the foundation of respect for families is the same in all approaches.

Courtesy of Chris Zahn.

Taylor, Age 5

FROM PARENT INVOLVEMENT TO PARENT ENGAGEMENT

Most of the literature on parent involvement relates to four main goals: (1) to educate parents, (2) to provide parents with the opportunity to influence or control the programs in which their children are involved, (3) to provide for the greatest possible continuity of care between home and centre, and (4) to empower parents, a goal that was strongly encouraged by experts in the 1980s and 1990s (Couchenour & Chrisman, 2011; Powell, 1989).

Underlying the goals of parent involvement was the desire to support parents in their child-rearing roles. Strategies for parent involvement aimed to benefit everyone in early childhood programs—children, parents, and staff alike.

›› Perspectives

Professor Lilian Katz, who was the editor of ERIC Clearinghouse on Elementary and Early Childhood Education, has been a dominant force in early childhood education for over two decades. She was interviewed about her views on parent involvement, and her thoughts are summarized here.

Many educators pay lip service to the idea that all parents know their children best, while unfortunately, we too often see results of parenting that indicate otherwise.

Early childhood educators have knowledge about what is best for children and should be using this knowledge in their interaction with parents. We must have confidence in our knowledge and understanding. Just as a teacher stands before a classroom because she knows more about the subject matter than the students do, early childhood educators should have some authority, based on their knowledge, that comes into play in their interaction with parents.

Although the relationship with parents is important, the primary consideration of the early childhood educator should be what is best for the client rather than what makes the client happy, and the two do not always coincide. (Powell, 1989)

Although these words were written by Lilian Katz many years ago, they still ring true today. Educators still struggle to understand their place and role with families.

Parent Education

Historical Perspective

Parent education is probably the oldest form of parent involvement. We can trace it back to the early 1900s, when day nurseries (the precursors of child-care centres) were first established to serve poor and needy families. Mothers were instructed about health and hygiene and about how to raise children in ways that would keep their children from falling into lives of crime.

Parent education became extremely popular during the 1960s and 1970s with the development of Head Start programs, where family involvement and early childhood education were believed to make a big difference in the lives of children and families living in poverty. A number of parent education formats evolved, including group meetings, home visits, and attendance by parents (usually mothers) at the preschool to learn from the teacher appropriate ways of interacting with children. The primary focus of many of these programs was teaching parents to interact with children in ways that would promote children's intellectual development (Couchenour & Chrisman, 2011).

At the same time, many other kinds of parent education programs were being implemented. Nursery schools, churches, community centres, and other organizations were forming parent education groups. These groups were often inspired by the works of such psychologists as Haim Ginnott (2003). They generally focused on communicating effectively with children, discipline, and related topics, and most of the parents attending were middle class.

Parent education programs have traditionally been directed at two audiences: one for the poor, disadvantaged, or at risk, and another for the middle class and affluent. In fact, parent education has often been imposed on people living on assistance, immigrants, teen parents, and single parents. In other words, receiving welfare benefits or a space in child care has been conditional on parents' attendance at parent education programs. The under-lying premise of parent education is that an expert will provide resources, advice, and sup-port to parents, who are often in need. These programs have largely provided instruction to parents and have focused on parenting. On the other hand, middle-class parent education has been voluntary and based on discussion rather than on instruction (e.g., discussions of sibling rivalry or techniques for guidance and discipline). More recently, there has been a movement to "normalize" parent education so that people understand that parenting can be challenging for all parents, and that all parents, from time to time, may need support.

Today, many early childhood educators believe that educating parents is an ongoing process that best occurs through regular communication rather than in formal education programs. However, both early childhood educators and parents have stated that efforts that attempt to educate parents in this manner are often futile.

Does Parent Education Work?

While many parent education programs have undergone rigorous evaluation, we must be care-ful not to assume that all parent education programs have demonstrated their effectiveness. There is generally little evidence to support specific types of parent education (Couchenour & Chrisman, 2011). Although many studies have shown that parent education classes have influ-enced parents' attitudes or knowledge about child-rearing, there is much less evidence to sup-port the claim that real changes occur in families as a result of parent education programs.

It's difficult to understand just what kind of parent education is effective, but there is some consensus that successful programs share the following features:

- Treatment of parents as partners (Jago et al., 2013)
- Empathic interaction with parents (Jago et al., 2013)
- Education delivered by someone known and trusted (Mytton, Ingram, Manns, & Thomas, 2014)
- Respect for time issues and child-care needs (Mytton et al., 2014)
- Facilitation of peer support (Axford, Lehtonen, Kaoukji, Tobin, & Berry, 2012; Jago et al., 2013)
- Engagement of fathers (Jago et al., 2013)

Today, it's more common for educators to collaborate with programs offered through family resource centres to meet parent education needs; it's less common for preschool staff to deliver parent education programs. Almost all the helping professions today engage in parent education. Nurses, psychologists, teachers, early childhood educators, social workers, clergy, and even people with no related professional background now offer parent educa-tion. Families and family relations are the focus of many professions, and the different disciplines can enrich one another's perspectives.

Parent Effectiveness Training (PET) and Systematic Training for Effective Parenting (STEP) are popular packaged parent education programs. Early childhood educators fre-quently recommend PET and STEP resources to parents. It's important to note that educa-tors don't see their role as necessarily teaching "parenting skills"; that is, they are aware of the expertise and experience of other professionals, such as health care professionals and family program professionals, in this regard.

A Parent's Confidence

One caution about parent education: some believe that it may undermine mothers' beliefs in their ability to parent. In the chapter on family roles (Chapter 2), we discussed the confusion caused when different experts give different advice, and the same point applies to parent education programs. Parent education does not have to undermine parents' confidence. The intention, in fact, is just the opposite: to help parents gain confidence in themselves and thereby become better parents. Awareness of the potential impact on parents' self-image and a sensitivity to and appreciation of different parenting styles will help early childhood educators ensure that parent education meets its goal.

Information Sharing

The concept of parent education has also been criticized because it implies a one-way sharing of information: the "experts" provide the required information to the parents without ever asking for their opinion. Parents do, however, have a wealth of information about their children, and this knowledge is every bit as valid and important as the contents of child development courses (Gonzalez-Mena, 2009). The point is to develop the space that recognizes that parents have something to offer as "sources of knowledge and bearers of cultural capital" (Bernhard & Gonzalez-Mena, 2005, p. 22). The socio-cultural approach that recognizes the valued space families play in the lives of children is relevant. Therefore, many early childhood educators have moved away from parent education as part of their practice, and rather, look for opportunities to *share information* because sharing implies a two-way communication process that inherently values families.

SCENARIO

WHO IS QUALIFIED?

Marsha, a recent graduate of an early childhood education training program, expressed the view that she did not consider herself qualified to be an educator of parents. "In my training, I learned a lot about child development and about how to care for children in a group. But I did not learn about parenting; I'm not a parent; I haven't brought up my own children. I can't teach parents how to do their job."

The sort of discomfort Marsha felt over being asked to provide parents with guidance and advice when she was not a parent herself is common among young early childhood educators. Some parents do readily look to early childhood educators for guidance about parenting. Other parents do not. Similarly, some educators believe that their role includes teaching parenting skills to parents, while others are uncomfortable in this role. The question, then, of whether early childhood educators should engage in parent education, is rooted in values and beliefs, as well as in the confidence and experience and readiness of the early childhood educators.

Parental Influence and Control

Beginning in the 1970s, early childhood education researchers proposed that an important goal of parent-involvement strategies is to acknowledge the rights of parents to control, or at least to influence, policies and programs that affect their children (Wilson, 2010). Families may be considered as "consumers" who have made a considerable investment in their children. On the one hand, in tuition-based early childhood education programs, parents expect to influence policies and how their children are cared for and educated (Couchenour & Chrisman, 2008; Wilson, 2010). On the other hand, early childhood professionals, backed by research, are beginning to assert their knowledge and authority in their practice and programs.

This is a very sensitive issue for many early childhood educators. Through education and training they have acquired values, beliefs, and a considerable degree of knowledge about what is good for the children in their care. They spend much time and effort developing programs for the children based on those beliefs. It's not always easy to let parents influence decisions about the program. For example, the following incident occurred not long ago in a child-care centre.

SCENARIO

WHO KNOWS BEST?

Marcy, the centre director, regularly scheduled large blocks of time for free play because she firmly believed it to be the most important learning opportunity for children. A group of parents expressed the concern that the children were not learning enough, and they pressed the centre to teach children their ABCs and numbers and to encourage worksheets. The parents were not convinced by Marcy's argument that play is the most appropriate way for very young children to acquire knowledge and skills. The staff members were upset that parents ignored their expertise, and parents felt that their views were not being respected.

This all too common scenario illustrates one of the difficulties that might arise in parents' influence on centre programs. Research has consistently and unequivocally pointed to play as the foundation of children's learning, yet parents continue to question its value in favour of "traditional" teaching practices that they believe will prepare their children for school. Parents may, for example, state that they're not paying for their child to play. Early childhood educators have to articulate clearly their foundational beliefs and principles and, thus, which areas of programming can't be compromised. Literature published by professional associations—for example, the NAEYC, the CAYC, and the CCCF—are vital resources for staff whose beliefs and practices are being questioned. Curriculum frameworks built on a solid foundation of early learning theories and philosophies are another source for educators. The involvement of parents in the decision-making process is complex, and early childhood professionals need to consider carefully how they can encourage parent participation in a way that will benefit everyone involved. Although parent-based programs are common, early childhood professionals are moving toward establishing the context and engaging with parents without compromising their beliefs. Consider the following scenario.

SCENARIO

HAVING CONFIDENCE IN CONVICTIONS BASED ON RESEARCH

Shelley has been the owner and director of a small community preschool program for 20 years. She started working in the preschool when her aunt owned the program. The program then was theme based and included very structured activities such as worksheets, prepared crafts, and alphabet and number learning activities. Shelley completed an early childhood program, which emphasized that learning through play is the foundation of early childhood education. When she took over as director of the preschool, she maintained the academic focus because that is what parents wanted. Over the years, Shelley became stronger in her convictions related to the importance of play-based learning and child-centred practice based on research. As a result, she adapted her program accordingly. She has learned how to effectively explain her principles to new parents, and most parents understand her new program focus. However, when parents are insistent that their children should spend most of their time in the kind of highly structured activities that were offered in the previous program, Shelley suggests to these parents that they may find that another program better suits their needs.

The view that play-based learning and child-centred practice are important has taken time to develop, but these approaches are now being adopted in more and more early learning programs. The introduction of curriculum frameworks, mandated by provincial governments, has also influenced this trend. However, the fact remains that community-based programs often have parent boards, and parents may be in positions of control and influence over programs. Such situations can be challenging. Educators' confidence in their knowledge and values about early learning, as well as excellent communication skills, are helpful in these situations. So too is the realization that changing attitudes takes time and effort, and results are not always immediate. In the next chapter, strategies for communicating with parents who may have conflicting views will be covered in more depth.

Continuity of Care, or "Creating Bridges"

As stated earlier, continuity of care between home and centre has received much attention in early childhood literature on parent involvement. Continuity of care, or seamless child care (Baker & Manfredi-Petitt, 2004), is based on the premise that there should be some degree of similarity between the home and the centre (Couchenour & Chrisman, 2008; Wilson, 2010). This argument reinforces the belief that ongoing communication between parents and program staff is essential (Baker & Manfredi-Petitt, 2004; Wilson, 2010).

Wendy, who worked for years as an early childhood educator before she became an instructor of early childhood students at a community college, made the following observation about continuity of care.

SCENARIO

ONE DEFINITION OF CONTINUITY

"When people talk about the importance of continuity of care, they refer to grand notions of home and centre doing things in a similar fashion or responding to the child in similar ways. Educators like big phrases like 'continuity of care.' This is unrealistic. My job is to make the child feel welcome in the child care. Often, he'll talk about something relating to his home—his sick goldfish, or his brother's new shoes. If I know a little bit about those things (from talking with his parents), it's easier for me to talk with him about them and make him feel more comfortable at the centre. It's that simple. That's what I mean by 'continuity.'"

Continuity for this early childhood educator meant nothing more complicated than ensuring that she knew enough about the child's home life that she could help the child make sense of his experiences throughout the day and feel more comfortable at the centre. Continuity, then, is based on principles of respect and mutuality.

Continuity of care can have added significance if children are experiencing stress in their home environment. This idea is reflected in the following remarks by Elizabeth, an early childhood educator.

SCENARIO

WHAT YOU NEED TO KNOW

"You need to know things that happen in the children's homes. If Mom and Dad have suddenly split up, I think it's important that we know that. We don't want to know who or why, but it's important to know that maybe Daddy left or Mommy has gone for a while. That's important because it's going to affect the child's behaviour, and we need to know what kind of support the child will require."

If continuity of care, or seamless child care, is to happen at all, it presupposes that information about the centre will be taken home to the parents, and that information about the child's home life and family will be made available to the centre. However, such disclosure requires a level of trust and openness that may not always be present. Some parents feel very strongly that their private life is not a concern of the early childhood educator. The following remarks made by one mother are typical.

SCENARIO

ONE PARENT'S VIEW

"Of course I'll inform the early childhood educator of any sudden change in our family life, but only the bare details. All families have ups and downs, and I don't want to feel pressured to discuss these with my child's educator. It's not that I don't trust her; it's just that I didn't choose her, as I would a counsellor or psychologist. So if my husband walked out on me, I'd mention that John was no longer living with us, but I'd leave it at that."

Other parents, though, do look on the early childhood educator as a prime source of support, as someone with whom they can discuss family concerns. Sometimes this kind of support leads to important actions, as the following scenario illustrates.

SCENARIO

SOME TIMELY ADVICE

An early childhood educator asked to speak to a mother whose child seemed to be under a lot of stress. The mother tearfully related that she was indeed having difficulty with the child just then. The little girl had just turned 4, an age that the mother associated with excruciating memories of the abuse she experienced as a child. The educator listened attentively and encouraged the mother to go to counselling at a nearby centre for adult victims of child abuse. Several years later, the mother recalled how it was the caring early childhood educator who facilitated the beginning of a healing process for herself and her family.

The value of continuity of care can't be denied or minimized. The transition from home to child care or school can be a major transition for some children, which will affect those children and their classmates, their families, and their educators. Continuity of care requires an atmosphere of respect, where both the parent and early childhood educator are sensitive to each other's rights and values. It is pivotal to our practice with children and families to ensure the best quality of care possible.

The practice of bridging home and family comes with some cautions, which are outlined in the box that follows. Note the emphasis on the "two-way street" that is vital for success.

Bridging Centre and Home: A Two-Way Street

1. For some families, privacy is a highly esteemed value. Respecting parents and families will help you decide what is absolutely necessary to know about the family's life, and what is not essential, and this will, in turn, help you to respect the privacy of the family.

2. Early childhood educators are not trained to be counsellors or therapists. Parents may disclose highly personal information to the early childhood educator, who will then feel a strong

desire to be helpful. However, knowing your professional limits is extremely important. Being able to refer parents to appropriate sources of support is critical to your professional role.

3. Unfortunately, educators who believe in continuity of care often translate it to mean "This is the way we do it at the centre, and therefore parents should do it this way at home as well." Bridging home and centre must be a two-way street. It includes incorporating ideas in the centre that reflect or recognize how things are done at home, as well as sharing with parents how things are done at the centre.

4. It is important to consider using varied types of communication, including both one-way and two-way communication. Exploring ways to engage parents in meaningful conversation and dialogue is vital.

5. It is also important to consider the congruity of values and expectations between home and centre. Many factors can influence congruence (e.g., culture, income level, education level). These factors or differences need to be openly discussed between the parent and early childhood educator.

SCENARIO

TEACHER'S HELPER ON HALLOWEEN

Halloween is celebrated across Canada as a fun day for children, who dress up in costumes and typically go trick or treating. It is an event with pagan origins, and thus some families prefer that their children not celebrate it. Yoshua's parents spoke with Anne, the teacher, about their preference that Yoshua not participate in the centre's Halloween celebrations. Together, they found a solution that worked for everyone. Yoshua would be the "teacher's helper" on that day and help the teacher prepare packages of treats to deliver to the local food bank, as charity seems to be a tenet of many if not all religions. That way, Yoshua was able to participate in class in a way that was congruent with his family's religious preferences.

Bridging home and centre is easier if educators gain an understanding of the different traditions, religions, and culture of the children in the centre. See Chapter 9 for further discussion on culturally diverse families.

Empowering Parents

Empowerment is a term that has become popular in the helping professions (Addi-Raccah & Ainhoren, 2009). It denotes a move away from the traditional way of working with people, where an "expert" was assumed to know what was best for her or his clients (Addi-Raccah & Ainhoren, 2009; Couchenour & Chrisman, 2008). Empowerment is a process by which families and communities increase their influence and control over their own circumstances. In an early childhood setting, the empowerment approach includes the following:

- Understanding that families commit to their child's lifelong well-being
- Nurturing children and families to reach their full potential
- Validating children and parents as an important part of community

This approach de-emphasizes the expert role and gives parents, in collaboration with professionals, the power to make and implement decisions that will be in the best interest of their children. The following scenario looks at empowerment from a parent's point of view.

MOTHER MAY KNOW BEST

"When I had my first child, I was a young single parent. I thought I knew nothing about children, and I just waited for the early childhood educators to answer my questions and tell me what to do.

"When my little girl 'graduated' into the toddler room, I met Elcira, her early childhood educator, and continued to ask her questions. Elcira would listen to my questions, but then would say things like 'What have you been doing about that up to now? That seems to have worked well.' Sometimes she would ask me what I thought would be the best way. Other times she would recommend a book to read.

"At first I was annoyed with her. 'Can't she just answer my questions?' I thought to myself.

"Gradually, I came to understand that she was giving me the message that I really do know what is best for my child and that I could rely more on my own knowledge and intuition. That was an important thing for me to learn."

All of the strategies discussed so far in this chapter can be pursued in a way that empowers parents. First, parent education can empower parents if it's done in a manner that goes beyond just delivering reams of advice and information. Such an approach will empower parents to trust their own feelings and responses to their children. Second, parents can be empowered by actively participating in the early childhood programs at both the planning and implementation stages, where there is a genuine openness to parent influence. Third, parents can be empowered by many of the strategies that encourage seamless child care or continuity of care.

Parent empowerment was reframed by the Reggio Emilia approach (Malaguzzi, 1994). Loris Malaguzzi, the founder of Reggio Emilia's educational philosophy, developed a charter of rights for parents in 1993, which states the following:

> It is the right of parents to participate actively and with voluntary adherence to the basic principles in the growth, care, and development of their children . . . Parent participation enables a communication network that leads to fuller and more reciprocal knowledge, as well as a more effective shared search for the best educational methods, content and values. (Malaguzzi, 1994, p. 59)

> *Source:* Loris Malaguzzi and the Schools of Reggio Emilia: A Selection of His Writings and Speeches, 1945–1993, Routledge.

THE FAMILY-CENTRED APPROACH

The term *family-centred* has also become popular in early childhood care settings (Scott & Arney, 2010; Wilson, 2010). Use of this term represents a movement away from the traditional approaches, where the "expert" designs and implements interactions without input from family members. This movement has grown from respecting the rights of families and from the ecological perspective, which recognizes the multiplicity of factors that influence development. In addition, evidence suggests that involving families more respectfully and fully is beneficial to families and children (Scott & Arney, 2010).

> Family-centered practice is based on beliefs and values that (a) acknowledge the importance of the family system on child development, (b) respect families as decision makers for their children and themselves, and (c) support families in their role of raising and educating their children. (McBride, 1999, p. 62)

Family-centred, culturally sensitive care incorporates the following beliefs:

- Family is key in the lives of children.
- Each family has its own strengths, resources, and ways of coping.
- Each family must be respected without judgment or preconceptions.
- Cultural, ethnic, and religious diversity must be honoured.
- Programs must support families, and practices need to embrace diversity.

Defining and refining family-centred practice is an evolving process. Awareness of and access to community resources has become increasingly important in finding flexible services to meet the unique needs of children and families. Early childhood educators have a solid foundation and rich traditions of working with families from which to continue to grow and develop more family-centred practices. The family-centred approach is not a new fad or phenomenon—it encompasses the best practices of early childhood educators and a realistic perspective on families.

Family-centred practice includes elements of a strengths-based approach that has also become more common. In a strengths-based approach, educators discover individual and family strengths and work with these unique talents and skills as one way to address unmet needs. This approach also includes elements of relationship-based practice, a framework that promotes optimal parent–child interactions through parent–educator relationships. When educators use this approach with parents to demonstrate behaviours and attitudes, it is assumed that these parents will feel more comfortable using the same approach to support their children. Relationship-based practice includes the ability to observe, the ability to be aware of your own values and beliefs and how those might impact others, the ability to be reflective, and the ability to be strengths based.

This conceptual framework provides educators with a way to focus on and emphasize the strengths and functioning of the family or parents. The family-centred approach is built upon a foundation of respect, and it is most commonly used with families with young children. This approach is also commonly adopted in relation to services for children with special needs.

HOW TO APPROACH PARENT ENGAGEMENT

How are early learning educators expected to engage with parents (and other family members who share responsibility for raising children)? As this chapter has shown, educators have a variety of approaches to draw upon. All of these approaches are used in specific contexts with specific populations, and one is not predominant across early learning programs in Canada. However, a socio-cultural perspective that situates families as central to practice commonly underlies new curricula, and educators are finding ways to intentionally and meaningfully engage parents and families in the lives of the children.

Educators need to thoughtfully reflect on their role with parents as well as their values and beliefs regarding parents. In addition, they need to consider the vision and goals of the program they are part of in relation to parent engagement. Some programs may have access to funding for specific parent strategies, such as home visits or parent effectiveness programs. Educators must also understand parents and their needs. Some parents will actively seek support and ways to become engaged, while others will not. With this understanding, educators can determine individualized approaches and begin to set goals. Early childhood professionals can draw on the different perspectives presented in this chapter to develop their own strategies.

Marjory Ebbeck and Manjula Waniganayake (2003) suggested four key purposes for collaborating with parents and families:

1. To bridge the gap between home and the service, and ensure consistency and continuity for children

2. To plan more effectively for children based on their individual needs, interests, and abilities

3. To model cooperative social skills to children, in teaching them the real meaning of being a member of society

4. To ensure accountability and service satisfaction to children and parents who have chosen to use your professional services (pp. 84–85)

The CCCF has proposed a number of easy steps to strengthening your partnership with parents and families (www.cccf-fcsge.ca/wp-content/uploads/RS_86-e.pdf).

CONCLUSION

To work with parents in a way that supports them and their children, early childhood educators need to understand the interrelated concepts that impact their interactions with families. The family systems model (see Chapter 3) reminds us that whatever changes occur in the child and/or parent are likely to have an impact on the entire family system. The ecological model recognizes that a child is part of a family and that family is part of the child's life, and that the kind of services available to families, including early childhood frameworks and other support systems, are vital to the well-being of children and families. Our understanding of the impact of change and trauma and interrelated factors that pose deep challenges for families struggling to provide a good life for their children will assist in establishing the positive empathic relationship that is the basis for all interactions with family. The socio-cultural perspective affirms the centrality of families in the lives of children. Family-centred practice provides another perspective that puts families in the centre of our practice. Beliefs about parent engagement lead us to consider how we can provide education for parents and families as well as continuity of care. An emphasis on empowering parents has led us to consider how parents can be supported in their role as parents and thereby strengthen family at its core. All of these approaches provide the educator with a multitude of ways to interact with families. They also underline the importance of considering the child in the context of the family and recognizing the impact of the family on the well-being of the child.

Chapter Summary

- This chapter has focused on the importance of working and engaging with parents in a meaningful way.

- We explored the concept of parent engagement as it relates to perspectives prevalent in early learning, including family systems and ecological models.

- We examined parent education and issues related to parental influence and control. Early childhood educators need to consider the importance of supporting families and developing goals related to parent engagement.

- We discussed engaging with parents from a socio-cultural perspective, where the family is central to practice.

RESOURCES

Canadian Child Care Federation:
www.cccf-fcsge.ca

Centre of Excellence for Early Childhood Development:
www.excellence-earlychildhood.ca/home.asp?lang=EN

Child Care Information Exchange:
www.childcareexchange.com

Positive Behaviour Supports for Children (Mount Royal University):
www.pbsc.info

EXERCISES

1. In your own words, write a definition of the term *parent engagement*. How does parent engagement differ from parent involvement? Parent participation? Parent collaboration?

2. Ask two early childhood educators to give you their definitions of the term *parent engagement*. Summarize their responses in writing.

3. Ask two parents what they feel the term *parent engagement* means. Summarize their responses in writing.

4. Compare the responses of the early childhood educators and the parents you interviewed with your own definition. What are the similarities, and what are the differences? What do you think accounts for these?

5. Consider your image of the family. How does it relate to your image of the child? How does your image of the family impact your practice with children? With families? With children and families together?

6. What do you think parents find meaningful? How might you determine what is most meaningful to them?

7. Brainstorm a list of reasons you might have for making a home visit. What are some things you could do in advance to ensure a successful home visit? Discuss the ethical considerations involved in home visiting.

CHAPTER 6

Enhancing Parent–Educator Engagement

- To consider the approaches pertinent to engaging with parents

- To provide guidelines for planning activities with parents

- To suggest activities that are congruent with the goals of parent engagement

- To highlight special considerations in planning collaborative strategies

Cathy, a recent graduate of an early childhood education program, sighed in desperation after a parent meeting she had organized was poorly attended. "I don't know why I even bother," she said. "Parents just aren't interested in coming." At the same time, Adele, a parent who did not attend the meeting, was thinking, "I wish they [staff] would give me more notice about parent meetings. Three days isn't enough time for me to arrange a babysitter. They probably think I don't care."

WHY BUILD PARTNERSHIPS?

Over the many years of writing and rewriting this textbook, there has been a noticeable shift in thinking about how educators should work with families. As noted in Chapter 1, family involvement consisted of keeping parents happy and informed. The literature espoused many approaches required for family involvement or partnership with families. A variety of words were and continue to be used in the literature to describe the relationship between educators and families: *partnership, collaboration, empowering parents,* and *working with parents* (Ebbeck & Waniganayake, 2003). In some jurisdictions, there was a period of time where parent participation was mandated by programs; that is, funding bodies required parents to be part of a program's decision-making processes. There was a period where the expert model dominated services for children and parents, and parent education was an essential part of child-care services—especially for vulnerable families, who were expected to attend parent education programs. This was followed by a time when parent communication received greater emphasis; educators were to share information with parents during times of interaction. Later, the accountability of educators to parents as consumers moved to the forefront of the educator–parent relationship (Ebbeck & Waniganayake, 2003). During this time, program staff were required to maintain contact as an essential part of service provision. Toward the turn of the century, genuine partnerships with parents became a part of practice because it was recognized that working together was necessary to ensure optimal growth and development of the child. Today, the socio-cultural perspective has become the predominant perspective in early childhood education; it considers development within the context of the family, not as an individualistic venture. Accordingly, in recognition of the vital role parents and families play in a child's education, the educator's role has evolved to include engaging with parents and families. More recently, we have witnessed a change to working with families or working alongside families in meaningful ways.

ENGAGEMENT WITH PARENTS

Chapter 1 emphasized the vital role of educators in the engagement of parents and families, and subsequent chapters were devoted to better understanding families, and strategies for supporting families based on that understanding. As we have noted, neuroscience research has inspired new understandings of the importance of the early years, as well as greater awareness of the vital role of the early childhood educator in children's development. When the profession of early childhood education adopted the socio-cultural perspective, it moved toward recognizing the influence of socio-historical practices, beliefs, and experiences of the family and community into which the child is born. (Edwards, 2003, p. 39). As well, taking a strengths-based approach has impacted educators' image of the child and the family, and the types of supports educators need to provide (Center for the Study of Social Policy, 2017). The profession's adoption of the early learning framework, where educators make "teaching" visible and critically examine and reflect on their practice, has made the knowledge and expertise educators bring to their practice evident to parents. All of these factors have led to a re-examination of how early childhood educators can practise in a way that meaningfully engages parents. Chapter 5 reviewed models on parent engagement that were used in the past and touched on those currently used. This chapter will focus on additional contemporary approaches and best practices.

A variety of factors influence the impact of parent engagement activities. They include having a clear understanding of goals, having a repertoire of approaches and activities, considering the practical aspects beforehand, and having in place some way of evaluating the success of the parent engagement program on an ongoing basis. We refer to these considerations as the "why, what, and how" of working with parents and families.

Parent engagement is not always easy. Educators play multiple roles in a day, with obligations sometimes extending long beyond their hours of employment. The diversity of families, program structures, and program finances led to the development of a range of family-engagement approaches. For example, some programs require home visits, other programs mandate parent education programs, and still others require documentation in multiple formats. This chapter includes approaches to enhancing parent engagement. You will need to determine which are best suited for your philosophical underpinnings, your program goals, and the needs of your families.

THE PRACTICE OF RELATIONSHIPS

Early childhood educators are engaged in the practice of relationships.

> A *practice of relationships* describes the complex and dynamic relationships with diverse community members and begins as you learn with and alongside children and families. When you engage in a practice of relationships, you create *places of vitality* in early learning communities with children—as *mighty learners and citizens*—and their families. (Makovichuk, Hewes, Lirette, & Thomas, 2014, p. 50)

When educators understand the significance of family for the child, they foster a relationship with families alongside their relationship with children. Just as educators' image of the child will influence how they interact with children, their image of the family will influence how they interact with parents.

> In a similar way to the image of the child, the image of the family is also constructed within social, cultural, historical, economic and political contexts. . . . When you value family connections and contributions, you are more likely to engage families in open,

respectful, and reciprocal dialogue to share and generate ideas, solve problems, and learn more deeply about children. (Makovichuk et al., 2014, p. 50)

Educators starting from this belief will engage parents in meaningful ways in all aspects of caring for the child. Knowing about family routines is paramount as young children move into child-care settings. Understanding what, when, and how the child eats and how the child falls asleep are important pieces of information to begin with. Educators can then generate many planning ideas specific to the child that parents share. Similarly, educators can suggest ideas and activities to families for their child. The following scenario demonstrates how educators and families can work together to build on the interests of children in meaningful ways.

SCENARIO

WORKING TOGETHER TO BUILD ON CHILDREN'S INTERESTS

Jack spent part of the weekend with his grandparents. They went for a walk in the local park and saw a family of owls with young chicks nesting in a tree. As they watched, Jack collected feathers from the young chicks and the adults that had fallen on the ground. He took them to preschool the following week to show them to the preschool teacher. She asked Jack to bring the feathers to the carpet and to share what he knows about owls and owl babies. She built upon Jack's interest by bringing out art materials and creating opportunities for children to learn about owls. She had the children make binoculars out of toilet paper rolls and explained to other parents where the birds were located in the local park. Several parents made a point of walking in the park (with the binoculars) to find the owl nest. After several excited children (and parents) came back, she decided that the preschool group should also go for a walk to see the nest in the park.

THE "WHAT AND HOW" OF PARENT ENGAGEMENT: CLARIFYING GOALS

Once educators understand that building mutual relationships with families is the foundation of their practice, it seems appropriate that our discussion should begin with the "what and how" of practice with families.

In this chapter, we will also focus on practical approaches (the "how") that early learning educators can use to engage with families. We will begin with more natural, organic, simple ways of interacting—in person at drop-off or pickup—based on the child, who early childhood educators know best. From there, we will present approaches that may require more planning and organization. As early childhood educators, how we work with parents will vary greatly depending on our own beliefs and goals. It's important to understand where we wish to go before we determine how we will get there. For example, in the following scenario, a mature staff member admits that in the beginning of her career, her feelings influenced her more than her knowledge.

SCENARIO

APPREHENSION ABOUT PARENTS

"In the beginning, I couldn't bring myself to initiate a discussion with parents. I would quickly say hello and then busy myself with the children to avoid further contact. I knew I should be telling them about Johnny's artwork or about a new book we had in the centre, and asking them about his trip to his grandmother's over the holiday. But every time I tried, I was overwhelmed by the fear that they wouldn't really want to hear what I had to say."

It may be helpful to consider goals from the different perspectives of the child, the parent, the family, and the educator. Although it's common to think of goals as one dimensional, the goals of parent–educator collaborations should be viewed as multidimensional to recognize the different perspectives of those involved. For example, let's say that you invite parents to volunteer on a field trip with the goal of enhancing their engagement with the program. When parents sign up to accompany the class on the field trip, you have reached your goal. However, this kind of parent engagement can have other benefits; for example, children can have exposure to a new and interesting adult, the child of that parent may feel very special, and some staff members may value the assistance that a parent can provide on a field trip.

Consider the following scenario, in which a mother discusses her view of parent–teacher nights.

SCENARIO

JUST SHOWING INTEREST IS IMPORTANT

"I always go to parent–teacher nights at school. I don't ever expect to learn very much because it's always so busy there and the teachers have so many parents to deal with. I go just so that the teachers will know that I care about Jimmy's education. Then I make a separate appointment to discuss any concerns with the teacher."

One might assume that the teacher's goal in holding a parent–teacher evening is to provide parents with information or an opportunity to discuss concerns. However, the parent's goal in the preceding scenario was quite different: she simply wanted to show the teacher that she cared and wanted to stay current.

In Chapter 5, we presented an overview of the most prevalent goals of parent involvement: parent education, parent influence or control, continuity of care, parent empowerment, and family-centred practice. Further, we have seen that there may be other purposes. It's important to realize that any one activity can meet a number of goals.

SCENARIO

MULTIPLE GOALS COVERED BY ONE ACTIVITY

When planning an "open house" evening for parents, siblings, and grandparents, staff members found they had different ideas about what goals could be accomplished by such an event. "This will give us a chance to talk informally about the importance of free play with parents," said one staff member (i.e., parent education). "It'll give parents a chance to see all the new community-resources pamphlets we've got on our bulletin board," said a second staff member (working within the ecological model). "My biggest concern is that parents feel welcome and able to make suggestions about the room arrangement," said a third (i.e., parent influence and control). "It'll be nice when parents see the new playground and can talk to their kids at home about it," said another (i.e., continuity of care). The program supervisor was excited that parents would have the opportunity to see all of the things their child does in a day so they have a framework to talk about the child's day and perhaps, the parent can add new ideas (i.e., parent engagement and empowerment). The director was anxious to hear the parents' reaction to the documentation that was completed for the open house. Janet, a parent who had come in late and overheard the conversation, smiled and remarked, "The goal for me will be to come to a place where I'll be served a cup of coffee while the kids are busy playing" (i.e., family centred).

It's probably true that if an activity is designed to incorporate more than one goal, it's more likely to be well attended and well received than if the goals are too narrowly defined.

START WITH THE CHILDREN

Parent engagement activities can begin with early childhood educators' area of expertise: the children. Educators often have ideas, activities, and events that are appealing for young children that have sound developmental outcomes. Parents sometimes struggle with activities in which to engage their young children. As a result, they might appreciate educators' ideas on how to engage their children or the opportunity to attend events that showcase the abilities and interests of their children. Such events might include an arts and crafts evening, a family dance, or a family outing. These types of events provide an excellent opportunity to communicate with parents while engaging children. It may be easier for early childhood educators to consider parent engagement from the starting point of what they know best.

SCENARIO

FROM THE CLASSROOM TO THE HOME

As a class assignment, early childhood students were asked to develop some type of presentation for parents. One group of students was especially apprehensive, so it was suggested that they plan something based on their own area of expertise. One member of the group, an accomplished singer, decided to record the songs sung in the program; she and the children could sing all the songs, and the parents could take a CD home if they liked. The evening was planned and turned out to be a hit. Many parents remarked that their child was often frustrated because he or she didn't know the words, but now they could all happily sing the child's favourite songs at home. Another student set up a "goop station" to coincide with departure time at the end of the day. She set out playdough, goop, and other sensory materials children could play with, along with easy recipes for parents to try at home. The children got to show their parents what goop was, and parents had the opportunity not only to experience the activity but also to replicate it at home.

Although singing may not be everyone's talent, early childhood educators often have many developmentally appropriate ideas to share, such as the goop station, books to read, and art activities. Parents are usually thrilled to engage in learning some of these ideas or having them on hand for a rainy day. These ideas may be the perfect starting point for parent engagement activities.

THE IMPORTANCE OF COMMUNICATION

Once educators understand the impact of creating relationships with parents, it's essential to develop good communication skills. Effective communication is the framework for establishing and maintaining any kind of collaboration with parents. Although it seems logical that early childhood educators should be able to communicate easily with parents and adults, this is not always the case. In fact, in early childhood education programs, little training is directed at working with adults. It's important to recognize that messages can be interpreted in unexpected ways. For example, when the educator remarks, "He's been so good all day," the parent might interpret that to mean, "I know how to handle him better than you do," leaving the parent feeling undervalued. Communication skills can be learned and can be improved, and early childhood educators can commit to further training in this area.

As we have repeatedly emphasized, good communication begins with self-knowledge, that is, with an awareness of one's own beliefs and values (Wilson, 2005). Educators who examine their image of the family will understand the importance of reciprocal relationships with families and develop open communication skills to enhance sharing. A good communicator is careful not to pass judgment and is open to receiving new information (Vuckovic, 2008).

The ability to build effective communication with parents requires a rapport and trust, which serve as a foundation for all work with parents. Creating rapport and fostering trust take time and effort on the part of the educator. In addition to self-awareness and a nonjudgmental attitude, good communicators acquire a repertoire of verbal and nonverbal behaviours (e.g., listening, paraphrasing) that facilitate good communication. Good communicators also learn to ask questions that provide direction for the conversation and solicit more information from the speaker. They do so with sensitivity and without prying. Relationships between parents and educators can be complicated: some parents willingly share the details of their family lives (some too much!) and others are reticent to share. Educators may be left in a quandary when a crisis occurs because little has been shared.

Sometimes educators use technology to communicate with parents, especially busy parents who often rely on their electronic devices. In a world connected by text messages, email, and social media, early childhood educators should consider using multiple ways of communicating with parents. While electronic communication does not decrease the importance of face-to-face communication skills, early childhood educators can use electronic communication to enhance parent–staff communication (Liang & Chen, 2009; Miguez, Santos, & Anido-Rifón, 2009).

Since communication skills are so essential for effective work with families, it's recommended that early childhood educators continually assess and improve their skills in this area. Many continuing education programs hold courses and seminars in communication strategies.

Communicate a Welcoming Attitude

Embracing a welcoming approach can take two forms. The first occurs when a child and family enter the program. The second occurs as part of ongoing practice.

Administrators and educators need to intentionally plan for children beginning their first experience away from home. Separations are a stressful and exciting time for children, parents, and educators alike. Ensuring that parents have the information they need and feel comfortable with the program is a good place to start. Some programs provide opportunities for parents and children to spend time in the program prior to the first day or have a staggered entry approach. Providing information on and discussing the challenges of program entry with parents beforehand are essential. Often the first separation is an intense emotional experience for child and parent alike. Parents may be apprehensive, experience guilt, and feel helpless and scared. The more information they have about the program and their child's day, the better they will be prepared to handle the moment.

As the educator, you will need to be prepared to support the parent and the child at the beginning of the program. The first few days in child care or an unparented program can be distressing, to say the least, for the child. A child may react to the parent with tears, harsh words, or clinging which, in turn, evoke an emotional reaction from the parent. The educator may want to ensure that extra support is available in the playroom so that he or she can dedicate time to the transition as needed. Suggesting that the parent stay for a short period of time may be helpful, but the educator needs to be prepared to assist the parent in exiting soon after. Sometimes delaying the inevitable departure creates more tension than it diminishes. It's helpful for parents to develop a transition ritual at home, when entering the program, and when leaving. For example, before leaving, a parent might say, "I will read one story, then I need to go." In the following scenario, one parent describes her feelings about the ritual she used when leaving her daughter at her program.

It's important that the educator acknowledge the child's and parent's feelings but provide a positive perspective on the day. Perhaps, the educator can let the child know that her friend is waiting for her, describe the first activity of the morning, or share what is planned for snack. Children may need reassurance during the day and then again upon departure, when another separation is about to occur. Often departure evokes fewer emotions, but parents may be troubled when their child does not want to go home!

Change is difficult for everyone involved. Educators will be better able to support the child and the family when they are prepared to intentionally do so. When planning is not intentional, challenges may result; for example, an educator may have to scramble to find a way for a parent to leave the program after a difficult separation. Educators need to continue to observe and monitor children and families, as both may vary in the time it takes their separation tensions to ease.

Educators also need to consider their role in the transitions that children make at the beginning of every fall. Changing from one educator to another or changing from one playroom to another may cause tension and stress. Finding ways to support children and families in these changes is vital. For example, an educator in a child-care program began a portfolio for each child who entered the program. The portfolio incorporated all of the key events and milestones in the program. Before the child moved to another playroom or educator, the educator wrote a page or two about the child, starting with the image of the child and then chronicling significant moments and memories from the child's time in the program. This addition to the portfolio served as an introduction to the new educators and a wonderful keepsake for the child and family.

On an ongoing basis, early childhood educators need to ensure that parents feel welcome and know that their involvement is valued in an environment of acceptance (Halacka Ball, 2006). A number of parents don't feel welcome in their child's play space. Even small things, such as how the room is set up, can convey this message.

Communication between staff and parents and parent engagement will occur more readily if parents feel welcome. Keeping parents informed and providing them with opportunities to participate, to share opinions, and to be involved in multiple ways will all serve to promote a welcoming partnership (Reedy & McGrath, 2010). Communication needs to be frequent, clear, and two-way as often as possible (Reedy & McGrath, 2010).

SCENARIO

CREATE A RESPONSIVE ENVIRONMENT

A director and staff were exploring the early learning framework in their child-care program and chose to focus on responsive environments. They spent time observing different aspects of the day and schedule to determine what changes to the environment could make it more responsive to children and families. As part of these observations, they noticed that parents were not actively engaged in the program. Many educators had expressed frustration at the consistent lack of parent interest. In their observations, they noted that the sign-in sheet was located so that the parents never needed to enter the playroom. As a result, the director and staff moved the furniture around so that parents would have to enter the playroom to sign in their children. This change didn't seem to increase the amount of time parents spent in the playroom, so they moved the sign-in sheet to the back of the playroom. That way, parents would have to walk right through the centre of the playroom to sign in. Shortly after this change, parents not only happily walked the extra distance, but also sometimes stopped to see what their child was playing with. One day, a father sat on the couch for 10 minutes just watching his child play.

IDEAS FOR COLLABORATING WITH PARENTS

Once staff members have reflected on their attitudes toward parents and their goals for working with them (and once they have the necessary communication skills), the stage is set for the development of a broad range of plans to implement parent–staff collaboration. We must stress, though, that there will always be a tremendous diversity in parents' interests and availability (Halacka Ball, 2006). Early childhood educators should consider the spectrum of needs of parents from various linguistic, cultural, and educational backgrounds that have children in their program. In this chapter, we discuss a number of ways to engage with a variety of parents. The approaches and activities presented are *ideas* that you may wish to consider and discuss with colleagues. They are not meant to be exhaustive but rather to provide a starting point or some new options to try. Program staff must be willing to consider options to collaborate with parents in light of their program goals and the needs of their families. Develop as many options for collaborating with parents as possible, and then allow parents to choose or to offer feedback for future planning. It's not important to have perfect attendance for all program events, but rather to have each parent involved in something on a regular basis. We begin with the kinds of activities that should be ongoing and may exist as part of your practice, and then we will consider approaches to collaboration that require additional thought and planning.

Verbal Communication

Daily Conversations

All early childhood educators attempt to greet children and parents each morning and at the end of each day (Invest in Kids, 2010). Children, especially young children, usually require assistance during these transition times, and educators often try to build this short interaction and conversation into their daily routine. This is the most common and frequent type of parent engagement activity (Wilson, 2005). These informal contacts and exchanges are also, perhaps, the single most important aspect of parent engagement (Reedy & McGrath, 2010).

However, the intention to speak to each parent each day is not always as easy to carry out as it seems. Parents often arrive all at the same time, and one small disaster (e.g., wet pants, lost shoes, a crying child) can inhibit even the best of intentions. Transitions for children may be stressful, and both parent and educators may need to focus on making the transition as smooth as possible and forgo conversation at this time. Parents are sometimes tired or stressed at the end of the day, just as educators are. Moreover, rotating shifts often mean that the child's primary caregiver is unavailable for discussion.

Lynn Wilson (2014) reported that communications last less than one minute and parents spend, on average, just over one minute in the playroom. Furthermore, most of the exchanges consist of social exchanges (e.g., greetings, small talk, sharing information pertinent to the child) rather than sharing information that might lead to decision making. The amount of time parents spend engaging with educators decreases as children grow older; that is, parents rely less on educators for information the older their children are. It's unlikely that meaningful relationships can be built within the parameters of these short exchanges. Therefore, while ongoing face-to-face interaction seems on the surface to be the best way to communicate, it rarely occurs consistently or productively. Safeguards are needed to ensure that communication occurs regularly. Early childhood educators may want to keep a record of conversations with parents and review this record periodically, perhaps at the end of every week. If regular, meaningful contact with parents does not occur at arrival and departure times, educators should make other arrangements.

Phone Calls

Phone calls can be an effective way of communicating, provided that they occur at a time convenient for both parties (Reedy & McGrath, 2010). Staff should try to organize times when they are free to leave the playroom and let parents know when it's convenient for them to take calls, if this is a possibility within the structure of the program. Some parents enjoy receiving phone calls that are made simply to keep in touch and relate information about the child rather than just the bad news. One mother said that it made her day when she got a call from the centre with a funny story about her toddler's new accomplishment. Other parents may wish to communicate by phone only if there is a specific need, for example, to request extra clothing or in an emergency.

Written Communication

Communication with parents doesn't need to take place face to face or by phone exclusively. Written communication can meet some of the objectives of parent–staff collaboration and can be used to reach either individual parents (e.g., through documentation, communication books) or groups of parents (e.g., through newsletters). The following ideas can serve as one- or two-way communication vehicles to (1) share information with parents, (2) provide a mechanism for parent input, or (3) help parents gain access to wider community networks.

Documentation has become more prevalent in early learning practice and can serve as an excellent vehicle to communicate and engage with parents. Although bulletin boards, parent corners, and newsletters are usually considered strategies for sharing information, they can meet other goals at the same time. Parent participation in these activities furthers their engagement and interest at the centre. As well, the information shared may help parents form their own networks of support and access wider-reaching community resources. Sharing information through bulletin boards, parent corners, and newsletters may very well help parents bridge the distance between children's child-care experience and home experience. Moreover, reading about a field trip in the newsletter or learning about a new book or toy in the playroom may provide a forum for parents to communicate with their children about daily experiences.

Documentation

As educators, administrators, and programs bring early learning frameworks into practice, they begin to challenge their values, beliefs, and practices with children and with the environment, both physical and social. A key foundation for many frameworks is documentation. This documentation is broad based and incorporates many approaches, the most well known of which is the learning story. However, documentation serves diverse purposes and can take a multitude of formats, depending on the audience and purpose (Stacey, 2015). Documentation forces educators to make learning visible as they record their teaching. Early childhood educators have not, for the most part, been asked to produce documentation in the past. The documentation process can be difficult and may seem to be a monumental task. However, as educators become more practised, their confidence increases and they are better able to intentionally engage parents in meaningful ways around a photo or a documented moment. Often, the first time educators share documentation with a parent or colleague or a learning story, they experience an "aha" moment and see something in the child or practice that they had never considered previously. Parents are typically overwhelmed by the first piece of documentation and find that they see their child in a new light and, more important, see the educator from a new perspective (i.e., as a professional).

SCENARIO

THE POWER OF DOCUMENTATION

A director spoke passionately about a moment with a parent in her program. A mother was reading a new piece of documentation on her daughter, which was posted at the entrance of her daughter's playroom. The documentation focused on the educator's image of her daughter's disposition to learn. The director, whose office was across the hall, was watching the mother's reaction and noticed that the mother was crying. She approached the mother to ask if there was a problem, and the mother stated that she wasn't concerned about her daughter learning numbers, letters, or shapes because she knew that that would happen in school. She was just overwhelmed to see that her daughter was learning to be independent, caring, creative, and a problem solver.

This moment consolidated everything that this director hoped for in her program. The educators were documenting the children's learning in meaningful ways for parents.

The process of documentation leads to very natural and organic ways to share children's significant moments during the day with parents, for example, via photos of the day or a book at sign-in. This method of sharing leads naturally to receiving input from parents. For example, educators can ask parents to share their thoughts, to contribute to an area of interest children have created in the program, or to share related items from home.

SCENARIO

ENGAGING THROUGH DOCUMENTATION

A child-care director tells the story of how one playroom began to post one picture a day along with a description in a book format. Sometimes the description consisted of one or a few words; other times it consisted of a lengthier description (e.g., focused on the children's learning). The book was on a shelf right beside the sign-in/sign-out sheet, making it easily accessible to parents. At first, parents glanced at the book and rarely made comments or added ideas, which left the educators feeling unsure about the book's impact. The educators contemplated removing the book, thinking that it was not important for parents. The director urged them to maintain the book because she

continues ▶

▶ *continues*

had heard parents occasionally make comments about the day's activity depicted in the book, most often in relation to their child. To make it easier for parents to provide feedback, the educators added a whiteboard next to the book. There, they listed their planning ideas and dedicated space for parents to provide input. It didn't take long for parents to start adding their ideas.

Observation guided by specific goals can create unexpected changes. Through each one of these pieces of documentation and shared experiences with families, the educator's image of the family changes, as does the parents' image of the educator. It's important for educators to find ways to genuinely interact with families that are natural and authentic rather than arbitrary and disconnected. Approaches to family engagement are more meaningful when they start with the child.

SCENARIO

ASKING PARENTS TO WRITE THEIR REFLECTIONS

A preschool program set a goal to use documentation intentionally to engage families. At an open house during the year, the educators filled the playroom with different types of documentation, including panel boards of their study on where animals live, projects the children had worked on, and many learning stories. Scattered throughout the room were large pieces of paper with questions for the parents that invited their feedback. For example: "How do you see your child's relationship with the educator?" "How does this impact the child's image of the self?" "What does this piece of work tell you about your child?" "What does this piece of work tell you about how your child learns?" Parents circulated and added comments to each of the sheets. The number and thoughtfulness of the comments shared with the teachers was remarkable.

When documentation is part of practice and educators come to understand its value, making it a platform to engage parents can be easy. Educators can share simple photos, learning stories, or projects with parents in person or online.

Bulletin Boards

Bulletin boards can be an excellent way of making a wide variety of information available to parents, and they can also serve as an effective public relations tool for the program (Reedy & McGrath, 2010). Bulletin boards can relay information about the entire program or specific aspects of it; these boards can also include pamphlets from community agencies, book reviews, community events, and excerpts from magazines. Another part of the bulletin board can focus on centre activities, such as samples of children's artwork, photographs, information about daily activities, and lost-and-found notices.

We must remember that bulletin boards are useful only if parents actually read them (Reedy & McGrath, 2010). Therefore, information should be presented in an organized and appealing manner, such as by using pictures of the children to capture parents' attention (Essa & Young, 1994). The information should also be updated consistently. Parents may also have information they want to share on the bulletin board and should be welcome to make use of it for this purpose. Whenever possible, early childhood educators should represent different languages and have translations available for parents who do not read English.

Ideas for Bulletin Boards

1. Provide a bright, colourful background. Cover the board with an eye-catching background colour or design. Trim the board with a contrasting colour.

2. Choose a spot where parents will see the board every day, either near an entrance area or parent corner or near the sign-in sheet in individual playrooms.

3. Provide some type of sign so that parents know the information is specifically for them—for example, PARENTS.

4. Keep information current by displaying topics that have a direct effect on the children or families, for example, tips on summer safety or on coping with time changes. Make sure parents know when information has been updated or changed by using a new sign or a change of colour.

5. Provide information regarding upcoming family events in your community, especially if they are free.

6. Provide take-away information (e.g., pamphlets, articles, recipes, local child magazines) or a sign-up sheet so that you can make copies for those interested in the information.

7. Provide some humour in the use of pictures, cartoons, special messages, or thoughts for the day that would appeal to parents and bring a smile to their faces at the end of a long day.

8. Provide space for parents to post and exchange information with one another or with you (e.g., child-care needs, interesting articles).

9. Attach a pen and paper to the board in case parents wish to jot down information.

10. Change information on a frequent and regular basis.

11. Avoid posting information that would more appropriately be delivered individually (e.g., overdue fees).

12. Avoid visual clutter.

13. Interactive boards that encourage parent input may help to connect families.

14. In addition, programs may want to consider creating a separate bulletin board that introduces staff, perhaps accompanied by a recent photo. Displaying staff biographies or information will help families get to know individual staff members better and may serve as a way to share relevant information (e.g., education, experience). This may be an easy way to introduce new staff in the program or to highlight the accomplishments of existing staff (e.g., recipient of an award).

Parent Corners

As an extension of the bulletin board, many centres set up a parent corner with a bulletin board and a table for displaying information. This can be an effective way to communicate how much you value learning and the sharing of resources. A few comfortable chairs and a coffee pot can be a sign to parents that they are welcome to stay for a few minutes to look through the material. Even though the times parents are in the centre (usually for dropping off and picking up their children) seem rushed, sometimes they can be introduced to valuable sources of information during those few minutes. Parent corners may provide early childhood educators with a vehicle to provide information in sensitive areas without pointing fingers at a particular family, parent, or child.

SCENARIO

UNFORESEEN CONSEQUENCES

A parent dropped off her two preschool-aged children at the child-care centre. On her way out, she noticed an advertisement on the bulletin board in the parent corner for a meeting of Alcoholics Anonymous, which was being held in the same building during the evening. This small, innocuous posting prompted her to attend the meeting. Twelve years later, when her new baby began at the same centre, she recalled fondly that the bulletin board had played a significant role in changing her life.

Parent corners may also provide sufficient space for parents to advertise (e.g., for lost items, for a toy or clothing exchange, for articles they want to sell). Offering space for this purpose may also encourage parents to share information and resources with other parents.

Ideas for a Parent Corner

1. Provide a special room, section, or corner for parents to call their own. This space should be well defined, easily accessible, and inviting to parents. In an infant centre, this space may be used as a convenient, quiet spot for mothers to breastfeed their babies throughout the day. Think about the diversity of families when designing the parent corner.

2. The area should include the parent bulletin board, comfortable adult-sized chairs or a sofa, a table, and coffee, if possible, so that parents are encouraged to stop and relax for a moment.

3. Start a parent information library in this area. Include books that may be borrowed and articles or pamphlets that may be taken home or copied for personal use. Community newspapers or magazines that focus on children and families could also be provided.

4. Set out a picture album of happenings in the child-care centre for parents to look at. Add new photographs or children's art regularly so that parents can stay up to date on daily activities. Make sure to represent all the playrooms and all the children.

5. Learning stories or updated pieces of documentation can be posted here where parents may have a few minutes to stop and look. If this is set up in an area where the children can view it alongside their parent, have sticky notes or a whiteboard so that parents can jot down their reaction or their child's thoughts.

Daily Notes

In many cases, brief notes sent home with the children can provide parents with very important information. Notes can take on a variety of forms and serve many purposes. Many parents of infants and toddlers will want to know how much their children ate and slept, and whether or not they had a bowel movement. Small, prepared, fill-in-the-blank notepads can facilitate this communication process. This type of information can also be delivered to parents via email or text message to ensure that parents have the information. As the children get older, notes can contain other kinds of information, and the child may also wish to add a message with a picture or a scribble, again to enhance the communication. Many programs have tablets or digital cameras in each room to facilitate documentation. Educators are quite comfortable taking and uploading pictures, so photos may be the focus of what is shared. Educators may be reluctant to write or create learning stories, especially if they feel their written proficiency may be under scrutiny. However, photos on their own or with one-word captions may be sufficient for parents to see what happened and start a dialogue.

Example of a Daily Note

My Day

TODAY: Leanne was very busy playing at the water table with her new friend, Casey. She played with blocks, made a castle, and dressed up as a princess.

LUNCH: Leanne ate half a sandwich and some apple pieces, and drank two cups of milk.

TOILET: Leanne did not have a bowel movement today.

NAP: She napped for two hours. Leanne had a bit of trouble getting settled but slept soundly.

EDUCATOR COMMENTS: Do you think that if Leanne had a special cuddly or blanket, she might be more comfortable at naptime? Let me know if you have any other ideas.

When using daily notes, as with all other forms of written communication, staff should take into account whether the parents will be able to read English. In some cases, it may be possible to have a daily communication form with pictures or in a bilingual checklist format. Then staff could check off the relevant entries in English and the parents would be able to read them in their own language. In programs for infants and toddlers, this information is often presented on a whiteboard/chalkboard so that information can be readily updated for parents. Educators should remember that the writing proficiency of parents may prevent them from responding to photos or written documentation. Just as educators may feel judged, parents may as well.

Communication Books

Two-way correspondence can enhance communication in that parents and early childhood educators are seen as equals, both contributing valued information (Couchenour & Chrisman, 2011). A notebook that goes back and forth with the child provides the opportunity for the educator to write pertinent information to parents or to ask parents questions. Parents can then respond and ask staff any questions they may have. Topics may include eating, sleeping, a new accomplishment, and upcoming events. One drawback is that communication books can become a one-way vehicle for communication, going from the centre to home but with no information returning. Early childhood educators can enhance the two-way nature by asking questions, by seeking information or clarification on a matter of concern, or by asking parents to share details of the child's life at home (e.g., "Ken says that you went to the farm this weekend. What did he enjoy the most?").

SCENARIO

A COMMUNICATION AID

Two-year-old Miguel came home from the centre one day, looked at his mother, and said, "Boat." "Did you read a story about a boat today?" asked his mother. Miguel shook his head no. His mother tried several more guesses, but each time her guess was wrong. Miguel seemed more frustrated, so she tried to distract him. That evening she wrote in the communication book that Miguel had been saying "boat" and she wondered if the staff knew what he was trying to tell her.

The educator wrote back that the class had gone to the swimming pool and had watched the canoe practices there. The next evening, Miguel's mother asked him about the canoes, and both Miguel and his mother seemed highly satisfied with the conversation.

Communication books may include parts of posted documentation or learning stories that may be of interest to parents and provide a reason to respond.

ENGAGING BASED ON CHILDREN'S INTERESTS

An educator was walking to the local park with a group of children when a firetruck came by and stopped close to a hydrant. Typically, children are fascinated by the sight of a firetruck or firefighters. This group of children was intrigued by the fire hydrant. Upon return to the preschool, the educator asked the children about what they saw, and all of their questions were about the hydrant. She investigated the topic further with the children by walking along streets close to the centre, looking for fire hydrants. The children discovered that some fire hydrants were painted with interesting designs. The educator wrote about the children's interest in fire hydrants in the children's communication books, and asked parents to find fire hydrants in their neighbourhood and bring in photos. Soon, the documentation panel was full of photos of fire hydrants and some interesting topical information from parents.

Communication books can be delightful for parents and staff, but they can also become a burden. Parents will vary in the enthusiasm of their responses, and they should not be judged if they do not write back. One mother was asked why she did not write in the communication book and responded as follows.

WHO HAS THE TIME?

"After work I rush to the centre to pick up Kaitlyn, then to the after-school program to pick up the boys. Supper, playtime, dishes, baths, teeth brushing, and a bedtime story for each child leave me pretty exhausted by the time they've all gone to bed. I just don't have the energy to write in the book."

Some parents do not write in the communication book because they are concerned about the impression they will give by using poor grammar and spelling, so staff must demonstrate sensitivity in this area. Perhaps it's easier to follow up with a verbal exchange with parents rather than wait for a written response. When a parent does write in the communication book, it's vital for the staff to continue to respond, especially when parents are not in the program regularly (e.g., because children are bussed or dropped off by someone other than the parents).

Considerations for Communication Books

1. Provide children with a small notebook that will easily fit in their diaper bag or backpack.
2. Start with a picture, if possible, to give the parent an idea of what the child's day included.
3. Write legibly about the children's day, what they did, and how they responded to routines, such as naps, meals, or toileting. Include information about what parents will want or need to know, especially for younger children who may not be able to communicate this information. Remember, however, that older children may forget or answer every question from the parent with an "I don't know," so passing along information will still be considered useful. Include information about development or play. Check with families to ensure that the information they want or need is included.

4. Include questions for parents so that they know you want them to respond. Try not to ask too many questions, and phrase the questions in such a way that they require more than a yes or no in reply.

5. Ask parents for information about what they have done as a family, which will help you talk to the child and increase continuity of care.

6. Respect the parents' varying need or ability to write in the book.

7. Maintain confidentiality at all times.

8. Date and sign each entry.

Examples of Communication Book Entries

January 3, 2018

Martha: Jeff had a great time outdoors today. He was really interested in building a snowman, and said he wanted to build one at home to show you what he can do.

He ate a good lunch and napped for about an hour (must have been all the fresh air).

He's really coming along with dressing himself, especially his snow pants and boots. He's much less frustrated.

Jane [mother]: We haven't had time to build a snowman, maybe on the weekend. I have noticed that he is getting better at dressing; he doesn't give up as easily. Could you please make sure that he wears his hat outside this week? He seems to be getting a cold again.

January 9, 2018

Martha: We made sure that Jeff wore his hat and kept it on outside today. His nose was running quite a bit and he seems more tired than usual. He didn't sleep as long today—he woke up after a half hour all plugged up and couldn't get back to sleep. Hope he isn't getting another ear infection. He ate some of his lunch and played quietly for most of the afternoon.

Jane: Jeff seems to be feeling better. His grandma is visiting and would like to come and spend some time with him in the child care to see what he does there. I'll call to arrange a time with you.

Newsletters

Newsletters are a common means of sharing information with parents (Wilson, 2005). A newsletter provides a different format for sharing much of the same kind of information that can be available on bulletin boards and in parent corners. The advantage, of course, is that parents can take the newsletter home and read it at their convenience. Newsletters are usually more effective when they have a personal touch and include entries from the centre director, board members, staff, and parents. Some parents will be interested in reading about child development, others may want ideas for birthdays or recipes, and still others may be more interested in learning about the resources in their community, so it's important to have a good mixture of information (Couchenour & Chrisman, 2011). The best way to learn what parents want to read about is to ask them! It's also a good idea to find out whether the parents themselves would be willing to contribute or help in the production of the newsletter.

Having spots in the newsletter where children can be involved may enhance parents' interest and serve to improve communication between parents and children. One child-care centre's newsletter always left one blank page where children could draw a picture of something special that happened to them that week or on that day. When the newsletter arrived home, the child could describe the picture and event in more detail to the parent.

Alternatively, the newsletter could be sent out to parents via email, which some parents may prefer. The choice of whether to distribute the newsletter electronically depends on parents' employment and whether they prefer paper or electronic documents in general. Early childhood educators should ask parents how they want to receive the newsletter. For those who want to receive it via email, it may be worthwhile to create a distribution list for this purpose. Parents often prefer the email option because they can easily transfer the calendar of events to their mobile devices. Some parents may still prefer having a calendar that hangs on their fridge.

Developing a website for the centre, which involves technological skills that many educators have acquired, may be another means of providing parents with timely information. Working parents may take the time to browse a website regularly, especially if they know that information is often updated. A website may be a good way to ensure that parents have access to parent handbooks and policies, and notices. As well, posting back issues of the newsletter on the centre's website could serve as a useful means of storing information for parents.

Considerations for Newsletters

1. Newsletters should be published and sent home on a regular basis.
2. Always include contact information about the child-care centre, including phone number and address. Another page can be more specific to a particular playroom or age group.
3. Include a title—something catchy or more personal than "A Monthly Newsletter." Ask parents for suggestions.
4. Use coloured paper if possible.
5. Try to have the information typed or keyboarded so that it's easier to read. Be sure to proofread it for spelling and grammatical errors.
6. Try to match the reading level or language to that of the parents. If language differences exist, enlist the assistance of a translator for pertinent sections.
7. Get everyone involved in contributing information. Include the director, early childhood educators, cook, parents, and children.
8. Have a section where the children can draw a picture.
9. Have spaces for parents and community groups to add information as well.
10. Include messages from important people (e.g., the owner or director) and updates about the program and staff. A page dedicated to each playroom can serve to focus on the developmental needs of the children in each age group and particular noteworthy areas for parents.
11. Include activities, books, and toys that may be of interest to parents, and demonstrate the developmentally appropriate knowledge early childhood educators have.
12. Include a calendar of upcoming events and activities; a calendar is helpful for families in their planning.
13. Provide digital copies via email or on the centre's website.

NEW IN ROOM 3!

Classroom Newsletter

Where Is the Curriculum?

We welcomed lots of new children to our classroom this month and it has been a joy watching new relationships form. This month has been full of learning about each other and our families, learning about the classroom culture we want to create, and learning how we all fit together in our new classroom community.

As I sit and reflect, I find myself being reminded of Reggio Amelia's philosophy: that the day-to-day living is the curriculum in a classroom.

But what does that mean? How can our daily routines and functions be our curriculum?

Artemeva Juliya/Shutterstock

Roxanne is gardening.

I have come to realize that children enter our classroom as three-year-old toddlers and leave a year later as four-year-old children. Our days are filled with living together and the self-help skills associated with our classroom functionality. Together we learn to dress ourselves for the weather and how that weather can affect what we wear outdoors.

We learn helpfulness in setting the tables for lunch, sweeping or mopping up spills, and helping our peers with that especially tricky puzzle. We learn about color mixing too.

Changes to Our Classroom

We are sorry to say goodbye to Thomas as he moves up to Room 1, but we know that he's ready for new and exciting learning.

We would like to welcome Lily and Feroze to Room 5! We are so excited to have you join us!

Dates to Remember

Gardening: August 2nd, 16th & 28th

Library Visit: August 3rd & 17th

Centre Closures: August 7th & 25th

Field Trips: August 21st

Reminders to Families

- Please ensure your child is dressed for the weather with a sun hat and has had sunscreen applied before arriving to daycare.
- Please leave all snacks at home or in your car as we are a NUT-FREE environment.
- Please provide an extra set of clothes during field day trips.

Thank You, Students!

Special thanks are due to the following students:

Jacob Silver for helping to clean up after baking day and to **Shauna Ettinger** for sharing her blocks at recess.

Source: Based on Lynleigh Keat, Mount Royal University Child Care Center.

Ideas for Newsletter Content

- A Note from the Director
  - Review of policy
  - Staff changes
  - Calendar of Upcoming Events
  - Meetings
  - Potluck suppers
- Parents Contributions
  - Ask parents to share information, ideas, or concerns that would be pertinent to other parents
  - Thank yous
- Cook's Corner
  - New recipes
- Classifieds
- Primary Educator's Contributions
  - Update about what is going on in the room
- Children's Contributions
  - Pictures
  - Stories
- Parent Information (related to parents with children in this age group)
  - Courses/workshops (for parents and children)
  - Book reviews

- Room changes
- Welcome to new families

- Field trips

- Menu changes

- Requests for donations

- Jokes
- "Dictated" stories

- Child development information
- Ideas for "to-dos" with children
- Coping strategies

Online Communication

Online communication, particularly the use of social media, is prevalent in our society. The potential for providing one- and two-way communication, resources, marketing, advertising programs, and a sense of community is endless. Educators appreciate the relative ease, currency, and cost efficiency associated with sharing information with parents in this manner, and parents appreciate the real-time information, the child-care program's responsiveness, and the readily available sources of support. However, caution must be exercised. Educators must be cognizant of their ethical responsibilities and remember that anything posted has the potential to be viewed by a worldwide audience. Administrators attempting to deal with their staff's appropriate use of social media (e.g., Facebook postings) are well aware of the cautions that may be required; for example, the Canadian Child Care Federation (2004) has developed guidelines for using the Internet safely. In a program, developing policies and rules for online communication may be a necessary first (and continuing) step. Program staff need to look beyond the short-term time-saving benefits to ensure that program goals and family needs are met.

Many educators are being asked to move into the digital age, and others are asking how technology can enhance communication with parents.

How do we balance the use of technology as we become mindful digital citizens while nurturing responsive, and engaged relationships with the children, their families, and the professional community around us? How Early Childhood Educators build these authentic and responsive relationships is unique to both the educator and the organizations they work with in. There is a movement amongst educators, in support of creating more meaningful connections between "Home & School," towards the use of technology in communicating development and curriculum with families. This leap into a new pedagogical practice is often unknown territory for many educators, and can leave them with many questions. (Lalonde, 2015, p. 7)

As noted, social media can present hazards in terms of confidentiality, and programs must establish clear guidelines for their use. It's relatively common for day home providers to use social media with small groups of children in their care. However, many programs don't permit social media use because it's difficult to manage and control. Email and text messaging are used more commonly because they are more secure ways to communicate. Some programs have adopted online photo-, video-, and story-sharing services such as Storypark and Hello Mama. These online services are private and offer a safe, convenient way to share daily information and learning stories. They also provide opportunities for two-way communication between educators and parents.

Educators have shared positive stories about their use of online services like Storypark for parent engagement. Some report that parents are absolutely thrilled to share "in the moment" with their child. Parents have related how they share a photo from that day with the child at home, and it becomes a powerful way to engage with the child. Many online services provide a mechanism for parents to respond and make comments or even share photos, videos, and moments in the child's learning with extended family members. Creating meaningful connections between children and their families is a significant part of child-care practice and has contributed to the identity of the profession. Yet barriers of time, support, comfort, and resources can make it a challenging goal. The use of technology in practice can be both exciting and intimidating, and technology can allow educators to share openly with families and be contributors to innovation in practice.

At the same time, however easily accessible technology is, some programs have opted not to use it as a tool for recording and sharing children's learning. Many educators feel that the expectation to take digital photos and create online documentation for each child on a regular basis is too overwhelming and not supported by planning time in the majority of child-care programs. Other educators report that they never really know whether parents read the emails or the other online documentation they send since they don't get a response. Many educators prefer face-to-face communication, during which they can experience and respond to parent reactions.

SCENARIO

ENGAGING WITH PHOTOS

A child-care program began the practice of setting out an exploration book beside the sign-in/sign-out sheet. Each day, the educators would take one photo, print it off, and add it to the book. Some days, they would add a one-word description ("Fun!!!"). Other days, they would provide a description of the activity or learning that took place. At first, the educators created this documentation occasionally, but when they observed parents' and children's reactions, they decided to continue this practice daily. Although time was a constraint, they realized how valuable this photo was in their relationship with children and families.

SCENARIO

REFLECTING ON HOW TO BEST USE TECHNOLOGY IN PARENT ENGAGEMENT

After a community forum, program directors talked about their approaches to using online communication. One director was hesitant about using it because she felt that if parents received messages

continues ▶

▶ *continues*

and information during the day, they would not take the time to talk face to face with the educators. She felt it was an easy out for parents. Another director said that his program used online communication to relay the basic information that parents want: for example, the length of the child's nap, what the child ate, and the child's demeanour during the day. He stated that doing so freed the educators and parents up to talk about significant events rather than the mundane. Other directors discussed their use of private online services for all parent communication and stated that parents were happy to have documentation and learning stories they could access any time of the day or night.

The preceding scenario demonstrates that program staff must be willing to discuss and determine what is best for their programs and for their parents in relation to technology use. What is easiest may not necessarily produce the most desirable results. Educators need to examine their goals, be willing to try new approaches, and enter into dialogue with parents to monitor and understand what works best for everyone involved.

Travelling Goodie Bags

Most children derive great pleasure from being able to share their experiences with their parents. A "goodie bag" that contains prized possessions from the child-care centre may be a way of bringing a little piece of the centre home for an evening. For example, the children in one class each brought home a stuffed animal for the weekend, and then they drew pictures or wrote in a journal about what they did over those two days. The pictures and writing were then shared in class. Family theme bags (Helm, 1994) involve more comprehensive planning of activities, songs, crafts, and stories around a particular idea, but they also give families an opportunity to spend some quality time together. Literacy bags that contain a story and a variety of associated literacy activities such as songs, fingerplays, or art ideas may provide a means for parents to build on a child's interest. Portapacks (Wilson, 2005) consist of a small portable package of play materials that can be taken home or used in vehicles. These packs might include sensory objects (e.g., feely bags) or simple cause-and-effect toys. Goodie bags and family theme bags may have special merit for low-income families, where toys and books can be shared. The families could keep some of the items (such as playdough and craft supplies).

The goodie bag can be assembled by the child, and the educator can add to it according to her or his professional judgment. Sometimes child-care staff are concerned that the contents of the goodie bag will not be cared for or returned to the centre. It has been our experience, however, that families and children usually value this sharing and return the contents in good condition. Just as bringing a piece of the centre home can be enjoyed by children and their families, the reverse is equally important. Children are often thrilled to take a "piece of home" to the centre, in the form of picture albums of family as well as toys and objects.

But early childhood educators need to be cautious. If, for example, a family is in the throes of the divorce process, they might appreciate a book that explains divorce in language a child can understand. However, such a gesture may also be viewed as a criticism or an intrusion into family life.

Parents as Volunteers in the Child Care

In the 1970s, a large number of centres and preschools relied on parent "volunteers" to participate and assist. Today the realities of work and family mean that it's much more difficult for parents to be involved in this fashion. Many programs no longer require that parents volunteer regularly. However, volunteers are always appreciated, and parents who volunteer gain valuable insight into their child's day. With advance planning, parents may still be available to attend the centre. For example, many parents enjoy celebrating their children's birthday with their friends there. As well, parents can play a number of roles within the playroom—as a special helper, an extra guide for a field trip, or a guest speaker to talk about their job or a hobby (police officers and firefighters seem to be among the most popular). Early childhood educators should remember that children may have other special people in their lives who may be available to volunteer. A grandmother who will come and sing or a grandfather who reads to the children can be a welcome addition to the playroom, especially to the individual child. Parents need to feel welcome, and they may require sufficient notice to plan for such a day. Volunteers may be hesitant and not sure where to start or what to do. Providing guidelines and a range of ideas where they may become involved is often helpful.

SCENARIO

MAKING IT EASY

"I was really hesitant to spend time in the toddler room, since I'd never really spent time with little children except my own, and I've never been with a big group. But from the moment I walked in the room, the early childhood educators were so nice—they showed me where stuff was and let me spend time with Gabi until I was comfortable. Then it was suggested that I shift over to the housekeeping centre where many of the children played, including Gabi. They made it so easy—and now I'm not sure why I was so nervous!"

The educators provided this parent with many ideas on how she could participate. The educators were mindful that she was hesitant and were ready to intervene if she felt uncomfortable or found it challenging disengaging from her own daughter.

The benefits of parent involvement are clear. Parents can benefit from participating in their children's lives at the centre and from meeting their children's friends. This experience may also heighten parents' understanding of the complexity of the educator's role and the demands of the job. Moreover, early childhood educators can often learn much about the children by observing their interaction with their parents. Educators must remember, though, not to make hasty judgments based on a single observation of child–parent interaction. A parent might not feel comfortable enough to act naturally at first; therefore, the behaviour you see may not be at all typical. They may be hesitant as they feel you are observing them. Because of the many demands on parents today, educators must not judge negatively those who are not able to participate in this way. Instead, the educator needs to find other opportunities or activities for involvement that are more suited to that parent.

Ideas for Parents Visiting the Room

1. Welcome parents and thank them for coming.
2. Provide parents with an information sheet that welcomes them and gives some directions about what they can do in the room.
3. Invite parents to hang up their coat with their child's and then to feel free to observe or follow their child to the activity of their choice.
4. Be sure that you are observing and are readily available to suggest alternatives. Parents who feel uncomfortable may stay close to their child, unsure of how to get involved.
5. If parents want to be assigned tasks, you can suggest that they assist in the art area by putting children's names on their work or help organize a play area. You can also help them engage with a group of children if they are comfortable doing so.
6. Invite parents to join in any games, dramatic activities, or play that may develop, since the children will enjoy their participation.

continues ▶

▶ *continues*

7. Be sure that parents are enjoying their time in your playroom, and check regularly that they feel comfortable and at home.

You may wish to talk with parents before they visit your playroom to find out if they have any preferences of how to be involved or if they have anything they would like to share from their own family traditions or culture.

Before- and After-Work Activities

For parents who are unable to come to the centre during daytime hours, activities before or after work may provide the only opportunity they have to be actively involved in the centre.

Evening hours are often precious to staff and families, so early childhood educators should recognize their efforts to ensure successful evening events. Planning breakfast or lunch-hour events (e.g., in workplace centres) may be another alternative that better fits families' schedules. These activities may include celebrations, social activities, or speakers. Any of these events presents an opportunity for fundraising. At a family picnic or carnival, parents won't be averse to paying a nominal fee if they know that the money will be used within the child-care centre. Parents may actually be more willing to contribute and be involved in a social event than in other fundraising activities (e.g., selling merchandise or tickets). Early childhood educators should always consider families' ability to pay and should provide a choice if payment presents concerns for some children or families.

Celebrations and Social Activities

Social activities may include informal gatherings such as afternoon or evening tea or coffee parties, potluck suppers, or fundraising dinners (e.g., spaghetti nights, pancake breakfasts, barbecues). Parents may enjoy evenings planned around children's activities at the centre, such as art shows, or, if the children are old enough, performances of songs or plays. Even though some early childhood educators may have concerns about children performing, parents and grandparents treasure these moments.

SCENARIO

A CREATIVE IDEA

The director of a child-care centre was getting tired of constantly having to dispose of children's artwork and of cubbies filled to the brim. She decided to stage an "art exhibition." All pieces of artwork were labelled and displayed. Families were invited to view the children's accomplishments and share refreshments and snacks. The children took great pride in showing off their artwork. The evening ended with each child leaving with his or her pieces of art—this alone fulfilled the director's goal for the evening, but the enjoyment experienced by the children and their families was a pleasant bonus.

Many preschool programs hold an evening where the daily program is simulated so that parents can actually experience "a day in the life of a child at the centre." "Special people" may be invited to attend, and even though fathers might be the most commonly invited guests, these can also include siblings, grandparents, cousins, and friends.

Holidays and special occasions are often good motivators for get-togethers between families and the centre. Halloween parties, Mother's and Father's Day celebrations, and cultural awareness evenings are often popular. Fundraising events such as games nights, cakewalks, or carnivals can provide families with a fun night out and at the same time give them an opportunity to support the centre. The ideas are endless, but you never know which idea will attract parents.

Early childhood educators need to arrange activities to fit parents' schedules and needs. For example, parents who need child care in the evening will be more likely to attend family events or activities that begin earlier in the day (e.g., at pickup time) or that have child care built in. However, parents with other young children at home will likely find these arrangements more difficult. Parent input will help guarantee a higher attendance rate. Educators should be careful to include diverse families in all events; for example, a Father's Day event or craft may serve to alienate those children who come from divorced families or single-parent homes. Ensure that children know they have the option of inviting a special person or of making the craft for that person.

Speakers

Engaging a speaker to discuss a topic of interest with a group of parents is one activity that is often well received. The speaker may be from a related profession, such as a doctor, nurse, psychologist, or social worker, or may be one of the staff. Sometimes early childhood educators don't give their own expertise enough credit, and the parents might very well prefer listening to the educator—who has daily contact with their children—discuss such topics as discipline or development. Many communities have parent programs that may be interested in partnering with the centre to provide speakers for an evening. In addition, educators should remember that parents themselves have a wealth of knowledge and information and may be invaluable as "guest" speakers. Students from a local university who attend an early learning program may be willing to present on a topic they are well informed about. These events require considerable planning, and input from parents is necessary to ensure that they are sufficiently interested and able to attend. Parents' attendance may be improved by providing child care during a parent education activity.

An experienced early childhood educator recently relayed the following story about her journey in parent engagement.

SCENARIO

ENGAGING PARENTS IN MEANINGFUL WAYS

"Years ago, we held parent education events. We always had food and provided child care and always had a smattering of parents. We abandoned the idea when we realized that parents were very busy and an after-hours event was too much. In our inner-city multicultural program, we recently reinvented the idea of a parent education evening, but with a twist. We still always provide food and child care and we usually have a small activity to engage in, like making worry dolls or painting rocks. But the major difference is that we have a question for the parents. Our latest was 'How should we rename our playrooms?' (rather than the typical 1, 2, 3). The parents engaged in discussing the question and then continued to educate us about their culture, their traditions, and the things that were important to them and their families. The difference is that the parents are educating us, and all we have to do is be there and listen. We still only get small numbers of parents, but we learn so much that the staff can hardly wait until the next event."

Sample Parent Meeting Agendas

Agenda I

5:00–5:45   Supper with the children in the out-of-school care room (chili and toast—vegetarian substitute available)

continues ▶

5:50	Parents adjourn to the lounge for the meeting (child care provided in the 3- to 4-year-old room)
6:00	Meeting begins

1. Welcome from the director
2. Guest speaker—Mary Adams: Topic: Guiding Your Child's Behaviour
3. Centre update
   - Playground
   - Fees
   - Licensing inspection
4. Questions and feedback

7:30	Adjournment

Agenda II

5:00–5:45	Dinner in the main gym
5:50	Children can move to Room 3 for activities
6:00	Meeting begins

1. Welcome from educators and director
2. Discuss celebrations to highlight from now until June
3. Update on new project (and sign consents)
4. Questions

7:30	Adjournment

Home Visits

Home visits have traditionally been used as a form of parent–educator involvement (Wilson, 2014). Some educators note that there can be advantages to these visits. They can give the educator a very different perspective on the child and family. Children often talk about the "time you came to my house!" long after the visit. If the intent of a home visit is clear, it can be a very positive strategy for building relationships. However, home visits can be problematic. For example, some parents feel they are intrusive. Many families value the privacy of their home and are uncomfortable at the thought of a visit by an educator, who they feel is there to make judgments about their family, lifestyle, or parenting. Moreover, children may not understand the reason for the visit and misinterpret the intent. Early childhood educators have also observed that, given the demands of their work, the time required to visit the parents of all their children is unrealistic. For many reasons, then, home visits have waned in popularity and are seldom implemented these days, except in the case of children with special needs or vulnerable families. If home visits seem like a worthwhile strategy, it's essential that the goals of the visit are clear to both staff and parents and that all parties are comfortable with the visit.

SCENARIO

TENSION DURING HOME VISITS

"One day our daughter's preschool teacher came to our home for a visit. We lived in the same community and had been friends for some time before she became my daughter's teacher, so we were expecting a pleasant visit. My daughter felt strange calling her 'Mrs. Smith' instead of 'Sandy' and taking her on a 'tour' of her room. I felt that some of Sandy's questions weren't as casual and were about my parenting."

This anecdote highlights the boundary issues involved in home visits. Usually people who visit are friends, and a home visit by an educator can sometimes be stressful. The problem can be partially resolved by both sides having a clear idea of the purpose of the visit.

Parent Meetings and Conferences

Parent–teacher meetings tend to be more formal and are a way of ensuring that regular communication occurs. Typically, meetings are held in the early learning setting. These meetings may also be called *conferences* or *interviews*, depending on the program or affiliation (e.g., programs affiliated with school systems may refer to these meetings as *conferences*). Just as the school system schedules regular meetings or interviews with parents, so do some child-care centres. Meetings can be called for a special purpose (e.g., to discuss a concern, to develop a joint plan for toilet training), or they can serve to update the parents on the children's experiences at the centre.

Parent meetings can be stressful for early childhood educators. Some staff actually freeze up at the idea of having to discuss problem behaviour with parents. Parents, too, can view the meeting with trepidation ("What bad news am I going to hear this time?") because of previous bad experiences that ended in misunderstandings (Nalls, Mullis, Cornille, Mullis, & Jeter, 2009).

Good rapport and effective planning are essential ingredients for successful parent–teacher conferences. Conferences should always begin and end on a positive note (Nalls et al., 2009; Wilson, 2010). Effective planning also includes gathering documentation from other staff members, organizing the material to be shared with parents, and being prepared for questions from parents. It is just as important to listen to the parents' perspective as it is to make the points you want to convey.

SCENARIO

A SUCCESSFUL CONFERENCE

Jennifer, an educator, decided to ask Norman's parents to come in for a meeting. Norman had been so restless at naptime that the early childhood educators had had trouble settling him down for a sleep. When Jennifer discussed this matter with his parents, they said that bedtime at home had been difficult, too. Norman's parents thought he was having strange fears at night, which is quite usual for children around the age of 3. His parents had found that a nightly ritual of looking under the bed and placing a stuffed animal "on guard duty" seemed to alleviate his fears. The staff suggested that the parents bring the stuffed animal to the centre so that it could guard Norman at naptime as well. This input from the parents was most helpful.

Planning effective conferences with parents requires careful consideration of who should come, when they will come, what will be discussed, and how the discussion will be organized. Planning may be particularly important with parents from diverse cultural or linguistic backgrounds or when children present special concerns.

Considerations for Parent–Educator Conferences

1. Be prepared.
   - Have a clear idea about why you are holding the conference and what you hope to achieve.
   - Consider which staff members would be the most appropriate to involve in the conference. These will most likely be the primary early childhood educators, but consider including others (e.g., family members, professionals) as well.
   - Familiarize yourself with the child and parent by reviewing the child's records, if needed.

continues ▶

2. Set the stage.

■ Choose a time that is mutually convenient for both parents and educators. Try to ensure that no one is rushed, either getting there or during the meeting itself.

■ Let the parents know what you'll be discussing ahead of time so that it won't come as a surprise and they have the opportunity to organize their thoughts and ideas.

■ When the parents arrive, make them feel comfortable. Provide adult-sized chairs in a quiet area, and offer refreshments, if possible.

■ Have all the necessary information with you so that you won't have to disrupt the meeting.

■ Attempt to start every conference on a positive note.

■ Begin with something personal about the child—an anecdote or a picture.

■ Share relevant and current documentation.

3. Lead the way.

■ Inform the parents about the child's life at the centre by sharing, throughout the conference, observations, anecdotes, and specific examples of what the child is doing.

■ Speak in plain, clear English. Avoid the use of jargon and terms with which parents may not be familiar.

■ Listen to the parents and try to understand their perspective, their concerns, and their interpretation of what you're telling them. Be open to learning more about the child from the people who know him or her best.

■ Present child behavioural problems as challenges requiring joint problem solving.

■ Be prepared to offer parents ideas, resources, or referrals.

■ Work out a plan of action with parents that will be in the best interest of the child, planning subsequent meetings or forms of communication, if necessary.

■ Close the conference on a positive note. Summarize what has been discussed and the plan of action, if there is one. Set a time to review progress, if necessary.

■ Thank the parents for coming and for their input.

■ Follow up after a few days with a note of thanks, a summary of the meeting, or a progress review.

Parent Boards

Many nonprofit child-care centres and preschool programs are run by a volunteer board of directors. The centre's director is accountable to the board of directors and reports to it regularly on all aspects of the centre, including finances, personnel issues, and programs. Often the board of directors consists of community members who have knowledge and talents in particular areas, such as accounting, fundraising, law, health, or human resources. When parents volunteer to be on the board of directors, their involvement gives them the opportunity to learn more about the program and to influence, and even control, the policies that govern the centre and its staff.

Parent boards can be difficult to manage. Early childhood educators may find it difficult to accept that they are accountable to people who are not trained in their discipline, and may feel that decisions, particularly about daily occurrences at the centre, should be made by people who have appropriate training. Directors and educators need to include parents thoughtfully. This may start with a workshop on board governance that will assist in determining the roles and responsibilities of board members. It may be worthwhile to have parent board members sign a code of conduct that stipulates that their focus is on child care and not the centre or their individual child (or finances). Parents may need to feel that they can opt out of discussions and decisions where they are challenged to step out of their parent role and act in accordance with the program needs (e.g., a budget increase). These discussions can be tricky and may need to be handled by someone external to the board. Sometimes, staff and parents may need to negotiate areas of control. For example, the parent board could be responsible for areas such as finances and public relations, while staff maintain control of the day-to-day activities of the centre. The division of duties may work in some programs, but not in all. Early childhood educators will need to be knowledgeable in their field and confident in their abilities to negotiate successfully with parent boards or seek outside assistance if needed.

Parent Advisory Committees

Advisory committees have less power than boards of directors, and members may assume a variety of roles, from advising to helping with daily setup and snack time, with social events, or with hands-on assistance with the children in the classroom. All parents have the opportunity to be involved, but the type of involvement has been predetermined by the staff and is therefore usually very helpful to the early childhood educators.

BEYOND THE CENTRE: WORKING WITH WIDER SYSTEMS

Sometimes families require assistance and support that goes beyond the time limitations or professional boundaries of the early childhood professional. Many families have adequate support networks and can access required assistance without the help of the centre. However, for others, assistance provided by the centre in accessing community support networks can be invaluable (Daro & Dodge, 2009; R. Freeman, 2010).

Early childhood educators should be aware of the different types of resources their community offers. This knowledge will help them provide accurate information to parents about resources that can meet their particular needs. Parents' ability to make choices on their own must be respected, and sometimes the role of the educator is simply to provide information about existing resources so that the parents can independently decide what action to take.

There are a number of services in each community that provide support for a wide range of family or individual problems. When investigating and updating information related to community services, centre staff should gather specific and detailed information to ensure that their recommendations are appropriate.

Considerations for Community Resources

- Is the agency a self-help group run by people with similar problems, or is there professional support? For some parents, self-help groups are invaluable, but for others, professional counselling and guidance will be their only choice.

- Is there a cost for the services, and can the costs be claimed (e.g., through insurance policies or deducted from income tax)? Does the agency have a sliding fee scale where clients are charged according to their income? Providing alternatives may prevent the awkward situation of parents having to admit that they cannot pay for such a service.

- Does the agency have entrance criteria? Often agencies have to limit the number of people they deal with by imposing criteria based on age, disability, or type of problem. Sometimes the agency will openly state criteria, but in some cases guidelines will be vague and the early childhood professional will need to clarify.

continues ▶

► *continues*

- Does the agency have expertise in working with preschool children? Because most early childhood educators reading this book will be working with preschool children, a good question to ask is whether the agency has past experience in this area.

- What is the involvement with the early childhood professional? Some agencies work very closely with early childhood staff and invite observations and opinions from the educators who are with the children on a day-to-day basis. Other agencies will not be able to work in active collaboration with the centre or even to keep staff informed of what is happening. Depending on the organization, its structure and purpose, the nature of the problem, and the wishes of the family, the desirability of centre involvement will vary.

- How does one access the agency? Some agencies require a referral from a family physician, child welfare worker, or social worker. Other agencies are based on self-referral. A family in stress does not need to make extra phone calls. Finding out the appropriate way to access services and facilitating access may be helpful.

- Is there a waiting list? Some agencies have a waiting list of six months or more, while others will see people in crisis immediately. This information is vital to have.

- What kind of support does the agency offer? Some agencies provide group structures for people with problems, some work with families together, and some do individual counselling. Some offer "crisis intervention"—that is, short-term intensive support—while others may offer less intense support over a longer period of time. Many agencies offer a variety of formats.

Once the information is available, consider how best to pass it on to parents and how to assist them, if required, to "take that first step." You might display pamphlets from different agencies in the parent corner or on the bulletin board, write a short article in the centre's newsletter, or, through your personal relationship with parents, encourage them to seek outside assistance.

Community Participation

There are often issues in communities that may affect the well-being of children, and over which both educators and parents share concern. Those issues could be a lack of recreational facilities, the need for crosswalks, or issues related to early learning (e.g., the need for full-time child care or affordable care options). Some educators are willing to go beyond their day-to-day work at the centre to join parents in advocating on behalf of children, or even facilitating such efforts. Many communities and municipalities have joined the effort to focus on the early years. These initiatives more often involve the whole community or different aspects of the community coming together rather than one program. These groups may stem from recent developments in neuroscience or the need for play, but they typically share a common goal to create environments that are responsive to the needs of young children and their families, especially when young families struggle with a lack of support (Lombardi, 2017).

In an attempt to influence developmental outcomes for children at risk in Alberta, Alberta Education funded a project called the Early Child Development Mapping Project (ECMap) from 2009 to 2014. The purpose of the project was to conduct a province-wide population-based study of early childhood development and then share the findings with community-based coalitions to help them better respond to local needs. Many coalitions included representatives from health, schools, libraries, and Parent Link centres; parents; community members; and students. Educators also engaged in this community project. The coalitions were able to be truly responsive to the needs in their specific communities because there were no expectations for strategies or approaches or outcomes. In this way, community coalition members were provided a forum to engage in meaningful ways (ECMap, 2014).

MAKING COLLABORATION WORK

Even with the best intentions, early childhood educators who overlook certain considerations can hamper effective collaborative strategies, which can sometimes result in parents' negative feelings toward the centre. Here are some considerations that should apply to the planning of all attempts to collaborate with parents.

Cultural Awareness and Inclusion

Sometimes, even though it may happen inadvertently, certain people are made to feel left out. The following scenario provides an example.

SCENARIO

ENSURE INCLUSIVITY

Staff at a child-care centre put up a poster in the parent corner that advertised a new indoor park in the city's downtown. The poster featured a photograph of people sitting on benches in a lovely area full of plants and flowers. The poster's written message was "Relax together in your garden." One educator, who had attended a workshop on multicultural awareness, took a good look at the poster and remarked that its photo included no people who are visible minorities, no people in wheelchairs, and no older adults. Everyone in the photo was well dressed, white, middle-aged, and appeared to be fairly well off. The staff member felt that the poster subtly excluded many people from feeling they had been invited to "relax together in your garden."

The words and pictures we use carry strong messages, and early childhood educators should be sensitive to this matter. Are the pictures and posters that invite parents to participate inclusive? Do they reflect the different family structures, such as single-parent and step-parent families? Do they include extended family members? Do they include parents and children with disabilities? Is the language level used suitable (e.g., little jargon)?

Some centres have made the effort to have their written material translated for parents who have difficulty with English. This process is time-consuming and sometimes expensive, but when there is a commitment to the principle of inclusion, it's possible to find a way. Sometimes parents who are fluent in a second language are happy to help out, and immigrant-serving agencies are often able to assist as well.

Imagine what it would be like to be invited to a parent–teacher conference at 5:00 p.m. on Christmas Eve, a time when your family has a traditional get-together every year. This happens all too often to families who celebrate their festivals and holy days at different times throughout the year. Several multicultural calendars are now available, and early childhood educators should ensure that parent activities don't conflict with special days from any of the religions and cultures represented at the centre. If in doubt, it's always better to ask than to plan without consulting parents.

Other Considerations

Bringing food to a potluck dinner may be a luxury that some families can't afford. Attending a picnic with little to put in a picnic hamper may be so humiliating for some families that they may choose not to attend. Having to pay for child-care arrangements may make evening activities too expensive for some parents to attend. Even extra bus fare to attend an evening session may not be available. Awareness of the cost implications of parent activities is important to consider in planning.

One mother related the following incident.

BE CONSIDERATE

"Last Wednesday I was invited to a parent discussion evening at the centre. I worked behind the cash counter until 5:00 p.m., rode home on a crowded bus, and quickly went through the children's supper, bath, and bedtime routine. Then I jumped into the shower, dressed, and ran out the door to catch the bus to the centre. When I got there, I almost broke down into tears. The little chairs that the children sit on were arranged in a circle, and we (the parents) were expected to sit on them and listen to an expert tell us about reading stories to children."

In addition to location, the physical arrangements of the space in which parent activities are held should be given careful consideration. The arrangement of chairs can appear formal (in rows, as in a lecture), or the space can be arranged comfortably and informally.

Cautions

It's important to remember that educators often struggle with family engagement. All educators would wholeheartedly agree that family engagement is essential, but many will have hesitations. Educators must be mindful of several factors.

The first and crucial consideration in planning collaboration with parents is the staff's time. It's not yet standard practice in the early childhood field for educators to have paid planning time, especially beyond time for the planning required in the playrooms. Many early childhood educators may volunteer time, after working for eight hours a day with children, to organize and attend meetings with parents. While their commitment to working with parents is honourable, it should not be taken advantage of. Educators need time to meet and plan, and they need to either be paid for their work or given time off in lieu of it. Centre directors and staff need to balance the demands of the program with the physical and emotional well-being of the staff.

Second, there may always be parents who don't engage, no matter what the activity or the timing of the activity. Parents with young children are often in the busiest time of their lives, and the time to interact and collaborate may present a challenge to many families along with the logistics (e.g., children of different ages with different activities, distance from the child-care centre). Although educators will always attempt to find some activity for parents to be engaged in, it's important that they not become discouraged when parents don't engage.

Lastly, educators may need to be flexible and even set aside their own values in some instances.

Meira recounted an incident that occurred when she worked in a community-health-based preschool program many years ago.

BEING FLEXIBLE

"The preschool I worked in was located in an inner-city community and had a strong parent participation component. The program focused on health and development in the early years. One family attended on a regular basis, but Mom was reserved and not actively involved. She typically sat at the back of the room and interacted readily with her son, Declan, but not with the other children. She rarely volunteered to assist or bring snack. One day, Declan ran excitedly into the room and declared that his mom had snack. I responded with excitement until I saw that snack consisted of a bottle of Coke and a bag of chips. I thought, *What is more important, one snack or one instance of family engagement?* I said, 'Oh that looks wonderful, thank you so much.' The look on Declan's and his mom's faces said it all. I realized that setting aside my values for a moment was more important to fulfill the family-engagement goals of the program. After all I know now after many years of practice, I would do the same thing."

How would you have reacted if you were Meira? Would your goals for family engagement overrule the objectives of the program? Would you set aside your personal preferences, beliefs, and feelings to achieve your program's goals for family engagement? These are hard questions, but ones that you will face in practice.

PARENT ACTIVITIES COME IN ALL SHAPES

Educators need to be mindful that a variety of activities can engage parents, as the following scenario demonstrates.

SCENARIO

ENGAGEMENT HAS MANY FACES

In discussing options for parent engagement, one student explained that in her centre, parents were expected to come in two Saturdays per year for a major cleanup and organizational day. The main rationale was cost saving. If parents didn't assist, extra fees would need to be gathered to hire cleaning staff. The student explained that the day was a major social event for parents: they planned well in advance, brought pizza, and had the opportunity to share with their child's educator and the parents of their children's friends. The event had been taking place for many years. It seemed clear that if parents found this type of activity engaging, a variety of activities could be successful with the right amount of planning.

Get Input from Parents

It is believed that parental time constraints are the major barriers to effective engagement (Duffy, Induni, & Moiduddin, 2010). Therefore, engaging parents early and appropriately is essential. Formulating the goals of parent–staff collaboration should always be done in conjunction with the parents. Co-creating opportunities for collaboration with parents would be ideal. Early childhood educators need to provide opportunities to promote parents' choices and decision making (Wilson, 2005). It is disempowering to have others decide what is best for you. In addition, there is little point in planning an activity if parents don't feel that it would be a valuable use of their time. Informal conversations with parents and a parent questionnaire or survey may give you ideas on the type, length, and scheduling of activities. For example, parents may be more willing to engage in social activities as fundraisers rather than commit to fundraising events throughout the year. When parents feel they have some input in activities, they will likely be more committed to them. Moreover, when parents see that their input is taken into account, they may be willing to increase their involvement. If a questionnaire is used to collect feedback on potential activities, bear in mind that, in responding, most parents will choose to support only those activities with which they are familiar; they will not have the benefit of discussion or of hearing about others' experiences with other options before they fill out the questionnaire.

EVALUATION

Evaluations of early childhood programs should be seen as an ongoing tool for improving the quality of the centre. Many accreditation tools also expect evaluation of parent–staff collaborations. After all, this collaboration is an essential ingredient of a quality program and should be evaluated just as the other program components are.

Evaluation should be considered as a means of gathering information and promoting discussion to help ensure quality care and good practice (Wright & Stegelin, 2003). Evaluation will also help staff and parents implement strategies that can lead to an enrichment of staff–parent relations and to successful collaboration between parents and staff.

Deciding What to Evaluate

Parent–staff relations, support for parents and families, and collaboration with parents are all multifaceted, subtle, but important aspects of a program. Therefore, determining how these areas should be evaluated and what information is to be collected should be the starting point in any evaluation. Early childhood educators must consider the many perspectives and variables when gathering and analyzing the data received.

Points to Consider

1. Consider the philosophies or beliefs of parents and educator.
2. Consider the different goals of parents, educator, and the centre.
3. Consider your purpose for the planned activity.
4. Consider which aspects of collaboration should be evaluated, such as
   - timing (e.g., evenings, Saturdays, after work)
   - location (e.g., Will parents have to travel back?)
   - child-care arrangements
   - parent versus family events
   - other considerations (e.g., length, time of year)
5. Consider who the stakeholders are.
6. Consider both parent and educator interests.

SCENARIO

HOW DO YOU MEASURE SUCCESS?

A local association for children with special needs hosted a guest speaker who discussed sleeping disorders. The parents who regularly attended were not impressed by the talk since their children, for the most part, were older and past this developmental period. However, one new parent came to the meeting precisely because her 18-month-old child with special needs was experiencing major difficulties in sleeping. This parent was extremely grateful for the information and support that resulted from this evening. She left feeling confident that her severely handicapped son would be able to learn to fall asleep on his own.

In the multicultural centre scenario "Engaging Parents in Meaningful Ways" presented earlier, the director informed us that one family always attends the parent education evenings. One child, 5-year-old Zenab, loves the family night and begs her mother to attend every month. Her mom explained that they mark the event on the calendar at home, and Zenab gets so excited when the time has arrived. Zenab loves that she can take her mom to her child care, and they can go together and spend time with her friends and teachers.

Program administrators and educators need to consider what success means to them. Is a full house most important? Is it essential to have 80% of parents attend? Can the event be meaningful if a handful of parents attend and deeply engage so that they, or the educators, come away with a better understanding of one another? Success can be measured in many ways, so be sure you understand what is important to families, your program, and the children.

THE "WHY" OF PARENT ENGAGEMENT

Now that we have considered multiple ways that educators may choose to engage or collaborate with parents, we will consider why this engagement is important.

Different people often have different perceptions of the benefits of an activity, and any single activity may have different benefits for the participants. Early childhood educators may wish to consider the positive value for themselves as professionals, for parents, and ultimately for the child. When benefits are seen from multiple perspectives, efforts made toward parent engagement may be seen as more worthwhile.

Benefits for the Child

■ Children whose parents support the program are better motivated and their self-esteem enhanced.

■ Children may feel more secure knowing that their parents trust and are involved with the centre.

■ Parents and early childhood educators may develop realistic goals to maximize the child's growth.

■ Parent engagement increases the children's self-confidence and makes them pleased and proud that their parents are interested in what is happening in their lives.

■ Collaboration provides information and knowledge of cultural or religious influences that may allow for a better understanding of the children and their families.

Benefits for the Parents

■ Collaboration strengthens families by helping them to have shared interests and goals and can give parents something to talk about or be engaged in with their children.

■ Collaboration increases parents' self-esteem by making them feel more confident of their parenting skills.

■ Access to resources and information helps parents develop knowledge.

■ Parents form new friendships and develop supportive networks with other families.

■ Parents have the opportunity to observe new or different parenting techniques.

■ Parents can see other children the same age as well as their own children in the developmental context of their peer group, which may help them set more realistic goals.

■ Parenting can be overwhelming. Having a reciprocal relationship can provide parents with much-needed support.

■ Parents may come to appreciate and value the efforts of early childhood educators.

■ Engagement through documentation provides parents with a means to better understand their child's development and educators with opportunities to seek input from parents.

Benefits for the Educator

■ Collaboration provides another opportunity to find out more about the children they are working with, so they can develop more child-centred experiences.

■ Understanding children's families helps educators understand the children.

■ Families may provide new ideas to explore in the program with all children or provide different perspectives on experiences.

■ Early childhood educators have more time when a parent takes responsibility for or works alongside with them in certain jobs (e.g., snack preparation, fundraising, field-trip supervision).

■ Making teaching and learning visible helps educators see themselves as professionals. Sharing their knowledge with parents helps parents see educators as skilled, knowledgeable professionals.

■ Having their work valued and respected is important to early childhood educators' sense of professionalism.

■ When strong relationships are established, staff morale is improved.

ONE ACTIVITY, TWO DIFFERENT GOALS

A child-care centre hosted a guest speaker for the evening. Parents arrived throughout the informal discussions and asked few questions, but after the meeting a lively debate ensued over coffee and doughnuts. One educator was quite upset at the low turnout and thought the late arrivals showed a lack of interest in the speaker. Another educator was pleased with the event since a significant number of parents did in fact attend (albeit not on time) and engaged in animated debate and socializing after the lecture. The first educator thought the goal of the evening was to provide information to the parents through the guest speaker. The second educator's goal was to provide parents with the opportunity to socialize with and support each other.

Clarifying criteria for success is an important part of evaluation. Early childhood educators need to bear in mind the vast differences in the parents' interest levels, their available time, and the ways in which they want to become involved. "Success" may not always be determined in terms of the number of parents involved in a particular event or how long they stayed, but rather in how this information can be used for change or improvement.

Engaging Fathers

The role of fathers is changing. Due to cultural and economic situations, fathers are becoming more involved in the lives of their young children. Fathers are more likely to be part of the drop-off or pickup routine and to be part of their children's activities (e.g., sports, child care, school). Many fathers consider work–life balance as important and seek ways to ensure that family time is included in their schedules. Early learning programs have begun to pay more attention to fathers as more fathers have become engaged in their children's education.

FATHER PARTICIPATION

One child-care centre monitored parents' participation in scheduled activities for a period of several months. They noticed with concern that few fathers attended. One staff member commented that perhaps parent activities were more geared to mothers than to fathers; for example, every Mother's Day, children and staff hosted a tea party. Events that are planned during the day may be more problematic for men's workplaces. This simple observation provided the impetus for staff to plan an activity geared specifically to fathers (e.g., soccer, hockey, video) once a month right after work. The activities were flexible enough that fathers could come and go according to their own schedules, and the children loved this time with someone special.

It's important to ensure that the environment of a program is welcoming for fathers and provides opportunities for them to become involved in day-to-day activities. Doing so may involve checking the program to ensure that positive images of men are included and that activities that fathers may choose to get involved in (e.g., sports, building) are available. Educators may want to self-reflect on their interactions with mothers and fathers. Do you tend to engage with mothers more than fathers? Do you speak to mothers and fathers differently? Do you share different information with mothers and fathers? Do you have different expectations of mothers and fathers? These questions may be a good starting point to better understand the role of fathers within your program and how to make changes, if needed.

CONCLUSION

This chapter has made a number of suggestions for enhancing collaboration with and engagement of parents. The ideas in the following box can serve as a reminder. Staff and parents will have their own suggestions to add to this list.

Methods of Parent–Educator Collaboration

Direct Communication:

- daily conversations
- emails, text messages

- phone calls
- learning story–sharing sites

Written Communication:

- documentation
- bulletin boards
- daily notes
- newsletters

- parent corners
- communication books
- travelling goodie bags

Volunteering or Visiting at the Centre

Evening Activities:

- speakers
- fundraisers

- family or social events
- discussion groups

Home Visits

Parent Boards

Parent–Educator Conferences

Parent Advisory Committees

Beyond the Centre

- referrals to community resources

- parent advocacy

The first step in planning successful parent–staff collaboration consists of understanding your own attitudes toward it and then making a commitment to its success. The next step is to intentionally commit time to building strong relationships with the families you work with. This will include developing good communication skills and a repertoire of strategies that can be adapted to individual situations. With careful planning, sensitivity to parents' needs and concerns, and the assistance and input of parents, many positive results can be attained. To ensure that parent–staff collaboration is maintained over time, staff must continually evaluate their efforts.

Evaluation need not be too time-consuming, nor should it be very complex. If staff members are committed to an ongoing process of asking for, analyzing, and acting on the feedback they receive from families, their success at planning engaging activities will likely increase. This ongoing dialogue with parents may well serve as the basis for each side getting to know one another better and thereby strengthening their relations. In addition, educators and parents will feel more comfortable when questions about collaboration are raised in accreditation review processes. Parents will feel more comfortable since they know the program and have input, and staff will have a better idea of where parents stand on issues affecting their child's care.

Chapter Summary

- In this chapter, we have provided an overview of approaches for early childhood educators to plan parent engagement activities.
- We have also given an overview of a variety of different activities and strategies that might be used, including strategies to engage parents that begin with the child and communication strategies that will assist early childhood educators in working with parents.
- We reviewed the importance of evaluating educator–parent engagement ideas on an ongoing basis and identified perspectives to consider when gathering and interpreting results.

RESOURCES

The Canadian Association of Family Resource Programs:
www.frp.ca

Canadian Child Care Federation:
www.cccf-fcsge.ca

Canadian Child Care Federation, "Families Building Partnerships with Practitioners":
www.cccf-fcsge.ca/?s=families+building+partnerships+with+practitioners

National Association for the Education of Young Children:
www.naeyc.org

Parents2Parents:
www.parents2parents.ca

EXERCISES

1. Interview three parents about what types of communication they find to be the most effective and why.
2. Role-play the following scenario. It may be a good idea for the "players" to switch roles after their first performance to get the benefit of the other perspective.

> **You are Ms. Renaud, director of the South East Child-Care Centre.**
>
> Billy Blake, aged 4, has been in your centre about six weeks. He has adjusted well and appears to be an active, happy child. He participates in most activities, asks interesting questions, and particularly enjoys the block area and water play. He is less interested in the story corner, but seems really to enjoy playing with the other children. This morning when Mr. and Mrs. Blake dropped Billy at the centre, Mrs. Blake asked for an appointment to speak with you this evening. You don't know the Blakes well, but they seem pleasant and genuinely interested in hearing about what Billy does at the centre every day. Mrs. Blake is a lawyer, and her husband is a co-owner of a small construction firm.
>
> Draw up a plan for the best way of preparing for this appointment.

You are Mrs. Blake, a lawyer with a large Edmonton firm.

Your husband is co-owner of a construction company. Your son, Billy, aged 4, has been in the child-care centre for about six weeks. Although the child-care director, Ms. Renaud, and the staff seem pleasant and friendly and although Billy seems to enjoy his time at the centre, you and Mr. Blake have serious reservations about it. You don't think Billy is learning anything. He is a bright child and should be learning to read and write, not just playing with blocks or at the water table all day. This is a competitive world; if Billy is to get into a good university, he must have a good start. These early years, when he is so eager to learn, are being wasted.

You have decided to talk to Ms. Renaud, the director, and this morning you made an appointment with her for when you pick Billy up this evening. (*Note:* Forget everything you know about the value of play, and don't make this easy for Ms. Renaud.)

3. Design a poster, brochure, or short video that explains the benefits that parent–staff collaboration offers for
   - the child
   - parents or families
   - early childhood educators

4. Interview parents and staff about a particular event or issue affecting them in the child-care centre. Gather the information first by using a random sampling and then by using a purposeful sampling. Compare the results. How are they similar and how are they different? Which type gave the most useful information?

5. Describe a situation in which you have worked with parents through sharing information and coordinating plans. How did you feel? How do you think the parents felt? What happened for the child?

6. Interview a family agency using the format suggested in this chapter (pp. 115–116). Present the information in a pamphlet form that would be practical for families to use.

7. The following information was taken from questionnaires that evaluated staff–parent engagement strategies. Based on this information, formulate some strategies and goals for your own program for the upcoming year.

   All seven staff responded. Of 40 parents surveyed, 38 responded. The responses were as follows:
   - Twenty-eight parents felt they did not know the staff very well.
   - Fourteen parents disliked evening meetings.
   - Thirty-five parents appreciated their children going on field trips.
   - Most staff members felt that field trips were not supervised well enough.
   - Thirty-seven parents needed care earlier than 7:00 a.m., and two needed care later than 6:00 p.m.
   - Seven parents enjoyed coming to the centre for lunch.
   - Nineteen parents were willing to contribute to snacks or lunch.
   - Some staff members did not know what to do when parents were in the room.
   - Some parents did not know what they were supposed to do in the room.

8. At a staff meeting, consider all the possible ways of engaging families. Which ones do you tend to use most often? What are the benefits for you, your program, the children, the families? What are the downfalls? Which other approaches may be interesting ways to engage families?

9. Keep a journal of parent engagement ideas that you have used and have heard about. You never know when you will want a new idea or approach.

CHAPTER 7

Resolving Conflicts and Tensions

OBJECTIVES

- To understand that conflicts and tensions may exist in some relationships with parents
- To examine the sources of some of these conflicts
- To discuss strategies that may help prevent or resolve situations where conflicts or tensions arise

Thelma, an early childhood educator at a centre in Calgary, went to see her supervisor at the end of a day that she referred to as "a day in purgatory." She was on the verge of tears, and just needed to "let off steam" and get some support. One of the staff members had left early that day because she wasn't feeling well, and it was impossible to find a replacement, so Thelma stayed on for three hours after her shift was supposed to end. In those three hours, almost everything that could go wrong did go wrong. The children couldn't play outside because a recent flood in the town damaged the playground; one child suddenly didn't feel well and needed to be tended to, and more than the usual amount of squabbles between the toddlers required more than the usual degree of intervention! At the end of the day, all but one child had been picked up by their parents. Thelma noticed that the child was a bit anxious and a bit sad, and offered to let the child sit on her lap and look at a picture book together. When the mother finally arrived, she barely apologized for being late, saying that she had a harrowing day at work, and added that she would change jobs with Thelma if she could—because she would love the opportunity to sit and look at a picture book and get paid for it at the same time.

Educators have probably heard this comment or others like it, such as "I wish I could just play all day like you do!" from parents.

UNDERSTANDING CONFLICTS AND TENSIONS

Almost all parents want what's best for their children, and of course early childhood educators are also committed to the children's well-being. This common goal should provide a sound basis for developing a positive relationship between educators and parents. Yet studies consistently substantiate what conversations with educators have suggested: that working with parents is often the most complex part of the educator's role (Ebbeck & Waniganayake, 2003; Wilson, 2005). It's also often the part with the least amount of support.

Many early childhood educators describe parents as helpful, understanding, and cooperative. They find that collaborative relationships with parents can be a major source of mutual support for both educators and parents. However, the relationship between two or more unrelated adults who share responsibility for, and a commitment to, the well-being of children is not simple. Because parents and educators have different roles and areas of responsibility, different perspectives, different experiences, and different expectations, it's not unexpected that tensions or conflicts will arise.

According to Lynn Wilson (2014), conflict in early learning settings may take one of two forms. One may be a sudden outburst that seems, for all intents and purposes, unprovoked. The other is an outburst that seems to have been simmering over a period of time. Sometimes tension without an obvious source remains beneath the surface, causing discomfort and stress for the educator and/or parent. It can be frustrating when neither side understands the cause of tension or is willing to deal with it, which can in turn create further tension. In fact, when the cause of tension isn't obvious, it's even more difficult to understand and resolve.

As we have noted, engaging families is part of the educator's practice (Ebbeck & Waniganayake, 2003). Early childhood education programs have an increased emphasis on engaging families in their curricula. Educators understand that early learning is the practice of relationships and that building strong, collaborative relationships with families is fundamental. Experienced early childhood educators expect that conflicts with parents will arise occasionally and know that avoidance or blame is not the best solution. Instead, they know that efforts can be made to resolve conflicts in mutually acceptable ways. Early childhood educators are expected to demonstrate a commitment to initiating and nurturing relationships with parents, and dealing with conflicts is part of the role (Gonzalez-Mena, 2002).

When educators begin from a place of relationship building, deepen their understanding of families, work from a place of respect, and take time to understand the sources of tension and conflict, they can then ensure a strong relationship with parents. In this chapter, we will concentrate on identifying and understanding the sources of potential conflict between educators and parents. We will also emphasize the importance of establishing relationships and good communication with parents in preventing and resolving conflicts. Understanding the sources of tension and conflict will help educators to consider conflict as an opportunity for change rather than a crisis to avoid.

SOURCES OF TENSION

Over the years, researchers have examined sources of tension between educators and parents (e.g., Curwin, 2013; Eldridge, 2001; Katz, 1980; Shimoni, 1992). Some sources of tension are related to technical matters that can be resolved easily. However, others run deep and are related to normal emotional responses that arise when closely working with children; misconceptions, different world views, and different perceptions of the role of the early childhood educator; and child-care centre policies that are either misunderstood or difficult for parents to uphold. Addressing sources of tension in a meaningful way often requires reflection and possibly challenging deeply held attitudes and beliefs.

Logistical Matters

Availability of Parents and Educators

Time pressures and mismatched schedules between parents and educators can create conflicts. Schedules in child care may mean that different educators are with the children at departure than at the start of the day. Arrival and departures can be frantic times of day for parents and educators alike. Parents may choose not to engage with educators because they feel that all is well, while educators may interpret this lack of engagement as parents ignoring them. On the other hand, some educators feel that parents who insist on talking with them at drop-off times take them away from their primary role, which is to greet the children and help them begin their day on a positive note. However, many of the tensions between parents and early childhood educators may stem from simple logistical problems, which may lead conflict to erupt over other seemingly minor issues (e.g., dirty clothing, lost items). Busy parents and busy educators are often unable to find suitable times to communicate, and thus misunderstandings arise. Many educators have little time outside of playrooms, so they have few opportunities to communicate with parents at the beginning or end of the day due to their work commitments. Parents are typically anxious to get to work in the morning, and the end of the day tends to be a time when both parents and educators are stressed and tired, and the possibility of meaningful interactions may be limited.

Emotional Responses

Judgment and Blame

Educators and parents judge each other all the time (Curwin, 2012). However, often these judgments are based on insufficient information and a lack of understanding. Educators may judge parents based on superficial traits such as dress, social skills, hygiene, or behaviours (e.g., dropping off a child late). On the other hand, parents may judge educators based on personal traits such as age or appearance. We all know how easy it is to blame others. When a child comes home unhappy, parents may assume that the educator isn't taking proper care of the child. When a child behaves in an unacceptable manner while in the program, the educator may assume that the parents are indulging the child or lacking in parenting skills.

Often judgments and blaming are related to our beliefs. For example, if an early childhood educator truly believes that mothers should stay at home with their babies and toddlers, this view may filter through to interactions with parents. Parents may be judged as neglectful when their preschool-aged child arrives with his or her hair uncombed, face unwashed, and wearing a strange assortment of clothing. However, the child's appearance may reflect nothing more than the morning rush, the parents' inability to engage in another battle to clean up the child, or the child's own quest for autonomy in choice of clothes. Some parents have expressed their feeling that educators blame them, often telling them about a problem with the child that they must "do something about." The opposite is also true: often educators feel that parents blame them for the child's lack of progress or behavioural problems (Curwin, 2012).

Affection

Traditional views of professionalism have, as one of their cornerstones, objectivity and a lack of emotional involvement with clients (Dahlberg & Moss, 2005). This view came under criticism in the 1990s because it doesn't take into account the mostly female-dominated professions, such as nursing, rehabilitation therapy, and early childhood education, in which caring and nurturing are paramount (Baxter, 1998). However, the fact remains that many early childhood educators do feel somewhat uncertain about the emotional bond that often forms between themselves and the children in their care. Parents are expected to show affection to their children, but professionals are not. In many minds, there is a fine line between attachment and favouritism.

Professionals are trained not to become emotionally involved because doing so will affect their professional objectivity. For example, students are taught to write "objective" observations and leave out their "subjective" interpretations. Professionals in human services often don't come to fully understand the "caring" part of their professional practice. As a result, many human service professionals feel conflicted about this expectation. How does the nurse working with terminally ill patients not become emotionally involved? How does the professional working with children with special needs in a home setting not become emotionally involved? How does the child-care worker who interacts with young children all day, caring for their most intimate and personal needs, not engage in caring? The fact is that early childhood professionals *do* become emotionally involved because of the very nature of their work. The crux of the dilemma is this: it's difficult to provide a child proper physical and emotional care without actually *caring for* that child both physically and emotionally. Parents who expect early childhood educators to be objective and detached and not become emotionally involved may find themselves in conflict when the child hugs the educator at the start of the day or expresses distress at having to leave the educator at the end of the day. These demonstrations of affection between child and educator may be misunderstood by the parent, and it may be difficult for the educator to understand this reaction.

Jealousy

In spite of the theoretical differentiation between the affection toward the child expressed by the parent and the educator, feelings of jealousy sometimes emerge.

SCENARIO

A TODDLER'S UNEXPECTED REACTION

At the end of the day, Mary rushed into the centre to pick up her toddler, Sam. She had to leave work in the middle of a meeting and battle traffic to finally arrive at the centre. She was anxious to receive the hug that she was expecting. When she arrived in Sam's room, she found Sam sitting in the story corner with Sheila, her early childhood teacher. As she saw her mother approach, Sam clung to Sheila and said a firm "no" to her mother, who was reaching out to her with open arms.

Educators and parents are human beings, and feelings of jealousy are part of being human. Parents naturally feel possessive about their children, but early childhood educators can also become attached to the children in their care (and vice versa). Competition for the child's affection can occur between parents and educators because children are likely to become attached to educators as well. As a result, both parents and educators may become insecure (Gonzalez-Mena, 2009). Most often, it's the parent who worries about being replaced by the educator in the child's affection.

SCENARIO

CONFUSION

A young educator was caring for a group of children who ranged in age from a few weeks to 12 months. One day a toddler, who had just begun to talk, very loudly and clearly called the educator "Mom" several times. When the child's mother arrived, the educator told her what had happened—and was surprised when the parent responded with tears instead of laughter.

Parents may have serious reservations about placing their child in care in the first place, and these feelings will be heightened if they feel they are missing any of their baby's firsts, or that the child's early childhood educator will replace them in their child's affection. This then increases any feelings of guilt or inadequacy they may have as parents, and feelings of jealousy or competition may result. Again, these negative emotions can usually be traced back to the original ambiguity about roles and responsibilities.

JEALOUSY

A parent had her 4-year-old daughter in a family day home operated by her sister, the child's aunt. The child would call the early childhood educator "Auntie Debbie" during the day and would often call her mother "Auntie Mom" in the evenings. The parent initially thought this was cute, but then began to question it.

Every parent knows that it's impossible to be objective about their own children. Nobody thinks it's a bad thing for a parent to admit that he's "crazy" about his child. The strong emotional bond between parents and children is natural and desirable. We hope that every child is a special child to his or her parents. However, the early childhood educator must be equally available to all children. If the educator acts differently with one child, the other parents interpret this difference as favouritism.

In addition, parents become "ego involved" in parenting. When there is failure, of whatever sort, the parent might experience low self-esteem and guilt and react accordingly (e.g., attempt to solve the problem or change the outcome). Early childhood educators are expected to be completely rational in their planning, observations, and interactions with the children in their care. Because they are not as emotionally involved, they can deal with failure in a more rational way.

Emotional responses are natural reactions, and some are hard to avoid. The self-awareness and ability to reflect on emotional responses that are part of professional behaviour can go a long way to mitigating conflict with parents.

Preconceived Ideas and Misconceptions

Parents often hold preconceived ideas about early childhood educators, who also hold preconceived ideas about parents (Invest in Kids, 2010; Wilson, 2005). These ideas or prejudices may interfere with establishing or maintaining a good relationship.

⟫ Perspectives

Mercy and her family immigrated to Canada seven years ago. As a young woman, Mercy had completed her teacher training at a college and worked as a teacher in an elementary school. At present, she is employed as an early childhood educator in a child-care centre and has one of her own children in another room at the same centre. Here are Mercy's comments about potential areas of conflict between parents and staff at child-care centres.

"As a parent and a teacher, I was rather disappointed in the lack of awareness of some of the staff about cultural differences. Several children at the centre are from countries where the diet is very different from here. My children, for example, were used to spicy food and found some of the meals here literally hard to swallow. I was disappointed to learn that my child had been punished for not finishing his main course. His dessert was taken away from him.

"Some children at the centre had never seen a child with dark skin before. I was pleased with the way staff in the playroom talked to the children in a matter-of-fact way about how some people have light skin and some have dark skin. I would have liked, however, to see more toys and dolls and books that had pictures of visible minorities. On the other hand, I wouldn't want my child to be singled out in every possible discussion as a representative of a minority group. Staff members need to stress the similarities among all children and not just the differences.

"Sometimes I've felt that people assume I'm less educated than they are because of my skin colour and accent. I sometimes get tired of having things explained to me two

continues ▶

▶ *continues*

or three times, or in 'easy English.' The truth is that I probably have more education than many of the people I work with and many other parents of children in the centre.

"There were no child-care centres where I lived in India. Grandparents often take care of the children while parents go to work, and often parents take the babies with them to work if they own their own business. I do remember, however, that there were excellent relations between the nursery school teachers and the parents. Most parents believe that teachers deserve a lot of respect and that if they treat the teachers well, the teachers will treat their children well in turn.

"I wear two hats—a parent of a child in child care and an early childhood educator in a child-care centre. Of all the strategies for enhancing relationships between parents and staff, I believe the most important one is mutual respect. I want my children's teachers to treat me as an enlightened and caring parent who may have different ways of doing things. As a staff member, I want parents to know that I'm committed to high professional standards and the well-being of their children. I'm open to their ideas and want to listen to them, but they need to understand that I'm not their personal nanny but an early childhood educator."

Below are examples of the common misconceptions that parents and early childhood educators may hold.

Parents May Think That Early Childhood Educators Have an Easy Job

As the scenario at the beginning of the chapter shows, parents sometimes believe that the early childhood educator has an easy job, thinking that all the educator does is play all day with children. They have little understanding of the complex factors underlying the educator's "easy" job—the planning, organizing, and preparation required in a group-care setting. This view may lead some parents to ask for small extras ("Could you braid her hair?" "Please try to find his blue snow pants"). They may not realize, for example, that on busy days clothing will sometimes not get changed or that toys will go missing. Parents who have never spent extended periods of time with groups of young children may truly not comprehend the complexities of the job and may make mistaken assumptions about the educator's role.

Early Childhood Educators May Think That Children Are Not the Parents' Priority

Consider the following scenario, which focuses on a discussion that took place recently in a family course.

SCENARIO

FLEX FRIDAYS

Students were sharing the challenges they experienced in their practicum settings. Several students in city-centre practicum sites where "Flex Fridays" are common expressed their dismay over parents who brought their children to child care on their Fridays off. The tone of the conversation among students (many of whom were not parents) was somewhat disrespectful. One student, who was a parent of a school-age child, listened and then offered her perspective as a parent.

As the preceding scenario demonstrates, both early childhood students and professionals question the intentions of parents leaving their children in child care while they take the day, or part of it, off. Many students are shocked when they hear tales of parents who use child care so that they can spend time without their child. However, they may not consider that those 20 minutes may be the only alone time a parent has all day or night, that it's more efficient to grocery shop without a 2-year-old in tow, and that it's better to spend quality time after errands and the grocery shopping are done. Sometimes the day off is better spent cleaning, studying, and organizing home lives so that the parent is free to concentrate on her or his children when they are at home.

Early Childhood Educators May Think That Parents Treat the Child-Care Centre as a Dumping Ground

Some educators believe that sometimes parents treat the child-care centre as a "dumping ground." Parents, they reason, are free to drop off a sick child, to control the payment of fees, or to dictate the child's pickup time. Even though many centres have policies or guidelines stating that children should be in care for no more than 10 hours per day, parents choose the length of the day based on their needs.

From the parents' perspective, their hurried comings and goings may seem entirely reasonable. Parents are frequently rushed in the mornings; if they are to be able to fight traffic and be on time for work, they have little time to linger at the child care's front door. The end of the day poses the same problem because the parent is often in a hurry to pick up other children or to get home and start supper. Some parents may simply be overwhelmed by day-to-day survival issues (Pelo & Davidson, 2003); for example, some parents may be struggling to balance work and family responsibilities. On the other hand, parents may be satisfied with the level of care and the child-care centre itself, and thus feel that they really have nothing to report on or query at each arrival or departure. This lack of communication may be their silent message that all is well (for now, at least), so it's important not to misinterpret parents' intentions. Early childhood educators, however, see staff–parent communication as being very important and are frustrated when parents don't engage (Wilson, 2005).

Different Values, Beliefs, or World Views

Conflict is likely to occur, considering the divergent cultural backgrounds, approaches, styles, and values that can exist between early childhood educators and parents (Gonzalez-Mena, 2009). Parents and educators may have different values and beliefs about children and parenting, which may be based on their own experience, on how they were raised as children, or on cultural or religious background. Sometimes, we are not even aware that we have these ingrained beliefs until we are confronted with a belief or practice that is contrary to our own.

SCENARIO

LEARNING ABOUT CULTURAL PRACTICES

Brianna, a new educator in a preschool program with 4-year-old children, was helping to change a child after he had an "accident." As she undressed the child, she saw a series of bruises along the child's back. She was shocked at the sight and called her supervisor over to prepare for documentation as she had been taught. The supervisor looked at the bruises and reassured Brianna that the marks were a result of cupping, a cultural wellness practice, and that the marks could be seen on several children in the program. Brianna had never heard of cupping and was thankful she checked before making a report to children's services.

Prejudgments may also result from cultural or religious differences (Gonzalez-Mena, 2009; Pelo & Davidson, 2003), although many factors can account for different values and world views. Joseph DeVito, Rena Shimoni, and Dawne Clark (2015) reviewed some essential differences in world views related to culture that potentially have a strong impact on parenting. The most relevant of these differences relates to individualism versus collectivism. The dominant cultural world view in North America is individualistic. The individualistic world view emphasizes achievement, self-reliance, and competition, whereas the collectivist world view emphasizes behaviours that contribute to the greater good of the group. Independence is highly valued in an individualistic society, and interdependence is highly valued in a collectivist society.

These two cultural world views can manifest in the child-rearing style of parents. For example, some parents may believe that it's important for their child to be strong and independent and, as a result, may feel it unnecessary to spend a lot of time easing the child through the daily separation. Early childhood educators may judge these parents as cold and unloving, while the parents see themselves as teaching their child an important life lesson about independence. Whereas some parents may promote independence, others who adhere to a more collectivist approach may promote interdependence. While independence is often reinforced in child care (e.g., children learn personal care and are rewarded for independence in this area), some parents may seem to always do things for their child. Early childhood educators may judge these parents as overprotective, while the parents see themselves as teaching their children values that are congruent with cultural norms relating to helping and interdependence.

Cultural differences may also be observed in relation to family roles. Most educators think of parents as the primary caregivers of the children and expect to communicate with them if any issues arise concerning the child. This view may cause difficulties in cases where extended families are integral to parenting, and aunts, uncles, grandparents, or older siblings take more responsibility for the child.

Divergent Approaches to Learning

Parents and early childhood educators may have very different approaches and ideas as to how children should learn. This difference is often due to the fact that early childhood educators have an in-depth understanding of child development and a firm commitment to learning through play. Parents typically have a different kind of understanding. In addition, they are subject to endless information and marketing regarding what is considered to be good education. The most common discrepancy occurs in educational or developmental goals, when parents, concerned about achievement, want to see their preschool children "educated" (Pelo & Davidson, 2003). The media are replete with convincing messages about different ways to create a genius, and these messages are hard to resist. In fact, marketing experts are learning that mothers are primary targets for digital marketing, particularly about activities for children, and ideas for how children learn numbers and language (Ray, 2015). It's likely then, that parents want their children to learn numbers and letters, likely in the same traditional learning style they recall experiencing at school (e.g., sitting at desks, memorizing) or through technology-based learning toys that are said to foster reading and number skills. Early childhood educators are also focused on learning, but know that learning happens best through play, discovery, and exploration. Parents may not understand or value a play-based, child-centred emergent approach. These methods are sometimes seen as mutually exclusive: parents want their children to learn the skills needed to be ready for school and may not understand that play-based learning may be a better way to achieve the same goal. Thus, the parent complains that the child "plays all day" rather than spends time learning. This discrepancy in perceptions of how young children best learn may lead to tensions if the parent believes that the early childhood educator is not fulfilling his or her duty to teach the child.

SCENARIO

A PARENT'S VIEW

Carolyn placed her 4-year-old in a preschool program that had a strong academic focus. Her reasoning was based on her child's need to be ready for school and know specific skills. More important, she felt it to be a waste to pay for her child to play all day. She could provide those experiences for free.

Developmental expectations and behaviour may be a source of conflict between parents and educators as a result of differing expectations. For example, parents are understandably unhappy when their child is hurt or bitten by another child, and they want corrective action taken immediately. Educators likely already have a strategy in place to address such behaviours, but the strategy may take time to have an effect. Parents who expect immediate results may perceive the educators' approach as a sign of lack of concern for their child, which can lead to conflict. Moreover, when educators notice differences in development, they may feel apprehension about sharing their observations with parents. In the same way, the educator's view of development may differ from the parents' and cause tension or conflict.

These few examples illustrate the importance of understanding parents' actions in light of possible differences in values, world views, and cultural norms. Establishing open communication with families of diverse backgrounds can be a major challenge for educators (Bernhard & Gonzalez-Mena, 2005), but when educators do, there is often a significant decrease in misunderstandings and tension.

Differences in Power and Status

Ascribed or Achieved Status and "Who Knows Best?"

Sociologists differentiate between "achieved status" and "ascribed status" (Crossman, 2017). Achieved status is status that a person gains on the basis of merit; it's a position that's earned and often reflects a person's abilities and efforts. By contrast, ascribed status is status that a person is either born with or is given by society.

Early childhood educators choose their career and achieve their status by hard work and study. They expect to enjoy the freedom and authority to practise in ways they choose. Parents, on the other hand, have an ascribed status, that is, status that's assigned to them by society rather than achieved solely through their own efforts. Parents can't choose what their children will be like: they have no control over their sex, temperament, abilities, or disabilities. In addition, there are no clear guidelines or practice standards for good parents, as there are for professionals.

The discrepancy between an ascribed and an achieved role may be at the root of some of the tension and conflict between the early childhood educator and the parent. For example, the educator may have more success in dealing with a child who presents behavioural challenges because he or she has chosen to work with this type of child, has developed professional expertise related to this type of work, and can go home after eight hours of work and leave the child with someone else. By contrast, the parent didn't choose to have a child with behavioural difficulties, may not understand the child's behaviour, and may not have the specific personal or professional skills needed to handle the child. Nor is the parent able to leave the child after a long day of work and several exhausting hours of interaction.

While the "achieved status" of the educator is based on specific education and credentials in preparation for the role, some parents don't recognize this achievement, and may never come to view the child-care staff as a professional (Wilson, 2010), despite the fact that early childhood educators often have more training and applied education in child development than many parents have in their area of specialization, including law, commerce, engineering, arts, and science. Parents' knowledge of child-rearing comes predominantly from family, friends, books, media, the popular press, and their own experience. Nevertheless, parents often consider that their sources of child-rearing information carry more authority than those of educators. This attitude can lead parents to feel that two-way communication with educators is unnecessary, and educators can interpret this lack of sharing as a reflection of their lower status in the mind of parents.

A PARENT'S PERCEPTION OF STATUS

Elaine had two children who attended a child-care centre attached to the college where she worked as an instructor. When interviewed about differences in the status and power of child-care workers and parents, she had this to say: "I'm going to be honest with you. When I want something to happen for my children at the child-care centre, I wear my business suit, walk in holding my briefcase and looking very professional, and make it very clear that I expect to have my own way. But you know, even though I think my status as a professional exceeds that of the child-care worker, in the long run, it's the educator who really holds the most power. At the back of my mind I always know that if they don't like me, the staff might, probably not even consciously, take it out on my child."

Ironically, just as early childhood educators sometimes feel that the parent has the upper hand, it's not uncommon for parents to feel that educators do. Parents see and hear that the child "loves" their preschool teacher and comes to question their relationship with the child, especially when the child and the teacher spend so many fun-filled hours together. Fear of criticism and of being judged can be a barrier to effective relationships (Pelo & Davidson, 2003). Parents may feel left out of the decision-making process when the teacher presents himself or herself as the expert (Wilson, 2010). Parents may fear the opinions or judgments of professionals, especially mothers looking for external validation of their parenting (Wilson, 2010). Fear of reprisal against their children may serve to silence parents. Who knows what really happens, a parent might think, when I'm not there? The following scenario vividly illustrates this fear.

WHO REALLY HAS THE MOST POWER?

One father, who himself was a university professor specializing in early childhood education, published a letter to his daughter's teacher, saying all the things he couldn't say to her directly. The father commented that, in all our professional wisdom, we haven't made it safe for parents to communicate honestly. Here is the letter:

> It has been a humbling experience, and a frightening one, for me to discover how little the accumulated wisdom in our professional literature really speaks to the circumstances of parents like me, parents who have discovered that the stakes are too high to open this particular conversation with this particular teacher. When I actually meet with her, I will temper my points, modulate my voice, tread so very carefully. Much will remain unspoken because I am so acutely aware of just how vulnerable my child is in this affair. My first agenda is the agenda of every parent: I must not make the situation worse. So where will parents' voices really be heard by teachers? Can parents' voices be heard in the professional literature without being encapsulated in someone else's study, framed by someone else's commentary; can parents be heard speaking on their own behalf? Sometimes they can, but still, not often. (Nuttall, 1993, p. 6).

While respect for the profession of early childhood education is growing, some educators still may feel that parents don't value or appreciate them (Invest in Kids, 2010), or just consider them as babysitters.

RESPECTED PROFESSIONAL OR HIRED HELP?

A parent had been complaining regularly to her daughter's early childhood educator about issues such as soiled clothing, missing items, and reports of being hit and bitten by the other children. These allegations were for the most part untrue, and the educator tried to explain the situation and reassure the parent that all was well. One morning, the parent arrived upset about yet another minor incident the preceding day. When the educator attempted to explain, the parent silenced her by saying that she was paying for a service and that she wanted things to change. At that point, her expectations were very clear. She expected to be treated as a consumer purchasing a service, and she believed she had hired the staff to provide that service.

Over two decades ago, researchers wrote about the phenomenon of "role ambiguity" between parents and early childhood educators (Katz, 1980; Kontos & Wells, 1986; Shimoni, 1992a). Early childhood educators tended to feel uncertain about their role, especially as it relates to parents. An increase in the educational requirements for early childhood staff seems to have decreased this phenomenon: educators today are more confident in their professional knowledge and skills. However, some parents still consider themselves as consumers of a service and treat staff as providers of a service rather than as professional educators. Other parents still treat early childhood educators as babysitters (fortunately, this trend is in decline).

The overall status of early childhood education in our society may well contribute to the perception of early childhood educators. In addition to status, salaries and working conditions in early child care continue to be problematic across North America. These factors may lead early childhood educators to feel that they are treated as inferior to parents or think that parents are uninterested in their observations or views, particularly in the area of developmental concerns (Wilson, 2010). As well, these factors may lead some parents to believe that early childhood educators are not true professionals.

Different Roles and Scopes of Function

Put simply, the parents' responsibility for the child is a 24/7 issue, regardless of where the child is at any given moment. Parents have all-encompassing responsibilities in the family: everything is their business, and they are never off duty. Early childhood educators, on the other hand, have fixed hours, and their scope of function is more specific and limited, even if they are extremely invested in the well-being of the children in their care. Parents are deemed responsible for how their children turn out and are emotionally invested. Educators are not invested in the same way. As a result, the two sides look at their child-care responsibilities from completely different world views, which can cause conflicts.

Additionally, because of their different scopes of function, parents and educators have different kinds of knowledge about each child. Early childhood educators usually see the child in one setting, where the child interacts with same-aged peers as well as adults. Parents see the child in other settings, in interactions with a range of different people—especially extended family members and siblings. The perspective from which the parent or educator views the child provides the framework for the way that person knows the child. The lack of opportunity to view the child in other contexts makes it difficult to understand the other person's view.

Thus, when parents report certain behaviours, skills, or abilities of their child, educators may find this information difficult to believe because they have never seen the child act that way or in that setting. Likewise, parents often can't understand educators' concerns about their child's interaction with other children. In both of these examples, the perspective from which an individual views the child provides the framework for the way that person knows the child. The lack of opportunity to view the child in other contexts makes it difficult to understand the other person's view.

The Individual or the Group

As mentioned earlier, differences in perspective relating to individualism or collectivism (the relative importance of the individual or the group) often are relevant to the differences sometimes perceived. However, regardless of world view, it's natural that parents, for better or worse, are concerned exclusively with their own child and therefore have distinct perspectives, concerns, and requests. For example, parents may request special consideration regarding schedules, snacks, or play for their child (requests that don't necessarily work well for the other children in the group).

By contrast, the early childhood educator is responsible for all the children under his or her care and must balance the needs of the individual in that group with the needs of the group as a whole. Sometimes meeting the child's needs can be accomplished on an individual basis (e.g., each child is changed when wet or dirty), and sometimes this is best accomplished as a group (e.g., in drawing up snack and lunch schedules). When the focused perspective of the parent clashes with the broader outlook of the early childhood educator, conflicts may arise surrounding care.

SCENARIO

WHY SHOULD ONE CHILD ENJOY SPECIAL PRIVILEGES?

A child-care centre opened at 7:00 a.m. each morning, and children arrived steadily through to 9:00 a.m. One mother worked a late shift in a grocery store; as a result, she went to work later and arrived home later in the evening. She would let her son stay up until 10:00 or 11:00 p.m. so that she would have time to be with him. She would then let him sleep in until whenever he woke up and take him into the child-care centre between 10:00 a.m. and noon. The early childhood educators found the child's schedule extremely difficult to plan around, since they didn't know when he would arrive and felt that they could not leave the playroom until he did so. The child, in turn, found the arrangement trying because he often had to search to find his group in the morning and join them partway through an activity. He felt that he was missing out on the fun, and the other children had difficulty making room for him midway through their play. The parent's perspective was that she wanted to spend time with her son and fit care into her schedule, while the early childhood educators felt that the child should conform to the schedule everyone else followed to ease the child's transition into, and interaction with, the group.

SCENARIO

CHILDREN INSIST ON BEING TREATED EQUALLY

One parent consistently brought in her 3-year-old child after the scheduled breakfast time. The child did not eat beforehand, so the parent and early childhood educators agreed that the parent could bring breakfast from home because it would be impossible for the centre to prepare it for him. This seemed to be a satisfactory solution until all the other children began asking for breakfast too (again). It seemed the arrangement created more problems than it solved.

In both of the preceding scenarios, the early childhood educators' view of group care came into conflict with the parents' perspective of what is best for their child. When parents have not been involved in group-care settings themselves, the difficulties they create may not even be apparent to them because they are acting according to the needs of their own child and their family. The potential for conflict here is obvious. While early childhood educators may find it difficult to accommodate the wishes of all parents, they should keep in mind that all children need a parent who cares about them more than anyone else.

Sources of Knowledge About the Child

Early childhood educators usually see the child in only one setting, where the child interacts with same-aged peers as well as adults. Their knowledge of child development and keen observation skills provide them with vital information about the child. However, we know that people often behave very differently in different contexts (e.g., at work, home, and school), and children are no different. Parents see their child in other settings, in interaction with a range of different people—especially extended family members and siblings. Sometimes parents may not see their child function much with other children of the same age, but the educator does on a daily basis. On the other hand, parents see their child in a range of situations and interactions that would not be available to the educator.

As noted earlier, when parents report certain behaviours, skills, or abilities of their child, educators may find this information difficult to believe because they have never seen the child act that way or in that setting. Moreover, parents often can't understand educators' concerns about their child's interaction with other children. As the following two scenarios show, the perspective from which an individual views the child provides the framework for the way that person knows the child.

SCENARIO

IT'S ALL A MATTER OF PERSPECTIVE

Judy's early childhood educator and mother were in the middle of an unpleasant conflict. Her mother didn't want Judy to nap for more than half an hour so that she would not be up late at night. Her mother needed the time after 8:30 p.m. to devote to Judy's older sibling, who often required help with homework. The early childhood educator, however, found that with such a short nap, Judy was fussy and cranky for the rest of the afternoon. The mother's observations were quite different. On weekends, when Judy didn't nap at all, she was fine until the early bedtime. It could very well be that, in the quieter home setting, Judy didn't need a nap to cope with afternoon activities, whereas in the noisier, busier child-care centre, a nap was required. However, neither adult had the opportunity to observe Judy in both settings.

SCENARIO

THE EFFECT OF CONTEXT ON PLAY

Faizal, an early childhood educator, carefully explained to Abdul's mom that Abdul had been hitting and hurting other children for some time and that it was an issue in the playroom. "He is so gentle at home and with our friends that I find this is hard to believe," his mom stated. When Faizal asked questions about the types of interactions and relationships in these settings, she learned that Abdul was largely in the company of adults and older teenaged children. His mom, in fact, had never had the opportunity to see her son play with children of the same or similar age. The educator suggested that Abdul's mom spend time in the playroom to see Abdul as he played. After the second visit, she better understood that even though Abdul interacted well with older children and adults, he struggled in interactions with children of his own age.

Unclear Policies

Most child-care centres attempt to provide parents with as much information as possible, both during their initial orientation and on a daily basis. Nevertheless, conflicts still arise when parents claim that they were never informed about one thing or another. Parents may receive pages of policies and procedure information but not read it, or they may read it and not remember it. It's also possible that they will be given details at the end of the day when the only thing on their mind is getting home. This apparent lack of communication is quite common and can result in conflicts between early childhood educators and parents, either on a short-term or long-term basis (Wilson, 2005). The transition from home to child-care centre can be a stressful time for parents; therefore, it's probably not the best time to ask them to remember various details about centre policies.

SCENARIO

UNCLEAR POLICIES?

A huge fluorescent green sign had been posted for a week on the front door of the child-care centre, reminding parents that fees were due on the fifth day of the upcoming month along with the penalty for nonpayment. On the morning of the 6th, some parents were informed that their children would no longer be able to attend because their fees had not been paid. All the parents affected responded with, "We didn't know."

While most of the sources of tension reviewed above focus on interactions between the educator and the parent, tension and conflict often emerge when the policies of the child-care centre are unknown or not understood by parents. Uncertainty and/or disagreements about child-care policies are a source of tension and conflict.

Child-care centres typically have clear policies about children who are ill, yet often these policies are a source of conflict. Parents may have no option but to bring their unwell child to the centre in the morning and may not realize the extent of their child's illness (e.g., if the child is slow or not wanting breakfast). Parents are in the precarious position of balancing work and family responsibilities, and achieving this balance may prove to be a challenge. Many workplaces and municipalities have no option for caring for sick children, and workplaces may not accommodate parents' absenteeism to care for sick children. The child-care centre or preschool has no provisions for sick children: it typically doesn't have extra staff or separate areas. As a result, it's not uncommon that dropping off a sick child at a child-care centre or preschool will cause tension.

Rules are often put in place by programs to manage all of the logistics associated with the services they offer. When these rules are broken, conflict is the result. Early learning programs work hard to minimize rules, develop clear policies, sometimes writing and rewriting policy manuals. But it's often the small things that create stressful situations (e.g., lost clothing, not bringing outdoor clothing, habitual lateness) (Wilson, 2014).

A Summary of Typical Sources of Conflict and Tension

As discussed, there are a number of potential sources of conflict and tension between educators and parents. In many cases, parents and educators don't clearly perceive that a difference in perspective exists, and this makes understanding the inevitable conflicts that much more difficult. Both sides may then attempt to rationalize their feelings (e.g., "She doesn't like me" or "He doesn't like my child"). We believe that an awareness and recognition of these sources of conflict can facilitate the development of more positive relations or, at a minimum, provide a basis for understanding the conflict. Having an understanding of sources of conflict doesn't mean that the "problems" will be automatically solved, but it will help early childhood educators consider the parents' requests from another perspective. For example, when educators recognize that it's natural for parents to advocate for their own children, it will be easier to avoid misinterpreting parents' requests. It will also be easier to think about complementary solutions and about how educators and parents can work together in the best interests of the child and the other children.

Sources of Conflict and Tension in the Parent–Educator Relationship

1. Logistical matters
   - Schedules and shortage of time make dialogue between children and staff difficult.
2. Emotional responses
   - Parents and educators often make judgments about each other that are based on superficial observations.
   - Often parents and educators blame each other when there is a concern about the child.
   - Expressions of affection and jealousy may contribute to tension or conflicts.
3. Preconceived ideas and misconceptions
   - Some parents believe that early childhood educators have an easy job.
   - Some early childhood educators believe that children are not really the parents' priority.
   - Some educators believe that parents consider the child care to be little more than a dumping ground for their children.
4. Different values, beliefs, or world views
   - Many differences in world views and values stem from cultural differences.
   - Individualism and collectivism are strong culture-based orientations that affect parenting.
   - Parents and educators often have different views regarding best strategies for educating children.
5. Differences in power and status
   - Parents have an "ascribed" status, while early childhood educators have "achieved" status.
   - Some parents find it difficult to view early childhood educators as professionals.
   - Both parents and educators can be uncertain of the early educator's role.
6. Different roles and scopes of function
   - Parents and educators have different scopes of function in relation to child care.
   - Parents will be chiefly concerned with their own child, while early childhood educators have to think about what is best for the children in their care as a group.
   - Owing to their ties of natural affection, parents are thought to interact with their children in a way that is primarily emotional. Early childhood educators, on the other hand, are expected to react with the children in their care in a cool, rational manner.
7. Unclear policies
   - Policies that are in any way unclear or ambiguous are a potential source of conflict.

We have examined the many ways that conflicts and tensions can arise between parents and early childhood educators. While understanding the roots and sources of conflicts is an important first step in resolving them, this understanding needs to be followed by action. The remainder of the chapter will focus on general guidelines for preventing conflict or dealing with conflict when it arises.

STRATEGIES FOR DEALING WITH CONFLICT

Dealing with conflict can be stressful and overwhelming. Educators must begin by reflecting on their values and beliefs. A foundation of socio-cultural practice, a strengths-based approach, and family-centred practice set the tone for interacting with families in positive ways and finding ways to engage parents in meaningful ways. Even within these values and beliefs, conflict may arise—sometimes for silly or random reasons, sometimes for more deeply rooted concerns. Early childhood educators need to be prepared to deal with conflict.

Techniques for Conflict Resolution

1. Take time to build and nurture respectful, positive relationships with parents and family members.
   - Understand and respect families, including their cultural and religious traditions.
   - Recognize that each family is unique, and develop strategies that allow you to empathize with different families.
   - Understand that conflict exists in meaningful relationships.
2. Expect conflict, and realize that skills for resolving conflict must be learned.
   - Understand that there may be differences in values and beliefs between the early childhood educator and parents.
   - Provide parents with up-to-date written policies and guidelines to try to minimize confusion or conflict.
3. Create opportunities for communication to occur on a regular basis.
   - Keep parents informed and provide them with opportunities to become involved in the centre's program.
   - Work to bring differences out in the open (rather than avoiding them).
   - Attempt to resolve conflicts using a problem-solving approach in a way that makes it a win-win situation for the parent and the early childhood educator. Develop effective ways to communicate in all situations.
4. Acknowledge your own resource limitations. Educators need to understand their role and scope of function. Sometimes tension or conflict requires support or resources beyond the scope of the program (e.g., social worker, counsellor).

Building Strong Relationships

The foundation of practice for educators is to build a strong, respectful, professional relationships with parents. Chapter 6 explores the parent–staff relationship in more depth. It's critical to remember that conflict may be inevitable given the type of work engaged in. Conflict can provide an opportunity for growth and change or can result in harmful words and actions. As professionals, educators must act in a respectful manner and manage a developing crisis. Once conflict occurs, it's easy to get enveloped in the strong emotions that come forth (e.g., anger, frustration, and disappointment). Educators must develop skills to manage conflict when it occurs, but, more importantly, build a solid relationship so that potentially conflictual situations can be dealt with in a professional manner.

Ask yourself the following questions, and write out your reply to each one.

■ What is your image of the family? Of mothers? Of fathers? How do these images impact your relationship with families that you engage with?

■ What do you think are the qualities of a good parent?

■ What values and attitudes do you have regarding children and their needs?

■ Being as honest as you can, try to define your attitude toward parents in general. Do you judge them harshly or leniently?

■ What is your attitude toward discipline and punishment within the family? Have you known parents who were harsh disciplinarians and who favoured the use of corporal punishment, such as spanking? How did you feel about them?

■ Does your attitude toward parents change based on any of the following factors: ethnic background, religious affiliation, income, lifestyle choices or marital status?

■ What behaviour do you associate with a caring attitude toward children?

■ List all the characteristics of the type of family with which you would have challenges working. Beside each characteristic, list the reason why you would find it troublesome. When you are finished, write a brief analysis of what this list tells you about yourself.

Examining the answers to these questions may help you recognize how you feel about parents and parenting. Once early childhood educators are aware of their own beliefs, they may take the first step in understanding and improving their relations with parents (Galinsky, 1988; Wilson, 2014). Your beliefs or values will not necessarily be altered, but perhaps you will understand why your relationship with Harry's mother is not like your relationship with the other mothers. At the very least, it may alert educators to those situations or occasions where they need to check their attitudes before responding.

Early childhood educators need to realize that conflict is inevitable in any relationship. Working through conflict may produce positive changes. Educators will need to deal with many different types of parents, and so they need to feel confident that they have the ability to resolve problems (Wilson, 2010).

Understanding Parents

First and foremost, early childhood educators need to be aware of their own beliefs, values, and attitudes and of how these may affect their interactions with parents (Gonzalez-Mena, 2002). They may then have to determine how they will continue to show respect for parents and interact with children despite differences of opinions and backgrounds. Sometimes, it may be helpful to take a moment to understand the situation from parents' perspective (e.g., they have had a long, hard day, they hear only unpleasant things at the end of the day about their child, they hear from you only when there is a complaint or demand). Sometimes understanding the backstory (Wilson, 2014) can be of value in these situations. However, educators understand the complexities involved in getting information about families.

SCENARIO

ACHIEVING A COMPROMISE

A young mother and an early childhood educator were at odds about toilet-training practices. The mother believed that children should be trained by the time they were 1 year old. Everyone in her family had been successfully trained by that age. The educator believed that children should be trained when they are developmentally ready, when they show interest, and at their own pace. The educator had difficulty understanding the mother's position until they discussed their beliefs and attitudes. Their different beliefs remained, but a compromise on practice was achieved.

UNSPOKEN ATTITUDES

An older early childhood educator in a baby room believed that mothers should really stay at home with their babies. That was the way that she had been raised, and that was the way she had raised her own children. Although she never expressed her views verbally, they were clear in her approach with the babies and mothers. She was often curt and cold to the parents, nonverbally communicating her lack of support for their actions. On the other hand, she was very cuddly and warm with the babies and viewed herself as the mother's replacement. Several of the parents complained to the director, claiming that the educator's need to be "a good mother" made her insensitive to the needs of the babies' real mothers. The real difference was in beliefs, and the educator's behaviour clearly portrayed her underlying attitudes about babies in child care.

Once early childhood educators become aware of their own beliefs in relation to parenting and families, they may also come to realize that the source of the conflict lies within their own values and beliefs. This understanding will be the first step in helping to ease strained relations (Couchenour & Chrisman, 2011) and in developing more family-centred practices. The next step will be to discuss differences openly (McIntyre & Phaneuf, 2008) to develop an understanding of the situation. Once early childhood educators recognize the diverse nature of families, they may acquire more appreciation of different cultures and then involve parents accordingly.

Making Policies Clear

As we noted earlier, a centre's policies must be phrased in clear language and be communicated to the parents in a way they will understand. Here are a couple of guidelines to help implement this idea.

First, early childhood educators must initiate a thorough orientation meeting at which they review and explain to each parent the centre's philosophy, policies, and procedures, especially those that may be more contentious (Wilson, 2010). In this way, parents will become aware not only of the policies but also of the rationale for each of them. They will also get to know the important people in the child-care centre, such as the director. Parents need to know how they can handle challenging situations (e.g., they can set up a meeting with the director).

Second, early childhood administrators typically develop a policy manual for parents, which they should make available as a paper copy or online to parents for their own reference. Updates and changes will be required from time to time; when they occur, changes should be communicated to parents. Some programs will have parents sign off on policies and their updates, indicating that the parents are aware of or have read the updated policies. Providing parents with this information should reduce the potential for conflict at the centre. For example, parents will know beforehand that only certain snacks are allowed in the child-care centre, and they will understand procedures regarding clothing, lost items, and pickup times. Providing opportunities for parents to have input in developing and adapting policies may also serve to help them understand the rationale behind the rules and increase their willingness to work with early childhood educators and centres.

Informing and Involving Parents

The importance of two-way communication between parents and the centre is paramount. The more ongoing communication that occurs with parents and the more parents are informed about and involved in the programs, the less likely it is that conflicts and

Courtesy of Chris Zahn.

Taylor, Age 5

tensions will arise. In addition to the guidelines presented here, Chapter 6 provides a number of strategies for enhancing communication and collaboration with parents on an ongoing basis.

Working Toward a Win-Win Solution

Resolving conflicts usually involves creating a situation in which both parties win. This begins with the understanding that conflict is inevitable and that avoidance is not the best solution. In fact, educators may learn about themselves, their program, or the child when conflicts are well managed. A problem-solving approach (i.e., be part of the solution, not part of the problem) rather than a power approach is usually more effective (McIntyre & Phaneuf, 2008). Ask yourself the following question: "What needs to happen so that the parent can walk out of here with her dignity intact and so can I?" If only one person wins, the other usually feels humiliated or victimized. Even though winning may feel good in the

Chapter 7 Resolving Conflicts and Tensions **135**

moment, it's rarely satisfying in the long run, if only because the conflict usually resurfaces in some other form. Early childhood educators need to act thoughtfully and develop relationships with parents based on professional rather than personal issues.

When a conflict does develop, early childhood educators need to adopt a problem-solving approach (McIntyre & Phaneuf, 2008; Wilson, 2005). Problem-solving strategies focus on solutions and resolutions, not on assigning blame. Such strategies may result in changing the situation (e.g., providing developmental information regarding toilet training) or recognizing that the situation will likely remain unchanged because of religious or cultural differences in child-rearing. The following suggestions reflect a problem-solving approach:

- Allow the parent to express his or her feelings without interrupting. Try not to speak first so that the parent can articulate the issue and feel like he or she has been heard (Wilson, 2014). Conflicts can be easily escalated if one party (the parent in this instance) doesn't feel like his or her concerns are being listened to.
- Try to remain calm and focused on the situation. Concentrate on lowering your voice, focus on your breathing. Check the tone of your voice: Do you sound defensive? Angry?
- Sustain eye contact to maintain your feeling of confidence.
- Don't get defensive or escalate the problem. When parents feel respected and in control, they are more likely to respond in a similar unemotional fashion. Remember that parents genuinely care about their children and attempt to do what is best for them, and that they may become passionate about issues concerning their child. Attempting to work with the parents toward this common goal is more effective.
- Clearly define the issue and ensure that all aspects are included.
- Allow all participants to voice their perspectives.
- Review relevant policies and rules.
- If you have made an error, apologize and explain. Truthfulness will serve to increase trust in your relationship. Being defensive and making excuses may harm it.
- Work toward solutions for all. Perhaps ask the parent what he or she would like to have happen. Sometimes the parent may just need to know that you have heard and are willing to deal with the complaint.
- Acknowledge the parent's feelings openly. Use an "I" statement such as "I understand that you are very angry."
- Practise empathy. For example, if a child has been hurt by another child, acknowledge that it was very upsetting for everyone.
- Understand that it might be necessary for another person to step in when a situation escalates. A supervisor or director may need to set the tone by stating that it's inappropriate to yell or speak disrespectfully in the child-care centre or in front of the child. This intervention may provide the opportunity for a break so that the issue can be discussed when everyone is calm and better prepared. Educators need to feel that they can be supported by someone in these situations.
- Inform all parties of resolutions.

Recognizing the absolute importance of family and working in respectful and supportive ways form the foundation of good child-care and family-centred practice. This does not mean that early childhood educators must act in a subservient manner or apologize every time something goes amiss. If an apology is warranted, provide it. If it's not, provide a clear explanation of what happened. The parent may have to go home to reflect on the situation, but your manner of handling it without reacting emotionally or being defensive will help the process.

Respecting Cultural and Religious Differences

A Multicultural Approach to Conflict Resolution

Educators across Canada are likely working with a more diverse population of children than ever before. As noted earlier, conflicts may arise inadvertently as a result of differing cultural or religious beliefs. Chapter 9 provides several strategies for enhancing intercultural communication. These strategies include:

- reducing your ethnocentrism
- confronting your stereotypes
- not making assumptions

Understand that resolving difficult situations requires time and patience.

Katie Shonk (2017) noted that when attempting to resolve conflicts across cultures, we need to recognize that each person brings to the discussion different behaviours, communication styles, and norms. These differences may result in misunderstandings that only deepen the conflict. She further noted that when we confront cultural differences, we tend to rely on stereotypes that are often pejorative (e.g., people from country X are always late). However, understanding some of the *prototypes* (behaviours that are likely to be common in a particular culture) may help in resolving conflict. For example, if we recognize that certain behaviours are more typical in a particular culture, it may help us enhance our understanding of that culture. Here is an example: in North American culture, using time "effectively" is valued. In other cultures, the building of a trusting relationship (which often takes time) is more important. If we know that, we may understand that when we thought that a parent was avoiding a discussion of a disagreement, they may have been taking the time to build the relationship, which they see as a necessary first step.

Developing Empathy

Empathy is the cornerstone of effective work with children and with parents. It's not difficult to feel empathic with a person with whom you have a positive relationship and with whom you agree with on important issues. However, in a conflict situation, empathy is much more difficult to achieve. It is possible, though, and essential. Development of empathy takes practice, especially when you need to be empathic to someone with whom you are in conflict. Empathy is the simplest way to demonstrate caring, and parents will react positively to it. Empathic educators are better able to respond and find ways to engage a family in meaningful ways based on the family's strengths. It takes practice and commitment to develop empathy, but it's well worth the effort. There are several ways that this can be done.

The first way to develop empathy is fairly simple. Use the knowledge that you already possess and try to imagine what it would be like if you were in the same situation as the parent. What would it be like, for example, to go to work every morning having had no sleep because of a crying baby? What would it be like having to worry about where money for the next meal was coming from? What would it be like to lose an entire social network with the ending of a marriage?

Sometimes it's easier to empathize with people who are in the midst of a serious crisis or in unfortunate circumstances than it is with people who seem to be successful. Therefore, try to imagine also what it would be like for a mother of young children who has invested heavily in her career and is now struggling to juggle the demands of a job and family. Imagine the stress such a mother will feel when she has to be at work to negotiate a major contract she has spent months preparing and finds that her child has come down with chicken pox. Even if you think that a career should be secondary, try to consider this from her perspective, and imagine her frustration in such a situation.

A second way to develop empathy is to listen to and talk with people who are in similar situations. Talk to single mothers about the stresses in their lives; listen to fathers who are trying to be nurturing parents but have had no one in their own lives to act as a model.

A third and more sophisticated way of developing empathy is to find parallels in your own life that can help you identify with the feelings of parents. Suppose, for example, that you are having trouble understanding what it would be like for a new immigrant to Canada. Perhaps you can remember changing schools when you were little, or moving houses, or travelling in a foreign country where people did not speak the same language as you. In these and other ways, you may learn to empathize with parents rather than to blame or judge them.

Knowing Your Limits

All human service professionals want to provide the best and most inclusive services possible. In keeping with this desire, early childhood educators must recognize the limits within which they work. They need to know when to say yes, when to say no, and when to refer to other resources. Furthermore, educators need to feel confident in saying no. They also need to recognize the stress of their chosen career and ensure that they have supports in place for themselves. As well, because it's so easy to create conflict unwittingly with parents and with others, they need to work within clear professional boundaries and limitations.

SCENARIO

BOUNDARIES

Sam was an early childhood educator in the 4-year-old room. She began to babysit after work hours and on weekends for McKenzie, whose parents had just divorced and whose dad was really stressed. McKenzie often stayed after hours until Sam was ready to leave, and she also spent time at Sam's apartment. McKenzie would come in and tell the other children about Sam's place and what they did. Soon the other children began to ask if they, too, could come to Sam's house, but McKenzie told them that only she was allowed to go with her dad. The other early childhood educators began to feel that McKenzie was being favoured and thought that there might be something more between Sam and McKenzie's dad than just babysitting. The situation became more contentious when other parents expressed their belief that one child had special privileges, and also began to request after-hours care.

We can see in the preceding scenario how the lack of professional boundaries in this all-too-common situation can lead to confusion and conflict, not only between parents and early childhood educators but also between educators and children. The role educators play and the fact that they are typically caring people who want the best for the children in their care can lead to conflict and tension. Early childhood educators need to be aware of these potential areas of concern and deal with them in a proactive manner, before problems result.

As demographics change, so do the demands of communicating with different types of parents. In recent years, for example, students have posed questions related to communicating with older, more professional parents. It appears that many families with two professional parents have recognized the need and value of child care for their preschool-aged children—so much so, in fact, that educators have often expressed the difficulty in meeting the needs of these "demanding" parents. This perception may (or may not) be accurate, and of course educators will often need to cope with the requests of demanding parents of all varieties. Again, educators need to be reminded that parents typically have the best interests of their children at heart. Listening to parents is critical, and developing a relationship of trust and mutual respect can take time. When educators feel overwhelmed by these demands, they may wish to check out local supports and resources (e.g., community colleges) for courses that may assist them. For example, a course on effective communication, conflict resolution, or mediation techniques may be extremely helpful to your practice.

Caring for the Educator

We want to end this chapter with a reminder of the importance of self-care. Self-care is vital for everyone, but especially those in the caring professions. It's even more essential when dealing with the stress of conflict situations. When we are tired, stressed, or feeling uncomfortable, it's very difficult to harness the empathy and the skills required for resolving conflicts. To be competent professionals in all areas of their work, early childhood educators need to learn to care for themselves, and the importance of self-care can't be overstated in relation to working with parents and avoiding or dealing with conflict situations. The days of coming to work sick have passed, and taking "mental health" days or personal days is seen more favourably (when appropriate). Workplace stress is recognized as real, and it's expected that educators will care for themselves in appropriate ways to ensure that the best interests of the child are always first. Child care can be physically and emotionally exhausting, so caring for oneself is of paramount importance.

More recently, researchers in human services have begun to write about compassion fatigue. This topic has been discussed most commonly in relation to workplace interactions with vulnerable children and families, but it has also become an important concern for early childhood educators. Educators, who spend their days in caring interactions and creating and maintaining compassionate environments, may find themselves exhausted at the end of the day, especially if they have had to deal with conflict. Although compassion fatigue is expressed differently by each individual, there are some common signs. Physically, compassion fatigue can be manifested as exhaustion, headaches, and being more susceptible to illness. Behaviourally, it can be conveyed through irritability, lack of patience, use of alcohol or drugs, absenteeism, and compromised care of children or families. Psychologically, it can appear as holding a negative image of oneself, trying to distance oneself from work, or being less able to feel empathy. Any or all of these signs may lead an educator to feel inadequate as a professional and may diminish his or her sense of satisfaction in working with children or families (Mathieu, 2017).

Compassion fatigue may be a contributing factor to the high rate of turnover of early childhood educators. Recognizing that the work you do can and does have a physical, emotional, and psychological toll may be the first step in dealing with compassion fatigue. Educators need to seek support in their workplace and beyond to ensure that burnout and compassion fatigue doesn't become overwhelming. Supports need to be in place in childcare programs as one measure to attract and retain high-quality staff. This is an ongoing dilemma in child care, where supports are typically not in place. However, educators commonly experience compassion fatigue and feelings of being overwhelmed and unsupported. Educators must recognize the potential for compassion fatigue and associated feelings and be prepared to cope in positive and effective ways.

CONCLUSION

The early childhood profession has made great strides in the past decade in articulating the professional role of early childhood educators and teachers. Collaboration with parents is part of the definition of quality care. The importance of educators establishing and maintaining ongoing professional contact with families has been well established. However, the conflicts and tensions described in this chapter often present obstacles to successful fulfillment of the early childhood educator's role. Understanding the sources of conflict and developing strategies to prevent and overcome them will ultimately enhance the relationship between educators and parents and benefit the children in their care.

Educators understand the value of establishing and maintaining relationships with families. Educators understand the value to children, families, and to themselves. When confronted with unpleasant conflicts, it may be a good time to think deeply about your work with families. What are the benefits to the child? To the parent? To the family? To your practice? To your program? Sometimes your answers will provide a different perspective and a new way to consider the issues that you are facing. Moreover, it's important to remember that taking care of yourself may be one of the most critical components of dealing with difficult and stressful situations when working with parents.

Chapter Summary

- Early childhood educators must understand that conflict is inevitable in relationships. Rather than trying to avoid conflict, they must develop strategies and approaches to prevent and deal with it when it arises.

- Early childhood educators need to become familiar with the sources of tension that may arise when working with parents to be better prepared to understand a conflict when it erupts. As well, they need to be equipped with strategies and approaches to resolving conflict.

- Understanding the sources of conflict and developing strategies to enhance the relationship between educators and parents will benefit the children. Becoming aware of the different perspectives that parents and early childhood educators may have will also aid educators in their dealings with parents.

- Educators need to understand that the work of caring for children and their families may cause stress, burnout, and feelings of being overwhelmed. They should also be aware of and understand how to cope with the physical, behavioural, and psychological signs of exhaustion.

RESOURCES

Canadian Child Care Federation:
www.cccf-fcsge.ca

National Association for the Education of Young Children:
www.naeyc.org

EXERCISES

1. Check your attitudes by completing the following checklist regarding your feelings about working with parents.

   As an early childhood educator, I . . .   YES   NO

   a) feel that parents are more work than help.
   b) feel stress when parents enter my playroom.
   c) prefer to work alone.
   d) compare siblings from the same family.
   e) feel threatened by parents.
   f) view parents as a great resource.
   g) enjoy having outside people in the room.
   h) hold certain beliefs about certain groups of people.
   i) feel that parents use television to babysit their children.
   j) feel that parents are not interested in their children.
   k) work better with a social distance between myself
      and parents.
   l) believe parents are irresponsible for letting children
      come to child care in inappropriate clothing.
   m) feel that a close working relationship with parents is
      necessary.
   n) feel that developing this relationship is part of my job.
   o) am pleased when all the parents leave.
   p) anticipate parent conferences with pleasure.
   q) use written communication to avoid face-to-face contact.
   r) feel that parents have resigned from their parental role.
   s) feel that parents have their children overinvolved
      in activities.
   t) enjoy working with parents.

   Source: Adapted from a class exercise used at Grande Prairie Regional College in Alberta.

2. Identify your own areas of stress when working with families. List some of the factors outlined in this chapter that may help you or your colleagues work through some of these difficulties.

3. Plan a discussion around family values that includes topics such as discipline, sleeping arrangements, hygiene, illness, and expectations for play. Try to consider the multiple perspective that diverse families may have.

4. Read the following family situations, then
   a) determine your attitude or clarify your values toward the parents described in each situation;
   b) brainstorm ways to offer support to these families.
      i) Mr. and Mrs. Ban own their own small business and find it necessary to put in long days. It is difficult for them to spend time in their children's centre because of their business.
      ii) Mrs. Smith has not been seen at the centre for some time, and rumour has it that she has had a nervous breakdown. Her husband finally confirms this to be true. She is still interested in what happens to her daughter at the centre, but she is not ready yet for large groups or for attending meetings.
      iii) Wanda Green is a single parent and has expressed interest in attending parent meetings. She has no car, however, and would have difficulty affording the extra expense of a babysitter to attend.

iv) Mr. and Mrs. Gupta are new to this country and have just enrolled their son in your centre. They have told him that he can't participate in Halloween or Thanksgiving activities.

v) Jack Reed would like to meet more parents of the other children. He has approached the early childhood educator but has been ignored each time he suggests a get-together.

vi) Mona Perth is a very busy woman with three children and a full-time career. She feels that whatever happens during the day in the centre is the centre's problem and that the early childhood educators should handle it without bothering her.

vii) For craft activities, the child care uses a variety of food, including macaroni, flour, dried vegetables, and fruits. One parent, Mrs. Earl, has a lot of difficulty with this since she is trying to teach her children to value what they have and is very involved in international relief. She believes that using food as toys is in conflict with her values.

5. Empathy exercise—For each of the following remarks, write down what feelings you think the parent may be experiencing:

a) I'm not sure what I'm supposed to do when I come to the centre for the day.

b) All my child does here is play. He never brings home worksheets or drawings.

c) My son teaches every song he learns here to everybody in our family.

d) The children are going on another field trip?

e) My child's soiled pants were sent home, and I'd just like to know why you didn't get him to the bathroom on time.

6. Who can you talk openly with when you are feeling upset about a parent? How does talking to this person help you?

7. How do you feel when parents are present in the room? How do you think the parents are feeling? List some ideas about what you could do to help parents and early childhood educators feel more comfortable and welcome.

8. Ask people from different cultural backgrounds what their approach to conflict and conflict resolution is. How will this information assist you in your work with parents?

9. Develop a list of opening lines to use when a parent begins an uncomfortable interaction. For example, "I can see that you are very upset right now. Can you tell me what is causing you to be so angry?" Having a few phrases that can give you the opportunity to collect your thoughts and assume a calm approach will be handy if you are confronted by an angry parent.

10. List the signs that let you know you are starting to feel overwhelmed or exhausted. Do you get headaches? Do you book time off work because you just can't face another day? List the ways that you cope with stress in your life, including the positive ways and the less positive ways.

PART THREE

Family Diversity

Parts 1 and 2 of this book were intended to provide students with general knowledge about families and the ways in which early childhood educators can apply this understanding as they engage with and support families. This final part of the book takes a closer look at the diversity that exists in Canadian families. When we speak of diversity, we refer to differences in culture, family structure, social and economic factors, and the life events and processes of change experienced by families.

Each chapter in this part explores a different aspect of diversity and includes adults' and children's views as well as practical ideas that educators can use to support the child, the parent, and the family as a whole.

Chapter 8 provides an introduction to engagement with Indigenous families.

Chapter 9 provides insight into the cultural diversity of Canadian children and families, and information on some of the challenges associated with immigration and being a refugee.

Chapter 10 provides an overview of the impact of poverty on Canadian families, with the understanding that the impact of poverty may be relevant across all groups that are described in the chapters within this part.

We then examine different family structures and the processes of change and adaptation that accompany these families. The following topics are discussed: single-parent families (Chapter 11), families undergoing divorce (Chapter 12), blended families (Chapter 13), and families with teenage or adolescent parents (Chapter 14). Families who adopt and who foster children are reviewed in Chapter 15.

The unique challenges and strengths of families who have children with special needs are reviewed in Chapter 16. Many parents, too, have special needs, and this topic will be discussed in Chapter 17.

In recent years, educators have learned about the importance of understanding gender diversity in families, and Chapter 18 provides the latest understanding in this area.

We end this part with a focus on topics that are considered difficult to deal with. Chapter 19 explores the impact on children and families when there is a death in the family, and the final chapter (Chapter 20) examines abuse and family violence. This knowledge will help prepare early childhood educators respond to highly challenging and often stressful events and situations that arise with families in a competent manner.

CHAPTER 8

Indigenous Families in Canada

OBJECTIVES

- To gain an initial understanding of the impact of colonization on the Indigenous peoples in Canada

- To gain an initial understanding of some aspects of the cultures of Indigenous peoples in Canada

- To consider respectful ways of engaging with Indigenous children and families

An ancient Indigenous proverb states, "Treat the Earth well. It was not given to you by your parents; it was loaned to you by your children. We do not inherit the Earth from our Ancestors; we borrow it from our Children."

INDIGENOUS PEOPLE OF CANADA

Before reading this chapter, we ask you to stop and think deeply about the meaning of this ancient proverb. What do we, as early childhood educators, need to learn before we can engage with Indigenous parents to ensure that we can provide their children with the best education about the land we share?

As a starting point, we need to gain an understanding of the history of Indigenous peoples in Canada and the impact of Canada's colonial history and current policies, which are a product of colonialist conceptions, on Indigenous communities. Colonization has been explained as a form of invasion, dispossession, and subjugation of a people that dispossess those people of their lands and results in institutionalized inequality and racism (LaRocque, 2014; Truth and Reconciliation Commission of Canada, 2015a). The colonization of Canada by European settlers started in the 11th century. We touch on this history and its impact in the following section. Then, we attempt to share our appreciation for and understanding of some of the tenets of Indigenous cultures, their "ways of being, knowing and doing, their beliefs about children's learning, or Indigenous pedagogy" (Maher, 2012, p. 343). With this understanding, we can think about how we might invite collaboration with Indigenous families in a meaningful way. With a deeper appreciation of what all educators can learn from Indigenous cultures, we will be able to produce richer early childhood environments for children and stronger relationships with their families.

It's important to share with readers our reflections relating to the writing of this chapter. We are well aware of the fact that as settlers, our knowledge is based on what Indigenous people have shared with us through conversations and through writing, as well as on academic articles that we have read. We are also aware of the fact that Indigenous knowledge does not live in academic institutions, books, and articles, but in the lived experiences and languages of Indigenous peoples (Battiste, 2002).

As we reflect on what we have learned, we are also well aware that we are both products of a culture and education system that today we know has been inextricably influenced by colonialism, and colonialism and the legacy of colonialism have infiltrated much of what we know and do (Pacini-Ketchabaw & Taylor, 2015). We have grown up unaware of the myriad of policies, actions, and racism that infiltrated our culture, our education system, and our institutions. At the same time, we know that we, directly or indirectly, have benefited in some ways by colonization, at the expense of Indigenous people. The following statement by a journalist from the *Globe and Mail* reflects what many Canadians today are thinking.

Taking a Second Look at the Official Story

"I still remember passages in my Grade 9 Quebec history textbook that described the colonization of '*les sauvages*' by French settlers. Our first prime minister, Sir John A. Macdonald, also referred to the aboriginal peoples as 'savages.' I didn't have the moral courage to confront my history teacher about the offensive language, or the sanitized version of history taught in government-issued textbooks.

"I am ashamed to admit that for decades, I remained ignorant about the rich history, traditions, culture or contributions of our aboriginal brothers and sisters. I also had no knowledge of the terrible injustices inflicted upon them." (Khan, 2016)

While we are committed to trying to understand and respond to this entanglement, we know that the process of doing so is complex and ongoing, and we still have much to learn. Moreover, because we are aware of the fact that much of the existing research on and the stories of Indigenous people in Canada have been, by and large, not authored by Indigenous people themselves, these accounts are often characterized by racist stereotypes and images (Browne, 2003, 2005; Clark, 2007; Gilchrist, 2010; Neegan, 2005; Watters, 2007). Within the profession of early childhood education, there is growing awareness that much of the knowledge base in child development and family studies has been developed by scholars and researchers from the dominant cultures, with little or no regard for the cultures and voice of Indigenous people. Therefore, we have strived to base this chapter on writings by Indigenous people or on research that has been done in collaboration with, or at least cited by, Indigenous scholars. Meanwhile, we are committed to diligently challenging the "filter" of our own cultural assumptions and experiences. We know that in our attempt to contribute to an education in which we can learn, grow, and be inspired, we needed to write this chapter with the support of and under the watchful eye of Indigenous colleagues whose generosity we are most grateful for.

A BRIEF INTRODUCTION TO THE INDIGENOUS PEOPLES IN CANADA

Many Canadians are proud to be viewed as one of the most multicultural countries in the world. However, few are aware of the fact that less than 500 years ago, before this land was "discovered" by Europeans, the original inhabitants of this land—the First Peoples—spoke at least 53 different languages, and each group referred to itself by a specific name in its own language (Canada's First Peoples, 2007). Multiculturalism is not a recent invention!

Today, descendants of the original inhabitants of Canada, whose history in this land goes back thousands of years, are referred to as *Indigenous peoples*. In Canada, the term *Indigenous peoples* refers to different cultural groups. There are three distinct Indigenous peoples in Canada: First Nations people, Métis, and Inuit, each of which has unique histories, languages, cultural practices, and spiritual beliefs. There is also a rich diversity within those groups—particularly within the First Nations peoples, who form the largest group. What all

Indigenous peoples share is the fact that they are descendants of the people who lived here for centuries before the Europeans discovered, settled, and conquered this land (Canada's First Peoples, 2007). The number of Indigenous people living in communities throughout the country is approximately 1.8 million; this figure comprises over 600 First Nations bands, each with its own distinctive culture, language, art, and music (Statistics Canada, 2016b).

First Nations People

First Nations is a term used to describe Indigenous people in Canada who are not Métis or Inuit. While "First Nations" is used as a general term, First Nations peoples are more likely to define themselves as members of specific nations, or communities within those nations. For example, a Mohawk (Kanienkehaka) person from Akwesasne who is a member of the Bear clan may choose any number of identifiers, which would all be more accurate than simply "First Nations person" (Gadacz, 2015). It's also important to understand that First Nations peoples belonged to communities that were not delineated by national or provincial borders. For example, members of the Cree Nation, which has a population of over 200 000 in Canada, live largely north and west of Lake Superior in Ontario, Manitoba, Saskatchewan, Alberta, the Northwest Territories, and Quebec. However, they also live in the United States. Members of the Piikani Nation (formerly referred to as *the Peigan Nation*) live largely in Alberta and Montana (Government of Canada, 2013; Native Languages of the Americas, 2016). First Nations people developed many distinct cultures, all in harmony with the land. Each cultural group was made up of several nations with similarities in language and social structure, and similar ways of making a living from the environment they lived in.

It's virtually impossible to capture the rich diversity of the cultures of First Nations peoples, and generalizations are often misleading. However, First Nations' authorities emphasize that

> First Nations culture provides a rich essence that is intrinsically woven by the supportive threads of relationship: with one other, with the Great Spirit, and with the Earth. This is the kernel of First Nations wisdom, and the core value from which all expressions of cultures evolved—whether ritual, artefact, or ceremonial practice. Relationship, often expressed best (in the English language anyway), as "All My Relations" guides the development of all cultural practices, including language, oral teachings, prayer, music, dance, spiritual and social ceremonies, rites of passage, housing, even clothing, adornment, art, tools, and object creation. . . . The various nations . . . cultural practices, symbols and belief systems [are] coloured by their unique experiences on the land, and with each other, always conscious and connected with the Spirit world. (First Nations Pedagogy Online, 2009a).

More elements of First Nations' culture will be described later in this chapter.

The Métis

The Métis people trace their origins to about 1600. They were the children born of European settlers and their Indigenous wives. The beginning of their community was in the Red River region of present-day Manitoba. However, Métis communities spread west as the French Canadian fur traders moved west in the 1700s and 1800s. Today there are 350 000 to 400 000 Métis in Canada (Canada's First Peoples, 2008).

The Métis National Council defines the Métis homeland as the three Prairie provinces and parts of Ontario, British Columbia, the Northwest Territories, and the northern United States (Métis Nation, 2017). The Métis have a common culture, ancestral language (Michif), history, and political tradition, and they are connected through an extensive network of kin relations. Métis Family Services describes the Métis Nation as people who are united by their relationship to the land and to each other. They consider the land a resource rather than a possession. Métis are often referred to as "the rainbow people," for they are a people of many colours and shades. Métis are a community which celebrates two cultures (Métis Family Services, 2017). They are "the heirs of a rich heritage; descendants of the voyageurs. . . . [T]he explorative spirit of the Métis has left its mark across the whole face of North America, from the shores of the Great Lakes, to the shores of the Pacific; from the prairies of Saskatchewan to the bayous of Louisiana" (Métis Family Services, 2017).

The Inuit

There are four Inuit regions in Canada—Inuvialuit Region, Nunavut, Nunavik, and Nunatsiavut—collectively known as *Inuit Nunangat*. The term *Inuit Nunangat* is a Canadian Inuit term that includes land, water, and ice. Inuit consider the land, water, and ice of their homeland to be integral to their culture and way of life.

The majority of the Inuit population lives in 53 communities across Inuit Nunangat. Inuit Nunangat encompasses 35% of Canada's landmass and 50% of its coastline. According to Inuit Tapiriit Kanatami (the National Voice of the Inuit),

> We have lived in our homeland since time immemorial. Our communities are among the most culturally resilient in North America. Roughly 60 percent of Inuit report an ability to conduct a conversation in Inuktut (the Inuit language), and our people harvest country foods such as seal, narwhal and caribou to feed our families and communities. (Inuit Tapirit Kanatami, 2017)

Traditionally, the Inuit were hunters and gatherers who moved seasonally from one camp to another. Large regional groupings were loosely separated into smaller seasonal groups, winter camps (called "bands") of around 100 people and summer hunting groups of fewer than a dozen. Each band was roughly identified with a locale and named accordingly; for example, the Arvirtuurmiut of Boothia Peninsula were called "baleen whale-eating people" (M. Freeman, 2010).

With the arrival of the European settlers, traders, and missionaries over the last three centuries, Inuit culture has lost some of its traditional features, but Inuit culture persists. Moreover, the Inuit maintain a cultural identity through language, family and cultural laws, attitudes and behaviour, and their much-acclaimed Inuit art (M. Freeman, 2010).

TODAY'S INDIGENOUS PEOPLES

The population of Indigenous people in Canada is growing at a significantly higher rate than the population of other groups in Canada. Moreover, the Indigenous population is a considerably younger population than the rest of the population in Canada (Battams, 2013). Indigenous people in Canada share a harsh history of colonialization, beginning with the arrival of European settlers in the 11th century. However, today we see that in spite of this history, which will be described next, Indigenous peoples have grown and thrived. A growing number of Indigenous young people are visibly proud of their heritage and culture, and they are active in restoring their culture and contributing to Canadian cultures (Murphy, 2015). First Nations people, Métis, and Inuit of all backgrounds have served as role models in the Indigenous community and helped shape Canadian cultural identity (Ministry of Indian Affairs and Northern Development, 2000).

HISTORICAL PERSPECTIVE

An in-depth review of the colonial history of Canada is beyond the scope of this book (see Worokiak & Camfield, 2013). We highly recommend that students use the resources presented in this chapter and other opportunities to deepen their knowledge about Indigenous peoples and their central role in Canadian history.

Indigenous peoples have a history that far predates the arrival of Europeans in the 11th century (Indigenous and Northern Affairs Canada, 2017). Before Europeans landed, First Nations societies were well developed, highly organized, and stable, despite their diversity (Dickason & McNab, 2009; Mandell & Duffy, 2010). The newcomer colonists who conquered the land subjected the Indigenous people to injustices and cruelty that are difficult to imagine. They found Indigenous culture different and uncivilized and considered it a barrier to their goals of colonization, which were largely to own the land and gain from its riches. There was no question in their minds that their religion and culture were superior, and that it was they and their culture that would rule. They forced changes on Indigenous people that eroded their culture and livelihoods and family life (Joseph, 2016). Today, many people would cringe when they read how Canada's first prime minister, Sir John A. Macdonald, spoke of the Indigenous people in the House of Commons in 1883.

> When the school is on the reserve and the child lives with its parents, who are savages, he is surrounded by savages. . . . It has been strongly pressed on myself . . . that Indian children should be withdrawn as much as possible from parental influence, and the only way to do that would be to put them in central . . . schools where they will acquire the habits and modes of thought of white men. (cited in Truth and Reconciliation Commission of Canada, 2015a, p. 2)

A document by the Wellesley Institute of research and policy in Toronto (Allan & Smylie, 2015) outlines some of the key colonialist policies that Indigenous people were subjected to that caused them unimaginable damage. These policies included the following:

- The Indian Act (1876) and related policies and processes, which served to: 1) dispossess Indigenous peoples of land and disrupt traditional economies, thereby cutting off sources of food and manufacturing food dependence on colonial authorities (e.g., restricting hunting and gathering practices by restricting mobility) . . .; 2) give colonial authorities the power to determine who could be an "Indian"; 3) impede the transmission of identity and traditional knowledge . . .; and 4) undermine the roles and responsibilities of women in previously matriarchal and/or matrilineal societies. . . .

- The forced relocation of Inuit peoples and the imposition of permanent settlements, compounded for some communities by the mass slaughter of sled dogs. . . .

- The residential school system, which subjected generations of children to sexual, emotional, physical, mental, spiritual and cultural abuse.

- Historical and current child welfare processes, which have and continue to separate substantial numbers of children from their families and communities. (Allan & Smylie, 2015, p. 2)

The authors of this document make it clear that the impact of some of these policies, including racism that is still present in our society and its institutions, is still affecting the health and well-being of Indigenous people today, impacting access to education, housing, employment, and institutions related to health care, child welfare, and the criminal justice system (Allan & Smylie, 2015).

Residential Schools

Residential schools for Indigenous people in Canada date back to the 1870s. Over 130 residential schools were located across the country, and the last school closed in 1996. These government-funded, church-run schools were set up to eliminate parental involvement in the intellectual, cultural, and spiritual development of Indigenous children, which was the wish of Sir John A. Macdonald, prime minister of Canada, as quoted above. The schools forbade the use of Indigenous language, as well as the practice of their cultural teachings and traditions. Most of the children in the schools didn't have the opportunity to visit or even see their family members for months and years at a time. We know today of the unspeakable abuses that occurred at the schools, including physical abuse, neglect, torture, and sexual abuse, committed by staff hired first by religious orders who were running the school, and later by the government, which assumed control of the schools (Manitoba Trauma Information Centre, 2017). More than 150 000 First Nations, Métis, and Inuit children were placed in residential schools, often against their parents' wishes. While there are an estimated 80 000 former students living today, the ongoing impact of residential schools has been felt throughout generations and has contributed to social problems that continue to exist (Truth and Reconciliation Commission of Canada, 2015b).

The tragic legacy left by the residential schools is described in detail by the Truth and Reconciliation Commission of Canada "file:///C:\Users\Yakhin\Documents\Principles%20 of%20Truth%20and%20Reconciliation.pdf":

> Many students were permanently damaged by residential schools. Separated from their parents, they grew up knowing neither respect nor affection. A school system that mocked and suppressed their families' cultures and traditions destroyed their sense of self-worth and attachment to their own families. Poorly trained teachers working with an irrelevant curriculum left them feeling branded as failures. Children who had been bullied and physically or sexually abused carried a burden of shame and anger for the rest of their lives. Overwhelmed by this legacy, many succumbed to despair and depression. Countless lives were lost to alcohol and drugs. Families were destroyed, and generations of children have been lost to child welfare.
>
> The Survivors are not the only ones whose lives have been disrupted and scarred by the residential schools. The legacy has also profoundly affected the Survivors' partners, their children, their grandchildren, their extended families and their communities. Children who were abused in schools sometimes went on to abuse others. Some students developed addictions as a means of coping. Students who were treated and punished as prisoners in the school sometimes graduated to real prisons. (p. 103)

Source: Principles of Truth and Reconciliation, Truth and Reconciliation Commission.

Early childhood educators know very well the importance of providing an infant and child in their early years with a loving and nurturing primary caregiver or caregivers. Understanding the trauma of being removed from those primary caregivers and being placed in an environment where the emotional needs are ignored or violated makes it possible to understand how the trauma could last a life time and be transferred to subsequent generations. This is referred to as *intergenerational trauma.*

›› Perspectives

An instructor in the social work program related a moment of learning when a student in her class had the courage to share the following story with her fellow students.

"Many years ago, I was teaching a social work class at Mount Royal University. One of the students, a mature Indigenous woman who had returned to college to earn a diploma in social work after many years of, as she put it, 'being on the very edge,' shared with the class:

'By now most of you know about the residential schools—I was at one of those kids. You have heard the stories—the punishments, the abuse, the humiliation.

'But the worst for me was that I never learned how to be a mother. And I couldn't be a good mother to my own children, because all I knew was beatings, beatings, beatings.

'I caused my own daughter to suffer, but she has forgiven me. And now I am a grandmother and every day I bless and love that child.'

"That class happened over 20 years ago—but I will never forget that student—or what she told us—ever!"

Bill Mussell is a member of the Skwah First Nation. He is also a professional in corrections and a post-secondary educator, a president of the Native Mental Health Association of Canada, and Chair of the First Nations, Inuit and Métis Advisory Committee to the Mental Health Commission of Canada. Here are his words on the effects of colonization on caregivers in First Nations families:

> They know institutional, custodial care, but not the healthy nurturing of traditional family life. Many of today's parents and grandparents were deprived of an upbringing that would have:
>
> - enabled them to develop a relatively secure personal and cultural identity
> - transmitted and strengthened the relational nature of their lives—the connectedness with the land, its resources and all other things of the Creator
> - fostered growth and development that would facilitate meaningful bridging between cultures and nations. (Mussell, 2008)

In 2008, the federal government established the Truth and Reconciliation Commission of Canada to look at the impact and legacy of the residential school system on Indigenous peoples. In 2015, the Commission published its report (the executive summary can be found here: www.trc.ca/websites/trcinstitution/File/2015/Honouring_the_Truth_Reconciling_for_the_Future_July_23_2015.pdf). We encourage students to read this document to gain a deeper understanding of the history and impact of residential schools.

Concepts of Family, Children, and Child-Rearing

When we discuss the concept of family among Indigenous communities in Canada, it's important to keep three points in mind. First, our very understanding of the concept of family is rooted in our cultural meanings, which may not be the same as those of Indigenous people (Menzies, 2017). We know that the understanding of the concept of family is changing and is more inclusive today, as depicted by the Vanier Institute of the Family (2016). However, over the years, welfare agencies, the education system, and other institutions that interacted with Indigenous families definitely didn't have this inclusive view. Second, understanding Indigenous families can't be disconnected from the impact of colonialism on the organization of their communities. Third, there is great variety in families and community structures in the diverse Indigenous communities in Canada.

Any discussion of Indigenous cultures must bear in mind their diversity, understanding that one can't assume that what is true for one community is true for all. However, there are aspects of Indigenous cultures that are broadly shared. According to Patti LaBoucane-Benson (2005), the concept of family for early or traditional Indigenous peoples in Canada included a complex combination of biological ties, extended family members, clan membership bonds, adoptions, and economic partnerships (i.e., hunting partnerships between communities), which resulted in a strong network of relationships and sharing of responsibilities. This, in effect, created a vital safety net.

In Indigenous communities, more emphasis is placed on large, multigenerational families than on nuclear families, though there is great variety in the nature of these relationships. In every case, family networks of sharing and reciprocity continue as a crucial aspect of Indigenous society. The sharing of responsibility among family members for raising children is seen as a major difference between Indigenous and non-Indigenous families, the latter of which place almost exclusive responsibility on the parents as primary caregivers. In the past, the different approach taken by Indigenous people was misunderstood and misjudged by non-Indigenous people as parental neglect. Yet the emphasis on family networks has been, and is, a way to provide loving and committed care when parents work or are unable to care for children. Moreover, the experience of growing up in an extended family (e.g., in a family belonging to the Miqmak Nation) that is headed by a grandmother or an aunt provides children with an important opportunity to develop a sense of their identity (Menzies, 2017).

The fact that Canadian officials didn't recognize the strength of the extended family and its role in supporting children contributed to the removal of so many children from their families. Indigenous families were deemed inappropriate due to impoverished living conditions, to the fact that children were often cared for by grandparents who were seen as too old to care for children (Fournier & Crey, 1998), or to a perception of neglect of the children. The nuclear model of the family was forced upon Indigenous families through the actions of Family Services, even though this model didn't fit within the paradigm of the Indigenous extended family (Fournier & Crey, 1998). The enormous price paid for the lack of understanding of the Indigenous concept of family is only beginning to be understood today.

Loss of Language

"The history, passion, and soul of your culture lives in each word you speak in your native tongue" (Cuevas, 2016). Anybody who has experienced the frustration of being in a place where no one understands the language they speak will be able to identify with this quotation.

Language is more than a way of communicating with others. Imbued in it are the customs, traditions, and passions of a particular culture. Through language, the histories of a people and a way of life are passed down the generations in nuanced ways. The identity—the soul—of a group of people resides in the syncopated and unique vocalizations of their native tongue (Norris, 2004). For many Indigenous people, language is at the very core of their identity. Yet Indigenous children were robbed of their right to speak in their first language. When they lost their first language, they lost the connection to their families and to their cultures. As a result, today many first languages are disappearing (Norris, 2014).

While Canada has two "official languages" (French and English), today there are approximately 50 languages belonging to 11 Indigenous language families. These Indigenous languages reflect distinctive histories, cultures, and identities linked to family, community, the land, and traditional knowledge. As stated by Wab Kinew, musician, university vice-president, CBC broadcaster, and politician who comes from Onigaming First Nation in northwestern Ontario, "Language is one of the fundamental characteristics of nationhood, and it's one of the fundamental characteristics that defines your identity as an Indigenous person" (Macdonald, 2015). For many First Nations people, Inuit, and Métis, these languages are at the very core of their identity. Fortunately, today, efforts are being made to return first languages to the younger generation—and early childhood educators should play a role in supporting this effort. Concrete suggestions in this regard are provided later in this chapter.

Indigenous Family Traditions

Today, psychologists are telling us of the importance of rituals and traditions in enriching family and community life. Traditions include activities, events, and ceremonies that occur regularly and are conducted in a similar fashion over and over again. They vary in size and in scope, but they are different than regular daily activities. They usually (but not always) involve entire families and communities. The most well-known traditions are associated with religious practices and beliefs, such as Diwali, Christmas, and Ramadan. But other traditions, such as celebrations associated with major sports events, are also a key component of our cultures (Scully & Howell, 2008). Brett and Kate McKay (2013) define *family ritual* as "any activity you purposefully repeat together as a family that includes heightened attentiveness and something extra that lifts it above the ordinary ruts." Traditions, when done right, lend a certain magic, spirit, and texture to our everyday lives. Traditions and rituals provide us with a sense of identity, teach children their religious or cultural history, teach values, and bond families and communities together. Their predictability adds a sense of security and creates fond memories. It's no wonder that Ellen Galinsky, a leader in early childhood education and co-founder of the Families and Work Institute, found that when children were surveyed about what they would remember about their childhood, most kids responded by talking about family traditions (McKay, 2013). By contrast, many of the parents and grandparents of Indigenous children are not able to remember childhood family traditions because they were removed from family and community at a young age and, thus, from their traditions.

OVERCOMING THE IMPACT OF HISTORY

According to Karla Bell (2016), Indigenous children may be the most vulnerable segment of Canada's population, and the population who stand to benefit most from having access to high-quality care and education (Alwani, 2017). Indigenous leaders and scholars have asserted that, as a group, difficulties with parenting, mental health, addictive behaviours, and domestic violence are direct consequences of the ways Indigenous parents were negatively affected by colonization, including residential schooling (either as children forced to attend or as children of residential school survivors) (Canada, 1996; Dion Stout & Kipling, 2003; Fournier & Crey, 1997; Mussell, 2008; Wesley-Esquimaux & Smolewski, 2004). Jessica Ball (2008) has highlighted the risk to Indigenous children when poverty, marginal living conditions, and "overwhelmingly negative social stigma" create "formidable obstacles" to many Indigenous families as relates to bringing up their children (p. 8). Margo Greenwood (Greenwood & Griffin, 2013) describes how huge socio-economic and environmental disparities that are rooted in colonization result in persisting social inequalities and the poor health of Indigenous people. She also notes that Indigenous children bear the greatest burden of these inequities with an increased incidence of a variety of chronic and acute illnesses, including higher rates of suicide, heart and circulatory disease, fetal alcohol spectrum disorder, and injuries (Greenwood & Griffin, 2013).

Today, major efforts are under way in Indigenous communities to overcome these challenges. According to Mussell (2008), a first step is for Indigenous people to take positive control over their lives as individuals, families, and communities; build on who they are culturally; and understand history from an Indigenous perspective. Reclaiming and building on cultural strengths contributes to a secure personal and cultural identity. He also highlights the importance of grieving and healing of the losses suffered through colonization as a step toward collective wellness. He notes:

> More and more First Nations leaders and workers are calling for healing, family restoration and strengthened communities of care. These people promote a renewal of cultural practices and teaching history from an Indigenous perspective. They call for education and training that combines the best of mainstream and Indigenous knowledge, and for building the capacity of workers to improve the quality of life in their villages.

All Canadians have a role to play in mitigating the ongoing effects of this history. Mussell also states that it is vital to engage in a

> . . . process of consciousness raising [that] must occur within Canadian society, so stigma and discrimination against aboriginal Canadians can be eliminated, both on the personal and the structural levels of society. (Mussell, 2008)

Yet we are reminded that in spite of the many challenges and consequences of history, "there is, in fact, much to celebrate about First Nations families" (Menzies, 2017). In the general population, it's a shame that more awareness exists about the troubles and difficulties facing Indigenous communities than about Indigenous communities, cultures, and approaches to child-rearing and educating children. The next section provides a glimpse.

AN INITIAL UNDERSTANDING OF INDIGENOUS CULTURES

The website of an Indigenous research group at the University of Calgary explains that cultural differences relate to how "the world, psychological, social, and spiritual, is constructed, organized and interpreted" (University of Calgary, 2017a). It refers to a world view found in the culture's guiding story. While the guiding story of mainstream Canadians can often be understood in its Judeo-Christian roots, Indigenous people have their own guiding story. It must be stressed that there is considerable diversity within different Indigenous groups in North America, in terms of language, customs, and history. At the same time, their guiding stories are similar: they explain "the universe, its origins, its characteristics, and its essential nature" (Cajete, 2000, p. 58). These guiding stories serve as the foundation of all knowledge, and they're essential to understanding human development and behaviour and the patterns of meaning embedded in cultures.

The guiding stories of Indigenous peoples were passed down by Elders from one generation to another. That is how Indigenous children learned how the world came into being and that they, their values, and traditions were gifts from the Creator. One of the most important and most common teaching was that people should live in harmony with the natural world and all it contained (Battiste, 2011). This respect for the natural world was expressed in daily life, and through song, dance, festivals, and ceremonies (Battiste, 2011; Indigenous and Northern Affairs Canada, 2017). All First Nations believe that their values and traditions are gifts from the Creator (The Faith Project, 2015).

In oral stories and legends that Elders passed from one generation to another, Indigenous children learned how the world came into being and that they were a part of the whole of creation. People gave thanks to everything in nature, upon which they depended for survival and development as individuals and as members of their communities. First Nations treated all objects in their environment—whether animate or inanimate—with the utmost respect (Indigenous and Northern Affairs Canada, 2017).

Leroy Little Bear (2005, 2017), a member of the Small Robes Band of the Blood Indian Tribe of the Blackfoot Confederacy and a well-known educator and founder of the Native American Studies Department at the University of Lethbridge, notes that Indigenous people have an inextricable connection to their land. He explains that "there is enough similarity among North American Indian philosophies to apply the concepts generally, even though there may be individual differences or differing emphases" (Little Bear, 2000). Here, he describes the philosophy of the Plains Indians:

> Tribal territory is important because Earth is our Mother (and this is not a metaphor: it is real). The Earth cannot be separated from the actual being of Indians. The Earth is where the continuous and/or repetitive process of creation occurs. It is on the Earth and from the Earth that cycles, phases, patterns—in other words, the constant motion or flux—can be observed. Creation is continuity. If creation is to continue, then it must be renewed. Renewal ceremonies, the telling and retelling of creation stories, the singing and resinging of the songs, are all humans' part in the maintenance of creation. Hence the Sundance, societal ceremonies, the unbundling of medicine bundles at certain phases of the year—all of which are interrelated aspects of happenings that take place on and within Mother Earth. (Little Bear, 2000, p. 2)

INDIGENOUS SPIRITUALITY: WAYS OF KNOWING AND BEING

We often make the mistake of presuming that other people see the world and society in a manner similar to us, and that they share our goals and values. That is, we base our actions and interactions on many assumptions that we rarely question or are rarely aware of, because this is the way we were brought up to believe. More importantly, we often judge people according to those world views that we hold, some of which we are hardly aware of.

In much of the literature, key cultural values of Indigenous people are compared, as in the table below, to those of the dominant Western culture. Even though we may think that we don't agree with these values, we need to be aware of the fact that they have been deeply embedded in our education system and in many other of society's institutions (Indigenous Works, n.d.).

Differences Between Traditional Indigenous Cultures and Mainstream Western Culture

Traditional Culture	Mainstream Western Culture
Community is the foremost of all values	Individualism is the foremost value
The future tense is dominant	The present is the dominant tense
The world is understood mythically	The world is understood scientifically
Goals are met with patience	Goals are met with aggressive effort
Ownership is often communal	Ownership is reward for hard work
Gifts are regarded as social glue	Gifts are regarded as holiday issues
Work is often motivated by group need	Work is motivated by ambition
Aging is a source of wisdom	Aging is decay and loss
Eye contact is thought over-assertive	Eye contact is part of conversation
Silences are acceptable anywhere	Silences are a waste of time
Assertiveness is non-communal	Assertiveness is a basic social skill
Listening skills are prized	Communication skills are prized
Soft spoken words carry farthest	Emphasis carries the day
Nodding signifies understanding	Nodding signifies agreement
Handshake is soft, signalling no threat	Handshake is firm, assertive
Collective decisions are consensual	Collective decisions are put to a vote
A faith in harmony with nature	A faith in scientific control of nature
Family is extended family	Family is nuclear family
Responds to praise of the group	Responds to praise of the individual

Source: Used with the permission from Indigenous Works.

These beliefs are often presented as a dichotomy. However, not all those raised in Western culture hold the beliefs listed in the right column of the preceding table, and not all Indigenous people would adhere to beliefs listed in the left column. Perhaps some of us would answer that we believe in elements listed in both columns or a few elements in both columns. Such responses would not be surprising. Our different cultures don't exist in isolation from each other, and there are opportunities for people of different cultures to learn from, and be affected by, one another (Joseph, 2016). Of course, there is great cultural diversity in Canada today, and certainly among students of early childhood education; many students may have come from cultures that share many of the tenets of Indigenous culture, as opposed to the dominant beliefs of Western culture. Think about where your beliefs "fit" in the preceding dichotomy.

While it is interesting and informative to examine the differences in belief systems, leading Indigenous scholars today are inviting us to consider what we have in common. Dr. Willie Ermine (2007), for example, writes that an "ethical space" can be formed when groups with very different worldviews engage with each other and "the space in between them . . . contributes to the development of a framework for dialogue between human communities" (p. 193). The focus then shifts to building on what groups have in common. An excellent example of this kind of dialogue and "ethical space" can be seen in early childhood practice where the Reggio Emilia Aotearoa New Zealand approach was embraced by an Indigenous early child centre (Mohawk) in the development of a "culturally relevant curriculum whereby culture and Indigenous ways of learning would be seamlessly woven into daily practice" (Smith-Gilman, 2015, p. 53).

The View of Spirituality

For Indigenous people, religion or spirituality is not an "add on" to daily life, but "a way of living." Spirituality is "more a worldview than a set of practices" and "sacredness is interwoven through all dimensions of life," where "humankind strives for holistic, balanced and harmonious existence" (The Faith Project, 2015, p. 1). Indigenous culture is deeply rooted in spiritual traditions that include complex and diverse sets of customs within each community. These spiritual traditions enable members to engage with the sacred and supernatural (The Faith Project, 2015). Many stories highlight the origins of ritual practice, the cosmos, death, ethical actions, and religious institutions. These have been shared as part of an oral tradition. In spite of the diversity among Indigenous people, some basic principles are shared by most, including the following:

- "Human beings are created to live in harmony with the natural world. . . . The natural world is alive, intelligent and integrated with humankind.

- "There is a profound interconnectedness among all of creation. All animate and inanimate parts of the environment are endowed with powerful and mysterious spirits, and thus deserve the utmost respect.

- "Gratitude is a central concept in [Indigenous] traditions—humankind expresses gratitude to the natural world for abundant gifts." (The Faith Project, 2015, p. 1)

CEREMONIES AND RITUALS

Perspectives

As part of a capstone final assignment in an early childhood program, a student took on a project that was to create an early learning program for Indigenous children and families. The project was exploratory in nature to determine best practices for working with young Indigenous children. As part of her coursework, she had learned quite a bit about Indigenous culture. In several sessions, Indigenous Elders were invited to class to lead discussions with students on Indigenous ways of being.

One of these sessions was a circle and a smudge. The Elder asked each person to introduce themselves by telling where they came from (not what they had accomplished or what they had). This evoked quite an emotional response from the students as they reflected on their experiences growing up. One student divulged that she had Indigenous roots and was raised by her Indigenous grandmother. Afterward, she explained that she had never shared this information with anyone before.

After sharing, her role in the group changed. She was seen as someone who had knowledge and understanding not only about young children based on her education but also about the richness and challenges of Indigenous family life. It was interesting to observe the "hidden" part of her background become meaningful and important in her practice.

Ceremonies and tradition are a key component of Indigenous life. How unthinkable it is today that for centuries Indigenous people were forbidden to practise their rituals and traditions, as they were seen as "non-Christian." The following quotation from Christopher Ronwanièn:te Jocks (Kahnawake Mohawk and Brooklyn Irish) gives some indication of the devastation this caused:

> Traditional ceremonies and spiritual practices . . . are precious gifts given to Indian people by the Creator. These sacred ways have enabled us as Indian people to survive—miraculously—the onslaught of five centuries of continuous effort by non-Indians and their government to exterminate us by extinguishing all traces of our traditional ways of life. Today, these precious sacred traditions continue to afford [us] the strength and vitality we need in the struggle we face every day; they also offer us our best hope for a stable and vibrant future. These sacred traditions are an enduring and indispensable 'life raft' without which we would be quickly overwhelmed by the adversities that still threaten our survival. Because our sacred traditions are so precious to us, we cannot allow them to be desecrated and abused (as cited in Ontario Human Rights Commission, 2017).

Source: Christopher Ronwaien:te Jock, (2000). Spirituality for Sale: Sacred Knowledge in the Consumer Age, Vol. 20, No. 3/4, pp. 415–431

Some of the rituals and traditions of Indigenous communities are becoming known to non-Indigenous people in Canada. This chapter can't possibly do justice to the richness of Indigenous spiritual practices. The few examples included in this section provide only a tiny glimpse into some aspects of the very rich spiritual practices of Indigenous people that have been shared by Indigenous people. As a result of the generosity of many Indigenous people and communities, an abundance of information on Indigenous rituals and traditions is available on websites and YouTube, and in books and articles that provide us with an opportunity to deepen our knowledge and understanding.

A caution is noteworthy here. It's ironic that Indigenous people were denied the right to practise rituals that are so vital to their families and community strength in the past, but now we see some non-Indigenous people trying to copy some of these rituals. Some non-Indigenous people may be well intentioned (although misguided) and seek to copy Indigenous ceremonies as a token of solidarity with Indigenous people. Others have less noble motives, such as the desire to profit from Indigenous practices, for example, through marketing and selling objects that are associated with Indigenous traditions. Such actions are known as *cultural appropriation*, which is considered yet another form of racism and stealing of what rightly belongs to Indigenous people. Cultural appropriation of ceremonies and objects removes and distorts them and disassociates them from their original context. Sometimes, such actions result in gross caricatures that are a slap in the face to the original practitioners of ceremonies, with complete disregard for history. Early childhood educators need to be very conscious of cultural appropriation, especially when we seek to have our playrooms reflect cultural diversity. We must consult with Indigenous families before using ceremonial objects or exposing children to Indigenous traditions. Also, it goes without saying that the decisions about using ceremonial objects or sharing of traditions need to be made by Indigenous people (Unsettling America, 2011).

The ceremonies that tend to be better known outside of Indigenous communities include the following.

The Smudging Ceremony

Medicines such as sage and sweetgrass are used in a sacred manner, placed in a container, and burned. The smoke is taken in one's hands and rubbed over the body while prayers of gratitude and well-being are shared (First Nations Museum, 2016). "The smoke is traditionally fanned using the hand or a feather, and directed over a person or throughout a living space. The purpose is to wash away impurities, sadness, anxieties or unwanted energies or emotions" (Polizzi, 2017).

The Sweat Lodge Ceremony

This ceremony is usually used for healing, but each sweat lodge has a different purpose and each Elder or spiritual leader conducts the ceremony differently. One sweat lodge can be used as a place to work out family or community problems, while another handles health problems, or teaches and shares Indigenous traditions or languages (Aboriginal Tourism BC, 2014).

> Chief Ian Campbell of the Squamish Nation recently spoke about First Nation sweat lodges, saying that entering the dome-like structure and shallow earthen pit of a sweat lodge represented entering the womb of Mother Earth. "It is a place of transformation," he said. "As you participate in the ceremony, you are purified through breathing, meditating, and through the sharing of words, prayers, songs and storytelling.
>
> "Through this unique and profoundly personal experience, your body is cleansed of toxins, which aids in removing stress and the improvement of your mental, emotional, physical and spiritual well-being." (Aboriginal Tourism BC, 2014)

The Baby-Naming Ceremony

Baby naming ceremonies are very important in many indigenous cultures. For example, the Ojibwe Language and Culture Website provides the following information (http://ojibwelanguageandculture.weebly.com/naming-ceremony.html),

> The Naming Ceremony remembers the Original Man's sacrifice for naming everything. It requires a father and mother to ask a medicine person to seek a name for their child. The medicine person does the seek by fasting, meditation, prayer, or dreaming and the spirit gives the name. The medicine person burns an offering of tobacco and pronounces the name to the four directions. The people at the ceremony repeat the name when it is called out by the medicine person. After the name is announced the spirit world can then accept the name and recognize the child as a living thing for the first time. The Spirit World and ancestors guard the child and prepare a place in the spirit world for them when the end of their life comes. At the naming ceremony the parents ask for four men and four women to sponsor the child. The sponsors vow to guide and support the child.

The Medicine Wheel

The medicine wheel is perhaps the Indigenous symbol that is most often seen outside of Indigenous communities, although it's not used by all Indigenous communities. Yet, few people understand its meaning. The medicine wheel can take many different forms, such as a work of art or a painting, or a physical construction. The medicine wheel has been used by North American bands for generations. It's used for health and healing, and it embodies the Four Directions, Father Sky, Mother Earth, and Spirit Tree, all of which symbolize the dimensions of health and life cycles.

Movement in the medicine wheel (and in most ceremonies in Indigenous cultures) is circular, and typically sun-wise or clockwise in direction. The purpose is to align with the forces of nature, such as the rising and setting of the sun. The medicine wheel is interpreted differently by different bands; for example, it can be used to focus on the stages of life; the seasons; spiritual, emotional, intellectual, and physical aspects of life; or the elements of nature (U.S. National Library of Medicine, n.d.).

INDIGENOUS PEDAGOGY

One way of understanding cultures is to focus on how children are educated, both formally and informally, through family and community interactions. *Pedagogy* is a term that has many definitions, but we will use the following: "pedagogy is about learning, teaching and development influenced by the cultural, social and political values we have for children" (Child Australia, 2017, p. 1). Pedagogy provides a theoretical and practical base for what we do and how we teach and how we believe that children learn (Child Australia, 2017).

This approach to understanding cultures is particularly relevant to early childhood educators. It's unfortunate that until recently, most diploma and university programs in early childhood education have been based on dominant-culture theoretical models (Ball & Pence, 2006) that ignore the unique cultures of Indigenous communities. Western child developmental theory that is required as part of the early childhood education curriculum was developed mostly by Western psychologists who knew little or nothing of Indigenous culture, "ways of being," and ways of teaching children. Different from the pedagogy most early childhood practitioners have studied, the pedagogy of most Indigenous scholars and practitioners emphasizes holism as the central vision of Indigenous ways of thinking and learning. Indigenous knowledge and learning incorporate the spirit, heart, mind, and body, as well as the belief that we are linked with one another and everything around us through circular and relationship-based connections. Jo-ann Archibald (Q'um Q'um Xiiem), former associate dean for Indigenous Education and director of the Indigenous Education Program (NITEP) at the University of British Columbia notes, "Only when our hearts, minds, bodies, and spirits work together do we truly have Indigenous education" (Archibald, 2008, p. 12).

Marie Battiste and James Youngblood Henderson (2009) characterize Indigenous views on learning as sacred, holistic, and a lifelong responsibility. From an Indigenous viewpoint, every child is unique in his or her learning journey and knowledge construction (Battiste & Henderson, 2009). Further, ceremonies, traditions, and daily observations are all understood as essential to learning in Indigenous cultures, and the spirit-connecting process allows gifts, vision, and spirit to emerge from the individual.

The number of early learning centres that focus primarily on Indigenous ways of knowing and learning has grown in the East Coast of Canada. Young Indigenous children, ages 3 to 5 years, can be registered in programs, known as Head Start, both on-reserve and off-reserve, particularly on Prince Edward Island. "The structured program is also designed to prepare children for their school experiences. The early childhood educators strive to provide a balanced learning experience for the students, including Mi'kmaq Language and Culture, skill development, and health and hygiene" (Walton et al., 2009, p. 40.). This balance includes providing an inclusive learning space that allows for the hands-on, experiential learning that is integral to how Indigenous children learn, as well as a structured curriculum. By removing the linear and colonial way of learning, children can be more engaged with their educators, and the curriculum becomes something that has meaning to children's lived experiences. The early childhood educators in these centres are very focused on connecting with the family unit, so as to increase the understanding and trust of the children and their families. When meaningful contact is established and nurtured, children begin to thrive in their academic settings.

The Importance of Experiential Learning

Marie Battiste, a leader in Indigenous education, explains the importance of experiential learning for Indigenous people:

> The first principle of Aboriginal learning is a preference for experiential knowledge. Indigenous pedagogy values a person's ability to learn independently by observing, listening, and participating with a minimum of intervention or instruction. (First Nations Pedagogy Online, 2009b)

Experiential learning can be described as essential First Nations traditional teaching and learning since this process entails the making of meaning from direct experiences through reflection on doing or action. "Experiential learning, including learning from the land, Elders, traditions and ceremonies, community, parental and family supports, as well as the workplace, is a widespread and vital—but often unrecognized—form of Aboriginal learning" (First Nations Pedagogy Online, 2009b).

The qualities of experiential learning include the following:

- It is connected to the experiences of life.
- The "classroom" is the community and the natural environment.
- It is learning by doing.
- It is a community-based way to teach skills, attitudes, language, literacy, and knowledge.

Experiential learning in Indigenous pedagogy "includes the elements of Experiencing, Reflecting, Meaning Making, and Acting that reveal an engaged, deliberate, open and aware process" (Kaminski, 2012).

A comparison of some of the commonly held views of Indigenous and Western society concerning children and child-rearing was undertaken by Doug Dokis, a member of the Dokis First Nation in Northern Ontario, when he was an instructor in a program for Aboriginal Child and Youth Care Workers at Mount Royal University. He found that Indigenous pedagogy emphasized that children are unique, whole individuals, while Western pedagogy emphasized the need to mould children and direct them. Whereas the Indigenous view considers that children learn best by observation and experience, the Western view advocates learning through formal and planned activities. Western educators tend to see the parents as having primary responsibility for the child (and failing that, the government). By contrast, in Indigenous cultures, the extended family and the community have responsibility for the child. The approach of Western educators is to allow children to make mistakes once and then "correct" them by teaching consequences. However, the Indigenous view is that children make many mistakes until they learn.

The Importance of Understanding Indigenous Pedagogy

As we have indicated, understanding how Indigenous pedagogy views children, life, and education is important because this pedagogy is very different from the pedagogy in which mainstream Canadians have been educated.

Cultural misunderstandings have been the basis of many injustices toward Indigenous children and families, and the literature abounds with examples of teachers, welfare workers, and other officials making terrible decisions about Indigenous families based partly on these misunderstandings. Early childhood educators are now committed to attempting to ensure that this tradition of ignorance and misjudgment does not continue. Certainly, if we are committed to engaging with families, we need to do so with a genuine respect for the cultural traditions from which they come (Pacini-Ketchabaw & Taylor, 2015).

Yet there is another reason why it's vital for early childhood educators to gain an understanding of Indigenous pedagogy. The reason is that many educators today, especially in the world of early childhood education, believe that education should move away from the practices of yesterday and move toward a more holistic approach "with an emphasis on "critical thinking, creativity, collaboration and communication" (Munroe, Lunney Borden, Murray Orr, Toney, & Meader, 2013, p. 319). In fact, it has been pointed out that there is much in common between the beliefs underlying quality early childhood education models, such as Reggio Amelia, and Indigenous values and ways of knowing (Pacini-Ketchabaw & Taylor, 2015). As Munroe et al. (2013) concluded, what we consider newer ideas in learning and education are, in fact, "rooted in very old ideas embedded in Indigenous knowledges" (p. 319). This insight provides a wonderful basis for mutual learning and collaboration between early childhood educators and Indigenous people.

THE ROLE OF EARLY CHILDHOOD EDUCATORS

There is no question that early childhood educators, families, and the children in child care have much to benefit when educators and Indigenous families engage with each other. As a first step, it's vital to learn about the history and understand not only its impact on Indigenous peoples but also its impact on the lens through which we view our own knowledge and ways of practice. The strongest recommendation that we can make, besides the effort to enhance our own learning, is to invite or request help from Indigenous families in the effort to engage. Consider the perspective of an Indigenous childhood educator, presented in the following box.

Perspectives

Dianna is a 45-year-old mother of seven children. She was born and raised on a Blackfoot reserve and married into the Tsuut'ina.

"I come from a large family, five sisters and four brothers. My native language is Blackfoot. I attended boarding school from grade 1 to grade 10, and came to the city to finish high school. I recently completed a diploma in social work and am working in child welfare on the reserve. From my experience as an Aboriginal person, and as a parent, I see much that early childhood educators can do to enhance the relationship between us. What I'm saying is undoubtedly influenced by my own experiences of racism and discrimination, my sense that mainstream culture is sometimes very apathetic concerning what has happened to Native people, and my feelings that I and my children have not always been free to express our opinions about our values and beliefs.

"The caregiver should be aware of the children's ethnic and cultural origin, including their history, extended family, and community. Early childhood educators shouldn't just read books, which are often written by whites, but should actually talk to tribal members. First, I would educate early childhood educators a bit about my culture so that they may better understand the Aboriginal lifestyle.

"These are some of the customs we watch for:

- We don't let children go outside after dark, because of the night spirits.

- We teach them patience and respect for Elders.

- We teach them to respect and never abuse nature, for it has a life form in itself.

- We believe that children should never, ever be shamed, for shaming a human being is not acceptable in our culture.

"The caregiver should also be made aware of the communication patterns of the Native child. When Native children are asked questions, they often take time to respond. People sometimes think our children are dumb because they don't answer quickly. They don't answer quickly because we teach them to think carefully and formulate a precise answer before responding.

"Early childhood educators should know that, for many of us, grandparents and aunts and uncles have much responsibility for the children. In many cases, these extended family members take on lots of roles that you would assume belong to the parents.

"I would have been very happy to participate in activities in my children's child care, as I do in the schools today. Some of the activities I think suitable are storytelling by Elders, organizing cultural days, taking children on nature walks, and demonstrating Aboriginal arts and crafts. I would also suggest that Aboriginal parents help the child-care staff design and decorate the child-care centre so that it reflects Native culture as well as the cultures of other children in the centre."

Diana's words teach us much, although it's important to remember that she is speaking in her own voice, which is not intended to represent all Indigenous people.

Understanding and Empathizing

A first step in understanding and empathizing is to recognize how Canada's colonial history has impacted Indigenous peoples, and how it continues to "subject Indigenous peoples" (Joseph, 2017). For early childhood educators who have an in-depth understanding of the psychology of children, it should be possible to understand the trauma suffered by Indigenous parents and grandparents when, as children, they were placed in residential schools.

Imagine how you might feel as an Indigenous child when

- expectations for interacting are very different from what you are taught at home
- you are ignored or punished for acting the way you have been taught at home
- people expect you to act in ways that are not valued in your home or community

Imagine how you might feel as a parent when

- you are worried that your ways, values, and beliefs are not understood or valued
- you worry that your child will be teased or bullied because your child is Indigenous

Engaging Indigenous Families

To engage families from Indigenous communities, you might consider the following:

- Begin by examining your own attitudes. There are many myths and stereotypical images of Indigenous people in Canadian cultures. Be vigilant in questioning your own attitudes.
- Find Indigenous people to guide you and your program to help ensure relevance and authenticity for both Indigenous and non-Indigenous children. A new school and resource centre in Calgary has "Open Elder Time" in the school, during which Elders are available to respond to questions, not only from families and staff within the school but also from the broader community. Check the resources in your own community.
- In consultation with, and with the permission of, Indigenous families, invite Indigenous people to introduce Indigenous stories, songs, and dances in daily activities so that all children can come to appreciate traditional ways. Include outdoor play and opportunities for contact with plants and animals so that children may strengthen their appreciation of the natural world.
- Avoid making assumptions: ask, ask, ask!
- Take advantage of the resources available to learn about the "do's and don'ts" of interactions and communication with Indigenous people. Bob Joseph (2016) provides easy-to-understand guidelines that can help prevent embarrassment and pave the way for the development of positive relationships.
- Recognize how important it is for Indigenous children to learn the language of their people. We are reminded by Betty Bastien, in her book *Blackfoot Ways of Knowing: The Worldview of the Siksikaitsitapi*, about the inextricable connection between language and

culture (Bastien, 2004). As Indigenous people today are striving to revive languages that were, for so many years, forbidden, early childhood educators can find many ways to support families in this quest, such as asking parents to share key words and phrases that can be used in day-to-day interactions with the children.

SCENARIO

RESPECT

In a methods class, early childhood students were discussing activities that might be used to promote different cultures in respectful ways. This discussion began with stereotypical images and how these might be avoided. For example, making teepees can be a fun activity but can also be used to explore different types of living arrangements, how houses are built, etc. When one student mentioned that she had her 5-year-old children make dream catchers, an Indigenous student reacted with surprise and concern. Her perspective was that dream catchers are considered spiritual and have many traditional beliefs associated with them. She felt that it would be difficult to use this as an art activity respectfully without the spiritual association.

CONCLUSION

Working with Indigenous children and families challenges us to understand the world as culturally diverse. Taking a journey to deepen our understanding of cultural diversity often reaps meaningful rewards, the least of which is a greater understanding of our own roots and cultures. This chapter will end with a quote from professor Jo-ann Archibald, who reminds us about both the difficulty and the necessity of change:

> The theme of creating change reminds me of the story of Raven who initiated a major change or shift in the environment by bringing sun to the people who lived in darkness. The sun represents Indigenous teachers who bring together Indigenous Knowledge and other forms of knowledge that teachers require to be effective. Creating educational change that is meaningful, of high quality, and culturally relevant and responsive is difficult and demanding. But it needs to be done if we are to make significant improvements to Aboriginal education at all levels and in all contexts.
>
> We need to have Raven-like persistence, courage, and commitment to question what does not work and to develop many different educational strategies to bring the "sun" to places and people so that they have a better life. This NITEP Newsletter highlights many perspectives, hopes, and dreams for creating educational change in ways that would make both Elders and the Raven smile. (Archibald, 2012)

Chapter Summary

- Engaging with Indigenous families requires that educators become aware of the colonialist history of Canada and its impact on Indigenous families that is still a reality today.
- The residential schools were among many of the practices and the policies of the colonial government that deprived Indigenous people of their language, their traditions, their land, and the ability of families to raise and care for their children.

- Indigenous cultures are rich with traditions and symbols that are an essential and ongoing part of life, and spiritual beliefs. It's important to learn about them with respect, and never to use them without the permission of Indigenous people.

- Indigenous pedagogy entails many views of children and learning that are consistent with contemporary views of early childhood educators. Much can be learned from Indigenous pedagogy.

RESOURCES

The Aboriginal Head Start Association of British Columbia (AHSABC) hosts a website with a bulletin board for practitioners in culturally based programs and lists wonderful resources for drawing upon local cultures in programs:
www.ahsabc.com

The BC Aboriginal Child Care Association (BCACCS) is a resource and referral clearinghouse. This website lists and provides links to many documents about culturally based programming that can be downloaded for free:
www.acc-society.bc.ca/files_2/accs-publications.php

For an overview of the rich and varied religious beliefs and practices of Canadian Indigenous people, see:
www.thecanadianencyclopedia.ca/en/article/religion-of-aboriginal-people/

Early Childhood Development Intercultural Partnerships:
www.ecdip.org

Canadian Child Care Federation:
www.cccf-fcsge.ca/

Government of Alberta, "Walking Together: First Nations, Métis and Inuit Perspectives in Curriculum":
www.learnalberta.ca/content/aswt/#/kinship/observing_practice/a_relationship_model_of_kinship

Speaking My Truth: Reflections on Reconciliation and Residential Schools:
http://speakingmytruth.ca

Aboriginal Perspectives, film excerpts depicting the impact of colonization on Indigenous peoples (National Film Board):
www3.nfb.ca/enclasse/doclens/visau/index.php?mode=theme&language=english&theme=30662&submode=about

The Indigenous World View V. Western World View, video:
www.youtube.com/watch?v=hsh-NcZyuiI

Colonization and Racism, a National Film Board film featuring Emma LaRocque, a Plains-Cree Métis originally from northeastern Alberta, who is also a scholar, author, poet, social and literary critic, and human rights advocate:
www3.nfb.ca/enclasse/doclens/visau/index.php?mode=theme&language=english&theme=30662&film=&excerpt=&submode=about&expmode=2

Marie Battiste: Knowledge as a Key Site for Decolonization. This video is a must for instructors in early childhood education:

www.youtube.com/watch?v=Evxpt0u4tOU

First Nations Films—The Medicine Wheel, video:

www.youtube.com/watch?v=ffw15vmaWr4

EXERCISES

1. Ask for permission to attend an Indigenous ceremony or ritual at your college. What were your impressions? What did you learn?

2. Review the ceremonies described in this chapter or other ceremonies that you have learned about. Think about the rituals and traditions that you are familiar with in your own culture. What are the differences? What are the similarities?

3. What are the ways that you can demonstrate, in your daily work, your new understanding of Indigenous cultures?

4. Review the section on intersectionality and the section on trauma in Chapter 3. How do the perspectives described there relate to Indigenous families?

5. Read the calls to action from the Truth and Reconciliation Commission of Canada at www.trc.ca/websites/trcinstitution/File/2015/Findings/Calls_to_Action_English2.pdf.

6. How can you, as an early childhood professional, respond to these recommendations? What would you recommend to your professional association in terms of actions? How do you think early childhood education college and university programs should respond to the recommendations?

CHAPTER 9

Culturally Diverse Families

OBJECTIVES

- To understand and appreciate the cultural diversity that exists in Canada

- To understand the experiences of immigrants and refugees as they transition to life in Canada

- To discuss ways in which the early childhood educator can support new Canadian families

An educator was talking with her class about diversity and tolerance, and said, "We have to remember that we are all immigrants." One child pointed to the little boy sitting beside him, who he knew was Inuit. "He's not an immigrant," he said, "but all the rest of us are."

MULTICULTURAL CANADA

It can be said that except for the Indigenous peoples, in Canada the rest of the population are immigrants. Until the last few decades, most of the immigrants in Canada were from Europe. Although they spoke different languages, they shared a Western and Christian culture. This cultural map of Canada has been changing considerably over the past few years. People immigrate to this country for many reasons, and from all corners of the world. For some, it's the opportunity to participate in, contribute to, and enjoy the economic and social opportunities that life in Canada affords. For others, it's an opportunity to reunite with family and loved ones who have immigrated here in the past. For others still, Canada provides an escape and safe haven from war and other situations that are simply unimaginable to many Canadians. Canada has been lauded throughout the world for its humanistic approach to receiving refugees. In this chapter, we will discuss the cultural diversity of Canada, the experience of immigrating to Canada, and the challenges faced by immigrant children and families. As well, we will discuss the tragic impact of war and refugee status on so many new Canadians. Finally, we will consider the ways in which the early childhood educator can provide support to new Canadian families.

The following scenario serves as a reminder that we can't make assumptions about others' cultural experience.

SCENARIO

MAKING ASSUMPTIONS

Nathan, an 8-year-old boy, was listening intently as his social studies teacher was telling the children how the first railroad in Canada was built, by and large by Chinese immigrant labourers who were treated extremely poorly. As he listened, he began to show signs of anxiety and kept glancing at Jimmy, who was sitting a couple of seats away from him. His teacher noticed, and as the children exited the class, she asked him if he wanted to tell her what upset him. "Now Jimmy will hate me," he said, "because Canadians did not treat his great-grandparents very well."

The next day, the teacher decided to have a discussion with the children about how they think the great-grandchildren of the early Chinese immigrants might feel when they learn about the history of Chinese immigrant labourers in Canada. Several children looked at Jimmy, expecting him to answer. "Don't look at me," he said. "I have no idea. My parents came from Hong Kong and I was born here."

CULTURAL DIVERSITY IN CANADA

Historically, Canada has been one of the world's largest immigrant-receiving countries (Burnet & Driedger, 2011). In the early years, immigrants were expected to integrate into British or French societies, and those who didn't (either because they had a different religion or were people of colour) suffered from discrimination. Since the 1970s, Canada has welcomed immigrants from non-European countries all over the world. In 1971, then prime minister Pierre Elliott Trudeau declared a commitment to the principle of multiculturalism and worked on the development of policies to promote diversity to ensure that all Canadians have equal rights under the law. This principle was formalized in the Canadian Charter of Rights and Freedoms (1982). Jumping ahead more than three decades, we see that the 2011 census recorded more than 200 different ethnic origins: 21% of Canadians (6 775 800 people) were born outside Canada, and that number continues to grow.

Vast demographic changes are taking place throughout Canada. As of 2008, approximately 20% of Canadians were immigrants (Statistics Canada, 2008). Since 2005, about 250 000 immigrants have come to this country each year. Furthermore, it's estimated that by 2030, Canada's only source of growth will be through immigration, as the result of our aging population (Statistics Canada, 2010). A walk through any large city, many small towns, or just about any college or university campus reinforces the impression that Canada is largely a collection of many different cultures. Many cultural groups have been successful in preserving their identity and special traditions while contributing to Canadian society as a whole.

Accordingly, over the past decade, much emphasis has been placed on diversity in early childhood education. Twenty years ago, many articles, workshops, and chapters in books were entitled "Tolerating Diversity." However, public awareness of the possible negative connotations of that phrase led to a reconsideration. We then began to talk about "celebrating diversity," which better reflects the idea that Canadians are proud of their multicultural society. Canadian identity is considered a multicultural mosaic, with different cultures and groups within the mosaic influencing one another in a number of ways.

Canada's multitude of ethnically diverse groups is constantly changing. For example, between 2001 and 2006, approximately 60% of new Canadians were from Asia (Chui, Tran, & Maheux, 2007), whereas in the 1960s, Asians accounted for only about 6% of immigrants (Statistics Canada, 2016a). From 2001 to 2006, only 16% of new Canadians were from Europe, compared with close to 75% in the 1960s (Chui, Tran, & Maheux, 2007). These examples indicate the ongoing shift in demographics—a shift that will affect many aspects of society in the future.

While the phrases "embracing diversity" and "celebrating diversity" appear in many textbooks, many Canadians feel somewhat ambivalent about the societal changes diversity often brings. It may be easier to celebrate difference when those who are different are in the minority than when there is a concern that the traditional ways of mainstream Canadians may be challenged. Nonetheless, we have to be careful not to automatically assume that people are racist or prejudiced if they question how the changing landscape of Canada may affect their lives. Successful adaptation to change requires a strong commitment to mutual understanding and much dialogue. It's very important that, as professionals, we move beyond such slogans as "celebrating diversity" and "embracing diversity" and encourage dialogue to occur. A first step for educators is to learn about the culture of others and about the range of behaviours and values that reflect these cultures. A second (and no less important) step is to understand our own culture.

Religious Diversity in Canada

Early childhood education programs have integrated knowledge and skills related to multiculturalism and inclusion in most of their courses and programs. So important is our ability to successfully engage with culturally diverse children and families that many universities across Canada have developed undergraduate and graduate programs that prepare educators "in attending to socio-cultural differences . . . by listening, observing, and being prepared to respond to questions, ideas, and even conflicts related to diverse child-rearing . . . practices" (University of Calgary, 2017b).

Most early childhood educators, like most Canadians, welcome and celebrate religious diversity. There is a strong belief in inclusion and a true desire to find appropriate ways of celebrating the religious diversity that we see in our centres, schools, and institutions. Yet how to put the principle of inclusion into practice is a question that researchers in Canada, and all over the world, are trying to learn more about ("Religious Diversity in Canada: Secularism, Multiculturalism, Pluralism," with Dr. Peter Beyer, 2014).

In Canada today, the children in most schools and child-care centres are from different religious backgrounds. Those religious backgrounds include a variety of denominations of Christians, Muslims, Buddhists, Jews, Bahai, Sikhs, and other religious groups that are less well known. There are also many Canadians who adhere to no religion, such as those who consider themselves to be atheists. It's important to keep in mind that some people consider their religious beliefs and traditions as a private family or community matter, while others wish to share their traditions and celebrations.

While many educators approach their day-to-day work with children with cultural awareness and competence, some educators feel less confident when it comes to engaging with parents who come from different ethnic, religious, or cultural backgrounds. Some educators choose to deal with religious diversity by ensuring that the centre is "neutral"; that is, they don't address any religious celebrations.

Consider the following view of one educator, who highlights practical considerations about incorporating religious diversity in her program. All of these considerations can seem overwhelming. However, there is growing consensus that the benefits of being truly multicultural in our approach to working with children and families is well worth the effort.

SCENARIO

INCORPORATING RELIGIOUS DIVERSITY IN THE CLASSROOM

One early childhood educator told us, "I worry that celebrating a holiday belonging to one group will offend other groups with different holidays. There are so many different religious festivals from all the different religions, that we would be celebrating a festival every day of the year! And the different dates of holy days makes it difficult to know when to plan parent activities without excluding those who can't attend. I also need to think about the different dietary restrictions of different religious groups, which makes it difficult to know what is and what isn't allowed for the children."

Tolerance or Inclusion?

Former UN secretary-general Ban Ki-moon once stated, "Tolerance does not mean indifference or a grudging acceptance of others. It is a way of life based on mutual understanding and respect for others, and on the belief that global diversity is to be embraced, not feared" (United Nations, 2009).

Teaching Tolerance and Acceptance

The National Association for the Education of Young Children suggests that young children can, at an early age, be taught to become tolerant and resist bias (Derman-Sparks, 2005). Educators can help enhance the children's ability to empathize with one another and be more accepting of difference. It's still extremely important to "teach tolerance," but today Canadians recognize that there is much more to being a multicultural country than tolerance. There is understanding, there is learning from one another, there is celebration, and there is a mutuality that everyone can benefit from. The following scenario is about the first step: teaching tolerance and acceptance.

SCENARIO

TOLERANCE AND ACCEPTANCE

Janice, the teacher in a preschool classroom, overheard the following conversation between two boys, Mike and Raj. Mike asked Raj, "What's your last name?" Upon hearing a name that sounded very unfamiliar, the child started to poke fun at his friend. "That's a weird name." Upon observing that Raj was trying hard to hold back tears, the educator intervened and said, "Do you know that when we travel to other countries, the people there often think that our names sound very strange as well? Perhaps you could tell Raj that his family name is a bit hard for you to pronounce, but that you will keep trying. It's okay to say that, but if you laugh at the sound of Raj's name, it can be very hurtful and I know you wouldn't want to hurt his feelings, because he's your friend."

Joseph DeVito, Rena Shimoni, and Dawne Clarke (2015) provide a number of strategies to enhance communication between people of different cultures, which is referred to as *intercultural communication*. Because our cultural background influences both how we receive messages and how we communicate messages, the result can be misunderstanding or lack of understanding. To help avoid such results, take the following steps:

1. **Prepare yourself.** We can't become experts on every religion and every culture. However, we can be curious, we can search for information, and we can learn. There are so many sources to draw on: videos, magazines, and websites. Parents are often willing to share when they understand that learning about traditions is important for all children. Notice whether the material was produced by a member of the religion or culture being described, or by an outsider. Both perspectives will provide valuable information. Yet one of the best ways to learn about another religion or culture is by having good conversations in an open and caring atmosphere with someone different than you. One important thing to remember: there is much diversity within each religious and cultural group, and an individual may want to share only his or her personal or family's perspective, traditions, and beliefs. Beware of generalizing!

2. **Reduce your ethnocentrism.** Ethnocentrism is the tendency to judge others through one's own cultural "filters," assuming that the values, beliefs, and behaviours of one's culture are superior to those of others. As part of a major research study carried out in New Zealand, one early childhood educator described how she and her team recognized

the importance of having "inquiring attitudes, a willingness to be uncertain, and to investigate" because they knew that it was necessary to understand that many values are not universally shared, that understanding different family values is necessary, and that conscious thought needs to be given to how family values are catered to (Mitchell et al., 2015). This is how one supervisor explained to a researcher her effort to reduce ethnocentrism:

> From your little sheltered perspective everybody shares the same values and I think one of the first things in early childhood I learned was this idea of independence is not shared by everybody. That interdependence is also very important and so we started to alter a little bit the way we thought about values and trying to understand what our families were bringing, and integrate those into what we were doing. So— you know someone said to me, "Why does my child need to be able to dress themselves? I can dress them? That is my job." And so we started to think more about—okay, that's what they're doing at home, we need to think about how we, how we're fitting into their world. Instead of just expecting everybody that comes to us to subscribe to our value set. (Mitchell et al., 2015, p. 19)

This kind of commitment to multicultural practice is a very deliberate process to find out about the values of families and respect them.

A discussion with a group of post-secondary educators around the "image of the child" took an interesting turn. Several of the educators had engaged their students in this discussion and learned that there were diverse views and perspectives about children represented in the room. They then asked themselves this question: *Is it my job to change their image based on their values, beliefs, and experiences, or is it my role to understand the diversity of perspectives that educators can bring to their work with families and children?* Many admitted that this question presented a very real ethical dilemma for them.

3. **Confront your stereotypes.** We all hold stereotypes, that is, a fixed impression of a group of people. While there is enough multicultural awareness today to make people cautious about expressing these stereotypical views, they often exist below the surface. Once people become more conscious and aware of the stereotypes they hold about different cultural groups, they can make an effort not to prejudge people based on these stereotypes. It can be helpful to consider generalizations such as "most people of Christian heritage celebrate Easter," but stereotypes tend to be negative and often become a barrier to developing positive relationships.

4. **Don't make assumptions!** Just as the boy in the first scenario of this chapter made an assumption about his Chinese schoolmate, we need to be cautious about making assumptions about people with different religious or cultural affiliations. Sometimes we make these assumptions based on stereotypes or the very little information we have on a different culture. Not all Hindu people are vegetarian. Not all Jewish people follow the dietary restrictions of their religion. A number of Canadians of different religions celebrate Christmas because they see it as a lovely holiday. However, a number of Canadians don't celebrate it. The only way we can avoid making assumptions is to ask! Most people are more than willing to share their ideas.

5. **Attempt to reduce uncertainty.** Early childhood educators use effective communication strategies in communicating with all parents, but when communicating with a person from a different culture, it's helpful to remember and use some of the techniques of active listening, such as "perception checking." One educator we spoke with gave an example of how important this is:

> We had planned an outing to the swimming pool at the nearby community centre and sent a note home telling parents about the planned event, requesting that the children

come to school with bathing suits and towels. One of the mothers came up to me and said that her son must not swim. Because she was wearing a hijab, long-sleeved shirt, and long skirt, I wondered if she did not want her son to be at a swimming pool because of modesty traditions within her religion. I wasn't quite sure what to do—and hoped she wouldn't be insulted if I asked if she could explain to me why she didn't want her son to go to the swimming pool (checking my perception). "Oh," she said. "He had a bit of a cough last night, and just to play it safe I think he should not be going to the pool." I was really glad I checked my perception—as I had it all wrong!

6. **Be aware.** Be aware of differences in nonverbal communication styles. Eye contact, physical space, touch, and tone of voice are some of the differences that may lead to misunderstanding. In some cultures, for example, speaking in a loud voice, using large gestures, and standing close to the person one is speaking to is common practice. However, in Canada, these ways of communicating could be understood as aggression (CMAS Canada, 2013).

7. **Remember names; it's important.** Have you ever been unsure about how to pronounce someone's name but were too embarrassed to ask? What often happens is that we try to avoid using the name at all. It's much better to simply say, "I'm sorry. I didn't quite hear how you pronounce your name, and I want to make certain I got it right." This is a much better idea.

8. **Construct a customized calendar.** At the beginning of the year, construct (with parents' help) a calendar that notes important dates for families of the children in the centre. These dates could be festivals or days of worship that would preclude children attending the centre or the parents' participation in any activities. Then invite the parents to share their customs and traditions pertaining to these dates. This action enriches the children and makes the parents feel welcome and included. Be sure that the invitation is genuine, but not one that makes parents feel under pressure to participate.

9. **Involve the parents.** Ask parents if they can help by providing examples of stories, games, and traditions from their culture that could be integrated into the daily activities of the centre.

10. **Think about the difference between multicultural and intercultural.** *Multicultural* usually refers to one group learning about other groups, whereas *intercultural* refers to educators, children, and families having the opportunity to learn from one another (Artis & Telford, 2016). Think about some of the learnings you have gained from your relationships with people from other cultures. Similarly, think about what your culture has to offer to others!

    One intercultural program describes its activities as "activities that support children's cultural backgrounds and home languages that help them build a strong cultural identity at the same time as they encourage cross-cultural sharing and learning" (Intercultural Child & Family Centre, n.d.).

11. **Ask families to share.** Invite families to participate in the sharing of their celebrations. Hindi Diwali, Jewish Purim, Buddhist Visakha Puja/Wesa, and Chinese and Vietnamese New Year are but a few examples of colourful celebrations that children would enjoy. For those who fear the overabundance of celebrations, each year could focus on different ones.

12. **Enjoy.** Engaging with families that come from diverse backgrounds can have its challenges, but more often than not it's enriching, educational, interesting, and a lot of fun. Remember that engaging with families from different cultures is a two-way process with multiple benefits. It can help the children feel good about themselves, their families, and their communities, and it also exposes the children, the families, and the educators to ways that are unfamiliar and outside their own experience (Community Tool Box, 2017).

Courtesy of Chris Zahn.

Taylor, Age 5

IMMIGRATING TO CANADA

It's perhaps not surprising that Canada is an attractive destination for many immigrants. Canada has a high standard of living, good employment rates, and a health care system that ensures care to every citizen. Canadians are proud of their education system and their social programs. Canada is also a safe and beautiful country. As well, Canada is a multicultural country that embraces all cultures and religions (Evans, 2013).

The decision to immigrate is probably one of the most significant decisions that a family will ever make. Yet, even for the many immigrants who choose to come to Canada, there is usually a difficult period of adjustment. The review of the processes of change and loss described in Chapter 3 is very pertinent to immigrants. Even when immigration is a choice, it always involves loss. Immigrants lose their familiar surroundings, lose close contact with extended family and friends, and often lose status related to their level of education and employment. As noted by Kelley and Conner (1979), even when the move was a choice and a change for the better, people will undergo a predictable emotional cycle that occurs in five stages (Kübler-Ross, 1969, 2017). First, people who immigrate to Canada may be very excited about being here and experience "uninformed optimism." Second, they may encounter problems that lead them to feel letdown and experience "informed pessimism." Third, they eventually experience "hopeful realism" after they become more familiar with the new situation. Fourth, they experience "informed optimism," a phase in which they come to terms with the choice and feel more comfortable with it. The fifth stage is completion: they have worked through most of the problems and feel that the change is complete.

While we are able to summarize the cycle of change experienced by immigrants in a few short sentences, adjusting to a new life can take a considerable amount of time. It's a good idea to remember that within an extended family that has immigrated, the adjustment period may be very different in both its nature and its duration for each individual due to many factors. Reena, a woman who immigrated from India more than 15 years ago, shares her story in the following scenario.

SCENARIO

ADJUSTING TO A NEW LIFE

"My husband is an engineer who was classified by the Canadian immigration authorities as an 'HQP'—a highly qualified professional. He received much support in arranging for his credentials to be recognized here and to find a job. He felt wonderful the first days after we arrived. It was quite different for me. I was a school principal in India, had many professional contacts, and enjoyed the status and relationships that came with my position. My credentials were not recognized here. I had to take a job with a lower salary and much less responsibility than I was used to. I was quite depressed about it, and it took me a long time to 'reinvent' myself. I am now doing research to learn more about 'the wives of HQPs.' I want to learn how they are adjusting, and what might be done to help in that process."

It's often difficult to imagine the experiences of new Canadians as they build their lives in this country. For example, gender roles can change, and immigrant fathers often experience a shift in roles and responsibilities upon immigrating to Canada (Este & Tachble, 2009; Roer-Strier, 1999; Roer-Strier, Strier, Este, Shimoni, & Clarke, 2005). If a woman's earning potential is greater than her husband's, a woman's role may shift from a primarily domestic one to that of primary breadwinner, forcing the man to take on more "traditional" mothering roles (Kim-Goh & Baello, 2008; Remennick, 2017). The change in family roles and the status of family members has been described by many researchers (Roer-Strier, Kosner, & Shimoni, 2017). For example, in a study that focused on Russian immigrants, grandparents spoke about how they had changed from being the persons with authority in the family (authority based on wisdom and experience) to ones totally dependent on their children (Roer-Strier et al., 2017). This is just one example of the many changes that may occur upon moving to Canada. Even under the best of circumstances, moving to a new location, communicating in a new language, and encountering a profusion of new sensations, experiences, and people can be simply overwhelming.

The Challenges of Being an Immigrant

Based on research conducted with immigrants four years after their arrival in Canada, Statistics Canada (2005) surveyed the greatest difficulties they faced by recent immigrants. The biggest difficulty was related to finding an adequate job, followed by learning a new language. Others included getting used to the weather; missing support from the homeland; adapting to new culture or values; financial constraints; finding quality housing; and access to education, child care, and professional help.

The following box provides details on a number of risk factors faced by immigrant families. Some of these risk factors apply to many Canadian families, and some are unique to immigrants and refugees.

Risk Factors Faced by Immigrant Families

■ *Underemployment or unemployment*. Due to a number of factors, such as language barriers, different demand levels for occupations in various countries, and different qualification criteria, many immigrants don't find work in their own fields, despite arriving in Canada with education, experience, and professional qualifications (Este & Tachble, 2009; Schellenberg & Maheux, 2007; Spracklin, 2017; Statistics Canada, 2006).

■ *Language barriers*. Clearly, competence in the English or French language is necessary for success in Canada, and many efforts are made to help new Canadians focus on teaching and learning English (Spracklin, 2017). However, as Chud and Fahlman (1995) point out, people who required language training became labelled "ESL" (English as a Second Language), much the same way that children were labelled "special needs." The skills, talents, and potential of the adult and child are often overlooked when the label "ESL" is applied.

■ *Role reversal*. Often when new Canadians seek employment, women find jobs (often in childcare or domestic realms) more easily than their husbands, and the father becomes their children's primary educator (Deaux & Bikmen, 2010; Shimoni, Este, & Clarke, 2003). Some families find this role reversal very difficult, as fathers have not had the socialization or training to be the primary educator and nurturer of children (Williams & Vashi, 2007).

■ *Generational differences in immigrant families*. Generational differences between older immigrants and their children or grandchildren may also alter traditional family roles (Este & Tachble, 2009; Foner & Dreby, 2011; Roer-Strier et al., 2005). For example, adult immigrants may have arrived from a culture where daughters were expected to stay at home and help with domestic tasks, but their daughters, having grown up in Canada, may refuse this domestic role. Conflicts can and often do arise as immigrant families battle with "Canadian" values.

■ *Social isolation*. Feelings of isolation often intensify the social, psychological, and economic pressures that immigrants face. Immigrants of diverse religious and cultural backgrounds can feel excluded from mainstream social events, and sometimes experience discrimination and exclusion.

■ *Barriers to health and helping services*. Barriers may prevent new Canadians from fully utilizing community and health services that offer support to individuals and families (Dastjerdi, Olson, & Ogilvie, 2012; Spracklin, 2017). These barriers can include difficulty communicating in English, lack of knowledge and information about services, perceptions that help is unavailable or that professionals won't be able to help, fear of stigmatization and deportation, and lack of child care. Health care professionals have suggested additional barriers, such as fear of hospitals and clinics, professionals' lack of understanding of immigrants' cultural background, and agencies' inability to provide translators or workers who speak immigrants' first languages.

■ *Barriers to recreation*. A recent study found that immigrants participate less in recreation activity due to lack of awareness about available facilities, unfamiliar with Canadian sports, weather conditions, etc. (Curtin, Loitz, Spencer-Cavaliere, & Khalema, 2016; Spracklin, 2017).

■ *Loss, grief, and depression*. Many immigrants to Canada are grateful for the opportunity to live in this country and appreciate all the advantages that Canada offers. However, even if they are here by choice, it's normal to grieve the loss of family, friends, and a way of life that has been left behind. Depression has been noted as one of the common problems among immigrants. This has a major impact on the child-rearing capacity of immigrant parents, who, for extended periods of time, may be emotionally unavailable to their children. In addition, studies on immigrants report that many cases of depression go undetected due to cultural barriers and inappropriate services (Shimoni et al., 2003).

- *Racism.* Unfortunately, racism still exists in Canada, and immigrants encounter it far too often. Research suggests that this is felt most often in the workplace, where people with the same credentials as nonimmigrants are less likely to receive promotions, and often remain in work below their abilities and education. Racism has an impact on self-esteem and mental health. It also deprives the workforce of talent! (Fang & Goldner, 2011).

- *Trauma induced by war or enforced refugee status.* It's well known that refugees and other immigrants who have been affected by traumatic events require special intervention and attention. Adults who have suffered these kinds of trauma appear to need to move through several stages as they seek to restore mental health after being uprooted and displaced. Post-traumatic stress disorder is fairly common and can deeply impact a family's life.

- *Other barriers:* Lack of knowledge and experience and scarcity of school resources serve as barriers for the parents to support their children's academic work (Isik-Ecramn, Demir-Dagdas, Cakmakci, Cava-Tadik, & Intepe-Tingir, 2017).

Coping Strategies and Approaches with Parents

The previous description of the risk factors that apply to immigrant and refugee families may lead readers to the mistaken conclusion that the odds are high against successful immigration. The truth, however, is just the opposite. After an almost inevitably difficult beginning, most immigrant families acculturate and become successful Canadian citizens. As with many of the issues facing families with young children that have been described in this text, the appropriate support at the appropriate time can make a tremendous difference. For this reason, it's important to understand the risks facing immigrant families. It's equally important to understand some of the differences in child-rearing approaches and strategies so that we don't approach these families from an assumption of deficit. Effective support usually builds on the family's strengths.

Shimoni et al. (2003) describe the various coping methods used by immigrant and refugee families. Their study found that while all the parents wanted to support their children in becoming successful adults in Canada, they had different approaches. Some felt that it was vital to protect the culture of their former country, and to demonstrate that in their daily life. Others wanted to preserve some cultural practices, but in the privacy of their own home. Still others (though a smaller proportion) were happy to leave the "old ways" in their former country and adapt totally to what they saw as a Canadian way of life. These families will have different approaches to professionals. For example, some may be worried that professionals will interfere with their way of life, and some may feel disempowered as parents due to their own adjustment difficulties and may even go as far as abdicating responsibility for decision making to professionals such as teachers and nurses.

SCENARIO

DIFFERENT STROKES

Lee was doing his practicum in a family resource program in two locations in the city: one with predominantly young single mothers living in impoverished settings, the other with new immigrant families. One of his tasks was to plan play experiences for drop-in time in both locations. For the young mothers' group, he planned open-ended activities that children typically worked on while their mothers interacted or attended support meetings. In the other location, the play experiences were totally different. Parents often stayed with their children and directed them in completing the

continues ▶

▶ *continues*

tasks "right" for the "teachers." Parents often asked for models, sought clarification, and insisted that children complete their projects correctly. They joined circle time to ensure that their children paid attention and participated. Lee commented on the difference in his planning and how difficult this was for him, since he didn't really favour highly structured activities. However, he said that this was obviously important to those parents and that he would plan accordingly.

When immigrants move from one culture to another, they can either preserve the image of a successful adult from their home country or abandon it in favour of the image of the successful adult in their new country. In fact, it's never quite this clear-cut. Following immigration, many interrelated factors affect which image parents hold. However, in each case, immigrant families have to find ways to cope with the different norms, expectations, and values regarding children that are prevalent in the new country. These can surface when they interact with professionals at preschool and school, and with health and social services.

Refugee Children and Families

Canada has become known for its humanitarianism and efforts to provide a home for people whose lives have been in extreme danger due to wars. The ongoing conflict in Syria over the past few years has been referred to as the worst humanitarian crisis in the world today (Government of Canada, 2017). Canada's response to this crisis has been to develop a multifaceted strategy to ensure Canada's security, "stabilization, as well as its humanitarian and development assistance" (Government of Canada, 2017). The important role of early childhood educators in supporting children and families who are refugees can't be overstated (Doyle, Dotsch, Savazzi, & Awamleh, 2015). The program guide describes the plight of Syrian children who have

> . . . lost loved ones, suffered injuries, and witnessed violence and brutality . . . and) are at risk of becoming ill, malnourished, abused or exploited. . . . They face daily challenges, as their educators deal with the consequences of war and displacement and are unable to be as supportive as they once were. These ongoing stresses have lasting effects on children's well-being and their developing brains. (Doyle et al., 2015, p. 7)

We see more and more reports of toxic stress in Syrian children, and the long-term effects of this stress are a growing concern (Save the Children, 2017b; Sirin & Rogers-Sirin, 2015).

≫ Perspectives

Ilana is the mother of a 5-year-old girl who comes to a drop-in centre. Her husband was killed at the beginning of a war in their country, and the family spent almost four years as refugees, sharing a small apartment with extended family members.

"It was a time of poverty, loneliness, and sadness. Grief and loneliness seemed to be the only things I could feel. During our times as refugees, my daughter became extremely anxious when we were separated. She would cry at all times when I was out of sight. When we arrived in Canada, I wanted to look for work, or go to English classes, and tried to put my daughter in a child-care centre. Every

morning, as we approached the centre, my daughter started to feel ill, cried, and refused to stay. I was becoming so frustrated, and feeling a bit angry with my daughter.

"The staff at the centre helped me understand that my daughter had severe separation anxiety as a result of the life we had led as refugees. My daughter never really had the opportunity to play, and we were always so tense. They helped me understand how important it was for me to let my daughter play, with me nearby. After a long time, she was okay if I left for a while. I can't believe that now I can leave for several hours, and my little girl lets me go. Sometimes she still fusses again, but I see other Canadian children behaving the same way. I am thankful for the help we received."

We need to understand the challenges faced by many new Canadians who undergo the transition from country to country, some of whom have fled from circumstances that we can only begin to imagine. Young children who have experienced the trauma and horrors of war are often in need of extensive treatment and care. Imagine the impact of witnessing the torture or beating or killing of a sibling, parent, or relative; of being moved from place to place to hide; and of going for days without shelter or food.

A recent study of the trauma experienced by Syrian refugee children in a Turkish refugee camp found that nearly half of the Syrian refugee children surveyed had symptoms of post-traumatic stress disorder—10 times more than the rate among other children around the world who took the same survey (Sirin & Rogers-Sirin, 2015, p. 13). The experience of trauma and then a trying journey to a new and unfamiliar country are overwhelming for children. Parents, who usually provide support for children in stressful situations, may be so overwhelmed by their own reactions to trauma and grief that they are unable to provide emotional support and security to their children. It's no wonder, then, that refugee children commonly display signs of chronic sadness. They may seem excessively fearful or shy, and many develop symptoms of school phobia. The preceding box describes a very common occurrence: a heightened degree of separation anxiety that under normal circumstances would be considered inappropriate for the child's age. Regressive behaviour, learning disabilities, and poor school performance are often seen in refugee children. Hyperalertness or hyperaggressive behaviour are also common.

THE ROLE OF EARLY CHILDHOOD EDUCATORS

Working effectively with people from cultures different from our own requires a willingness to examine our own values and biases. Much has been written about diversity education and the importance of increasing the awareness and competence of early childhood educators in multiculturalism (Durand, 2010). Educators working from the perspective of socio-cultural practice will know that it's critical to understand the context of the child and family and their experiences. This understanding forms the foundation of care. While we can only touch on some of these principles in this chapter, we highly recommend that readers refer to the many resources on developing cultural competence available online. There are also many articles on multiculturalism in early childhood journals, on websites, and in newsletters and other resources for educators. A number of invaluable resources for supporting children and families who are refugees are available at https://cmascanada. ca/cnc/resources/. These resources provide information and numerous strategies. They also remind the educator, "you know your program best. Use only the ideas that work for the unique challenges and strengths of your program, children and families" (CMAS Canada, 2015).

Remember that early childhood educators can be a key factor in helping children develop resilience. As we know, close affirmative relationships, continuous and personalized caregiving, appropriate teaching and learning experiences, and an external social group with a supportive ethos and behavioural styles are all factors that protect children from developing maladaptive behavioural patterns (Rutter, Pickles, Murray, & Eaves, 2001). In addition, early childhood educators can and do support and promote resilience in families, and this may be especially relevant in supporting new families in Canada. As with many of the strategies suggested throughout this book for engaging families, we suggest beginning with an examination of your attitudes (Daud, Klinteberg, & Rydelius, 2008). Answering the following questions might help you clarify some of the areas you need to explore further.

- How do you feel about Canada's policies for welcoming immigrants and refugees?

- What challenges do you expect when working with people whose cultural background is different from your own?

- What does being Canadian mean to you? What does Canadian culture mean to you?

There are no right or wrong answers here, although there may certainly be strong opinions that support one view or the other. If you do feel strongly about your response to any of these questions, it may be helpful to examine how your own cultural background influenced your opinion, and how and why a person from a different cultural background may have a different opinion.

Understanding and Empathizing

Providing support to children and families who are immigrants or refugees requires the ability to empathize with their difficulties. Try to imagine what young children who are refugees might feel like when

- they witness the torture or killing of a loved one
- they live in fear and hiding
- they are hungry, exhausted, and confused

Try to imagine the experiences of an immigrant child who

- experiences strange smells, new sounds, and a very different home.
- doesn't see familiar people anymore, and doesn't understand why
- watches children behaving in very different ways from what he or she is used to

Understanding the experiences of people who are victims of war is very difficult. You might want to think about watching films or reading books that capture the experiences of victims of war or trauma (there are many current films and books on war and terror).

Think about how might you feel as a new Canadian when

- you feel that you have no right to complain, because you will be told, "If you don't like it, go back to your own country."
- you can't work in your own profession, even though you have the appropriate education and experience
- you can't help your children with their homework because the subject matter or the language was different in your home country
- you want your children to get along well in Canada, but see them forgetting about the things that were so important to your parents and grandparents

SCENARIO

CONSIDERING MULTICULTURALISM

When child-care accreditation was developed in Alberta, the evaluation framework included a section on multiculturalism as reflected in the child-care or family child-care program. This section caused much angst for many directors who had never really considered this component of their program. Directors began to create a "multicultural box" that was filled with different items that could be used for programs when it was time for accreditation. Although this box was created as a quick fix for accreditation, many programs actually realized that multiculturalism was a missing dimension in their programs and kept the contents of the box in the program and often added to it.

Multicultural strategies should not be quick fixes. Instead, they should be intentional features of early childhood programs. These strategies require thought and planning and, just as important, a commitment to inclusive child care.

Providing Support to Parents

You can provide support to parents who are immigrants and refugees in a number of ways:

- Provide them with easily accessible information about relevant resources. This would include information on preschools, child care, health care services, and social support and recreational services.

- Provide information in first languages. Many immigrant-serving agencies translate brochures, posters, and handouts into a number of first languages. This information is extremely helpful to parents who are struggling to learn English.

- Bring representatives of other agencies to the centre to meet with parents. The community nurse or social worker could make a short presentation at a parent evening. It may be easier for parents to make contact with new agencies after meeting these professionals at a familiar place.

Educators can help children who are new Canadians in a number of ways as well:

- Provide opportunities for staged entry into the program. As many immigrant and refugee children may feel insecure in a new setting, particularly if they do not speak English, they may need to spend a lot of time at the centre with their parents.

- Learn a few key words in the first language of the children. "Dolly," "lunch," "book," and a few phrases such as "good morning" may make a child feel at home.

- Find symbols that represent their home country and culture. Parents will be able to help you or perhaps bring something from home that will make new Canadian children feel that the centre is their home away from home.

- Be patient and work hard to develop a trusting relationship with the child. Children may be wary of new people in their lives, especially when they don't understand the language you speak. Try to be nearby, and watch for opportunities to provide support or to show the child something interesting. Gradually, a relationship will form (Doyle et al., 2015).

- Separation from primary caregivers can be particularly stressful for refugee families who have experienced trauma. Take extra care to allow time for gradual separation, and if possible assign one consistent person to work with a parent and child. Also, involve the parents as much as possible in planning the separation.

SCENARIO

OBSERVING AND LEARNING

In a child-care centre, a policy existed that children were not allowed to speak their home language as the parents had specifically made this request and enrolled their children to learn English. Manisha, the director, and Aisha, the assistant director, were observing in different playrooms where they came upon an interesting scene. Two children had dumped several bins of toys on the carpet area (which was another no in the program). However, the two administrators paused to observe and noticed that the little boy was sorting the manipulatives into piles by colour. As he did, he spoke their home language but then clearly said, "Blue." The

continues ▶

▶ *continues*

activity continued and the word "orange" was applied to a pile of orange toys, and then yellow. The administrators realized that the little boy was teaching the little girl the English words for colour. By taking the moment to observe rather than react, the two administrators learned something very valuable about their approaches and had a great discussion with their educators about strategies.

CONCLUSION

Working with children from diverse cultures challenges us to understand the world view of others and to empathize with challenges faced by many families. Deepening our understanding of other cultures often reaps meaningful rewards, the least of which is a greater understanding of our own roots and culture.

Chapter Summary

- Vast demographic changes are taking place in Canada. It's estimated that in 2031, the percentage of individuals belonging to a visible minority could exceed 40% in Ontario, compared with 3% in Newfoundland and Labrador. This difference would then be larger than the one observed in 2011 between British Columbia (27%) and Newfoundland and Labrador (1%) (Martel, 2017). It was also predicted that Canada would welcome over 300 000 immigrants in 2017 (CIC News, 2016).

- Immigrants to Canada face many challenges and stressors, even if immigration was by choice. These include role transitions, barriers to employment, and grieving the loss of what was left behind. Refugees face additional problems related to recovering from the trauma caused by war or other extreme conditions.

- Canada is providing a safe home for many refugees, particularly those from Syria. A number of Syrian children suffer from toxic stress, the long-term effects of which are a growing concern.

- Early childhood educators can play a vital role in supporting immigrant and refugee families and their children. This support includes helping families and children learn about their new home in Canada. It also includes providing emotional support and helping families and children develop the resilience skills required to cope with the stresses they encounter.

RESOURCES

"Welcoming Refugee Families," a highly recommended resource for working with refugee families from Syria:
http://cmascanada.ca/wp-content/uploads/2015/12/Supporting_Refugees/WELCOMING%20REFUGEE%20FAMILIES.pdf

Early Childhood Development Intercultural Partnerships:
www.ecdip.org/index.htm

Canadian Child Care Federation:
www.cccf-fcsge.ca

Government of Canada, "Immigration and Citizenship":
www.cic.gc.ca/english/index-can.asp

Health Canada:
www.canada.ca/en/health-canada.html

Instructors' manual for *Stand Together or Fall Apart* (2012), by Judith Bernhard, about working with newcomers:
http://standtogetherorfallapart.com

EXERCISES

1. Playrooms are often multicultural and include children from diverse cultural and religious backgrounds. How will you accommodate the different and sometimes conflicting perspectives and requests in your playroom (e.g., food requests, celebrations)?

2. Review the messages that a visitor to your centre would receive about culture. Look at toys, books, equipment, decorations, and information brochures and pamphlets on display. What cultures are represented? What would you change?

3. Consider different strategies you might use if children and/or their parents don't speak English or French.

4. What resources (translation services, multicultural training, etc.) are available in your community to help staff work more effectively with new Canadian families?

5. Consider the policies and guidelines that exist in your program (e.g., food, celebrations, special events). Do they fit all children and all families? Do they respect the cultural traditions of all?

CHAPTER 10

Families and Poverty

OBJECTIVES

- To describe the extent of poverty in Canada

- To examine the factors associated with poverty

- To examine the effects of poverty on families

- To examine values and beliefs regarding poverty and the poor

- To discuss the role of the early childhood educator in supporting children and families who are poor, including the homeless

"When my husband and I first split up, I talked to my kids about the changes that were going to occur. My older daughter would no longer be able to wear the same kind of jeans as some of her friends, and we probably wouldn't be able to afford many after-school activities. I wouldn't be able to chauffeur the kids, because I would no longer have a car. My younger daughter asked, 'Does that mean we're poor now?' I answered, 'Maybe, in a way, but it doesn't matter because we have each other.' That was four years ago. Now it's no longer a matter of doing without the extras—I can't even manage to buy the basic necessities. Now when my children ask me if we're poor, I say yes. But I can't say it doesn't matter anymore. It does matter. It matters a great deal."

WHAT IS POVERTY?

Discussions of the poor often lead to heated debates about what constitutes poverty (Fremstad, 2010). We hear stories of times gone by when there was barely enough food on the table, clothing was mended and handed down from sibling to sibling and family to family, and brothers and sisters had to share a bed at night: "We all worked hard, didn't feel sorry for ourselves, and shared the little that we had. We didn't think about being poor."

Does *poor* simply mean not having enough money to meet survival needs (food, clothing, and shelter), or does it mean not having enough money left *after* meeting basic survival needs to participate in a lifestyle that is viewed as "average" or "normal" in our society? In fact, both are important measurements of poverty. Poverty has both an *absolute* significance (i.e., there is not enough money for food) and a *relative* significance (i.e., there is not enough money to live as most North Americans do). No single definition of *poverty* has been adopted by the Canadian government.

According to the United Nations Human Rights Office of the High Commissioner (2017), "Economic deprivation—lack of income—is a standard feature of most definitions of poverty. But this in itself does not take account of the myriad of social, cultural and political aspects of the phenomenon. Poverty is not only deprivation of economic or material resources but a violation of human dignity too."

Being poor affects every aspect of family life and every family member (DeNavas-Walt & Proctor, 2015). It may mean getting food at a food bank, eating dog food to survive, or not having running water or heating. Being poor often means having only worn-out and inappropriate clothing. For many, being poor may result in homelessness and moving from shelter to shelter. Often poverty results in feelings of powerlessness, shame, isolation, helplessness, and hopelessness. Words such as "isolating," "humiliating," "traumatic," and "a brutal experience" are some of the ways that people struck with poverty describe their situation (Canada Without Poverty, 2017). Poverty is a fact of life for many Canadian families. It can have such an astounding effect on family life as a whole and on the growth and development of children that all professionals concerned about children's well-being must be committed to addressing the problems of poverty. Sociologists, statisticians, and social policy experts have used different methods to define poverty, but the essence of poverty lies in simply not being able to afford the basic necessities of life and to participate in society in a meaningful way—be that education, recreation, employment, and housing.

ATTITUDES TOWARD THE POOR

SCENARIO

STUDENTS' ATTITUDES

A class of early childhood students was asked whether they thought that people who lived on social assistance wasted taxpayers' money by drinking, playing bingo, and passing the days watching soap operas. The instructor expected the students to object to such obvious stereotyping, but to her surprise, at least half the class nodded their heads in agreement. She now starts every new class with the same question, and each time receives similar responses from the class. The instructor has realized that teaching facts about poverty is not enough. The assumptions and value judgments made about the poor have to be addressed as well.

MYTHS SURROUNDING POVERTY

A number of myths are often associated with negative attitudes toward any group of people. A myth in this sense is a widely held belief that is accepted uncritically, even when much evidence to the contrary exists. The prevalence of myths about poverty has in fact interfered with government policy initiatives that have the potential to alleviate some of the problems of poverty.

For example, a common belief in our society is that hard work pays off—and that if people work hard, they are likely to succeed in life. Perhaps because of these shared beliefs, many people who have never been poor feel at least a twinge of resentment toward poor people. "If they worked harder or wasted less money, they'd be able to make ends meet," some people say. This feeling is sometimes stronger among those who began their lives in poverty and through hard work have managed to overcome many obstacles to become successful. "If I did it, why can't they?" they wonder. When children arrive at the child-care centre or school without having had breakfast, all too often a bit of resentment toward the parents emerges. "Don't they care about their children? If they didn't waste all their money, the kids wouldn't have to come to school hungry."

Another offshoot of the belief in equal opportunity is the idea that people who are poor haven't tried hard enough and have only themselves to blame. The poor are often described as passive, as unable to delay gratification, and as believing in luck rather than hard work.

Yet it's evident that even some families with two wage earners live in poverty. In fact, 8.2% of two-earner families are living below the poverty line (Walberg & Mrozek, 2009).

One of the myths surrounding poverty centres on what we might call the self-sufficient family. If we believe that "each family is on its own," then we have no responsibility to help others. Yet in our society, no family is completely independent, and families that lack the means to acquire their basic needs must rely on others for help. Another myth assumes that families that seek help are incompetent. Underlying this idea are stereotyped notions that the poor are lacking in motivation or are deficient in personal qualities or values. We think, "There must be something wrong with those people" rather than considering that there may be something wrong with the economics or organization of our society. However, the causes of poverty are often not under the control of the individual. These causes include changes in economic forces, such as employment opportunities, rising costs of housing, sudden illness or death in the family, or unexpected medical needs. We must remember that a full-time job at minimum wage will not keep a family from poverty. This can be true even when there are two wage earners in the family (Beauschene, 2006).

A further prevailing myth is the belief that public assistance condones failure or takes away the will to be self-sufficient. We hear about "welfare bums" who would rather be on welfare than work. This generalization simply does not apply to many people who require financial assistance.

Many people are familiar with the concept referred to as "the welfare trap." People on welfare can't receive continued assistance (such as medical coverage or child care) if they find work. Parents whose first goal is to protect and provide for their children often reluctantly choose to stay on welfare rather than become part of the unprotected group of working poor. The following scenario exemplifies this dilemma.

SCENARIO

RETRAINING OR REGRESSING?

A single mother with three children, aged 1, 3, and 5 years, had been receiving social assistance for a number of years. When she became aware that the assistance included a retraining program, she eagerly signed up for the early childhood education program at a community college. She graduated, got a job, but quit after three months. Her net income, taking into account her child-care expenses, clothing, and commuting costs, was about the same as what she had received on social assistance. More important to her, she was away from her own young children for most of the day, caring for other people's children and coming home extremely tired and stressed. The bottom line for this woman was that she and her children were better off on social assistance.

Early childhood educators will inevitably come into contact with children whose families are struggling with poverty. If educators have an attitude of resentment or blame toward poor people, they will have to overcome that before they can work effectively with these children and their families. The next step is to become educated about poverty in our society and understand the effects that poverty has on families and children. The third step is to learn more about the role of early childhood educators in working with families and children who are poor, and to advocate for policies that will result in a reduction of poverty.

WHO ARE THE POOR?

If we return for a moment to the discussion of intersectionality that appears in Chapter 3, we can see how that concept relates to our understanding of families who live in poverty.

Intersectionality promotes an understanding of people as shaped by intersecting categories (Hankivsky, 2012). These categories include race, ethnicity, age, disability, and migration status. Simply put, inequity, or in this case poverty, is rarely the result of a single factor, but more often an outcome of the interrelatedness of several factors. As you read about the categories of those affected by poverty, it's important to note that many poor people could describe themselves as belonging to several of these categories.

Children

Over 20 years ago, the Canadian House of Commons unanimously resolved to "seek to achieve the goal of eliminating poverty among Canadian children by the year 2000." Yet more than 3 million children—one out of every five children in Canada—live in poverty (Canada Without Poverty, 2017). This figure is shocking for a country ranked among the wealthiest in the world. Canada ranks bronze on childhood poverty, with a rate almost six times that of Denmark (Conference Board of Canada, 2009). Children make up the largest single group of poor people in Canada ("Report Card on Child and Family Poverty in Canada," 2009). UNICEF rated Canada 17 out of 29 countries due to the number of children living in poverty in Canada (Canada Without Poverty, 2017).

Indigenous Peoples

While there is a wide variety in the social conditions of Indigenous peoples in Canada, poverty rates among Indigenous people (especially children) have been described as "staggering" (Hildebrandt, 2013). Indigenous people in Canada earn on average 30% less than other Canadians, and the poverty rates among Indigenous children are vastly higher than those of children in the rest of the population (Wilson & Macdonald, 2010). As a clear example of the interconnection between categories, being a child and a member of an Indigenous community increases a person's chance of being poor several fold. In fact, a recent report found that half of Canada's Indigenous children live in poverty (Wilson & Macdonald, 2010).

Women

In 2016, Prime Minister Justin Trudeau announced, "Poverty is sexist" (Thomson, 2016). He was referring to the well-known relationship between gender and poverty. The Canadian Women's Foundation provides statistics that show how being a woman makes the risk of poverty extremely high. It also notes that certain kinds of women are more prone to poverty than others (Canadian Women's Foundation, 2017). Looking at women's poverty from the perspective of intersectionality, we see that 36% of women who are Indigenous are poor, 28% of women who belong to a visible minority are poor; 33% of women with disabilities are poor; 21% of single mothers are poor; and 16% of senior single women are poor (McCullough, 2017).

Multiple reasons, both historical and sociological, explain these disturbing statistics, among them the lack of accessible child care and the time away from education and employment due to child-rearing (which is unpaid work, leaving less time for paid employment); and the fact that there is still a gender gap in wages—women get paid less than men even when their work is identical (Canadian Women's Foundation, 2017). YWCA community development coordinator Joëlle Favreau has said, "Women don't have a monopoly on poverty, but statistics clearly illustrate the face of poverty often is a woman's face" (McCullough, 2017).

Visible Minorities

Often referred to as "visible minorities" or "people of colour," people who are of non-European background or heritage, including Canadian-born people of colour and those who are newcomers to Canada, are much more likely to be poor. In 2017, it was estimated that visible minorities constituted approximately 20% of the population of Canada. The proportion of poor families is much higher among visible minorities than in Caucasian families, and that gap seems to be growing. Many factors explain this gap, but racism and prejudice have been identified as a major cause of poverty among these Canadians (The Colour of Poverty Campaign, 2007). For this reason, many scholars and experts refer to this group as "racialized" Canadians. Although most Canadians believe that Canada has overcome racism, it appears to still be a significant problem (Galabuzi, Casipullai, & Go, 2012).

EFFECTS OF POVERTY

Poverty is a complex, multidimensional phenomenon with a wide variety of effects. As early childhood professionals, we pay special attention to the impact of poverty on children, and some of these effects start before the child is born. Aspects of the ecological model are helpful in understanding the widespread and pervasive nature of poverty, and the interplay of factors on individuals, families, communities, societal values, and social policies (Gill & Jack, 2008). For example, how living in poverty may affect parent–child relationships is a microsystem concern; how poverty impacts the child's opportunity to participate in positive actions with others is a mesosystem concern; how perceptions about the poor may affect children living in poverty is a macrosystem concern; and how the length of time a family lives in poverty affects that family's ability to function is a chronosystem concern.

Effects of Poverty on Children

Children who are born to poor parents are more likely to be born underweight, which makes them more vulnerable to health problems throughout their life. Indeed, a key aspect of poverty is not having enough food, or having limited access to nutritious and healthy food (Canada Without Poverty, 2017). It has long been argued that socio-economic disadvantage experienced early in life is more damaging than that experienced later in life (Gupta, de Wit, & McKeown, 2007). Research has shown that the negative consequences of childhood poverty persist and affect adult well-being (Najman et al., 2010). This is particularly true when the poverty is of long duration or when it occurs during adolescence (Magnuson, 2013; Najman et al., 2010). The negative long-lasting effects of poverty are evident in all domains of a child's development, and the physical and mental health of children (Conway, 2016; Driscoll & Nagel, 2008; Magnuson, 2013). There is irrefutable evidence that poverty has an extremely negative impact on the educational achievement of children (Jensen, 2009). Najman et al. (2010) indicated that poor children experience less social support and have parents who are less responsive. They are read to less frequently and have less access to books. As early as preschool, children in low-income families have increased behavioural and cognitive problems (Scaramella, Neppl, Ontai, & Conger, 2008). In addition, children in long-term poverty are often more likely to experience such psychological consequences as anxiety and depression (Caughy, Nettles, & O'Campo, 2008).

A report by Save the Children (2016) summarized much of the research on the impact of poverty on children around the world. The impact of child poverty can be devastating, and it lasts a lifetime. The poorest children are most at risk for disease, malnutrition, and stunting. They're more likely to miss out on school or get a poor-quality education. Also, there's a greater chance they'll get married young and experience physical violence (Save the Children, 2017a).

Perhaps we can better understand child poverty by hearing from children about how poverty makes them feel. Save the Children (2016) summarized research from many countries on children's views of living in poverty. According to this research, children feel that they are invisible and that their voices are not heard. They feel exposed to stigma and discrimination, and feel excluded and humiliated. Moreover, these feelings often cause anger and frustration, as well as hopelessness. Children who live in poverty are more often the victims of bullying than children who don't. They are often forced to give up some of their childhood by taking on more responsibilities at home. Poverty can lead children and young people to "feel different and inferior," and it can cause "significant anxiety and sometimes depression" (Save the Children, 2016, p. 19). As one Irish child explained to a researcher: "Folk look down on them. They don't have the things that everyone else has like trainers, a nice school bag, a school bag with a name—names are important" (p. 19). Children living in poverty can feel left out; they may not go to a party "because they might not have enough money to buy a present" (p. 19). Depending on the environment that the child lives in, poverty can be felt by being hungry, wearing old clothes, or by not having a cellphone when all the other children in the class do. There is no question that not having the same material things as the other children often makes a child feel isolated, left out, and deprived.

Effects of Poverty on Families and Communities

The effects of poverty reach individuals, families, and communities ("The Effects of Poverty," n.d.). Poverty is associated with poorer health, lower participation in the labour force, family disintegration, and increased rates of suicide (American Psychological Association, 2017b; Health Poverty Action, 2017). Poverty is considered a key obstacle to parenting capacity (About Families, 2012; George & Levin, 2015). Viewed from the ecological perspective, the effects of poverty are felt not only because of limited financial resources, but also because being in poverty almost always encompasses a lack of social resources, higher stress, and the quality (or lack thereof) of neighbourhoods where children grow up (Canada Without Poverty, 2017). For example, low-income neighbourhoods often have less access to services, poorer quality schools and child-care centres, more crime, greater pollution, and higher rates of drug use, as well as high levels of violence, social disorder, and fear (Caughy et al., 2008; de Boer, Rothwell, & Lee, 2013). In addition, poor people have less sense of control over their life and work, suffer increased levels of stress and higher levels of depression (and face decreased mental and physical health in general), and have a poorer ability to take care of their children (Caughy et al., 2008). The stress felt as a result of poverty is chronic and strongly influences family well-being (de Boer, Rothwell, & Lee, 2013).

Communities and societies as a whole are affected by poverty, in both the long and the short term. Crime rates are higher in poorer neighbourhoods, and poverty becomes a major source of social tensions when there is great disparity between rich and poor. When the supports are not there to help families escape from poverty, it becomes a vicious cycle— and the negative impacts of poverty are passed on from one generation to the next (The Borgen Project, 2016). This is the key reason why ongoing serious efforts need to be made to alleviate poverty, both in Canada and the rest of the world.

Homelessness

The homeless are, not surprisingly, among the most destitute of the poor. Most of them have been poor or on the margins of poverty all their lives. While homeless people face many of the same risks and consequences as other poor people, educators are becoming increasingly aware of the devastation to family life caused by homelessness. Life tends to be unstable and irregular for families living in poverty, which, all too often, leads to homelessness for families with young children. Families are often homeless because of a lack of affordable housing, while some have left their homes because of domestic violence or abuse. The pathways into or out of homelessness vary for every child and family (Gaetz, Donaldson, Richter, & Gulliver, 2013; Gulliver-Garcia, 2016). Homeless people tend to be extremely vulnerable and lack the income and necessary supports to stay housed. The causes of homelessness reflect an "intricate interplay between structural factors, systemic failures and individual circumstances. Homelessness is usually the result of the cumulative impact of a number of factors, rather than a single cause" (Gaetz et al., 2013; see also Gaetz, 2013; Gulliver-Garcia, 2016).

The destructive force of homelessness should not be underestimated. Recent research has demonstrated that while many people become homeless as a result of traumatic issues, homelessness in and of itself is often considered a cause of trauma. Moreover, the ripple effects of the trauma of homelessness (largely experienced by single mothers, who are most likely to be homeless) include effects on the children, such as poor health, emotional and behavioural disorders, cognitive vulnerabilities, difficulties forming secure attachments, lack of school readiness, and poor school performance (Olivet, 2015).

Mothers in homeless shelters report having lost control over their environment and their lives, and having difficulty balancing their own physical and personal needs with those of their children. They don't have control over the daily routine, and they are unable to be effective parents because of the interference of house rules and shelter staff. Homeless children change schools often and are sick more frequently than other children (McCoy-Roth, Mackintosh, & Murphey 2012). They may suffer from inadequate nutrition, and their parents are often too stressed to help and guide them (Bassuk, DeCandia, Beach, & Berman, 2014). Homelessness can only be described as an immense trauma that leads to the disruption of social networks, family roles and routines, and emotional stability.

Homelessness is devastating at any age, but for younger children it's particularly disruptive. Gulliver-Garcia (2016), in a report on child homelessness in Canada, describes a day in the life of a homeless child:

> Imagine waking up in a strange place one morning and not knowing where you are, not recognizing any of your surroundings. Your mom takes you and your siblings to a cafeteria-style dining hall where you eat a bit of breakfast before taking a bus to school. After classes finish, your mom meets you in the schoolyard and you take transit across the city to another strange building for the night. This time, you are sharing a bed with your younger sister, your brother is on the couch and your mom sleeps on the floor of the living room. Yet you know you were lucky to be out of the shelter tonight and in a friend's house. Tomorrow you know the process will repeat itself. (p. 3)

If we consider the developmental needs of young children and the importance of security and consistency in building trust and autonomy in the early years, it's clear that the instability of homelessness can be highly detrimental. In short, homelessness deprives children not only of a decent quality of life but also of most of their future opportunities.

REDUCING POVERTY

In the past, the poor were at the mercy of their families, communities, or charities for assistance. Since about the time of World War I, however, governments in the West have taken various steps to address the problem of poverty.

The "Report Card on Child Poverty" ("Campaign 2000," 2000) concluded that Canada had made no progress in the last decade in reducing child poverty. More recent reports show a slightly more optimistic view, while still maintaining that much needs to be done (CBC News, 2011). Campaign 2000 developed five benchmarks against which to evaluate a jurisdiction's progress toward the elimination of poverty in Canada (Bassuk et al., 2014):

- increasing the availability of good jobs at living wages, raising minimum wages, facilitating the inclusion of immigrants, and providing better protection through employment
- creating an effective child benefit system that provides enough income support to keep working parents, including single parents, out of poverty
- building a universally accessible system of quality early education and child care to support optimal early development of children and enable parents to work or receive training
- expanding affordable housing significantly to end adult and family homelessness and enable parents to raise their children in healthy community environments
- renewing the national social safety net, with increased federal funding and increased accountability for provincially delivered social services

THE ROLE OF EARLY CHILDHOOD EDUCATORS

Each and every early childhood educator can make a huge difference in the life of a child and family living in poverty. As we emphasized in the chapter on resilience (Chapter 4), the special relationship between the child and the early childhood teacher can be one of the factors that contributes to the child's ability to cope with the stresses associated with poverty. There is much research to back up the belief that confirms the notion that high-quality (and the emphasis is definitely on quality) preschool can do much to fight the impact of poverty on children before they reach school (Lamy, 2013).

For early childhood educators to be effective in supporting children and families in poverty, it's important to examine our deep-seated attitudes and beliefs about the poor. Doing so will affect the way we understand the problems of poverty and the short- and long-term solutions that we promote to deal with these problems. It will also affect the way we relate to the children and families living in poverty. As members of the early childhood profession, we have an ethical obligation to accept and respect people regardless of their social or economic standing. Sorting out one's personal beliefs about people who are poor is an important first step.

Understanding and Empathizing

Providing support to children and families in poverty requires the ability to empathize with their difficulties. Try to imagine what young children might feel like when

- they can never be sure where they will sleep from night to night
- they go to a child care or nursery school, but don't know if they will be able to return the next day
- they have no space or toys to call their own
- they have no consistent routines, and may not have clean clothes or the opportunity to bathe
- they sense the feelings of hopelessness, despair, and frustration felt by their parents, and feel helpless themselves

    Now try to imagine what it might be like for parents who may

- be embarrassed about being homeless
- be unable to give their children even the most basic and simple provisions (snacks, a hot drink, or 50 cents for a hot dog for lunch)
- feel isolated and alone
- have no links with or support from their community

- fear having their children taken away from them
- fear being perceived as neglectful or abusive parents
- fear being perceived as vagrants or lawbreakers
- know that many judge them and their children by their appearance
- feel unprotected and vulnerable
- have no privacy for intimacy with their partner

It's important not to stereotype homeless people or to make assumptions. The preceding lists may apply to many people in such a situation, but not to all. It's also wrong to assume that homeless families are dysfunctional. They are enduring highly stressful circumstances, and extended periods of homelessness can indeed lead to family breakdown. We must be very careful not to "blame the victims," but rather to understand the circumstances that lead to poverty and homelessness.

For many children who are homeless or poor, the child-care centre or other early childhood programs can be a crucial source of stability and support. Recognizing the special needs of children and families in these circumstances can help staff meet these children's needs in a supportive and sensitive manner.

SCENARIO

UNDERSTANDING HOMELESSNESS FROM THE CHILD'S PERSPECTIVE

When Jimmy lay down for his afternoon nap, he insisted on taking his favourite toy, jacket, shoes, hat, and snack with him. On some days, there were so many belongings on his cot that there was no room for Jimmy. When the early childhood educator mentioned this to his mother, she learned that Jimmy's family had been evicted from their apartment; some nights they were staying with friends, and some nights at shelters. No wonder Jimmy was clinging to his belongings.

For children living in shelters, every hour can bring change, and that can be frightening. Use the information you have read in this chapter to try to imagine what special support you could provide. Think about routine care. Might the child need extra nourishment at meal and snack time? Might she need extra attention to help her settle down at naptime? Would it be helpful to have some extra clothing on hand should a change be necessary? Is it reasonable to assume that some children who live in shelters will be more hesitant to leave their personal belongings out of sight? Will these children sometimes require more individual time or small-group time than other children? A bit of extra thought and planning may go a long way to alleviate some of the stresses that homeless children may bring to the child-care centre.

SCENARIO

SENSITIVITY PAYS OFF

Staff members at an inner-city child-care centre were well aware that most children were coming in hungry and that the centre provided most of their nutritional needs. With some extra funding, they started a program in which extra food was prepared for lunch and snacks, and children were encouraged to take food home for a snack for themselves and to share with their siblings. Early childhood educators were sensitive to the needs of these families. The program was especially successful because poor children were not singled out. All the children enjoyed having the opportunity to take home things that they made or received at the centre.

A homelike environment that contains many private areas and personalized space with pictures, photographs, and personal cubbies is important to all children but will be vital to those who lack these elements in their lives outside the centre. Most important is the development of a trusting relationship with a staff member, who can anticipate some of the feelings associated with poverty and homelessness and who is willing to find many small ways to make children feel welcome, appreciated, and safe.

When we understand the long- and short-term devastation that poverty can bring to children and families, it seems clear that as professionals committed to the well-being of children, we must not ignore the need to advocate for ending child poverty in Canada. There are several organizations—local, provincial, and federal—that are committed to this goal. At the end of this chapter, we have included an exercise related to advocacy.

Supporting Parents of Poor and Homeless Children

Low-income single mothers often have fewer networks of support and are less likely to seek help from both professionals and informal support systems (Rios, 2015). Thus, early childhood educators play a role in supporting low-income parents in a nonjudgmental and dignified manner. As one parent in these circumstances noted, "The last thing I need is to come to a parent meeting and have someone try to teach me how to be a better parent." Little gestures, such as having coffee, juice, and a quiet place to sit for a while, can make all the difference. Practical supplies such as extra clothing, toys, books, and food for emergency use should also be on hand. Provision of snacks and meals might be a major factor in the selection of child care for families living in poverty.

SCENARIO

LOW-COST OR NO-COST ACTIVITIES

Several child-care centres working with disadvantaged children incorporated different ideas that would involve and benefit their families. One centre started a lending library of toys and books for children to take home to ensure that they offered stimulating, educational materials. Another centre organized an exchange of toys, clothing, and other belongings. Each family brought items they no longer used to trade for other items. Families were able to replenish toys, book, and clothing supplies while sharing resources with other families. Another centre accomplished the same thing by having a garage sale. Parents were able to purchase toys, clothing, and items for a token fee, and the centre was able to raise a few dollars to purchase art equipment. The common factor in all these activities was that families were involved at no extra cost and in a manner that did not differentiate between those who were poor and those who were able to make some kind of contribution.

It's important not to assume that poor or homeless parents don't want to or can't be involved in the program. They can be asked, without placing pressure on them, if they want to accompany the children on a field trip or help with serving lunch. One problem is that parent meetings held during evening hours often require that parents pay for a babysitter. Meetings during afternoon hours, with child care and food provided—if this is possible—are more likely to be attended.

Sometimes the centre can be a focal point for meeting with other parents in similar circumstances, for providing information about services and resources, or for simply providing a meeting place that is safe and where parents will be accepted and respected. This can be a most meaningful form of support. More important, these strategies may become coping devices for the families involved. Providing parents with this kind of framework can result in a sharing of resources and mutual support.

Tips for Providing a Sense of Security to Young Children

1. Provide a homelike environment with private areas and personal space.
2. Provide consistent routines and preparation for transitions.
3. Assure children that there is plenty of food at mealtimes.
4. Never use food as a reward, punishment, or play item.
5. Provide a consistent place for each child's cot at naptime and extra attention when needed to help children settle.
6. Provide an appropriate number of toy choices and help children decide.
7. Provide open-ended materials.
8. Ensure that each child receives some individual attention and that all children participate in small-group experiences.
9. Enlist volunteers (when appropriate) to provide more adult–child interaction.
10. Develop a relationship with the children by helping them to feel welcome, appreciated, and safe.

Beyond the Centre

At the beginning of this book, we described the family as a system that affects and is affected by other systems in society. The well-being of children is ultimately linked to the well-being of the family, and the well-being of families is inextricably connected to such societal factors as employment, housing, neighbourhoods, child care, and social assistance. Increasingly, experts in early childhood are pointing out the need to go beyond caring for children and families within the confines of the centre and to advocate actively for the eradication of poverty.

We can't underestimate the potential of quality early childhood programs in mitigating the effects of poverty (Magnuson, 2013). Investing in selected early childhood interventions appears to be a cost-effective way to reduce the effects of poverty over the long term, and current public investments in such programs appear to have helped in this regard. Therefore, early childhood professional associations such as the Canadian Child Care Federation lobby relentlessly for government investment in quality care. Many early childhood educators are involved in lobbying for community efforts to promote quality care as well. As one early childhood professional, Viktoria Bitto, who was recently honoured by the Canadian Child Care Federation, stated, "I never stop encouraging anyone that will listen, to learn to advocate for what they love or believe in. I believe in an affordable, accessible, high-quality child-care system. I believe that child care is a fundamental human right and that all children regardless of the situations they are born into deserve the best start to life" (McLaughlin, 2015, p. 28).

Early childhood educators should keep abreast of progress on eliminating poverty on a local, provincial, and national level. (Check the resources recommended at the end of this chapter.) There are many organizations committed to reducing poverty in Canada. Find one that fits your values and beliefs, whether it be a religious organization, a nonprofit organization (such as the National Anti-Poverty Organization), or a charity. Early childhood educators could join advocacy efforts through their local and national professional organizations.

As well, writing letters to editors, seeking media coverage, and writing to legislators about the problems of poverty are among the more specific strategies. Early childhood educator organizations might try to network with other professions, for example social workers, to develop a broad-based coalition, and could enlist community and business leaders to support the cause. As with any kind of advocacy and activism, early childhood educators must be well prepared and have accurate and up-to-date information at both the local and the national level.

Early childhood educators play a critical role in the lives of young children—all children, but especially children facing adversity. Along with awareness, educators need confidence in their abilities and the increasingly important role they play in the lives of children and families.

CONCLUSION

This chapter has explored the many dimensions of poverty and how each of these dimensions may affect families. Poverty has profound effects on family structure and parenting and puts every family member at risk. Families exist within a societal framework and are, therefore, affected by their neighbourhood, the available supports, and the quality of child care.

Educators can play a major role in providing support to children living in poverty and to their families. Regardless of our own experiences with poverty, our beliefs about its causes, and our opinions about dealing with it, we must acknowledge the urgency of the problem and the need to find solutions for the children in our care and the children of future generations as well.

Chapter Summary

- Despite Canada's wealth, more than 3 million children—one out of every five children in Canada—live in poverty.

- Children make up the largest group of poor in Canada. The rates of poverty in Indigenous children are higher than the rates for other children in Canada. As well, women, particularly single-parent women, tend to be poor.

- Poverty is a complex, multidimensional phenomenon that affects the physical and sociological health of individuals, parents, and communities at large.

- Poor children don't do as well as their peers on any measure of achievement or physical and mental health.

- Child-care services can provide support to parents by offering a comfortable, nonjudgmental space for parents to meet and share resources.

- Child-care services can support children who are poor by providing consistency, individual attention, and by being sensitive to some of the special needs of poor and homeless children.

- Early childhood educators should work toward the reduction or elimination of poverty on a wider system level, through individual advocacy and the combined efforts of organizations and associations that are committed to ending child poverty in Canada.

RESOURCES

Child Care Canada, "Poor-bashing Is Never the Answer":
http://childcarecanada.org/documents/child-care-news/04/08/poor-bashing-never-answer-ca

Canada Without Poverty:
www.cwp-csp.ca/

Raising the Roof, *Putting an End to Child & Family Homelessness in Canada*:
www.raisingtheroof.org/wp-content/uploads/2015/10/CF-Report-Final.pdf

Canadian Child Care Federation:
www.cccf-fcsge.ca

Child Care Canada:
www.childcarecanada.org

C. Rios, "7 Everyday Things Poor People Worry About That Rich People Never Do":
http://everydayfeminism.com/2015/05/poor-people-worries/

The Homeless Hub, *The State of Homelessness in Canada, 2014*:
http://homelesshub.ca/resource/state-homelessness-canada-2014

Child Poverty Action Group, "Ending Child Poverty" (one example of how poverty is addressed in the United Kingdom):
www.cpag.org.uk/ending-child-poverty-by-2020

EXERCISES

1. Write one paragraph summarizing your feelings about each of the following:
   a) Parents who bring their children to the centre poorly dressed and hungry
   b) Parents who spend social-assistance money to smoke, drink, and play bingo
   c) Parents who are social-assistance recipients

   Now write a brief analysis of your own attitudes toward poor people.

2. Brainstorm ideas about how you could help a child feel safe and secure in your centre. Review the chapter, list all the ideas suggested, and then add your own.

3. Help a child create a personal space of his or her own by using a cardboard box big enough for the child to crawl into. Make the box comfortable with a pillow or rug, cut out windows, and possibly a "door" for privacy. Take some pictures of the child, family members, and friends, and let the child paste them to the walls. Provide a flashlight, books, CDs, or other objects that will help make the child feel comfortable.

4. Provide a "personal bag" for every child in the program to store his or her treasures.

5. Research your community for resources that may be available for families living in poverty. Make sure to check the cost before recommending ideas (e.g., it may be better to recommend a babysitting co-op than paid babysitters).

6. Consider ideas for exchanges and sharing that the child-care centre could initiate or be a part of (e.g., clothing exchanges, buying bulk foods, making meals).

7. Check your local library or bookstore for books that may be suitable for children or their parents.

8. Check the Internet to find groups that advocate ending child poverty in Canada. What responsibility do early childhood educators have in addressing the problem of poverty in Canada?

CHAPTER 11
Single-Parent Families

OBJECTIVES

- To understand the nature and prevalence of single parents in Canada

- To clarify attitudes toward single-parent families

- To discuss the implications of single parenting for adults and children

- To consider the role of the early childhood educator in supporting single-parent families

A young single father made every attempt to attend preschool events with his 4-year-old son, Rahim. He regularly acted as a classroom volunteer and never missed a parent function. At the final windup party, the preschool teacher kept telling the children to show their moms this, or get their moms to help them with that. Jokingly, the single father would yell out each time, "And dad!" The last straw came when the teacher gave each child a year scrapbook and said, "Show this to your mom!" When she presented Rahim's book, he threw it down and began to wail for his mother. "Why can't she be here, I hate her!" he cried. At this point, the early childhood educator realized what she had done, but it was too late. A very upset father gathered his son and his belongings and left.

PROFILE OF SINGLE-PARENT FAMILIES

Single-parent families, sometimes called *lone-parent families* or *one-parent families*, are often referred to as a particular group in society, but in fact they are very diverse. Lone-parent families are those headed by a person who is single, separated, divorced, or widowed, and who cares for one or more children with no assistance from a spouse or partner (The Source for Women's Health, 2013). As well, a growing number of single women who have had a child through in vitro fertilization (single mothers by choice) would also be included in this category. According to the latest census data available, about 8 out of 10 lone-parent families are female and account for 12.8% of all census families, whereas male lone-parent families account for 3.5% of all census families (Statistics Canada, 2015a).

Most one-parent families result from divorce, and about a quarter of one-parent families are a result of nonmarital birth. Only a tiny proportion of single fathers have never been married; that is, they usually become single fathers following a marriage breakup (Beaupré, Dryburgh, & Wendt, 2010). The latest census data available indicate that almost 20% of children under the age of 14 are living in lone-parent families, but some scholars estimate that close to 50% of children live in single-parent families for at least a brief period in their childhood (Ambert, 2009).

The financial and social circumstances of single-parent families vary as well. Many single parents are women who are struggling to make ends meet financially and who are stuck in low-paying jobs that grant little satisfaction. In fact, the vast majority of single mothers suffer from economic disadvantage (Walberg & Mrozek, 2009). Single fathers seem to be at less risk of economic disadvantage than single mothers (Beaupré et al., 2010). Some single parents live with and receive emotional support from their extended families, while others live alone with their children and feel socially isolated. Some children of lone parents have ongoing positive contact with the nonresidential parent. In other cases, especially where there is continued animosity between the parents, children have little or no contact with their noncustodial parent. Some single parents may be living with partners who are actively involved with the children, and some may live alone. All of these differences, in addition to family background, personality, and coping styles, will have an impact on how single-parent families function and how the children in those families develop.

EFFECTS ON CHILDREN

As described above, there is so much diversity in the population of single parents that it's difficult to lump all the children of single parents together when considering the effects of single parenthood on children. A study by Kimberly Howard and Richard Reeves of the Brookings Institute found that children raised by married parents do better at school, have stronger cognitive and noncognitive skills, are more likely to go to college, and earn more as adults (Howard & Reeves, 2014). It's difficult to determine what effects living with a single parent may have on children, since any effect may be complicated by the factors of separation, divorce, and the absence of the noncustodial parent, all of which may have a cumulative effect on children. The existence of the single-parent family presents a different reality for children and may impact them in a variety of ways. In addition, families who are headed by a single parent due to death face different issues than families headed by a single parent by choice, divorce, or military service. Different issues are involved if remarriage is pending.

When considering these rather discouraging findings, it's vital to remember that the worrisome outcomes for children of one-parent families are almost identical to findings from studies on the impact of poverty on children (see Chapter 10). Children of one-parent affluent families don't show the same difficulties. Furthermore, the outcomes for siblings differ even when raised in similar circumstances (Dunn, 2004; Lansford, 2009), which suggests that genetics, child temperament, and personality may play a role as well. Thus, the outcome for children of lone parents seems to depend mostly on economic circumstances, but it also depends on the parent's characteristics, education, mental health, and social support.

The Brookings Institute study attempted to untangle some of the factors that explain the different outcomes in children of married parents versus children of single parents (Howard & Reeves, 2014). According to the study's findings, children from single-parent families are most likely to have less income and be less engaged in parenting. The gap in income is easily explained by the "two incomes versus one income" explanation, but marriage is more common among university-educated people to begin with. More income is related to better nutrition, better schools, and better neighbourhoods. Although the study's researchers make it clear that income is a highly significant factor in outcomes, it's not the only factor. They maintain that today, many couples who marry do so because of their joint commitment to raising a family. Moreover, simply put, two engaged and committed parents can provide more quality parenting time with children than can a single parent (i.e., more activities, such as reading and joint play, and more physical affection) (Howard & Reeves, 2014). The researchers of the Brookings Institute study, as well as those of other studies, stress that it's not the marriage per se that's key regarding the outcomes for children, but rather the higher income, the skilled parenting, and the amount of quality time spent with children (Wilcox & Lerman, 2014).

This understanding has important policy implications for supporting single parents and their children in ways that can close this gap.

SINGLE MOTHERS BY CHOICE

A recent social phenomenon is the increase of single women, usually in the 30–45 age range, who plan to have children without a partner (Lau, 2017). Termed *single mothers by choice*, these women are increasingly having planned births, through a known donor, an anonymous sperm donor, or adoption, raising the child or children on their own. Single mothers by choice are often women who would have wanted a traditional family, but career aspirations or other reasons meant that the traditional family didn't happen. Age (and women's "biological clock") is often the biggest factor in choosing single motherhood (Golombok, Zadeh, Imrie, Smith, & Freeman, 2016). This social trend began in the mid-1980s, as reproductive technologies made it possible for women to have children without having sexual intercourse with a male partner. Because this kind of single parenting is a relatively recent phenomenon, there are limited empirical studies describing the effects on children.

Outcomes for Children of Single Mothers by Choice

It's difficult to make any conclusive statements about the developmental outcomes for children of single mothers by choice, as this topic has not been widely researched. The following observation about choice motherhood from Choice Moms founder Mikki Morrissette is quite common:

> The kids I have talked to tend to be very secure and confident. As most child experts and teachers will tell you, being able to devote individualized attention to a child has an enormous impact on self-esteem. The downside to that is the relationship between mother and child tends to be intense, making it important to find healthy ways of separating. Boys in particular need outlets with male role models. But in general, Choice Moms are resourceful, independent women who raise children to be the same ("Defining Choice Moms," 2015).

The studies so far suggest that children raised by "choice" moms are secure and confident (Morrissette, 2008). Single mothers by choice often face a degree of criticism or skepticism from family and friends (Shechner, Slone, Meir, & Kalish, 2010). As is the case with "traditional" single parents, single mothers by choice are thought more likely to be stressed as a result of having fewer resources, such as time and parenting support (McDaniel & Tepperman, 2007; Shechner et al., 2010). Yet recent studies generally conclude that children of mothers by choice do quite well (European Society of Human Reproduction and Embryology, 2017). A small but very in-depth study of mother–child relationships and children's psychological adjustment found no differences among children conceived by donor insemination and those raised in a two-parent family (Golombok, MacCallum, Goodman, & Rutter, 2002). Nor did the study find differences in parenting quality or child adjustment. The study actually found that there was less conflict between the parent and child in the single mother by choice families.

Why then, do children of single mothers by choice appear, as a whole, to fare better than children of other single parents? For one thing, the process of becoming a mother through a donated sperm is usually a lengthy, difficult, and very expensive one. Women who make this decision are generally mature, fairly well established professionally, and highly motivated to become mothers. They make an active decision to become lone mothers—the children are "extremely wanted"—and this strong intention, along with the planning required before engaging in the process, could partly explain the positive parenting and related positive child outcomes (Golombok et al., 2016). This information reminds us that the structure of the family is not the key factor in healthy child development. Rather, how the child's needs are met with positive parenting is.

Courtesy of Arielle B.

Arielle, Age 3

ATTITUDES TOWARD SINGLE PARENTS

Single parents have often found themselves socially stigmatized. Even today, cultural values of most societies dictate that children be raised by two parents who are married or, at the very least, cohabiting (Amato, 2010; Livingston, 2014).

This stigma may still hold in parts of society today. Not too long ago, terms such as *illegitimate children* and *children from broken homes* were used in reference to children being raised by single parents. Families in which the mother and father did not live together were referred to as *broken*, implying that they were in need of fixing (Ward, 2006). There appears to be a difference in the acceptance of single parenthood for men and women, and one study has shown that single fathers generally face less approval in society and experience more role ambiguity than do single mothers (DeGarmo, Patras, & Eap, 2008; Goldscheider & Kaufman, 2006). However, a recent study suggests that single mothers are viewed less positively than single fathers (DeJean, McGeorge, & Carlson, 2012). There is still very little research available on single fathers, and the little that exists does not point to any dramatic differences between single fathers and mothers in regard to their contribution to their children's development. The research does suggest, however, that despite their increasing numbers, single fathers may experience more difficulty with regard to work–family balance and, as a result, experience more stress (Janzen & Kelly, 2012). In addition, there still seem to be fewer support services available to single fathers than to single mothers, and perhaps a greater reluctance on the part of fathers to access the supports that may be available (Janzen & Kelly, 2012).

Generally, there are indications that attitudes are gradually shifting, and that younger people (many of whom grew up in single-parent families) are more accepting the phenomenon of single parenthood (Cherlin, 2009; Goldscheider & Kaufman, 2006). Previously, the only kind of lone parents that seemed to escape moral judgment were widows and widowers. In spite of statistics that indicate that single parenthood is a prevalent family structure, many single parents feel that although their families may be different in structure from society's concept of a "normal" family, they are still just as intact and functional, and should thus be equally acceptable. However, society clings to old concepts, despite the decreasing gap between the number of single parents and the number of two-parent families.

Abandoning Our Preconceived Ideas

While we can't ignore the evidence that links single parenthood to economic disadvantage and the stress that results, we can and must overcome moral judgments that may interfere with developing a supportive professional relationship with single parents. We live in a society today that sends mixed messages. Divorce and sexual activity among nonmarried people are no longer condemned, but the resulting single parenthood is still somewhat stigmatized. We also need to remember that most single parents are highly committed to providing the best possible environment for their children, in spite of the obstacles and barriers described. Finally, we should remind ourselves that most of the research has been conducted from a "deficit model" that outlines the challenges and concerns. We have seen few studies that look at the strengths of single-parent families or that focus on children who have been raised in one-parent families. For all these reasons, early childhood educators might be better advised to shift the focus from asking which form of family is better to understanding the facts at hand. Early childhood educators can play an important supportive role with single-parent families, as with any other kind of family, if they develop an understanding of some of the challenges faced by single-parent families today.

THE CHALLENGES OF SINGLE PARENTHOOD

While the diversity among the single-parent population makes it difficult to generalize, there do seem to be some specific challenges associated with single parenthood that are worth considering for the early childhood educator. Care must be taken not to make assumptions, while at the same time early childhood educators must be sensitive to some of the areas in which support and understanding might be welcome. Although many parents indicate that single parenting presents no special problems, many others report that they do indeed face a considerable number of challenges.

The Economics of Single Parenting

The economics of one-parent families have been described briefly above. Canadian and American statistics on poverty lead to the inescapable conclusion that single parenthood and poverty often go hand in hand. A Statistics Canada report indicates that lone-parent families headed by women have, by far, the lowest incomes of all family types (Statistics Canada, 2016c). As a result, we should be aware of and sensitive to the financial burdens that complicate the lives of many single parents. (For more information on poverty and its impact on Canadian families, see Chapter 10.)

Barriers to Employment

Working is a necessity in single-parent families; however, many single mothers with pre-school-age children are not able to work because of the needs of their children. There are multiple barriers to employment of single parents, particularly single mothers, including issues of self-esteem and job readiness following a divorce, ambivalent social attitudes about women's roles in the labour force, and sexual harassment in the workplace (Chan, Lam, Chow, & Cheung 2008). Research has shown that the majority of single mothers would work if quality, accessible child care were available. Working mothers with school-age children are constrained by school hours and school holidays. The choices of child-care facilities may be limited by income, and such a large portion of the single parent's income may be used for child care that there is little left over for anything other than the most basic necessities.

Job opportunities may be restricted for single mothers due to limited, inflexible hours and single mothers' inability to work overtime. Even lone parents with good incomes will experience more economic strife than their married counterparts, who are either in a two-income household or not burdened by child-care costs because one parent is at home. Because of employment and child-care conditions, the only alternative for many single mothers is social assistance, the benefits of which typically don't provide an adequate standard of living and which come with a stigma attached.

Stress

Being a single parent can present many challenges. In Chapter 2, we looked at the "supermom" syndrome—that is, the pressure that many women feel to have successful careers while at the same time being excellent homemakers and child-rearers. However, single parents have to assume the roles of both mother and father, which requires patience and flexibility and may lead to role overload. As one single mother noted, "It's as if there is this obligation upon me to be a better mother than a mother in a two-parent family, since I'm also expected to be the father. I'm the breadwinner, I do the nurturing, I'm in charge of the household and finances, and I do a lot of the kinds of things that are normally associated with fathers, like sports and special outings."

Many of the concerns and challenges faced by single fathers are similar to those faced by single mothers. Although single-father families are much less likely to live in poverty (since the fathers tend to be better educated and better employed), many single fathers feel that they experience more social stigma than do women in similar circumstances. Single fathers report that they feel they are able to provide the daily care and affection required to "mother" and that they feel close to their children, although parenting styles can differ (Beaupré et al., 2010; Goldscheider & Kaufman, 2006; Lamb, 2010).

>> Perspectives

Ron is a 24-year-old single father. He recently attended a parent night at his children's child-care centre and discussed his experiences as a single dad.

"I come from a military family. My father was a commander in the Canadian Armed Forces, and he raised me and my two brothers in the 'army ways'—lots of discipline and a firm hand. My mother died when I was 11 years old, and it was really hard for all of us, especially my dad, who wasn't really good at talking about things that were bothering him. He never changed at home; he was still the boss, the disciplinarian, the commander.

"I joined the army as soon as I finished high school, just like my two brothers. It wasn't something we thought about; we just did it; it was expected. I got married and we

had two children; Amy was 13 months old when Andrew was born. I was a father just like my father—I set out the rules and was the commander at home. When the children got older, I decided to quit the army because it was too hard to balance work with my family life—the army is kind of like that. I quit and became a firefighter, which gave me more time at home. I don't really know what happened, but six months after that major change in my life, my wife decided that this was not the life for her and left me with a 3-year-old and a 2-year-old. I have never felt so scared and so alone in my whole life, and I had nobody that I could talk to about being a father. My dad and brothers didn't understand, my guy friends weren't used to sharing stories about bedtime routines and sick children, and single mothers were a bit unsure about this single father. I thought I knew what being a father was all about—I'd done it for three years and had a strong role model in my own father—but I had no idea how to be a mother.

"One of the first things I did was to quit my job, since it's hard to be a single parent on shift work. I found a job in an office—not what I want to do forever, but at least it's easier to manage a home life. I had to put the children into child care.

"When we started at the child-care centre, I was very quiet and very cautious. I really felt that I had to do it all. I didn't tell them very much and tried to pretend that our lives were normal. When the staff would ask questions or offer suggestions, I would get really bent out of shape. I remember once coming to pick Amy up at the end of the day. She was excited because her early childhood educator had French-braided her hair with ribbons. I was so angry because I saw this as a slap in the face—you can't do this, so we will. I blew up at Sally, the educator. She was shocked at my reaction and explained that all the staff try to spend individual time with each child. Amy had gotten up early from nap that day, and they'd had lots of time to spend together and play with her hair. It took me a long time, and other incidents like this, to realize that I couldn't do it all, and that I needed other people to help. Their mom wasn't coming back, finding a new mom wasn't a solution, and Sally was just trying to give Amy the things she needed, things I didn't have time for.

"Things are getting easier. Being a single parent will always be hard, but at least now I have some people I can count on, and I don't feel so alone and so scared—that's enough for now."

Social Support

We are living in a hurried culture. With a dramatically accelerated pace of change, most families experience "time crunches," where responsibilities for work and family cause anxiety and stress. Lone parents who work suffer from too many responsibilities with too little time to carry out those responsibilities (Daly, 2006). The responsibilities of work and child-rearing can make it very difficult for the single parent to find time to meet her own needs—for socializing and for support.

A primary concern for many single parents is the lack of emotional support. Emotional and social isolation are still cited as having a significant impact on the well-being of children and their single parents (Copeland, 2010; Copeland & Harbaugh, 2005). When single parents have good informal social networks for emotional support, child care, and financial assistance, their adaptation and experiences as single parents are more positive. Some single parents become very dependent on these informal supports, however, and then may have to deal with constant interference from family and friends. In addition, lone parents also report that they have difficulty depending on these supports for long-term arrangements. In such circumstances, feelings of isolation or loneliness are increased to the point where single parents need to reach out for support from social agencies.

Single fathers report that even less social support may be available to them, as the following scenario suggests.

SCENARIO

NO SUPPORT FOR SINGLE FATHERS

Jack is a single father of two children—Jillian is 3 years old and James is 18 months. Jack tells two stories that exemplify his experiences as a single father.

Whenever Jack is out with his children and they're upset, crying, or dirty, people repeatedly remark, "Where's their mom?" or "Your mommy will take care of you." He says that this happens so often that it clearly demonstrates society's views of fathers in general and single fathers in particular.

continues ▶

▶ *continues*

Soon after Jack's wife left, he knew that he needed help and someone to talk to about parenting. He did manage to find a local support group for single parents, but when he walked into the first meeting, all the single mothers stopped talking. He joined the group, but said, "I felt so uncomfortable, and it was so obvious that they were all uncomfortable that I left at the break." Next, he tried a men's support group, but his concerns about parenting were a foreign issue to this group. "The bottom line," he said, "was that I just didn't fit anywhere and I am truly on my own."

Time

Time is a precious commodity for everyone—but there seems to be a chronic lack of time for single parents. Most will have less time to spend with their children because all the other responsibilities of work and family life fall exclusively on them (Sawhill, 2014). Many parents talk about the need for having time for themselves. Although this is a yearned-for luxury among most parents, those who live without partners often find it even more difficult to get some time away from their children. A report by the Vanier Institute of the Family drives home the time crunch felt by lone-parent families: "Not surprisingly, those working the longest hours (10.9 hours of paid and unpaid work per day averaged over a 7-day week) are female lone parents aged 25–44 with full-time employment" (Sauvé, 2010, p. 140). "I can't call a babysitter if I just want to go for a walk for 15 minutes, and the extra cost of babysitters makes going out for an evening or weekend something I very rarely do," said one single mother we spoke with.

Child-Rearing

It used to be that single-parent families were characterized by lack of discipline or consistent control (Brooks, 2010). Earlier studies suggested that single mothers were less effective in discipline, were more negative in their comments, gave more commands, and were more hostile and dominating than mothers in two-parent families (Bank, Forgatch, Patterson, & Fetrow, 1993). Poor single-parent families seemed more likely to experience violence and abuse within the home (Bank et al., 1993; Jaffe, 1991). The biggest differences in parenting are attributed to lack of time and resources, compared with two-parent families, and the added economic strain that so often accompanies single parenthood (Amato, 2010; Howard & Reeves, 2014). Single parents who have social and emotional support find it easier to deal with authority issues in a consistent manner.

Different Gender Role Models

Earlier studies that focused on children's developmental need for role models of both genders are being challenged today, as gender roles are becoming blurred. As women engage in career activities that formerly fell within the exclusive domain of men, many men are taking on traditional female roles associated with nurturing and homemaking. Nonetheless, there are still gender differences in how women and men parent. According to Dubeau (2002), mothers are more repetitive and ask questions more, while fathers verbalize less and more frequently use the imperative form. Fathers apparently promote the child's integration in settings outside the home and are less tolerant of children's dependent behaviours. Fathers tend to play rough-and-tumble games with children more often and use unconventional behaviours (such as putting blocks on heads), which may help the child develop self-control. Dubeau notes that it's important to keep in mind that one type of interaction isn't necessarily better than the other; both parents contribute to the child's development by providing different types of learning experiences. In addition, while mothers and fathers do parent differently, the gender role model may be less significant than was previously assumed (Biblarz & Stacey, 2010). Research has highlighted the fact that differences in how men and women "rear children" are relatively minor and have little impact on children's development (Biblarz & Stacey, 2010).

It's worth noting that society is beginning to become more aware of the need to understand gender as a continuum rather than as a binary phenomenon. That is, the fact that most people are biologically male or female does not and likely should not dictate their personality traits. In fact, many women very likely respond to their children in a way that is expected of men, and vice versa. Thus, it makes more sense to try to understand what kinds of activities, interactions, and emotional responses are good for children and focus less on whether a male or female provides them.

Regardless of gender, in a family where two parents are present, children have the opportunity to observe different ways of communicating, solving problems, and resolving conflicts. They might also be exposed to a more diverse range of interests and talents than they would in a single-parent household. Therefore, some single parents do wish that their children had other close adults in their life, as models and support. The feeling that the responsibilities of parenting are easier if shared by two was succinctly expressed over two decades ago by K. Alison Clarke-Stewart (1988), and there is little reason to believe that this has changed: "One parent can model only one gender role, give only so many hugs, offer so much discipline, and earn so much money" (p. 71).

THE ROLE OF THE EARLY CHILDHOOD EDUCATOR

Clarifying Attitudes and Values

Perhaps the first step in providing support is to maintain a nonjudgmental approach. The way you answer the questions in the following box should reveal how you, as an early childhood educator, interact with single parents and their children.

> **Examine Your Attitudes**

- Do you think a single mother or father can do an adequate job of parenting?

- Do you feel the child of single parents is missing something?

- Does the language you use reflect your knowledge of single-parent families? (For example, the teacher in the vignette at the beginning of the chapter did not demonstrate an awareness of single-father families.)

- What social stigma, if any, do you attach to single parents?

Supporting Families

Providing support to single parents and their children should not be very different from supporting any other family. Early childhood educators must remember, though, that single-parent families may be facing the challenges of parenting in conjunction with additional stresses brought on by the absence of one parent. Three dimensions appear to be important for single-parent family adjustment (Garanzini, 1995). The first is the presence of resources within the family, including the parents' abilities, along with the presence of authority and communication. Environmental stress is the second dimension of single-parent family adjustment. This might include pressures outside the family (e.g., illness, transitions). The last dimension is the availability of social networks to the family. Such networks may include child care, role models, and economic help. Single parents facing economic pressure will appreciate sensitivity on the part of early childhood educators when they ask for extra fees for special events or for special equipment for the children. All parents who find the task of juggling jobs and family life difficult will appreciate being understood by educators. No family likes to feel that their parenting is being scrutinized and criticized by educators, but single parents who are sensitive about being socially stigmatized may react a little more defensively. Staff members need to bear this in mind and take care not to offend, either in words or in actions.

Any efforts to eliminate the stigma associated with single parents by seeing them as competent and their children as typical will go a long way in supporting lone-parent families. Recognizing that additional stresses may be present and that extra support may be needed is an important step in this process, but single parents should not feel they are being singled out or pitied. Ensuring that the information and support provided by the centre is addressed to single fathers as well as single mothers is very important. Whenever possible, accommodating single-parent families' complex schedules by arranging flexible hours or by organizing parent-involvement activities can help ensure that these parents are not excluded. Sometimes referring single parents to professionals can help link them to formal and informal community networks, such as support groups or short-stay relief homes.

Supporting Children

SCENARIO

CHOOSE YOUR WORDS CAREFULLY

An early childhood educator gave her group of 5-year-old children instructions for making Father's Day gifts. At one table, the children asked Amanda who she was making her gift for because her father lived far away. Amanda did not participate in the activity. At another table, Lisa declared that she was making her gift for her grandfather, because he took care of her when her mother worked at night. Her peers told her that she couldn't do this, because this craft was just for fathers.

In this scenario, the feelings of specific children could have been protected, and the understanding of all children enhanced, if the early childhood educator had been more careful with the words she used with the children. Explaining that the craft was for a special person would have helped include all the children in the activity.

Single parents and their children appreciate efforts to treat their family structure as normal. This normalization occurs when toys, books, and stories in the child-care centre reflect single-parent families as intact and typical. When early childhood educators read stories in which only traditional nuclear families appear, they can use the moment to explain that families are different, and then they can encourage discussion, if this is warranted. Sensitive educators should think carefully about events that are likely to make the child of a single parent feel left out. Mother's Day and Father's Day are just two examples.

Supporting children may also involve helping them understand the various types of families, and providing a range of experiences for them to think about. For example, the early childhood educator could provide books about different types of families or stories that feature male role models. Showing sensitivity in day-to-day activities may be the best starting point for developing a base of support.

Supporting Single Mothers by Choice and Their Children

Today's reality is that nontraditional families continue to outnumber traditional families. Early childhood educators have a responsibility to support children and their families regardless of the circumstances. Supporting nontraditional families means being inclusive and accepting while avoiding negative stereotyping. It means that early childhood educators must forgo their own preconceived notions of what "family" means and whether there is a right or wrong way to parent. Instead, educators need to focus on the best ways to support individual children and their families.

Educators may wish to review the website www.singlemothersbychoice.com, which characterizes some aspects of single motherhood. This website is not designed by an advocacy group, but rather as a support site which provides information. The site highlights the fact that single mothers by choice are women who have taken the initiative to become mothers, with all the entailed responsibility of raising a child on their own. Many of these women are well-off and well educated, and can thus provide for their children without public help. The site offers support for single mothers as well as a peer support group for their children. A further aim of this site is to clarify issues and enhance public understanding for single motherhood by choice.

CONCLUSION

Single-parent families are becoming more and more common in today's society. Nevertheless, they still face many challenges, some of which may come from the stigma attached to them by society, from increased stress, or from poor economic conditions. All single-parent families are different. Each has taken its own path and encountered different combinations of difficulties and challenges. Single-parent families need to be recognized as "normal" and as having the potential to raise healthy and well-adjusted children. Like all families, they may at times require support. The early childhood educator can play a supportive role by being aware of their strengths and difficulties and by maintaining a nonjudgmental attitude.

Chapter Summary

- Single-parent families, sometimes referred to as *lone-parent families* or *one-parent families*, are diverse. One-parent families are created when a couple separates and one of the ex-partners has custody of the children, when a woman gives birth to a child and does not live with the child's father or any other partner, when a father or mother is widowed, or when a single person adopts or chooses to have a child through reproductive technology.

- Single parenthood, when the parent is a woman, is often associated with poverty.

- Children from one-parent families, except for children from single mothers by choice, seem to fare less well than their peers from two-parent families on a number of measures, including academic achievement, behavioural problems, and health. These outcomes may be linked more to low income than to the fact of having one parent, as children from affluent one-parent families seem quite similar to those from two-parent families.

- Single parents still experience stigma today, as the perception that children should have two parents is still very prevalent in our society.
- Single parents face barriers to employment, lack of social support, and lack of time for themselves.
- Flexible hours, quality child care, and normalization of the single-parent family experience are ways that the early childhood educator can support single parents.

RESOURCES

Single Parent Canada:
www.singleparent.ca

Single Parents Network:
http://singleparentsnetwork.com

Parents Without Partners:
www.parentswithoutpartners.org

Single Mothers by Choice:
www.singlemothersbychoice.org

EXERCISES

1. Interview three single fathers and three single mothers. Ask them about the joys and the challenges of being a single parent and about the support networks available to them. Record their responses, and then compare them. Were there significant differences in the responses you received? To what do you attribute these differences?

2. Review the books in your child-care centre. How many of these reflect the single-parent family as "normal" compared with the images presented of two-parent families?

3. Check local community resources for support groups that may be available to single-parent families. Will the needs of single fathers be accommodated in these groups?

4. Are the policies and activities in your centre sensitive to the needs of single-parent families?

5. The outcomes for children of lone parents tend not to be as positive as those of married parents. The explanation for this difference focuses on fewer resources and fewer quality interactions between parents and children. How can social policies, both provincial and national, attempt to address these areas of concern?

6. How does the concept of intersectionality (as explained in Chapter 3) relate to single parents? What multiple social identities might single parents have? How might these identities interact? What results might these interactions produce?

CHAPTER 12

Divorce

OBJECTIVES

- To understand the prevalence of divorce

- To understand the potential impact of divorce on the child and family

- To understand the factors that influence adjustment to divorce

- To examine attitudes toward divorce

- To discuss ways that the early childhood educator can support children and families who have experienced a divorce

When Karen's mother brought her to child care one Friday morning, the woman was clutching an infant car seat and an overnight bag in her arms. "We just finalized our separation arrangement," she said matter-of-factly. "Please make sure that her dad remembers the car seat. He doesn't have one for his car and he'll need it." Gabriella, the early childhood educator, sighed and thought to herself, "I knew that something was going on at home because Karen hasn't been her usual happy self, but I had no idea this is what it was."

ASPECTS OF DIVORCE

Estimates of the prevalence of divorce in Canada over the past decade vary slightly, but it's reasonable to assume that approximately one in four marriages will end in divorce (Smith, 2011). However, statistics on divorce are not an accurate way of assessing how many families with children split up because so many households with children today are headed by couples who are not formally married.

For early childhood educators, the exact statistics are less important than the understanding that in every class there very well may be a child whose parents are considering splitting up, who are in the process of splitting up, or who have, in the not so distant past, split up. Therefore, it's important to consider the various aspects of divorce, how it affects the young child's perceptions and feelings, and how it affects the relationship between the children and their parents. Finally, we will discuss how the early childhood educator might provide support to children and families who are experiencing a divorce.

A MULTIFACETED LIFE EVENT

Even though divorce and separation are much more prevalent today than in the past, children and adults alike often consider it to be a major event or crisis that greatly disrupts their lives (Pickhardt, 2011; Wallerstein, 2005). As educators of young children, we need to pay close attention to the impact of divorce on children. We also need to offer support and help children develop coping strategies and resilience. Divorce is a process that occurs on many levels and over a fairly lengthy period of time. Inevitably, it involves stress, loss, and change. An understanding of these processes and their impact on the child and on the family as a whole will contribute to the ability of educators to offer timely and appropriate support.

Divorce can be a disorganizing process that extends over years, with lasting effects (Amato, 2010; Wallerstein, 2005). Many adults may recover after two or three years. However, two or three years in the life of a young child may have much more of an impact on that child's development. In the eyes of preschool children, the world consists almost entirely of the family, and divorce means that the family ceases to exist. These children must adapt to living with one parent rather than two and may experience a sense of abandonment by the parent who is not living at home. There may also be tensions associated with building a relationship with a "weekend parent." This visiting relationship will usually be an unfamiliar experience for both the parent and the children. Because of the frequent disruptions—the repeated need to say goodbye to each other just when they are renewing their relationship—hostility may develop on both sides. Moreover, there will likely be a substantial decline in the children's standard of living, as noted in Chapter 11 (Divorce-Canada.ca, 2017). All of these factors will prove to be of major significance to child development.

Effects of Divorce on Children

Research findings on divorce are highly varied, and they depend on when the study was conducted, the subgroup studied, and the angle from which divorce was examined. Often there are two extreme positions. The first is that the long-term effects of divorce have a significant negative effect on children's mental health, academic achievement, relationships, and more (Lansford, 2009). The second, at the other end of the spectrum, is that divorce does not significantly affect children (Lansford, 2009). More recent reviews of research relating to the impact of divorce on children qualify that most of the negative effects are seen more in the short term and that the "vast majority of children endure divorce well" (Arkowitz & Lilienfeld, 2013).

From the mid-1980s to the 1990s, as North American society was seeing rapid increases in divorce rates, several studies focused on the impact of divorce on children (Furstenberg & Teitler, 1994; Skolnick, 1992; Wallerstein, 1991). Some of these studies have been criticized for being too "one-dimensional," and today the focus has changed to look at broader structural issues and their impact on children. While there are negative effects that repeatedly emerge (Amato, 2010), many researchers are suggesting that these negative effects are not "as bad" as originally thought (Hetherington, 2005). For example, a study that looked at data from a survey of 5004 Canadian children concluded that divorce is unrelated to changes in parenting behaviour (Strohschein, 2007). This study showed that more similarities than differences exist in the parenting practices of married parents and divorced parents (Strohschein, 2007). Divorce has been associated with poor academic achievement, behavioural difficulty, poor self-esteem, aggression, and depressive behaviours (Ambert, 2009; Bee & Boyd, 2007). Researchers have recently noted that lower academic achievement has to do with the lower well-being of the child and general family functioning prior to divorce, rather than the divorce itself (Li, 2007; Potter, 2010). The magnitude of the effects appear to be related to children's temperaments and personalities, the quality of the parental relationships prior to the divorce, the adjustment by the custodial parent, and the parents' post-separation relationship (Ambert, 2009). It has therefore been suggested that early childhood educators (as well as researchers and parents) should look at divorce not in terms of specific outcomes, but with the expectation that children of divorced parents will experience certain adversities (Ambert, 2009).

Finally, it's important to consider that many of the negative effects of divorce have more to do with the effects of poverty than divorce itself, as we will discuss later in this chapter (Government of Canada, Department of Justice, 2015; Li, 2007). Comparisons with European countries, which have a wide social safety net for families, show that support and policies can mitigate the negative effects of divorce (Ambert, 2009).

There is great diversity in children's reactions to divorce (Dunn, O'Connor, & Cheng, 2005; Hetherington, 2003). Children who generally adapt to new situations with ease will likely have an easier time adjusting to the divorce than those who seem to need regularity and consistency, and who have trouble adapting to new situations. Children who have witnessed severe conflict between parents over a brief period prior to the divorce may experience divorce quite differently from children whose parents gradually grew apart and agreed to terminate the marriage. Similarly, children whose parents continue to demonstrate their love, commitment, and involvement with their children, and who relate to each other respectfully, will experience divorce differently from those children whose parents are involved in bitter post-divorce conflict (Hopf, 2010; Wallerstein, 2005). While environment plays a major role, research indicates that a certain gene, coupled with the environment of divorce, explains why some children are resilient and others are more vulnerable (Amato, 2010).

While most parents who divorce try to assure the children that both parents still love and care for them, it's not uncommon for children to feel that one or both parents have abandoned them. Feelings of abandonment, if not recognized and addressed, can have long-term implications on future relationships. For example, they can sometimes lead to over-clingy behaviour in adult relationships (Blood, 2017).

FACTORS AFFECTING ADJUSTMENT TO DIVORCE

Several factors have been identified as possibly affecting both adults' and children's understanding of and adjustment to divorce. Not all children will react in precisely the same way following a divorce. Throughout the divorce process, both adults and children experience emotional highs and lows that often resurface and intensify when a new crisis or transition occurs. Divorce is multifaceted, and children and families may be affected by a number of divorce-related factors, such as conflict, poverty, disruption of routine, or change of neighbourhoods (Bee & Boyd, 2007).

The length of time that situations like this one continue, and the intensity of the related mood swings, will vary from person to person. However, early childhood educators need to be aware that strain does manifest itself long after the actual decision to separate or divorce is made, and may intensify rather than diminish over time.

Factors Affecting Children's Adjustment to Divorce

- Amount of parental conflict
- Number of changes after the divorce
- Economic factors
- Absence of father or mother
- Availability of both parents
- Extra responsibilities placed on the child
- Custody arrangements

MISSING THE FATHER

Marcy had been divorced for two years. She had a well-paying job and had managed relatively well with her two children, aged 4 and 6. By the second summer after the divorce, she felt that she was ready to take her children on a vacation. In a holiday mood, they drove to their favourite campsite and began to set up camp. As she unpacked their camping equipment, she suddenly realized that the task of setting up the tent was all hers. As she tried to ready herself for this task, her 6-year-old noticed the look of despair on her face. "Daddy always did this part, didn't he?"

The Amount of Conflict

The amount of conflict that exists in the marriage is one factor to consider when gauging children's emotional adjustments (Hopf, 2010; Wallerstein, 2005). Conflict may exist before and/or after the separation. Evidence shows that low-conflict marriages that end in divorce can actually have a more negative impact on children, whereas enhanced-conflict marriages that end in divorce can sometimes be beneficial for children (Ambert, 2006; McDaniel & Tepperman, 2007). When children have been living in an environment with a high degree of conflict and much fighting, they may be better off living with one stable parent rather than with two parents who are constantly embroiled in conflict (Parke, 2006).

Circumstances may also exist where conflict escalates only after the separation or during the divorce process, as the parents attempt to divide their belongings and decide on custodial arrangements. The children then become central to the conflict, whereas previously the parents tried not to involve them in their problems. The chances of an easy adjustment are greatly hindered when the children become the focal point of the conflict, such as in a custody battle. This scenario works against the best interests of the children involved (McDaniel & Tepperman, 2007).

Changes in Relationships After Divorce

It's rare that separation and divorce result in the change of only one relationship, that which exists between the parent and child. For example, the loss of the father often leads to changes in the standard of living (Hopf, 2010). A stay-at-home mother may need to go back to work, leading to the need for child care, thus leaving the mother with less time for the child. Other relationship changes within the family may also occur. For example, the child may not continue to live with his or her siblings, and contact with grandparents, aunts, uncles, and cousins may lessen. If the divorce necessitates a change of residence, then friends, child care, school, and lifestyle may also change. The child may lose a pet with a change of residence. The more changes children encounter, and the more new factors they must learn to cope with, the more disorganizing the entire process is likely to be (Amato, 2010). Thus, it's possible for the child to feel an overwhelming sense of "accumulated loss"—a sort of chain reaction that began with the breakup of the parental unit (Dixon, 2017).

Emotional Availability of Parents

While in theory, parents can be instrumental in helping children cope with the sadness and other responses to the breakup, it's often very difficult for parents to provide that support in an ongoing and consistent manner. They are dealing with their own strong grief reactions, which affect their emotional availability to their children. However, research has shown beyond any doubt that parental responsiveness to children's sadness is one of the key predictors of positive outcomes for children (Poon, Zeman, Miller-Slough, Sanders, & Crespo, 2017). All the more reason, then, that supporting parents through the process of divorce can play an important role in facilitating their ability to support the children.

Economic Factors

The most problematic and enduring change for mothers and their children is the decline in economic conditions (Hopf, 2010), which will often last for an extended period, particularly if the mother remains a lone parent. One likely reason is the difficulty for mothers with children, especially preschool children, to find and maintain employment. This problem may be compounded by the fact that women earn lower wages than men in most occupations and by irregular child support payments from fathers (Ha, Cancian, & Meyer, 2007; Institute for Women's Policy Research, 2017). Withholding child support payments may be associated with the ongoing conflict between spouses and the frequency of visits from the noncustodial parent. The reality is that most families need two incomes to make ends meet. After the divorce, lone parents are faced with the same expenses for child care and (increasingly) with care for older family members. However, now the full burden is usually on them, and with only one income (Vanier Institute of the Family, 2010).

Custody Arrangements

In Canada, the law says that in most cases both parents have the right to raise their children and to make decisions about how the children are cared for (Family Law for Women in Ontario, 2013). Therefore, the onus is on the parents who have separated to make plans about the child's life, and where the child will live. Many parents are able to make these decisions on their own, but often these arrangements are done with the help of mediators or lawyers. When there is no agreement, either parent can apply to the court for custody (Family Law for Women in Ontario, 2013). This is a change from earlier times when it was more likely in North American culture that the mother would get custody of the children. In 2006, amendments to the Divorce Act were instrumental in moving toward the change to joint custody (shared parenting). Joint child custody is becoming the most common arrangement for children of divorce. A US study (Bauserman, 2012) found that children from divorced families are better adjusted when they live with both parents in different homes or when they spend significant time with both parents (joint physical custody), as compared with children who interact only with one parent (sole physical custody). The study suggested that children in joint-custody arrangements had fewer behavioural and emotional problems, higher self-esteem, and better family relationships compared with those in sole custody arrangements. In fact, in terms of their developmental outcomes, "joint-custody children" were no different from children living in an intact family situation.

Nonetheless, it should be remembered that, especially for young children, it can be very difficult to understand and make the necessary adjustments to living in two homes. The children will have to contend with two different homes and with two different sets of rules, expectations, and routines. Just as they become accustomed to one, it will be time to change to another. Moreover, if parents live in different neighbourhoods, children lose a sense of continuity with their friends and neighbourhood activities. The day-to-day problems of keeping track of their belongings and other aspects of their lives lead most children to think of one place as home, as their permanent residence (McDaniel & Tepperman, 2007; Skolnick, 1992). Indeed, some people believe that dual residence arrangements penalize children.

The Bauserman (2012) study emphasized that the influential factor in custody is not where the child lives, but rather the amount of time the child spends with each parent. Children from divorced families who either live with both parents at different times or spend certain amounts of time with each parent fare better than children who live and interact with just one parent. Decisions about living arrangements in child custody arrangements should depend on the particular needs of the child—and these needs will change as the child grows and develops. For younger children who alternate between two homes in this manner, the child-care centre might be the most consistent environment in their lives.

Given the difficulties inherent in divorce and in finding a solution that will work best for all parties involved, the most common basis for determining custody arrangements has been called "the best interest of the child" principle (Lansford, 2009). This process includes consideration of the parents' wishes, the expressed wishes of the child, the child's relationship with both parents, the length of time in residential custody with the one parent, the child's adjustment during the separation period, and both the financial and emotional ability of either parent to provide for the child's needs (Skolnick, 1992). Any past history of neglect, abuse, or addiction may also be relevant in determining custodial arrangements. Needless to say, custodial arrangements are by their very nature controversial. The bottom line is that long-term legal battles full of conflict are ultimately not in the best interest of the child. In Canada, there are now many programs for divorcing parents that focus on the interests of children.

In summary, many factors influence children's eventual adjustment to divorce. Children must cope with the accumulation and interaction of many stressors at the same time (Bee & Boyd, 2007). When there are a greater number of stressors, poor coping mechanisms, and few resources, children are more at risk for serious adjustment difficulties (Olson et al., 1983). There is a growing body of research showing that most children from divorced families end up fine (Hetherington, 2003; Rutter, 2009). Others argue that effects are neutral (Li, 2007). "Most researchers have come to the conclusion that divorce has some negative effects on children's adjustment but that these effects may be small in magnitude and not universal" (Lansford, 2009, p. 140). Recent research argues that we shouldn't ask whether or not divorce affects children, but how and under what circumstances it affects children either positively or negatively (Amato, 2010). Factors like the parents' relationship, socio-economic status of the family pre- and post-divorce, marital quality prior to divorce, and the quality of parenting have more of an effect on children's experience with divorce than the act of "divorcing" itself (Lansford, 2009). Technologies like Skype can be helpful for divorced families as children can have the opportunity to see and talk to a parent who may be living elsewhere.

In addition, the growing body of research that highlights both risk factors and factors that promote protection and resilience in children has led to improved interventions aimed at helping children of divorce (Kelly & Emery, 2003). Such interventions often employ a systems approach by addressing families as well as broader social and legal systems. This approach attempts to contain parental conflict, to promote closer relationships between children and both parents, to (when possible) include children in post-divorce arrangements, and to enhance economic stability (Kelly & Emery, 2003). In societies (such as Sweden) that have highly liberal policies for nontraditional families, and that support divorced parents, divorce produces fewer stress-related outcomes (McDaniel & Tepperman, 2007). This shows that the effects of divorce can be mitigated by supportive government policies and other social supports.

CHILDREN'S PERCEPTIONS OF DIVORCE

Young children know more about divorce than is commonly assumed (Ebling, Pruett, & Pruett, 2009). The child's level of cognitive and emotional-social development will influence his or her reaction to a separation or divorce. Infants or toddlers may not react to a separation or divorce simply because they have no understanding of the implications of the separation. That is, infants will not comprehend the changes that have occurred. Infants or toddlers may, however, react to any change in the quality of caregiving from the mother or the father. For example, since the mother is preoccupied with her own stresses related to the divorce, she may be less attentive to her children's needs. Babies may cry more, want more cuddling, or change eating and sleeping patterns as a consequence of this change in the mother. Children's attachment to the departing parent may be at risk. In situations where the father is the nonresidential parent, it is he who frequently feels excluded and, as a result, decreases contact over time (Ebling et al., 2009). Divorce also impacts children's definition of family. Children affected by divorce at a young age often have vague and confused definitions of both "family" and "divorce" (Ebling et al., 2009).

Toddlers may be just as affected as infants by the change in caregiving from a distressed or resentful parent. Toddlers may not yet have the time concepts to realize that Daddy has been gone for a long time; thus, their reactions will be similar to those of younger children. However, since toddlers are moving from the developmental stage of acquiring trust or security to independence, this transition may be threatened as they experience a loss of security in their world (Ebling et al., 2009). Achieving autonomy and independence may be much more difficult for such children under these circumstances.

Preschool-age children have developed fairly clear ideas of their own families, and divorce is disruptive because it destroys those concepts. Divorce is a devastating event for young children because they don't yet have the cognitive or language capacity to fully understand this kind of change. For example, such children may ask, "How long will Daddy be gone?" or "What do you mean Daddy is gone?" Regressions to earlier forms of behaviour are common (Ebling et al., 2009) and may include crying, clinging, separation anxiety, bedwetting, or needing a soother, bottle, or blanket again. Preschool children, who see the world from their own perspective and have difficulty separating reality from their own thoughts, can experience guilt, confusion, and self-blame (Amato, 2010). For example, a little girl may tell herself, "If I'm a good girl, Mommy will come back." It's common for young children to have fantasies of their parents or families reuniting (Ebling et al., 2009). When divorce occurs, classic childhood fears may become more pronounced because the home base is no longer secure (Johnston, Roseby, & Kuehnle, 2009). Fear of abandonment by adults, leading to clinging, is common in young children (Johnston et al., 2009). While acknowledging the confusion that preschool children experience, Hetherington (2003) suggests that their cognitive immaturity may actually be beneficial over time, since they tend to forget the conflict and their own feelings about it rather quickly.

Children aged between 5 and 7 are considered to be more vulnerable (Wallerstein, 2005) because they understand more about the implications of divorce but don't yet have ways to cope or a means of arranging activities that give them some relief. Children at this age may feel sad, deprived, angry, and lonely; they may be more demanding or disobedient; and they may often experience fears (Johnston et al., 2009), including the fear of abandonment or loss of love. For example, children at this age may reason that "Mommy loved Daddy and Mommy loved me. Now Mommy doesn't love Daddy, so maybe Mommy doesn't love me either." Although adults may not understand this fear, it can be very real for children.

Preschool and school-age children are likely to view divorce from their egocentric point of view (Amato, 2010) and, therefore, believe that they are to blame (e.g., "I should have cleaned my room better" or "If I didn't fight with my brother, this wouldn't have happened"). In addition, since children are often not provided with all the details or given all the information about the divorce, they try to make up their own understanding of it by piecing together bits of information. Adults are sometimes puzzled by children's understanding or conceptualization of the situation, but it's important to remember the child's developmental stage and reasoning abilities. Helping children to understand and cope with divorce requires seeing the situation from their perspective, bearing in mind how children think and feel at different developmental stages, and providing them with age-appropriate information.

Grieving the Loss

Reactions to grief and loss are inevitable for a young child whose parents are divorcing. The child may at times express feelings of anger and sadness. At other times, the child may act as if all is well and that the separation is just temporary. Not all children will react in the same way, and often many of these emotions don't last for long periods of time (e.g., they're sad until they need a peanut-butter sandwich). However, parents and early childhood educators should recognize the importance of these emotions and not minimize them merely because they are short-lived. On the other hand, children may feel a recurring sense of loss because the "departed" parent still comes by. In summary, children may experience one emotion or a range of emotions that may last for a long time or be short-lived. No matter how long they last, though, these feelings have a powerful impact on children.

THE IMPACT OF DIVORCE ON PARENTING

Because parents are enmeshed in their own problems and need for support, the needs of their children are sometimes forgotten, and it becomes increasingly more difficult to provide a consistent environment for them. Due to the crisis, parents may be unable to respond to the emotional needs of their children. Several studies have noted that the quality of the mother–child relationship is more likely to suffer because of her personal emotional needs at the time, her anxieties associated with being single, and her self-involvement (Hetherington, 2003). All of these effects on the adult have corresponding effects on children, as well as on parenting.

Often, as both parents become immersed in their own situations and the wide range of emotions involved, the first and most significant result is that the amount and quality of communication between parents and children declines (Amato, 2010). This effect is due partly to the parents' inability to verbalize their feelings and thoughts to their children in a way that they will understand. How do you explain love, infidelity, or a change of heart in terms that children will understand when these things are difficult even for adults to grasp? This feeling of helplessness often leads to less and less communication, because parents automatically assume that young children won't understand, or because they feel it's crucial to protect their children from the crueler aspects of life.

However, young children usually do know that something is going on, and they often think that since no one will talk about it, it must be *really* bad. If we also consider children's way of thinking (i.e., the egocentric thinking, the self-blame, and the guilt) and the disproportionate fears they often have, we realize that children may perceive the situation to be much worse than it actually is.

In the period of transition after a divorce, parents of preschool children are often much less effective and consistent in their discipline, communicate less (and less effectively), and hold changing expectations for their children's behaviour (Hetherington, 2005). When the parents feel able to cope, they are attentive to the needs of their children (e.g., "It's time to take a bath" or "Tidy up your toys" or "Eat all your supper"). When parents are in a period of emotional upheaval, these day-to-day activities may not be completed. It's also common for the remaining parent to spend extended periods of time alone or on the telephone, and for the children to be left to fend for themselves or shuffled from babysitter to babysitter.

As parents experience a range of emotions, they may respond to their children in inconsistent ways. There may be times when they make few demands for appropriate behaviour, while at other times their expectations are very high. These conditions may alternate without their children understanding the cues that govern the particular situation. For example, one request for a bottle may be met with a quick response while the next is met with reprimands (e.g., "You're too old for a bottle" or "Stop acting like a baby" or "Daddy doesn't like babies"). Children begin to fear that there will be a negative reaction every time

Courtesy of Chris Zahn.

Taylor, Age 5

they approach the parent, and communication again is diminished. Although these things do happen in all families, it's likely that they happen more frequently when a family is experiencing high levels of stress, as in a divorce.

The last factor to consider is that, under the demands of the situation, parents may be less able to listen to their children. This failure is partly the result of parents' self-preoccupation, but it also stems partly from their children's cognitive representation of the situation. Children ask the same question over and over (e.g., "When will Daddy come home?") in an attempt to increase their understanding of the situation ("Never is a long time; it's more than one sleep"). Children also put together pieces of information in ways that seem incomprehensible to adults, which further reinforces the parents' belief that their children cannot grasp even the least complex aspects of the situation. Children may express strange ideas (e.g., "You were angry and yelled at Daddy and he had to leave, so if you get angry with me, I'll have to leave, too") or may begin to play out the happenings at home (e.g., the fights, the threats, the separation). Sometimes, children direct their anger at the custodial parent ("I hate you" or "You can't make hamburgers like Mom" or "I like Dad's stories better"). The parents may think their children's coping mechanisms are inappropriate or indicate a lack of acceptance, rather than trying to understand how children think and express themselves.

SUPPORTING FAMILIES

Early childhood educators can utilize their knowledge and understanding related to loss and change as they consider how they may support families who are in the process of divorce. The divorce process entails considerable stress on each member of the family. As we are aware of the danger of prolonged stress to the child's development, the early childhood educator's support to the child, and directly or indirectly to the parent, will make a significant difference.

- Do you think children are better off with one parent than with two who fight?

- Is divorce always traumatic for children?

- In your opinion, can children ever get over the divorce of their parents?

- Can divorcing parents keep the interests of their children in focus?

- Should custody always be awarded to mothers?

- Can divorce have positive effects for children and families?

- Do you believe that parents should sacrifice their personal happiness and gratification to keep the family together?

As early childhood educators whose primary concern is for the well-being of the children in our care, we sometimes find it difficult not to feel angry when we see children deeply distressed because their parents have decided to divorce. These feelings may be exacerbated if the divorce brings forth associations from our own lives, rekindling memories we find painful. If, for example, your father abandoned your family for another relationship, there may be some carry-over of personal resentment to the present situation. On the other hand, your parents' divorce may have been a relief for you. If this sort of memory interferes, you may not be as aware of the impact of divorce on the children in your care.

SCENARIO

PERSONAL EXPERIENCES CAN AFFECT OUR SENSITIVITY

Dianne was an early childhood educator in a playroom of 5-year-olds. Her earliest memories were of her mother and father fighting constantly. Often, her mother was physically abused. When her mother decided to leave, the fighting and beatings stopped. Dianne felt a sense of relief and thought that divorce was a good thing. So when 5-year-old Jessica was sad because her daddy had left, Dianne tried to explain that this was good and that her life would be much better now. Jessica felt otherwise and stopped talking about her feelings about the divorce. Because the circumstances were entirely different, Dianne's personal experience interfered with her ability to respond with sensitivity to the child.

Sometimes religious or cultural values prohibit divorce. Sometimes, even when we have the most liberal views, seeing children suffer can encourage us to view the parents as selfish.

SCENARIO

AN EARLY CHILDHOOD EDUCATOR'S PERSPECTIVE

Shauna, an early childhood educator at a child-care centre, admitted that she had negative feelings for Bernice's parents. Bernice was a well-behaved, happy child until her parents separated. They arrived at a joint-custody agreement that meant Bernice spent one week at Mom's and then one week at Dad's. Both parents felt that this was the best possible arrangement for all concerned. Shauna saw Bernice every day of the week and had a different impression. On Mondays and Tuesdays, Bernice was unsettled and cried at transitions and any change in plans for the day. Wednesdays and Thursdays, she was more settled and calm, but by Friday she was anxious, clingy, and unsettled again. Perhaps the weekends were fine for the parents, but Shauna indicated that she was lucky to have one or two good days a week with Bernice.

While there is no easy way to overcome these feelings, it's important to recognize and be aware of them, show empathy for parents, and offer practical advice when appropriate. Some reminders may be helpful:

1. Remember that there are two sides to every story and that you may not be hearing the whole story. The family is a complex system and many factors may lead to divorce. Although painful, the divorce may very well be in the best interest of the whole family.

2. Never take sides. You may have heard one partner's version, but it may differ substantially from the other partner's version. As a professional, you must remain concerned about the child's best interest without becoming involved in the parents' conflict.

3. When appropriate, provide information to parents that may help them support the child, for example, the development of a parenting plan that both parents agree on and that allows a child to have as much stability as possible in both homes, taking into account the child's friends, siblings, afternoon activities, and religious events, and that is flexible to allow a child to remain at one home for special events.

4. Provide lists of websites that provide information to parents on helping children cope with divorce and custody arrangements.

5. Examine your own beliefs and attitudes toward divorce and how these will translate into interactions with the young children and families with whom you work. Try to remember that divorce can have positive effects, especially for families in which divorce may represent an escape from an abusive situation or an opportunity for a second chance.

Perspectives

Lea is a 44-year-old divorced mother of two children, Rebecca, aged 9, and Grant, aged 5. Lea was recently talking about her divorce with several of her colleagues.

"I grew up in a small town in Saskatchewan in a strict Catholic home. I went to convent schools for all my education, and our family was very religious at home. I left for Saskatoon to continue with university. I worked very hard at my studies and then later at my teaching career. Consequently, I didn't marry until later in life. I met Pascal, who was also a teacher and a devout Catholic, at a church fundraiser. We were both actively involved in the church, and our love grew from there. We married when I was 33 and he was 37.

"I think we both realized that our marriage was in trouble when I was expecting our second child. I was having a difficult pregnancy, and Pascal wasn't as supportive as he'd been when our daughter was born. We had a major argument the day I arrived home with Grant, and I remember thinking, 'What am I going to do?' Divorce was just not something we could consider—the church forbids it, and my parents have been married 44 years and Pascal's parents were married 46 years before his father died.

"I stuck it out—I think we both stuck it out because we felt that we had no options. I tried seeing a counsellor, who suggested joint sessions, but Pascal figured that I had the problem, not him, so I didn't continue.

"Last year, things became unbearable. I knew that Pascal was seeing another woman, although he denied it. I finally broke down and issued him an ultimatum—either me or her. To my utter surprise, he chose her and left.

"I can't say that I'm proud of my behaviour over this last year. I've been mean, vindictive, have used the kids to get at him, and have blamed all our problems on him. Needless to say, he also blamed all our problems on me. Now that the air has had time to clear, I know why I did what I did. First, I was hurt and I wanted him to be hurt, too. But I also realize that my Catholic upbringing played a role. Divorce wasn't allowed, so I couldn't let the problems be my fault—if the breakup was his fault, then it was his sin and I wouldn't need to feel guilt. I did feel guilt, and some of my behaviour was a result of it, too, I guess. I blamed him for everything, everything was his fault, he was always the bad guy so that I could carry on with a clear conscience. I realize that much of my behaviour was influenced by my traditional religious and family beliefs."

Working with the Child

Children of divorce often understand far more than adults in their lives think they do (Ebling et al., 2009). While young children are aware of the changes going on in their family, they may express frustration at either or both parents and at others. It's important that early childhood educators are aware of this and are prepared to help and support children as best as possible during this time.

Lack of stability typifies the lives of children whose parents are in the process of divorce. Therefore, the early childhood educator must try to maintain as stable an environment as possible. If circumstances permit, it may prove beneficial to have a primary early childhood educator assigned to such children to ensure this constancy. It's important to maintain consistent expectations for these children, to maintain firm yet reasonable limits, and to try not to overprotect or to indulge them. Although it's true that children may need more attention and affection, consistent limits will usually be helpful. For example, children can't come to believe that it's okay to hit or act out frustration, or to expect extra privileges because of what is happening at home. Nevertheless, these feelings of anger and frustration must still be acknowledged and validated. There are a number of helpful Internet resources for supporting children of divorce and their families.

Children need to be listened to in an honest and nonjudgmental way. Sometimes children say hurtful things like "I hate you, Mom." It's difficult not to respond in a way that makes the child feel guilty or ashamed. However, when a child says something like "I hate my mom," the responsive early childhood educator can say, "You're feeling pretty angry at your mom, right?" Listening to the child can provide the early childhood educator with some insight into what might be happening at home so that further support can be offered. Listening in this way includes observing what the child does in interactions with other children, with adults, and with toys. Often children are reluctant to share their true feelings for fear of hurting a loved one. Let them know that whatever they say is okay. If they aren't able to share their honest feelings, they will have a harder time working through them (Kemp, Smith, & Segal, 2017).

It may be possible to help children of divorced parents gain an understanding of their situation both cognitively and emotionally. Give these children information through discussion, by reading stories, or by sharing information—other children may have had similar experiences. Recognize that children may experience a variety of emotions and may need to grieve the loss of a parent or of their family. Provide them with opportunities to work through their feelings. This means allowing each child some time to spend alone, providing them with a variety of activities like art, playdough, physical activity, or dramatic play to work through their feelings.

Minimizing the Risks of Divorce for Children

There is much that the early childhood educator can do to minimize risk factors and promote protective factors when a family is experiencing a crisis such as divorce. However, every family will differ greatly in the kind of help it wants or is able to receive. Timing may be a critical factor. If parents, for example, are experiencing intense emotional turmoil, it may not be the most appropriate time to supply information about how to talk to their children. Although parents may find it helpful to be informed about their children's possible reactions, they will also find information difficult to digest or use under conditions of duress. It may be best to pass along this information at another time, but soon enough to prepare the residential parent for the child's "I hate you" screams when they come.

Bearing in mind the vast individual differences among parents in their need for and ability to act upon information, the following suggestions are cautiously offered. At a minimum, supportive information may consist of reassuring the parents that their child's needs will continue to be met at the child-care centre or day home. Sometimes just acknowledging the possibility of positive parent–early childhood educator communication will smooth the way for such communication to occur. There may be times when the early childhood educator is certain that something is happening at home but will not actually be told anything until much later, usually when raising a concern about the child's behaviour (see this chapter's opening vignette). All parents are different; some are open and willing to divulge all information, while others believe that divorce is a private issue. These feelings must be respected and deferred to in future communications. Early childhood educators must convey to parents that their place is not to judge but to offer support.

As well, early childhood educators need to be sure that clear boundaries are established when working with families experiencing a divorce. While early childhood educators possess a firm foundation of knowledge concerning children and some knowledge about families and family dynamics, they must also be prepared to acknowledge the limits of their expertise. Early childhood educators are not marriage counsellors and must be careful about which aspects of the divorce they discuss with parents. They need to understand these boundaries and know when to refer the parent to appropriate community resources.

The following scenario demonstrates how one early childhood educator offered support within the context of appropriate professional boundaries.

SCENARIO

DEALING WITH A DISTRAUGHT PARENT

Mrs. Kortright approached Guadelupe, the early childhood educator, at the end of the day. She had tears in her eyes and seemed to be on the verge of sobbing. "Everything seems to be falling apart," she said. "My ex-husband disappeared two weeks after the divorce." Shanda, her 3-year-old daughter, was wetting her bed every night and then couldn't get back to sleep. Steven, her 9-year-old son, had been called to the principal's office three times that week for fighting with the other children. "I feel like I'm going to collapse," Mrs. Kortright said.

The educator responded with empathy, acknowledging that there were a seemingly endless number of pressures Mrs. Kortright had to face. "Perhaps I can offer some ideas that may help you and Shanda through this difficult time. It's often helpful in times of crisis to have contact with a trained counsellor who specializes in helping families cope with divorce. I know that things may seem overwhelming now. Would you like me to give you the names and phone numbers of some counsellors? Their services are offered on a sliding fee scale, so cost shouldn't be a concern. Also, I know that a counsellor will be available immediately. We'll continue to do all we can here at the centre to help Shanda through this difficult period."

Note that the early childhood educator responded with nonjudgmental support and empathy, outlined clearly the boundaries of her professional expertise (i.e., the preschool child), and referred the mother to more appropriate resources that she had checked out ahead of time. She also reassured the mother that her child would continue to be cared for at the centre.

Early childhood educators must be very careful not to take sides with one parent against the other. Parents embroiled in custody disputes may try to put the early childhood educator in a difficult position by using comments made against the other parent in court. Early childhood educators must recognize this possibility and try to remain neutral.

It's very important that the child be assured that both parents love him or her and will be part of the child's life. Parents can be gently reminded that speaking poorly of an ex-spouse in front of the child is not in the child's best interest, and that arguing in front of the child should be avoided when possible. Remember that parents will be grieving, and some will need to vent negative feelings. However, the child shouldn't be subjected to this venting to the extent that this is possible (Kemp et al., 2017). Early childhood educators should keep their director or supervisor updated about families going through divorce so that an informed neutral person is available if needed. Educators may also want to discuss potential situations, such as the scenarios provided earlier, to ensure that they'll know in advance how to deal with future situations.

Early childhood educators should have the expertise to explain to parents how their children may be perceiving the divorce and to prepare them for reactions or behaviours their children may exhibit. Such behaviour may include, for example, more crying, increased need for cuddling, more resistance, strange explanations, and constant questioning. Children may also play out the divorce. Assure parents that their children need to be listened to, and suggest trying to talk about what is happening in their family and home. It may also be helpful to encourage parents to talk openly to their children to reassure them that the divorce is not their fault and that both parents still love them. The early childhood educator may help the parents by suggesting they use simple words or explanations that children may understand, by providing them with books or videos to promote discussion, and by providing concrete activities that may enhance planning (e.g., "You'll see Daddy in four sleeps"). Make sure that the parents understand that children also need to grieve and to express their anger. Children may ask the same questions over and over ("When is Daddy coming back?"), and although this may be difficult, parents need to provide answers and reassurance ("Daddy still loves you"). Children need to feel safe, and for this reason they need time to adjust to the situation emotionally.

Children's need for stability becomes apparent when transitions occur from one situation to another. Both parents and early childhood educators may have to be more aware of the need to warn children in advance. Although it seems odd, early childhood educators may want to let the children know when they're about to move to another group of children, or to make a transition to a new playroom at the end of the year, so that the children don't come to think that everyone leaves them.

Resources may be useful for both children and parents going through a divorce. Books such as *Two Homes* (Masurel & Denton, 2001) and *Standing on My Own Two Feet* (Schmidt, 2008), among others, can be instrumental in helping parents promote discussion with their children, or in helping children realize that divorce is a normal experience for many families. A simple Internet search or visit to the local public library shows that there are countless books, DVDs, and other resources designed for both parents and children to help them cope with divorce. In addition, parents can be referred to local social agencies that may provide emotional support for them or for their children. Awareness of the resources available in your community will be most helpful to families in this time of need.

How You Can Support Families That Experience a Divorce

1. Be aware that the child-care centre may be the most constant factor in the child's life. Maintain consistency in early childhood educators, settings, expectations, and routine as much as possible.
2. Listen to the child. Be nonjudgmental and help the child to express feelings and questions openly.
3. Share developmentally appropriate information about divorce with the child.
4. Provide the child with opportunities and play experiences for self-expression (e.g., play-dough, art, physical activity, dramatic play, or a place to be alone).
5. Be respectful of the parents in their crisis and try to support them.
6. Establish clear boundaries with parents.
7. Provide resources and referrals for families as requested.
8. Encourage the parents' understanding of their child's reactions. Encourage parents to talk openly with the child about divorce, to discuss feelings and impending changes or plans.

CONCLUSION

For some families, divorce can proceed smoothly, but for others, it's a time of crisis for adults and children. Parents may be experiencing their own loss and associated pain, while the children are suffering the loss of the familiar family structure and secure home base (Amato, 2010). This change may include the permanent loss of one parent and, at least temporarily, a lessening of the availability of the remaining parent. Communication can easily break down because parents become involved in their own concerns, but also because they may think that their children are incapable of understanding or that they need to be protected from the harsher realities of life. Early childhood educators can play a key role by maintaining a safe and stable environment for the child, one where it's okay to talk and express feelings. They can also help by providing parents with the support and information they may be ready to hear (Amato, 2010). Empathetic and knowledgeable professionals can offer stability and support during this difficult time for both the child and parent.

Chapter Summary

- The impact of divorce can be seen as a disorganizing process for children and adults, which can endure over years and have lasting effects.
- There is great diversity in the way children react to divorce, including poor academic achievement, poor self-esteem, aggression, and depressive behaviours.
- Factors that affect a child's reaction to divorce include the amount of parental conflict, the number of changes after the divorce, economic factors, the presence or absence and availability of both parents, the amount of extra responsibilities placed on the child, and the custody arrangements.
- Early childhood educators can support children by listening with empathy, maintaining a stable environment for children, and maintaining consistent expectations.
- Early childhood educators can support families by finding the appropriate time to provide parents with helpful information on the child's needs, reassuring the parents that the child's needs are being met while at the centre, and referring parents to community resources when appropriate.

RESOURCES

Single Spouse: A Community for Single Parents:
www.singlespouse.com

HelpGuide.org, "Children and Divorce":
www.helpguide.org/articles/parenting-family/children-and-divorce.htm

Divorceinfo.com, "Preschool Children and Divorce":
http://divorceinfo.com/chpreschool.htm

Berkeley Parents Network, "Advice About Divorce":
http://parents.berkeley.edu/advice/family/divorce.html

KidsHealth, "Tips for Divorcing Parents":
http://kidshealth.org/parent/positive/talk/divorce.html

The Spruce, "Disadvantages of Joint Child Custody":
www.thespruce.com/disadvantages-of-joint-child-custody-2997602

EXERCISES

1. Role-play or consider your responses to the following situations. (Early childhood educators may not be confronted with any or all of these, but a thoughtful response to any unexpected situation may cause less stress and conflict than making an inappropriate response on the spot.)

   a) One parent asks you for information about the other parent.

   b) The custodial parent puts you in the position of telling the noncustodial parent that the weekend visit has been cancelled.

   c) The parent wants to tell you everything about the divorce.

   d) The child refuses to go home with Mom. He says he hates her because she made Daddy go away.

   e) The father is attacking the quality of care at the child-care centre. You find out that if Dad has custody, the child will stay at home with a full-time nanny. If Mom has custody, full-time child care will be required.

   f) The mother lies to the child and says, "Daddy isn't here because he didn't want to see you this weekend."

   g) The parent tells you that what happens at home is none of your business.

2. Check community resources for those that deal with divorce-support groups for parents and programs for children. They will vary from community to community, so it may be useful to know in advance what is available.

3. Check your local library and bookstore for books about divorce. Are there any you would want to recommend for parents? Are there any that would help parents understand divorce better from the child's perspective? Is there a book that might stimulate conversations about divorce with the child? Would this book be appropriate for parents to share with their children?

CHAPTER 13

Blended Families

OBJECTIVES

- To consider the challenges involved when new families are formed

- To discuss children's feelings about becoming part of a blended family

- To discuss parents' reactions to their children during the blending process

- To discuss the role of the early childhood educator in supporting parents and children

Frank, a 50-year-old man who had been divorced for 15 years and whose children were grown up, made the following comment shortly after his marriage to Margaret, a 42-year-old woman who had a 5-year-old son. Margaret and Jordan had moved into Frank's condominium while they were all waiting to buy a new house. "When I came home from work the other day, I tripped over Jordan's toys as I entered the front door. Jordan heard the beginning of a string of profanities, which I controlled as soon as I realized that I was not alone in the house! I guess there are a lot of things that I'm going to have to get used to, not the least of which is having to share my living room with a 5-year-old and his toys!"

PERCEPTION OF STEPFAMILIES

Remarriage has become much more common today. In fact, according to the 2011 census, stepfamilies are becoming the new norm, representing about one in eight couple families with children ("Step-families," 2012). Statistics Canada reports that the number of new families in which one or both partners have children from previous unions has increased, as has the number of step-parents who are having children together (Vézina, 2015).

Nevertheless, the view still exists that stepfamilies are incomplete or inferior, a view that is reinforced by negative stereotypes, myths, and media representations. The adjustment to a parent's remarriage is a complex process that plays out differently in different families (Dupuis, 2007). This adjustment is often complicated by the fact that, as a society, we don't yet have norms or realistic expectations for how this type of family should operate or for how the new roles and relationships should be defined (Dupuis, 2007). Step-parents themselves may be oversensitive to family problems due to the stigma related to stepfamilies. People often assume that stepfamilies are more susceptible to problems than two-parent biological families. Researchers have noted that there is a lack of quality assistance available for remarriage and stepfamily preparation. Traditionally, few family professionals have been trained to work with stepfamilies, although this is changing (Dupuis, 2007). The tendency to consider stepfamilies as nontraditional, atypical, or pathological, however, has been decreasing in recent years (Dupuis, 2007).

Many terms are used to describe what results when previously distinct families come together. Examples include *reconstituted*, *blended*, or *stepfamilies*, as well as *The Brady Bunch* or *Yours, Mine & Ours*. Some of these terms seem to carry with them negative implications. *Step-parents* may bring forth images of Cinderella's wicked stepmother, and the myth that stepmothers are evil has significant consequences for both the self-esteem of the stepmother and the relationships she has with family members (Fanning, 2008; Planitz & Feeny, 2009). The term *blended families* has to a large extent replaced the term *stepfamilies*. Margorie Engel, president and CEO of the Stepfamily Association of America, opposes this change. She claims that the term *blended* is misleading, and that "couples with 'blended' as their objective tend to have the most problematic households because some or all of the members won't buy into the blended concept" (Engel, 2002). Whatever they are called, the myths are still very much with us. What we will see in this chapter, though, is that the "blending" is different for each family, and in some cases there may not be much blending at all after a remarriage.

There is great variability in the makeup and structure of "blended" families. In some of these families, both spouses will have children from previous marriages; in others, only one spouse will have children. As well, new children may be added after the remarriage, or the new couple may have no children together. In some cases, one of the spouses has never been married before and thus has no experience with young children, or, if there is an age difference between the couple, a new stepmother who has had no experience raising adolescent children may have difficulty stepping into a parental role (Hull & Mather, 2006). Thus, the experiences of step-families may be very different because of the great variation in structure that exists among them.

When two families join together to form a new family, the end result is often a positive one. Remarriage can offer each spouse emotional and financial security, and it can result in having another adult to share parenting duties, intimacy and sexual satisfaction, and the happiness that comes from having a successful relationship (Daniel, 2012). For all of these reasons, the task of parenting itself may seem easier, partly because step-parents may enrich the child's life and provide an extra measure of emotional security. After divorce or single parenthood, parents may perceive this union as a welcome relief. However, most step-parents will attest to periods of friction and doubt with their stepchildren. They will also point out the need for patience and support from within the family, as well as for external support. In this chapter, we will consider the challenges facing blended families, both from the adults' and the children's perspectives, and the role of early childhood educators in supporting families in this major transition period.

CHALLENGES FOR STEPFAMILIES

Stepfamilies face many challenges in the context of the couple relationship, in the new parent–child relationship, and in extended family systems. Other challenges may be related to previous family histories. We will explore these various challenges in more detail.

Myths About Step-Parents

One of the co-authors of this book tells the following story about her daughter.

SCENARIO

THE EVIL STEPMOTHER

"One day I was driving with my 4-year-old daughter. She repeatedly asked to have the window wipers turned on, even though it wasn't raining. After I refused her request for the third time, she said that if I didn't turn on the wipers, I would be a stepmother. My daughter has never met a stepmother and doesn't understand what one is, but she obviously has her own idea of what a stepmother must be like."

We can assume that the daughter's perceptions have been shaped by stories or television, and that if she were to become part of a blended family, that perception would have an impact on the development of her relationship with a new stepmother.

The wicked stepmother myth is alive and well in our culture today, and stepmothers attest to the challenge it creates in their new role. However, there are other prevalent myths that will, at least in the initial period, often be directed toward the step-parent (The Step and Blended Family Institute, 2017).

Children can develop myths about their step-parents—either positive or negative. On the one hand, they may have unrealistic expectations that the new step-parent will "fix everything." For the child who has had an absent father, or for the child who has experienced parental conflict prior to divorce, the hope is often that the new step-parent will be the "rescuer" who will undo the damage done in prior relationships. Obviously, this is an unrealistic expectation, and when it isn't met, the child can feel deeply disappointed. Some children believe that the step-parent will replace the nonresident biological parent, thus recreating the two-parent family (DeAngelis, 2005). This expectation may create "romantic notions of instant love" and "one big happy family" that may be exceedingly difficult to live up to. According to The Step and Blended Family Institute (2017), it's important to debunk these myths as early as possible, as they can place significant strain on the family unit, as well as the couple relationship.

On the other hand, the new step-parent is often blamed for causing all the changes that the child faces. The child may have to move to a different neighbourhood, change schools, and possibly lose friends. In these circumstances, it's common for children to feel hostility and resentment (Hull & Mather, 2006). Several authors (Claxton-Oldfield, Goodyear, Parsons, & Claxton-Oldfield, 2002; Ward, 2006) have described additional myths about stepfamilies. The first is that "step is less" (Wald, 1981). This myth entails the belief that a nonbiological or step-parent can never love a child as much as a biological parent does.

ROLES AND EXPECTATIONS

One of the challenges facing blended families is that when the new union is formed, the members of that union don't have shared histories or a mutual understanding of the way things should be done (Facts for Families, 2015). If we recall the importance of family roles and rules, both spoken and unspoken, in family systems (see Chapter 3), working out these new roles and rules is a process that takes time and occasionally requires "trying on" a role and then adapting. Sometimes step-parents are seen as "mature friends" for the children of their spouses, who play with the children but don't participate in discipline or in making major decisions. However, in a shared household (as in the scenario at the beginning of the chapter), this role may be difficult to maintain. Is the new parent to become a partial replacement for a noncustodial parent? If so, in what aspects of parenthood should the step-parent engage—financial commitment, discipline, or recreational activities?

Often one or both step-parents wonder who is responsible for managing money, and who will discipline whom. Stepmothers may face the challenge of a societal expectation that they will take on the major responsibility for raising the children, which can be very difficult, especially if they are not readily accepted by their stepchildren.

One of the factors that can contribute to or impair healthy family development in a newly blended family is the relationship with the ex-spouse (The Blended and Step Family Resource Center, 2013). Often there is animosity, and the ex-spouse may have serious concerns about the way the new spouse relates to his or her children. The biological parent and the step-parent may share in the care of the child, but may not share approaches to discipline and child-rearing. When the ex- and current spouse have shared the same partner, it's likely that boundary issues could be quite complex. We have little research to date on these factors, but plenty of anecdotal stories exist in movies, magazine articles, and conversations between people who are in these situations. Former in-laws can complicate matters, as can unresolved past issues that may interfere with a partner's ability to trust the new spouse (Blended Family Success Network, 2013; Coleman & Ganong, 2004). We also know little about how extended family members impact the new blended family; they can either be supportive or an added stressor.

Complexity of the Family Structure

We don't have well-established norms for depicting the many kinds of relationships that evolve when a marriage dissolves and a new one is formed. The result of new or unclear family boundaries is often "role ambiguity" (Carroll, Olson, & Buckmiller, 2007). Examples of this ambiguity could relate to the "grandparents" (parents of the step-parent), to the relationship between the siblings and stepsiblings, as well as between the ex-spouses and the new spouses, who may need to relate to each other over matters of child care. Children have been known to ask "Which dad?" when an adult asks them a question about their father.

SCENARIO

WHEN STEPCHILDREN ARE TREATED DIFFERENTLY

Sam and Marina married when Marina's two daughters were aged 14 and 16. A year after their marriage, they had a son, Steven. When Steven was 2, Sam's mother invited the family to a Christmas dinner. As the gifts were opened, Steven gasped with delight when he opened his generous gift from his grandmother. The stepgranddaughters tried to hide their hurt feelings when they opened their token gifts. In discussing this later with a family counsellor, the two girls were embarrassed about their reactions. "We know she's not our 'real' grandmother," said the 19-year-old, "and it's very childish of me to feel hurt. But it's kind of hard being 'family' but not really part of the family."

In a further complication, blended families often have different values and traditions, and even when core values are the same, those values may be played out quite differently in different households (Davis, 2000; Henry & McCue, 2009). Little things, such as how birthdays are celebrated or which holidays will now be celebrated when two cultures join, may cause confusion. Families may be at very different stages in the life cycle. One parent may have adolescent children and may be dealing with the associated concerns and parenting issues, while the other parent brings an infant or toddler into the remarriage, introducing a completely different life cycle into the blend. All of these factors add complexity and perhaps play a role in the adjustment of all family members. Blended families may also struggle with complicated financial arrangements as well as conflicting practices and priorities (Gold, 2009).

The Couple Relationship

A new intimate relationship is usually a source of joy to both partners. As they begin to explore the physical and emotional aspects of their new relationship, they can be hampered by the presence of young children. Generally, when newlyweds begin their life together, they have time to adjust to their changing roles in this union before they become parents. With stepchildren, they have to adjust to parenting roles at the same time (Focus on the Family, 2017). Again, there are few guidelines for blended families regarding boundaries between children and parents and for prioritizing the couple relationship. On the one hand, if the new spouses take the time to be on their own to enhance their relationship, the supervision and support of children may falter. At the other extreme, the couple relationship could suffer if the children are always the top priority and if guilty feelings about the remarriage distort the parents' perceptions about reasonable expectations of the child.

SCENARIO

ADJUSTING TO THE PRESENCE OF YOUNG CHILDREN IN A REMARRIAGE

A single mother with a 4-year-old daughter had been involved with a young man for a few months when they decided to marry. He had not been previously married, and had become very fond of the young girl. When they decided that the three of them would go on a honeymoon together, it did at times seem strange to the young man to hear his future stepdaughter discuss her honeymoon plans with her friends.

Sometimes step-parents may feel that their needs come second to the needs of their partner's biological children. On the other hand, the relationship between the couple is legally binding, as in any marriage, but there is no such binding relationship between the step-parent and stepchildren. A remarriage does not require that the new partner take any financial or social responsibility for the stepchildren.

Planning the blending process by taking into account these potential difficulties might help to reduce their intensity. For example, steps can be taken to foster the development of the relationship between the step-parent and children before the marriage, and agreements regarding household task-sharing can be discussed during this preliminary stage. The development of new boundaries between subsystems in the new family will be one challenge that will require some thought (Sweeney, 2010).

One newly remarried parent confided the following: "I read all the books, and I knew all the 'recipes' for successful blending. Then I did everything practically the opposite of what I had planned to do." Experts often forget that emotions do sometimes interfere with the implementation of their advice or that advice may not be available until it is too late. When conflicts appear, parents may encounter feelings of guilt, self-blame, helplessness, or confusion. Children's reactions to the new situation, which we will discuss in the next section, can increase these feelings, thereby putting further stress on the marriage and on the task of parenting.

Children's Reactions

The results of research on the effects of remarriage on children are ambiguous. It's difficult to separate the effects of the "blending" from other factors that will have impacted children's lives ("Remarriage and Stepfamilies," 2012). Earlier studies indicated that both divorce and remarriage put children at risk for developing social, psychological, behavioural, and school problems (Hetherington, 2005). Children in blended families were more likely to be described as aggressive and noncompliant, to display acting-out behaviour, to be disruptive in social relationships, and to have adjustment difficulties. Behavioural problems were more prominent in the early months after the remarriage, when the family was consolidating. The educational achievement of children from blended families seems to be lower than in children of two-parent families (Case, Lin, & McLanahan, 2000). On the other hand, some writers suggest that behavioural problems, common after remarriage, may result from reduced involvement with the noncustodial parent and may not be a result of the remarriage per se (Hetherington, 2005; Sweeney, 2010). In addition, some authors argue that behavioural problems and educational differences may be the result of previous marriage dissolution and the experience of single parenthood prior to remarriage, as opposed to remarriage itself (Sweeney, 2010).

James Bray, past president of the American Psychological Association, conducted a study that looked at different types of stepfamilies and their relative success over a nine-year period (DeAngelis, 2005). The most successful type was what he called the "neotraditional" family, where parents formed a solid committed partnership so that they could nurture their marriage and the children, and didn't get stuck on notions of what an ideal family should be like. The second most successful type was what he called the "matriarchal" family, where the mother married for her own companionship and didn't expect her new husband to take on a significant role in child-rearing. This type of family seemed to work as long as the new husband didn't want to play a greater role. Finally, the most divorce-prone type of family was what he called the "romantic" family, in which couples had unrealistic expectations and wanted to create a "perfect" family atmosphere.

Children's reactions to this transition, as with other major life changes, will be related to their own developmental level and their ability to comprehend. Their responses will be influenced by the way in which they are prepared for the event, by their experiences prior to the blending of families, and by the number of changes that accompany the remarriage. Besides adjusting to a new parent, children have to adjust to new rules, new traditions, new extended families, new siblings, and a new way of life. We also know that the relationship between the biological parents impacts the relationship quality and contact between the step-parent and child. If there is conflict between the biological parents, the stepfather–child relationship has been shown to suffer (DeGarmo, Patras, & Eap, 2008). Furthermore, the degree to which stepchildren are monitored will influence the outcome for the child. The research suggests that children may be monitored more closely in homes with two biological parents. Thus, higher levels of monitoring of children in step-parenting households will likely lead to better outcomes for children. Also, influences such as friends, neighbours, and schools can be very helpful for children throughout this transition (DeAngelis, 2005).

A stepfamily typically comes together after a loss, such as divorce (Facts for Families, 2015). Children need to grieve this loss and to bid goodbye to the dreams they carried

Courtesy of Chris Davin B.

Davin, Age 5

about their first family, which can take up to two years or longer (Favazza & Munson, 2010). Remarriage may shatter children's fantasies that their original family will reunite or that their parents will reconcile (Goldenberg & Goldenberg, 2008). Children may lose their status as the oldest child, the baby, or the only child when other children enter the stepfamily. They may also lose a valued role with their biological parent. For example, a mother and daughter may have had a close relationship in which they confided in each other about everything, which may be lost within the new stepfamily. Similarly, children who have been raised in single-parent families may feel that they are losing a unique relationship with their parent, and may feel that they are losing some of their independence and autonomy.

The early stage in stepfamilies involves coping with the loss of the old family. During this time, a new co-parenting style must emerge while all family members need to accept the new family dynamics and feel comfortable in both houses. The middle stage represents a time of adjustment and rebuilding. An understanding and appreciation of the new family, and the way each parent behaves, develops during this period. The later stage involves the continued reorganization of rules and boundaries as all family members, particularly children, grow and develop.

Long-term adjustment is related to the personality of the child, the number of new stresses encountered by the child, the quality of the new blended family's home environment, and the resources available to support the child (Hetherington, 2003).

OBSTACLES IN STEP-PARENT–CHILD RELATIONS

The establishment of the step-parent–child relationship can be challenging, and several obstacles appear to be common.

Discipline and Child-Rearing Issues

Even when the new couple shares basic values, they may not share the same ideas about daily living. It would be quite miraculous if the two families that came together had exactly the same practices for guidance and discipline. Children may react strongly to a change in expectations of their behaviour, and may respond with strong statements such as "I hate him!" In a family with two biological parents, the reaction of parents might be something like, "I know you're angry at Daddy now, but I'm sure you'll get used to the new rule." In a new blended family, the reaction is more likely to be one of stress, guilt, and concern about the future of the relationship.

When the new parent undertakes the role of disciplining and guiding the children, it's sometimes a matter of trial and error. While all parents make "mistakes," a step-parent does not have the long-standing bond of unconditional love that forms over the years between parents and children. While the biological mother may overreact to a cup of spilled milk and speak harshly to her daughter, an apology and a cuddle might set things straight. However, if the step-parent overreacts to the same incident, it's harder afterward to resolve the hurt feelings (Hetherington, 2003).

Divided Loyalties

In many cases, new step-parents, usually stepfathers, will have children of their own who live with their ex-spouse. It's not uncommon in such a case for guilty feelings toward the biological children to interfere with the development of positive relations with the stepchildren. In families where the children of both marriages reside together, jealousy and rivalries between the stepchildren are not uncommon. A new stepmother who tries to establish a bond with her stepchildren may feel disloyal to her own children. A stepfather may need to decrease involvement with his biological children to make his new marriage and stepfamily work. Stepmothers often feel caught between their love for their husbands and guilt for remarrying against their children's wishes (Hart-Byers, 2009). Not surprisingly, women seem to be more deeply upset about stepfamily problems than men are (Hart-Byers, 2009). It's not uncommon for all the members of newly reconstituted families to feel pulled in many different directions.

Just as the parents may feel torn between bonds of loyalty toward various members of the new family, children, too, often experience this dilemma (Goldenberg & Goldenberg, 2008). Attachment to the step-parent may cause the children to feel disloyal to their biological parent. A simple issue such as what to call the new father can be a source of major concern and trigger many emotions. When the new step-parent assumes a role in discipline and guidance, children may feel that compliance involves disloyalty to their biological parent. It's difficult for children to ascertain where their loyalties should lie or how to divide those loyalties among all the players.

Sexuality

SCENARIO

WILL AFFECTION BE MISINTERPRETED AS SEXUAL ABUSE?

A newly remarried mother of a 4-year-old girl was talking to a family counsellor about how her husband seemed to be unresponsive to the child. Upon further investigation, it became apparent that the new stepfather was deeply concerned about any intimacy with this young girl being perceived as sexual abuse. "If I cuddle her on my lap before bedtime and kiss her goodnight, how will this be viewed? And if a hug and cuddle are okay at the age of 4, are they at the age of 5, 6, and 7?"

This man's anxiety was well founded. There is a higher incidence of sexual abuse in stepfamilies than in biological families (D'Alessio & Stolzenberg, 2012). While most step-parents are not abusers, fears surrounding this sensitive, seldom-discussed issue can impede the development of affectionate relations. Certainly, it's also true that, as children grow older, stepsiblings can be attracted to each other and will need guidance and protection in this regard. Stepfamilies that include adolescents may need to consider this issue before moving in together (Hetherington, 2003).

Finances

Although the blending of families often results in improved living conditions (Gold, 2009; Hetherington, 2003), money can become a source of conflict in some cases (Gold, 2009). Some studies have suggested that financial strains are more frequent in remarried couples (Lebow & Newcomb-Rekart, 2007). Typically, financial matters are more complicated, with issues to be resolved such as support payments to children. Moreover, since there are no norms regarding the obligation of step-parents to offer financial support to stepchildren, problems often arise regarding decisions as to who pays for what. These problems are more likely to occur when the children get older and questions such as who will pay for post-secondary education arise. However, there are many expenses involved in the rearing of young children, and issues of financial responsibility need to be carefully worked out.

Idealized Images of the Non-Step-Parent

Children often idealize the parent who no longer lives with them. Although this is more likely to occur after the death of a parent, it does happen after divorce as well. When the shadow of an "ideal" real parent looms large, it's difficult for children to form an attachment to their step-parent. "Mommy would never get mad at me for doing that" and "My real daddy always played with me after supper" are difficult ideals for the new step-parent to live up to.

As well, children may become jealous of their parent's affection for the new partner and new stepsiblings. Children may view the new adult as a threat to their established parent–child relationship (Hetherington, 2003). This perception may be more pronounced for the only child of a formerly single parent, who may not be used to sharing parental attention with anyone, and who may have had a special relationship with that parent (e.g., "You used to tell me everything; now you only ever talk to him"). When we bear in mind that the parents may be very involved in their own relationship, it's understandable that the child may feel left out and jealous.

SUPPORTING BLENDED FAMILIES

Sometimes children who are in the process of blending into a new family are undergoing so many changes in their lives that the child-care setting or preschool becomes a secure haven for them. There is currently much more recognition that appropriate intervention, parent education, and counselling can be highly significant in preventing divorce in blended families (Higginbotham & Adler-Baeder, 2008; Higginbotham & Myler, 2010; Higginbotham, Skogrand, & Torres, 2010; Hull & Mather, 2006; Sobon, 2005). Providing stability for the child and support for families may be the most important way early childhood educators can help blended families. Structured, predictable environments may offer much-needed stability at a time of major changes at home. It may be especially beneficial to provide the child with a primary early childhood educator, if possible. The constant reassurance of having a caring and trusted adult with whom the child feels secure can play a strong role in providing that extra bit of support that the child may require at this time of transition.

Empathizing with the tensions that the family may experience is an essential component of supporting families. Our attitudes and beliefs about step-parenting will affect our ability to empathize and offer the necessary support. One of the most helpful things an early childhood educator can do, if the step-parents are open to having this discussion, is to encourage work with a therapist who has expertise in working with stepfamilies, and possibly to help them in accessing information about where such therapists may be found. Early childhood educators can universalize the experience by sharing their knowledge about the challenges faced by all or most blended families, which can relieve some of the guilt and stress that parents may feel.

Check the following "Examine Your Attitudes" box to see whether any of the myths about blended families influence your thinking. It would also be a useful exercise to think of how you would address the step-parent in a letter or in a face-to-face exchange. In this way, you may be better able to empathize with any feelings of awkwardness the stepchild is experiencing.

>> **Examine Your Attitudes**

- Do you view the step-parent as the "wicked stepmother (father)" or as a "white knight" who rescues the stepchildren from an uncomfortable situation?

- Do you think that mothering comes naturally to women and that there will be "instant love" between a stepmother and her stepchildren?

- Is a stepfamily something less than a "real family" in your view?

- Do you believe that a stepfamily is automatically a better situation for children than a single-parent family?

- Do you think blending is an easy process that just naturally happens when people love each other?

Sharing Information with Parents

Bearing in mind our hesitations about giving advice, we still believe that there are times when providing parents with information can be helpful. The three major issues most likely to be raised in a blended family are (1) establishing discipline and parental authority for children, (2) forming a strong marital relationship, and (3) developing ongoing arrangements with the noncustodial parent. Early childhood educators may be able to provide this type of support and information. It's important that the information shared not be interpreted as criticism of the parents or as an expectation that they will implement the advice. We must also bear in mind that the advice we have to give is tentative, since we too have much to learn about what works and what does not. In addition, we must remember that blended families form a diverse population; therefore, not all suggestions will be appropriate to all families.

New Territory

A review of the challenges and problems involved in the blending of families should not be interpreted as a warning against remarriage. In fact, second marriages tend to last. The age of couples at their first and second marriage is a factor, with greater success for older couples than for younger ones (Clark & Crompton, 2006). As well, social support seems to be a decisive factor in the success of the second marriage (Clark & Crompton, 2006). We have a lot to learn about how different kinds of reconstituted families work out ways to face their challenges and become familiar with ways that may be quite different from the biological nuclear family. Today, there is much information on the Internet that is intended to offer support and advice to new step-parents.

SCENARIO

DIFFERENT FAMILY BACKGROUNDS

Charlene and Lauren were talking in the back seat of the car. Lauren was explaining that she was going to spend part of the summer with her real mom and Bill, her new stepfather. She would see her old stepfather and stepbrother for a week, and then spend the rest of the summer with her real dad and her stepmother and her children. Charlene had trouble following the conversation and tried to understand by describing her family with her one dad and one mom. Lauren sat for a minute and then remarked, "That means you only get one birthday present from your mom and dad. Wow, that's too bad."

This conversation between children from very different families shows that children often accept their lives as being normal or typical once they grow accustomed to them. Lauren was surprised by the news that her friend would only get one present because she had only one set of parents. By helping children to recognize and appreciate the differences in routines, expectations, roles, and other aspects of family life, early childhood educators can help children adjust to blending.

E. Mavis Hetherington (2003) suggests that stepfamilies need to give up the fantasy image of the happy, nuclear family to adjust. When they let go of this ideal, they will become more flexible, more realistic, and better able to cope. They may need to establish more flexible boundaries with the many people involved with the blended family, including the noncustodial parents, rather than closing in like the nuclear family.

Time

Some step-parents might appreciate being reminded that, just as they are exploring the new territory of a remarriage and blended family, so too is society at large only beginning to learn about this increasingly common phenomenon. Stepfamilies may need encouragement to give the adjustment period more time, and may require professional help in establishing new norms and boundaries for the family (Facts for Families, 2015; Hull & Mather, 2006).

Sometimes step-parents feel pressured to "make it work," and they become frustrated when the bond between them and their stepchildren does not develop as well or as rapidly as they had hoped. They may find it helpful to be reassured that these relationships often take time. Emotional attachments between the step-parent and child may take longer to develop because this relationship is not as binding as the marriage is and because integration into a family can take time (Goldenberg & Goldenberg, 2008). Children may need some time to adjust to all the changes and to the new parent. Step-parents can't be expected to like or love their stepchildren automatically, and, likewise, demands can't be placed on children to accept or love their new parent (Hetherington, 2003; The Step and Blended Family Institute, 2017). Newly blended families will gradually learn what works for them and what doesn't and then be able to establish their own expectations.

In the early stages, stepfamilies are typically made up of two subsystems: the "absorbing" or "veteran" family members and the "newcomer(s)" (Hull & Mather, 2006, p. 264). Eventually, the subsystems become less distinct, but it takes time.

Time is also a factor for the parents' relationship. It's important for a newly married couple with children to have time alone together. Early childhood educators can help alleviate parental guilt by demonstrating an understanding of their need to be alone and by helping them explain this to their children.

Permission

We described earlier the problem of divided loyalties that many children experience during the transition to a new family structure. Children may not be comfortable calling the new parent "Mom" or "Dad," but they may be more comfortable with first names or an original title. One early childhood educator told her class that she was called "Mom Number Two" for many years after she became a step-parent. Another said that she was called "New Mom."

It may in fact be easier for children to adjust to the new situation if the adults in their lives give them explicit verbal "permission" to maintain their loyalty to their biological parent. Communication between early childhood educators and parents can ensure that children's decisions about how they refer to their biological and step-parents are reinforced both at home and in the centre.

Communication

Studies have shown that major improvements take place in behaviour, child adjustment, and self-esteem when communication occurs between step-parents and the children (Braithwaite, Bryant, & Wagner, 2004; Halford, Nicholson, & Sanders, 2007). Communication involves open and frequent discussions about family roles, boundaries, shared identity, adjustments to the family, diverse expectations, conflicts, and feelings. Communication seems to be the key to adjustment for a stepfamily (The Blended and Step Family Resource Center, 2013; Braithwaite et al., 2004; Golish, 2003; Halford et al., 2007). Sometimes early childhood educators can help parents formulate these role clarifications in simple language, at the child's level of comprehension. For example, "When Mommy isn't home, John will give you supper. If you don't want to finish all your food, you don't have to. You can have a snack later when Mommy gets home. When Mommy's away, John will be in charge."

Activities

With all the new arrangements and attempts to blend, families sometimes lose sight of the joy of being together. Joint fun activities can go a long way in helping the development of positive relationships. Early childhood educators may be able to suggest child-care activities or community events for families. Sometimes a gentle reminder and permission to let go and laugh can be very helpful.

ADJUSTING EXPECTATIONS

A child in nursery school was having a difficult time getting used to living with his new father. His mother had remarried four months previously, and his new dad had never been married or had children. One of the first activities they participated in as a family was a picnic at the nursery school. Afterward the parents remarked that the event had been special because it was the first they had enjoyed as a family and because the father was finally able to see what other 3- and 4-year-old children were like. He could now readjust his expectations for his stepson's behaviour.

New Family Traditions

Family traditions and rituals can be seen as binding agents that help hold families together (Hutchinson, Afifi, & Krause, 2007). Newly reconstituted families can be encouraged to develop new family traditions to replace the ones that the members may have left behind, or to adapt rituals and traditions from the previous household. These new family traditions could be as simple as the stepfather making a pancake breakfast each Sunday or the family watching a movie together at home every Saturday evening. New traditions could also involve more elaborate events like celebrating the anniversary of the family's move to their new home. Establishing such traditions can add to children's sense of security and identification with the new family.

Sometimes, newly remarried parents suffer from "super parent" syndrome. They may feel that the world (and their children's teachers) are judging them, and that it's important to demonstrate that all is well. An empathetic early childhood educator somehow gets the message across that parents will not be judged and that the door is open to discuss issues that concern their child. If parents express concerns that go beyond the professional boundaries of the early childhood educator, they should be referred to community resources such as support groups for stepfamilies or family-counselling agencies. Early childhood educators may also be able to suggest books for children or adults that may be helpful. When parents understand that early childhood educators can be counted on to listen and, if necessary, to provide resources, then both children and parents can adjust much more easily to their newly blended family.

CONCLUSION

Each stepfamily is different from every other one, and each faces many challenges. Families may include different people from various extended families, each with his or her own histories. There may also be complicating factors, such as the need to deal with noncustodial parents. Stepfamilies are still subject to societal pressure, as is evident in the many myths that still exist about stepfamilies and in the common belief that the most successful stepfamilies are those that most closely resemble the nuclear family. The mere fact that these myths are so commonplace puts an enormous amount of stress on the blended family. However, the literature suggests that, over time, children do adjust and that stepfamilies do integrate successfully (Hetherington, 2003). When families understand the problems they may have to deal with and know about the support systems available, successful adjustment is more likely. Early childhood educators can play an important role in promoting resilience and adjustment in children and parents of blended families.

Chapter Summary

- Stepfamilies are becoming the new norm: in the 2011 census, they represented about one in eight couple families with children.
- Challenges for blended families include societal myths, unclear role expectations, and the complexity of the new family system.
- The effects of living in a blended household are difficult to extract from the effects of other life events that the child has undergone (e.g., divorce), but they seem to be linked to lowered academic success, increases in noncompliant and aggressive behaviour, and disruption in social relationships.
- Positive and frequent communication about changes, boundaries, and feelings seems to be a key ingredient for success.
- Early childhood educators can offer support, encourage blended families to enter into counselling or therapy, and provide the child with a secure and stable environment.

RESOURCES

National Stepfamily Resource Center:
www.stepfamilies.info

The Step and Blended Family Institute:
www.stepinstitute.ca/index.php

The Stepfamily Foundation:
www.stepfamily.org

Blended Family Success Network:
www.blendedfamilyfocus.com

EXERCISES

1. List some of the challenges a new blended family might face. Discuss strategies that might help the family overcome these challenges.
2. What beliefs do you hold about blended families? Try to identify how you might have acquired those beliefs. How might your particular beliefs hinder you in providing appropriate care for the children of blended families?
3. How would you explain blended families to a group of young children, all of whom come from nuclear families?
4. Check out community resources and support groups that relate to blended families. Which would you feel comfortable recommending to parents? Under which circumstances?
5. Check your library for books pertaining to blended families. Make a list of those that would be appropriate for children and those that would be beneficial for their parents.
6. Review the books in your centre. How many of these show blended families to be as normal as two-parent nuclear families?
7. Consider ways in which noncustodial parents may stay involved in a child's life. Is this possible? Desirable? Discuss.
8. The theories of loss and change discussed in Chapter 3 are particularly relevant to blended families. How can an understanding of these theories help step-parents and children adjust to the new blended family?

CHAPTER 14

Teenage Parents

OBJECTIVES

- To examine the complex sociological and psychological issues related to teen parents

- To examine attitudes toward teen parents

- To discuss the risks to the teen parents and child

- To discuss the role of professionals in supporting teen parents

"I resent being singled out as a bad mother. I had my first baby before I turned 16 and my second child two years later. My children have always been well cared for, and they are just as well adjusted as any of the other children I see around me!"

(An early childhood student who was a teen mom.)

THE CHALLENGES OF TEENAGE PARENTING

The comment in the opening vignette came from a student who had sat quietly through a lecture on the sociology of teen parents. She felt that the lecturer had dealt with the subject in a judgmental fashion, particularly when he outlined the risks faced by the babies of teen mothers. In fact, many early childhood students have commented on the negative tone associated with the study of teen parents, claiming that they have teenage friends who are marvellous parents. Many young mothers do, in fact, respond to the challenge of rearing their children with commitment, courage, and determination, and they have positive relationships with their children. They must deal with many of the same risks and challenges that all parents do. Yet, as we discuss in this chapter, teen parents face a number of specific challenges, and research indicates that the children of teen parents face a number of very real risks. It's important to keep in mind that, despite common challenges, teenage mothers exhibit a broad range of parenting behaviours and abilities (Best Start Resource Centre & Sex Information and Education Council of Canada, 2007).

As early childhood educators who work with families, we should be aware of the special challenges and risks facing any particular population. Perhaps our first concern should be to determine what risks to the baby are associated with teenage pregnancy, and how these risks can be reduced. Since we know that the well-being of the family and the child are inextricably connected, we should also be concerned with the potential risks faced by the mother. Will she be able to complete her schooling or participate in job training, or is she likely to be economically disadvantaged? Does becoming pregnant as a teen affect one's chances for a stable marriage? What is the likelihood of a second pregnancy? How does having a baby affect the young mother's own personal development?

In the following discussion of teen parents, we will bring to light some of the difficulties that young parents encounter. Our main objective will be to enhance our ability to provide appropriate support when needed rather than to single out anyone for judgment. Our contention is that early childhood educators may be better able to anticipate and support the needs of parents if they are aware and informed. It's important to use this information sensitively and not stereotype or jump to conclusions. This chapter begins with a review of the prevalence, risks, and challenges of teen parenthood, and then looks at the role of the early childhood educator in supporting these families. We avoid stereotyping by reminding ourselves that whatever we have learned from research only informs us of general probabilities. It does not predict anything for a single individual.

THE PREVALENCE OF TEENAGE PREGNANCIES

In Canada, the overall rates of teen pregnancy have been on a steady decline since the mid-1970s, with variations across provinces and territories. A consistent overall decline of more than 15% was noted between 2001 and 2010 (Bielski, 2013; McKay, 2013). However, during this same period, the pregnancy rate increased in Newfoundland (+23.9%), Yukon (+19.5%), New Brunswick (+17.6%), Nova Scotia (+12.8%), and Saskatchewan (+1.6%) (McKay, 2013, p. 165). These increases have been attributed to socio-economic factors; that is, a greater number of pregnancies result in locations where teen girls have fewer educational and employment opportunities (Bielski, 2013). According to Alex McKay, research coordinator with the Sex Information and Education Council of Canada, "Young women who feel optimistic about their futures with respect to access to education and career tend not to get pregnant. Young women who are starting to feel discouraged about their employment and education opportunities are more likely to get pregnant. That is a straightforward correlation that persists, wherever in the Western world you go" (Bielski, 2013). Teen pregnancy continues to be a significant concern in specific populations, in particular, socio-economically disadvantaged groups. The rate of teen pregnancy in Indigenous populations continues to be much higher than the rate in other populations in Canada (Luong, 2008).

The United States has the highest rate of teen pregnancy in the developed world and considers this phenomenon to be a serious social problem (Best Start Resource Centre & Sex Information and Education Council of Canada, 2007). Interestingly, the teen birth rate in the United States is over twice as high as the rate in Canada. However, it too has been declining steadily (Bielski, 2013; McKay, 2013). For example, in 1990, the birth rate per 1000 teen girls was 59.9, and in 2014 it was 24.2 (U.S. Department of Health & Human Services, 2016). Researchers suggest that this decline can't be attributed solely to policy changes or funding of programs directed at preventing teen pregnancy, but to other factors. One factor is the American reality TV series *16 and Pregnant*, which focuses on teen parents (it began in 2009), and another is technology. Social media have provided youth with more accurate information about sexuality and the implications of teen births. Moreover, teens may be spending more time on social media and less on face-to-face physical relationships (Guldi & Herbst, 2015).

Factors Associated with Teenage Pregnancy

Why do teens become pregnant? First, it's assumed that teen pregnancy results from inadequate sex education and lack of access to contraceptives and health services (Best Start Resource Centre & Sex Information and Education Council of Canada, 2007). While most young people are aware of the need to use contraception and are knowledgeable about its availability, many don't use it, especially when sex is unplanned. Alcohol and being "in the moment" are key factors that diminish the likelihood of contraceptive use (Brown & Guthrie, 2010). In addition, there is an irrefutable link between teen parents and poverty. When teen pregnancy rates are compared between economically advantaged and disadvantaged youth, there is a huge discrepancy. However, teen pregnancy is not a simple social problem that can be fixed with sex education and access to health services. It results from complex socio-economic and cultural factors. "Growing inequity in rich countries, lack of opportunities for disadvantaged youth, cultural norms and alienation from schools are all factors that can increase the likelihood of a teen pregnancy" (Best Start Resource Centre & Sex Information and Education Council of Canada, 2007).

A recent review of the literature on teen pregnancy found that of the 36 US and UK studies examined, none indicated whether the pregnancy was wanted or unwanted (Best Start Resource Centre & Sex Information and Education Council of Canada, 2007). In some cultures, and where youth have a family history of early child-bearing, teen pregnancy may be considered normal. In areas where early child-bearing is expected, families tend to be supportive and teen pregnancy is not viewed as a social problem.

The majority of research on the effects of teen pregnancy prevention programs has been conducted in the United States, where, as we noted, the rate of teen pregnancy is high and considered to be a social problem. Many other countries don't label teen pregnancy as such. It's critical to remember that teen pregnancy is a complex social issue that is affected by a multitude of socio-economic factors and is still subjected to a range of moral judgments.

THE RISKS OF TEENAGE PREGNANCY

Risks Associated with Teenage Pregnancy

- Teen parents are often socio-economically disadvantaged.
- Teen parents often don't complete their education.
- Teen parents are likely to be single parents or have marital difficulties.
- Teen parents may have limited knowledge about child-rearing.

The challenges faced by teen parents are multifaceted. Some researchers report dire outcomes, while others are more moderate. US-based research from the 1970s and 1980s consistently documented significant negative effects on teen of teen pregnancy; for example, teen mothers were more likely to be socially and economically disadvantaged throughout their lives, less likely to complete their education, and less likely to find a job with high wages (Luong, 2008).

More recent research suggests that the link between teen pregnancy and socio-economic disadvantage is not causal but more likely related to the teen mother coming from a disadvantaged background. However, Luong (2008) suggests that lower educational achievement among teen mothers leads to reduced labour force participation and contributes to more teen parents living in poverty.

Researchers have sought to determine what outcomes can be attributed to the teen pregnancy alone rather than to the broader environment that the teen lives in. Teen mothers often face many disadvantages based on the communities and families they live in. Their families typically have lower incomes, their public schools are weak, and their communities have fewer amenities and supports (Hoffman & Maynard, 2008). Poorer outcomes can be attributed to a teen mother's living conditions and the early age of parenting. The outcomes for teen mothers whose pregnancy is unintended and unwanted are of particular concern (Best Start Resource Centre & Sex Information and Education Council of Canada, 2007). Looking at the lives of many adolescent mothers, researchers have consistently noted a higher accumulation of adverse life events.

Several studies conducted in the 1990s and the 2000s suggest that child-bearing in adolescence is not a causal factor in the poor outcomes of adult women who were teen mothers.

The consequences of teen pregnancy were partly due to the rate of high school graduation. For example, a recent US study found that by 22, only 50% of teen mothers achieved a high school diploma compared with 90% of adolescents who did not parent early (Centers for Disease Control and Prevention, 2017). Pregnancy and birth were significant contributors to dropout rates for teen mothers. Moreover, the number of years spent as single mothers tends to be longer, which is associated with a lower annual income ("Teen Pregnancy," 2017).

Being a teen father also has an impact on educational achievement: teen fathers have a 25% lower probability of graduating from high school, which compromises their future earning potential ("Teen Pregnancy," 2017). Teenage fathers who choose to marry the teen mother appear to spend more time at work to support their families. It has been suggested that males who postpone fatherhood are likely to have higher average incomes over their lifespan ("Teen Pregnancy," 2017). Overall, research has repeatedly suggested that teen pregnancy and childbirth have a significant impact on educational outcomes of teen mothers and teen fathers.

Alternative Perceptions

Many qualitative studies where the teen voice is captured describe pregnancy as a positive influence (Best Start Resource Centre & Sex Information and Education Council of Canada, 2007). Some young women report that pregnancy motivated them to plan for the future and cease destructive behaviours (e.g., drug and alcohol abuse). Although these teens reported that they did not plan to get pregnant, their pregnancy forced them to think about their future educational and employment goals. Other researchers state that young women from economically disadvantaged backgrounds were challenged by teen pregnancy, but their desire to succeed in life was not compromised. In fact, the pregnancy became the reason why certain young women pursued their goals, not the reason their goals were abandoned (Best Start Resource Centre & Sex Information and Education Council of Canada, 2007).

Physical Risks Associated with Teenage Pregnancy

Many of the physical risks associated with teen mothers and their children are related to the fact that teen mothers typically don't access prenatal care early enough or frequently enough. In addition, the children of teen mothers are more likely to suffer from health risks associated with low birth weight and/or prematurity. Researchers have noted a higher accumulation of adverse physical risks over time.

The physical problems associated with pregnant teens can stem from a number of factors. Sometimes teen mothers don't know or don't admit to being pregnant until the pregnancy is very visible—in other words, well into the second trimester. It's well known that the development of the fetus during the first three months can easily be affected by poor nutrition, smoking, and drug or alcohol abuse. Because many teens are already involved with substance abuse, the problems associated with it are more commonly found in teen pregnancies than in those among the population at large. Many teen mothers are unaware of these risks, and so substance abuse, as well as other dangerous behaviour, continues during pregnancy.

In addition, maternal stress is thought to have an effect on the unborn child. A pregnant teen will not only experience the normal stress associated with pregnancy but may also experience tension with parents, the boyfriend, and peers, as well as having to make difficult decisions for the future.

All of these factors suggest that teen pregnancy presents serious risks for teen mothers and their children. Teenage mothers face a significant risk for depression, specifically postpartum, which may be related to a lack of social support and poor partner relations (Savio Beers & Hollo, 2009).

THE TEENAGE MOTHER

When considering how the birth of a child might affect a 13-, 14-, or 15-year-old adolescent, it's helpful to consider the adolescent from a developmental perspective, and to think about the nature of the changes taking place in that period of life. The first is the psychosocial change of identity versus role diffusion (Erikson, 1963). At the same time puberty, the second change, is taking place, complicated by pregnancy. The third change is caused by the physical, emotional, and temporal demands of the new maternal role. Let us consider each of these changes in more detail.

Adolescence in North America is usually a time when young people try to establish their individual identity. This process is referred to as "identity versus role confusion or diffusion" (Erikson, 1963). Teens reflect on their own past, on who they are in the present, and on who they may turn out to be in the future. A sense of identity involves, first of all, a sense of independence from parents. Adolescents attempt to inform parents, in many different ways, that they are grown up and autonomous, an assertion that often puts them in conflict with their parents. In the quest for independence, adolescents tend to be very responsive to their social environments. Peers are probably more important and more influential during the teenage years than in any other stage of life. Teens' emotional and psychological immaturity can also lead to a lack of understanding of the real nature of parenthood.

During pregnancy, teens are also dealing with issues associated with puberty, including hormonal changes, body changes, and the formulation of a sexual identity. Many parents joke about the hours that teenage girls spend gazing at themselves in the mirror. This preoccupation with the body and body image is part of the growing-up process. Teen mothers have the added burden of dealing with changes to their bodies and with body image as well as the hormonal changes associated with pregnancy.

Bearing in mind the developmental tasks facing adolescents, how might a pregnancy affect a teen mother's development? Becoming a parent will likely make the quest for individual identity exceedingly difficult, since her world is changing so rapidly, and plans for the future are at least temporarily interrupted. Just at the point when she is attempting to become independent, the pregnancy can put her in a position where she is forced to depend on her parents for increased financial and emotional support. The physical changes that occur throughout the pregnancy can also be quite difficult for teenage mothers, since they complicate their attempts to define their sexual identity and sense of self.

Demands of the Maternal Role on the Teenage Mother

Becoming a parent can result in alienation from one's peer group, and we have already stressed the importance of peers in this developmental stage. A teen mother's needs and life are so different from those of her old friends that they no longer associate with her. When the baby is born, child-care duties, time demands, and limited finances can interfere with her social life and lead to feelings of isolation. Finding a new peer group is not always easy.

The very nature of adolescence, combined with the physical, social, and economic stressors associated with pregnancy and childbirth, is thought to pose a risk to the parenting abilities of teen mothers. Teen mothers, like many other mothers and parents, are unaware of the demands and developmental needs of very young children. On the one hand, they may expect some skills to emerge earlier than they do; for example, they may be impatient for the baby to begin walking, self-feeding, and toileting.

MISREADING THE BABY'S NEEDS

Fifteen-year-old Jenny frequently took her 12-week-old son, Dylan, to a McDonald's restaurant with her friends, and reported that Dylan loved McRib sandwiches. When the child-care staff questioned her, she pointed out that the ribs were big enough that he wouldn't choke on them, and hard enough that they wouldn't break into pieces. From her perspective, she had considered the baby's needs. Early childhood educators at Dylan's child-care centre were having a difficult time convincing Jenny that the baby was not ready for spicy barbecue sauce. When the baby turned up his nose at infant cereal, Jenny felt her choice of food was reinforced. "See," she said, "he likes barbecue sauce!"

On the other hand, teen mothers are often unaware of the need for language or cognitive stimulation, for close attachment to the mother, and for praise and encouragement. They may not provide the stimulation required for all areas of development or may not realize the child's need for a close attachment, thus demanding independence earlier. These issues arise with mothers and parents of all ages, but teen mothers may show resistance to learning, perhaps because of the stage of their development and need for independence. Teen mothers also are very aware of the attitudes of other people toward them. They often believe that older adults assume that they are incompetent and irresponsible and that they are not prepared for the responsibility of parenting (Best Start Resource Centre & Sex Information and Education Council of Canada, 2007).

A MOTHER'S DEFENSIVENESS

Because of the increasing prevalence of child abuse, hospital emergency staff and medical staff in clinics have been trained to look for and investigate any signs of abuse. A teen mother was told by the child-care staff that her 8-month-old daughter had a slight temperature that should be monitored, and that the baby should be taken to the emergency clinic if her fever worsened. The young mother avoided going to the clinic for two days. When she returned to the child care with her baby on the third day, the baby was very ill. The early childhood educator asked the mother why she hadn't followed the staff's advice and gone to the clinic. The mother finally admitted that she hated going to emergency clinics because the staff there always assumed that she wasn't a good mother and that whatever was wrong with her baby was her fault. The educator realized how difficult it must have been for this young mother to deal with such a situation, so she accompanied her to the clinic to provide support.

The preceding scenario shows that, despite the health care professionals' positive intentions, their attitudes and response to the mother made her feel defensive. She had likely been exposed to these negative attitudes in many instances before, which led her to avoid places where judgments would be forthcoming.

TEENAGE FATHERS

So far, we have discussed teen mothers and their babies primarily. So, what do we know about the role of teen fathers? The truth is that only recently has the role of teen fathers been given much consideration. Like teen mothers, teen fathers often have unrealistic expectations about support, and this is one reason that males are likely to give up involvement with the baby soon after birth. In their study of how teen fathers matter for children, Stefanie Mollborn and Peter

Lovegrove (2011) found that 30–50% of children born to teen mothers have an acknowledged teen father. More teen women have children with adult men, whereas few teen men have children with adult women (Mollborn & Lovegrove, 2011). It's common for teen males to be shut out of the decision in the case of abortion or adoption. Recent studies indicate that teen fathers may be involved in relationships with the mothers of their children, but only a few of those relationships result in marriage or long-term cohabitation (Mollborn & Lovegrove, 2011).

The Mollborn and Lovegrove (2011) study also found that only about half of teen fathers lived with the mother of their children, compared with 9 out of 10 adult fathers. It's notable that the teen fathers were involved in playing with and caring for their children similarly to adult fathers. In addition, "adolescent fathers reported feeling more attached to their child than adult fathers did in terms of both talking and thinking about the child" (Mollborn & Lovegrove, 2011, p. 16). The study also found that despite usually having a lower socio-economic status, a significantly lower rate of marriage, and lower residency with their children, teen fathers had a father–child relationship similar to the father–child relationship experienced by adult fathers (Mollborn & Lovegrove, 2011). Not surprisingly, teenage fathers typically come from more disadvantaged groups than adult fathers. While teenage fathers paid significantly less in child support than adult fathers, no significant difference in the amount of other monetary help (i.e., toys, health care) was provided by teen fathers as compared with adult fathers. Notably, among teen fathers, "levels of informal, irregular financial support of children were surprisingly high" (Mollborn & Lovegrove, 2011, p. 15).

David Long (2011) conducted a study of teen fathers and concluded that the overall lack of support to teen fathers in everyday life and educational achievement leads teen fathers to live in and stay in poverty. The relationship between education, occupation, and income determined short- and long-term consequences for the young father's ability to support his family. Young fathers overwhelmingly indicated that they felt stigmatized regardless of their maturity, education, or ability to support their children. Generally, young fathers felt "being a young father makes them a bad father" (Long, 2011, p. 3). Deficit-based perspectives lead people to blame young fathers for their choices and problems. In Long's (2011) study, young fathers indicated that services, supports, and financial support were available primarily for teen mothers.

Studies of intervention programs involving adolescent first-time fathers indicate that participation in a support network (such as parenting classes or meetings with social workers) can have a positive effect. These support groups are becoming increasingly popular and are an effective way of engaging fathers (Long, 2011).

›› Perspectives

Carlos is a social worker in his early fifties. He came to Canada as a refugee from El Salvador in 1984 with his wife, Rosa, two sons aged 11 and 12, and a daughter aged 7. Both Carlos and Rosa were teachers in El Salvador. Once they settled in Canada, Carlos felt that he could be more effective helping immigrants, so he retrained and has been a social worker for several years.

"When we left our home and came to Canada, my main goal was that my children complete their education and be healthy, happy, contributing members of society, while at the same time maintaining a strong sense of identification with their Spanish culture. Religion doesn't play a big role in our lives, but the beliefs are there in the background. My children all attended a Catholic school.

"When my son was 19 and a student at college, he fell in love with a 16-year-old girl from El Salvador. Although we'd hoped he would concentrate fully on his studies, we noticed that he seemed sad and withdrawn and seemed to be avoiding us. One day, my daughter heard from some friends that he was planning to get married. We were absolutely shocked, because he hadn't said a word about this to us. Normally, we talked a lot; we had a good relationship with lots of communication between us. Shortly after that he came to us and said, 'Dad, Mom, I need to talk to you. You'll be very angry with me. My girlfriend is pregnant.' Our first responses were 'We're here to help you' and 'Are you planning to get married?' and 'What about finances?' At that time, he said he didn't think they should get married because neither of them had any money.

"We decided to speak with his girlfriend's mother, and we all came to the conclusion that it was probably best for them not to marry, and for the girl to live with her mother until they finished school. We would help them financially, if necessary, and of course my son wanted to be involved with the baby. But marriage just didn't seem feasible. However, the next time we saw each other, my son told me that they had decided to marry. We think his girlfriend's mother was desperate to see her daughter settled and officially part of our family, as she herself hadn't really integrated into Canadian life and hoped to return to El Salvador, confident that we would take care of her daughter. Part of me felt that I was losing my son, and not to the best of circumstances. It was quite sad.

"We held a family meeting. I said that we needed, as parents, to support our children. We didn't want our grandchild to suffer. The young couple was very emotional, and many tears were shed.

"They got married, with my son still in college and my new daughter-in-law at a high school for pregnant teens. Our biggest concern was that he stays in school. After all we'd been through, the thought of our son ending up uneducated and employed in some menial job was hard to bear. With some social assistance and a summer job, they managed to get an apartment in a municipal housing project, and six months after their marriage Juan Carlos was born.

"My wife gave up her part-time job to look after the baby while my daughter-in-law finished high school and my son attended college. Maybe it's a cultural bias, but we feel that babies should be looked after by loving family members. We both love the baby dearly, but Rosa at times felt burdened by the responsibility. My daughter-in-law loves her baby, but we worried that at times she seemed a bit careless about food and other matters. You can understand that—she's a young girl; she wants to go to parties and be like her friends. It must be quite a conflict for her. I think she regrets being in this situation, having such a big commitment. I believe that my son is a caring and responsible father and very proud of his little boy. He's working and studying full-time but tries to spend as much time as possible with the baby. He is still very connected to us. He calls or visits almost every day. Their marriage seems to be okay—they seem to love each other. I sometimes suspect that my son is being manipulated a bit, but that might be a biased perspective.

"Two years have passed now; my son has almost finished his education, and my daughter-in-law has completed high school. We feel now that it's time to pull back a bit. Rosa wants to have some time to herself again. I hope that soon my son will get a good job. We've been giving them financial support up to now, and that has been a bit of a strain. We've worked hard for many years and want to be able to think about our retirement. We also hope to return to El Salvador for a while so that I can spend some time with my own parents before they die. I think it will be a bit hard for them—finding care for the baby, and so forth.

"My son and daughter-in-law's unplanned pregnancy changed all our lives. It hasn't been an easy time for us. But always our first thought has been 'We must do what's best for the child.' We must support our children so that they can be good parents."

THE CHILDREN OF TEENAGE PARENTS

Researchers have consistently noted issues with children born to teen mothers. Babies tend to be at a higher risk for low birth weight and infant mortality (Youth.gov, 2017). They tend to have cognitive delays and be less prepared to enter kindergarten. Typically, they are described as having behavioural problems and are more likely to have chronic medical conditions. As adolescents, they typically have lower academic achievement and are at a higher risk for not completing high school (Hoffman & Maynard, 2008). They are more likely to become teen parents themselves and have higher rates of unemployment as adults.

Studies have also concluded that young children are more likely to be placed in foster care and are almost twice as likely to be reported for abuse or neglect (Youth.gov, 2017).

However, these results must be considered in the context of the situation; that is, socioeconomic and living conditions must be factored in. Although the results may be definitive, the circumstances and layering of factors may contribute to very different results. Your role as an educator is critical in the early years for all children, including the children of teen parents. Your expertise and deep understanding of young children will prepare you to provide the best care and learning environment possible.

THE ROLE OF THE GRANDPARENT

As many adolescent mothers live with their parents following their child's birth, it's not surprising that grandparents play an important role in the lives of teen parents (Savio Beers & Hollo, 2009). Mothers of adolescent mothers, for example, often provide housing, food, educational support, and parenting support, in addition to continuing to parent their adolescent children (Savio Beers & Hollo, 2009). While research has shown that adolescent mothers gain more ability and confidence in their parenting through a positive relationship with their own mothers, these grandparents often face high levels of stress (Savio Beers & Hollo, 2009). In addition, grandparents run the risk of becoming so involved in their new role that the teen parent does not experience all aspects of parenting. For example, if grandparents are "built-in babysitters," the teen never has to worry about child care. When grandparents pay expenses for the teen and the baby, the teen may not come to understand financial responsibility. Often, the extended family needs to walk a very fine line between being supportive and letting the teen parent take responsibility and experience parenthood fully.

Compared with the relationship between maternal grandmothers and their adolescent daughters, researchers found far greater variability in relationships between maternal grandmothers and teen fathers (Savio Beers & Hollo, 2009). For example, grandmothers may limit a father's access to his child, so when the teen mother and baby live with the maternal grandmother, father involvement tends to decrease (Savio Beers & Hollo, 2009). However, paternal grandparents can play an important role in mitigating this. When the teen father is encouraged to stay involved and is supported by his own parents, his involvement may increase (Mollborn & Lovegrove, 2011).

SUPPORTING TEENAGE PARENTS AND THEIR FAMILIES

To work effectively with young parents, as with the members of any population, early childhood educators must consider their own beliefs and responses. On a professional level, they must make a concerted effort to avoid being judgmental and to determine the areas where they can provide support. Moral convictions about premarital sex and other religious and culturally based beliefs make it difficult for some educators to accept teen parents in an objective fashion. In addition, there seems to be a general tendency to view teenagers as irresponsible, rowdy, and generally quite disagreeable. High school and college students commonly report incidents where they were wrongly accused of shoplifting or of other misdemeanours simply, they think, because they were young. Teen parents are thought to be irresponsible and pregnant only because they tend to be socio-economically disadvantaged and members of a marginalized group (e.g., Indigenous people, Hispanic population).

SCENARIO

WHAT ARE YOUR FEELINGS ABOUT TEENAGE MOTHERS?

After seeing a film about a 14-year-old new mother who was having trouble keeping her patience with a cranky baby, students were asked to jot down some of their feelings. Some said they felt sorry for the young mother and her baby; others were honest enough to admit that they felt quite angry. Why didn't she use birth control in the first place? Didn't she know that having a baby wasn't going to be like playing with a doll? Another student, a teen mother herself, said that she remembered feeling the frustration expressed by the mother in the film, but reminded the class that any mother, regardless of age, might feel frustrated with a baby who cries incessantly.

People often assume that children born to teen parents are unwanted and are largely the result of a mistake or promiscuous sexual behaviour. "Really? How could she? How could she not know to take precautions? How stupid!"—these are comments commonly made about the teen mother. This lack of understanding of teen parents and their particular situation can lead to the teen's feeling isolated, as if she were an outcast.

Methods of Support

Despite the stereotype suggesting the opposite, the "consequences" of child-bearing in the teen years may not be as set in stone as once believed (Savio Beers & Hollo, 2009). Teen parents can be and often are very successful parents, especially if they have appropriate support from the child's father, both families, and the community (Savio Beers & Hollo, 2009). In fact, researchers are now suggesting that teens who are also parents are not significantly different from peers of the same socio-economic status.

Supporting teen parents can best be viewed from the ecological perspective (see Chapter 3). Although early childhood educators work primarily and directly with the teen mother and her child, other systems, such as the extended family, peer group, schools, and employers, all need to be considered in supporting the teen. After examining their personal beliefs about teens and teen parents, early childhood educators should become knowledgeable about the stressors and risks facing these families, and support them in a nonjudgmental fashion. Educators will need to work from a family-centred approach that is strengths-based to fully consider the multitude of factors that may affect the lives of the teen parents and their child. The lives of teen parents are often layered with defining factors that may put the teen at a disadvantage; those factors include socio-economic status, education, employment, and being marginalized. Being supportive in practice means not making any assumptions and recognizing the strength and potential in young mothers as well as the difficulties they may face. It's particularly important to ensure that the young parent does not sense any disapproval or judgment on the part of the professional.

Providing the babies of teen parents with nurturing, responsible, and stimulating care while the young mother completes her schooling can enhance the life chances of both the baby and the mother. A teen mother who can complete her education stands a much better chance of achieving economic stability and a reduction in all the adverse effects of poverty (Youth. gov, 2017). Early childhood educators can give demonstrations of appropriate care and invite young parents to spend time at the centre to observe and learn. Extra care needs to be taken to help young parents feel at ease and to reassure them that they are not being constantly observed and judged. Young parents may benefit from information about development, discipline, health, and nutrition, as long as the information is not transmitted in a threatening manner that may elicit defensiveness and possible resistance to accepting advice and information.

Many community and high school-based programs are currently available in Canada to assist teen parents, teaching them how to be effective parents and giving them an opportunity to continue their education (see the "Resources" section at the end of this chapter). Successful programs combine social, psychological, and educational support for the teen mother, her baby, the teen father, and the extended family. This support may include on-site child care, flexible hours, child-care classes, child development classes, prenatal care, social workers, counsellors, and so on. All professionals in such programs work together with the teen. These comprehensive programs are thought to be effective in promoting the well-being of both the young mother and the baby (Artz & Nicholsen, 2009) and even in decreasing the likelihood of another pregnancy during the teenage years. Finally, early childhood educators should be aware of online forums, virtual support groups, and websites that teen parents can use for support and education (Kauppi & Garg, 2008).

Supporting the Child

Early childhood educators provide high-quality care to all children. This fact is especially important for families who are faced with social conditions such as poverty, poor living conditions, or few community supports. Teen parents may experience these conditions and special challenges as teen parents. Accordingly, your role as an educator is significant in providing children in your care with learning opportunities to ensure continuous growth and development.

Attendance at a high-quality child-care centre can act as a protective factor for children as their young parents develop their parenting skills. A good child-care centre can ensure adequate nutrition and can also monitor the health and development of the children in its care. A child's ongoing interaction with early childhood educators in the context of a secure and responsive environment can facilitate the cognitive, language, motor, emotional, and social development of the child. Such care is important for all children; however, if the young age of the parent and accompanying social conditions have a negative impact on parenting, the importance of having the highest quality of care is accentuated.

CONCLUSION

In essence, the needs of teen parents for information, support, and guidance are not very different from those of other parents. However, young mothers face a daunting challenge in needing to simultaneously integrate different life roles and expectations in an accelerated fashion. These include their life roles as teenager, daughter, student, partner, and mother. It's, therefore, vital for the early childhood educator to understand these additional challenges faced by teen mothers, who must deal not only with the challenges of motherhood but also with the developmental tasks of adolescence. Professionals should offer support and assistance in an accepting, nonjudgmental, and nonthreatening fashion.

Chapter Summary

- The overall prevalence of teen mothers in Canada has been declining steadily since the mid-1970s, although there are regional variations. While many risks are associated with teen mothers and their infants, there are many individual differences between mothers. Many teen mothers are devoted and committed to their children in spite of the obstacles.
- Teen parents by and large come from socio-economically disadvantaged families and groups that are marginalized (e.g., Indigenous people, Hispanic population).

- Becoming a teen mother is associated with ongoing economic difficulties and accumulated negative life circumstances.

- Infants of teen mothers may have higher rates of low birth weight, cognitive delays, and behavioural issues

- Teen fathers are likely to give up involvement with the baby soon after birth. This decision is influenced by family support, professional help, and an expectation of inclusion. However, teen fathers may choose to be involved and will also require support.

- High-quality child-care programs that support and encourage a teen mother's return to school and school completion can significantly reduce the risks to the teenage mother and the child. Responsive child care will enhance the development and growth of skills for the children.

RESOURCES

Active Parenting Canada:
http://activeparentingcanada.com

Government of Canada, "Teen Pregnancy—Information for Teenagers":
www.canada.ca/en/public-health/services/health-promotion/childhood-adolescence/stages-childhood/adolescence-13-19/teen-pregnancy.html

Youth Law (Alberta), "Teen Pregnancy and Child Support":
http://youthlaw.ca/teen-pregnancy-and-child-support/

Best Start Resource Centre:
http://en.beststart.org

The Sex Information & Education Council of Canada (SIECCAN):
http://sieccan.org/wp/

Raising Children Network (Australia), "What Parents Mean to Teenagers":
http://raisingchildren.net.au/articles/family_relationships_teenagers.html

EXERCISES

1. Reflect on your own level of maturity at the ages of 13, 15, and 18. In what ways would you have been ready to become a parent, and in what ways would your level of development have hindered your ability to parent? How typical do you think you were at those ages?

2. Draw up a list of your preconceived ideas about teenage parents. After you have done so, ask yourself if these ideas could also apply to the following: new parents, parents over the age of 40, parents who are poor, or parents who are experiencing family problems. Can you identify a pattern of stereotyping in your attitudes toward parents?

3. Check community resources to find those that may be used to support teen parents and their children.

4. Check your local library and bookstore to find out which books might be helpful to teen parents in raising their children.

5. What risks do teen parents face? What is the potential of teen parents?

6. What are the most important supports that teen parents may need from family? From the community? From their friends? From their peer group? From the child-care centre?

7. How does the concept of intersectorality (as explained in Chapter 3) help us understand the complex challenges faced by teen parents? Consider how challenges may become layered.

8. How might you encourage teen fathers to engage with their young child? What might you plan in your program to support fathers?

CHAPTER 15
Adoptive and Foster Families

OBJECTIVES

- To deepen our understanding of adoptive families and foster families

- To discuss some of the challenges faced by these families

- To discuss how early childhood educators can support these families

When 5-year-old Ming returned from preschool, she asked her mom, "Where's my real mom?" and said "I want a sister that looks like me!" Faye was not sure how to respond. They had created a story about Ming's journey to their home, starting at the time that they first met in the orphanage. Ming knew that she had been chosen by her adoptive family and that every milestone had been journalled in the story. The next day at drop-off, Faye learned that the topic of family had come up in preschool when another child had shared the news that he had a new sister. One of the children had asked Ming why she didn't look like her mom and dad. Faye and the preschool teacher chatted about this question and came up with a plan to open up the topic of different kinds of families with the children.

NONTRADITIONAL FAMILIES

Within the diversity that exists among Canadian families, adoptive and foster families may be less accepted as "real" due to dominant societal perceptions and beliefs. These perceptions and beliefs may be inaccurate, inappropriate, or based on myth. Many adoptive and foster families face unique challenges, some of which relate to being different or devalued. More often, the challenges result from a lack of knowledge or understanding by mainstream society. It's important to consider the particular issues faced by nontraditional families because these issues can become stressors that can impede positive child–parent relations and healthy child development. Beyond having to deal with societal perceptions, parents who adopt or foster children must contend with considerable legal procedures and the involvement of social services or private agencies, which is typically not required in other kinds of families. If we work toward increasing understanding and eliminating stigma and prejudice, and if we provide appropriate support if and when required, children in these families can thrive.

It's equally important to remember that not all families described in this and other chapters necessarily require support. Many families survive and thrive despite the potential and actual stresses in their lives. However, when families are experiencing stress, as educators we may be able to support them or provide developmentally appropriate support to the child in our care.

ADOPTIVE FAMILIES

Years ago, adoptive families were not always considered "real" families. Although this view has changed somewhat, children and parents in adoptive families still face stigmatization that may cause extra pressure or stress in their lives.

Adoption is defined as "the legal and permanent transfer of parental rights from a person or couple to another person or couple. Adoptive parents have the same responsibilities and legal rights as biological parents" (Adoption Council of Canada, n.d.a). The five types of adoption are as follows:

1. Adopting an infant, child, or youth from the Canadian child welfare system (Public)
2. Adopting an infant or child (Private)
3. Adopting a child from another country (International)
4. Adopting a stepchild/children
5. Adopting a birth relative (Kinship adoption) (Adoption Council of Canada, n.d.a)

Source: Adoption Council of Canada; retrieved from http://www.adoption.ca/faqs

In Canada, the provinces and territories oversee and regulate adoption. Accordingly, the rules and regulations are different, depending on where the family lives.

Adoption is a complex process and experience, involving at least three sets of participants: the birth family, the adoptive family, and the adoptees. Members of this adoption triangle may share some feelings and experiences, but they may also differ in how they experience adoption. This situation is the result of several factors. Fewer infants are available for adoption because of the availability of abortion, young parents have more support services, and single or teen parenting carries less of a stigma, so fewer children are put up for adoption (Khoo, 2015). There is still not a high need for adoption, however. In fact, one Canadian agency cited that 30 000 children in Canada are currently awaiting adoption (Adoption Council of Canada, n.d.b). Adoption is a lengthy process, and the number of newborns and very young children who await adoption is somewhat limited.

International adoptions grew in popularity as the number of domestic adoptions decreased. In Canada, there was a steady upward trend in international adoptions chiefly from China and Ethiopia since 2006. However, in 1993, the Hague Adoptive Convention was established following allegations of sales and trafficking of young children under the guise of adoption. The Convention set global standards to ensure that the proper consents for adoption were secured and the rights of children and families were maintained. Over 100 countries have signed the Convention, which puts stricter laws and policies in place and requires that adoption agencies be certified. As a result, international adoption is now a much lengthier and more difficult process (Khoo, 2015). In Canada, the number of international adoptions declined from 1 660 in 2010 to 905 in 2014, a 45% decrease (Khoo, 2015). In the United States, the number of international adoptions declined from 22 991 in 2004 to 6 441 in 2014, a more than 70% decrease (Haubursin, 2015). Today, the children adopted internationally tend to be older (i.e., 3–5 years old) and often have special needs. The process can take one to four years. In addition, countries have imposed their own restrictions; for example, some countries don't allow parents to be over 40 years of age, while others don't allow adoption to same-sex couples.

Children adopted internationally may face additional challenges. Often they lived in an institutional care setting for some period of time, which may have led to developmental delays. Depending on the age at adoption, children may have begun to develop their first language. For the majority of children, English is an entirely new language that must be learned. As well, there may be cultural differences that the new family may need to be aware of, especially in relation to older children. For example, in some cultures, eye contact is not made in conversation, whereas in Canada it's expected. New families may need to recognize that the child is making a transition from one culture to another and support the change by gathering information and explaining cultural differences to the child (Canada Adopts!, 2014).

COPING WITH THE UNEXPECTED

Sharma and her husband agreed to adopt a child internationally after many years of struggling to have children. Her husband was hesitant but finally agreed. They completed all of the paperwork, home visits, and requirements expected of them and eagerly awaited the arrival of their new baby. Sharma travelled alone to pick up her new daughter. She remembers that the process was very rushed and hurried: there was little time to visit with her new daughter and no one spoke English, so she received very little information. The baby was very quiet and docile all the way home and for several weeks after. When Sharma took the baby for her visit to the family doctor, she was told that the baby had severe developmental delays that were evident even though she was only 3 months old. Sharma, who knew little about how babies develop, was in shock. Like many parents of a child with a disability, it took Sharma and her husband time to adjust to this reality and grieve the loss of the "perfect child" that they had hoped for. With help and support from the family, the preschool, and the social services agency, today mom, dad, and child are all doing very well.

People may assume that adoptions take place as a second choice when a couple has difficulty conceiving or is unable to conceive a child. Couples may have experienced loss through repeated miscarriage or disappointment through repeated infertility treatments (U.S. Department of Health & Human Services, 2015). These events undoubtedly take an emotional toll on prospective adoptive parents. Families are in a precarious situation because of this second-best idea. Many feel that they have failed in their ability to conceive their own children, and then have failed again because their adoptive family is only "second best." Adoptive parents must often deal with complex feelings about their infertility, feelings complicated by the assumption that a biological tie is a prerequisite for bonding and attachment. Because of these stereotypes, many adoptive families never feel truly comfortable in seeking assistance, and so for the most part deal with issues after adoption on their own. Although it's important to take these factors into account, they are not necessarily true for all adoptive families. It's also important to note that many families who adopt may already have their own children, or may have made the decision not to have their own children owing to their belief in and commitment to sharing their lives with children who are much less fortunate or need a family.

Until the 1980s, formal adoptions were almost always closed. Typically, the birth mother had "made a mistake" that brought shame to her family. She was instructed to give up the child because that was "best for the baby." The commonly held view was that if a birth mother received no information about the child and the adoption, she would be better able to get on with her life and forget about this "mistake." Adoptive parents were given little or no information about the child's history, and records were often sealed. Denial of the child's background was used as a strategy to encourage the development of a primary attachment between the child and the adoptive family. Adopted children were told that they were chosen and therefore special. Many were never told at all. They were thus expected to suffer no consequences.

Over the past few decades, professionals recognized that secrecy and anonymity actually created difficulties for all parties involved. For example, secrecy can disrupt the child's development of trust and capacity for intimate relationships. The result of this awareness has been a trend toward open adoptions. Adoptions now can be considered along a continuum from completely closed or confidential, where there is no contact between the birth and adoptive families, to completely open or fully disclosed, where there is ongoing contact. In the middle is mediated adoption, where the adoption agency facilitates the exchange of information but there is no direct contact (Siegel, Smith, & Donaldson, 2012). The extent of contact within the adoption can range from minimal to a continuous, long-term relationship.

Open adoption has been gaining popularity in Canada and the United States since the 1990s. Personal experiences with open adoption suggest that it can be very positive for all involved—the child, the biological parents, and the adoptive parents. Most parents report positive experiences and greater satisfaction with more open options. The primary benefit is having access to the medical and family history of the child. Adolescents report that this information helps them better understand the reason for adoption, which helps them come to terms with adoption easier. Knowing their history is also beneficial to their identity formation (Siegel et al., 2012). Adoptive parents report that they felt a high level of comfort with adoption, which was connected to more open communication about adoption with their adopted children. However, certain factors have been noted to making open adoption more successful, one of which is counselling (Siegel et al., 2012).

SCENARIO

COMMUNICATING YOUR EXPECTATIONS

When Glen and Petra agreed to an open adoption, they weren't sure what to expect. They went to their first interview with an expectant mother and were denied. They were denied two more times as well. The fourth expectant mom, Ginger, chose them as prospective parents and started to share experiences about the pregnancy (e.g., when the baby started kicking). Glen and Petra got excited as the birth date arrived. When the baby arrived, they went to the hospital and found Ginger to be cold and aloof. She said that she had seen her baby and held her and wanted a few days to be sure she was ready. She would have the social worker call when she was ready. On the ninth day, the social worker called to say that Ginger had changed her mind and was keeping the baby. They were heartbroken.

After some time, they agreed to put their portfolio back into the mix and were chosen by another expectant mother. This time, the adoption happened and they set guidelines with the birth mother for the future—sharing pictures for birthdays and significant events, etc.

Glen and Petra's relationship with their daughter's birth mother has existed for eight years, and the openness has been a wonderful experience for all. Glen and Petra are not worried about their daughter's reaction when she wants to know more about her birth mother or her past. Although this adoption happened on the heels of a major disappointment, both Glen and Petra agreed that the first experience helped them set more realistic expectations.

Impact of Adoption on Children

We know that children in adoptive families face some challenges. One challenge may be a feeling of loss and uncertainty (Child Welfare Information Gateway, 2013a). This feeling may be characterized as an ambiguous sense of loss that may recur over the years, particularly at life's milestones. This feeling may lead to questions about personal identity. Identity formation may be impacted by adoption as the child may have many unanswered questions (e.g., Do I have siblings or grandparents? What is my medical history? What is my family history?). Issues related to identity development may lead to compromised self-esteem and self-confidence (Child Welfare Information Gateway, 2013a). In addition, the lack of genetic or medical history may create issues for adopted adults as well. Studies have shown that adolescents tend to become somewhat preoccupied about adoption, more so when it's closed. This preoccupation may impact family dynamics within the adoptive family.

Children may act out after the adoption is finalized and may continue to do so long after the adoption. Children may engage in inappropriate behaviour for different reasons. They may be seeking to create feelings of anger or pain in the adoptive parent. This type of testing may be the child's way of saying that they are feeling comfortable enough to communicate their feelings. When inappropriate behaviour persists, it may be a sign of trauma. Trauma is an emotional response to an experience where the child feels threatened (e.g., by separation, multiple moves). The child may perceive separation and transition as traumatic because they trigger an emotional response from the past. Some children may have learned to cope with the trauma they experienced, while others may be overwhelmed by it. Signs of trauma include irritability, difficulty calming, and acting out traumatic events in play or in conversation (Child Welfare Information Gateway, 2015). Some children may have gone through multiple separations and transitions from foster care to adoption. Other negative early experiences such as maltreatment may result in trauma for the child. Parents and educators need to be aware of this potential reaction and be prepared to develop resilience in young children.

Children coping with separation or multiple separations may have attachment issues. When a child experiences a significant separation or separations in the early years, his or her ability to develop attachments may be impacted because children need consistent caregivers to help them learn to establish secure attachments. Adoption or foster care may lead to disruption in attachment and lead to challenges with emotional regulation and social relationships (Child Welfare Information Gateway, 2015). These issues may be noticeable at the time of adoption or may manifest later in life. Sometimes children can perceive changes as abandonment, which may lead to attachment issues. Attachment issues may also appear later in development as reactive attachment disorder, which can arise when the child has been unable to form healthy bonds with others in the early years (Traster, 2014). Parents and educators can provide the child with multiple opportunities to engage and interact (e.g., physical touch, talking, playing together), which support the development of attachment.

SCENARIO

IT TAKES TIME

Four-year-old Jan had been in foster care with foster parents Heinz and Vita for two years, staying one or two days per month. He always seemed quite happy and content on his weekend visits. When Heinz and Vita adopted Jan, they saw major changes in his behaviour after six weeks. They both admitted that their foster care experience and the first six weeks had been such an easy transition that they never expected issues and were mystified. Vita mentioned the change in behaviour to Shannon, the preschool educator who had come to know him over the school year, and she had noticed no changes. Vita was surprised and thought that maybe Jan didn't like her and her husband, but Shannon replied, "Maybe he just wants to be sure that you want to keep him—no matter what." Vita thought about the significant changes in Jan's life and thought that maybe she would try spend more time with him to let him know that he was wanted and loved. Several weeks later, Vita reported back to Shannon that the sweet, quiet Jan had returned!

It should be noted that the majority of studies of adopted children show no significant differences in the outcomes of adopted and nonadopted children. Moreover, although adopted adolescents and adults may seek professional support more often, they don't necessarily have higher rates of mental health issues (Child Welfare Information Gateway, 2013a). Some researchers have attributed the perception of differences between adopted and nonadopted children to "adoption-coloured glasses." In other words, parents, teachers, and others tend to see issues as the fault of the adoption as opposed to the result of typical developmental behaviour (Corbin-Dwyer & Gidluck, 2009).

Recently, research has begun to address the possible effects of transnational adoption on child development. However, most research attributes any major differences in typical

Courtesy of Chris Zahn.

Taylor, Age 5

developmental behaviour to the way adoptive families are treated by society at large (Yngvesson, 2010). We are living in times when the adoption of children from war-torn or poverty-stricken countries, or from countries where natural disasters have struck, has gained considerable media attention. It's very likely that the excessive media attention, rather than the adoption per se, will be a significant factor in these children's lives. It's important to remember that children lack the ability to fully comprehend what is going on around them, so processing changes in their lives can be quite difficult.

Supporting Children Who Have Been Adopted

The most important thing an educator can do to support young children who are adopted is to help them, when necessary, accept the range of emotions they may express. All children occasionally feel angry, hurt, or rejected by their parents, but children who are adopted may need reassurance that it's natural to feel that way sometimes. Stories and dramatic play that include adopted children help normalize adoptive families. All children fantasize about wicked step-parents, abandonment by parents, and other themes that may be exacerbated for the child who is adopted. Being aware of this and providing reassurance that they are special and loved by their adoptive parents can be very helpful to children.

Books recommended for preschool adopted children include *A Koala for Katie* by Jonathan London (1997), *Horace* by Holly Keller (1991), and *In My Heart* by Molly Bang (2006).

Some children may feel anger at their adoptive parents, believing that they are preventing them from being with their *real* parents. Children who are adopted later (i.e., not as infants) may have undergone traumatic experiences prior to the adoption, and care needs to be taken to help these children develop a sense of security, trust, and belonging.

The following recommendations may help support children and families of adopted children:

1. **Create a photo album or "adoption lifebook"** that shows in pictures where the child is from. This will help provide a story for the child and promote inclusion as part of the family. It may also help the child remember their past through pictures and words. Be sure to follow the child's lead—some children may not want to remember.

2. **Establish family rituals and traditions to build the concept of family.** This may include special celebrations and events centred around becoming a family.

3. **Establish routines and family guidelines.** The more clarity and consistency there is in expectations, the easier it will be for the child to adjust. Be careful to ensure that the expectations are age appropriate, and minimize the rules to a few at a time so that the child is not overwhelmed.

4. **Give the time needed to develop a relationship.** Remember that children who have experienced crises prior to adoption may be reluctant to receive affection.

5. **Understand that children who have been adopted from countries after disaster or war may have habits that seem strange to us.** Habits may include hoarding food, being very vigilant, and being afraid to fall asleep. Show that you understand, and model ways of behaving.

6. **Give children time and space to grieve.** Understand that they may have lost more than most of us can imagine: family members, a home, a language, and a way of life. Remember that they are grieving someone important or the life they lost. Talk about caregivers the child had in the past or have pictures available. Allow the child to feel sad or miss them.

7. **Build attachment.** Provide the child with many opportunities to feel secure and trust in their environment. Provide the parents with ideas and activities. Attachment is a powerful tool to building resilience.

8. **Build resilience.** Finding multiple ways to build resilience within the child and family will be helpful.

Supporting Adoptive Parents

In many cases, completing the adoption process is considered the most difficult aspect of adoption. However, post-adoption issues may exist for adoptive parents. Adoption will create stress and tension, and most of these feelings will resolve as parents and children adjust to their new lifestyle. Parents may need time to adjust to being new parents. Sometimes there is a moment when the adoptive parent truly feels like a parent, while at other times, the feeling comes from the day-to-day routines of caring.

Understanding the stresses that families may have endured prior to the decision to adopt and demonstrating support when needed can make a remarkable difference. Making it easy to ask for advice and guidance, assuring parents that their parenting abilities are not being judged, and emphasizing that all parents struggle with parenting at times can also make a real difference. It's sometimes recommended that adoptive parents join support groups with other adoptive parents. However, it's important to respect the adoptive parent and child's right to privacy, and parents don't need to discuss the circumstances of the adoption with the school or centre if they choose not to.

Support groups have proven very helpful to some adoptive parents, as they provide a framework for validating their experiences, a social group with whom to celebrate the joys and share the concerns, and a mechanism for sharing resources and ideas. Most important, perhaps, is that such a group can reduce the feelings of isolation that are sometimes experienced by adoptive parents (Adoption Council of Canada, 2014).

To create a sense of belonging among family members, parents may find it beneficial to create a family storybook that includes the background and personal journey of each new family member. Families may also connect with the child's birth culture as a way to develop a deeper understanding of the child and create a sense of belonging. Professionals also suggest establishing family traditions or rituals that promote a sense of belonging for all family members. For example, marking special days for the family (e.g., the day the adoption was finalized) is a way to reinforce the family's identity.

FAMILIES WHO FOSTER CHILDREN

Foster care refers to the provision of substitute family care when the child is unable to be cared for by his or her own family. Foster parents provide nurturing and supportive environments for children and are considered to be a vital part of the child welfare team. According to the 2011 census, over 47 000 children were in care across Canada, and most of the children in care were under 14 years of age (Child Welfare League of Canada, 2012). In Canada, there has been a decline in the number of foster homes for many years (Bissett, 2016). The Child Welfare League of Canada has suggested that foster care is in crisis for a variety of reasons, including the changing needs of children and the level of services required for foster care. This organization's report, entitled *Canada's Children*, makes recommendations for the recruitment and training of foster parents, as well as the resources foster parents need (e.g., respite services) (Child Welfare League of Canada, 2012).

Foster families often face challenges similar to those faced by adoptive families. In particular, they struggle to be seen as "legitimate" families. This challenge is exacerbated by news headlines following an incident of neglect, abuse, or both in a foster home. There is a wide range of arrangements for foster care, from very short term to almost permanent. There is also a wide variety of approaches that foster families take to foster care. For some, foster care becomes a substitute for the biological family. Others provide a warm, caring, supportive environment designed to be a support for the biological family in the hope that the child will be returned. Whatever the approach, the misconceptions and myths surrounding foster care can be a real barrier faced by children and foster parents alike.

In addition to the stereotypes and preconceived notions about foster families as "second choice" is the lack of permanency felt in many foster care families. Foster care is often short term, which can affect the parent–child relationship and level of attachment (Riggs, Delfabbro, & Augoustinos, 2008). However, as for adoptive families described earlier, these areas are affected by how foster families are treated in comparison with biological families. Researchers have noted that foster parents may feel "role ambiguity" within their parenting role, even in long-term (12 months or more) foster families (Riggs et al., 2008). Furthermore, foster families often struggle to claim a family identity (Riggs et al., 2008; Thomson & McArthur, 2009). Finally, children placed in foster care more often come from highly conflicted, disrupted homes. Many of the children entering foster care have faced multiple adversities, such as parental substance abuse, poverty, violence, and abuse. Often, children have faced multiple moves. The children have more likely faced traumatic events in their development and need support to work through them.

Nonetheless, foster care families can provide a safe haven for children who have experienced adversities, giving them a chance to "start fresh" in a loving, caring family. Both foster mothers and foster fathers play an important role in caring for children (Riggs, Delfabbro, & Augoustinos, 2010). For example, one study has shown that while foster mothers are expected to be the *nurturers*, foster fathers are often more nurturing or motherly than expected in traditional fathers (Riggs et al., 2010). In addition, foster fathers who model positive parenting and family behaviours can counter earlier abusive experiences in birth families, and help break negative parenting patterns experienced by children (Riggs et al., 2010). This change (the positive parenting change) could be because foster fathers are more likely to exhibit both authoritative, rough-and-tumble parenting (the traditional expectation of fathers) and nurturing behaviour.

Foster parents perceive their role in different ways. In some cases, foster parents provide care to children while keeping very much in mind that the child is placed with them temporarily. Their role is to help provide interim support until the child can be returned to his or her parents or a permanent placement is found. In others, foster parents continue to provide care over a number of years and see themselves as real parents.

Foster parents face many challenges. The biological children of foster parents often struggle with adjusting to the changes in their home and family. Many foster parents feel that they don't receive the appreciation and support that is due to them. There is a chicken-and-egg situation whereby children who spend time in foster care are often very troubled, but then often it's the foster care that is blamed when these children get into trouble or are unsuccessful. For example, a recent national survey on youth homelessness reported that out of the 1103 homeless youth surveyed across Canada, 47.2% had spent time in foster care (Gaetz, O'Grady, Kidd, & Schwan, 2016). Although it's unfair to conclude that these youth are homeless because foster care was inadequate, that is the conclusion many people make. It's no wonder, then, that there is a current shortage of families willing to become foster families.

Efforts are currently being made to reduce the misunderstandings about foster care, about who can or should become foster parents, the financial aspects of foster care, and many other related issues. The Government of Alberta's Caring for Kids webpage (http://caring4kids.ca) explains many of these misperceptions. It also describes what foster children are like:

> Some foster children have been mentally or physically abused. Others have been abandoned, or can no longer stay with their families because their natural parents don't have the skills to look after them. But almost always, these children are hurt, confused, angry, frightened, and in desperate need of care and stability. (Caring4kids.ca, 2006)

Foster parents are highly likely to adopt children in their care. However, foster parents have not always been considered as the best option for adoptive parents. Prior to the 1980s, foster parents were considered temporary caregivers only. Often there were regulations that prevented adoption from foster care. Although it has taken time, the value of foster parents becoming permanent parents has been recognized in society and reflected in adoption policies.

Supporting Foster Families

Foster families can be supported both individually and systemically. Early childhood educators can help by showing their appreciation for the commitment foster families have to the children, and their empathy for the difficulties they face. Educators should provide these families with as much information about resources as possible (Riggs et al., 2008). In addition, early childhood educators should recognize foster families as legitimate families, and focus on using inclusionary language (Riggs et al., 2008). For example, ask the foster parents how they want to be addressed—by name? As the child's mom/dad or foster mom/dad? Early childhood professionals can also help by advocating that governments and community groups provide foster families with appropriate, high-quality education, training, and ongoing support (Caltabiano & Thorpe, 2007). Studies have suggested that foster parents often desire more information and resources but are denied in many jurisdictions (Child Welfare Information Gateway, 2013b; Child Welfare League of Canada, 2012). Educators can be a source of information regarding development and expectations for behaviour as well as community based resources.

Supporting Children Who Are in Foster Care

Like most children who have experienced loss and trauma, many of the children in foster care will need extra support to build trust and to feel secure. Normal setbacks in toileting, eating, and sleeping habits can be expected, and need to be addressed with patience, understanding, and support.

It's important for educators to consider that these children may be grieving, and to explain this to the child in an age-appropriate manner while stressing that the situation is not the child's fault.

It must be stated that children in care is an ongoing area of concern in Canada. The media often report on tragedies within the foster care system. Moreover, there is a lack of sufficient support for foster parents, a significant number of foster care children with special needs, and challenges with the family reunification process. Many early childhood education students may learn alongside child and youth care students who have chosen to focus their learning on providing support to children in care and their families.

Of major concern is the disproportionately high number of Indigenous children who are in foster care and the relatively small number of Indigenous parents who could raise these children within their own cultural context. Indigenous writers have highlighted two main causes of this problem: residential schools and the Sixties Scoop. As described in Chapter 8, residential schools have had a significant influence on Indigenous people's parenting skills. Based on prejudice and a lack of understanding of Indigenous families, Indigenous children were forcibly removed from their homes, parents, and communities and placed in church-run, government-funded boarding schools. During the 1960s, social workers who lacked the resources to address the poverty, cultural loss, and grief experienced among Indigenous families supported removing children from their homes and placing them with non-Indigenous families. The removal of Indigenous children occurred on such a widespread basis that it was termed the *Sixties Scoop* (Child Welfare League of Canada, 2012). It's estimated that over 110 000 children were removed from their families and adopted into non-Indigenous homes between 1960 and 1990 (Child Welfare League of Canada, 2012). Provincial and territorial governments have evaluated and changed policies since that time. However, foster care, especially in Indigenous communities, continues to be a major concern. More recently, many groups have worked toward developing foster care within Indigenous families. Band councils and governments have worked together in an attempt to change policies related to Indigenous foster care and to deal with the issues of Indigenous children in the foster care system. For example, in 2014, premiers across Canada directed provinces and territories to work collaboratively with Indigenous communities to create solutions. Their directions included understanding the causes of children in foster care based on social determinants of a health model, early intervention, and developing a broad range of supports in the foster care system. Cindy Blackstock provides excellent information on the work conducted across Canada. Visit her website at https://fncaringsociety.com.

CONCLUSION

One of the greatest challenges facing adoptive and foster parents is being accepted by mainstream society. An abundant amount of research shows that such parents are perfectly capable of providing strong, nurturing, and consistent care for their children.

As educators, it's important that we provide support to children and families touched by adoption or foster care. Children may require extra support to understand and to come to terms with their living situation. Educators may need to be mindful of building resilience in children and in families. A strengths-based family-centred approach will serve adoptive and foster families exceedingly well. Educators may be in a position to provide a deeper understanding of young children, their needs, and their behaviours to parents and provide resources and support.

Chapter Summary

- In Canada, an estimated 30 000 children in Canada are currently awaiting adoption. At the same time, the number of international adoptions has decreased as a result of stricter policies and regulations.

- The psychological needs of adoptive children ought to be deeply understood. The children may experience trauma from separation and transitions. It's equally important to understand the psychological and social challenges faced by adoptive parents and to support parents.

- Foster care is a temporary placement for children, although it can sometimes last for years. Foster parents may feel "role ambiguity" within their parenting role. Foster families often struggle to claim a family identity. Foster parents vary in their perception of their role, from feeling like real parents to feeling like temporary caregivers. Many children have suffered trauma and abuse before entering foster care, and require consistent care and stability.

- Foster care has been challenged by the high number of children with behavioural and developmental needs, the lack of education and support for foster families, and concerns with the family reunification process. Indigenous children continue to be over-represented in the foster care system. Children in care continues to be an ongoing area of concern across Canada.

- Educators can provide support to foster and adoptive parents by implementing resilience-building strategies for children and families.

RESOURCES

Adoption Council of Canada:
www.adoption.ca

Canadian Foster Family Association:
www.canadianfosterfamilyassociation.ca

Child Welfare League of Canada:
http://www.cwlc.ca

Waiting to Belong, "Adoption Basics":
http://waitingtobelong.ca/topics/adoption-basics

Kids in the House, "Adoptive Struggles":
https://www.kidsinthehouse.com/adoption/parenting-adopted-children/related-issues/adoptive-struggles

EXERCISES

1. Try to imagine how young children may have experienced the 2010 earthquake in Haiti, first losing their family, and then being transported to an eager and loving family in Canada. Try to describe what they may have felt as they entered a Canadian home. Do you think there may be parts of this experience that could be extremely frightening? What might they be?

2. What are some strategies you could implement in your child-care centre to support adopted children and their new adoptive parents?

3. You have a new child in your centre who has recently been removed from his biological parent and placed in a foster home. The child is having a difficult time at the centre and is prone to hitting other children. What are some steps that you can take? What kind of conversation would you have with the foster parent?

4. Describe how children may experience trauma in foster care or adoption. What signs of trauma will you look for? What aspects of trauma-informed practice will be relevant for you to understand when caring for these children?

5. Consider resilience for adoptive children and families. What aspects of resilience will be most important in your practice?

6. Consider resilience for foster care children and families. How can you provide ongoing support to foster parents while building resilience? What aspects of resilience will be most important in your practice?

CHAPTER 16
Children with Special Needs

- To understand the challenges faced by parents of children with special needs

- To understand how parents' reactions affect their interactions with their child who has special needs

- To understand how the family system and all its members are affected by the special needs of a family member

- To understand the role of the early childhood educator in supporting families with a child who has special needs

A support group for parents whose children had Down syndrome invited an early childhood educator to speak at an information session called "Choosing Quality Child Care." The speaker described all the important components of a high-quality centre. At the end of the session, one parent approached the speaker and remarked angrily, "You didn't even talk about children with Down syndrome." The speaker replied that certainly parents in this group would need to examine the additional aspects of a program related to the special needs of their children, but that it was important to remember that their children, like all children, required a caring and responsive social environment, a developmentally appropriate physical setting, and nutritious meals and snacks. "Sometimes," the speaker added, "we focus exclusively on meeting the 'special needs' and don't pay enough attention to the aspects of a program that are crucial to all the children."

Another parent was listening thoughtfully to the discussion. She commented, "A year ago I would have been just as angry, because I could see only how my child was different from all the other children. I know that Marcy will always have special needs, but I've learned that children with disabilities must be viewed first and foremost as children."

SEEING THE CHILD FIRST

All expectant parents look forward to the birth of a "normal" and healthy baby. When a child's health or development is impaired, families often enter a period of intense crisis, which is followed by a lengthy and difficult process of adjustment. The preceding scenario describes two parents who are in different stages in the process of adjusting to the birth of a child with special needs.

Many educators understand the fundamental importance of "seeing the child first" rather than focusing on the child's special needs. In fact, many educators in Canada who work within new curriculum approaches have gone through a reflective process based on "the image of the child," during which they think deeply about children with special needs and their role with them from different perspectives. The "seeing the child first" perspective provides a way of looking at all children, including those with special needs, against a backdrop of beliefs and rights. This perspective has changed the way educators approach children with special needs and engage with them in their programs. These changes may appear in early learning programs in different ways. However, it's important for educators to bear in mind that parents and families may have a different view of their child and his or her needs. For this reason, it's essential that educators also understand the child with special needs from the family's perspective.

Early childhood educators can fulfill a vital role in facilitating the family's adjustment to the special needs of their child and can also help enhance the family's ability to provide for the child's optimal development. To do that, early childhood educators need to understand the profound effect that the special needs of a child can have on the family. They also need to be sensitive to the initial and ongoing reactions of parents during the process of adjustment, and they should be aware of the challenges faced by all families whose children have special needs.

DEFINING SPECIAL NEEDS

The term *special needs* is sometimes confusing, because every child has unique and special qualities that are often identified as needs. Some people prefer to use the terms *exceptional children*, *developmentally delayed*, *handicapped*, or *atypical*. More recently, the term *children with special rights* has been used as well. Professionals have long debated both the advantages and disadvantages of using any label at all to describe children, as well as the pros and cons of each particular label.

We use the term *children with special needs* in this book for three reasons. First, this is the term most commonly used in the early childhood literature. Second, we know that some children require extra support so that they can develop their abilities to the maximum. The term *special needs* can apply to all children who need extra support, whether or not they are exceptional or have a particular disability. Third, we use the term as a reminder that we always need to consider the child first.

Special needs are usually described in terms of atypical development. For example, cognitive development may be delayed or accelerated (as with gifted children). The special needs may relate to physical development, with atypical motor development (such as cerebral palsy), or sensory development (such as visual or hearing impairments). The special needs of some children relate to the social-emotional domain, for example, emotional or behavioural problems or conditions such as autism. Some children have special needs in the area of language, resulting in delayed speech or a stutter. As well, some children have special needs due to a chronic health condition such as epilepsy, diabetes, or severe allergies.

We will consider *special needs* in the broadest sense of the term—that is, as they relate to any child who presents specific concerns to his or her parents, and who requires extra support to integrate successfully into early educational programs. Often, special needs are diagnosed at birth. However, sometimes special needs are identified only later in the child's development. In most settings, an official diagnosis (usually given by a medical doctor) is required to qualify the child and family for professional or financial assistance.

There are many children who, although not officially labelled as having "special needs," still warrant special consideration. For example, some children are extremely challenging for parents to raise due to a particular combination of temperamental traits. These children have been called many things, ranging from hyperactive children to children with behavioural problems to simply "difficult children."

The notion of the "difficult child" stems from the pioneering work of Thomas and Chess (1977), who described a number of traits or characteristics that people are born with and that remain fairly consistent over time. Examples of such traits are *activity level* (some people seem to need to be in constant motion, while others are content to sit still), *adaptability* (some people adjust easily to new situations, while others find change difficult), and *regularity* (some people have very regular sleeping and eating patterns, while others seem to thrive on an irregular schedule). For example, a child who is very active, who does not adapt easily to new situations, who does not establish eating and sleeping routines, and who gets fussy when exposed to different textures or sounds may pose difficulties for parents. This is particularly true if the parents' own temperaments differ greatly from their child's (Turecki & Tonner, 2000). Although these children may be considered completely "normal," the fact that parents find them difficult to raise can create challenges within families. Educators must try to understand this in the context of the child and family in an attempt to support the family and child.

SCENARIO

TEMPERAMENT CLASHES

Varda, an instructor in an early childhood development course, was introducing students to the work of Turecki and Tonner (2000). She asked the students if they could provide examples of temperament clashes they had witnessed between parents and children. Almost all of the 30 students in the class raised their hands. Three students shared personal experiences:

■ "My parents were the quietest people you could meet—all they wanted was peace and quiet—and I could never sit still for a minute!"

■ "My daughter always fussed when I tried to zip up her jacket in cold weather. I didn't realize that she was simply very sensitive to sensory stuff."

■ "One of my daughters just marched into preschool on the first day and acted as if she owned the place, and the other clung to me for dear life for the longest time."

At the end of the class, a number of students stayed behind and said how they wished they had known about Turecki and Tonner's ideas when their children were little. At the end of the year, the instructor got a lovely thank-you letter from a student telling her that the class on temperament helped her understand her toddler so much better and resulted in a wonderful year!

When children are diagnosed early on with a health condition, the diagnosis will provide many challenges for families: the need to understand new information, an increase in professional interactions, the need for support, the experience of heightened emotional responses, and increased stress in managing daily routines. When children are diagnosed early on with a lifelong health condition (e.g., diabetes, epilepsy), families may need to learn a whole new skill set (e.g., how to give insulin injections) and may have to adjust routines and lifestyle (e.g., diet, sleep patterns). In the early years, parents may take much time learning the complexities of the condition and how to cope with it. This process creates immense tension for families. In addition, the health condition may require hospitalization, so the child may miss child care for short or extended periods of time (which may impose additional strain on the child and his or her development).

SCENARIO

SHIFTING ROUTINES

Nineteen-month-old Malak was diagnosed with type 1 diabetes. After many short visits to the hospital when he was in crisis (e.g., highly elevated blood sugar, low blood sugar, or seizures), the family felt that it was beginning to cope. However, just as the routines around diabetes became part of their lives, something would happen (e.g., a stomach flu) that required a shift in what they were doing and how they were reacting.

In addition, families will learn to be ever vigilant, observing the child and changing routines in response. There may be sleepless nights, missed meals, or forgotten events as parents cope with the day-to-day issues that come along with understanding the impact of the condition. Children may be affected as well by late-night trips to the hospital and medication.

When children with health conditions come to child-care or preschool programs, parents may make requests that educators feel are unreasonable. Part of the reason parents do so stems from their need to be vigilant and to ensure that the child is stable in child care while maintaining their full-time employment obligations. Parents may ask for extended nap time (or no nap), for special dietary requests, for less or no time outdoors, or for more or less activity, depending on the child's needs. Educators who are coping with 10 or more children with their own unique needs may struggle with these requests.

SCENARIO

CONCERNS WITH RESPONSE TIMES

Deroda placed 2-year-old son, who has cystic fibrosis, in a child-care program after he had been home with a nanny. During the first week, she spent large portions of her day viewing the videocam that had been placed in the playroom and lunchroom by the child-care centre. She would note how long it took the educators to respond to her son, if they were delayed with his medication or treatment, how long he slept, etc. At pickup time, she would then go through the list and demand that these things not happen. The educator, who was experienced, felt overwhelmed by the mother's requests and wondered whether the child should perhaps be at home with the nanny so that the level of support needed could be maintained. She asked her director to talk to Deroda with her to assure the mother that they too were learning to cope with unique needs and needed her support.

No matter the underlying nature of the "special need" the child comes to the program with, it's highly likely that parents are attempting to cope with additional stress in their lives. Parents may make unreasonable demands based on high expectations of educators, but such interactions are yet other opportunities for educators to understand the family and offer support.

REACTIONS OF PARENTS

Parents' reactions to the news that their child has special needs has been compared to the grief cycle experienced after a death. This cycle can also apply to families where a mental health diagnosis has been made (Kostouros, 2003). Parents struggle to cope with the loss of their "wished for" or "normal" child or with a symbolic loss—that is, the loss of hope and the perceived loss of potential (Kostouros, 2003). Parents have described this event as heartbreaking and traumatic. Overall, most parents begin with a strong emotional reaction.

Early childhood educators who have learned to accept and respect each child's uniqueness sometimes have difficulty understanding the intensity and duration of parents' responses. When educators are sensitive to the possibility that parents may be grieving, they are in a better position to offer support (Gray & Robinson, 2009). As reviewed in Chapter 3, reactions to loss and grief are processes that people go through with different intensity, at different paces, and in different ways. Each family's inner and outer resources and coping styles are unique. However, there is some commonality in the way families experience the grief cycle, and this understanding may help educators appreciate the parents' point of view and empathize with their emotions. Early childhood educators must remember, however, that people don't generally progress through the following stages in this particular order and that emotions may resurface.

Understanding the Grief Cycle in Relation to Parents of Children with Special Needs

Shock

Often parents are completely unprepared for the birth of a child with special needs. Couples don't usually consider, mention, or discuss the possibility during the pregnancy, and child-birth preparation classes usually avoid the topic as well. When the birth of a child with special needs does occur, almost all parents react with shock (Penzo, 2008). The parents may experience such emotions as numbness (the inability to feel anything at all) and denial (thinking that the doctor can't be right; there must be a mistake).

Guilt and Shame

Many myths about children and adults with special needs exist in society today. Although these myths have been proven untrue, they continue to influence people's views. For example, a belief stemming from the 1940s was that a child's disability was somehow the parents' fault. In the case of psychological or psychiatric disorders, there has been a tendency among professionals to blame mothers.

Some religions can reinforce parents' guilt or shame by teaching that a disability is a consequence of the "sins of the father." Although it has been demonstrated that these beliefs are, for the most part, false, some people still harbour them. These beliefs sometimes live on within extended families and may create challenges for new parents. Thus, when parents receive the news of the disabling condition, they must question whether they hold these beliefs and attitudes themselves and learn to deal with their feelings of guilt and shame. The fact that some disabilities are linked to heredity or the parents' state of health at conception and during pregnancy can reinforce the sense of shame and guilt. Most societies expect that parents will love their children. When a child with special needs is born, the parent may experience negative emotions (e.g., rejection) and then experience guilt (Penzo, 2008).

A Period of Intense Emotions

Following the first stage of shock and denial, there is a period of intense emotions, including confusion, depression, loneliness, anxiety, and anger (Penzo, 2008). These emotions can be very strong and are often directed at a wide range of people (e.g., guilt can be directed at oneself; anger might be directed at the spouse, the doctor, or God). Parents often attempt to bargain with God or the doctor as their way of dealing with or denying the diagnosis. Parents may experience fear: fear of the unknown and fear for the future (McGill Smith, 2003). Fear may be especially intense when the diagnosis is lengthy or delayed. Parents may feel a sense of powerlessness, and their interaction with professionals is heightened.

These intense emotional responses can affect parents' well-being. The confusion resulting from the diagnosis may lead to sleep interruptions and additional stress. If parents are hearing words and terms they never heard before, they may find it difficult to make sense of and cope with the overload of information.

These intense emotional responses can also affect parents' ability to interact with the child. We know, for instance, that parents who are depressed will interact less with their children. In addition, the baby, due to his or her disability, may have a reduced ability to interact or to give parents positive feedback. Initial contact between baby and parents is sometimes limited because the baby is in an incubator, is attached to feeding tubes or other equipment, or simply does not respond well to cuddling. This lack of positive, rewarding interaction could hamper the bonding and attachment process. Moreover, if the baby is ill, parents sometimes restrain themselves from becoming attached, fearing that the baby may not live. Given the importance of bonding and attachment to the social development of all children, the effects of these initial reactions can be significant in the long term.

While early childhood educators need to be sensitive to the intensity and potential risks involved in these initial phases of the grieving process, it's just as important to note that most parents do manage to move beyond these stages (usually with a few setbacks) to adjustment and acceptance. However, families may not come to closure after a period of time but, rather, may move back and forth between periods of emotion and adaptation. For example, families often move back to strong emotions as new milestones are missed (e.g., first day of school, graduation).

Adaptation and Reorganization

When the intense feelings begin to subside, the stage of adaptation begins; during this period, the parents usually feel better able to care for the child. This leads to the last stage, reorganization and acceptance (Penzo, 2008; Turnbull & Turnbull, 1990), when the parents reach a positive, long-term acceptance of their child's condition. This stage is marked by the parents' attempts to find suitable services and to organize their lives with their child's disability in mind. Penzo (2008) and Seligman (1991) talk about this stage as one of realistic acceptance in which parents love their children despite their disabilities but would still prefer, if they could choose, that the child not be disabled.

Parents vary in the intensity and duration of their grief as well as the order in which they experience their reactions. The emotions experienced may intensify or change over time. At the beginning, many parents relentlessly seek a cure for their child's problem. When it becomes apparent that there is no such "miracle" solution, parents often try to provide their child with a series of educational opportunities—they will teach this child everything he or she needs to know. When parents stop shopping for a cure or if they begin to think teaching is of little value, they often feel that they've lost control over their child's life—that they're powerless, without a plan. In time, families usually reach a stage where they no longer hope for miracles or can make the problem go away, but feel they can help the child develop to the best of his or her ability.

Factors That Affect the Grief Cycle

The parents' adjustment may depend on a number of factors, such as how and when they learn about their child's disability, the presence or absence of support, the reaction from others, the severity of the child's needs, and often, the parents' religious and cultural beliefs.

Breaking the News

Adjustment may depend partly on when and how parents are told of the disability (McWilliam, 2010). The birth of a baby with a disability is often perceived as a "failure" for the parents and for the doctor as well (McWilliam, 2010). There seems to be an unwritten rule that if you do everything the doctor says, all will be well. When this is not the case, the medical profession is often at a loss. Sometimes medical professionals think they're helping by putting the new mother in a room by herself so that she can have extended visiting hours and time alone to deal with the situation. From the parents' point of view, though, this can lead to feelings of suspicion and isolation (Beattie, 2009).

SCENARIO

IGNORED AT THE HOSPITAL

A mother was in a private room with her newborn baby, who had been diagnosed as having Down syndrome. Due to concerns for their health, the mother and child stayed in hospital for four days. The mother reported that she was left pretty much to herself. She would wander the hallways and

continues ▶

▶ *continues*

go in and out of the nursery, where she frequently heard nurses exclaim, "What a cute baby. Isn't he adorable?" She realized that no one had commented on her own baby until she was leaving, when the receptionist took notice and told her how sweet her new baby was. This lack of interaction with medical professionals was so noticeable that it had a significant effect on this new mother.

As the preceding scenario makes clear, the attitudes of the doctors, nurses, and other professionals involved can provide the parents with hope, or they can be subtly discouraging.

Sensitive professionals can assess a parent's need for support and information, and although they can't (and shouldn't try to) diminish the parents' sorrow, they can facilitate the adjustment process.

Delayed Diagnosis

Children may be diagnosed with difficulties immediately after birth or a traumatic event (e.g., head injury), or the diagnosis may be delayed (Gallo, Angst, Knafl, Twomey, & Hadley, 2010). When the diagnosis is not immediate, the parent is usually the first to notice that something is wrong with the baby's development. Anxiety often increases as parents read more books about development; as they attempt to compare their child with others of the same age; and as they discuss development with their family doctor. When this stage continues for a lengthy period of time, parents often report a feeling of relief upon hearing the diagnosis (Gallo et al., 2010). They feel that their concerns have finally been heard and their suspicions confirmed. This sense of relief is usually short-lived, though, as the parents adjust to the reality of the situation and as the quest for more information and services begins in earnest.

Religious and Cultural Beliefs

Earlier, we suggested that some religious beliefs can reinforce a sense of guilt or blame or contribute to different notions of the disability. Sometimes, these cultural beliefs live on and can interfere with how the parents cope. However, many parents have attested to the critical role their religious beliefs have played in helping them accept their child. The following scenario is an example of how one parent's religious beliefs helped her adjust to the birth of a child with special needs.

SCENARIO

RELIGIOUS BELIEFS AS A FACTOR IN ACCEPTANCE

Ann was raised as a Christian and was devoted to her religion. Her third son was born with severe developmental delays and major health problems. He was in intensive care for three months before he was physically well enough to go home. Ann seemed to deal with her son's condition extremely well. She didn't appear shocked, deny the condition, exhibit anger, or blame others or herself. When questioned by the early intervention worker, Ann explained that in her religion, a child with a handicap was considered a gift. She believed that God had chosen her and her husband as special parents because he felt that they were able to cope with the child. Her beliefs helped her and her family make the transition directly to acceptance.

ONGOING ADJUSTMENT THROUGHOUT LIFE

As noted earlier, the grief cycle may repeat itself at different times in the child's life. Although parents may have apparently adjusted to their newborn child's special needs diagnosis, they may re-experience strong feelings of grief or crisis at transition times. These feelings may arise, for example, when the child reaches the age to begin school (Baxter & Read, 1999), or when other children become more independent and attend functions outside the home during their early school years. These transitions in development or family life cycles may either produce a mild reminder of their child's needs or launch the parents back into the emotional ups and downs of the grief cycle as they learn to cope with the difficulties and realities that each new stage will bring.

As the child grows older, the family once more realizes what a serious, long-term commitment they've made to daily care; they may have to renew their awareness of what social resources are available and the best ways to advocate for their child. Parents may be at a stage in their own lives when their friends are beginning to experience the freedom that comes with having older children; although the child with special needs may be the same age, he or she may not be able to cope without supervision or help. Again, the parents are likely to feel tied down and somehow restricted by their child's needs. Throughout the life cycle, parents are reminded of their child's disability, of their long-term commitment, and of the lack of support (e.g., respite care or babysitting) available to families with children like theirs.

Children with a chronic health condition typically adjust to the routines and medical regimes associated with the condition (e.g., diabetes). However, there may be changes associated with growth (e.g., puberty) or with increased independence (e.g., the child can now go to a friend's house or the mall unaccompanied). In addition, they may feel different and perhaps excluded from their peers, which can complicate the condition and the care that is needed. In other words, when the child feels different or excluded or needs special attention, peer relations may be affected.

SCENARIO

SHARING INFORMATION WITH OTHERS

A grade 1 teacher agreed to spend time with 6-year-old Aashi to assist her with monitoring her blood glucose prior to lunch and then help sort out which foods she should have from her packed lunch. As part of this routine, Aashi would check her blood glucose level. While Aashi stayed behind, her three closest friends went off to the lunchroom but were curious about why she had to stay with the teacher. One day, one of them saw Aashi with a needle. The three friends started to avoid Aashi, and when the teacher observed this, she mentioned it to Aashi's mother. Aashi's mother was adamant that the other children didn't need to know about Aashi's diabetes and likely wouldn't understand. When the teacher explained how it made her different and her friends thought there was something scary happening (that involved the teacher), the mother agreed to come in and provide an explanation with the teacher about what was happening. The three friends are now Aashi's strongest allies and supporters.

THE IMPACT ON FAMILIES

As we have seen, parents of young children with special needs are confronted with many stresses and strains at a time that is likely to be emotional for everyone involved. The birth of a child with special needs can change families dramatically. Stresses, both long and short term, can affect the entire family, in what has been referred to as the ripple effect (Turecki & Tonner, 2000) or the domino effect. We must be aware that families who have a child with special needs are likely to deal with more stress than most families on an ongoing basis (Berns, 2010; McDaniel & Tepperman, 2007). Consequently, these families are likely to be at greater risk for marital difficulties, and the mothers are more likely to be subject to depression (McWilliam, 2010). There is a disproportionately high number of children with special needs living with neglect and emotional, verbal, and physical abuse, and with a greater sense of disruption in family life (McWilliam, 2010). Stress is also related to the severity of disability and whether the responsibility (or blame) is placed on one particular family member (McGuire & Shanahan, 2010). Parenting children with disabilities is more complex and can often cause increased levels of stress in parents, which may cause difficulties in all interactions within the family (Berns, 2010; McDaniel & Tepperman, 2007).

However, while recognizing these stressors, research on families with children suggests that the experience of parenting a child with special needs isn't "as bad" as traditional disability research suggests (McDaniel & Tepperman, 2007). In the long term, the family has a generally positive experience, and successful coping with the disability is usually the case (Van Riper, 2007). Not surprisingly, this is significantly affected by the type and amount of available support (Van Riper, 2007).

Let us now examine how different aspects of the family might be affected by the presence of a child with special needs or behavioural challenges.

Parents

We have described the intense emotional responses that parents of children with special needs experience and how the bonding and attachment process may be affected. Parents may be impacted personally and in their role as parents. Parents may feel isolated and that they are totally alone in their journey. This feeling can be reinforced as parents search for services and supports for their child, only to find that few services exist for the needs of their child. Family members and friends may be unavailable to provide support to the parent or family for many reasons, and parents may find themselves in a position where they must find new sources of support.

Many parents talk about the difficulty associated with dealing with the reactions of other people.

SCENARIO

UNEXPECTED REACTIONS

A student shared this story with her classmates: "My son, Harper, is on the spectrum. He is now 8, but when he was young, we were still trying to figure out what he reacted to (both positively and negatively). We always wanted to stay active as a family, but this became difficult in public. My daughter, Tasha, had a school Halloween party when she was in grade 2. In a packed, loud gymnasium, Harper began to spin, quietly at first and then quite violently. He knocked into several children and, when we tried to make our exit, he got on the floor and began to bang his head. This was truly one of the first major incidents we had experienced, and we had no idea how to handle it. Everyone stopped and stared. You could just see and feel everyone in the room move away and then look at my husband and me as if to say 'do something,' not understanding we had no idea how. When Harper started to settle, we made a hasty exit, much to our daughter's chagrin as it was her celebration. This event sticks out in my mind because it was a turning point for us. The people that I associated with from the school no longer had time for us. My daughter's friends were no longer allowed to come to our house for play dates. Everyone seemed to think that Harper was out of control or a danger and that we were totally inadequate as parents. Little did they know that we were struggling and needed support, not exclusion from the people in our community. This changed our family as well—we no longer took him to Tasha's events, and we really questioned whether we wanted to take him out in public anymore."

Or, parents may feel that they don't have the time for social activities for themselves or their families due to the time required to provide care for their child. This leads to a sense of further isolation.

When the child has challenging behaviour, other factors may contribute to the parents' experiences. In North American culture, where mothers still carry the major responsibility for raising children, they are also most often blamed when things go wrong. When a child throws a tantrum at the supermarket checkout counter, most people still think, *Why can't that mother control her child in public?* Many mothers believe that they should be able to raise and parent their children well, and that they should love and like their children. So when children exhibit difficult behaviour, the mother is left questioning her abilities, her intentions, and her effectiveness. It's not uncommon for mothers to feel emotions such as guilt, isolation, depression, embarrassment, or denial. A mother may overprotect her child or become overinvolved as a means of ensuring that the child is successful.

Mothers often have difficulty interacting with the child consistently and effectively because they don't understand the child's behaviour and may inappropriately ascribe motives to it (e.g., "He's doing that to bug me," "My child hates me") (McGuire & Shanahan, 2010).

SCENARIO

MISINTERPRETING BEHAVIOUR

At a preschool picnic, Monica was trying to get her 2½-year-old son ready to leave. She had given several warnings that they were getting ready to go. When she finally called him to leave, he screamed and ran off in the other direction. She waited for several minutes, then called again. He looked at her and followed a group of children in the other direction. She called again and he screamed back "No!" The mother tried twice more before the educator approached. "See," she said to the educator, "he hates me."

Such failure to understand a child's behaviour may result in ineffective or inconsistent discipline. One day the mother may be restrictive; the next day she may be too tired to argue, and so will allow the child to run freely. She may then attempt to regain control by using harsher discipline techniques, which can make the behaviour worse. Punishment often seems to be immediately effective, which reinforces the parent's decision to use it; however, punishment is effective in the short term only because the child has not learned a better way to behave. This vicious cycle of control and behaviour leads to a lowering of self-esteem for both the child and the mother. Breaking out of this cycle can be a difficult process (McGuire & Shanahan, 2010).

In traditional families, the father may either present the solution for breaking out of the leniency/punishment cycle or contribute to its continuation. Dad may arrive home at the end of the day to provide Mom with a welcome respite and help re-establish her authority, or he may not understand why the child acts the way he or she does or why the mother reacts the way she does. His questioning of her actions may be interpreted as criticism or as a lack of confidence in her parenting techniques.

The father may be put unwillingly into the role of the disciplinarian or left out of the parenting process altogether because he doesn't agree with the mother. In the past decade, researchers noted that fathers of children with special needs are often estranged from the parent–child relationship (McDaniel & Tepperman, 2007). The mother may sense this lack of support or feel jealous because the father has a conflict-free relationship with the child. He, on the other hand, may feel that he's not permitted to be part of the parenting routine and may spend more time away from home to avoid further conflicts. This dynamic may be changing as fathers become more involved in the care of their young children. For example, a quick Internet search of "fathers of children with special needs" leads to story after story by dads of children with special needs.

Stress on Parents

So far, our discussion has focused on the traditional family. However, we can see the same stressful effects of a family member with special needs in all kinds of families. Families with two working parents, a single parent, or a noncustodial parent will experience additional stress associated with raising a child with special needs as well. These parents may also find themselves without any supports to provide them with a much-needed respite or to restore balance within the household.

It's important to understand that parents may show resistance or appear to be unwilling to listen to educators when they express concerns about their child, as the following scenario shows.

SCENARIO

COPING WITH THE STRESS OF INCLUSIVE TREATMENT

A resource team provided assessment and inclusive treatment for children and their families within the child-care centre. All parents were informed that a speech therapist and physiotherapist would be spending time in the playrooms at the beginning of the program year. (A few parents refused to sign the consent form for their child to be observed.) In mid-October, the resource team and educator would meet with parents as needed to provide them with strategies and plans for their child. The strategies and plans might involve speech therapy, additional physical activity to strengthen gross or fine motor skills, etc. These meetings were often very stressful for parents, some of whom did not want to hear matters raised about their child. The team leader remarked that for meetings where the resource team might not be enough, they arranged for someone who could support the parents, to be present.

Parents may spend time searching for answers or strategies to find a solution for the child's difficulties. Autism spectrum disorder (ASD) is complex and can present very differently in each child. Children often look completely "normal" but may act very differently. Parents have searched for and researched many different approaches to understanding and supporting their children's needs. Many parents of children with autism believe that this condition was caused by inoculations that their children were given. Although all scientific evidence points to the contrary, the belief is still widespread.

Parents who have a child with special needs may have diminished opportunities for social activities due to time constraints and may feel that they have lost their friends and supports. The result may be feelings of isolation and loneliness. In addition, parents may not have the time or energy to care for themselves (or other members of the family). Lack of self-care may lead to many other problems (e.g., illness, mental health concerns). Perhaps this is why the various support groups for families of children with special needs are seen as vitally important.

The Adult Relationship

The stresses involved in raising a child with special needs can put a great deal of strain on a relationship. A partner may feel left out of the relationship with the child and may even feel left out of the relationship as well, since the other parent may be too exhausted for intimacy. It's not uncommon for the parent who takes on most of the care and management of the child to direct some of her intense and negative feelings—anger, anxiety, or resentment—toward the less involved partner. This can result in even further withdrawal and decreasing his involvement in child care, and a vicious circle results in an even wider rift between the parents. If the rift grows wide enough, it may lead to a breakdown of the relationship. However, while separation and divorce continue to be disproportionately high in families with a child who has special needs, these outcomes are not always the case. In fact, some families report feelings of renewed closeness after the birth of a child with special needs (McGuire & Shanahan, 2010).

Siblings

Siblings may also be affected by the child with special needs (Kilmer, Cook, Taylor, Kane, & Clark, 2008). It may be that the siblings of children with special needs feel that they are favoured by their parents over their special needs siblings, while other siblings of children with special needs may feel that their special needs sibling is preferred. One or both parents may have less time for their other children and may place higher expectations on them. These expectations may be in the form of day-to-day responsibilities or in expectations that they will achieve goals that their sibling with special needs is not able to attain. Siblings may find it difficult to talk about the situation or even to gain clarification about the disability (Berns, 2004; Kilmer et al., 2008). The University of Michigan's medical school (Boyse, 2009) describes the often conflicting feelings that a sibling may feel at different times:

- worried about their sibling
- jealous of the attention their brother/sister receives
- scared that they will lose their sibling
- angry that no one pays attention to them
- resentful of having to explain, support, and/or take care of their brother/sister
- resentful that they are unable to do things or go places because of their sibling
- embarrassed about their sibling's differences
- pressure to be or do what their sibling cannot
- guilty for negative feelings they have toward their sibling or guilty for not having the same problems

Later in life, siblings report either that the experience was positive and that it made them more accepting, tolerant, and understanding or that the experience created feelings such as shame, guilt, resentment, and jealousy (Berns, 2010; Kilmer et al., 2008). This difference in feelings can be attributed to several factors, including the attitudes of the parents, supports available to all family members, religion, culture, family cohesiveness, and the severity of the disability.

SCENARIO

DOING CHORES

Two students in a disability studies class were comparing their siblings, both of whom had special needs. Nina explained that her severely mentally challenged sister was always treated as a member of the family. She had her own chores to do, which were well within her capabilities—she set and cleared the table, and she loaded and unloaded the dishwasher daily. Even though she had special needs, there were expectations for her, just as for anyone else in the family. June responded that her asthmatic brother was treated very differently. Since no one was sure when he would have an attack, he was never expected to help out around the house, and his sisters did all his chores for him. Their mom woke him, prepared his meals, and protected him from the other children. As June and Nina talked, their lasting impressions of how their siblings affected them and their families became very clear. While Nina was quite accepting of her sister, June was resentful of her brother's needs and of the effect they had on her.

Siblings may also be affected by the presence of the child who is difficult to manage or who requires a lot of parental time and attention. Either or both parents may thus have less time to spend with the siblings, who may come to resent the difficult child, resulting in jealousy or competition. Siblings could decide that the only way to get attention is to be perfect or to get into trouble. These reactions can, of course, lead to further difficulties within the family.

Taylor, Age 5

Chapter 3 contained a brief overview of the family systems model, which emphasized the interconnection between members of the family system. Examples like those described above illustrate the domino or ripple effect, whereby one source of stress ends up affecting the entire family. The child with special needs presents a situation that entails different tasks, responsibilities, and emotions for each family member. The emotions felt by the primary caregiver in learning to cope may affect the interactions with the child with special needs, with the spouse, and eventually with other children in the family. Sometimes the ripple effects are even felt beyond the nuclear family, reaching the extended family and friendship networks as well (Turecki & Tonner, 2000). Again, however, despite the greater degree of stress associated with parenting an exceptional child, research suggests that many parents today show resilience in adjusting to the presence of a child with special needs in their family (Gerstein, 2009).

CHALLENGES FOR FAMILIES WHO HAVE A CHILD WITH SPECIAL NEEDS

As noted earlier, in addition to coping with their own grief and with the stressors within the family unit, families who have a child with special needs often encounter difficulties in their interactions with "the outside world." These difficulties usually relate to common prejudices in our society about people with special needs. Sometimes parents are faced with negative and insensitive beliefs about people who have disabilities from other parents and from professionals (as the following scenario shows). Parents report that other parents can be judgmental or pitying, or consider them as special parents with amazing qualities. As well, parents note that certain language (e.g., sexist or homophobic) may not be tolerated in society, but many people will use terms such as "retard" or "spaz" to refer to their children. Parents face many barriers, and the barriers from other parents and society in general can provide many additional challenges to families (Moorhead, 2013a). Educators may be in a position to support families and provide information to other families in the program so that parents who have a child with special needs feel supported.

SCENARIO

IGNORANT REMARKS

The parents of Donny, a 5-year-old boy with severe mental and physical challenges, worked closely with the child-care staff in an attempt to get Donny ready for school. Since he was noticeably cross-eyed, staff recommended that the parents have his eyes examined. Donny's parents made an appointment with an optometrist, but returned from it absolutely devastated. The optometrist had matter-of-factly declared that since correcting Donny's eyes would make no difference to "his condition," why would they want to spend the money?

Incidents such as these reflect a fairly widespread attitude, one that parents of children with special needs come up against all too often. In some cases, the negative attitudes may be less blatant, but parents still find themselves interacting with people who have very unclear expectations about the potential of children with disabilities.

These negative attitudes are usually based on ignorance, and the ignorance is usually a result of the fact that many people have limited interactions with those who have special needs. Therefore, they don't know what to expect or what potential a particular child may have in the future.

SCENARIO

LACK OF INFORMATION AMONG MEDICAL STAFF

A woman described an experience she had as a new mother, 20 years ago. She had just given birth in a hospital to a baby with Down syndrome. First, the obstetrician came to deliver the news. This visit was followed by one from the family doctor and a pediatrician, both of whom described the child as someone who would grow physically to a normal size but would always have the mind of a 2-year-old.

Although this scenario occurred 20 years ago, this kind of ignorance can still be seen today. In fact, researchers have noted that parents continue to express dissatisfaction with how medical staff communicate with them (Carbone, Behl, Azor, & Murphy, 2010). The kind of conversation illustrated above could be extremely frightening for parents who have had little contact with people who have special needs. Furthermore, it's often very difficult to ascertain at an early stage what the full potential of any child will be, and many children with Down syndrome attain a fairly high level of competence. Although professionals should not be unrealistically optimistic, nor should they err on the side of pessimism.

Interaction with Professionals

One of the most stressful factors reported by the majority of parents of children with special needs is the necessity for increased interaction with professionals (McWilliam, 2010). Parents who have had little contact with professionals may suddenly be required to deal with doctors, nurses, dietitians, physiotherapists, speech therapists, psychologists, and social workers. What makes these interactions so difficult is that the parent usually has a strong emotional reaction, while the professional normally does not. Parents may feel isolated and overwhelmed and not know where or how to begin their search for supports (Brown, Goodman, & Kupper, 2003).

Many parents interacting with medical professionals have reported that they feel a loss of control over their child's life and treatment (McWilliam, 2010) and that they feel disempowered by their constant struggle. Parents may attempt to challenge a professional's authority, but this is a difficult task indeed. Parents and professionals, especially medical professionals, often operate at different status levels, which in itself commonly makes interaction and communication difficult. Parents may not understand the terminology or jargon or may receive conflicting messages from different professionals. And since each professional typically focuses primarily on a particular aspect of the child's development (e.g., the physiotherapist is concerned with physical abilities, the speech therapist with speech development), the "whole child" may sometimes be forgotten. Consequently, parents may be required to learn a new set of skills so that they can better obtain information and act as advocates on behalf of their child. Parents have come to rely on the Internet to increase their understanding of the condition and to find alternate treatments. Unfortunately, there is a lot of information available that may be questionable due to lack of evidence. However, they offer hope to parents in their time of need. This may result in conflict between the parent and medical professional who do not sanction certain practices. Parents may rightly believe that it's their role to advocate on behalf of their child, but this sometimes creates problematic situations with professional staff.

SCENARIO

CONFLICTING ADVICE FROM PROFESSIONALS

Jan was the mother of Kaitlin, a 2-year-old girl with cerebral palsy who attended a hospital-based early intervention program. The program included a speech therapist, a physiotherapist, and a social worker, all of whom provided Jan with guidance and direction. The physiotherapist explained the absolute necessity of changing Kaitlin's position regularly and completing daily range-of-motion exercises. The speech therapist explained that Kaitlin was at the developmental stage when hearing speech and having many opportunities to communicate with her mother would be crucial to her development of language skills. The social worker closed by explaining that it was important for Jan to plan time off from her caretaking duties, and that she shouldn't become overinvolved in Kaitlin's care. Needless to say, Jan felt a little confused by the end of the session, as she couldn't possibly do all that was required of her and also take time off for herself!

This sort of confusion can be further complicated by the rapid turnover of professionals that sometimes occurs. One social worker may be replaced by another as the child grows older, or other professionals may be transferred or promoted. With each new professional the parents often feel that they have to "start all over again," building the relationship, explaining the history, and sometimes being confused by conflicting messages of the past and current professional. This represents another challenge for the parents and the child, and these continual changes can be extremely stressful.

Interaction with professionals often involves interaction with social agencies that provide specific care and assistance to children with special needs. Unlike universally accessible systems for normally developing children (e.g., playschool or the public school system), a range of services are available for exceptional children, each with its own criteria for admittance and subsequent service. These criteria may be based on age, developmental level, severity of the disability, type of disability, proof of disability, and income. If parents wish to gain access to these services, they must acquaint themselves with what is available and with each service's particular set of rules. Whenever parents request something a little different for their child, such as inclusion in the neighbourhood school, their communication and advocacy skills are truly tested.

Professionals should try to provide support based on the needs and desires of each individual family. They should also try to remember that families with children who have special needs also have many other interests and concerns and complex lives. For this reason, it's important to treat the family as a unit rather than singling out or focusing exclusively on the child with special needs (McWilliam, 2010).

» Perspectives

Jody is now a single parent of two boys: 12-year-old Ryan and 13-year-old Xenon. She works as a full-time college instructor.

Jody and her former husband, John, adopted Xenon, who, at 3 weeks old, had major heart surgery to correct a congenital heart defect. At that time, the doctor told them that children with this condition may develop on "both sides of normal," but that Xenon's progress was excellent thus far. In addition to the surgery, Xenon was on Phenobarb for a period of time to control seizures, and had serious respiratory problems, with the possibility of cystic fibrosis. The list of medical conditions seemed to go on forever: auditory discrimination problems, memory problems, visual motor problems, mild myopia, poor tooth enamel, bowel and bladder problems, and asthma. If you were to meet Xenon, you would think he looks just like everyone else, but when all these "little" problems are added together, he has definite special needs. The frustrating part is that each problem is treated by a different doctor, specialist, or teacher, who doesn't know or think about the other problems. So one medication will treat one set of symptoms but cause an unpleasant interaction with another medication or affect Xenon's behaviour in some way that causes difficulties at school or in learning.

"As a parent, I always feel that I walk a fine line in what to tell to whom. On the one hand, I don't want Xenon singled out as the child with special needs, but I also don't want him to be labelled as lazy or having a bad attitude because people don't understand that, given his medical problems, his performance can't always be optimal.

"Xenon always has been, and still is, in a regular school with supports. So far, the schools and teachers have been great in meeting his particular needs, but sometimes they don't realize the impact that some of their statements, although likely quite innocent, have on Xenon or me. For example, one teacher explained to me that completing a certain assignment should be easy because 'even Xenon can do it.' I think I know what she meant, but Xenon was devastated by her comments and so was I, knowing how hard he tries to get things done. On one occasion, when Xenon was left behind on a class outing due to health concerns, he thought he wasn't allowed to go because he'd been bad. It took a lot of convincing by me and the teacher to reassure him that this wasn't true.

"Maybe my experiences have made me a little oversensitive, or maybe, because I know Xenon—a kind, gentle, caring, whole person—I'm a little more sensitive about what people say. Anyway, I hope that all the professionals and specialists who come into contact with Xenon see him for the person he is, not today's problem or symptom."

Unrealistic Expectations Placed on Parents

Over the past three decades, professionals have made great strides in the treatment and education of children with special needs. They have learned through research and practice that intervention initiated in the early years is most effective in treating the disability as well as in preventing secondary problems that may result from the disability.

In addition, a number of earlier research studies led to the belief that the parent should be the child's primary teacher, and this became the cornerstone in many early intervention programs (Katz, 1980). Many intervention models were developed in which the professional would "teach" the parents to carry out a wide range of exercises and individualized programs with their child. Sometimes this put tremendous strain on families. Parents were instructed to teach their child at every possible moment, to have a wide assortment of professionals into their homes, and to always have the best interest of the child in mind. With such expectations placed on parents, some began to wonder when they would be able to relax and "just be a parent." When would they have time to cuddle and spoil their baby rather than always being the teacher and therapist? These expectations put additional pressures on the families of children with special needs. On top of all the other emotional stresses, the expectation that parents be available for constant teaching may have placed excessive demands on them. Although this type of approach occurred in the 1980s, it has persisted as professionals, for a variety of reasons, believe that parents must be involved. In the past 30 years, however, things have changed, and now a more inclusive model, in which communities, educators, and families work together to support children with special needs, is largely the norm (Bruder, 2010).

Work and Parenting Children with Special Needs

Many parents face challenges trying to maintain employment and family responsibilities. When the family includes a child with special needs, there may be additional challenges in terms of extra expenses, changes in employment income, and stresses due to inadequate child care and supports in the community and workplace (Bruder, 2010). Sometimes the demands of the special need may vary, for example, doctor visits in the middle of the day or extended hospital visits.

Researchers (Hope Irwin & Lero, 2004) in one report found that a significant number of parents were unemployed, underemployed, or worked fewer hours to meet the demands of their child with special needs. This finding was confirmed in a more recent American report, which reported that 30% of parents of children with special needs either quit or significantly cut back on their employment, which results in financial hardship (Turrell, 2014). Typically, mothers' employment was affected. Unsurprisingly, these families felt that they experienced economic strains (e.g., extra expenses and loss of income in addition to increased stress). As well, 88% of parents said they felt tired and overloaded, and 90% said they were stressed about balancing work and family obligations. A major cause of stress was the lack of access to appropriate, affordable, licensed child care, along with workplace and social supports.

SUPPORTING FAMILIES WITH A CHILD WITH SPECIAL NEEDS

The presence of a supportive family will undoubtedly be a major influence in the life of the child with special needs. The child may require additional support from his or her family in daily routines and in developing new abilities. In addition, the child with special needs may be ridiculed and teased by other children in school and on the playground. A strong family unit provides the child with a solid foundation to face present and future challenges.

The educator plays a key role in helping the family recognize that the child may have special needs, suggesting the appropriate resources for assessment and support, and providing ongoing support to the family.

An early learning program may be the first place the child engages with others beyond the family. This engagement may occur at infancy or a very young age. Accordingly, the educator may be the first person to observe differences in the child's development. Through their studies of child development and their experience with groups of children in the early years, educators are often in a position to recognize a developmental or behavioural problem (McWilliam, 2010). Although this early identification is important, it can put educators in a precarious situation with parents, and so it may be helpful for educators to have professionals (e.g., speech therapists, occupational therapists) who can support their observations.

For children with health conditions, educators may work alongside parents to better understand the child's condition (e.g., routines, how medication affects the child, the need for exercise). As educators spend many hours and routines with children, they too will make observations about the child or condition and then may share their perspectives with the family. In doing so, educators and parents may come to realize that they want to learn more.

The second role is to offer support to family members as they come to cope with the new reality in their lives. Early childhood educators can help such families in their continual struggle to maximize opportunities for their child with special needs. By attempting to understand and empathize with what families may be experiencing and feeling, early childhood educators may be better able to provide these families with support. For families who are stressed, this show of support and empathy may be what the family needs to carry on.

Changing times have altered the role of early childhood educators who work with parents of children with special needs. Professionals generally believed for many years that problems could be eliminated by direct and early intervention with the child (Gallagher, 1993). Thus, they thought that working with the child in a certain program would be sufficient to deal with that child's special needs. More recently, it has become evident that families need to be considered as a unit, and that early childhood educators may play a valuable role in facilitating families' strength and in developing their support networks (Bruder, 2010; McWilliam, 2010). Family-focused programs serve to ensure that the child with the disability is not seen in isolation but as part of the family, which helps strengthen the entire family (Bruder, 2010). Family-centered practice or strengthening families approaches embody this perspective. When early childhood educators are sensitive to a family's particular needs and provide appropriate support, the family develops a sense of control and empowerment over its world (Bruder, 2010) which benefits the child and the family.

>> Examine Your Attitudes

Negative attitudes—fear, prejudice, dislike—often influence people's reactions to the parents and siblings of children with special needs. After you ask yourself each of the following questions, consider it again for a person with one of the following challenges: cognitive, physical, visual, hearing, and mental health.

- Do you think people with special needs can't learn, or do they learn in different ways and at different rates than other people?

- Do you believe that people with special needs contribute to society, or are they unproductive members who sap medical and financial resources while contributing nothing themselves?

- Should people with special needs be educated together in special classrooms, or is it better to "mainstream" them?

- Is it true that parents are always directly responsible for their children's behaviour? Is bad behaviour the result of parents' failure to discipline their children?

- Have you found that parents of children with special needs are reluctant to work with professionals? If so, have you discovered a reason for this reluctance?

- Would you work with a staff person who had special needs in your child-care centre? Would you expect as much from him or her as from the other staff members?

- What do you believe is your scope of practice related to health conditions? What types of procedures would you be willing to do or learn about?

Now that you have examined your attitudes, consider your image of the child with special needs. Perhaps, in the course of your studies, you have considered your image of the child. Is your image of the child with special needs the same? Different? In a recent second-year early learning course, a professor asked students to write about their image of the child with special needs. Their written work included the same words and overtones that they had for all children. However, as over the course of the term and many discussions, it became clear that their image was quite different—these children needed "help" and were challenging. Their image of the family was impacted by children's needs as well. Parents of children with special needs were considered demanding, unreasonable, or as asking for way too much from educators. While in some cases this description may be accurate, it would not be fair to make this generalization. It's important to ask ourselves how the image of children with special needs can be as close to the image we hold for other children. What needs to happen in the setting? What attitudes and notions need to be addressed? The same can be asked of the educator's image of the family.

Identifying Special Needs

When the early childhood educator suspects that a particular child may have special needs, the most difficult task will be in sharing this information with the parents (McWilliam, 2010). Many staff members feel anxious about facing parents in this situation.

Early childhood educators may first want to collect documentation rather than making their suspicions known to parents with little supporting information. It may be helpful to ask a colleague to observe the child to see if he or she reaches the same conclusion. When bringing up the concerns with the parents, discussing the observations clearly and honestly, face to face, is often a better approach than discussing them over the telephone or using jargon that parents may not understand (McWilliam, 2010). Talking to parents can often be easier when information is shared; therefore, early childhood educators should be prepared to share ideas and resources. For instance, they can help parents decide what the next step will be, or they can provide a list of potential services to consider. Bearing in mind the stages of shock, denial, and intense feelings discussed earlier in the chapter, early childhood educators should also expect the parents to react intensely, sometimes with anger and vociferous denials, and be prepared to deal with such emotions (McWilliam, 2010). Sometimes, a parent will actually be relieved to have this conversation, as they suspected that their child was "different" but did not really know what to do about it.

SCENARIO

BREAKING BAD NEWS TO PARENTS

Martha, a fairly new early childhood educator, had decided to conduct focused observations on one of the children in the group because he seemed to display a range of difficulties in play and had more outbursts of withdrawal and crying than was normal for that age group. After several days of observations, she thought that there was a chance that the child had fetal alcohol spectrum disorder (FASD), which could explain the behaviour, emotional, learning, and attention problems that she saw. Martha was quite distressed and consulted with her supervisor, saying, "How can I tell the parents that I think their child might have FASD? How can I give that message without blaming the mother? I have no idea how to handle this." Her supervisor made it very clear that it's beyond the role of the educator to provide a diagnosis, and it would be highly inappropriate to do that. However, she definitely should share with the parent her observations about the child's behaviour and her concern that the child be assessed by a qualified professional, and assure the parents of her support through that process. The supervisor also suggested that she could meet with the parents if Martha didn't feel confident, or she could accompany Martha to the meeting. Martha decided that she could handle the meeting on her own and reported back to her supervisor. She told her that she found out that the parents were actually adoptive parents, which she hadn't known, and that they were sad but not surprised at the concerns, and that they actually suspected that the child may have FASD.

Providing Ongoing Support

Once the diagnosis has been made and the reality of the special needs or behavioural concern is evident, parents may require support on an ongoing basis. Early childhood educators may assist parents in many ways. First, they can share information regularly. This means not just describing what the child is doing, but also asking parents to share their own information, since they play an important role in creating a positive learning environment (Crowther, 2006). Parents know the child from a different perspective, one that early childhood educators rarely get to see. Make sure that, along with the not-so-pleasant details, parents hear positive things about their child. In the busy activity of the day, it's easy to overlook the positive aspects of the child's development and remember only the difficulties presented. Parents need to hear about both, and if they are having difficulty coping, it may be beneficial for them to hear more positive than negative statements. Sharing documentation with parents may be one way to let the parent know that the child is included in activities and routines in the playroom.

Interpreting Information

The early childhood educator may also play a role in helping parents interpret information. For instance, parents may be unable to ask the specialist or therapist for an explanation of terms because these professionals are too busy or because the parents feel awkward admitting that they don't understand the terminology. In this case, providing information in understandable terms and in relation to this particular child may be of real benefit to the family. And even if the educator is unable to interpret the information, he or she can still play a valuable role in helping parents obtain information that's more readily understood (e.g., by giving them reading material, or finding a credible website or the number of another professional to call). This may be the first step in helping the family to build a support network.

SCENARIO

DIFFICULT TERMINOLOGY

Tony's mother was invited to a case conference with the speech therapist, physiotherapist, grade 1 teacher, and psychologist. She asked if Tony's educator from the child-care centre would come along because she felt intimidated by all these people. The conference began with each professional providing the most recent assessment results. The speech therapist talked about Tony's "inability to form fricatives and his lack of occlusion." The physiotherapist described his "poor motor control in the prone and supine position and total lack of balance and coordination." At this point, the mother left the room in tears. When the educator found her in the bathroom, she said she understood two things very clearly. First, her son wasn't capable of doing anything. Second, she was too stupid to understand what it was exactly that he couldn't do.

Educators may support the family by providing or interpreting information whenever possible. They may also escort the parents to meetings and help them listen and ask appropriate questions. Or they may simply listen to the parents and act as a sounding board as they determine their course of action. When early childhood educators establish a good working relationship with parents, the particular course of action can be worked out together.

Customizing Resources

There are numerous support groups and other resources on the Internet for parents, other family members, and early childhood educators, some of which are listed in the Recommended Websites at the end of this chapter. Educators need to be sure that the resources and support provided is credible and does not endorse a particular method (e.g., which may require fees). Today there is such an abundance of information available on the Internet—information for fathers, mothers, and siblings. However, this abundance can make it difficult to find the appropriate and relevant information. Sometimes it can be so helpful to say something like "Just by chance, I came across a very informative website that deals with helping siblings adjust to the special needs of their brother or sister."

Sharing Coping Strategies

Early childhood educators can also play a role in making parents aware of ways to deal with difficult behaviour. Role-modelling effective strategies may be beneficial to parents. For example, the early childhood educator may help by intervening in and breaking the cycle of negative reactions with a temperamentally difficult child simply by giving the child time to settle down when the child and parent are embroiled in a conflict. Educators need to be cautious when they report their own "successes" with the child, since the parent may interpret this to mean that he or she is a failure in parenting. Educators may provide resources related to parental support or suggest "computer-mediated support groups" as a way to share coping strategies (Bragadóttir, 2008).

SCENARIO

ESTABLISHING NEW ROUTINES

An educator observed that when Shane arrived in the morning, his mother was usually in a rush. She would carry him in and help him remove his jacket, and then he would cry and cling. She would react with harsh words, and he would cling more. Whenever the early childhood educator attempted to intervene, both the mother and Shane would get upset. Finally, the educator realized that she needed to intercept the situation before it occurred. So the next morning she arranged with the other staff in the playroom that she would wait for Shane at the door. The moment Shane and his mother walked in, she greeted the two by saying, "Good morning! I know your mommy is in a hurry. I'll take you from here, so let's give her a big hug and kiss goodbye and say, 'Have a good day at work, Mom!'" There were hugs, kisses, and a cheery goodbye. The next day, the same procedure was repeated. By the third day, a new morning routine was in place.

Sharing Information

Sharing information about the problems typical of children who are difficult or have special needs may be the first step in helping families cope. Often, it's not necessary for the child's behaviour to change; rather, everyone involved learns to deal with the behaviour. For example, if the child does not cope well when tired, every effort can be made to begin bedtime routines long before tiredness sets in. The child who does not adapt well to new settings may require more time and patience on the part of the parent and educator and will also appreciate warnings that activities are about to change. Changes in the parents' reactions may thus serve as a catalyst for the child's behaviour to improve. Parents may need to understand that it may be the child's temperament that leads to certain behaviours, not the disability. When parents can understand this, they may begin to see their child beyond the disability.

Respecting the Family's Needs

Early childhood educators must remember that each family they deal with has a life extending beyond the child with special needs or difficult behaviour.

So much of the family's time and effort will be expended in caring for the child that other needs and perspectives may be neglected. Educators can easily fall into this trap themselves by urging parents to try a new idea or carry out a program at home.

If early childhood educators consider the entire family unit, they may be able to support the family in such a way as to benefit them as a whole. For example, providing information about accessible activities in the community may give the whole family the chance to do something together. This may also help each family member feel as if they are part of a "normal" family and give them a chance to relax and enjoy recreational activities together. Or educators may provide support for the child with special needs to attend family events to ensure all family members feel included. Families often feel that all activities revolve around the child with special needs, providing alternatives may be beneficial.

Providing Emotional Support

Early childhood educators may also play a role in providing families with emotional support. Families will experience many different emotions and cope in many different ways. The educator may be able to provide different perspectives, approaches, or resources for families to consider. Sometimes parents simply need to have their feelings validated or be given permission to feel angry or disappointed. Providing emotional support requires understanding that each family will respond to circumstances in a unique way and will have different strengths and different needs.

Helping Families Access Resources

Parents of children who are difficult or who have special needs often benefit from support groups that consist of parents in similar circumstances (McGuire & Shanahan, 2010). Educators can play a fundamental role by offering leadership, support, and practical assistance. In this way, parents can share their fears and experiences and offer each other support and encouragement. They may need reassurance about parenting decisions they make or require specialized information and advocacy skills. These specialized needs can often be met effectively by other parents of children with special needs (McGuire & Shanahan, 2010).

SCENARIO

THE USEFULNESS OF SUPPORT GROUPS

A mother with a successful professional career had adopted two young children. The older child was 2 when the second baby arrived. It soon became apparent that the second child had severe special needs. The mother experienced a range of emotions, but felt that, since she was highly trained and skilled, she should be able to cope. When the child was 2, the child-care staff told the mother about a meeting whose topic of discussion was diet and nutrition for preschool children. Understanding her reluctance to seek support, the staff didn't emphasize that the presentation was for parents of children with special needs, nor did they coerce her into attending. The mother decided to go because her daughter experienced extreme feeding difficulties. After the meeting, she met other parents who had children with similar disabilities. They shared hopes, disappointments, and practical ideas. This was the first time this mother had been involved with other parents in similar situations, and she found it to be truly beneficial.

However, support groups may not be a good alternative for all parents. For example, a mother with a severely mentally and physically disabled baby was encouraged to join a local Moms and Tots program that met one morning a week. When she decided to attend, she was depressed to see how advanced the other babies were. The experience had been so depressing, she said, that she never returned and would never join another parent group.

Parents are probably the best judges of how appropriate a support group may be for them. Early childhood educators can provide parents with information about support groups, and then leave the decision about whether to participate up to them.

Working Alongside Parents

Many parents are new to the world of disabilities. Some may feel awkward sharing information and be unsure of their role in the child-care program.

SCENARIO

EDUCATION OF SPECIAL NEEDS

Sharleen was a child amputee and was enrolled in her local kindergarten when she was 5 years old. Her mother was adamant that she wanted Sharleen to be just like the other children and would not offer "excuses" for her daughter. The teacher saw that the children were quite curious about Sharleen, but she felt helpless to provide information since she had not been given an explanation or permission to share information by the family. She accessed information on amputees and attempted to provide learning about physical disabilities within the classroom by adding special supports in the housekeeping centre (e.g., glasses, an old hearing aid) so that children could begin to understand what a disability could be. Sharleen's mom was horrified by the focus on disabilities at first, but when the teacher explained that the children were curious and wanted to understand, she agreed to come in and share information about Sharleen. The mom brought several of Sharleen's old prosthetic legs and permitted the children to touch them. She also told the children that Sharleen was just like them. She was surprised at how interested the children were, and once their questions were answered, Sharleen indeed became just one of the children.

Educators will need to develop a strong relationship with parents to understand how the parent is coping. Family members may not understand the context of group care for children and may be able to work alongside families to support the child's needs in a positive and supportive manner.

Providing Advocacy and Education

The ecological approach (see Chapter 3) reminds us that for a child with special needs to develop optimally, factors beyond the child and the immediate family must be considered. These factors include attitudes in our society toward people with special needs, legislation that protects the rights of people with special needs, and the kinds of support services available to children and families. Research demonstrates that early childhood educators are critical in providing inclusive learning opportunities that promote development (Crowther, 2006).

Early childhood educators may find it necessary to teach others about children with special needs. This can happen in a number of ways. It may involve demonstrating to other children how to interact or play with the child who has special needs, and more broadly, establishing norms of acceptance and equity for all children within early childhood programs. As an extension, educators may find themselves in the role of educating other parents in the program who are unfamiliar with the child's special needs. Early childhood educators may also play a role in helping parents become effective advocates, or they may engage in direct advocacy themselves, which could include writing letters, making presentations, and providing information. Early childhood educators can assist by providing leadership and supporting autonomy. Educators need to consider how to empower parents, what supports may be useful, and how parents can help themselves and each other. Through advocacy and education, early childhood educators can contribute to the well-being of children with special needs by promoting their acceptance and inclusion in all aspects of society.

CONCLUSION

Early childhood educators need to be aware that although parents may be experiencing their unique emotions and grief even many years after the diagnosis, most parents' love for and commitment to their children help them overcome many obstacles. Extra understanding and appreciation of their struggles is always warranted.

Although the strategies for working with parents discussed in the final portion of this book will be just as relevant for these families, early childhood educators may have to search for resources, services, and information suitable to a particular child's and family's needs. It's important to remember that the child with special needs or behavioural concerns is part of a family and to consider and support that family whenever possible.

Chapter Summary

- ■ Working with families that have a child who is difficult to raise, has a particular disability, or has chronic health problems will pose particular challenges for early childhood educators.

- ■ Parents may experience a range of emotions when a child with special needs is born. Professionals need to understand their reactions and support families.

- ■ There is growing understanding of the impact on siblings when a child in the family has special needs.

- ■ All family members may be affected in some way. When early childhood educators use interaction and helping strategies, they need to take all family members into consideration.

RESOURCES

The Offord Centre for Child Studies Centre of Knowledge on Healthy Child Development:
https://offordcentre.com/research/knowledge/

SpeciaLink: The National Centre for Child Care Inclusion:
www.specialinkcanada.org

National Association for the Education of Young Children, *Including Children with Special Needs* (includes a "Preschool and Kindergarten Inclusion Readiness Checklist"):
www.naeyc.org/files/yc/file/200903/BTJWatson.pdf

Michigan Medicine, "Siblings of Kids with Special Needs" (includes resources related to siblings):
www.med.umich.edu/yourchild/topics/specneed.htm

National Responsible Fatherhood Clearinghouse, "Dads of Children with Special Needs" :
www.fatherhood.gov/toolkit/work/special-needs

EXERCISES

1. Review the following case study, and discuss how you would present your information and concerns to the parent involved. Role-play this situation with a partner who can respond as a parent might. Have one person observe the role-playing to provide feedback about your role.

> ## CASE STUDY
>
> Rhanda came to your centre at the age of 3 months. She was a very easygoing child who demanded little attention. As she grew older, she was quite content amusing herself with toys and activity centres and with watching the other children play. You noticed that she was usually the last child in the playgroup to achieve milestones, such as rolling over or sitting up, but she still did progress. Over time, more things became noticeable. At 16 months, she was just beginning to walk, relying far more on crawling. She seemed to be quieter and not playing with sounds and words as much as she used to. Sometimes, it seemed as if she didn't hear people calling her or was oblivious to noises in the room.

2. Check your community centres and local government offices to determine what types of resources exist for children with special needs and their families. Determine whether these resources are run by parents or by professionals (since parents may want a parent support group rather than adding more professionals to their list). Check to make sure that all the resources can provide support to children with special needs (e.g., a local Big Brother program might not accept children with special needs; a support group for difficult teens might not deal with children labelled as having behavioural problems). Keep your list updated so that you'll be prepared if a parent requests information.

3. Role-play the following situations or discuss them with a classmate or colleague. It might be helpful to write out a list of possible responses beforehand.
   a) You want to discuss a child's development with her parents because you believe that the child isn't progressing as are the other children in your group.
   b) A parent arrives after a case conference at the hospital and yells at you for not providing adequate information to her and adequate programming for her child.
   c) A physiotherapist has just asked you to develop and implement a program with one of the children in your care that will take "only" 45 minutes three times a day. The parent can't understand why this would be a problem.
   d) A parent wants major changes to her child's routine (e.g., eating more frequently or at set times, different napping schedules, no outdoor activity). The parent reminds you that she is paying for you to care for her child.

4. You have just found out that, owing to funding cutbacks, support services for the integration of children with special needs in schools have been eliminated. Write a letter to the editor of the local newspaper explaining how these cuts may affect children and their families.

5. Choose two of the perspectives for understanding families from Chapter 3 (e.g., family systems theory, ecological theory, theories of loss) and describe how these theories help in understanding the challenges and needs of families who have a child with special needs.

CHAPTER 17

Parents with Special Needs

OBJECTIVES

- To gain an understanding of the effects on children when parents have special needs due to chronic health conditions, addictions, or mental health issues.

- To understand the impact of chronic health conditions, addictions, and mental health issues on family well-being.

- To understand the role of the educator in supporting children whose parents have special needs.

- To understand the role of the educator in supporting families.

One day, as Maria, the educator, greeted Adele and her mom when they arrived in the child-care centre, she noticed that Adele looked as if she had just woken up and had been crying. Her mother appeared to be very distressed. She handed Adele over and left without saying a word, something that had happened regularly over the last few months. Maria had tried on more than one occasion to gently inquire whether she was okay, but Adele's mom didn't seem to want to share any information. Adele didn't show any signs of stress and seemed fine after she settled in to the morning routine. At the end of the day, Maria shared her concerns with the director, who talked to Adele's mother the next day. The director reported back that Adele's mother had gone through a long diagnosis process and was now starting treatment. This information helped explain what had been happening, and now Maria could try to support Adele and her mom.

SUPPORTING PARENTS FACING CHALLENGES

It's well known that parents play a major role in the development of their children. Parents' personal histories, including how they themselves were parented and their patterns of attachment, will influence how they parent their children. Moreover, a parent's current psychological functioning can influence his or her children's development. For example, if a parent is stressed (e.g., going through the experience of a divorce), his or her parenting will likely reflect this.

Today, Canadian families are experiencing increasing levels of stress. Approximately 23% of Canadians indicate that most days are stressful. Perceptions of stress peak for people between the ages of 35 and 44 and are generally higher for women (Vanier Institute of the Family, 2010). In addition, many Canadians are feeling overwhelmed by the demands of paid and unpaid work. If this is true for the average Canadian parent, imagine the extra struggles a family might have when a parent is afflicted with a chronic health condition, an addiction, or a mental health concern. Such conditions increase the level of stress families have to deal with, and the level of stress families have to deal with can often lead or contribute to poor physical and/or mental health. Many parents with whom early childhood educators interact may be experiencing high levels of stress, which in turn can lead to health concerns (e.g., high blood pressure, heart disease) and, in some cases, to the use of drugs or alcohol to help cope.

It's sometimes difficult for early childhood educators to know how and when to support families when parents have physical or mental health challenges. Part of the reason for this is that parents are often reluctant to share their situation with educators because of the stigma attached to chronic conditions, particularly those related to mental health. Moreover, when the problem is related to an addiction, the stigma is often worse.

This chapter will explore how chronic health conditions, addiction issues, and mental health concerns experienced by parents may affect the child and the family. Although these conditions are quite distinct in their manifestations, they can all negatively affect the consistency of care and the stability of routines in the home, and thereby be detrimental to a child's healthy development. For this reason, it's vital for educators to gain an understanding of these conditions to be more effective in supporting both the child and the family.

It's important to emphasize that it's beyond the scope of the profession of early childhood education to diagnose or label parents, or to provide therapeutic counselling. However, by understanding what may be happening in the life of the child at home, educators will be better able to determine how they can support both the child and the parents. As with all aspects of the professional relationship between educators and families, the basis of a respectful relationship requires an examination of one's own attitudes toward chronic illness, addiction, and mental health.

EFFECTS ON CHILDREN WHEN PARENTS HAVE SPECIAL NEEDS

The emotional health of young children is closely related to the emotional characteristics of their environments, including parents, other family members, and child care. Children who grow up in homes where there are addictions or mental illness face major threats to their emotional development, along with threats to development in general. Early childhood educators focus on developing intellectual, physical, language, and social skills. However, emotions play an integral role in the development of all skills, and, therefore, enhancing emotional development is crucial as well. There is still much more to learn about the dynamics of emotional development and resilience and how these skills may be developed.

Recent brain research suggests that child development, specifically from birth to 5 years old, sets the foundation for future development (National Scientific Council on the Developing Child, 2007). Brains begin to develop before birth and continue to develop into adulthood. Good early experiences lead to a sturdy, healthy foundation for development. Toxic stress, which includes chronic stress caused by poverty, abuse, or maternal depression (National Scientific Council on the Developing Child, 2010a), can be harmful to the brain and to brain development. Brains require supportive, interactive relationships to grow and develop, and young children need stable, caring relationships to ensure that healthy brain development can occur. Quality care, which includes warm, caring educators in child-care settings, is noted for influencing the development of social, cognitive, and behavioural skills in young children (National Scientific Council on the Developing Child, 2004). These relationships have been shown to influence both school adjustment and school achievement.

Recent research has also suggested that early exposure to situations that produce fear and chronic anxiety can affect children's development, including development of the brain (National Scientific Council on the Developing Child, 2010b). Exposure to abuse produces the most noticeable effects on a child's development, but excessive stress is also problematic. When a person is faced with a threatening situation, stress systems are activated to cope with the threatening event. Exposure to stress and anxiety can trigger extreme prolonged activation of the stress response system. Very simply, when the stress system is activated for prolonged periods of time, the body responds in one of two ways. It anticipates everything as threatening, so the child responds to every event in his or her environment as potentially harmful. Alternatively, the body habituates so that the child comes to see nothing as threatening, and so responds inappropriately to danger.

In the 1990s, research on health and addictions demonstrated that prolonged exposure to stress in early childhood can lead to lifelong health concerns (Felitti, 2004). In particular, the Adverse Childhood Experiences (ACE) study investigated childhood abuse and neglect and later-life health and well-being. This study, which involved a survey of over 17 000 participants, suggested that adverse childhood experiences are relatively common but often unrecognized or concealed and can manifest years later as health or mental concerns or social impairments. It also purported that psychological stress associated with childhood experiences can lead the person to seek chemical relief (e.g., through smoking, alcohol, drugs) as a way to cope. These behaviours typically begin in adolescence and continue through adult life, even though the health risks are known, because of the short-term benefits they offer. This research led to an explosion of literature focused on brain development—in particular, toxic stress and how to disrupt it. It also led many to revise their conceptualization of addictions and, therefore, ways to address addictions. The Alberta Family Wellness Initiative (AFWI) has an extensive library of research on the ACE study and on building resilience in children and families. Resilience has relevance for early childhood educators who have the opportunity to provide support to young children to cope and build resilience.

The *Canadian Incidence Study of Reported Child Abuse and Neglect* (Public Health Agency of Canada, 2010) reported that adverse conditions that affect parents may have an adverse effect on children. For example, there is a relationship between parental mental health and suspected child abuse. Moreover, the study found that in 78% of child maltreatment investigations, the primary caregiver had experienced at least one risk factor, for example, being a victim of domestic violence, mental health issues, alcohol abuse, or substance abuse (Public Health Agency of Canada, 2010). It's important that early childhood educators understand that these risk factors may exist for parents so that they can be better able to support children and parents as necessary.

We know that young children are highly vulnerable to adverse conditions in the home, especially mental health issues and family violence. If the child's home environment is characterized by stress and chaos, the child may need a stable, interactive child-care environment to ensure that healthy brain development can continue. Furthermore, it has been documented that young children can benefit from forming secure relationships with multiple caregivers, including child-care educators, and that this will not interfere with the attachment to their parents.

PARENTS WITH CHRONIC HEALTH CONDITIONS

Although it may be uncommon for young parents to experience chronic health concerns, it does occur. In fact, research shows that 18% of adults with newly diagnosed cancer are parenting children under the age of 18 and that up to one-third of these children are under 6 years old (Hutchison & Allen, 2010).

Chronic health conditions are labelled as such when symptoms have lasted three months or more and/or there is persistent pain. Examples of chronic health conditions include diabetes, asthma, migraines, heart disease, and cancer. Along with symptoms of the illness, families often need to cope with difficulty accessing services, associated costs, treatment, and the quality of care. Families that have a parent with a chronic health condition may experience a range of practical, financial, and emotional stresses (Diareme et al., 2007). The parent may deal with fatigue, pain, or mood changes that may make him or her inaccessible or unavailable to the children. When there is remission, uncertainty and fear may continue to haunt the family. Needless to say, chronic health conditions can be very difficult on all family members.

It can be challenging for families to meet the developmental needs of the child in conjunction with the needs of the parent with the chronic health condition (Diareme et al., 2007). The stress related to cancer in particular can be overwhelming. Cancer can be understood in three phases: crisis, chronic, and terminal (Rolland, 2005). In the crisis phase, the parent and family are faced with diagnosis and initial coping. The chronic phase is focused on day-to-day living, including ongoing treatment and its changes. The terminal phase includes preparation for loss. Very few resources exist for the patient and the family in the terminal phase. The majority of supports for families experiencing cancer are directed at school-age children and older, and very few exist for younger children.

The developmental age of the child influences how the child perceives a parent's chronic health condition. While infants may react to the unavailability or inconsistencies in parenting, toddlers may view absence of the parent as abandonment or punishment. Although preschool-aged children may have some understanding of the illness, they may believe that they are the cause of the illness and may engage in wishful thinking about making the parent well again.

Beyond the personal stress of the illness, parents with a chronic illness likely experience stress from worrying about how the condition is affecting their children. Parents with a chronic illness are most likely actively trying to treat, manage, and cope with their health concern while they may be actively parenting young children. Their concerns can vary greatly, from how to tell their children to how to protect them and how to parent while being treated. Parents also may experience guilt about their decreased ability to parent effectively. In addition, they may feel they are receiving little or no support from their health care professionals in helping them deal with their young children. There are often additional costs associated with treatment that affects families, as well as stress on the healthy spouses who attempt to take on both parenting roles.

A common problem faced by people with chronic health problems is stigma. Some chronic conditions, such as arthritis, may be completely invisible to outsiders yet prevent that person from actively participating in many activities. People with physical health issues are often accused of being lazy, unhelpful, or simply unpleasant because others are not aware of the disabling condition. Furthermore, some conditions result in chronic pain or persistent feelings of unwellness. Under these conditions, it's sometimes quite difficult to behave in a friendly and social manner, and this sometimes results in being labelled as unpleasant, "crabby," or simply not a nice person. All in all, coping with chronic health issues can be extremely stressful on parents.

SCENARIO

PARENTS HAVE STRESS, TOO

A new family brought their 4-year-old to a preschool program. At first there were no concerns with Aiden and his mother, but a few months later, drop-off and pickup times became quite erratic. Aiden's mother was late or early and reluctant to let staff know her schedule. One day when she was particularly late, the director was on hand and decided to speak to her about her irregular schedule. Aiden's mother was visibly upset, and began the conversation by saying, "I guess *you'll* ask us to leave too? Aiden was asked to leave the preschool last year because I couldn't always be there on time to pick him up. They tried to put me on a contract so he could stay, but that didn't work." She went on to explain that she struggled with Crohn's disease, which meant that some days were fine and she coped well, but other days could be a challenge. "Sometimes I'm ready to leave and everything is okay and then I run into problems. I really do try because I know Aiden loves it here and he needs to be in preschool, but some days I just can't control how things will work. It's really embarrassing to have to explain to people why I'm always late," she added.

Families with chronic health conditions have several features in common, since it affects the whole family. Often, family life revolves around the condition. Things happen on good days, and things don't happen on bad days. Children may arrive at the child-care centre early on good days and be late or absent on bad days. Life may be centred around medical needs and protocols—for example, doctor's appointments, treatments, and eating schedules around treatments. Routines and schedules may affect young children more when they are unable to influence the situation. Older children may be able to dress and get something together for lunch and even get to the bus stop or school, but this is very difficult for younger children.

Changes in the home environment will affect not only the stability of day-to-day routines but also the psychological environment. For example, parents may not be able to be consistently attentive to their child's psychological and emotional needs. Young children may react to changes in the environment with regressions (e.g., need for a bottle at bedtime) or "acting out."

Parents often want to protect children, and so they may not provide information to the children about their condition. In addition, it may be very hard to provide accurate information to young children without unduly scaring them. For example, young children may not understand what surgery or chemotherapy is. However, it's well documented that children cope much better when they understand (Diareme et al., 2007; Kazemi, 2013; Rauch, Muriel, & Cassem, 2002). It may be helpful to answer questions as simply and honestly as possible. If it's feasible, have the child visit the hospital or clinic where others may also be able to provide information and be exposed to medical treatments if the child chooses and health care provider agrees. Supportive medical professionals view the patient in the context of family and may be able to offer helpful and appropriate information for the child. Many health services have adopted a family-centred approach to manage illnesses in a family, both for the child and adult. Explaining to the child, for instance, that the parent may be in hospital for a few days and who will be taking care of him or her may help the child to cope. Although it's frustrating for parents, allowing children to ask the same questions over and over—even if "I don't know" may be the only answer a parent can provide—is helpful for children to build understanding.

When information is limited, children will attempt to create their own answers. Young children see the world from their own perspective and may think that they created their parent's illness from their actions or thoughts (Rauch et al., 2002). When information is not forthcoming, children may assume that the illness is even worse than it is, and imagine many dreadful and often unrealistic scenarios (Centre for Addiction and Mental Health, 2003). Children need to understand that they did not create the illness and that they will (likely) not get it. It's important that adults have these conversations so that children understand as much as possible and don't develop unnecessary fears. If parents and educators are able to talk about how to explain the parent's condition to the child in a way that is appropriate for the child's level of understanding, this would be a very meaningful way of offering support.

It's better for the child if the parents attempt, as much as possible, to maintain routines within the home. Child care or preschool may be one of these important routines. Parents can be reminded to allow the child to have time away from the illness and to have fun. Preschoolers will often feel that it's inappropriate to have fun or play when the mood in their household is serious or somber.

THE ROLE OF THE EARLY CHILDHOOD EDUCATOR

Early childhood educators may find themselves in a difficult situation with regard to the child of a sick parent. There may be a period of time—for example, while waiting for a new diagnosis—when very little information is known about the parent's condition and anxiety is high. Treatment schedules and regimes may change, responses to treatment may vary, altering family life. Major transitions may occur, for example, a parent needing a wheelchair for the first time. It's not uncommon that information will not be shared with young children or with the child-care centre. However, changes in stress and anxiety levels in parents and children will be noticeable.

A child who has a family member with a chronic health condition will most likely need additional support while in your care. Consistent routines and schedules at home and in your care will be extremely important. While it's important to be understanding, educators want to be sure to maintain the same level of expectation of children. For example, it may be easy to explain the child's inappropriate behaviour based on the situation at home, but the child will need to learn ways to cope rather than ways to use the illness as an excuse for misbehaving. Young children may have difficulty expressing their feelings in words, and so you may see them expressing their feelings through play or inappropriate behaviour. Children may express frustration or anxiety in how they play with objects or other children. It's possible that children will play more aggressively or have more difficulty getting along with their peers. Educators will need to be aware that these changes in behaviour may be a result of the child's situation at home, and will need to assist him or her in finding coping strategies.

Communicating with children as much as possible will be helpful. This doesn't mean you will have answers or that parents will have information to pass along, but listening to the child—to his or her perspective and potential fears—is a good starting point. Educators may wish to warmly attend to a child's questions without having an answer immediately; for example, "That's a good question, maybe I can ask your Mom or Dad." It's always a good idea to check with parents, and you will need to respect their views even if they choose not to share information with the child. You may be able to support the parent in these conversations. Many support groups have books that may be suitable for younger children.

Supporting Parents with Chronic Health Conditions

Educators may be in a precarious situation when a parent experiences a chronic health condition. The educator may not be aware of the health concern or accommodations within the family home and may misinterpret the parent's behaviour (e.g., "The parent is never willing to help out or support us," "The parent is not interested in what her child is learning"). Some families may be willing to share information, while others may not.

Typically, when a parent has a chronic health concern, his or her needs are met by a team of medical personnel, which may include a psychologist or social worker for emotional support (e.g., for ongoing persistent pain or cancer). It's unlikely that the parent will need further support from the educator focused on their medical needs. The most significant role an educator may play is to ensure that the child is well cared for and that the child's needs are met. Parents will want to be assured that their child's physical, emotional, and developmental needs are met consistently and that the child is not missing out on important milestones in their lives. Educators may support parents by taking photos or videos of events or projects that the child can share at home. Educators may also be able to provide simple explanations about the condition or treatment and support children's understanding. These explanations would be based on information the parent has provided. Educators may need to feel comfortable saying, "I don't know" and supporting the child to seek answers.

PARENTS WITH ADDICTIONS

Addiction is defined as an uncontrollable compulsion to repeat a behaviour regardless of its negative consequences. Alcohol, prescription or nonprescription drugs, and food are common substances to which people can become addicted. Symptoms include an increased physiological tolerance for the substance and, in its absence, withdrawal—which can vary from mild cravings to severe illness, such as shaking, vomiting, and even death. Most addiction-forming substances initially result in a form of pleasure or a reduction in pain. For example, adults may begin to consume alcohol to experience a feeling of well-being, a common effect of alcohol. However, drinking heavily over a long period of time can lead to health problems such as stomach ulcers, liver disease, and many kinds of cancer. Excessive drinking is often responsible for problems within families and with employment.

Most people are social drinkers; that is, they drink alcohol in a social setting in a responsible way. However, some people are problem drinkers in that they may be physically addicted to alcohol and not be able to function adequately without it. Other people are binge drinkers: they may not consume alcohol for long periods, but then consume large amounts. The risk of accidents, impaired driving, and health problems (e.g., seizures, stroke) increases with binge drinking.

In homes where there is alcohol abuse, there tend to be several unwritten rules that family members abide by (Alberta Alcohol & Drug Abuse Commission, 2010)—namely, that the issue of over-drinking is not to be discussed, and that feelings are not to be indulged in but instead suppressed. Families with alcohol addictions tend not to trust outside help. Living by these "rules" is harmful to everyone, especially children.

Drug abuse can include a wide range of drugs, both prescription and nonprescription. No one plans to become addicted to drugs. A person may start using drugs because he or she is curious, feels the need to fit in, or is trying to deal with physical or emotional pain. Drug use may continue for other reasons, for example, group pressure or dependence on the drug. Problems can occur quickly or gradually—when the person takes a drug too much, too often, over too long a period of time, or in combination with other drugs. Drug use is considered harmful when it causes physical, mental, social, or financial problems (Alberta Alcohol & Drug Abuse Commission, 2010). People are considered drug dependent if they experience discomfort when they try to stop using it. Drug abuse affects the user as well as his or her family and friends.

Recently, more attention has been paid to addictive behaviours such as a gambling addiction, eating as an addiction, and an addiction to sex. These behaviours are every bit as problematic in terms of the risk to the addicted person and his or her family. For instance, many people buy lottery or raffle tickets, go to the racetrack, or enjoy an evening of bingo, and once the game is over, they carry on with other, nongambling activities. However, others find that gambling becomes a need, which can be problematic. The consequences of a gambling addiction can range from small, short-lived problems (such as difficulty paying rent or bills) to a serious, ongoing negative impact on the person and his or her family (such as chronic depression, financial devastation). Signs that gambling may be becoming a problem include spending a lot of time gambling, placing bigger, more frequent bets, hoping for the "big win," denying that gambling is a problem, promising to cut back, and refusing to explain behaviour.

For many years, research has suggested that children living in a home where there is drug or alcohol abuse are at risk for emotional, behavioural, and cognitive problems (National Institute on Alcohol Abuse and Alcoholism, 1990). In fact, parental mental health concerns are one of the top reasons for reporting children to protective services (Huntsman, 2008). Children from these homes are more likely to need mental health, welfare, and special education programs. Many children have difficulties in school and display more behavioural problems. They often have more psychological difficulties, including depression, anxiety, and stress. They also tend to have more relationship problems and display more anti-social behaviour (National Institute on Alcohol Abuse and Alcoholism, 1990). Some behaviours (e.g., acting out) are noted as early as 2 years old. As Dr. Bruce Perry points out, 90% of brain development occurs prior to 3 years old (Perry, 2010). Early experiences shape the brain for a lifetime. Consistent, caring environments will lead to healthy brain development, whereas chaotic, neglectful, or inconsistent environments will increase the likelihood of health problems, psychological problems, and substance abuse. In this way, homes that deal with addiction are similar to homes that deal with chronic illness in that they both create stress and disruption.

SCENARIO

EFFECTS OF ALCOHOL ABUSE ON CHILDREN

Sylvan was 5 years old and had been in the same child-care centre since he was a baby. Over the years, the staff who worked with him suspected that there may be issues at home. Sometimes he would be clean, cared for, and happy to be in the centre, but at other times he was tired, wore the same clothes over and over, and couldn't wait to eat. Repeated attempts to get information from his mother or father were met with silence. When Sylvan turned 5, his father left the home, and Sylvan began to talk about how his home life had changed; for example, "Now we eat supper every night," and "I sleep better now, because my mom and dad aren't fighting." Sylvan's mother did eventually tell the staff that his father had left due to alcohol abuse, and she described the effect it was having on her and Sylvan. This explained a lot to the educators who had worked with him over the years.

Parental drug addiction can affect children's development in two ways. The first is caused by the impact of the drug or alcohol abuse itself. Parenting may be inconsistent, routines sporadic, and care occurring irregularly. Children may be further impacted by an increased incidence of divorce, ongoing parental anxiety, and discord in the family. The second impact comes from what children are learning from adults. Children of drug- and alcohol-addicted parents learn different strategies for coping. As Jerry Mo (2010) points out, children who live with adults who cope by using drugs and alcohol may learn to cope using drugs and alcohol as well.

Resilience has been studied in relation to children in homes impacted by addiction. Research has shown that these children can be quite resilient, and that more than 50% of children grow up without experiencing difficulties (Buddy, 2016). Children who showed resilience growing up in a home impacted by addiction had the following characteristics in common:

- the ability to get attention
- good communication skills
- average intelligence
- a caring attitude
- the desire to achieve and do well
- a belief in self-help (Buddy, 2016)

It's important for educators to be aware of the role they can play in the development and resilience when children may be impacted by addiction (Buddy, 2016).

Once again, it's relevant to discuss the long-term effects of adverse childhood experiences reported by the ACE study (Felitti, 2004) discussed earlier in this chapter. Exposure to toxic stress in the early years can lead to physical and chemical disruptions in the brain that will have lifelong consequences. When children are exposed to these experiences, they will find ways to cope. As children, this may manifest in behavioural changes (e.g., acting out or withdrawing). As children get older, they may find ways to deal with the turmoil they are experiencing in other ways (e.g., using tobacco, alcohol, overeating).

The Role of the Early Childhood Educator

It's important to understand that a person who suffers from a serious addiction may be unable to meet the needs of his or her children, since the need for the substance or behaviour is so strong that it overtakes any other thoughts or emotions. This can result in a serious decline in family income, quality of life, and even safety.

Supporting Parents with Addiction

Educators may find it challenging to work with parents with addiction. First, parents may not divulge this information, so the educator makes educated guesses based on limited interactions with the parent. Sometimes these guesses may lead to misinterpretations or assumptions. Second, if the educator is reasonably sure that an addiction is involved, it may be extremely difficult to approach the parent and have a conversation. Again, educators are not counsellors and may not be in a program where there is access to support personnel to work with parents.

Early childhood educators may find themselves in a very awkward situation when working with families impacted by addiction. One possible scenario is the parent arriving at the child-care centre after using drugs or alcohol. Educators have an ethical and legal obligation to protect children, and so they may need to contact social services, which can provide immediate support to the child. Most child-care programs will have a policy outlining how to handle such a situation, which will help educators follow through. As difficult as responding to such a situation is, the safety of the child is absolutely paramount.

In another possible scenario, children may tell you things about what is happening at home that you may question or be unsure of how to handle. In the presence of parents, you may have no concerns; that is, they may seem attentive, caring, and interested in their children. However, parents and family members may not realize that they have a problem or may choose not to disclose it. As an educator and as a caring adult, you may wish to intervene and support the family as much as possible, but the family may not necessarily provide an opportunity to do so. Young children have little or no choice but to adapt to the environment and the family they are part of. Although it may be difficult to provide support or to change the environment at home, it's important to support the child in your care. Of course, if you have reasonable grounds to suspect abuse or neglect, you have a duty to report your suspicions to social services.

Ultimately, the role of the educator may consist of showing understanding and caring, as difficult as this role may sometimes seem. Educators will need to put and maintain firm boundaries in place regarding the safety and well-being of the child, which may be a difficult balance to maintain.

Supporting Children

Educators can support children in two ways. One is by engaging in good child-care practices that foster growth and development for all children. This includes the following:

- developing and maintaining daily routines and schedules
- maintaining as much consistency in the environment as possible
- ensuring that the child has access to the necessities of life—adequate food and sleep
- ensuring that the environment is healthy and safe
- providing a caring, supportive environment where healthy brain development may continue to occur
- creating and be mindful of opportunities to promote and develop resiliency

Children develop in an environment of relationships (Center on the Developing Child at Harvard University, 2010). It's well accepted that attachments to parents are primary, but children can benefit from relationships with responsive caregivers outside of the home

(Center on the Developing Child at Harvard University, 2017a). Therefore, it's important for educators to engage in high-quality, consistent care and interactions with children.

The second and related role for early childhood educators is to build programs and practices focused on resilience, as these are areas where educators can impact children in deliberate and thoughtful ways. Children may need support to develop the capacity to adapt and thrive when living with adversity. This can be accomplished through the presence of one reliable supportive relationship, which is you, the educator. Educators can intentionally teach and model skills related to individual resilience in all aspects of their environments. For example, educators typically teach communication skills such as how to get attention in appropriate ways. Educators model caring or self-help and can assist in developing skills such as empathy and problem solving. Being intentional about resilience for children and families will be paramount for children living in adverse circumstances.

PARENTS WITH MENTAL HEALTH ISSUES

Prevalence of Mental Illness in Canada

The very term *mental illness* often evokes fearful images. In this chapter, we use the term *mental illness* to encompass clinically diagnosable disorders and difficulties that interfere with a person's daily functioning (Huntsman, 2008).

Here are some facts that may influence how you perceive mental illness:

- One in five Canadians will experience a mental illness during their lifetime (Centre for Addiction and Mental Health, 2012c).
- By 40 years old, one in two Canadians have or have had a mental illness (Centre for Addiction and Mental Health, 2012c).
- Three percent of Canadians, or nearly 1 million, live with a severe and persistent mental illness (Lamoure, 2013).
- Seventy percent of mental health issues arise during childhood or adolescence (Centre for Addiction and Mental Health, 2012c).
- Mental illness is the second leading cause of hospital admission among youth (Mental Health Commission of Canada, 2013).
- The World Health Organization estimates that by 2020, depression will be the leading cause of disability in developed countries (World Federation for Mental Health, 2012).
- Large numbers of people with mental illness are living on the streets (Centre for Addiction and Mental Health, 2012c).

Despite the prevalence of mental illness in our society, people with mental illness face so many kinds of stigma that they may deem it preferable not to disclose their condition to anyone. According to a 2008 survey, only 50% of Canadians stated that they would divulge to friends or co-workers that they have a mental illness. Moreover, 42% of Canadians were unsure about whether they would socialize with a co-worker with a mental illness (Centre for Addiction and Mental Health, 2012c). The stigma surrounding mental illness can make it much more difficult to access treatment and support. Most mental illnesses today are treatable, some with medication and others with therapy, and often with a combination of both. Among the most common mental illnesses are mood disorders such as depression and bipolar disorder, anxiety disorder, and schizophrenia. The Centre for Addiction and Mental Health (CAMH) provides good information on these and other disorders. The symptoms and the severity of symptoms vary widely. It's important to keep in mind that most people with mental illness can't control their symptoms on their own. When a person is depressed, for example, we often hear people saying things like

"She just needs to pull up her socks, get busy, and stop feeling sorry for herself." This is both inaccurate and unhelpful.

Among the one in five Canadians who will develop a mental illness at some point in their lives (as listed above), 1% are likely to have a serious or continual mental illness (Centre for Addiction and Mental Health, 2012c). Mental health issues are often associated with alcohol or drug use, especially prior to diagnosis as the person attempts to deal with his or her change in mood or anxiety with drugs or alcohol (e.g., self-medicating). It may take a long time for some people to be diagnosed, as they come to understand that the reason for their feelings can't be helped with drugs or alcohol. This realization may be preceded by a significant event (e.g., a breakdown, breakup, or job loss) or prolonged difficulties that never seem to be resolved. Often, friends and family recognize that there may be a problem but are unsure of how to intervene. Early childhood educators may witness some of these issues or concerns in parents as well.

As we discussed previously, the early years are critical to development, especially brain development. Healthy brain development requires that the child be cared for; protected from illness, hazards, and excessive stress; and provided with predictable routines and schedules. Mental health problems in parents can be a source of fear and anxiety in children and can affect development (National Scientific Council on the Developing Child, 2010b). Parents may be less able to provide care; there may be neglect or abuse and exposure to other forms of stress that will have consequences on development.

Depression and Bipolar Disorder

Depression is a type of mood disorder. It has a variety of symptoms that vary in intensity, duration, and number, depending on the person. Depression becomes an illness, or clinical depression, when the feelings described below are severe, last for several weeks, and begin to interfere with one's work and social life. Depressive illness can change the way a person thinks and behaves and how his or her body functions. These are some of the signs to look for:

- feeling worthless, helpless, or hopeless
- sleeping difficulties
- changes in appetite and eating
- having difficulty concentrating or making decisions
- irritability
- loss of interest in taking part in activities, people or sex
- overwhelming feelings of sadness or grief
- feeling unreasonably guilty
- loss of energy, feeling very tired
- thoughts of death or suicide (Centre for Addiction and Mental Health, 2012b)

Depression in mothers has been documented as highly problematic in terms of the effect on children (Center on the Developing Child at Harvard University, 2009). The effects of maternal depression on attachment have been well documented. Depression can manifest itself in inconsistent and problematic parenting that doesn't foster the "serve-and-return" interactions required for healthy brain development (Center on the Developing Child at Harvard University, 2009). Depression often occurs in an environment of other adversities (e.g., unemployment, poverty, poor housing).

Bipolar disorder is another type of mood disorder. Bipolar disorder, also known as *manic depressive disorder*, is a brain disorder in which people experience extreme mood swings. It typically consists of times when the person is in a high state (mania), when they are feeling low (depression), and periods of wellness or feeling normal in between (Centre for Addiction and Mental Health, 2012a). In the manic state, signs may include the following:

- excessive talking
- less need for sleep
- racing thoughts
- increased activity
- feeling invincible

It's not difficult to understand how very difficult it is for someone who experiences depression or serious mood swings to be a responsive and attentive caregiver of a young child.

Mood disorders can be short-lived or more chronic in nature. Depression is even more prevalent in families experiencing poverty, with one in four of these families affected (Centre for Addiction and Mental Health, 2012a). However, often only a small number of those experiencing depression will seek and obtain professional care. Depression will have a significant impact on children's development if it occurs during the prenatal environment or the first few years of life. The effects of paternal depression and mental illness have been studied much less, and the impact is less known.

Anxiety

Key features of anxiety disorder include the following:

- irrational and excessive fear
- apprehensive and tense feelings
- difficulty managing daily tasks and/or distress related to these tasks (Rector, Bourdeau, Kitchen, & Joseph-Massiah, 2005)

Although a certain level of anxiety is normal, excessive anxiety can lead to changes in thinking and physical changes (e.g., increased heart rate, sweating, and behavioural changes). When these changes are persistent or severe, anxiety may be considered a disorder.

It may be easy to see why parents may be more demanding, stressed, or concerned about their child and perhaps place more demands on you when you understand anxiety disorders. Parents are often anxious about their children and the care their children receive. Having excessive anxiety may cause a heightened response or demands from parents.

THE ROLE OF THE EARLY CHILDHOOD EDUCATOR

Depression and anxiety issues typically occur in the context of other family issues. According to the Center on the Developing Child at Harvard University (2009), "mothers experiencing depression are often also young, socially isolated, economically or educationally disadvantaged, and burdened by more family conflict and stressful life events than mothers who are not depressed. Mothers who experience deep or chronic depression are also more likely to have experienced intimate partner violence, to be in poorer health, and to have problems with anxiety or substance abuse" (p. 4). However, it's important to note that depression can and does affect people across social and economic groups.

Healthy development is based on interactions with the environment, in particular, caring adults. An example of mutually responsive serve-and-return interaction (Center on the Developing Child at Harvard University, 2009) is when the baby smiles at the parent and the parent returns the smile or says a kind word back. Recent research has shown that these repeated interactions—involving words, gestures, touch, or attention—are critical to brain development. Children can be particularly at risk when their primary caregivers don't engage in these interactions. Parents can undermine the serve-and-return pattern in two ways. They may serve in ways that are difficult for the child to return—for example, when parents are intrusive or hostile. Or the child may serve and the parent doesn't return—for example, when the caregiver doesn't respond to the infant's cues consistently. Both of these possibilities arise when mothers experience mental health issues, especially depression.

Early intervention is critical. Hence, there has been a major focus on postpartum depression and dealing with the symptoms early. In addition to medical approaches (i.e., medication) and counselling, many programs have been developed that focus on parenting, especially on mother–child interactions. For example, many provincial and regional programs offer home visitation and support programs that focus on improving interactions. The promotion of positive parenting practices has been shown to have excellent results for children and families. Interventions that focus on reducing the mother's symptoms alone have not shown the same results in long-term outcomes for children or parents (Center on the Developing Child at Harvard University, 2009).

Mental illness continues to be highly stigmatized in North American society. The predominant coping strategy is secrecy or hiding the diagnosis (Hinshaw, 2005). Mental illness can be concealed, but this can lead to additional concerns: "Who do I tell? How do I let people know?" When parents are dealing with a mental health concern, having to also deal with the attached stigma may affect their parenting in that they may not be willing to seek support to cope as a family. Yet parental mental illness is a documented risk factor for mental health concerns in their children. This increased risk may result from the parent's lack of responsiveness, inconsistent parenting, or parental modelling (Hinshaw, 2005). Hopefully, as knowledge and understanding of mental illness and mental health increases in society, parents will come to understand the critical role they play in the early years.

Since the fear of stigma may be one of the main reasons that parents avoid sharing information about their physical or mental health conditions, it's important to find different ways to communicate to parents that staff are knowledgeable and unbiased. The Canadian Mental Health Association and other organizations offer materials about mental health and mental illness.

Mental health issues are complex and can be challenging. Again, educators may find themselves in the position of having access to no information and making guesses about the parent's behaviour. These may lead to assumptions or misinterpretations. Educators, who interact with parents regularly, may notice significant changes in the parent or related to the care of the child. It's essential that educators observe and document these behaviours and interactions and consult with professionals for information. When parents share their concerns, assure them of your support and encourage them to seek help. This may be one of the times that parents require more support and understanding from the people in their children's lives. Attending to the child's needs so that the parent knows the child is well cared for may be extremely important for these families. Parents who seek support and care in earnest may show improvements and will be excellent parents.

SCENARIO

LIFELONG SUPPORT

Enza struggled with bipolar disorder from an early age but was not diagnosed until she was in her last year of high school. She was very fortunate to access medical support and medication that worked for her. When she married and decided to have children, she was concerned that the medication may be harmful to her unborn child. She consulted with her psychiatrist and family doctor to develop a plan to ensure that her baby would not be put in harm's way. She required additional support from her family to cope with the changes in her medication through her pregnancy, but managed well and is a wonderful, caring mother to her adorable son.

It's common for parents to have a second or third child when one child is in child care or preschool. As educators are in the position to observe and talk with parents daily, it may be helpful to be aware of the signs of post-partum depression. Although many parents in Canada take a full year of maternity leave, some parents return to work and enroll their child in a child-care program earlier. Educators who engage with parents (typically mothers) every day may be in a position to observe and provide support if needed. Some parents may choose to keep a child in child care or family child care when a younger sibling arrives to ensure the child maintains social relationships. This will provide the mother additional time to spend with her newborn while the social and emotional needs of the older child are being met.

The following scenario demonstrates the importance of observing parents and listening to them. When educators take the time to truly listen, information may be gained.

SCENARIO

THE IMPORTANCE OF LISTENING

Shino had her first son in the child-care program from the age of 19 months. When he was 5 years old, Shino had a second child; she brought the baby in shortly after he was born and was quite excited. Anika, the program director, didn't see Shino for a while, and when she did see her daily, Shino never stopped to say hello. The time Shino spent dropping off her son and picking him up got longer, and one day she popped into the office to ask whether babies really needed to have their diapers changed so often. She explained that her mother-in-law was here for an extended visit, and as Anika engaged her further in conversation, Shino divulged that she was being treated for post-partum depression during the evenings in a hospital setting but was at home during the day to bond with her baby. They were able to talk about places that offered support and how the centre itself might provide support with Shino's older son. From that time onward, Anika watched a little closer and tried to engage Shino whenever she could.

The preceding scenario may occur in any child-care centre at any time, which is why it's so important for educators and directors to observe and take the time to engage with parents. In this situation, a mother's innocent question opened the door to her gaining the program director as another pillar in her support system.

Brochures and posters about health issues at the centre will give parents the message that educators are open to communicating about these topics. Taking a few extra minutes to ask a parent how he or she is feeling and responding with empathy and concern will provide parents with the opportunity to express a need for help or support. It's also important to have a good knowledge of resources for parents handy and available, including the contact information for local associations and support groups for different conditions.

SCENARIO

REPERCUSSIONS OF A STIGMA

Joline, a 30-year-old student in a social work program, related the following story to her classmates after a lecture on bipolar disorder. Her story provides a moving example of how the stigma connected with mental illness can have devastating effects.

"I was an A student in high school and had plans for preparing for architecture school. But on my 18th birthday, my life began to fall apart. My personality seemed to change drastically; I became aggressive, irresponsible, and even began to have paranoid delusions. Following that, I fell into a deep depression that ended in a suicide attempt. I was so lucky to have the support of my family and good medical care, and I managed to pick up the pieces and finish university. I got married and am now the mother of two children. Two years ago, my husband started drinking, and although he's never been physically abusive, he is emotionally abusive and refuses to get help for his addiction or go to counselling. I want to leave him, I know that now, but I'm afraid that with my diagnosis, I may not get custody of the children even though I've been well for many years now."

>> Examine Your Attitudes

- Do you think parents with mental health concerns are capable of parenting effectively?
- Do you think that mental illness will affect their child?

- Do you think children should be protected from parents with addictions? Mental health concerns?
- Do you think addictions will affect the child?

Once you have examined your attitudes, you will need to consider how you will interact with the child and the family. Children will need your support and understanding. Parents may require additional support as well. For example, when educators understand the struggles a parent may face, they may be more flexible. Educators may further support parents by providing books or resources that may be appropriate to help young children understand. CAMH and provincial mental health organizations have resource sheets available for parents to talk to children. Many of these resource sheets have been developed for school-aged children, so educators may support parents by providing more age-appropriate language or concepts. Parents may need to be reminded that children may appear to not understand (e.g., by asking the same question over and over) and may need constant reassurance.

CONCLUSION

New research in brain development tells us that the early years are even more important than previously known, and that responsive, reciprocal caregiving is the foundation for healthy brain development. Parents' mental and physical illnesses, as well as their addictions, may negatively impact the child's development through inconsistency of care. Yet research also tells us that young children can cope with multiple caregivers without compromising their attachment to their parents. Therefore, the role of the early childhood educator in ensuring healthy development should be seen as critical in helping families face such issues. Educators who are knowledgeable about resilience and bring resilience into their practice with young children can provide long-term benefits to the lives of these children. Family-centred practice that respects the child and family is essential when families are struggling with addictions, mental illness, or chronic health issues. Although dealing with these matters may be difficult, educators will need to remember to follow a strengths-based approach.

Parents with chronic health concerns will evoke caring emotions. Educators can understand and empathize with a parent struggling with physical health problems. Educators may face very different emotions with a parent with addictions or mental health issues. Assumptions and fears may be part of the initial reaction—assumptions we make about people who are addicted and fears we hold about mental illness. As professionals, we must face our fears or prejudices and seek information to be informed on all aspects of the challenges these parents may be facing. It may be necessary to seek support from a supervisor for approaches and seek expert advice. There may be challenges within the family, and parenting may be impacted. However, it's essential to remember that parents, no matter the issue, want what is best for their child. If the educator can provide extra support to the child during this challenging time for parents, that may be the best approach while parents cope with their issues.

The family situations we have discussed in this chapter all share one feature: they result in less time and ability to provide the nurturing, interactive relationship that is so critical for a child's development. The educator may be in a situation where, for a variety of reasons, little information is forthcoming from families in which parents have special needs. Nonetheless, the role of the educator is to provide the child with a rich, stimulating, nurturing, and responsive environment conducive to continued development and learning. In doing so, the educator may help alleviate the stress and anxiety experienced by parents who feel that their parenting may be inadequate or feel that the child is missing out on critical early experiences. This may be the best support an educator can offer to parents. Providing information about community resources and supports may also be helpful, but parents may need to feel ready or able to benefit from such information.

Chapter Summary

- Parents living with a special need (chronic health condition, addiction, or mental health concerns) may affect children and their development in a number of ways.

- Recent research suggests that the home environment is extremely important for early brain development, and that high levels of stress can be particularly detrimental. Young children need stable, interactive relationships to develop optimally.

- Each type of special need is associated with some type of stigma that may hinder or prevent the parent from seeking support and treatment. In addition, parents may be reluctant to share information with educators.

- It may be difficult for educators to gather information to obtain a clear picture of what may be happening in the home. However, it's always critical that educators provide young children with a stable, caring environment filled with positive, intentional interactions so as to ensure that their development continues.

- Supporting parents with special needs may be more difficult, but being understanding and providing support will still be necessary.

- No matter what the presenting issue is, educators must be respectful of parents and families. Doing so includes respecting a request for privacy or confidentiality, not making assumptions and providing support to the child and family in meaningful ways.

RESOURCES

Alberta Family Wellness Initiative:
www.albertafamilywellness.org

Canadian Mental Health Association:
https://cmha.ca

Centre for Addiction and Mental Health:
www.camh.ca

Center on the Developing Child at Harvard University:
https://developingchild.harvard.edu

National Institute on Alcohol Abuse and Alcoholism:
www.niaaa.nih.gov

Health Canada:
www.canada.ca/en/health-canada.html

EXERCISES

1. Search online for current information related to mental health agencies (e.g., the Canadian Mental Health Association or provincial organizations) for addiction support or health concerns.

2. Consider how stigmatization may affect people's behaviour. Talk with friends, family, and colleagues about their perceptions of parents who have addictions or mental health issues. In what ways will you be able to support families who are dealing with these perceptions?

3. Check community-based resources that support adults with addictions or mental health concerns. Are there community supports that a parent with a chronic health condition may be able to access (e.g., home nursing care)? Do these supports entail any associated costs?

4. Role-play the following situations. What might you watch for, and which actions might you take (now or after observations)?
   a) A father comes to pick up his child, and he appears to be "high."
   b) A child reports that Mommy sleeps all the time at home.
   c) A mother with a 2-year-old in your program decides to keep her in care after she has her second baby. After four weeks, the mother becomes quite unpredictable and less talkative.
   d) The parents of a 3-year-old have separated and take turns caring for him. During the father's week, the little boy is on time, well cared for, and settles in easily. But when it's the mother's week, the child's hours are chaotic, he arrives in the same clothes and is unclean, and his behaviour is less settled. You suspect the mother may be struggling, but you don't want to create more challenges for the couple.

5. How might you support families struggling with chronic illness? What supports might children need? What are some of the more common health concerns parents may encounter?

6. Find books that provide explanations for children under 6 years old about chronic health conditions (e.g., cancer, multiple sclerosis); mental health issues (e.g., depression, bipolar disorder); and addictions (e.g., alcohol, drug use). How would you use these books with children?

7. Find resources in your community to support young children living with a parent with chronic health problems.

CHAPTER 18
Gender Diverse Families

OBJECTIVES

- To enhance our understanding of gender diversity

- To highlight the need for strategies to ensure that early childhood frameworks are inclusive in regard to gender diverse families

- To consider strategies for supporting gender diverse families

Three-year-old Stephen came to the centre wearing red sequined shoes. His educator greeted him and asked him if he was playing dress-up at home before coming to the centre. "No," said Stephen. "These are my new shoes. They are not dress-up." "Well, they are very pretty," responded his educator. Later on in a conversation with Stephen's parents, the educator learned that one parent is in the process of coming out as transgender and that the parents are bringing up Stephen to feel comfortable in clothing that is both traditionally for "girls" and "boys."

THE COMPLEXITY OF GENDER DIVERSITY

A recent book on gender diversity tells us that the variety and number of nontraditional families has grown. Therefore, we need to find new models of family and parenthood and to realize that it's possible to "live, love, and form a family in an astounding variety of ways" (Ruspini, 2015).

This chapter will provide an introduction to gender diverse families and discuss the ways in which early childhood professionals can contribute to a welcoming and supportive atmosphere for lesbian, gay, bisexual, transgender, transsexual, Two-Spirit, and queer (LGBTQ) families (University of Toronto and Centre for Addiction and Mental Health, 2017).

A mother of two young children made an interesting observation. She noted that in our society today discrimination is not tolerated. Yet, she explained, when she goes into a department store, she sees that there is a separate "boys' section" and a "girls' section" for children's clothing and shoes, and the toy section definitely separates the toys that target little girls, such as the dolls and cooking corners, and the more "masculine" toys for boys. While there is no sign saying "Boys not allowed" in the girls' shoe section, most parents would feel uncomfortable if their little boy wanted to try on pretty red shoes that were in the girls' section. This mother asked why, in a country that doesn't tolerate discrimination, are these subtle and not so subtle methods of discrimination so prominent in our society? They give children clear messages about expectations for behaviour and images to portray that are associated with masculine and feminine (Huberdeau, 2014).

While most Canadians would support equality between men and women, as well as gay and lesbian unions, we as a society are only beginning to understand the complexities of gender in all its diversity (Killermann, 2013). Early childhood educators in particular will need to expand their knowledge of gender diversity, certainly in regard to their work with children, but also as part of the knowledge base for effective work with families. As the Positive Spaces literature of the Ontario Council of Agencies Serving Immigrants explains,

> Regardless of your personal beliefs, all service providers have a commitment to provide respectful, relevant and effective service to clients . . . [in] an atmosphere that respects human rights, and is positive for . . . [all]. This is not about changing your beliefs—it's about becoming more aware so that you can do a better job" (Best Start Resource Centre, 2012b, p. 10)

Genuine inclusion of families who are LGBTQ requires reflection, understanding, and action (Ontario Council of Agencies Serving Immigrants, n.d.). A good place to begin this process is by learning about gender—what it is and what it means. In fact, many people are confused by the very notion of gender. What is it—and what is the difference between gender and sex?

UNDERSTANDING GENDER AND GENDER DIVERSITY

Sam Killermann, a leading educator in relation to gender, explains three components of gender (Killermann, 2013):

1. Gender identity, which refers to how people think of themselves
2. Gender expression, which refers to how people behave, dress, and their demeanour
3. A person's biological sex

While biological sex is generally thought of as male or female, based on physical features such as a penis and vagina, there are people who are born with ambiguous genitalia or with sex organs of more than one sex. For example, a person can have testes that haven't descended where fallopian tubes were otherwise expected. This fact makes it clear that biological sex is not always simply one or the other. These components don't line up in straight lines for many people. A person can feel like a woman but act and dress like a man. A person can be a woman biologically but dress like a man and sometimes feel like a man and other times like a woman. Moreover, each of the categories relating to gender is fluid, and not a clearly determined one or the other. In addition, gender identities and gender expression are highly influenced by culture and can and often do change over time (Killermann, 2013). Given these facts, Killermann wonders how anyone thought it possible to take the whole population of this planet, some 7 billion people, and divide them all into two simple categories: male and female! In many if not most of the world's cultures, being a male is associated with characteristics such as aggression and strength, and being a female is associated with passivity and submissiveness. The idea that there are only two genders—man and woman—and that people can only be one or the other and stay that way all their life is called *gender binarism* (Best Start Resource Centre, 2012b).

Gender Diverse Terminology

This gender binary view is increasingly being understood as wrong, as evidenced by the customizable gender option used on Facebook (Bell, 2015). Terms such as *agender* (people who don't identify with any gender), *gender fluid* (people whose gender identity fluctuates), and *gender queer* (a person who does not subscribe to conventional gender distinctions but identifies with neither, both, or a combination of male and female gender) are becoming more familiar to the general population, but there are many more terms to understand (Genderqueer and Non-Binary Identities, 2011). It's important to keep in mind "that language and terms change over time, and are used differently amongst individuals and communities" (Best Start

Resource Centre, 2012b). However, there is also a fair bit of ignorance about the meanings and definitions related to sexual preference and gender. The following list provides some of the basic terminology that is important for educators to become familiar with:

- *Sexual orientation:* A term for emotional, physical, romantic, sexual, and spiritual attraction to another person. Examples: gay, straight, bisexual, lesbian, pansexual.

- *Lesbian:* A woman whose primary sexual/romantic attractions are to other women.

- *Gay:* A man whose primary sexual/romantic attractions are to other men. Is sometimes used by lesbians, . . . but many lesbians and bisexual people do not feel included by this term.

- *Bisexual:* A person whose sexual/romantic attractions are directed towards individuals of more than one gender, although not necessarily at the same time.

- *Heterosexual:* A person who is primarily attracted to people of the "opposite" sex.

- *Pansexual:* Someone who is attracted to other people regardless of their gender or sexual orientation.

- *Queer:* A term that has traditionally been used as a derogatory and offensive word for LGBTQ people. Many have reclaimed this word and use it proudly to describe the identity and/or as an umbrella term for LGBTQ people or communities. It is not accepted by all LGBTQ people.

- *Questioning:* Someone unsure or exploring their sexual orientation and/or gender identity. (Best Start Resource Centre, 2012b, pp. 11–12)

As this list makes clear, people's gender identification and way of life can no longer be seen in terms of "one or the other" or "binary." Researchers are currently trying to gain a better understanding of the dynamics of sexual- and gender-minority people, how their families function, and the unique challenges and strengths of this population (Tornello, 2015). Early childhood educators are learning to better understand families that are led by people who identify as LGBTQ, as well as families who may have members whose "dress, behaviour," or identity does not match traditional gender norms. This learning, not surprisingly, begins with an examination of our own gender identity and our attitudes toward gender diversity.

›› Examine Your Attitudes

It's useful to reflect on the gender and sexuality norms we grew up with and question them (Best Start Resource Centre, 2012b; Ontario Council of Agencies Serving Immigrants, n.d.). Doing so may not be as simple as it sounds, and can be uncomfortable. "At times it can feel like you are going against your own upbringing, against your family, or even against your moral beliefs, religion or culture" (Best Start Resource Centre, 2012b, p. 5). However, this kind of self-reflection will help us develop a truly inclusive attitude toward children and their families.

- How would you feel if your son wanted to go to school wearing a skirt?

- Do you believe that gay and lesbian people should have the right to parent?

- If you were a judge making a decision on an adoption case, would you favour a heterosexual couple over a same-sex couple, all other things being equal?

- Do you think children will be damaged by learning that their parents are LGBTQ?

ABOUT LGBTQ FAMILIES

It's estimated that between 5 and 15% of the Canadian population identify as LGBTQ. However, this estimate may be low because many people don't disclose their sexual identity for fear of negative consequences (Best Start Resource Centre, 2012b). There is more information available about same-sex couples than about other gender diverse groups. It's inherently difficult to enumerate trans people, as some may identify as transgender or as a trans female or trans male while others may identify as male or female. Same-sex parents have existed for many years, often in the context of, or following, heterosexual relationships (Mendez, 2009).

Statistics on the actual number of gay and lesbian parents have only recently been gathered. Canadian census data didn't begin to officially capture statistics on gay and lesbian families until 2006, one year after gay marriage was legalized in Canada (Woodford, 2010). The 2006 census reported that 45 345 couples in Canada identified as same-sex couples, of which 7465 (16.5%) were married couples (Statistics Canada, 2007a). The number of same-sex couples surged by 32.6% between 2001 and 2006, five times the pace of opposite-sex couples (Statistics Canada, 2007a). Approximately, 9% of same-sex couples had children aged 24 years and under living in the home in 2006; more females (16.3%) than males (2.9%) had children living in the home (Statistics Canada, 2007b). It's important to note that in both Canada and the United States, statistics on same-sex households are not accurate, as many same-sex families don't report their sexuality (Mendez, 2009). For example, some argue that the 2000 census in the United States underestimated same-sex households by 62% (Mendez, 2009).

Notably, over the past several years there has been a dramatic increase in the number of planned same-sex families through adoption or artificial insemination in both Canada and the United States (Mendez, 2009). However, the legal battle to allow same-sex couples to parent has been an ongoing challenge. Canada was only the fourth country in the world to recognize same-sex marriage (Woodford, 2010). Same-sex marriage was legal in 11 countries in 2010, and by 2017, that number grew to 25 (Pew Research Center, 2017). Still, even in countries where legal recognition of same-sex marriage has been achieved, lesbian and gay people must fight for their right to parent. Same-sex-parent–headed families are often not considered to be "real" families, and, like adoptive and foster families, often have to deal with stigmas and myths. Although there is great diversity among same-sex parents and their children, they often face homophobia, resulting in isolation, prejudice, discrimination, and invisibility in relation to society as a whole (Mandell & Duffy, 2010; Trawick-Smith, 2010). Homophobia faced by same-sex families is both systemic (i.e., policies discouraging adoption, legal recognition) and individual (i.e., interpersonal interactions) (Brown, Smalling, Groza, & Ryan, 2009).

>> Perspectives

An Individual's Story

We can learn much by reading one individual's story. This story is an example of the self-reflective and sometimes painful journey of an individual who chose to share her transition from a male to a female, to live as honestly and authentically as she can.

"The exact beginning of my transition is difficult to pinpoint in time, though I realize now that my transition had begun before I was fully aware it had. I began seeing a psychologist in early 2012. I was uncertain about the exact nature of challenge that prompted me to reach out for professional help, but in time, the focus of my therapy centred on gender expression. As signals grew stronger, I started to pay more attention, for the first time. I began the process of

listening to my heart and mind, and giving the tension inside the attention it merited. I went through a long process of contemplation and self-reflection. Later that year, I gave myself permission to explore, providing myself with the space required to begin a deliberative journey that facilitated both profound insight and profound challenge.

"One of my primary interests was to simplify my life. I didn't want to compartmentalize my gender expression, whereby I would explore at home and present as a cis in other contexts, such as in the workplace or online. [*Cis* is a term that refers to people who are not trans and less likely to experience tension about their gender and assigned sex at birth.] I understood that I needed to be me in all contexts, not just in some parts of my life. I also felt it important to be open about what I was going through, even though I

continues ▶

▶ *continues*

lacked the words to describe the tension and joy that moved me to action.

"In the fall of 2012, I began to wear women's clothing in a modest way to ensure I could continue along the path of living my truth without attracting unwanted attention. I also began growing out my hair and wearing cosmetics. In essence, I presented as androgynous. I also allowed photos of myself to be posted online, and I began sharing links to articles on gender diversity. With each new step, I put greater distance between the person I had been and living my truth. There was no turning back, yet I was uncertain about my destination.

"I would like to describe the participation of my partner, Beatrice, in my journey. Beatrice and I pay active attention to fostering a relationship and marriage in which we can be both vulnerable and safe. At each point when there was a clear signal of tension or desire of feminine expression, I was open with Beatrice. We discussed, contemplated, and sought clarity together. For several years, these moments of clear signal seemed fleeting, unconnected, and context specific. Neither of us saw a pattern or a nascent journey unravelling before us.

"In 2012, when my journey became much more deliberate, I brought Beatrice in at the earliest of stages to co-create the space we needed to look for meaning and seek answers to many questions but one in particular: 'Is Brett trans?' We also began the difficult discussion on what a firm answer to that question could mean for our relationship and family. I am not naïve, and I understood that my transformative journey might be too big a strain and too much a paradigm shift. But being trans is not a choice. My truth was emergent.

"Nothing I dare contemplate would bring me more grief or despair than the dissolution of our family unit. Beatrice and I explored my journey and its potential destination at great length, and we returned to the subject as often as needed. It seemed at times we were discovering the parameters of our relationship and testing its resilience—but we now understand that our process and attention to each other's hopes and aspirations brought us closer together and strengthened our foundation. We arrived at a deeper appreciation for the family we want to be.

"My declaration, 'I am trans,' was met with tears. We both cried and hugged each other tightly and for an extended period. Beatrice looked up at me. My eyes fixed on hers, which were made a deep ocean blue from her tears, and with unblinking lids she said reassuringly, 'I love you, and I support you. Samuel (our son) and I want to be on this journey with you, wherever it takes us.'

"I am trans. My preferred pronouns are *she* and *her*. Call me Brett."

GROWING UP IN A FAMILY WITH LGBTQ PARENTS

There are many myths about same-sex parents. Some include beliefs that children are more likely to turn out gay or lesbian, that children will not have a proper male or female role model, or, shockingly, that gay fathers are more likely to molest their children.

There is also a commonly held view that children of same-sex couples will be teased and ostracized by their peers, and that this will cause distress for the child and interfere with his or her ability to build and maintain friendships. Children may be impacted by the need for secrecy, the fear of exposure, and social isolation. Certainly, some children may experience this, but studies have suggested that no differences in friendships were evident. Moreover, while the experience of being teased or ostracized was significant, it may in fact build resilience and strength in children (Mandell & Duffy, 2010).

Most of the common reactions against same-sex parents are continually disputed in research. So far, there is virtually no evidence that suggests parents play any role in children's sexual orientation (Mendez, 2009). Nor are there differences between gay and heterosexual adoptive families, or in children's behaviour (Averett, Nalavany, & Ryan, 2009). To date, there is no evidence showing that same-sex parents are less effective parents, that they organize their home and family differently, or that children develop differently (Averett et al., 2009).

There is, however, evidence that children are less confined to traditional notions of "boy" and "girl" roles, that children see women as independent human beings, and that, despite the homophobia experienced in society at large, gay and lesbian parents provide a strong, loyal family unit and an extended support network and community (Mendez, 2009). Gay and lesbian families are less confined to traditional gender norms and often use more innovative

Courtesy of Chris Zahn.

Taylor, Age 5

approaches to parenting (Dunne, 2001). In addition, there appears to be a more equal division of labour in lesbian and gay families than in heterosexual, two-parent-headed families (Patterson, Sutfin, & Fulcher, 2004). Because of the lack of norms surrounding gay parenting, gay- and lesbian-headed families have the opportunity to renegotiate, redefine, and recreate roles and responsibilities (Dunne, 2001). Research on trans parenting has found that children of trans parents tend to bring an increase in their parents' happiness and well-being, leading to better parenting, improved child relationships, and increased open-mindedness (Brown & Rounsley, 1996; Burdge, 2007; Canfield-Lenfest, 2008; Hines, 2006).

CHALLENGES FACED BY LGBTQ FAMILIES

Social support for lesbian and gay parents is slowly increasing. Canada's liberal same-sex legislation may suggest that Canadians are highly supportive of gay and lesbian parenting. However, a recent report highlights that close to 50% of the Canadian population doesn't believe that gays and lesbians are capable of parenting effectively (Vanier Institute of the Family, 2010). In addition, such institutions as schools and organizations within communities can be discriminatory toward same-sex–headed families (Brown et al., 2009) and many same-sex parents claim to face a general lack of acceptance (Brown et al., 2009).

A common mistaken assumption that lesbian and gay families face is the perceived problematic nature of raising children without a male or female figure. Notably, this assumption is faced more often by gay men, as many people struggle to accept men's capacity to parent without women (Vanier Institute of the Family, 2010). There is little current research on challenges for LGBTQ parents, but early research conducted with respect to gay fathers suggests that we still have a long way to go before we can congratulate ourselves on being a truly inclusive society. The experience of being a gay father is not without challenges. Rachel

Epstein and Scott Duggan (2006) interviewed a number of gay men in Toronto and found that they were concerned with the extreme invisibility of gay fathers, especially in terms of programs and services and other formal elements of support. They also found that Canadian society is still largely disapproving of gay fathers, exhibiting negative stereotyping about gay men and parenting, and that homophobia (both systemic and individual) was a major issue faced by gay parents. Finally, it remains difficult for gay men to acquire children, owing to barriers in legislation and to an ongoing struggle for legitimacy as parents. For gay men, the process of acquiring children is often emotional, time-consuming, and expensive (Epstein & Duggan, 2006). While these studies were conducted over a decade ago, there is no solid evidence that suggests that these obstacles have been significantly mitigated.

The issue of children "needing" role models that are male and others that are female is in itself problematic, although almost all studies on gay and lesbian parents indicate that these parents actively provide role models for their children who are of the opposite sex (Vanier Institute of the Family, 2010). Rachel Epstein, a well-known Canadian gay rights activist and scholar, highlights the deeply gender-based notion of this critique, a notion that assumes women and men are homogeneous groups simply due to biology, while ignoring the diversity and degree of masculinity and femininity within categories of women and men (Vanier Institute of the Family, 2010). Epstein argues that instead of worrying about the presence of male or female role models, we should be asking, "What do kids need and how can we best provide these things, regardless of biological sex?" (Vanier Institute of the Family, 2010).

Lesbian and gay parents who overcome society's barriers tend to be highly motivated and committed parents. For example, in families with lesbian parents, children are treasured because child-bearing is a conscious, and often very challenging, choice that requires considerable effort (Mendez, 2009). Likewise, a recent study shows, unsurprisingly, that gay foster fathers show a strong commitment to parenting and are reworking the definition of what it means to father, as many gay fathers exhibit maternal properties.

LGBTQ parents have said that one of the ongoing challenges they face is that people simply don't feel comfortable with them (Ross, Steele, & Epstein, 2006). Some talk about feeling invisible. That is, as they don't always have recognizable signs of being LGBTQ, many aspects of our culture make them feel excluded. Moreover, some intake forms don't offer options that would allow them to identify themselves, posters on the walls of early childhood spaces typically portray only heterosexual couples in families, and some service providers "do not recognize the partners or co-parents or even their right to have a family" (Best Start Resource Centre, 2012b). The Ontario Coalition for Better Child Care highlights the fact that despite a growing awareness of the ability of LGBTQ parents to raise children, and the inclusion of LGBTQ rights in family law, many heterosexual people still don't consider LGBTQ people as suited to parenthood (Ontario Coalition for Better Child Care, 2017). Unfortunately, in spite of all evidence to the contrary, some people believe that persons who identify as LGBTQ are sexual predators (FindLaw, 2013). The implications of this falsehood are quite astounding. Imagine how a child and his LGBTQ parents might feel if some of the neighbours will not let their child play with, or visit with, a child because his parents are LGBTQ.

At the time of writing of this chapter, much political discourse on transgender people was taking place in the American media. As one example, the question of whether trans women should have access to women's bathrooms was a hot topic of debate. Those against this access argued that trans women are a threat to the safety of girls and women. This kind of argument is harmful because it makes it more difficult for trans women, trans people, and gender diverse people to exist in public spaces; because it denies them access to public washrooms; and because it brands trans people as predators. The transgender bathroom issue has been driven by proposed bills on the matter and by groups who sometimes resort to violent tactics in the name of "protecting" women's spaces. Imagine what it must be like for a trans woman who wants to take her daughter into a ladies' washroom and is not permitted to do so!

THE RISKS OF BEING OPEN

Verna and Amira are a lesbian couple who have lived together with Verna's daughter, Janne, for more than five years. As Janne began to approach her teen years, they were experiencing a fair bit of tension at home. Amira suggested that the three of them see a family counsellor. Verna replied that she was reluctant to do so, since it could be interpreted as an admission of failure. "I always feel as if we're on trial," she said, "and if anything goes wrong, I may lose custody of my daughter."

SUPPORTING CHILDREN OF LGBTQ PARENTS

It's important for educators to treat the children of LGBTQ parents the same as all children, and to teach children from a very early age that there are many kinds of families. Prevailing myths should be countered with facts, showing that children of LGBTQ parents are known to be in warm, loving families (Johnson, 2010). Most children at one time or another bear the brunt of negative interactions and teasing, and it's likely that children of LGBTQ parents will be no exception. The advice here is the same as for any other kind of negative interactions: we try to teach children to avoid hurtful behaviour, while at the same time reassure them that adults in their life will protect them should there be a need (Johnson, 2010).

SUPPORTING LGBTQ FAMILIES

A student who had recently "come out" as a transsexual once told her instructor after class: "I sometimes feel like my friends can't get it right. On the one hand, I want them to know that I am no different than they are—I have the same goals, the same good and bad habits, and share their values about children and families. But on the other hand, I want them to know that I am not the same. I belong to a group that faces unique challenges, celebrates unique joys, and think that many could benefit from learning about this unique journey that I have been on." Many members of minority groups share this dilemma. On the one hand, they don't want to be singled out as "different." Yet on the other hand, they don't want to hide the fact that they are in some ways different and would welcome the opportunity to share some of "their world" with others.

There are many things that unite all parents of young children, and this commonality helps develop strong bonds between parents of young children. However, for LGBTQ parents, becoming a parent is often a long and thoughtful process, sometimes with a heavy financial burden, and full of challenges related to their lack of acceptance—factors that make them a unique group. For early childhood educators who attempt to ensure that they are inclusive and supportive of LGBTQ parents, the lesson here is to find a balance. Find the common challenges, dilemmas, and joys that parents share, and ensure that LGBTQ parents are included. On the other hand, gain an understanding of the unique challenges and strive to support families in meeting these challenges. We see this dilemma of "unique versus universal" in the research findings. Some theorists critique the uniform identity of gay and lesbian parents, since it discredits the diversity within gay families (Berkowitz, 2009). Like heterosexual or one-parent families, there are considerable differences within gay families and no "one-size-fits-all" way to support them (Berkowitz, 2009). It's important to recognize individual families and their unique needs, while also being aware of the large, systemic challenges facing LGBTQ families, including struggles with policies and access to system-wide support (Mendez, 2009). It's also important to recognize that LGBTQ families are likely to run into bias and discrimination, and to make very certain that they are treated with respect and can participate in the welcoming environment of the child-care centre.

The Atkinson Centre for Society and Child Development published *Building Bridges: Queer Families in Early Childhood Education*, which is an excellent resource for early childhood educators (Janmohamed & Campbell, 2009). This document provides many ideas for supporting both children and families and for ensuring that the centre is truly welcoming and accepting. Examples include displaying rainbow stickers and triangles to symbolize a welcoming environment; referring to "parents" rather than "mom and dad" in communications from the centre; and integrating books with LGBTQ families into the reading corner.

Other concrete ways the centre can support LGBTQ families are as follows:

1. Suggest that staff all have the opportunity to learn about LGBTQ families, and then consider how to ensure that LGBTQ parents are welcome.
2. Redesign intake forms to be inclusive.
3. Ensure that there are posters that reflect an array of family structures (Best Start Resource Centre, 2012b)

Parents may also need reassurance of the commitment to diversity and inclusion at the child-care centre. It may be appropriate to occasionally remind all parents of this commitment, especially if there is a complaint of disrespectful behaviour toward an LGBTQ parent from another parent or staff member. It's possible to share your knowledge of research that indicates that children from secure loving families can thrive, regardless of the particular structure of the family (Johnson, 2010).

CONCLUSION

While there has been growing awareness and acceptance of same-sex parents, few people today understand that gender is not just "male" and female" but encompasses a broad range of identities. Many LGBTQ people today feel that society has a long way to go in terms of understanding them and reducing the negative stereotypes that persist. One of the harmful stereotypes relates to their ability to be good parents. All existing research suggests that the children of LGBTQ parents do very well. Early childhood educators are encouraged to use the available resources to learn about LGBTQ children and families, and to use this knowledge to ensure that their programs are truly inclusive.

Chapter Summary

- Canadians are known to be a liberal open society, but there is much ignorance and misinformation about LGBTQ individuals and families today.
- LGBTQ individuals who wish to become parents face barriers that are based on widely held beliefs that children will suffer. These beliefs have been disproved by research.
- Because of the difficulties facing prospective LGBTQ parents, those who decide to pursue parenthood tend to be highly committed to their children.
- Children of LGBTQ parents have been shown to be more liberal in their attitudes toward family roles, and more open minded than other children.
- Early childhood educators can support LGBTQ families by being very purposeful about strategies for inclusion.

RESOURCES

The following resources will help you gain a deeper understanding of LGBTQ children and families.
Gender Diversity Education & Support Services:
www.genderdiversity.org/wp-content/uploads/GenderDiversity_brochure.pdf

It's Pronounced Metrosexual, "The Genderbread Person" model for understanding the social construction of gender:
http://itspronouncedmetrosexual.com/genderbread-person/#gp3

It's Pronounced Metrosexual, "Activities & Classes" (activities and classes focused on learning about LGBTQ people):
http://itspronouncedmetrosexual.com/activities-classes/#sthash.zAQH4Kja.dpbs

Best Start Resource Centre, *Welcoming and Celebrating Sexual Orientation and Gender Diversity in Families, from Preconception to Preschool*:
www.bccf.ca/static/media/uploads/Resource%20PDF/lgbtq_resource_book.pdf

Humber College, "Tips for Teachers: Class Room Climate for LGBTQ Students":
http://humber.ca/lgbtq/resources/tips-for-teachers

British Columbia Teachers' Federation, "LGBTQ Resources for Teachers":
https://bctf.ca/SocialJustice.aspx?id=17990

LGBTQ Parenting Network, "Trans Parents & Family Law":
http://lgbtqpn.ca/wp-content/uploads/woocommerce_uploads/2014/09/TFL-Tip-Sheet.pdf

Sam Killermann, *Understanding the Complexities of Gender: Sam Killermann at TEDxUofIChicago* [video]:
www.youtube.com/watch?v=NRcPXtqdKjE

Pamela M. Malins, *Gender and Sexual Orientation in the Elementary Classroom: Teachers Negotiating Critical Literacies and Queer Pedagogies* (Master's thesis):
http://ir.lib.uwo.ca/cgi/viewcontent.cgi?article=2058&context=etd

Samantha Allen, "It's Absurd to Claim That Trans Kids Are Being 'Rushed' into Transitioning" (*Daily Beast*):
www.thedailybeast.com/its-absurd-to-claim-that-trans-kids-are-being-rushed-into-transitioning

Mehak Anwar, "7 TED Talks That Will Change the Way You Think About Gender & Gender Equality" (*Bustle*):
www.bustle.com/articles/147600-7-ted-talks-that-will-change-the-way-you-think-about-gender-gender-equality

EXERCISES

1. a) List the traits that you believe are associated with "male" and those associated with "female." Which of the traits do you believe are the result of "nature" and which are the result of "nurture"?

   b) Think of three people that you know fairly well and list each person's traits. How do the traits of each person correspond with the "female" and "male" traits you listed in part "a" of this exercise? What does this exercise tell you?

2. In what ways do you think the media and advertising contribute to stereotyped ideas about gender?

3. How does the concept of intersectionality (as explained in Chapter 3) relate to LGBTQ individuals?

CHAPTER 19

Death in the Family

OBJECTIVES

- To describe the impact that a death in the family has on family members

- To explore the grief process for children and adults

- To discuss the importance of helping children cope with a death in the family

- To highlight the role of early childhood educators when a death occurs in the family

Sylvia was a 4-year-old girl whose father was tragically killed in a car accident. He had been a musician who performed in bands during evening hours and had played a major role in her care and nurture during the day. For several months, Sylvia would play "funeral" in the doll corner. It was a daily ritual, to which she would invite the other children in the child-care centre. One day Marie, the early childhood educator, said to her supervisor, "That child has a problem. She seems so morbid." The supervisor reflected for a moment. She had noticed that when Sylvia first began enacting the funeral, her face was tense and it was obvious that she was deeply distressed. As time passed, the funeral play became lighter, and Sylvia clearly enjoyed arranging flowers, singing, and telling the other children where to sit. In the end, the supervisor told Marie that Sylvia's play seemed a healthy and natural way of coping with her father's death.

EXPERIENCING A DEATH IN THE FAMILY

Despite North Americans' long life expectancy, many children in preschool programs do in fact experience the death of a loved one. It could be the loss of a grandparent or, less commonly, a parent or sibling; the death could be the result of violence, accident, or illness. For many children, even the loss of a pet can be devastating. Responses to death are influenced, in part, by the nature of the relationship with the deceased. It would not be an exaggeration to say that the experience of losing an intimate family member has a profound and pervasive effect on the entire family that often lasts for many years. In addition, religion and cultural beliefs play a major role in people's conception of death.

Discussing death often causes discomfort. In many parts of our modern world, deaths occur in hospitals, away from the family (Child Development Institute, 2015; Walter, 2010). Although hospice care is well established in Canada, some authors suggest that societal discomfort with death is still evident in the way dying people are often treated (Walter, 2010). Many people today have never witnessed the death of a person, and just thinking about that image can be stressful. Death today is considered an unnatural event or accident (Walter, 2010).

Television provides confusing images of death (Woodthorpe, 2010). Cartoon characters die, yet they regularly rise again for the next blow. News shows flash endless images of death, so much so that we may have become desensitized or fail to understand the true meaning of what is perhaps the most traumatic event in the course of a family's lifespan.

» Perspectives

Glenna is an Indigenous social work student at a community college. During a discussion of grief counselling, she described how death is explained to young children in the Stoney culture.

"In the old days, children were kept away from the person making his final journey. Children were not told about death. They were forbidden to attend the wake services and the burial grounds. They never looked at a deceased person.

"The purpose of not telling a child about death was to alleviate the disturbing emotions and to respect our traditions. It was said that a child's soul is sacred, and therefore children should not be near a dead person, for the dead may be in need of a holy soul to lean on. Once the soul has been dominated by the dead spirit, the child's spirit will be possessed through eternity. The only way to bring the child's spirit back into the body is for a powerful medicine man to perform a sacred ceremony, which our forefathers say isn't easy; only some are successful. Therefore, children were kept away from the dead person during the two nights and three days of the wake service and right up until after the body was buried.

"Nowadays, since we're living in a new generation and shifting into a new style of life, this kind of tradition can't be maintained. Some people who prefer to attend church services take their children with them. There a child learns about our Saviour, how He died and His promise of a new world, a paradise called Heaven where all the nations in this world will eventually meet. Children realize that the dead aren't living in the ground permanently, but are merely awaiting His calling.

"But for some who still practice the traditions, some things have changed. Upon the loss of a loved one, the eldest member of a family—someone well respected—is the one who does the explaining to the children. It must be done before the children can look at the deceased, or even before they hear about it from someone else. If children hear from another person, they say, they will have ambivalent feelings, and it will take a long time before the children accept the loss or heal."

MULTIPLE ASPECTS OF DEATH

Death often has multiple impacts on family life that go beyond the members' emotional responses. If a spouse dies, the family income can decrease significantly. This may necessitate a temporary or long-term change of residence. Many widows slide into poverty when their husbands die. Men often experience more difficulties since they typically rely on their wives for emotional support. Feelings of loneliness and social isolation and a perceived need for major changes in lifestyle often accompany the loss of a spouse (Anderson, 2010). A long illness before a death can deplete the family resources and take an emotional toll. The death of a grandparent can result in a number of changes in the family, particularly when the surviving grandparent can't live on his or her own. These changes may impact children as well.

Unclear Norms Regarding Death

People sometimes don't know how to behave when there is a death in the family. In our society, there are few guidelines or rules concerning appropriate length of time for mourning, dress, behaviour, and remarriage (Anderson, 2010; Walter, 2010). Grief is allowed only at specific times, usually in private (Jenkinson, 2004; Walter, 2010). Some would say that society does not recognize the individual's right or need to grieve or the child's capacity to grieve (Murray, Toth, & Clinkinbeard, 2005). The lack of norms is even more noticeable for nontraditional families: Cohabiting partners or same-sex couples may feel that although their grief is as intense as that of a traditional spouse, they lack the support of the community.

Courtesy of Chris Zahn.

Taylor, Age 5

The death of an unborn child through miscarriage or stillbirth is another area where people are uncertain of how to respond. For the parents (sometimes only for the mother), the loss of a fetus may be as devastating as the death of any other close family member. The mother may experience extreme guilt along with many other emotions associated with grieving. The parents often feel isolated in their grief because family members and friends did not have a chance to know the baby, and therefore they don't feel the loss in the same way.

Whatever guidelines do exist have not kept pace with social changes, as illustrated in the following scenario.

SCENARIO

WHO GOES TO THE FUNERAL?

Leslie had been divorced from Norman for two years. They had two teenage children, Anna and Peter. Norman remarried a year after the divorce and had a child with his new wife, but he maintained regular contact with his teenage children. Shortly after the birth of this new child, Norman was in a tragic accident and died. His children, Anna and Peter, were devastated and wanted their mother, Norman's ex-wife, to accompany them to the funeral. Norman's widow did not want Leslie to attend. Leslie felt that, even though she was the ex-wife, she, too, had lost the father of her children and her ex-spouse. "There is no acceptable way for an ex-wife to mourn," claimed Leslie.

ADULTS' PSYCHOLOGICAL RESPONSES TO GRIEF

Elisabeth Kübler-Ross (1974) identifies five stages in the grieving process: denial, anger, bargaining, depression, and acceptance. The stages identified by Kübler-Ross have often been interpreted as distinct phases that succeed one another until the process of grieving is complete.

However, Kübler-Ross and Kessler (2014) suggest that human beings rarely follow precise formulas, and this is especially true for people in acute emotional pain. Grief reactions are highly individual; they may occur in different sequences, and the components of the grief response can occur and recur in an unpredictable fashion (Anderson, 2010). Kübler-Ross and Kessler (2014) explain that the five stages "are a part of the framework that makes up our learning to live with the one we lost. They are tools to help us frame and identify what we may be feeling" (p. 7). Grief reactions can last for minutes or hours, and a person may have one reaction and then move on to another in an unpredictable manner. Certain events can evoke strong emotions and grief years after the death has occurred. Bearing in mind that these stages are meant to help frame and identify feelings, they are useful in understanding some of the most salient components of responses to grief (Prigerson & Maciejewski, 2008).

Shock and Denial

Shock is usually the initial reaction following the death of someone close. Denial often begins with shock and can be accompanied by a feeling of numbness (Kübler-Ross & Kessler, 2014). Essentially, this initial response to a death helps the person to survive the loss. Denial involves the inability to believe that the death has occurred: *Did this really happen? Was it a dream?* One man said that as he was coming up the steps to his apartment after his wife's funeral, he was expecting her to be at the door so that he could tell her who attended. People may tell the story over and over or ask questions ("Why?"). Through this stage, the finality of death becomes reality.

Anger and Protest

The second stage of grief typically begins with anger, but it may also include protest or guilt. Anger is necessary in the healing process. The anger may be directed at the person who died ("Why did you leave me?"), at the doctor or nurse who cared for the deceased ("They didn't do enough!"), at the person who caused the accident (e.g., drunk driver), or at oneself ("Why didn't I see this coming?") (Kübler-Ross & Kessler, 2007). The person may be angry at the loved one for leaving him or her behind. People may express anger at God. In this stage of grief, the mourner may cry a lot or have a difficult time sleeping. People can also experience guilt, which is anger turned inward (Kübler-Ross & Kessler, 2014).

Bargaining

Bargaining is perhaps often more common before the death has occurred (Kübler-Ross & Kessler, 2014). Pleas directed at God, at the dying person, or at the doctor may include statements such as "Please just let him live to see his daughter graduate" or "Please let him live and we'll never fight again." After death, there may be bargaining that involves ending the misery. The person dwells on "what ifs" in an attempt for life as he or she knew it to return. This negotiation keeps people living in the past as they attempt to adapt to the new situation.

Depression and Despair

When the person's focus moves to the present, a period of despair or depression is common among those in mourning. Depression can be deep and feel like it will last forever. This experience often involves feeling apathetic, being disorganized, and lacking purpose and direction. Behaviour sometimes regresses, and people in this stage of mourning may want to sleep excessively. Feelings of hopelessness and helplessness are common. It's important to remember that depression is a normal and appropriate response (Kübler-Ross & Kessler, 2014). It can't be stopped or hurried along.

Adjustment and Acceptance

This phase is not necessarily about feeling good about what has happened. Rather, it's about adjusting to and accepting the reality that the loved one is gone permanently and learning to live with it. In the adjustment phase, people begin to feel a sense of hope and some mastery over their lives again. They begin to loosen the psychological ties with the deceased and to reorganize their lives. In this stage, people attempt to find ways to maintain the memories of their deceased loved ones while moving forward with their own lives. With this adjustment and with time comes acceptance. Acceptance may entail having more good days than bad and realizing that we can't replace what has been lost, but we can create new experiences and memories (Grief.com, 2013).

CHILDREN'S RESPONSES TO DEATH

Children's grief responses are in some ways similar to those of adults (Dyregrov, 2008; Webb & Doka, 2010; Willis, 2004). However, their different cognitive abilities and relative lack of experience limit their understanding of death and thus their response to it. For example, children may experience many of the same stages of grief as adults, such as shock or disbelief. Children may protest and feel apathy. They may demonstrate grief more actively by expressing anger, which may be directed at the person who died, at "God," at the doctors, at the parents, or at themselves. There may be feelings of sadness that may include crying or isolation. Yet, because children are learning about their emotions and are in the process of learning how to regulate them, the nature and intensity of their reactions may vary. One minute the child may be inconsolable, and the next minute he or she may want to play or request a snack.

SCENARIO

A CHILD'S REACTION TO DEATH

A 30-year-old man relayed this story about the time his sister died when he was 7 years old: "I was there when the doctors told my mom and dad. I couldn't follow and really didn't understand but knew something bad had happened. Two days later, I remember my teacher phoned. I think she wanted to know if I was okay. I answered the phone and she said, 'This is Mrs. Jones.' I said, 'Guess what, my sister died!' I am still haunted by my reaction that day and have no idea why I said that to her."

Concepts of irreversibility, finality, causality, and inevitability need to be understood to comprehend death fully (Webb & Doka, 2010). Children's understanding is often intermittent or sporadic, sometimes referred to as a "short sadness span" (Dyregrov, 2008). Often children don't immediately react with strong feelings; for example, they may not cry. Adults may be concerned about this apparent lack of feeling, but it's a normal shock reaction and may help the child to cope with the extreme emotions.

In earlier generations, it was common for children to be present when a family member died, to participate in the funeral preparations, and to be involved in the funeral itself. Children in modern society, by contrast, don't have much opportunity to experience death naturally as part of the life cycle of families or in nature (Webb & Doka, 2010). They often live away from older relatives, and when a death does occur, it often takes place in a hospital, without the presence of children (Jenkinson, 2004). Children miss out on what happens and subsequently miss many of the rituals associated with death.

Many adults find it difficult to explain death to children, either because they think children should not have to think about death, their own conception of death is unclear, or they are not sure how to explain it to a child. Yet adults often underestimate children's capacity to understand or empathize (Webb & Doka, 2010). Children often talk about death in a much less inhibited fashion than adults do, *until* they learn that death is not a topic for discussion or that it's improper. In fact, children are naturally curious about death (Dyregrov, 2008; Way, 2010). They are fascinated by dead insects, they pretend to kill each other, and they may enjoy retelling morbid descriptions (e.g., of worms eating the eyeballs of a corpse). These are children's ways of learning about what happens, and about the irreversibility and permanence of death. When children are denied these opportunities, or when a dead pet is immediately replaced, they are deprived of an opportunity that helps them understand and cope with death.

Children's Developmental Understanding of Death

Babies and Toddlers

The way children perceive death depends largely on their developmental level (Dyregrov, 2011; Way, 2010). Babies have no understanding of death per se, but from a very early age they will be disturbed by being separated from a family member to whom they had an attachment (Way, 2010), as evidenced in their behaviour (e.g., poor eating and sleeping, increased crying, more difficulty settling). Toddlers seem to relate to a deceased member of a family more in terms of missing someone who is no longer around rather than by attaching any particular meaning to death. Generally, children under the age of 3 sense an absence or miss a family person.

Preschoolers

Many preschoolers, on the other hand, understand death in specific, concrete terms (Himebauch, Arnold, & May, 2008). Preschoolers can't understand the finality of death and tend to believe that the dead person or animal will come back and be able to move again (Dyregrov, 2008; Himebauch et al., 2008). They lack time concepts, and researchers have suggested that the concept of death develops for children along with the concept of time. Children don't understand *forever*. They believe that death is reversible, and they talk about the deceased person as if he or she were still alive.

SCENARIO

IS DEATH FOREVER?

A 6-year-old boy named Lucas watched a television drama in which the main character, a 9-year-old boy, died of AIDS. Lucas was moved by the show and asked his parents many questions about death and dying. Three weeks later, he was watching a weekly television serial in which the same actor appeared. Lucas couldn't understand how the boy could be dead and then alive again. Perhaps death didn't really last forever as his mother had told him. Lucas's mother realized that he was confused and that she'd have to explain death to him once again.

Because children lack a full understanding of how the body works, they may ask questions related to the well-being of the deceased (e.g., "Will they stay warm?" "Do they have a nice bed to sleep in?"). Another characteristic of preschoolers is their fascination with details, which is sometimes disconcerting for adults, who view this as morbid curiosity. Typical questions children may ask include "How will Gramma be able to go to the bathroom?" "Does she have her glasses to see?" Such questions reflect young children's natural curiosity about all the concrete and practical aspects of death. Young children need to ask questions over and over again and to revisit feelings and thoughts through each new stage of development (Himebauch et al., 2008). It's through this repetition that they come to understand death.

SCENARIO

UNDERSTANDING DEATH AT DIFFERENT AGES

A student relayed the following story regarding her early experience with death: "When my grandma died, my mom told me that her mother had 'gone to work.' I was 4 years old at the time and didn't really think about what that meant—it just meant that Grandma wasn't around to spend time with me. When I was in grade 1, my mom announced that she was going to work. I remember being scared and pretty confused—when Grandma went to work she never came back—but at 6, I understood a little bit more about death than I did when I was 4."

Young children may, egocentrically, assume that they are responsible—that their thoughts and feelings have caused the death. Atle Dyregrov (2008) refers to this idea as "magical thinking": the child believes that he or she is at the centre of all things and can control what happens. Accordingly, young children are at risk of feeling responsible or guilty in relation to the death (Silverman & Kelly, 2009); for example, they may think, *Daddy died because I was bad.*

Preschoolers may also associate particular places with death. For example, they often think that hospitals or the ambulance cause death. As children move toward 5, they begin to understand more about the body and how it works. Around this age, they will understand the effects when organs no longer function (e.g., the heart stops beating).

Preschoolers, like Sylvia in this chapter's opening vignette, often act out the funeral or dying in pretend play. Acting out this script may seem morbid, but it's a natural way of attempting to understand, to make sense of what has happened. Preschoolers may also exhibit a "short sadness span" (Dyregrov, 2008). They may be extremely sad when they hear of the death but then seem to forget about it shortly after, often while engaged in play. Then hours, days, or even weeks later, they will display signs of sadness again. These types of reactions are typical for this age group and may explain why young children may have little or no reaction and react emotionally after a period of time.

Children often have grief responses that look different from those of adults. The shock or denial typical of the adult grief response may look like an inability to comprehend finality in the child. "Mommy will come home" is something that would not be uncommon for a 5-year-old child to believe. A death in the family may cause certain bodily reactions, such as stomachaches, lack of appetite, headaches, or changes in sleeping habits. Loss may also evoke a sense of loss of security. As a result, preschoolers may become clingy or more demanding (Himebauch et al., 2008). Regression to earlier behaviour may also occur, for example, thumb-sucking, bedwetting, or the need for a security item (Silverman & Kelly, 2009). A child's anger is often directed at the loved one who died, and he or she may make comments such as "Mommy is bad for dying" or "I hate her."

Children who are beginning to understand the finality of death may be stricken with feelings of genuine panic, wondering who will love them and care for them. Children may also idealize the family member who has died. For example, a child may remember his mother as being "perfect in every way." This, of course, makes it very difficult for someone else to attempt to fill the role of the deceased person.

5- to 9-Year-Old Children

Children between the ages of 5 and 9 begin to understand that death is permanent and irreversible. Closer to 7, children start to understand that death is universal, but they think it's not a possibility for themselves. For example, some children in this age group think that old people die because they can't run fast enough when "Mr. Death" approaches (Silverman & Kelly, 2009). Children will still have fears about death. Children at this age are often very curious about details particularly related to dying and what happens after death. Children of this age group are less egocentric and can understand the perspective of others more clearly. Therefore, they are more empathic to others (Dyregrov, 2008). Given their moral development, children are preoccupied with feelings of fairness or unfairness (e.g., "It's not fair," "He was a good coach").

10 Years Old to Adolescence

About the age of 10, children come to understand the finality, irreversibility, inevitability, and causality of death (Corr & Balk, 2009) because they are now beginning to think in abstract terms (Corr & Balk, 2009). They realize that death is a natural part of life. At this age, children are vulnerable to the effects of the loss and more likely to experience strong emotions to death. They are also likely to understand the family problems that result from a death, such as the loss of income, a move to a new neighbourhood, and the effect of the death on other family members (Corr & Balk, 2009). Yet children at this age, like younger children, rarely have the resources, abilities, or independence required to give them some sense of relief from their grief. They can't simply decide that they want to spend time with a friend, for example, and make arrangements on their own to do so. Such arrangements would require involving family members who are often too busy to respond to the requests of the child.

Grieving in Children

Young children may display other reactions. Because of their lack of understanding of finality, they test reality until they come to accept the fact that the person has died. For example, the child may continue to get Grandpa's fishing rod ready at the beginning of fishing season. Children deal with memories. They may want to hear stories about the deceased and look at their pictures over and over. It's thought that children hold visual memories more so than language-based memories (Dyregrov, 2008). Children may engage in fantasy play about death or the funeral or have dreams or nightmares related to death or dying. As well, children may look for someone to replace the dead person. More than occasionally, a child might look for a family member or friend to take the place of the deceased. One mother we spoke with related the story of how her 5-year-old asked the gardener if he could come and be the new daddy.

Young children may also experience anxiety and fear. If the person who died was close to the child, his or her sense of security may be affected. The child may worry that something may happen to Mom or Dad. Anxiety can also manifest as clinginess or a reluctance to make separations, especially from parents. Difficulty sleeping may be related to fear and anxiety as well, especially if the death has been described as "sleep." Often children will have more time to think and recollect as they fall asleep, which may contribute to difficulty falling asleep or waking up with nightmares. Dyregrov (2008) postulates that children who are provided with opportunities to process the trauma of death during the day in play or conversation are less apt to process these types of thoughts at night and will have less sleep disturbances. Many people believe that children should not be told about or be given details on a death because it will upset them, because they won't understand, or because they need to be protected from such news (Corr & Balk, 2009; Jenkinson, 2004). Others believe that children will adjust more smoothly when they know, understand, and have the opportunity to cope. Furthermore, Goldman (1996) argues that information can help reduce the fear children may experience.

Cultural Perspectives

Research suggests that children's understanding of death is quite similar across cultures (Dyregrov, 2008). The difference is in the manner that young children are informed about causes and how children are included in the rituals associated with burials. Open and direct communication can result in a different level of understanding. In addition, it's important to note that children who have emigrated from war-torn countries or from countries with widespread famine may have had more exposure to death, so they may have different perceptions of death.

THE FAMILY DYNAMICS OF GRIEVING AND MOURNING

Grief is not only a personal process but also a family one. When children are reacting to the death of a loved one, their close adult family members are likely mourning as well. Parents may not be emotionally available or may be too preoccupied with their own grief to provide the children with the support they need. Sometimes, parents may even feel that children should be protected from the harsh reality of death and the grief it brings. Or they might believe that the child would not understand even if the situation were explained, or that the child may ask the parents to respond to such inevitable, difficult questions as "Will I die?" or "Will you die?" When children ask the same questions over and over, parents assume that they don't understand. Reluctance to explain or to confront the issue directly can contribute to the child's confusion. Although children feel the death of a loved one intensely, their grief spans are short and intermittent. While it's uncommon to see adults act lightheartedly soon after the death of loved one, children do move in and out of mourning. They may be extremely sad and then shift quickly into a play situation. Parents often misinterpret this behaviour as confirming the belief that children are less capable of feeling and understanding the loss. Attention-seeking behaviour and withdrawal are similarly misinterpreted. Yet the depth of the grief children experience should not be underestimated or ignored and parents, experiencing their own reactions, may misinterpret the child's understanding and reactions.

THE ROLE OF THE EARLY CHILDHOOD EDUCATOR

When a death occurs in the family of one of the children in your care, there is much that you, as an early childhood educator, can do to help both the child and the family. In this instance, it's particularly important to understand how your own views and feelings about death can affect your ability to provide support (Holland, 2008).

SCENARIO

THE FEAR OF SHOWING GRIEF

A class of early childhood students volunteered for a play program for young children with disabilities. One of the children in the program was Arial, a 4-year-old girl with cerebral palsy. This little girl was often sick, and she died after the sixth week of the program. The students decided to go to the funeral together. However, Valerie, the student who'd worked most closely with Arial and who had babysat for her family, refused to attend, feeling she couldn't handle it. After the service, the parents graciously thanked each student for coming and noticed that Valerie wasn't there. When they asked about her, one of the students explained that Valerie hadn't come because she was afraid she'd find the funeral overwhelming. The parents looked surprised and replied, "What about us?"

Dealing with families who are grieving can often bring one's own grief issues to the surface. For example, one early childhood educator confessed that she had great difficulty dealing with a family who had lost a child. After counselling, this woman realized that she still had many unresolved feelings about her grandfather's death. Early childhood educators who possess this self-awareness will be better able to provide empathy and support to families, as well as concrete suggestions that will help parents deal with their children during this stressful and confusing time. Perhaps most important, parents will appreciate any extra efforts made by the early childhood educator to help their child at a time when their own grief has affected their ability to meet the challenges of parenting.

≫ Examine Your Attitudes

The scenario about Sylvia in this chapter's opening vignette indicates that some adults are uncomfortable discussing death. If this is the case with you, it could impede your ability to help others who are grieving. Early childhood educators working with children and families should be aware of their own feelings about death and dying.

Answering the following questions might help you clarify your own thoughts and fears about death. If your answers indicate a high level of discomfort with the subject of death, you may wish to consider this discomfort in the context of professional development. Open and thoughtful discussions with counsellors, religious leaders, friends, and family members often help to alleviate much of the fear and discomfort people feel about death.

- Does the topic of death frighten you, or do you find it interesting to speculate about death and what it means?

- Have you ever experienced the death of a loved one? If so, did you attend the funeral or did you avoid it?

- Do you think children should be sheltered from the reality of death? Should they be kept from attending funerals?

- Do you view death as a release from earthly suffering, or does the idea of not thinking or feeling after death frighten you?

- Would you prefer to be told if you had a fatal disease, or would you rather be kept in ignorance for as long as possible?

Supporting Parents

It's important to put the role of early childhood educator in perspective from the beginning. Death is a major life crisis, and the educator is not in a position to counsel children or families.

However, it is relatively uncommon for the death of a significant family member (e.g., a child or parent) to take place while young children are in your care. More often, children will experience the death of a grandparent or perhaps a family pet. This kind of event will be traumatic to the family, and the family will require support. This will be one of the occasions in which educators will need to recall to promote resilience in the child and family. Moreover, families will likely need some empathy and time to cope, which may translate into some flexibility and extra caring on the educator's part.

Early childhood educators, like everyone else, may feel uncomfortable in approaching the subject of death with a parent. Yet simply by offering condolences and expressions of empathy, they can help parents to feel supported. A simple exchange like "Hi, Mrs. Dixon, I was sorry to hear of your mother's death. This must be a difficult time for you. Please let us know if there's anything we can do to help you" is much better than avoiding the issue, as we are often tempted to do. Some parents may respond by talking about their feelings, while others may acknowledge this offer of sympathy with a simple thank-you or nod of the head.

Although early childhood educators are not therapists and should not attempt grief counselling, they can listen with empathy. If parents seem to require more than this, or even if they seem to need extensive periods of time to talk, they should be referred to religious or counselling agencies. If a grief reaction seems too prolonged or too intense, it may be better to consult with a professional counsellor. Again, educators need to be aware of their boundaries in working with parents.

Often, early childhood educators can help by taking care of the technical details. They may ask another parent to drive the child home or prepare snacks for the day. Sometimes when people are in crisis situations, every small detail seems like a tremendous burden. Having an extra pair of hands may be just as welcome as the emotional support early childhood educators can provide.

Helping Parents Help Their Children

Early childhood educators should understand how children may respond to a death in the family, and they should also understand how caring adults can help children to cope with death. Sharing this information with parents can be extremely important. Two points should be remembered, however. First, for many people death is a taboo subject or, at the very minimum, one that causes discomfort. Therefore, parents may not ask for information prior to a death or at a time when they need it most. Then when the situation arises, parents may feel at a loss as to how to communicate with a young child. Second, even if this information is shared with parents, their own grief responses may interfere with their ability to apply it. Therefore, the early childhood educator may need to communicate information in a variety of ways—for example, through modelling and discussions, or by providing books and pamphlets on the subject.

At the same time, early childhood educators may need to understand and empathize with parents who may not be able to interact optimally with their children because of their grief. The two main areas that parents may want information about from early childhood educators are (1) how to talk to children about death and (2) what to do about children attending the funeral.

Talking to Children About Death

Open communication is the most effective way to deal with death (Dyregrov, 2008). When children are included in the grieving process and participate in associated rituals, they gain a better understanding of death. Young children need rituals and tangible ways to express their grief. Common mistakes adults make are to assume (1) that children shouldn't be exposed to a discussion about death because it will upset them and (2) that children don't understand the explanation provided because they keep asking the same questions over and over. However, when children are not engaged in conversations about the death, their imagination often takes over, and what they imagine may be more frightening than the truth. Therefore, when children are helped to understand how and why someone died, their fears may actually be alleviated. In addition, children shouldn't be required to withhold their feelings (e.g., tears). As stated earlier, children need opportunities to process the trauma in their waking hours through conversation or play. When children don't have such opportunities, they may experience nightmares or may suppress their feelings. Dyregrov (2008) suggests that boys in the preschool years may withhold their grief or be unwilling to talk about it because their reaction has been influenced by society (i.e., they may think that boys shouldn't cry).

Many adults are unsure of how they should talk about death with children. Adults will inevitably bring to their explanation their own thoughts and feelings about the subject. Cultural and religious factors also play an important role in determining how we perceive death. Not only do we have to be aware of our own perceptions, we also have to take care to be sensitive to the various cultural contexts in which children and their families might be experiencing grief (Corr & Balk, 2009). It is absolutely critical that educators talk to parents prior to offering explanations to ensure they fit with the family's beliefs. The following points may serve as useful guidelines in many cases.

Explain Death as Part of the Life Cycle

Children seem to appreciate the logic when death is explained as part of the life cycle of all creatures and as something that is therefore inevitable. Many children's stories about animals, plants, and people support this theme. Young children (under 5) who are developing an understanding of the biological aspects of life may not understand death as clearly as children over 7 who do understand fundamental principles of biology (e.g., when the heart stops beating, the person dies because it will not start again). Biological explanations may help curb children's fears and guilt—they may stop feeling that someone, either themselves or the bogeyman, was directly responsible for the death. Children do, however, need some assurance that it's unlikely they will die soon. It's truthful to tell children that usually people die only when they are very old, and that children (and their parents) will not be old for a long time.

Avoid Euphemisms

Adults often speak about delicate or taboo subjects by using euphemisms. That is, they use vague and inoffensive terms to substitute for the actual word. These ambiguous responses may create confusion or fear for the child (Edgar-Bailey & Kress, 2010; Fearnley, 2010). Death has been described to many children, for example, as "a long sleep" or "a long journey." If a grandmother's death was referred to as "a long journey," can you imagine how frightened a child might be the next time her mother goes on a business trip? Children may become fearful of getting sick if they were told that Granny died because she was sick. This feeling may be intensified if the symptoms are similar to the person who died (e.g., if Mom gets sick after the grandparent has died). It's difficult for children to sort out the difference between serious and common illnesses and their symptoms. Therefore, early childhood educators would be best to talk about death using accurate words. Using *died* is more understandable than *passed away* or other euphemisms. Educators may wish to check words with parents so that the explanations are as similar as possible.

Encourage Talking

In a discussion of death with children, early childhood educators should bear in mind children's curiosity and fascination with details, and establish an environment in which children feel free to ask any questions they may need answered. It's acceptable for adults to admit that they don't have all the answers. Educators should try to answer children's questions as honestly as possible, even if the response is "I don't know" or "Some people believe that . . ." or "Let's ask your dad when he picks you up." Differences in religious or cultural beliefs may be handled in this way.

To prevent mixed messages, early childhood educators should maintain a dialogue with parents about what was said and what the child was told and what is appropriate to tell children (e.g., the parents may not want a biological explanation but rather want the child to hear their faith-based explanation). Children don't need to understand the answers fully; just talking to them and letting them know that people will respond may be sufficient (Corr & Balk, 2009). Children need to know they can ask questions over and over again. Adults need to know that children will ask the same questions over and over and need to process the information over time. Adults discussing death with children should bear in mind how much information children are able to integrate. Young children may create misconceptions about death. It may be helpful to stress certain points:

- The doctors could not prevent death.
- The person loved the child.
- The child is not responsible.
- The child is loved and cared for.
- All feelings are okay, and the child may feel sad.

While children need the opportunity to discuss death and their fears about it, at the same time early childhood educators can encourage them to focus on the living and on the pleasant memories of the person they have lost. Reading and talking about books that deal with death can be an additional way for children to cope. Devereaux Poling and Julie Hupp (2008) suggest that children's literature is a place where children can seek consolation and gain recognition that death is a part of life.

Attending the Funeral

Often parents will ask early childhood educators whether they think the child should attend a funeral. Again, there will be differences of opinion based on culture, religion, and the particular circumstances of the families involved (Dyregrov, 2008; Silverman & Kelly, 2009). We noted earlier that children often have vivid imaginations. Funeral attendance may have positive results. Sometimes actually seeing a dead person or attending a funeral is much less frightening to children than the images they may create in their imagination. Fantasies of reunions or of dead people coming back to life are often minimized with funeral attendance. A funeral is an event full of tradition and ritual in most cultures and a time for family gathering (Ward, 2006), and children need rituals to help them cope (Corr & Balk, 2009). Although the following scenario goes beyond funeral attendance, it does attest to the ability of young children to understand and cope when provided support.

SCENARIO

SAYING GOODBYE

Jonathan was 5 years old when his grandmother died. Although he knew she was very sick and had seen her the day before at the hospital, it surprised him very much when his mother told him that Grandma had died. His first question was "Are you sure she's stopped breathing and her heart isn't thumping?" His mother tried to assure him that the doctors had checked all this. Jonathan still felt very unsure and cried that he needed to see for himself before she was buried. His mother brought him to the funeral home before the service and was amazed at the coolness he displayed while looking at his deceased grandmother. He touched her hand and face and placed his small hand over her heart to check if it was still thumping. He nodded his head and said a prayer. As he and his mother were leaving, Jonathan asked if he could just go back and say one more goodbye on his own. Upon arriving home, the first thing he told his father was that Grandma was okay because he had checked everything. He had experienced a meaningful closure.

Seeing the mourners express their emotions may help children express their emotions as well. The funeral is a means of sharing memories among family and friends. Children can observe this and participate in the sharing of memories. Being part of this release may help children realize that they are not alone in their feelings.

Attending the funeral may also help children to say their final goodbye to a loved one, since this is typically the culturally accepted way of saying farewell. This culturally accepted ritual can be very important for children to participate in.

SCENARIO

NOT ATTENDING THE FUNERAL CAN BE PAINFUL

In a discussion of death in an early childhood classroom, students were asked if they remembered attending funerals when they were young. Many students recalled the funeral as a sad but memorable experience. Others claimed that their most vivid memories were of not being allowed to go to the funeral, and of the resentment they felt for not getting the opportunity to participate in the final goodbye. Many of these students reported years later that the anger, sadness, and fears they felt about the person's death were heightened by their not attending the funeral.

On this topic, it's important for educators to bear in mind that a child's parents may be unavailable to the child during or after the funeral and unable or uncomfortable to answer questions, which may increase the child's distress. The possibility of attendance must be discussed openly and honestly with parents prior to the funeral.

Preparing for the Child's Attendance at the Funeral

Children attending funerals should be prepared in advance in age-appropriate ways (Silverman & Kelly, 2009). They can be told what the funeral setting will look like, how people may be acting/grieving, and whether the deceased will be buried or cremated. Since the people who normally provide support for the child may be consumed by their own grief at the funeral, it may be appropriate for the child to be accompanied by an adult who is less directly and emotionally involved and who will be able to provide the child with support. Educators may help support families to find a person who can be there to support the child. They should be reminded that children are unlikely to be able to sit still throughout an entire service; they may need to leave to go to the bathroom, or to go outside to run around for a bit. Children need to know that it's okay for them to cry or to leave if they need to. If such arrangements can be made beforehand, the child is likely to benefit from the experience.

Remember that you, as educators, may also be experiencing death in a personal way and have your own feelings to cope with, as you will see in the following scenario.

GRIEF AFFECTS US, TOO

A part-time student who works in a child-care centre shared this story about the unexpected death of the mother of a 5-year-old boy. The boy had been in the centre since he was a baby, and his older brother had been there as well, so the news of the mother's death came as a shock; it was a traumatic event for all the staff. The centre decided to close for the afternoon of the funeral, and all parents were given advance notice of the closure. One father read the notice, became very angry, and demanded that the centre find alternative care for his 5-year-old. The student and her team partner stood in shock and didn't know how to respond, which only made the father angrier. The student felt she hadn't handled the situation well, but commented, "I was dealing with a 5-year-old little boy who'd lost his mom, I was dealing with his dad who'd lost his wife, and I was dealing with my own feelings about losing someone who I had interacted with every day."

Alternatives to Funeral Attendance

When children decide not to attend the funeral, they need to be supported in that decision. If adults decide the child should not attend, then an alternate could be planned. The parent can be supported to arrange or find a caring adult who can arrange a "special ceremony" for the child. For example, one child made a special scrapbook about his grandfather. Another made a bouquet to take to the grave; another planted flowers. Children often have their own ideas about how they want to remember a loved one, and a caring adult can help them implement those ideas.

The Role of Early Childhood Educator

Most families will find comfort in the fact that their child's needs are being met by concerned and caring early childhood educators. A child who is mourning may require some extra attention, a few moments longer in the educator's lap, or extra flexibility at naptime and at other transitions during the day. Educators need to remember that the child may be reacting directly to the loss of a loved one, to a changed atmosphere at home, and to the parents' distress. The family-centred approach and the ecological model (see Chapter 3) will lead to this conclusion. Change and loss are multilayered and experienced in different ways, and many issues may intersect for the child and family at this time. The stability provided by the centre's routine and

Helping Children Cope with Death

1. Listen carefully to children as they talk about death. Try to understand their conceptions and misconceptions. When children don't talk, reassure them that you are available if they have questions or want to talk or just need a cuddle. We all avoid topics that we find uncomfortable, and a special effort needs to be made to ensure that we are not discouraging children, either through our body language or by avoidance of the subject altogether.

2. Try not to be overprotective of children. Whether it's seeing a dead bird or overhearing an adult conversation about someone who died, these experiences can be used to enhance the child's understanding of death.

3. In explaining death, avoid euphemisms such as "gone on a trip," "lost," or "sleeping." Children take such terms literally and may become fearful of sleeping or going on trips, or, if it sounds beautiful, children may want to join the deceased person. It's best to use the terms *dead* or *died* and, if necessary, explain to the young child what that means in a physical

sense. For example, "Grampa's heart isn't beating anymore; he can't breathe." Be sure to check with parents first to ensure they are using similar language and explanations.

4. Be prepared to support the attendance of children at funerals, unless there are religious or other factors that prohibit this. Ongoing discussion and collaboration with parents is necessary to clarify such a matter.

5. Be aware of children's short grief span, and ensure that this is not misinterpreted as denial. Ensure that parents also understand how children grieve to prevent misinterpretation of a child's behaviour and in so doing, providing support to parents.

6. Be aware of hidden fears, such as Grandma dying in the hospital, which may cause the child to think he or she will die if hospitalized. Explain the circumstances of the death, such as a serious illness, old age, or a car accident. Also, children need information and reassurance about what would happen and who would care for them if their parents died.

7. Consider developmentally appropriate information. Give the child as much as he or she wants and is able to handle. Check regularly if the child needs or wants more information.

8. While children should be encouraged to share their feelings, they should not be pressured to do so. Give children permission to feel sad or confused, or to cry if that is what they want to do, or to go and play if they want to. We must take care not to interpret a child's feelings incorrectly. For instance, a little boy may be crying because another child took the ball away from him. We must not assume that those are tears of sadness due to his uncle's death.

9. Provide children with many opportunities to express themselves through play or creative expression, such as art or music. Children will need to process the information over and over through words and in their play. Books and stories about death that are developmentally appropriate should be available to but not imposed on children. Parents may also find such resources valuable in explaining concepts to their child. Let parents know about any good, age-appropriate resources.

10. When adults working with children have firm beliefs about death and the afterlife, they must be cautious not to impose them on others. Children may come from families with very different belief systems, and early childhood educators must treat all of their beliefs with the utmost respect. Collaboration with the child's parents will be critical, and early childhood educators should encourage them to share their beliefs with their children. If you are unfamiliar with the specific traditions of mourning in a different culture, be sure to ask about them. Most people would rather be asked what is appropriate in their culture, and they will probably appreciate your interest. Parents may not always realize that your customs and beliefs differ from their own.

11. Remember that there is no universally accepted way to grieve and mourn, and that people vary widely in the time it takes to recover. In modern society, we have few built-in rituals to help with our mourning, and there often seems to be a rush to "get back to normal." Families and children may need more time than is formally allotted (compassionate leave at work, etc.) to recover from their loss. The patience and ongoing support of those who care about the bereaved family will be appreciated.

12. Perhaps most important, you should remember the tremendous impact that a death in the family can have on every family member. Early childhood educators might want to go that extra mile for a bereaved family. For example, you could allow for extra flexibility in arrival and pickup times or agree to be flexible in the centre's rules in other ways that would make things easier for the grieving family.

Source: Based on material from Canadian Child Day Care Federation, n.d. Helping children understand death. By G. Garvie. Resource Sheet No. 10. Ottawa: Canadian Child Day Care Federation. Retrieved from http://www.cccf-fcsge.ca/wp-content/uploads/RS_10-e.pdf.

the warm interaction with early childhood educators may be the single most critical factor during this time. In addition, the guidelines listed above can help early childhood educators support children who are trying to understand death and mourning the loss of a loved one.

CONCLUSION

The death of a family member usually begins a period of crisis in the lives of the surviving family members. The time following a death will be a time of mourning for all. Children may appear to understand death in different ways than adults do and may have different reactions. Early childhood educators must put the child's reactions into context to better understand and help children cope. By doing so, educators can also provide assistance to parents supporting their child in this difficult time. Children need rituals, so participating in ceremonies and traditions like funerals and memorial services can often help children overcome their fears and misconceptions about death. The early childhood educator can play a valuable role not only in providing support to children but also in supporting parents in their interactions with their young children.

Chapter Summary

- Early childhood educators need to be aware of the impact that death has on all family members, especially children.
- It's important that early childhood educators understand grieving in children and adults.
- Early childhood educators can better understand children's reactions based on development.
- Early childhood educators should consider ways to help children cope and should assist parents to help their children as well.
- Understanding resilience and how to build resilience in children and families will be useful information during this time.

RESOURCES

Canadian Child Care Federation:
www.cccf-fcsge.ca

Public Health Agency of Canada, *Responding to Stressful Events*:
www.phac-aspc.gc.ca/publicat/oes-bsu-02/pdf/helping-child-cope_e.pdf

KidsHealth, "Helping Your Child Deal with Death":
http://kidshealth.org/en/parents/death.html

EXERCISES

1. Discuss death and burial rituals with a number of different people from different cultural backgrounds. Compare their traditions and their beliefs with your own.

2. The TED website includes several talks on death (see www.ted.com/topics/death). Review one or more of these talks and discuss the implications for your own beliefs and in your role as an educator working with children and families with different beliefs.

3. An interesting TED Talks article discusses the funeral traditions in a variety of countries. Review these different traditions and discuss the concept of death as understood in the different cultures. The article is available at http://ideas.ted.com/11-fascinating-funeral-traditions-from-around-the-globe/.

4. Discuss funeral attendance with a number of people. Do they have pleasant or unpleasant memories? Can they explain why? How has it affected their beliefs today?

5. Practise what you might say in response to a 3-year-old's questions about death. What if the same questions were asked by a 5-year-old? How would your answers differ?

6. If one child in your playroom experienced a death, what would your response be to the other children? Would you tell them? Would you talk about it? Would you let the parents of the other children know?

7. Check your local community for people who may be able to provide information or expertise in dealing with death (e.g., mental health agencies, funeral directors). Check whether the information is suitable for children under the age of 5 and whether the professionals working there have experience with young children. Many professionals specialize in grieving but may not have expertise in applying it to young children. Funeral directors also often have information specifically related to young children and families.

8. The resource sheet "Helping Children Understand Death," published by the Canadian Child Day Care Federation to aid parents, makes the following suggestion:

   > Touring a neighbourhood funeral home and/or cemetery can be an excellent way to give your child accurate information about what happens to the body after death and the funeral process. Many funeral directors are experienced in answering children's questions, and often parents find such a tour extremely informative and interesting as well.

   Discuss this suggestion with your classmates and colleagues. Would you consider it? Why or why not?

9. Review information regarding resilience. What aspects of individual and family resilience may be most compelling at this time.

10. Death is likely a loss that will have the most significant and deep impact on children and family. Consider all the aspects of loss (major and minor) that the child may experience. What changes may occur (both short-term and long-term changes). How might you support the child in these times of change and loss?

CHAPTER 20
Violence and Abuse in the Home

OBJECTIVES

- To examine different types of abuse and neglect of children

- To examine the myths and characteristics associated with the perpetrators and the victims of abuse

- To examine the role of the early childhood educator in monitoring and reporting abuse

- To examine the role of the early childhood educator in preventing abuse

- To describe strategies for supporting children who are neglected or abused

- To examine the role of the early childhood educator in supporting families in which abuse and neglect occur

Maria, an early childhood educator, shared the following incident with her co-worker:

> "After I saw the bruises on Johnny's buttocks, I thought I'd faint when his father walked into the room at the end of the day. I wanted to scream at him, 'How dare you hurt this innocent child!' Instead, I took a deep breath and approached him as calmly as I could. 'Good morning, Mr. Smith,' I said. 'Would you please come with me to Mrs. Atari's [the director's] office? There's something she'd like to discuss with you.' I accompanied him to the director's office door; then I left. But I couldn't do anything when I got back into the playroom. I was trembling so much that I couldn't even speak."

UNDERSTANDING THE IMPACT OF ABUSE AND NEGLECT

The most difficult aspect of being a member of the early childhood profession is coming face to face with child abuse. Child abuse strikes at the very core of our professional commitment to children's well-being. It's in polar opposition to all we believe about how children should be nurtured, respected, and protected. At the moment when we discover that someone in the home or someone the child trusts hurt a child, the idea of being accepting and nonjudgmental can seem like nothing more than a meaningless theory. However, in many cases, the signs of neglect or abuse may be ambiguous and the process of confirming abuse may take a long time. This is a fundamental concern in child welfare intervention—there is no universal way to define abuse or maltreatment, nor is there one accepted framework for intervention (Stith et al., 2009; Ward, 2006).

Although in many jurisdictions adults are legally compelled to report incidences of abuse, educators must decide when it's appropriate to seek and provide families and children with additional support, either from the centre or from community resources, and when and if reporting to child protection is required. This process and decision can be agonizing for even the most seasoned professional.

Violence and abuse within the family are not new phenomena. Abuse and maltreatment have existed throughout history and across cultures (U.S. Department of Health & Human Services, 2017). According to Statistics Canada, 59% of instances of sexual and physical assaults against children and youth were committed by parents in 2009. Moreover, young child victims (under 3 years old) were most vulnerable to violence by a parent (Statistics Canada, 2015b). Sometimes it seems as if violence within the home is more prevalent in today's society than in the past. However, the increase may be attributed to the increase in attention abuse has received, in people's willingness to discuss it, and in the availability of better reporting procedures. We should note, however, that family violence is still under-reported (Stith et al., 2009; Vanier Institute of the Family, 2010) and that prevalence rates with children continue to be difficult to determine because children are dependent on others to detect and report on their behalf. Children younger than 5 are over-represented among young people living with domestic violence (Baker & Cunningham, 2009), and while the prevalence of abuse is reportedly four times higher for young girls than young boys, young boys are more likely to experience physical injuries (as opposed to emotional or sexual abuse) (Statistics Canada, 2008).

In this chapter, we will examine both abuse and neglect of children in the home and discuss their effects on the adults and children involved. We will also review domestic violence, as research has shown that this kind of violence and abuse within families (e.g., spousal abuse, sibling abuse) constitutes a serious problem with devastating and long-lasting effects on family members and particularly on children. It should also be clear that, even if children are not the direct victims, they are harmed as a consequence of any violent or abusive situation in a family. The chapter will close with a discussion of the role of the early childhood educator in relation to this very serious problem.

Key Points for Dealing with Children Who Have Been Exposed to Violence

- Ensure that you are aware of your local policies and procedures for reporting abuse and protecting the child as well as the other children in your program.
- When you think a child may be experiencing abuse but are not certain, consult with a peer or your supervisor. Don't ignore your suspicions.
- Document frequently, precisely and always report abuse promptly.
- Ensure that the child is provided with a nurturing and stable environment while in your care.
- Provide support to parents and provide information on community support services.
- Make certain that you have your own support network.
- Understand that involvement with family violence can be emotionally draining for staff.

DEFINING AND UNDERSTANDING ABUSE

To begin, we shall try to arrive at a clear and practical definition of the terms that are used in this chapter, since they so often seem to be open to interpretation. What one person considers abuse (e.g., corporal punishment), another may consider an appropriate response to bad behaviour (Health and Welfare Canada, n.d.). Increased awareness of and sensitivity to cultural differences have raised many questions as to how to determine whether culturally sanctioned practices are legitimate forms of discipline (Ward, 2006).

Child abuse "is any form of physical, emotional and/or sexual mistreatment or lack of care that causes injury or emotional damage to a child or youth. The misuse of power and/or a breach of trust are part of all types of child abuse" (Canadian Red Cross, 2017). *Abuse* usually refers to a situation in which a more powerful person attempts to exert control over a less powerful person (Ward, 2006). It includes any physical force that exceeds reasonable discipline. Abusers use threats and actions to maintain control over their victims, which result in physical or psychological harm to the child (Health and Welfare Canada, n.d.). *Maltreatment* refers to "intentional harm or endangerment of a child including unkindness, harshness, rejection, neglect, deprivation and/or violence" (Berns, 2004, p. 160). Being a *witness to violence* in the family refers to when children see, hear, or are aware of violence by one family member to another (Baker, 2009; Canadian Red Cross, 2017).

Understanding Abuse

Different types of abuse have been defined in a variety of ways. Before looking at specific definitions, it's important to stress that one form of abuse seldom occurs in isolation. More often, two or more types of abuse occur simultaneously. Thus, although the categories of abuse can serve as guidelines, in certain cases we may need to use them in a flexible way (Berns, 2010). In addition, early childhood educators must be mindful that behaviours may be attributed to other factors, so it's important to consider the context and look for patterns of behaviour.

Abuse can be divided into the following categories:

1. *Physical abuse* means that a person of trust purposefully injures or threatens a child (Canadian Red Cross, 2017). It has also been described as the deliberate application of unreasonable force (Royal Canadian Mounted Police, 2012). Physical abuse can occur with or without verbal abuse.

2. *Emotional abuse* involves depriving the child of affection, love, and acceptance. Verbal abuse, a common form of emotional abuse, entails belittling and humiliation. Emotional abuse may also include intimidating, exploiting, or terrorizing.

3. *Sexual abuse* involves the sexual exploitation of individuals against their will. It may involve contact such as touching, forcing the child to touch, or forcing sexual acts such as intercourse upon the child. It can occur by force, by tricking, or by threatening the child. It may be noncontact such as exposure to the sexual parts of another person's body or watching pornographic material.

4. *Neglect* describes a situation in which the child's necessities are not met by the adult to such an extent that it interferes with the child's emotional or physical development (Royal Canadian Mounted Police, 2012). Physical neglect occurs when there is a failure to meet medical, dental, nutritional, sleep, or dress needs. Emotional neglect occurs when the child's needs to feel loved, worthy, and secure are not met. Neglect is the least likely of all forms of abuse to be reported yet is the most common type of child abuse (Royal Canadian Mounted Police, 2012). Neglect typically receives less attention because it's less noticeable and the effects less obvious. Society continues to associate neglect with poverty (Berns, 2010), but neglect can exist without poverty.

Many documents define and provide indicators of child abuse and neglect. The indicators of abuse in the box that follows are from *Protocols for Handling Child Abuse and Neglect in Child Care Services*, published by Alberta Children's Services (2006). Indicators of abuse are presented with descriptions of physical and emotional signs that may be detected in the child. Behaviours that you may see in the adult abuser are also listed. For instance, one of the most common signs of abuse or violence consists of the strained interaction between the abuser and the victim. An early childhood educator who knows a child well will usually notice whether the child behaves strangely around certain adults, especially when the behaviour involves an obvious withdrawal from a person who is closely related to the child.

Child Abuse: What to Look For

Indicators of Neglect

The child may:

- be underweight, dehydrated, emaciated, or have a distended stomach
- show improvement of developmental delays following proper stimulation and care
- demonstrate signs of deprivation: cradle cap, severe diaper rash, diarrhea, vomiting, anemia, recurring respiratory problems
- be consistently dirty or dressed inappropriately for weather, or wear torn clothing
- often be hungry or thirsty
- often be tired or listless
- demand much physical contact and attention
- assume role of parent or adult in the family
- lack proper medical and dental care
- have poor hygiene
- have unattended medical or dental problems such as infected sores, decayed teeth, lack of needed glasses

The adult may:

- maintain a chaotic home life with little evidence of personal care routines
- not supervise child for long periods of time or not supervise when child is involved in potentially dangerous activity
- leave child in the care of inappropriate persons
- give child inappropriate food, drink, medicine
- consistently bring child early and pick up late
- be apathetic toward child's progress, be hard to reach by phone, and fail to keep appointments to discuss child and concerns
- overwork or exploit child
- show evidence of apathy, feelings of futility

Indicators of Physical Abuse

The physical signs might include:

- unexplained (or poorly explained) bruises and welts
- a number of scars in a regular pattern
- bruises of varying colours in the shape of an object (cord, rope, belt, buckle, clothes hanger)
- bald spots or missing teeth
- human bite marks
- unexplained burns, such as the following:
  - cigarette-shaped burns
  - immersion burns (e.g., glove-shaped, sock-shaped)
  - electric iron or burner-shaped burns
- unexplained (or poorly explained) fractures, sprains, dislocations, or head injuries
- inflamed tissue suggesting scalding
- symptoms of consumption of a poisonous, corrosive or non medical, mind-altering substance

continues ▶

▶ *continues*

The child may:

- be wary of physical contact with adults
- seem afraid of parent or other person
- be frightened in the face of adult disapproval
- be apprehensive when other children cry
- show extremes of behaviour—aggressive/withdrawn
- be over-anxious to please
- approach any adult including strangers
- be defensive about injuries
- have low self-esteem
- wear clothing that covers body even though the weather is warm
- not tolerate physical contact or touch
- run away often
- be unable to form good peer relationships
- be reluctant to undress when others are around

The adult may:

- be angry, impatient; frequently lose or almost lose control
- appear unconcerned about child's condition
- view child as bad or as the cause of life's problems
- resist discussion of child's condition or family situation
- view questions with suspicion
- use discipline inappropriate to child's age, condition, and situation
- offer illogical, contradictory, unconvincing, or no explanation of injuries
- show poor understanding of normal child development (e.g., may expect adult-like, mature behaviour from a young child)

Indicators of Sexual Abuse

Physical evidence of sexual abuse is rare. Often with young children, abuse is not intercourse but touching, which may leave no physical signs. Where physical evidence is present, it may be:

- torn, stained, or bloody clothing
- pain or itching in genital area or throat, difficulty going to bathroom or swallowing
- bruises, bleeding, or swelling of genital, rectal, or anal areas
- vaginal odour or discharge
- stomach aches, headaches, or other psychosomatic complaints

The child may:

- use language and make drawings that are sexually explicit
- fantasize excessively
- show fear of closed spaces
- resist undressing or diaper changes
- masturbate excessively
- exhibit seductive behaviour

- express premature or inappropriate understanding of sexual behaviour
- display inappropriate, unusual, or aggressive sexual behaviour with peers or toys
- be excessively curious about sexual matters or genitalia of others or self
- wet pants (in a previously trained child)
- soil pants
- have eating disturbances (over-eating or under-eating)
- have fears/compulsive behaviour
- have school problems or significant changes in school performance
- display age-inappropriate behaviour, pseudo-maturity or regressive behaviour, such as bed-wetting and thumb-sucking
- be unable to concentrate
- have sleep disturbances, such as nightmares, fear of falling asleep, and sleeping long hours

The adult may:

- often be domineering but emotionally weak
- suggest or indicate marital or relationship difficulties with adults
- indicate own social isolation, loneliness, especially as a single parent
- cling to child, both physically and emotionally; hold and touch the child in an inappropriate way
- tend to blame others for life's problems and child's sexual behaviour—may even accuse child of causing sexual abuse

Indicators of Emotional Abuse

Child's appearance may not indicate or suggest the extent of the difficulty. The child may appear clean, well-groomed, and well-nourished. Child's facial expression and body carriage may indicate sadness, depression, timidity, or held-back anger.

The child may:

- appear overly compliant, passive, shy
- show episodes of very aggressive, demanding, and angry behaviour
- fear failure, have trouble concentrating or learning, and give up easily
- be either boastful or negative about self
- constantly apologize
- cry without provocation
- be excessively demanding of adult attention

The adult may:

- blame or belittle child in public and at home
- withhold comfort when child is frightened or distressed
- treat other children in the family differently and better, showing more acceptance and love and less criticism
- tend to describe child in negative ways: "stupid," "bad," "trouble-maker"; and predict failure for child
- hold child responsible for parent's difficulties and disappointments
- identify child with disliked relatives

Source: Alberta Human Services, "Protocols for Handling Child Abuse and Neglect in Child Care Services," January, 2006. Reprinted with permission.

Early childhood educators should try to find a publication that provides written guidelines and other information for their own use and use by others in the child-care centre. These are often available from local child welfare offices, which provide specific information related to local legislation. In addition, national associations and clearing-houses that disseminate information exist in both Canada and the United States. Documents such as the one quoted above are intended to be used only as guides. Many of the indicators listed above characterize children who are experiencing problems, yet are not abused or neglected. Therefore, it's important to be vigilant and observant over an extended period of time and open to new information. It's particularly important to consult with local child welfare agencies or other specialists in child abuse when suspicions of abuse arise.

WHY ABUSE OCCURS

In this section, we will attempt to highlight some common characteristics associated with child abuse. The factors that contribute to child abuse are "complex and deeply rooted in the family, community, workplace and broader social systems" (Government of Canada, 2004). Note that some of the characteristics focus on the situation of the child and the attributes of the abuser, while others focus on social factors that make abuse more likely to happen. Abuse involves an interplay of characteristics and events and typically not just one factor (Administration on Children, Youth, and Families, 2008; Government of Canada, 2004).

Social Conditions Associated with Abuse

Research suggests that a key contributing factor for abuse is low socio-economic status (Administration on Children, Youth, and Families, 2008; Government of Canada, 2004). Abuse may occur due to the large number of stressors involved in living in poverty. However, some researchers have suggested that such a disproportionate representation may reflect the fact that abuse in low-income families is much more likely to be reported than abuse in middle- or high-income families. Possible reasons for this higher reporting may be because low-income families are more likely to be involved with social service agencies, low-income families may have fewer support systems to rely on, or people may simply be more willing to report such families (Administration on Children, Youth, and Families, 2008).

Research indicates that a number of factors related to parents may contribute to high rates of abuse, especially physical abuse, emotional abuse, and neglect. Factors include childhood experiences of abuse, violence in the home, parent mental health issues, substance abuse, and lack of social support (Government of Canada, 2004).

Children in single-parent homes have a higher risk for abuse (Stocks, 2011). There are two plausible and interrelated explanations for this phenomenon, both of which are based on the ecological approach (see Chapter 3). First, the single parent experiences a high degree of stress in meeting the demands of child-rearing alone and have no one to turn to when the situation escalates. Second, stress levels are further aggravated because many single parents live in deprived economic conditions. This is but one example of how economic and social factors may interact to produce conditions in which the probability of abuse is high.

Other social factors associated with abuse are social values and norms of behaviour. Cultural traditions do exist that condone and even contribute to family violence (Este & Tachble, 2009). Such traditions are strong in societies in which men are taught that they are in control and have the right to control others, especially their wives and children (Este & Tachble, 2009).

Nita is a 32-year-old married woman with two preschool-age children. She shared this story in an early childhood class she was taking in the evenings.

"My parents emigrated from Lebanon and worked very hard to set up a business and raise a family in Canada. I have two older brothers and three younger sisters. We've always been a close family, keeping our religious and cultural heritage in this new country. Just like back home, my father was the undisputed head of the house—he demanded respect and obedience, he set out all the rules according to tradition, and he dished out the discipline.

"I can't say when the abuse started; I can always remember being hit by my father when something went wrong or when I was bad. I know that my brothers and sisters were beat up too, but we never, never talked about it, because it was something that happened at home and stayed at home. I do remember that my father began to abuse me sexually when I was 12 years old. I never told anyone; it was his right as the head of the house, or so we were told. I think my mother knew, because she started to ignore me and was really distant. He came to my bed at night until I was 16 and couldn't stand it anymore. I ran away from home and the small community we lived in to the big city. I worked the streets for a few years—what the heck, I'd been doing it since I was 12, and now guys would pay me money, and they were nice, too.

"One day I was in the welfare office and met this really nice guy named Nick. He was in bad shape, too, and trying to start all over, so we tried together.

"That was five years ago. Now we're married, Nick works full-time as a baker, and we have two children. Domenica is 19 months and Marguerite is 3 years old. I still see my family, except for my father. Funny, everybody knew what Dad was doing, and he was doing the same thing to my sisters.

"I haven't talked about this much and haven't got any professional help. Maybe someday I will. But one thing I know for certain is that those things will never, never happen to my children. I'll never let my children go through the hurt like I did, and I'll do anything to make sure that it doesn't happen. My hurting will never go away, but it will always be a reminder of what kind of parent I should be."

Personal Attributes of the Abuser

Abuse is a complex issue, and there is no one factor that leads to it but rather multiple sources of stress that affect parents' ability to provide for their children.

Many myths surround abusers and victims of abuse. The two most common myths are that abusers fit one particular profile and that their victims somehow asked for or deserved the abuse. Both myths are untrue.

Abusive adults do, in fact, come from every walk of life—from every cultural group, socio-economic level, and educational background. No single description or profile fits all abusers. They do, however, share some common characteristics.

First, abusers who use physical force tend to be male, and their victims tend to be women and children (Ontario Ministry of the Status of Women, 2015). Power continues to be the cornerstone for violence (Ambert, 2006), which may be attributed to a number of factors. Fathers have always been perceived as more authoritarian than mothers. When it becomes evident that the use of violence can be effective in gaining and maintaining control of both women and children, its use is perpetuated. Again, there may be cultural sanctioning of the use of force in abusing women or disciplining children (Ambert, 2006; Este & Tachble, 2009). Women, on the other hand, are more likely to engage in corporal punishment (e.g., spanking) (Ambert, 2006; Global Initiative to End All Corporal Punishment of Children, 2016).

Possible explanations for why some mothers abuse their children or allow their children to be abused by their partners focus on the relative lack of power and control some women experience. Many women continue to live in situations in which they themselves are abused because they are financially dependent or have been socialized to believe that they can't make it on their own (McDaniel & Tepperman, 2007). Women are also often socialized to believe that their relationship with their spouse is the most important thing that can happen in their lives and that they are responsible for its success (McDaniel & Tepperman, 2007). Although gender differences can't adequately explain abuse, the socialization of men and women in our culture does contribute.

The second common characteristic of abusers is that they frequently have difficulty dealing with their emotions (Eshleman & Wilson, 1995; Stosny, 2015). Men have been socialized to believe that displays of violence are normal and to be expected.

A third characteristic of abusers is that they often blame other people or external situations for the violence they cause. For example, stress, alcohol, work, a messy house, or noisy children may trigger a violent reaction when they arrive home at the end of the day.

High Stress Levels and Few Coping Mechanisms

Abusive adults, whether they are mothers or fathers, tend to be under a great deal of stress (Krug, Dahlberg, Mercy, Zwi, & Lozano, 2002). Stress may come from events at work, at home, or from any other source. In addition, abusive people have few resources for coping with stress (Guterman, Lee, Taylor, & Rathouz, 2009; Schachter, 2015; Seng & Prinz, 2008). Abusers tend to be more socially isolated and have fewer connections (Schreiner, 2014; Seng & Prinz, 2008). They often lack access to good support systems, and even if they do have access, they seem reluctant to use them (Family Resource Center, 2017; Health and Welfare Canada, n.d.). Lack of social support, inadequate means of coping with stress, and the perceived cultural support for the use of force in disciplining children can all contribute to the creation and perpetuation of abuse within families (Guterman et al., 2009; Seng & Prinz, 2008).

Part of the Abuse Cycle

Researchers have established that many abusive adults were themselves abused as children (Moorhead, 2013b). In addition, researchers have found that violence and family turmoil are reproduced across generations of mothers and daughters, in what some researchers believe to be an "emotional archive" of gendered violence (Kenway & Fahey, 2008). The rate of abuse among those abused as children is 30%, which is significantly higher than the 2% expected in the general population. It may be that as children, abusive adults learned that violence was an apparently effective way to solve problems, or it may be that, as children, they were made to feel unloved, unworthy, and unwanted (Health and Welfare Canada, n.d.). Abusive adults perpetuate negative self-perceptions when they abuse others, thus reinforcing to themselves that they are no good. Perhaps they had poor role models as children or they are unable to meet the needs of their child just as their needs were unmet by their parents (Dixon, Hamilton-Giachritsis, Browne, & Ostapuik, 2009).

However, not all abused children go on to abuse their children or spouses, and, in fact, studies suggest that there is no increase in subsequent generations (Ambert, 2006; O'Grady, 2015). These studies conclude that the transmission of violence is complex and that many dimensions are likely relevant, not just that abusers were themselves abused as children.

Poor Parenting Skills

Abusive parents often think of parenting as stressful and have difficulty understanding the child's perception of the world (Government of Canada, 2012; Stith et al., 2008). They may believe that they have little control over their children. When a parent uses force or violence to control, there are immediate short-term effects (i.e., the problematic behaviour ceases), but the parent doesn't consider the long-term negative effects. The child misbehaves again and the parent uses force to control the situation once more, with the amount of force possibly increasing. This often leads to the creation of more stress and less control in parenting, and, before long, the cycle of abuse has become established within the home.

Abusive parents often have unrealistic expectations about their child's development and behaviour (Berns, 2010; NoBullying.com, 2015; Palusci, Crum, Bliss, & Bavolek, 2008). They demand physical, social, and emotional abilities that are well beyond the child's developmental stage (e.g., demanding that the toddler not cry when Mommy leaves or expecting a baby to sleep through the night). When the child doesn't display these expected abilities, the parents may feel further frustration, or they may look upon abuse as the discipline necessary to ensure compliance. Inappropriate parenting is characterized as being based on parents' needs, and so they accordingly ignore the child's needs, don't provide basic care or support, and use extreme discipline methods (Berns, 2010; Palusci et al., 2008).

Relationship Problems

Eighty-five percent of children who are sexually abused know their abuser (Canadian Red Cross, 2017). Sexual abuse is more likely to occur with family members than it is with strangers (McDaniel & Tepperman, 2007; Saffron Centre, 2015). In fact, it's far more common for children, especially girls, to be sexually abused by a person that they know and trust (McDaniel & Tepperman, 2007; Parents Protect!, n.d.). There are some common characteristics of families in which sexual abuse occurs. The adult is usually isolated and has difficulty in relationships in general but predominantly in emotional and sexual relationships. The presence of stepfathers is also a factor (Collin-Vezina, Daigneault, & Hebert, 2013). As well, abuse is more likely to occur in families that are socially isolated and appear very close and traditional. They often have poor communication patterns and blurred boundaries between family subsystems, with role confusion or reversal. Parents in abusive homes tend to suffer from emotional deprivation and are therefore emotionally needy. Sexual abuse usually occurs in situations where there is some form of inequality; for instance, males typically abuse younger females.

Characteristics of Victims of Abuse

Vulnerability

Children who are subjected to abuse also display particular characteristics. They usually know their abuser and may have an emotional relationship with that person. In the case of sexual abuse, the abuser may be the only person to show the child affection, making the child more vulnerable to being taken advantage of. Children have been taught to obey and be polite to adults, and not to question their actions or behaviour. In addition, children are generally unable to protect themselves from an adult, particularly one using physical force. Children are dependent on adults and so may be vulnerable to intimidation. Children may blame themselves for abuse and may believe that they may cause further harm (e.g., separation or divorce) if they say anything. Many abused children don't have well-developed social and emotional relationships with other people. This lack of support makes them feel isolated. Children may think they will not be believed or may have been told that no one will believe them. All of these factors leave the child highly vulnerable to abuse.

Special Needs

Research indicates that children who have special needs are more likely to be abused (Sullivan, Knutson, & Asford, 2009). These children include those who have developmental delays, physical disabilities, or chronic health problems, or whose temperaments make them difficult to raise (Sullivan et al., 2009). Children living in foster or adoptive homes and those living with blended families or single parents (especially when the child was not wanted) are also at a higher risk for abuse (Health and Welfare Canada, n.d.).

WITNESS TO VIOLENCE

In the past, it was thought that children living in families with spousal violence were simply witnesses of the violence. However, it has been found that witnessing domestic abuse can result in negative consequences including emotional, psychological, social, or behavioural concerns. Some studies suggest that young children display the most negative effects from witnessing violence (Sinha, 2015). It has been suggested that the effects of observing violence in the home may be similar to the effects of physical abuse.

Children may be the victims of abuse when they are directly involved in or when they hear or see domestic violence (Baker & Cunningham, 2009). Children who witness violence in the home are more likely to display aggressive behaviour and become desensitized to aggression. Witnessing parental violence can shape gender roles in young children. They may pick up messages from violence that shape their definition of what it means to be female or male, such as that men deserve to get what they want, or that women should be submissive (Baker & Cunningham, 2009). In addition, children who witness domestic violence can develop negative beliefs about themselves, become isolated from support, internalize the abuse, and come to believe that violence in the home is "normal" (Baker & Cunningham, 2009). One study noted that young children may experience traumatic stress reactions such as anger, fear, or grief, and may cry, act out, throw temper tantrums, or constantly worry about danger (Baker & Cunningham, 2009). Often (although not necessarily) inter-parental violence is coupled with poverty and substance abuse, which can heighten the effects of violence (Baker & Cunningham, 2009; O'Campo, Caughy, & Nettles, 2010).

Children have no ability to remove themselves from the situation. They are typically not cared for, either physically or psychologically. Such children no longer perceive the home as a safe refuge. Parents, experiencing their own struggles, may be less available to the child at a time when the child is likely in need of increased emotional support. Many parenting roles may be unavailable to the child when parents are concerned with their own basic safety, so neglect may be the result (Baker & Cunningham, 2009). In addition, children witnessing abuse between parents may wonder who can be trusted or loved. Children may not understand why their lives are different from others' or why they have family secrets, can't bring friends home, or have no one to protect them. Children may have strong ambivalence toward the parent who is violent—feelings of affection and resentment.

Children living with domestic abuse will often experience physical health problems, such as weight, eating, or sleeping problems; acting-out behaviours; low self-concept; anxiety; aggression; social isolation; or difficulties interacting with other children (Ambert, 2006). Children who live in high-conflict homes tend to respond to conflict more readily and with more intensity. Whereas boys tend to react more externally (e.g., with aggression and behavioural outbursts), girls tend to react with anxiety and depression. Children who have been abused often have an uncanny ability to adapt and to perceive the mood, feelings, and needs of significant others in their immediate environment and then act accordingly (O'Campo et al., 2010). Children have also been labelled as *hypervigilant*; that is, they constantly maintain vigilance over their environment so that they are prepared. Although this may be adaptive at home, it may interfere with learning (e.g., in school where the child maintains vigilance over the environment rather than focuses on the task at hand).

The adult abuser may use children as a control tactic against his or her spouse (Baker & Cunningham, 2009). For example, the adult abuser may say that the child is to blame for the violence. The perpetrator may threaten the child with violence in an attempt to control the abused spouse or may talk negatively to the child about the abused parent.

DEVELOPMENTAL EFFECTS OF CHILD ABUSE

Recent neuroscience research has determined that stress in the early years may have negative effects on developing brains. In particular, toxic stress results from "stressful events that are chronic, uncontrollable and/or experienced without the child having access to support from caring adults tend to provoke these types of toxic stress responses" (National Scientific Council on the Developing Child, 2014, p. 2). Toxic stress can impact the architecture of the brain. One of the most serious forms of toxic stress results from neglect and maltreatment. The effects on brain development can last long after the child has been removed from the source of neglect or abuse. Research also suggests that the presence of responsive educators can create a buffer against stress in young children. Furthermore, the quality of care in early learning programs also plays a significant role in buffering toxic stress. All in all, the role of sensitive, caring educators providing quality care is a critical component of child care for all children, but especially for those living with neglect or abuse (National Scientific Council on the Developing Child, 2014).

Exposing children to violence is not considered a criminal activity. However, it is considered a form of maltreatment, which means that child welfare systems are obligated to investigate incidences of domestic abuse to ensure the safety and well-being of children in the home (Sinha, 2015). Exposure to violence in the home has long-term effects on child development (Sinha, 2015).

Children who have been exposed to sexual and physical abuse or high rates of domestic violence report lower academic and social success at school, increased rates of depression, low self-esteem, and increased alcohol and drug usage in adolescence and adulthood (Baker & Cunningham, 2009; O'Campo et al., 2010). They may feel shame and isolation and be unable to talk to anyone about their experience (Hornor, 2008). The abuser may have told them to be silent, that no one will believe them anyway, or may have threatened them (Health and Welfare Canada, n.d.). Children who have been exposed to abuse or violence have demonstrated increased rates of negative and aggressive behaviour, anti-social behaviour, withdrawal, depression, fearfulness, and disruptions in eating and sleeping patterns, constant worry, difficulty concentrating (Baker & Cunningham, 2009; Christoffersen & DePanfilis, 2009). They may also experience nightmares, bedwetting, difficulties controlling emotions, insecurity, fears, or anxiety (Christoffersen & DePanfilis, 2009).

While school-age children have the ability to develop coping mechanisms, preschool-age children are more limited since they have not yet developed the cognitive capacities necessary for problem-focused or action-oriented coping. They are in the stage of cognitive development where they make sense of the world through generalizations, basic levels of categorization, and concrete thinking, so instead of being able to cope effectively, they must mentally, emotionally or behaviourally disengage (Baker & Cunningham, 2009). Fear and inconsistency may inhibit exploration, play, and developing independence. Children may use more aggression in their interactions and begin to associate gender roles with violence and being a victim (Baker & Cunningham, 2009).

SCENARIO

STORMY MONDAY

A new early childhood educator was starting in the child-care centre on a Monday morning. A 5-year-old who had just been dropped off by his mother began acting out. He threw his backpack and coat on the floor, kicked the articles around, lay down, and began to kick the floor. Other violent behaviour followed. The staff appeared to be watching but not reacting to this display. When the new educator questioned what was going on, the child's educator replied, "It's Monday." Further probing revealed that the child's mother had been a victim of spousal abuse for a long period of time. This was a typical display of behaviour for the child after having been home for two full days on the weekend and witnessing the violence.

Disruptions in development occur when children are victims of abuse. Infants may have difficulty developing a sense of trust when their parents are unable to provide consistent, predictable care (Baker & Cunningham, 2009). Continual abuse produces chronic stress. Over the long term, children will have to deal with the loss of self-esteem, trust, and security in their family life and with the reinforcement of inappropriate means of dealing with stress and problems in their own lives. As discussed earlier, children may become hypervigilant and overreact to threats or perceived threats in their environment (Hornor, 2008). Children often become passive as they learn that being quiet/invisible helps to avoid abuse (Gilbert, 1995). Regression is common, as are poor peer relationships (Baker & Cunningham, 2009).

The effects of abuse are far-reaching and have serious consequences on the child's development, possibly resulting in criminal activities, mental health problems, or developmental delays (Currie & Widon, 2009). We know that victims of abuse are at a higher risk of becoming abusers themselves, since they take their unmet needs from childhood to adulthood (Ambert, 2006; Hornor, 2008). In addition, we must not forget that child abuse may result in the death of children. By understanding more about the abuser and the abused, the early childhood educator may be better able to assist the family through this crisis by not prejudging the abuser or blaming the victim. Understanding in a more objective way may help the early childhood educator provide support to the child and to the family.

SUPPORTING FAMILIES

Throughout this book, we have tried to highlight the interrelatedness of the well-being of the child with that of the family. Indeed, from the standpoint of the early childhood educator, support provided to families is based on the belief that such support will directly or indirectly contribute to the well-being of the child. In the case of child abuse, however, the equation becomes more complex. Supporting a family in which child abuse is occurring often begins with reporting the family to the appropriate authorities. This step can lead to legal action against the abuser that culminates in investigation, the removal of the child from the abuser's care or a prison sentence. While many families who are helped by professional intervention may ultimately come to appreciate the person who first reported the abuse, it's unlikely that most perpetrators of abuse will be pleased initially. Regardless of how the parents view such intervention, though, when a child's psychological or physical safety is at risk, early childhood educators have a moral and legal responsibility to intervene.

SCENARIO

DIVIDED LOYALTIES

A young mother and her daughter's early childhood educator developed an excellent relationship over the two years when Jamie was in the child-care centre. The mother had worked hard to overcome many of the difficulties associated with being a single working parent and was committed to taking excellent care of her daughter. One day, she told the educator that her boyfriend had hit Jamie and that she was worried he would do it again. She asked the educator to promise not to tell anyone, since this was the first serious relationship she had had in several years. She was sure that once her boyfriend got used to having a young child around, things would work out and her dreams of getting married would finally materialize.

Of course, the early childhood educator has an obligation to document and report if the abuse continues, but we can't ignore how difficult this situation may be. It helps in this and similar situations to remind ourselves that protecting children must be our primary consideration, but also that reporting is often required by law and is the first step in the long and painful process of helping, healing, and breaking the cycle of abuse.

> ## Examine Your Attitudes

Do you agree or disagree with the following statements?

- Anyone who abuses children should be locked away.

- A parent who knows that abuse is occurring but does nothing deserves to be punished.

- Children should be removed from homes where there is domestic abuse.

- Victims of abuse deserve what they get.

- I would report child abuse only when I was absolutely certain that abuse was occurring.

- There are circumstances where I would exercise caution in reporting abuse.

With your instructor as moderator, organize a classroom debate on these questions and be prepared to defend your responses.

Dealing with the Early Childhood Educator's Emotional Response to Abuse

For people involved with early childhood care, abuse evokes many deep emotions. Some early childhood educators experienced abuse as children, or they witnessed abuse. Coming into contact with an abusive parent, or a parent who allows abuse to occur, can trigger unresolved anger or feelings of helplessness. When this happens, it's very important to recognize and discuss these feelings with a counsellor or therapist. Even after successfully receiving treatment, people who have been abused often carry psychological wounds that require treatment at various times throughout their lives.

For people who have not experienced abuse, it's sometimes difficult to understand or empathize with the abuser or the victim. Accepting someone who abuses children is not easy for anyone to do, but it's especially difficult for those people who have chosen a career in early childhood education because of their strong commitment to children and upholding the rights of children.

There is no easy solution to this dilemma. We maintain that it's important to remember several points. First, many characteristics, events, and experiences may contribute to abuse (e.g., stress, lack of support). Second, there are people who abuse and then feel deep sorrow, remorse, or feelings of failure, but they feel powerless to change their behaviour. Accepting the perpetrator of abuse does not mean that we accept the abuse itself; it only means that we try to see him or her as someone who is in need of help and who has the potential to be helped. It's sometimes difficult to take a strengths-based approach with families where abuse occurs.

It's also sometimes very difficult not to blame an adult who is either a victim of abuse or does not actively prevent the abuse from happening, as in domestic violence. "How can she be so stupid?" we say. "Doesn't she care about her children?" Again, while protecting the child has to remain our top priority, trying to empathize with the victim or to understand the circumstances surrounding the situation is also important. Imagine what it would be like to live with such fear. Try to imagine how it would feel to have no safe place to run to. Try to imagine feeling trapped. Try to imagine being raised in a situation where violence is considered normal. These and other considerations may help in developing empathy and may also help counter negative attitudes we might hold against the adult.

Strong negative feelings toward the abuser, lack of sympathy for the victim, or even blaming the victim are common attitudes that interfere when working with families in which violence occurs. Once again, it's important to remind ourselves that developing empathy and understanding is a process that is an ongoing part of professional development.

Monitoring Potentially Abusive Situations

When an early childhood educator suspects that a child is being abused or neglected, he or she must monitor and document the situation consistently. Systematic monitoring and documentation will help establish patterns for symptoms of abuse or neglect that are not immediately obvious. It may be the pattern or change of behaviour that is relevant. For example, the appearance of a bruise may provoke further observation and monitoring but not necessarily a reporting of the incident. The appearance of bruises over a period of time may warrant a reporting. Sometimes the child may verbally report something that happened or you may witness different interactions with the parent. All of these observations may be relevant, and so should be documented.

We must also take care not to judge too hastily. For example, could the impression of neglect we have formed be due to something as innocent as the child's desire for autonomy or the result of a simple lack of time on the parent's part? A boy may choose to wear summer clothing, such as shorts and a sleeveless top, in the middle of winter. We may misinterpret his quest for individuality here to mean that he does not have access to the appropriate clothing or that the parent is not paying sufficient attention to the child's well-being. Similarly, if a little girl arrives with her hair uncombed and face unwashed, this may be a result of nothing more than the parents' morning rush to work. When a child, however, is dressed in such a manner consistently, or his or her hygiene is so neglected that it poses a health risk, this needs to be monitored closely. We must be careful to maintain our objectivity and ensure that we focus on behaviour or situations that pose a real risk to the child. A careful record of each sign of abuse, giving the date, time of observation, and an accurate/objective description of the behaviour or symptom will be a crucial component of the assessment.

Bearing in mind that the well-being of the child is our primary concern, we must point out that often, if abusers suspect they are being monitored, they may withdraw the child from the centre. This often prolongs the abusive situation, since it may then go undetected for some time before the next child-care centre observes a situation or pattern of behaviour. Therefore, early childhood educators must be cautious until they have sufficient documentation and determined a plan of action. Being polite and acting as if all is well may not be easy, especially in light of the professional training that encourages open and honest relations with parents. Sometimes, however, this sort of conduct may be necessary and in the best interests of the child. During this time, seeking out and providing information or access to community supports may be crucial for this family.

Early childhood educators see young children every day. They see them in interaction with many different people, observe them as they engage in play, and are often involved in their personal care routines. From this vantage point, they can observe many things about the child. Educators need to document information on an ongoing basis in addition to making day-to-day observations. By doing this, the educator can make comparisons. For example, the educator is in a position to determine whether the child is unusually passive or pinpoint when the change of behaviour began; they can document regressions in behaviour. In addition, educators typically interact with a parent or parents on a regular basis. These interactions may also provide information regarding the relationship. Documentation will always be necessary if early childhood educators plan to report their suspicions to the authorities.

Reporting Abuse

It's not uncommon for early childhood educators to fail in reporting abuse for fear of making an inaccurate report, due to the lack of physical signs of abuse, or due to the feeling that child protective services may create problems for the families (Peter, 2009). Despite these factors, the obligation to ensure the well-being of all children under our care must not be forgotten. Early childhood educators must remember that a report is a way to express concern that warrants further investigation, and is not necessarily an accusation.

Protection of the rights of the child from violence and abuse are recognized under international and national laws and conventions (Sinha, 2015). In 1991, Canada ratified the United Nations Convention on the Rights of the Child, which recognizes that all children and youth have the right to protection from all forms of violence and abuse. The Criminal Code of Canada along with provincial and territorial laws ensure that these rights are enforced (Sinha, 2015). All provinces have mandatory reporting laws that compel professionals to report suspected cases of abuse to local child welfare authorities (Rankin & Ornstein, 2009; Sinha, 2015). In addition, legislation has been put in place that specifically protects individuals with disabilities at home or in care (e.g., Alberta's Protection for Persons in Care Act). Failure to report abuse can result in charges being laid against the child-care worker. In some jurisdictions, reports of abuse may be made on an anonymous basis. The authorities will then investigate and take further action if required. In other jurisdictions, the person reporting abuse must identify him or herself. Child and family services are responsible for protecting children and arranging care for children who are not safe at home (Gough, Shlonsky, & Dudding, 2009). In cases of suspected abuse, the child may be removed from the home as soon as possible if there is imminent danger to the child. In less severe situations, the child may not be removed from the home. In both instances, family services will provide resources and services to reduce risk and prevent harm in the home. Parental involvement may be voluntary or may be court ordered. It's critical that early childhood educators be aware of local policies to protect the children and themselves. Stop Family Violence, an initiative of the Public Health Agency of Canada, and the Child Welfare Information Gateway in the United States provide a wealth of information on child abuse for professionals. These organizations are good starting points for early childhood educators to obtain more information.

The following box provides an example of what to report in cases of suspected child abuse.

Reporting

When a person suspects a child is abused or neglected, the person must immediately report the situation to child welfare services. Any person who fails to report is guilty of an offence and liable to a fine.

A person must report to child welfare services, regardless of how the information was obtained and regardless of advice or direction not to report.

Provide the following information:

- name, age, birth date, sex, and address of child concerned
- the names and addresses of parents or guardians
- the names and addresses of the alleged perpetrator (if known) and any other identifiable information about that person
- full details of the incident or situation that precipitated your report. Try to be specific; include details, events, or behaviours that have caused concern. Include any previous dated documentation you may have collected.

No action will be taken against the person reporting unless the reporting is done maliciously or without reasonable or probable grounds for the belief.

Source: Alberta Human Services, "Protocols for Handling Child Abuse and Neglect in Child Care Services," January, 2006. Reprinted with permission.

Early childhood educators often worry about repercussions after they report suspected abuse. A report can lead nowhere or action may not be immediate. Patience, careful observations, and regular documentation can be most helpful in ensuring that this is not the case. In these situations, early childhood educators will require support from their peers and supervisors.

Responding to the Child's Disclosure of Abuse

It's probably an early childhood educator's worst nightmare when a child confides that a family member is doing bad things to him or her. How do you, as an educator, respond? We have seen what the professional response should be with regard to documenting and reporting, but how do you respond to the child in your care? Early childhood educators play an extremely important role in this situation. The child will have many needs at this time to which the educator will want or need to respond. At the same time, educators should be extremely careful when communicating with the child about abuse to ensure that he or she does not receive the wrong message or that words are not put into the child's mouth. The following box provides tips for the early childhood educator to use in this delicate balancing act.

Responding to a Child's Disclosure of Abuse

Remember these general guidelines:

1. The most essential foundation in preventing or responding to children is to ensure that all children have the opportunity to form a meaningful relationship with a caring adult. This can give children the opportunity to learn that there are people who care about them and will listen to them. Children may feel more comfortable and safe about confiding in someone if this relationship is established. This may be the only relationship outside of the home that young children have which makes nurturing strong trusting relationships so critical.

2. If a child begins to tell you about an abusive incident, the first thing to do is to *listen*. Young children may not know if it's appropriate to tell, and with older children, it's very likely that the abuser will have told the child not to tell anyone because no one will believe them anyway. By listening, you will let the child know that what he or she has to say is important. Listening may be enhanced by taking the child to a quiet place, away from the group, where you can listen without interruption.

3. Let the child tell you what has happened in his or her own words. Don't put words into the child's mouth by asking leading questions (e.g., "Did he hit you with his fist?"). If the incident is to be pursued by social workers or police, it will be questioned if the child uses an adult's vocabulary to describe events.

4. Follow the child's lead. If the child moves on to another topic or activity, don't pressure the child to talk or return to the issue. The child may be experiencing difficulty coping, as the circumstances may have changed or intensified and the child has come to a trusted person for support. When you respond in a supportive manner, children may come to understand that you are a person to be trusted and so may be more willing to share concerns in the future.

5. Let the child know that you believe what he or she has said. Children rarely lie or make up details about abuse, particularly sexual abuse.

6. Reassure the child. Tell him or her that it was a good thing to tell somebody. Reassure the child that you will do something to help.

---

7. Don't make promises to the child that you can't keep (e.g., "I promise s/he will never hurt you again" or "I will keep you safe"). This may well be the hardest thing for the early childhood educator to do. Because educators feel a strong emotional bond and want to protect children from harm, their first reaction is to promise the child that they will fix the situation. The professional must not promise the child that the abuse will not happen again or that she will not tell. Children will often begin their disclosure by saying that this is a secret and that they will tell if you promise to keep it secret too. The early childhood educator needs to let the child know that she will only tell to make sure that the child is safe and will only tell certain people (e.g., "I need to tell the director or the social worker, but I won't tell your mom"). Because this is so difficult for early childhood educators to do, it's important that they be aware of this potential situation and of what their response might be. The consequence of making and then breaking promises will be particularly devastating for the child who has already lost trust in adults closest to him or her. For the sake of the child, this must be avoided.

8. As difficult as this may be, it's important to remain calm and in control of your emotions. If you express disgust or horror, children may think they can't tell you all the details or may interpret your reaction as your belief that the abuse was their fault (e.g., "How could this happen?" "How could someone do this to you?"). Acknowledge the information and the child's feelings without overreacting to the situation.

9. Involve the supervisor as soon as possible to determine what the next step will be. This may require that a report be filed or that the child intervention authorities be contacted. Knowing the local regulations beforehand and having documentation available will be helpful at this stage, when emotions may be running high.

10. Early childhood educators may also require support for themselves and shouldn't feel that they have to deal with the situation on their own. You can discuss your feelings with colleagues or friends without disclosing confidential information.

11. Document, document, document. Document information on an ongoing basis.

12. If there are signs of severe abuse, call the police or child welfare authorities without delay.

Providing Ongoing Support to the Child

After the initial disclosure, early childhood educators will still need to be available to work with the child for a long time to come. Sometimes disclosure is just the beginning of a long and stressful process for the child and the family. Educators must ensure that they provide care and support throughout this period. The child's environment should remain as stable and consistent as possible, with regard to both the physical setting and the routines and expectations. The child and family may be going through many changes, and a stable setting may be of the utmost benefit to the child at this time (Baker & Cunningham, 2009; Hornor, 2008).

Provide the child with opportunities to enhance his or her sense of security. For example, provide the child with simple explanations for things that worry him or her and provide multiple occasions for the child to express him or herself. Children who have been abused will need to have contact with supportive adults who listen and allow them to express themselves. Being able to engage in self-expression in alternative ways, such as through art, music, and play, will be beneficial to them as well. Children in this situation may need to be exposed to good role models so that they learn how to behave in nonviolent ways. Again, in all of these strategies, early childhood educators must be cautious and sensitive about how they approach and react to a child who has been abused.

Working with Families

There are many different scenarios involved with abuse, and educators will need to be prepared to interact with the family as well as the child. It's not easy to talk about abuse, but as an educator, you may need to. You might begin by letting the parent know that you are concerned about the child's behaviour or change in behaviour. Be supportive of the parent. Providing resource information and supports to a parent may also be helpful, as the parent may be a victim as well. In other situations, child intervention workers may be more involved and provide guidelines to educators about the type and extent of involvement with parents.

Working with Other Professionals

In situations of abuse, several professionals are usually involved, and it's vital that they work effectively together. For example, doctors, social workers, psychologists, and counsellors may all be involved at some point. From the beginning, early childhood educators must understand the role that each professional plays. Will the child welfare worker keep you informed? Does the therapist want observational data from you? How would the parent like you to be involved and in what ways? Educators may be able to provide parents with resources and written materials (e.g., books, stories, videos) either for their own use or to share with their child. The level and type of support expected from the early childhood educator should be clarified. The nature and degree of involvement required may change over time. Therefore, frequent communication among the different professionals may be necessary. Establishing working relationships and protocols between relevant programs will make consultations, when necessary, easier.

Ongoing Professional Development

All early childhood educators would certainly agree that abuse and violence in the home are issues they hope never to encounter. Unfortunately, such incidents continue, and the likelihood of working with a child from an abusive or violent home is, therefore, also increasing. Educators can best assist if they are informed about local policies and practices—through discussion within the agency, through workshops, or through guest presentations—and are prepared for such situations. When educators are trained and prepared, they are better able to assist and be supportive at a time when emotions are high and likely to interfere. Many family support programs offer professional development opportunities. For example, women's shelters provide resources related to women and children living in domestic violence. Organizations such as the Sheldon Kennedy Child Advocacy Centre in Alberta, the Canadian Centre for Child Protection in Manitoba, and the Boost Child and Youth Advocacy Centre in Ontario provide professionals with resources in the areas of responding to and preventing child abuse.

Accessing Expert Help

Adults who abuse children are in need of professional help that is beyond the scope of the early childhood educator. In any situation, educators must recognize when outside intervention is required and be prepared to refer families to qualified experts. Highly qualified therapists who specialize in working with family violence have a good success rate in helping these families. However, the role of early childhood educators must not be undervalued because it's they who often have regular, front-line contact with children and parents.

Preventing Abuse

One of the key roles of the early childhood educator is the prevention of abuse. This may happen in a number of different ways. Many programs are available to teach children to protect themselves from potential abusers. They provide advice on how to say no, how to report that they were approached, and how to avoid dangerous situations. These programs or kits have excited much controversy. Some say that they are necessary; others adamantly insist that children should not be responsible for their own safety and that the protection of children should remain the sole domain of their parents or guardians. The potential hazard with the kits currently in use is that they are not all developmentally appropriate.

SCENARIO

STOP, DANGER!

The director of a child-care centre recounted how she had reluctantly agreed to let an expert on preventing abuse speak to the children at her centre. The expert told the children that, just as a red light means "stop, danger," when someone touches you and it doesn't feel right, it's like a red light. The 4-year-olds listened intently. The next day, one of the early childhood educators came dressed in a red sweater. "Stop, danger!" exclaimed the children. They had understood that red means danger, and the rest had gone over their heads.

Educators may support children and families by assisting in developing a safety plan in conjunction with child intervention. All educators must be aware of who can and can't pick up the child. It may be useful to have copies of court documents in the child's file. In addition, the plan may need to include what to do if the person who is not on the list attempts to pick up the child (e.g., someone should stay with the child, someone else should contact the parent or police if needed). Educators can provide general safety information to children, such as how to use the telephone in emergency situations.

Along with prevention, educators can help children and families develop resilience. The child's capacity to thrive in situations of adversity can occur in the presence of supportive relationships and "science now tells us that it's the reliable presence of at least one supportive relationship and multiple opportunities for developing effective coping skills that are the essential building blocks for strengthening the capacity to do well in the face of significant adversity" (Center on the Developing Child at Harvard University, 2017a). It's daunting to imagine that you, as the child's educator, could be the one significant relationship. These situations may provide a prime opportunity to develop individual resilience in the child (e.g., developing communication skills, teaching about emotions). Educators may support family resilience by providing access and information about local resources and supports. Community resilience may be supported as educators share their knowledge about children's learning and development to organizations that serve children and families (e.g., women's shelters).

CONCLUSION

Early childhood educators can play a role in the prevention of abuse. They may act as role models for parents by demonstrating guidance and nonviolent discipline techniques. Educators can model developmentally appropriate ways of interacting with children and provide guidelines as to what to expect of children at different ages. For example, they can demonstrate how to give the young child choices rather than expecting unquestioning compliance; they can let parents know that sitting quietly for extended periods of time may be difficult for younger children.

Early childhood educators can also be supportive of families by being aware of children's family situations and of stressful events that might be occurring in their lives. Knowing, for example, that the father has recently lost his job can be the signal that the family may be under additional stress and therefore needs more support. Developing and maintaining good parent–early childhood educator relationships before crises occur will be of the utmost importance in helping families feel comfortable in divulging such information.

As an early childhood educator, you may be able to create an atmosphere in which parents feel that they can confide in you when they things are falling apart. Sometimes just being able to let off some steam may be sufficient, but there will also be times when families need extra help. Being familiar with community resources, such as emergency shelters, relief homes, support groups, and telephone hotlines, may be useful. If abuse is associated with other problems, other support groups and services may also be pertinent. These are the times when you may be called upon to go that extra mile to prevent a crisis (e.g., check out resources). When good relations exist, early childhood educators can serve as an excellent support for children and their families.

Recent neuroscience research sends a strong message about the effects of abuse and neglect on children in the early years. Research clearly shows that the early years are pivotal for healthy brain development and that severe neglect can be more damaging to health and brain development than physical trauma (Center on the Developing Child at Harvard University, 2017a). In addition, prolonged stress or anxiety can lead to differences in how children learn to handle stress. Early childhood educators, then, provide responsive child care not only to meet children's developmental needs but also to ensure healthy brain development and build resilience.

Chapter Summary

- Early childhood educators need to understand the different types of abuse so that they know what to be aware of. Educators must know what to document and how.

- Early childhood educators should consider their own attitudes toward abuse and family violence so as to better understand and support children and families. They must also understand their role in preventing, documenting, and reporting abuse.

- Early childhood educators need to understand the characteristics of both abusers and victims.

- Early childhood educators must develop an understanding of abuse and the conditions leading to abuse for both the perpetrator and the victim of abuse.

- Educators should become aware of their jurisdiction's legislation and child intervention policies along with supports and resources in their communities.

RESOURCES

HelpGuide.org, "Child Abuse and Neglect: How to Spot the Signs and Make a Difference":
www.helpguide.org/articles/abuse/child-abuse-and-neglect.htm

Canadian Red Cross, "Violence, Bullying and Abuse Prevention":
www.redcross.ca/how-we-help/violence--bullying-and-abuse-prevention

Sheldon Kennedy Child Advocacy Centre:
http://sheldonkennedycac.ca

Canadian Centre for Child Protection:
www.protectchildren.ca

Boost Child and Youth Advocacy Centre:
https://boostforkids.org

McGill Centre for Research on Children and Families:
www.mcgill.ca/crcf/centre-research-children-and-families

Child Welfare Information Gateway:
www.childwelfare.gov

Child Welfare League of America:
www.cwla.org

Child Trauma Academy:
www.childtrauma.org

Center on the Developing Child at Harvard University:
https://developingchild.harvard.edu

Western Centre for Research & Education on Violence Against Women & Children:
http://learningtoendabuse.ca

EXERCISES

1. Find three resources (e.g., journal articles, reports, books, websites) that focus on the role of early childhood educators with children and families in abusive situations. What approaches do they suggest for supporting young children? What approaches do they suggest for supporting the family?

2. Based on the information in this chapter, review the following scenarios and discuss what you, as a director of a child-care centre, should do regarding reporting, responding to the child, and supporting the family.

SCENARIO 1

Bonnie (4 years old) comes from a nice home. She attends the centre regularly, is well fed, and is very well dressed. Her parents are reliable with their payments and follow up any of the centre staff's requests, but they have little involvement with the staff otherwise.

When Bonnie is at the centre, she is often apathetic and withdrawn. At other times, she will overreact or misbehave to get attention. One day, Bonnie confides in her early childhood educator that when she goes home, she always eats, sleeps, and plays in a closet so that she is out of Mommy and Daddy's way.

SCENARIO 2

Matt's mom, Mrs. Benning, is usually one of the last parents to pick up her child. She has to take a bus to the centre and then take two more buses to get home. She is often very rushed and hurries to get Matt ready as soon as she gets in the door.

One day, Matt wants to show her what he has done at the art centre. Mrs. Benning says that she has no time and tells Matt to hurry up. Matt deliberately moves very slowly toward his coat. Mrs. Benning becomes enraged and crosses the room, yelling, "I'll show you what slow means!" and proceeds to spank him on his bottom five or six times. She then gives him a firm shaking, grabs his coat, and drags Matt from the room.

SCENARIO 3

The staff members in the playroom for 3-year-olds have told you, the director, that Drew's mother has come late to pick her up three times this month. Each time, they could smell liquor on her breath. They ask you to stay in the playroom until she arrives this Friday after work. When she enters the room, it's obvious that she has been drinking, and she yells to Drew to hurry up because she's missing the party.

SCENARIO 4

Elaine is in the midst of a difficult separation from her husband. Her 5-year-old son, Shaun, has been unusually quiet and very reluctant to talk about what is happening at home. Late one afternoon, when most of the children have left, Shaun and the early childhood educator have just finished reading a story about a family of bears when Shaun remarks that he wishes his home was like that. When the early childhood educator asks him why, he explains that he wishes he could see his dad more and talk to his dad on the telephone and— At this point, his mother walks into the room and stares at Shaun. Shaun has a look of absolute terror on his face, covers his head with his arms, and then runs from the room in tears. Elaine declares that the conversation is over and never to be brought up again, and then leaves.

References

Aboriginal Tourism BC. (2014, November 12). The sweat lodge—An Aboriginal healing experience [Blog post]. Retrieved from https://www.aboriginalbc.com/blog/sweat-lodge-aboriginal-healing-experience/.

About Families. (2012). Parenting on a low income. Retrieved from https://aboutfamilies.files.wordpress.com/2012/03/about-families-briefing-3-parenting-on-a-low-income1.pdf.

Addi-Raccah, A., & Ainhoren, R. (2009). School governance and teachers' attitudes to parents' involvement in schools. *Teaching and Teacher Education, 25*(6), 805–813.

Administration on Children, Youth, and Families. (2008). Child maltreatment. Retrieved from http://www.acf.hhs.gov/programs/acyf.

Adoption Council of Canada. (n.d.a). Canada's waiting children. Retrieved from http://www.canadaswaiting-children.ca/.

Adoption Council of Canada. (n.d.b). Myths and realities. Retrieved from http://www.adoption.ca/myths-and-realities.

Adoption Council of Canada. (2014). Adoptive parent support group toolkit. Retrieved from http://www.adoption.ca/uploads/File/ACC_Post-Adoption_Toolkit_Part1.pdf.

Alberta Alcohol & Drug Abuse Commission. (2010). Get the facts. Retrieved from http://www.aadac.com/87.asp.

Alberta Children's Services. (2006). *Protocols for handling child abuse and neglect in child care services.* n.p.: Author. Retrieved from http://www.assembly.ab.ca/lao/library/egovdocs/2006/alchs/158779.pdf.

Allan, B., & Smylie, J. (2015). *First Peoples, second class treatment: The role of racism in the health and well-being of Indigenous peoples in Canada.* Toronto: The Wellesley Institute. Retrieved from http://www.wellesleyinstitute.com/wp-content/uploads/2015/02/Summary-First-Peoples-Second-Class-Treatment-Final.pdf.

Alwani, K. (2017). Indigenous-centred early childhood education in Canada: The facts. The Conference Board of Canada. Retrieved from http://www.conferenceboard.ca/topics/northern-aboriginal/nap-insights/alwani_ece-pt1.aspx.

Amato, P. (2010). Research on divorce: Continuing trends and new developments. *Journal of Marriage and Family, 72,* 650–666.

Ambert, A. M. (2006a). *Changing families: Relationships in context.* Toronto: Pearson Education Canada.

Ambert, A. M. (2006b). *One-parent families: Characteristics, causes, consequences, and issues.* Contemporary Family Trends. Ottawa: Vanier Institute of the Family.

Ambert, A. M. (2009). *Divorce: Facts, causes and consequences.* Contemporary Family Trends. Ottawa: Vanier Institute of the Family.

American Psychological Association. (2017a). Children and trauma. Retrieved from http://www.apa.org/pi/families/resources/children-trauma.pdf.

American Psychological Association. (2017b). Effects of poverty, hunger and homelessness on children and youth. Retrieved from http://www.apa.org/pi/families/poverty.aspx.

American Psychological Association. (2017c). The changing role of the modern day father. Retrieved from http://www.apa.org/pi/families/resources/changing-father.aspx.

Anderson, H. (2010). Common grief, complex grieving. *Pastoral Psychology, 59*(2), 127–136.

Archibald, J. (2008). *Indigenous storywork: Educating the heart, mind, body, and spirit.* Vancouver: UBC Press.

Archibald, J. (2012). Greetings from NITEP director Jo-Ann Archibald. Retrieved from http://aboriginal.ubc.ca/2012/03/26/greetings-from-nitep-director-jo-ann-archibald/.

Arkowitz, H., & Lilienfeld, S. (2013, March 1). Is divorce bad for children? *Scientific American.* Retrieved from https://www.scientificamerican.com/article/is-divorce-bad-for-children/.

Arpino, B., & Bordone, V. (2014). Does grandparenting pay off? The effect of child care on grandparents' cognitive functioning. *Journal of Marriage and Family, 76,* 337–351. doi:10.1111/jomf.12096

Artis, B., & Telford, J. (2016). Creating and celebrating diversity in preschool classrooms. Retrieved from https://osse.dc.gov/sites/default/files/dc/sites/osse/publication/attachments/DEL_Cultural%20and%20Linguistic%20Diversity_Creating%20and%20Celebrating%20Diversity.pdf.

Artz, S., & Nicholson, D. (2009). Documenting an integrated childcare program's ability to support at-risk young mothers and their children. Retrieved from http://Dspace.library.uvic.ca:8080/handle/1828/1421.

Åslund, O., & Grönqvist, H. (2010). Family size and child outcomes: Is there really no trade-off? *Labour Economics, 17*(1), 130–139.

Averett, P., Nalavany, B., & Ryan, S. (2009). An evaluation of gay/lesbian and heterosexual adoption. *Adoption Quarterly, 12*(3), 129–151.

Axford, N., Lehtonen, M., Kaoukji, D., Tobin, K., & Berry, V. (2012). Engaging parents in parenting programs: Lessons from research and practice. *Children and Youth Services Review, 34*(10), 2061–2071.

Bachman, H. J., & Chase-Lansdale, P. L. (2005). Custodial grandmothers' physical, mental, and economic well-being: Comparisons of primary caregivers from low-income neighborhoods. *Family Relations, 54,* 475–487.

Baker, A. C., & Manfredi-Petitt, L. A. (2004). *Relationships, the heart of quality care: Creating community among adults in early care settings.* Washington, DC: NAEYC.

Baker, L., & Cunningham, A. (2009). Inter-parental violence: The pre-schooler's perspective and the educator's role. *Early Childhood Education Journal, 37*(3), 199–207.

Ball, J. (2008). Promoting equity and dignity for Aboriginal children in Canada. *IRPP Choices, 14*(7), 5–12.

Ball, J. (2013). Indigenous fathers in Canada. In J. Pattnaik (Ed.), *Father involvement in young children's lives: Educating the young child.* Advances in Theory and Research: Implications for Practice 6. London: Springer Dordrecht.

Ball, J., & Pence, A. (2006). Supporting children and families with sustained community transformations. In *Supporting Indigenous children's development: Community-university partnerships.* Vancouver: UBC Press.

Bang, M. (2006). *In my heart.* New York: Little Brown.

Bank, L., Forgatch, M. S., Patterson, G. R., & Fetrow, R. A. (1993). Parenting practices of single mothers: Mediators of negative contextual factors. *Journal of Marriage and the Family, 55,* 371–384.

Bassuk, E., DeCandia, C., Beach, C., & Berman, F. (2014). America's youngest outcasts—A report card on child homelessness. Retrieved from http://www.air.org/sites/default/files/downloads/report/Americas-Youngest-Outcasts-Child-Homelessness-Nov2014.pdf.

Bastien, B., & Kremer, J. W. (2004). *Blackfoot ways of knowing: The worldview of the Siksikaitsitapi.* Calgary: University of Calgary Press.

Battams, N. (2013). Aboriginal families in Canada. Retrieved from http://vanierinstitute.ca/wp-content/uploads/2015/10/BTN_2013-08-00_Aboriginal-families.pdf.

Battams, N. (2016). A snapshot of grandparents in Canada. Retrieved from http://vanierinstitute.ca/snapshot-grandparents-canada/.

Battiste, M. (2002). Indigenous knowledge and pedagogy in First Nations education—A literature review with recommendations. Retrieved from http://www.afn.ca/uploads/files/education/24._2002_oct_marie_battiste_indigenousknowledgeandpedagogy_lit_review_for_min_working_group.pdf.

Battiste, M. (2011). *Knowledge as a key site for decolonization* [video]. Retrieved from https://www.youtube.com/watch?v=Evxpt0u4tOU.

Battiste, M., & Henderson, J. (2009). Naturalizing Indigenous knowledge in Eurocentric education. *Canadian Journal of Native Education, 32*(1).

Bauserman, R. (2012). A meta-analysis of parental satisfaction, adjustment and conflict in joint custody and sole custody following divorce. *Journal of Divorce and Remarriage, 53*(6), 464–488.

Baxter, J. (1998). *A qualitative study of caregivers* (Doctoral dissertation). University of Calgary.

Baxter, J. (2017). Stay-at-home dads. Retrieved from http://childcarecanada.org/documents/research-policy-practice/17/05/stay-home-dads.

Baxter, J., & Read, M. (1999). *Children first: Working with young children in inclusive group care settings in Canada.* Toronto: Harcourt Brace.

Baydar, N., & Brooks-Gunn, J. (1995). Does a mother's job have a negative effect on children: Yes. In R. L. DelCampo & D. S. DelCampo (Eds.), *Taking sides: Clashing views on controversial issues of childhood and society.* Guilford, CT: Dushkin Publishing Group.

Beattie, M. J. (2009). Emotional support for lone mothers following diagnosis of additional needs in their child. *Practice, 21*(3), 189–204.

Beaupré, P., Dryburgh, H., & Wendt, M. (2010). Making fathers "count." Retrieved from http://www.statcan.gc.ca/pub/11-008-x/2010002/article/11165-eng.htm.

Beauschene, E. (2006, July 20). Two wage-earners no guarantee against poverty. *Calgary Herald,* A8.

Bee, H., & Boyd, D. (2007). *The developing child.* Boston: Allyn & Bacon.

Bell, K. (2015, February 26). Facebook's new gender options let you choose anything you want. Retrieved from http://mashable.com/2015/02/26/facebooks-new-custom-gender-options/.

Bell, K. (2016). Diversity within and between people: A perspective on diversity efforts, campus climate and inclusion. Retrieved from http://sites.udel.edu/csd/2016/11/29/diversity-within-and-between-people-karla-a-bell/.

Berk, L. E. (2000). *Child development* (5th ed.). Boston: Allyn & Bacon.

Berkowitz, D. (2009). Theorizing lesbian and gay parenting: Past, present, and future scholarship. *Journal of Family Theory and Review, 1*(2), 117–132.

Bernal, J. G., & Anuncibay, R. (2008). Intergenerational grandparent/grandchild relations: The socioeducational role of grandparents. *Educational Gerontology, 34,* 67–88. doi:10.1080/03601270701763993

Bernhard, J. K., & Gonzalez-Mena, J. (2005). When family priorities differ from program priorities. *Interaction,* Fall, 19–22.

Berns, R. M. (2004). *Child, family, school, community: Socialization and support* (6th ed.). Belmont, CA: Wadsworth.

Berns, R. M. (2010). *Child, family, school, community: Socialization and support* (8th ed.). Belmont, CA: Wadsworth.

Best Start Resource Centre. (2012a). *Step by step: Engaging fathers in programs for families.* Toronto: Author.

Best Start Resource Centre. (2012b). *Welcoming and celebrating sexual orientation and gender diversity in families, from pre-conception to preschool.* Toronto: Author.

Best Start Resource Centre & Sex Information and Education Council of Canada. (2007). *Update report on teen pregnancy prevention.* Toronto: Best Start Resource Centre. Retrieved from http://www.beststart.org/resources/rep_health/pdf/teen_pregnancy.pdf.

Bibby, R. W. (2006). The future families project: A survey of Canadian hopes and dreams. Retrieved from http://www.vifamily.ca.

Biblarz, T. J., & Stacey, J. (2010). How does the gender of parents matter? *Journal of Marriage and Family, 72,* 3–22.

Bielski, Z. (2013, January 29). Why teen pregnancy is on the rise again in Canada (and spiking in these provinces). *The Globe and Mail.* Retrieved from https://www.theglobeandmail.com/life/health-and-fitness/health/why-teen-pregnancy-is-on-the-rise-again-in-canada-and-spiking-in-these-provinces/article7927983.

Bissett, K. (2016, June 21). Foster-parent shortage across Canada reaching a crisis point. *The Globe and Mail.* Retrieved from https://www.theglobeandmail.com/news/national/declining-number-of-foster-parents-across-canada-becoming-a-crisis/article30538343.

The Blended and Step Family Resource Center. (2013). Effective communication is the key to blended family success. Retrieved from http://blendedfamilyadvice.com/effectivecommunication-is-the-key-to-blended-family-success/.

Blended Family Success Network. (2013). Ex-partners & in-laws. Retrieved from http://www.blendedfamilyfocus.com/ex/.

Blewett, J., & Lamb, M. (2008). Changing role of fathers in their children's lives. *Community Care, 1721,* 28–30.

Blood, M. (2017). Abandonment issues. Retrieved from http://www.livestrong.com/article/69862-abandonment-issues/.

Booth, A. L., & Kee, H. J. (2009). Birth order matters: The effect of family size and birth order on educational attainment. *Journal of Population Economics, 22*(2), 367–397.

The Borgen Project. (2016). Effects of poverty on society. Retrieved from https://borgenproject.org/2016/08/03/howpoverty-effects-society-children-and-violence/.

Boyse, K. (2009). Siblings of kids with special needs. Retrieved from http://www.med.umich.edu/yourchild/topics/specneed.htm.

Bragadóttir, H. (2008). Computer-mediated support group intervention for parents. *Journal of Nursing Scholarship, 40*(1), 32–38.

Braithwaite, D. O., Bryant, L., & Wagner, A. (2004). Stepchildren's perceptions of the contradictions in communication with stepparents. *Journal of Social and Personal Relationships, 21,* 447–467.

Bright Horizons Family Solutions. (2017). Raising happy kids: Building resilience in children. Retrieved from https://www.brighthorizons.com/family-resources/e-family-news/2012-making-happy-happen-building-resilience-in-children.

Bromwich, R. (1981). *Working with parents and infants: An interactional approach.* Baltimore, MD: University Park Press.

Bronfenbrenner, U. (1979). *The ecology of human development: Experiments by nature and design.* Cambridge, MA: Harvard University Press.

Bronfenbrenner, U. (1990). Discovering what families do. In D. Blankenhorn, S. Bayme, & J. Bethke Elshtain (Eds.), *Rebuilding the nest: A new commitment to the American family.* Milwaukee, WI: Family Service America.

Brooks, J. B. (2010). *The process of parenting* (8th ed.). Toronto: McGraw-Hill.

Brown, C., Goodman, S., & Kupper, L. (2003). The unplanned journey. *NICHCY News Digest, 20,* 7–16.

Brown, M. L., & Rounsley, C. A. (1996). *True selves: Understanding transsexualism for families, friends, coworkers, and helping professionals.* San Francisco: Jossey-Bass.

Brown, S., & Guthrie, K. (2010). Why don't teenagers use contraception? A qualitative interview study. *The European Journal of Contraception and Reproductive Health Care, 15*(3), 197–204.

Brown, S., Smalling, S., Groza, V., & Ryan, S. (2009). The experiences of gay men and lesbians in becoming and being adoptive parents. *Adoption Quarterly, 12*(3), 229–246.

Browne, A. J. (2003). *First Nations women and health care services: The sociopolitical context of encounters with nurses* (Doctoral dissertation). University of British Columbia, Vancouver.

Browne, A. J. (2005). Discourses influencing nurses' perceptions of First Nations patients. *Canadian Journal of Nursing Research, 37*(4), 62–87.

Bruder, M. B. (2010). Early childhood intervention: A promise to children and families for their future. *Exceptional Children, 76*(3), 339–355.

Buddy, T. (2016). Challenges facing the children of alcoholics. Retrieved from https://www.verywell.com/challenges-facing-the-children-of-alcoholics-66636.

Burdge, B. J. (2007). Bending gender, ending gender: Theoretical foundations for social work practice with the transgender community. *Social Work, 52*(3), 243–250.

Burnet, J., & Driedger, L. (2011). Multiculturalism. Retrieved from http://www.thecanadianencyclopedia.ca/en/article/multiculturalism/.

Byrd, B., DeRosa, A. P., & Craig, S. S. (1995). The adult who is an only child: Achieving separation or individuation. In R. L. DelCampo & D. S. DelCampo (Eds.), *Taking sides: Clashing views on controversial issues of childhood and society.* Guilford, CT: Dushkin Publishing Group.

Cajete, G. (2000). *Native science: Natural laws of interdependence*. Santa Fe, NM: Clear Light.

Caltabiano, M., & Thorpe, R. (2007). Attachment style of foster carers and caregiving role performance. *Child Care in Practice, 13*(2), 137–148.

Campaign 2000. (2000). Retrieved from http://www.campaign2000.ca.

Canada Adopts! (2014). International adoption. Retrieved from http://www.canadaadopts.com/adopting-in-canada/international-adoption/.

Canada Without Poverty. (2017). Just the facts. Retrieved from http://www.cwp-csp.ca/poverty/just-the-facts/.

Canada's First Peoples. (2007). The First Peoples of Canada. Retrieved from http://firstpeoplesofcanada.com/fp_groups/fp_groups_origins.html.

Canada's First Peoples. (2008). The Métis. Retrieved from http://firstpeoplesofcanada.com/fp_metis/fp_metis1.html.

Canadian Charter of Rights and Freedoms. (1982). Part I of the Constitution Act, 1982, being Schedule B to the Canada Act 1982 (UK), 1982, c11.

Canadian Child Care Federation. (2002). Resource sheet #10: Helping children understand death. Retrieved from http://www.cccf-fcsge.ca/wp-content/uploads/RS_10-e.pdf.

Canadian Child Care Federation. (2004). Resource sheet #42: Managing the Internet. Retrieved from http://www.cccf-fcsge.ca/wp-content/uploads/RS_42-e.pdf.

Canadian Child Care Federation. (2008). Resource sheet #86: Building partnerships with families. Retrieved from http://www.cccf-fcsge.ca/wp-content/uploads/RS_86-e.pdf.

Canadian Red Cross. (2017). Definitions of child abuse and neglect. Retrieved from http://www.redcross.ca/how-we-help/violence--bullying-and-abuse-prevention/educators/child-abuse-and-neglect-prevention/definitions-of-child-abuse-and-neglect.

Canadian Women's Foundation. (2017). The facts about women and poverty. Retrieved from http://canadianwomen.org/facts-about-women-and-poverty.

Canfield-Lenfest, M. (2008). Colage: Kids of trans resource guide. Retrieved from https://www.rainbowhealthontario.ca/wp-content/uploads/woocommerce_uploads/2014/08/KidsofTrans%20Resource%20Guide.pdf.

Carbone, P., Behl, D. D., Azor, V., & Murphy, N. A. (2010). The medical home for children with autism spectrum disorders: Parent and pediatrician perspectives. *Journal of Autism and Developmental Disorders, 40*(3), 317–324.

Caring4kids.ca. (2006). Why become a foster parent? Retrieved from http://caring4kids.ca/text/.

Carroll, J. S., Olson, C. D., & Buckmiller, N. (2007). Family boundary ambiguity: A 30-year review of theory, research, and measurement. *Family Relations, 56*, 210–230.

Case, A., Lin, I. F., & McLanahan, S. (2000). Educational attainment in blended families. Retrieved from http://www.thelizlibrary.org/liz/case_blended_families.pdf.

Caughy, M., Nettles, S., & O'Campo, P. (2008). The effect of residential neighborhood on child behaviour problems in the first grade. *American Journal of Psychology, 42*(1), 39–50.

CBC News. (2011, November 23). Canada accused of still failing its poor. *CBC News*. Retrieved from http://www.cbc.ca/news/canada/canada-accused-of-still-failing-its-poor-1.1101140.

CBC News. (2012, September 18). Definition of family wide open, census may show. *CBC News*. Retrieved from http://www.cbc.ca/news/canada/definition-of-family-wide-open-census-may-show-1.1285678.

CBC News. (2015, January 12). Timeline: Same-sex rights in Canada. *CBC News*. Retrieved from http://www.cbc.ca/news/canada/timeline-same-sex-rights-in-canada-1.1147516.

Center for the Study of Social Policy. (2005). Strengthening Families. Retrieved from https://www.cssp.org/reform/strengthening-families/basic-one-pagers/Strengthening-Families-Protective-Factors.pdf.

Center for the Study of Social Policy. (2015). Introduction to Strengthening Families: A protective factors framework. Retrieved from https://www.cssp.org/reform/strengtheningfamilies/2015/StrengtheningFamilies101.pdf.

Center for the Study of Social Policy. (2017). Strengthening Families: About. Retrieved from https://www.cssp.org/young-children-their-families/strengtheningfamilies/about.

Center on the Developing Child at Harvard University. (2009). Maternal depression can undermine the development of young children. Working Paper No. 8. Retrieved from http://46y5eh11fhgw3ve3ytpwxt9r.wpengine.netdna-cdn.com/wp-content/uploads/2009/05/Maternal-Depression-Can-Undermine-Development.pdf.

Center on the Developing Child at Harvard University. (2010). The foundations of lifelong health are built in early childhood. Retrieved from http://developingchild.harvard.edu/wp-content/uploads/2010/05/Foundations-of-Lifelong-Health.pdf.

Center on the Developing Child at Harvard University. (2017a). 8 things to remember about child development. Retrieved from https://developingchild.harvard.edu/resources/8-things-remember-child-development/.

Center on the Developing Child at Harvard University. (2017b). Brain architecture. Retrieved from https://developingchild.harvard.edu/science/key-concepts/brain-architecture/.

Center on the Social and Emotional Foundations for Early Learning. (2017). Pyramid model. Retrieved from http://csefel.vanderbilt.edu/.

Centers for Disease Control and Prevention. (2017). About teen pregnancy. Retrieved from https://www.cdc.gov/teenpregnancy/about/index.htm.

Centre for Addiction and Mental Health. (2003). When a parent has bipolar disorder . . . What kids want to know. Retrieved from http://www.camh.ca/en/education/about/camh_publications/Documents/Flat_PDFs/WAP_Bipolar.pdf.

Centre for Addiction and Mental Health. (2012a). The clinical features of bipolar disorder. Retrieved from http://www.camh.ca/en/education/about/camh_publications/info_guides/bipolar-info-guide/Pages/The-clinical-features-of-bipolar-disorder.aspx.

Centre for Addiction and Mental Health. (2012b). Depression. Retrieved from http://www.camh.ca/en/hospital/health_information/a_z_mental_health_and_addiction_information/depression/Pages/default.aspx.

Centre for Addiction and Mental Health. (2012c). Mental illness and addictions: Facts and statistics. Retrieved from http://www.camh.ca/en/hospital/about_camh/newsroom/for_reporters/Pages/addictionmentalhealthstatistics.aspx.

Chan, D., Lam, C. B., Chow, S. K., & Cheung, S. F. (2008). Examining the job-related, psychological, and physical outcomes of workplace sexual harassment: A meta-analytic review. *Psychology of Women Quarterly, 32*(4), 362–376.

Cherlin, A. J. (2009). The origins of the ambivalent acceptance of divorce. *Journal of Marriage and Family, 71*(2), 226–229.

Child Australia. (2017). What is pedagogy? How does it influence our practice? Retrieved from https://childaustralia.org.au/wp-content/uploads/2017/02/CA-Statement-Pedagogy.pdf.

Child Development Institute. (2015). How to talk to kids about death. Retrieved from https://childdevelopmentinfo.com/how-to-be-a-parent/communication/talk-to-kids-death/.

Child Welfare Information Gateway. (2013a). Impact of adoption on adopted persons. Retrieved from https://www.childwelfare.gov/pubPDFs/f_adimpact.pdf.

Child Welfare Information Gateway. (2013b). Preparing and supporting foster parents who adopt. Retrieved from https://www.childwelfare.gov/pubPDFs/f_fospro.pdf.

Child Welfare Information Gateway. (2015). Parenting your adopted preschooler. Retrieved from https://www.childwelfare.gov/pubPDFs/preschool.pdf.

Child Welfare League of Canada. (2012). Canada's children. Retrieved from http://www.cwlc.ca/sites/default/files/CCv18-2-FINAL.pdf.

Christoffersen, M. N., & DePanfilis, D. (2009). Prevention of child abuse and neglect and improvements in child development. *Child Abuse Review, 18*, 24–40.

Chud, G., & Fahlman, R. (1995). *Honoring diversity within child care and early education: An instructor's guide* (Vol. 11). Vancouver: British Columbia Ministry of Skills, Training and Labour and the Centre for Curriculum and Professional Development.

Chui, T., Tran, K., & Maheux, H. (2007). *Immigration in Canada: A portrait of the foreign-born population, 2006 census.* Ottawa: Statistics Canada.

CIC News. (2016, October 31). Immigration plan 2017: Canada to welcome increased number of immigrants through economic and family sponsorship programs. *CIC News.* Retrieved from https://www.cicnews.com/2016/10/immigration-plan-2017-canada-increased-immigrants-through-economic-family-sponsorship-programs-108621.html.

Clark, P. (2007). Representations of Aboriginal peoples in English Canadian history textbooks: Toward reconciliation. In E. A. Cole (Ed.), *Teaching the violent past: History education and reconciliation* (pp. 81–120). Lanham, MD: Rowman & Littlefield and Carnegie Council for Ethics in International Affairs.

Clark, W., & Crompton, S. (2006). Till death do us part? The risk of first and second marriage dissolution. *Canadian Social Trends, Summer*, 23–33. Retrieved from http://www.statcan.gc.ca/pub/11-008-x/2006001/pdf/9198-eng.pdf.

Clarke-Stewart, K. A. (1988). Evolving issues in early childhood education: A personal perspective. *Early Childhood Research Quarterly, 3*, 139–149.

Claxton-Oldfield, S., Goodyear, C., Parsons, T., & Claxton-Oldfield, J. (2002). Some possible implications of negative stepfather stereotypes. *Journal of Divorce and Remarriage, 36*, 77–88.

Cleveland, G., & Krashinsky, M. (1998). *Our children's future: Child care policy in Canada.* Toronto: University of Toronto Press.

CMAS Canada. (2013). Tip sheets. Retrieved from http://cmascanada.ca/category/supporting-refugees/supporting-refugees-tip-sheets/.

CMAS Canada. (2015). Welcoming refugee families. Retrieved from http://cmascanada.ca/wp-content/uploads/2015/12/Supporting_Refugees/WELCOMING%20REFUGEE%20FAMILIES.pdf.

Coleman, M., & Ganong, L. H. (2004). *Handbook of contemporary families.* Thousand Oaks, CA: Sage.

Collin-Vezina, D., Daigneault, I., & Hebert, M. (2013). Lessons learned from child sexual abuse research: prevalence, outcomes, and preventive strategies. *Child Adolescent Psychiatry Mental Health, 7*(22). Retrieved from https://www.ncbi.nlm.nih.gov/pmc/articles/PMC3720272/.

The Colour of Poverty Campaign. (2007). Fact sheet #1—Understanding the racialization of poverty in Ontario. Retrieved from http://www.povertyinpeel.ca/pdfs/factsheet1-understanding-racialization.pdf.

Community Tool Box. (2017). Section 2. Building relationships with people from different cultures. Retrieved from http://ctb.ku.edu/en/table-of-contents/culture/cultural-competence/building-relationships/main.

Conference Board of Canada. (2009). Child poverty. Retrieved from http://www.conferenceboard.ca/hcp/details/society/child-poverty.aspx.

Conger, K. J., Stocker, C., & McGuire, S. (2009). Sibling socialization: The effects of stressful life events and experiences. *New Directions in Child and Adolescent Development, 126,* 45–59.

Conway, C. (2016, January 6). Poor health: When poverty becomes disease. *University of California San Francisco News Center.* Retrieved from https://www.ucsf.edu/news/2016/01/401251/poor-health.

Cooklin, A. R., Westrupp, E. M., Strazdins, L., Giallo, R., Martin, A., & Nicholson, J. M. (2014). Fathers at work: Work–family conflict, work–family enrichment and parenting in an Australian cohort. *Journal of Family Issues, 37*(11), 1611–1635.

Copeland, D. (2010). Psychosocial differences related to parenting infants among single and married mothers. *Issues in Comprehensive Pediatric Nursing, 33,* 129–148.

Copeland, D., & Harbaugh, B. L. (2005). Differences in parenting stress between married and single first time mothers at six to eight weeks after birth. *Issues in Comprehensive Pediatric Nursing, 28,* 139–152.

Corbin-Dwyer, S., & Gidluck, L. (2009). White mothers of Chinese daughters: Real mothers of real children. In S. Capporale Bizzini & A. O'Reilly (Eds.), *The personal to the political: Toward a new theory of maternal narrative* (pp. 71–85). Selsingrove, PA: Susquehanna University Press.

Corr, C., & Balk, D. (2009). *Children's encounters with death, bereavement, and coping.* New York: Springer.

Couchenour, D., & Chrisman, K. (2011). *Families, schools and communities: Together for young children* (4th ed.). Philadelphia: Shippensburg University of Pennsylvania Press.

Couchman, R. (1994). From cloth to paper diapers and back: Reflections on fatherhood during two generations. *Transition, 24*(1).

Cox, C. B. (Ed.). (2010). *To grandmother's house we go and stay: Perspectives on custodial brandparents.* New York: Springer.

Craine, J. L., Tanaka, T. A., Nishina, A., & Conger, K. J. (2009). Understanding adolescent delinquency: The role of older siblings' delinquency and popularity with peers. *Merrill Palmer Quarterly, 55*(4), 436–453.

Crenshaw, K. (2016). *The urgency of intersectionality* [video]. TED Talks. Retrieved from https://www.ted.com/talks/kimberle_crenshaw_the_urgency_of_intersectionality.

Crossman, A. (2017, August 6). Sociology: Achieved status versus ascribed status. *ThoughtCo.* Retrieved from https://www.thoughtco.com/achieved-status-vs-ascribed-status-3966719.

Crowther, I. (2006). *Inclusion in early childhood settings: Children with special needs in Canada.* Toronto: Pearson.

Cuevas, K. (2016, September 13). The importance of keeping your native language alive. *Odyssey.* Retrieved from https://www.theodysseyonline.com/the-importance-of-keeping-your-native-language-alive.

Currie, J., & Widon, C. (2009). Long-term consequences of child abuse and neglect on adult economic well-being. *Child Maltreatment, 15,* 111–120.

Curtin, K., Loitz, C., Spencer-Cavaliere, N., & Khalema, E. (2016). Challenges of being new to Canada: Considerations for physical activity. *Global Health Promotion.* Retrieved from http://journals.sagepub.com/doi/abs/10.1177/1757975916656347.

Curwin, R. (2013). Reclaiming children and youth. *Bloomington, 22*(2), 38–39.

Dahlberg, G., & Moss, P. (2005). *Ethics and politics in early childhood education.* Oxford: Routledge.

D'Alessio, S. J., & Stolzenberg, L. (2012). Stepchildren, community disadvantage, and physical injury in a child abuse incident: A preliminary investigation. *Violence and Victims, 27*(6), 860–870.

Daly, K. (2000). *It keeps getting faster: Changing patterns of time in families.* Ottawa: Vanier Institute of the Family. Retrieved from http://www.vifamily.ca.

Daly, K. (2006). *It keeps getting faster: Changing patterns of time in families.* Contemporary Family Trends. Ottawa: Vanier Institute of the Family.

Daniel, H. (2012). Benefits of remarriage. Retrieved from http://benefitof.net/benefits-of-remarriage/.

Daro, D., & Dodge, K. (2009). Creating community responsibility for child protection. *The Future of Children, 19*(2), 67–93.

Dastjerdi, M., Olson, K., & Ogilvie, L. (2012). A study of Iranian immigrants' experiences of accessing Canadian health care services: A grounded theory. *BioMed Central.* Retrieved from https://equityhealthj.biomedcentral.com/articles/10.1186/1475-9276-11-55.

Daud, A., Klinteberg, B., & Rydelius, P-A. (2008). Resilience and vulnerable among refugee children of traumatized and non-traumatized parents. *Child and Adolescent Psychiatry and Mental Health.* Retrieved from https://capmh.biomedcentral.com/articles/10.1186/1753-2000-2-7.

Davis, K. (2000, July). Making blended families work. *Ebony,* 128–131.

DeAngelis, T. (2005). Stepfamily success depends on ingredients. *PA Online, 36*(11), 58. Retrieved from http://www.apa.org/monitor/dec05/stepfamily.aspx.

Deater-Deckard, K., Dunn, J., & Lussier, G. (2002). Sibling relationships and social-emotional adjustment in different family contexts. *Social Development, 11,* 571–589.

Deaux, K., & Bikmen, N. (2010). Immigration and power. In A. Guinote & T. Vescio (Eds.), *The social psychology of power* (pp. 381–406). New York: Guilford Press.

De Azevedo Hanks, J. (2013). *The burnout cure: An emotional survival guide for overwhelmed women.* American Fork, UT: Covenant Communications.

de Boer, K., Rothwell, D. W., & Lee, C. (2013). Information sheets: Child poverty in Canada: Implications for child welfare research. Retrieved from http://cwrp.ca/infosheets/child_poverty.

Defining choice moms. (2015). Retrieved from http://www.choicemoms.org/about/about_choice_moms/.

DeGarmo, D. S., Patras, J., & Eap, S. (2008). Social support for divorced fathers' parenting: Testing a stress-buffering model. *Family Relations, 57,* 35–48.

de Haan, M. (2009). Birth order, family size and educational attainment. *Economics of Education Review, 29*(4), 576–588.

DeJean, S. L., McGeorge, C. R., & Carlson, T. S. (2012). Attitudes toward never-married single mothers and fathers: Does gender matter? *Journal of Feminist Family Therapy, 24*(2), 121–138.

DeNavas-Walt, C., & Proctor, B. D. (2015). *Income and poverty in the United States: 2014 U.S. Census Bureau. Current population reports P60-252.* Washington, DC: U.S. Government Printing Office.

Derman-Sparks, L. (2005). *Teaching young children to resist bias.* Washington, DC: National Association for the Education of Young Children.

DeVito, J., Shimoni, R., & Clarke, D. (2015). Messages: Building interpersonal communication skills. Toronto: Pearson Education Canada.

Diareme, S., Tsiantis, J., Romer, G., Tsalamanios, E., Anasontzi, S., Paliokosta, E., . . . Kolaitis, G. (2007). Mental health support for children of parents with somatic illness: A review of the theory and intervention concepts. *Families, Systems, & Health, 25*(1), 98–118.

Dickason, O., & McNab, D. (2009). *Canada's First Nations: A history of founding peoples from earliest times.* New York: Oxford.

Divorce-Canada.ca. (2017). The effects of a divorce on children. Retrieved from https://divorce-canada.ca/more-faq/the-effects-of-separation-or-divorce-on-children.

Dixon, L., Hamilton-Giachritsis, C., Browne, K., & Ostapuik, E. (2007). The co-occurrence of child and intimate partner maltreatment in the family. *Journal of Family Violence, 22*(8), 675–689.

Dixon, M. (2017, March 7). Changes in the parent-child relationship after divorce [Blog post]. Retrieved from https://www.goodtherapy.org/blog/changes-in-parent-child-relationship-after-divorce-0307175.

Doyle, T., Dotsch, J., Savazzi, H., & Awamleh, T. (2015). *Caring for Syrian refugee children: A program guide for welcoming young children and their families.* Toronto: CMAS. Retrieved from https://cmascanada.ca/wp-content/uploads/2015/12/Supporting_Refugees/Caring%20for%20Syrian%20Refugee%20Children-final.pdf.

Driscoll, A., & Nagel, N. G. (2008). *Early childhood education, birth–8: The world of children, families, and educators* (4th ed.). Boston: Pearson/Allyn & Bacon.

Drummond, J., Kysela, G. M., McDonald, L., Alexander, J., & Fleming, D. (1998). *Risk and resilience in two samples of Canadian families.* n.p.: Health Canada: Children's Mental Health Unit, National Health Research Development Program and Alberta Heritage Foundation for Medical Research.

Dubeau, D. (2002). *Contemporary family trends: Portraits of fathers.* Ottawa: Vanier Institute of the Family.

Duffy, S., Induni, M., & Moiduddin, E. (2010). *First 5 Contra Costa report on parent involvement.* Oakland, CA: Mathematica Policy Research. Retrieved from http://eric.ed.gov/PDFS/ED510423.pdf.

Duggan, M., Lenhart, A., Lampe, C., & Ellison, N. (2015). Parents and social media: Mothers are especially likely to give and receive support on social media. Retrieved from http://www.pewinternet.org/2015/07/16/parents-and-social-media/.

Dunn, J. (2004). Understanding children's family worlds: Family transitions and children's outcome. *Merrill-Palmer Quarterly, 50*(3), 224–235.

Dunn, J., O'Connor, T. G., & Cheng, H. (2005). Children's response to conflict between their different parents: Mothers, stepfathers, nonresident fathers, and nonresident stepmothers. *Journal of Clinical Child and Adolescent Psychology, 34*(2), 223–234.

Dunne, E. G., & Kettler, L. J. (2008). Grandparents raising grandchildren in Australia: Exploring psychological health and grandparents' experience of providing kinship care. *International Journal of Social Welfare, 17,* 333–345.

Dunne, G. A. (2001). Opting into motherhood: Lesbians blurring the boundaries and transforming the meaning of parenthood and kinship. *Gender and Society, 14*(1), 11–35.

Dupuis, T. (2007). Examining remarriage: A look at issues affecting remarried couples and the implications towards therapeutic techniques. *Journal of Divorce and Remarriage, 48,* 91–104.

Durand, T. (2010). Celebrating diversity in early care and education settings: Moving beyond the margins. *Early Child Development and Care, 180*(7), 835–848.

Dyer, K. (2002). Coping strategies for children. Retrieved from http://www.journeyofhearts.org/jofh/grief/kids_cope.

Dyregrov, A. (2008). *Grief in children: A handbook for adults* (2nd ed.). Philadelphia: Jessica Kingsley.

e! Science News. (2012). More grandparents fill caregiver role. Retrieved from http://www.childcarecanada.org/documents/child-care-news/12/09/more-grandparents-fill-caregiver-role.

East, P. L., & Siek, T. K. (2005). Longitudinal pathways linking family factors and sibling relationship qualities to adolescent substance use and sexual risk behaviors. *Journal of Family Psychology, 19*(4), 571–580.

Ebbeck, M., & Waniganayake, M. (2003). Early Childhood professionals: Leading today and tomorrow. Sydney, Australia: MacLennan and Petty.

Ebling, R., Pruett, K. D., & Pruett, M. K. (2009). "Get over it": Perspectives on divorce from young children. *Family Court Review, 47,* 665–681.

ECMap. (2014). Final report of the Early Child Development Mapping Project. Retrieved from http://www.ecmap.ca/.

Edgar-Bailey, M., & Kress, V. E. (2010). Resolving child and adolescent traumatic grief: Creative techniques and interventions. *Journal of Creativity in Mental Health, 5*(2), 158–176.

Edwards, O. W. (2003). Living with grandma: A grandfamily study. *School Psychology International, 24*(2), 204–217.

The effects of poverty on the health of those living in it. (n.d.). Retrieved from http://theeffectsofpovertyonhealth. weebly.com/relationship-between-poverty-and-health.html.

Eldridge, D. (2001). Parent involvement: It's worth the effort. *Young Children, 56*(4),65–69.

Engel, M. (2002). Stepfamily resources: Stepfamily Association of America. Retrieved from http://www.marriagepreparation. com/stepfamily_resources.htm.

Epstein, R., & Duggan, S. (2006). *Factors relating to parenting by non-heterosexual fathers (AKA gay fathers cluster).* University of Guelph Father Involvement Research Alliance (FIRA). Retrieved from http://www.fira. ugeulph.ca.

Erikson, E. H. (1963). *Childhood and society* (2nd ed.). New York: Norton.

Ermine, W. (2007). The ethical space of engagement. *Indigenous Law Journal, 6*(1). Retrieved from https://tspace. library.utoronto.ca/bitstream/1807/17129/1/ILJ-6.1-Ermine.pdf.

Eshleman, J. R., & Wilson. S. J. (1995). *The family* (Cdn. ed.). Scarborough, ON: Allyn & Bacon.

Essa, E., & Young, R. (1994). *Introduction to early childhood education.* Scarborough, ON: Nelson.

Este, D., & Tachble, A. (2009). Fatherhood in the Canadian context: Perceptions and experiences of Sudanese refugee men. *Sex Roles, 60*(7/8), 456–466.

European Commission. (2014). Proposal for key principles of a quality framework for early childhood education and care. Retrieved from http://ec.europa.eu/dgs/education_ culture/repository/education/policy/strategic-framework/ archive/documents/ecec-quality-framework_en.pdf.

European Society of Human Reproduction and Embryology. (2017, July 5). Children in single-mother-by-choice families do just as well as those in two-parent families: Family social support services are valued. *ScienceDaily.* Retrieved from http://www.sciencedaily.com/releases/2017/07/ 170705095332.htm.

Evans, L. (2013). Why choose Canada? Retrieved from http://canadianimmigrant.ca/guides/moving-to-canada/why-choose-canada.

Facts for Families. (2015). Stepfamily problems. Retrieved from http://www.aacap.org/aacap/families_and_youth/facts_ for_families/FFF-Guide/Stepfamily-Problems-027.aspx.

The Faith Project. (2015). Aboriginal spirituality. Retrieved from http://thefaithproject.nfb.ca/wp-content/ uploads/2015/03/TFP_Aboriginal_Dec2014.pdf.

Family Law for Women in Ontario. (2013). Child custody and access. Retrieved from http://www.onefamilylaw.ca/ doc/FLEW_legal_EN_05.pdf.

Family Resource Center. (2017). The causes of child abuse. Retrieved from https://www.frcmo.org/resources/resources-for-professionals/causesofabuse/.

Fang, M., & Goldner, E. (2011). Transitioning into the Canadian workplace: Challenges of immigrants and its effect on mental health. *Canadian Journal of Humanities and Social Science, 2*(1), 93–102. Retrieved from https://www.research-gate.net/publication/235228697_Transitioning_into_the_ Canadian_Workplace_Challenges_of_Immigrants_and_its_ Effect_on_Mental_Health.

Fanning, K. (2008, February 11). Blended families: Teens describe some of the challenges and rewards of living in a stepfamily. *Junior Scholastic.*

Favazza, P. C., & Munson, L. J. (2010). Loss and grief in young children. *Young Exceptional Children, 13*(2), 86–99. Retrieved from http://yec.sagepub.com/content/early/2010/ 01/12/1096250609356883.citation.

Fearnley, R. (2010). Death of a parent and the children's experience: Don't ignore the elephant in the room. *Journal of Interprofessional Care, 24*(4), 450–459.

Felitti, V. (2004). The origins of addiction: Evidence from the Adverse Childhood Experiences study. Retrieved from http://www.nijc.org/pdfs/Subject%20Matter%20Articles/ Drugs%20and%20Alc/ACE%20Study%20-%20 OriginsofAddiction.pdf.

FindLaw. (2013). Gay and lesbian adoptive parents: Issues and concerns. Retrieved from http://files.findlaw.com/pdf/ family/family.findlaw.com_adoption_gay-and-lesbian-adoptive-parents-issues-and-concerns.pdf.

First Nations Museum. (2016). The smudge ceremony. Retrieved from https://shop.slcc.ca/learn/the-smudge-ceremony/.

First Nations Pedagogy Online. (2009a). Culture. Retrieved from http://firstnationspedagogy.ca/culture.html.

First Nations Pedagogy Online. (2009b). Experiential. Retrieved from http://firstnationspedagogy.ca/experiential.html.

Flanders, J., Leo, V., Paquette, D., Pihl, R. O., & Séguin, J. R. (2009). Rough-and-tumble play and the regulation of aggression: An observational study of father–child play dyads. *Aggressive Behavior, 35,* 285–295.

Focus on the Family. (2017). Q&A How can I make the blended family transition smooth? Retrieved from https://www.focusonthefamily.ca/content/q-a-how-can-i-make-the-blended-family-transition-smooth.

Foner, N., & Dreby, J. (2011). Relations between the generations in immigrant families. Retrieved from https://faculty.washington.edu/dechter/classes/Soc352/Readings/Foner-Dreby_Relations%20Generations%20Immig%20Fam_AnnRevSoc_11.pdf.

Fournier, S., & Crey, E. (1998). *Stolen from our embrace: The abduction of First Nations children and the restoration of Aboriginal communities.* Toronto: University of Toronto Press.

Freeman, M. (2010). Inuit. *The Canadian Encyclopedia.* Retrieved from http://www.thecanadianencyclopedia.ca/en/article/inuit/.

Freeman, R. (2010). Home, school partnerships in family child care: Providers' relationships within their communities. *Early Childhood Development and Care, 181*(6), 827–845.

Fremstad, S. (2010). *A modern framework for measuring poverty and basic economic security.* Washington, DC: Center for Economic and Policy Research.

Furstenberg, F. F., & Teitler, J. O. (1994). Reconsidering the effects of marital disruption. *Journal of Family Issues, 15*(2), 173–90.

Gadacz, R. (2015). First Nations. *The Canadian Encyclopedia.* Retrieved from http://www.thecanadianencyclopedia.ca/en/article/first-nations/Historica/.

Gaetz, S. (2013). *Coming of age: Reimagining the response to youth homelessness in Canada.* Toronto: Homeless Hub Press.

Gaetz, S., Donaldson, J., Richter, T., & Gulliver, T. (2013). *The state of homelessness in Canada: 2013.* Toronto: Canadian Homelessness Research Network.

Gaetz, S., O'Grady, B., Kidd, S., & Schwan, K. (2016). *Without a home: The national youth homelessness survey.* Toronto: Canadian Observatory on Homelessness Press.

Galabuzi, G., Casipullai, A., & Go, A. (2012, March 20). The persistence of racial inequality in Canada. *Toronto Star.* Retrieved from https://www.thestar.com/opinion/editorialopinion/2012/03/20/the_persistence_of_racial_inequality_in_canada.html.

Galinsky, E. (1988). Parents and teacher-caregivers: Sources of tension, sources of support. *Young Children, 43*(3), 4–12.

Galinsky, E. (1990). Why are some parent/teacher partnerships clouded with difficulties? *Young Children, 45*(5), 2–3, 38–39.

Gallagher, J. J. (1993). The future of professional/family relations in families with children with disabilities. In J. L. Paul & R. J. Simeonsson (Eds.), *Children with special needs: Family, culture, and society* (2nd ed.). Orlando, FL: Harcourt Brace.

Gallo, A. M., Angst, D. B., Knafl, K. A., Twomey, J. G., & Hadley, E. (2010). Health care professionals' views of sharing information with families who have a child with a genetic condition. *Journal of Genetic Counselling, 19*(3), 296–304.

Garanzini, M. J. (1995). *Child-centered, family-sensitive schools: An educator's guide to family dynamics.* Washington, DC: National Catholic Educational Association.

Garris-Christian, L. (2006). Understanding families: Applying family systems theory to early childhood practice. *Young Children, 61*(1), 12–20.

Gauthier, A. (2002). The role of grandparents. *Current Sociology, 50,* 295–307. doi:10.1177/0011392102050002623

Genderqueer and Non-Binary Identities. (2011). What is "genderqueer"? Retrieved from http://genderqueerid.com/what-is-gq.

George, R. P., & Levin, Y. (2015). Family breakdown and poverty: To flourish, our nation must face some hard truths. *Education Next, 15*(2), 30–35.

Gerstein, E. D. (2009). Resilience and the course of daily parenting stress in families of young children with intellectual disabilities. *Journal of Intellectual Disability Research, 53*(12), 981–997.

Gilbert, K. R. (Ed.). (1995). *Annual editions: Marriage and family 95/96.* Guilford, CT: Dushkin.

Gilchrist, K. (2010). "Newsworthy" victims? Exploring differences in Canadian local press coverage of missing/murdered Aboriginal and white women. *Feminist Media Studies, 10*(4), 373–390.

Giles, R. (2017, February 13). The problem with mothers today. *Huffington Post.* Retrieved from http://www.huffingtonpost.com/entry/the-problem-with-mothers-today_us_58a1d4efe4b0e172783a9eb5.

Gill, O., & Jack, G. (2008). Poverty and the child's world: Assessing children's needs. Retrieved from http://cpag.org.uk/content/poverty-and-childs-world-assessing-childrens-needs.

Ginnott, H. (2003). *Between parent and child.* New York: Three Rivers Press.

Global Initiative to End All Corporal Punishment of Children. (2016). Corporal punishment of children: Review of research on its impact and associations. Retrieved from http://www.endcorporalpunishment.org/assets/pdfs/research-summaries/Review-research-effects-corporal-punishment-June-2016.pdf.

Gold, J. M. (2009). Negotiating the financial concerns of stepfamilies: Directions for family counselors. *The Family Journal, 17,* 185–188.

Goldenberg, I., & Goldenberg, H. (2008). *Family therapy: An overview* (7th ed.). Monterey, CA: Thomson Brooks/Cole.

Goldman, J. L. (1996). We can help children grieve: A child-oriented model for memorializing. *Young Children, 51*(6), 76–77.

Goldscheider, F., & Kaufman, G. (2006). Single parenthood and the double standard. *Fathering, 4*(2), 191–208.

Golish, T. D. (2003). Stepfamily communication strengths: Understanding the ties that bind. *Human Communication Research, 29*, 41–80.

Golombok, S., MacCallum, F., Goodman, E., & Rutter, M. (2002). Families with children conceived by donor insemination: A follow-up at age twelve. *Child Development, 73*(3), 952–968.

Golombok, S., Zadeh, S., Imrie, S., Smith, V., & Freeman T. (2016). Single mothers by choice: Mother–child relationships and children's psychological adjustment. *Psychology, 30*(4), 409–418. Retrieved from https://www.ncbi.nlm.nih.gov/labs/articles/26866836/.

Gonzalez-Mena, J. (2002). *The child in the family and the community*. Upper Saddle River, NJ: Merrill Prentice-Hall.

Gonzalez-Mena, J. (2009). *Strategies for communicating and working with diverse families*. Upper Saddle River, NJ: Pearson College Division.

Goodman, W. B., Crouter, A. C., Lanza, S. T., & Cox, M. J. (2008). Paternal work characteristics and father–infant interactions in low-income, rural families. *Journal of Marriage and Family, 70*(3), 640–653.

Gough, P., Shlonsky, A., & Dudding, P. (2009). An overview of the child welfare systems in Canada. *International Journal of Child Health and Human Development, 2*(3) 357–372. Retrieved from http://www.cwlc.ca/sites/default/files/file/resources/Overview_of_the_CW_Systems_in_Canada_Nov_09.pdf.

Government of Canada. (2004). Child maltreatment: A public health issue. Retrieved from https://www.canada.ca/en/health-canada/services/science-research/reports-publications/health-policy-research/child-maltreatment-public-health-issue.html.

Government of Canada. (2012). Distinguishing between poor/dysfunctional parenting and child emotional maltreatment—Risk factors for child emotional maltreatment. Retrieved from https://www.canada.ca/en/public-health/services/health-promotion/stop-family-violence/prevention-resource-centre/children/parenting-child/distinguishing-between-poor-dysfunctional-parenting-child-emotional-maltreatment-risk-factors-child-emotional-maltreatment.html.

Government of Canada. (2013). Piikani Nation—Connectivity profile. Retrieved from http://www.aadnc-aandc.gc.ca/eng/1357840941653/1360158689884.

Government of Canada. (2017). Global issues and international assistance. Retrieved from http://international.gc.ca/world-monde/issues_development-enjeux_developpement/index.aspx?lang=eng.

Government of Canada, Department of Justice. (2015). The effects of divorce on children: A selected literature review. Retrieved from http://www.justice.gc.ca/eng/rp-pr/fl-lf/divorce/wd98_2-dt98_2/p3.html.

Government of Ontario. (2007). Early learning for every child today. Retrieved from http://www.edu.gov.on.ca/childcare/oelf/continuum/continuum.pdf.

Gray, B., & Robinson, C. (2009). Hidden children: Perspectives of professionals on young careers of people with mental health problems. *Child Care in Practice, 15*(2), 95–108.

Greenwood, M., & Griffin, S. (2013). Social determinants of health and Aboriginal children. Retrieved from http://www.wabano.com/wp-content/uploads/2013/10/Margo-Greenwood-Wabano-Social-Determinants-of-Health-Spetember-26_13.pdf.

Grief.com. (2013). The five stages of grief. Retrieved from https://grief.com/the-five-stages/.

Gugl, E., & Welling, L. (2010). The early bird gets the worm? Birth order effects in dynamic family model. *Economic Inquiry, 48*(3), 690–703.

Guldi, M., & Herbst, C. (2015). Offline effects of online connecting: The impact of broadband diffusion on teen fertility decisions. Retrieved from http://ftp.iza.org/dp9076.pdf.

Gulliver-Garcia, T. (2016). *Putting an end to child & family homelessness in Canada*. Toronto: Raising the Roof.

Gupta, R., de Wit ML., & McKeown, D. (2007). The impact of poverty on the current and future health status of children. *Pediatric Child Health, 12*(8).

Guterman, N., Lee, S. J., Taylor, C. A., & Rathouz, P. J. (2009). Parental perceptions of neighborhood processes, stress, personal control, and risk for physical child abuse and neglect. *Child Abuse & Neglect, 33*(12), 897–906.

Ha, Y., Cancian, M., & Meyer, D. (2007). The regularity of child support and its contribution to the regularity of income. Institute for Research on Poverty, University of Wisconsin–Madison. Retrieved from https://www.irp.wisc.edu/research/childsup/cspolicy/pdfs/Ha_Cancian-Meyer_Task13B.pdf.

Halacka Ball, R. (2006). Supporting and involving families in meaningful ways. *Young Children, 61*(1), 10–11.

Halford, K., Nicholson, J., & Sanders, M. (2007). Couple communication in stepfamilies. *Family Process, 46*, 471–483.

Hall, D., & Pearson, J. (2003). Resilience—Giving children the skills to bounce back. Retrieved from http://www.reaching-inreachingout.com/documents/voices_for_children_report_-_resilience_nov_2003.pdf.

Hall, D., & Pearson, J. (2007). Critical abilities related to the development of resilience. *Interaction*, Spring. Retrieved from http://www.reachinginreachingout.com/documents/CCCF-Spring07-English.pdf.

Hancock, A. M. (2007). When multiplication doesn't equal quick addition: Examining intersectionality as a research paradigm. *Perspectives on Politics, 5*(1), 63–78.

Hankivsky, O. (Ed.). (2012). An intersectionality-based policy analysis framework. Vancouver: Institute for

Intersectionality Research and Policy, Simon Fraser University.

Hankivsky, O. (2014). Intersectionality 101. Retrieved from http://vawforum-cwr.ca/sites/default/files/attachments/intersectionallity_101.pdf.

Harrigan, S. (1992). Places everyone. *Health*, November–December, 67–71.

Harrington, D., Van Deusen, F., & Humberd, B. (2011). *The new dad: Caring, committed and conflicted.* Boston: Boston College Center for Work & Family. Retrieved from https://www.researchgate.net/publication/259266498_The_New_Dad_Caring_Committed_And_Conflicted.

Hart-Byers, S. (2009). *Secrets of successful step-families.* n.p.: Lothian.

Harvard Family Research Project. (2006). *Family involvement in early childhood education: Family involvement makes a difference: Evidence that family involvement promotes school success for every child of every age.* Battle Creek, MI: Kellogg Foundation.

Haubursin, C. (2015, April 7). Foreign adoption rates are plummeting. Here are 3 reasons why. *Vox.* Retrieved from https://www.vox.com/2015/4/7/8355241/foreign-adoption-rates-are-plummeting-here-are-3-reasons-why.

Health and Welfare Canada. (n.d.). *Child abuse and neglect.* Ottawa: National Clearinghouse on Family Violence.

Health Poverty Action. (2017). The power of conversation to end FGM. Retrieved from https://www.healthpovertyaction.org/news/end-fgm/.

Helm, J. (1994). Family theme bags: An innovative approach to family involvement in the school. *Young Children, 49*(4), 48–52.

Helmes, E. (2009, September 30–October 4). Stereotypes of older adults: Does status make a difference? In *The Abstracts of the 44th Annual Conference of the Australian Psychological Society.* Symposium conducted at the 44th Annual Conference of the Australian Psychological Society, Darwin, NT, Australia.

Henderson, T. L. (2005). Grandparent visitation rights. *Journal of Family Issues, 26*(5), 638–664.

Henry, P. J., & McCue, J. (2009). The experience of nonresidential stepmothers. *Journal of Divorce & Remarriage, 50,* 185–205.

Hetherington, E. M. (2003). Social support and the adjustment of children in divorced and remarried families. *Childhood, 10*(2), 217–236.

Hetherington, E. M. (2005). Divorce and the adjustment of children. *Pediatrics in Review, 26,* 163–169.

Higginbotham, B., & Adler-Baeder, F. (2008). The smart steps: Embrace the Journey program: Enhancing relational skills and relationship quality in remarriages and stepfamilies. *The Forum for Family and Consumer Issues, 13*(3). Retrieved from http://ncsu.edu/ffci/publications/2008/v13-n3--2008-winter/higginbotham-adler.php.

Higginbotham, B., & Myler, C. (2010). The influence of facilitator and facilitation characteristics on participants' ratings of stepfamily education. *Family Relations, 59,* 74–86.

Higginbotham, B., Skogrand, L., & Torres, E. (2010). Stepfamily education: Perceived benefits for children. *Journal of Divorce & Remarriage, 51,* 36–49.

Hildebrandt, A. (2013, June 19). Half of First Nations children live in poverty. *CBC News.* Retrieved from http://www.cbc.ca/news/canada/half-of-first-nations-children-live-in-poverty-1.1324232.

Himebauch, A., Arnold, R. M., & May, C. (2008). Grief in children and developmental concepts of death. *Journal of Palliative Medicine, 11*(2), 242–243.

Hines, S. (2006). Intimate transitions: Transgender practices of partnering and parenting. *Sociology, 40*(2), 353–371.

Hinshaw, S. P. (2005). The stigmatization of mental illness in children and parents: Developmental issues, family concerns, and research needs. *Journal of Child Psychology and Psychiatry, 46*(7), 714–734.

Hoffman, S., & Maynard, R. (2008). *Kids having kids.* Washington, DC: The Urban Institute Press.

Holland, J. (2008). How schools can support children who experience loss and death. *British Journal of Guidance & Counselling, 36*(4), 411–424.

Holtzman, M. (2006). Definitions of the family as an impetus for legal change in custody decision making: Suggestions from an empirical case study. *Law and Social Inquiry, 31*(1), 1–37.

Hope Irwin, S., & Lero, D. (2004). *In our way: Child care barriers to full workforce participation by parents of children with special needs—and potential remedies.* Wreck Cove, NS: Breton Books.

Hopf, S. M. (2010). Risk and resilience in children coping with parental divorce. *Dartmouth Undergraduate Journal of Science,* Spring. Retrieved from http://dujs.dartmouth.edu/2010/05/risk-and-resilience-in-children-coping-with-parental-divorce/.

Hornor, G. (2008). Child advocacy centers: Providing support to primary care providers. *Journal of Pediatric Health Care, 22*(1), 35–39.

Howard, K., & Reeves, R. (2014). The marriage effect: Money or parenting? Retrieved from https://www.brookings.edu/research/the-marriage-effect-money-or-parenting/.

Howe, N., & Recchia, H. (2008). Siblings and sibling rivalry. In *Encyclopedia of Infant and Early Childhood Development* (pp. 154–164).

Howe, N., & Recchia, H. E. (2014). Introduction to special issue on the sibling relationship as a context for learning and development. *Early Education and Development, 25,* 155–159.

Huberdeau, R. (2014). *Transgender parents* [video]. Retrieved from http://www.transgenderparentsdoc.com/.

Hull, G. H., & Mather, J. (2006). *Understanding generalist practice with families.* Belmont, CA: Thomson Brooks/Cole.

Huntsman, L. (2008). Parents with mental health issues: Consequences for children and effectiveness of interventions designed to assist children and their families. Retrieved from http://www.community.nsw.gov.au/__data/assets/pdf_file/0004/321646/research_parentalmentalhealth.pdf.

Hutchinson, S. L., Afifi, T., & Krause, S. (2007). The family that plays together fares better: Examining the contribution of shared family time to family resilience following divorce. *Journal of Divorce & Remarriage, 46*(3–4), 21–48.

Hutchison, C., & Allen, J. (2010, June 28). Parents with cancer: Millions of patients juggle chemotherapy and childrearing. *ABC News.* Retrieved from http://abcnews.go.com/Health/MindMoodNews/parents-cancer-million-parents-young-children-cancer-survivors/story?id=11013334.

Indigenous and Northern Affairs Canada. (2017). First Nations in Canada. Retrieved from https://www.aadnc-aandc.gc.ca/eng/1307460755710/1307460872523#chp2.

Indigenous Works. (n.d.). Differences between traditional Aboriginal cultures and mainstream Western culture. Retrieved from https://indigenousworks.ca/en/resources/getting-started/cultures.

Institute for Women's Policy Research. (2017). Pay equity & discrimination. Retrieved from https://iwpr.org/issue/employment-education-economic-change/pay-equity-discrimination/.

Intercultural Child & Family Centre. (n.d.). Our approach: An effective child care approach. Retrieved from http://icfc.ca/child-care-our-approach/.

Inuit Tapirit Kanatami. (2017). About Canadian Inuit. Retrieved from https://www.itk.ca/about-canadian-inuit/.

Invest in Kids. (2010). Answers for professionals: The power of parenting. Retrieved from http://www.investinkids.ca/professionals/answers-for-professionals.

Isik-Ecramn, Z., Demir-Dagdas, T., Cakmakci, H., Cava-Tadik, Y., & Intepe-Tingir, S. (2017). Multidisciplinary perspectives towards the education of young low-income immigrant children. *Early Child Development and Care, 187*(9).

Jaffe, M. L. (1991). *Understanding parenting.* Dubuque, IA: Brown & Benchmark.

Jago, R., Sebire, S. J., Bentley, G. F., Turner, K. M., Goodred, J. K., Fox, K. R., . . . Lucas, P. J. (2013). Process evaluation of the Teamplay parenting intervention pilot: Implications for recruitment, retention and course refinement. *BMC Public Health, 13*(1), 1–12.

Janmohamed, Z., & Campbell, R. (2009). *Building bridges: Queer families in early childhood education.* Toronto:

Atkinson Centre for Society and Child Development. Retrieved from https://www.oise.utoronto.ca/atkinson/UserFiles/File/Resources_Topics/Resources_Topics_Diversity/BuildingBridges.pdf.

Janzen, B. L., & Kelly I. W. (2012). Psychological distress among employed fathers: Associations with family structure, work quality, and the work–family interface. *American Journal of Men's Health, 6*(4), 294–302.

Jenkinson, S. (2004). Dying and children. *Interaction,* Spring, 24–26.

Jensen, E. (2009). Teaching with poverty in mind. Retrieved from http://www.ascd.org/publications/books/109074/chapters/How-Poverty-Affects-Behavior-and-Academic-Performance.aspx.

Johnson, R. (2010). How to support children with gay parents. Retrieved from about.com/od/gayparentingadoptio1/a/gayparent.htm.

Johnston, J., Roseby, V., & Kuehnle, K. (2009). *In the name of the child: A developmental approach to understanding and helping children of conflicted and violent divorce* (2nd ed.). New York: Springer.

Joseph, B. (2016, January 26). Indigenous peoples worldviews vs. Western worldviews [Blog post]. Retrieved from https://www.ictinc.ca/blog/indigenous-peoples-worldviews-vs-western-worldviews.

Joseph, B. (2017, September 22). Two examples of Indigenous education programs [Blog post]. Retrieved from https://www.ictinc.ca/blog/two-examples-of-indigenous-education-programs.

Kaminski, J. (2012). First Nations ways of knowing: Developing experiential knowledge in nursing through an Elder in residence program. Retrieved from http://firstnationspedagogy.com/EIR.html.

Katz, L. G. (1980). Mothering and teaching: Some significant distinctions. In L. G. Katz (Ed.), *Current topics in early childhood education* (Vol. 3). Norwood, NJ: Ablex.

Katz, L. G. (1994). Parent involvement—co-op style. *Young Children, 49*(1), 2–3.

Kauppi, C., & Garg, R. (2008). Development of cybermoms: A computer-mediated peer support group to address the needs of young mothers. *Currents: New Scholarship in the Human Services, 7*(2).

Kazemi, A. (2013). Chronically ill parents: Helping children cope. Retrieved from http://www.igliving.com/magazine/articles/IGL_2013-08_AR_Chronically-Ill-Parents-Helping-Children-Cope.pdf.

Keller, H. (1991). *Horace.* New York: Greenwillow Books.

Kelley, D., & Conner, D. R. (1979). The emotional cycle of change. In J. E. Jones & J. W. Pfeifer (Eds.), *The 1979 annual handbook for group facilitators.* San Diego, CA: University Associates.

Kelly, J. B., & Emery, R. E. (2003). Children's adjustment following divorce: Risk and resilience perspectives. *Family Relations, 52*, 352–362.

Kemp, C. (2003). The social and demographic contours of contemporary grandparenthood: Mapping patterns in Canada and the United States. *Journal of Comparative Family Studies, 34*(2), 187–212.

Kemp, G., Smith, M., & Segal, J. (2017). Children and divorce. Retrieved from https://www.helpguide.org/articles/parenting-family/children-and-divorce.htm.

Kenway, J., & Fahey, J. (2008). Melancholic mothering: Mothers, daughters and family violence. *Gender & Education, 20*(6), 639–654.

Khan, S. (2016, August 12). When an official story is a monstrous lie: The textbook history of Canada's Indigenous people. *The Globe and Mail*. Retrieved from https://www.theglobeandmail.com/opinion/when-an-official-story-is-a-monstrous-lie-the-textbook-history-of-canadas-indigenous-people/article31379104/.

Khoo, I. (2015, May 7). International adoption rates plummet in Canada. *Huffington Post*. Retrieved from http://www.huffingtonpost.ca/2015/05/07/international-adoption_n_7225150.html.

Killermann, Sam. (2013). *Understanding the complexities of gender: Sam Killermann at TEDxUofIChicago* [video]. TED Talk. Retrieved from https://www.youtube.com/watch?v=NRcPXtqdKjE.

Kilmer, R. P., Cook, J. R., Taylor, C., Kane, S. F., & Clark, L. Y. (2008). Siblings of children with severe emotional disturbances: risks, resources, and adaptation. *American Journal of Orthopsychiatry, 78*, 1–10.

Kim-Goh, M., & Baello, J. (2008). Attitudes toward domestic violence in Korean and Vietnamese immigrant communities: Implications for human services. *Journal of Family Violence, 23*(1), 647–657.

Kitzinger, S. (1978). *Women as mothers*. Glasgow: Fontana.

Kluger, J. (2006, July 10). The new science of siblings. *Time*.

Kontos, S., & Wells, W. (1986). Attitudes of caregivers and the day care experiences of families. *Early Childhood Research Quarterly, 1*(1), 47–67.

Kostouros, P. (2003). Major mental health systems. In D. Clark (Ed.), *Foundations of children's mental health: A Canadian perspective*. Calgary: Mount Royal University.

Kowal, A. K., Krull, J. L., & Kramer, L. (2006). Shared understanding of parental differential treatment in families. *Social Development, 15*, 276–295.

Kramer, L., & Conger, K. (2009). What we learn from our sisters and brothers: For better or for worse. *New Directions in Child and Adolescent Development, 126*, 1–12.

Krug, E., Dahlberg, L., Mercy, J., Zwi, A., & Lozano, R. (Eds.). (2002). *World report on violence and health*. Geneva, Switzerland: World Health Organization. Retrieved from http://www.who.int/violence_injury_prevention/violence/world_report/en/full_en.pdf?ua=1.

Kübler-Ross, E. (1969). *On death and dying*. New York: Macmillan.

Kübler-Ross, E. (1974). *Questions and answers on death and dying*. New York: Macmillan.

Kübler-Ross, E. (2017). On death and dying. Retrieved from http://www.ekrfoundation.org/five-stages-of-grief/.

Kübler-Ross, E., & Kessler, D. (2014). *On grief and grieving: Finding the meaning of grief through the five stages of loss*. New York: Simon and Schuster.

LaBoucane-Benson, P. (2005). A complex ecological framework of Aboriginal family resilience. Retrieved from http://www.cst.ed.ac.uk/2005conference/papers/LaBoucane-Benson_paper.pdf.

Lalonde, L. (2015). Documenting life: Connecting children, parents and educators in an online community with a child care documentation tool—Storypark. *Interaction, 19*(1).

Lamb, M. (2010). *The role of the father in child development*. Mississauga, ON: John Wiley and Sons.

Lamoure, J. (2013). *Psychopharmacology "boot camp" back to basics study review*. n.p.: EIM-CARE.org.

Lamy, C. (2013). How preschool fights poverty. Retrieved from http://www.ascd.org/publications/educational-leadership/may13/vol70/num08/How-Preschool-Fights-Poverty.aspx.

Lansford, J. E. (2009). Parental divorce and children's adjustment. *Perspectives on Psychological Science, 4*, 140–152.

LaRocque, E. (2014). Colonization and racism. Retrieved from http://www3.nfb.ca/enclasse/doclens/visau/index.php?mode=theme&language=english&theme=30662&film=&excerpt=&submode=about&expmode=2.

Lau, R. (2017, April 17). Single parent by choice: Women turn to sperm donors to conceive. *Global News*. Retrieved from https://globalnews.ca/news/3408726/single-parent-by-choice-women-turn-to-sperm-donors-to-conceive/.

Lawson, D., & Mace, R. (2010). Siblings and childhood mental health: Evidence for a later-born advantage. *Social Science and Medicine, 70*(12), 2061–2069.

Lebow, J., & Newcomb-Rekart, K. (2007). Integrative family therapy for high-conflict divorce with disputes over child custody and visitation. *Family Process, 46*, 79–92.

Lero, D., Ashbourne, L. M., & Whitehead, D. L. (2006). *Inventory of policy areas influencing father involvement*. Guelph, ON: Father Involvement Research Alliance, Centre for Families, Work & Well-Being, University of Guelph. Retrieved from http://www.fira.ca/cms/documents/22/FIRA-Inventory_of_Policies.pdf.

Lever, K., & Wilson, J. J. (2005). Encore parenting: When grandparents fill the role of primary caregiver. *The Family*

Journal: Counseling and Therapy for Couples and Families, 13, 167–171.

Lewis, C., & Lamb, M. E. (2010). The development and significance of father–child relationships in two-parent families. In M. E. Lamb (Ed.), *The role of the father in child development.* Mississauga, ON: John Wiley and Sons.

Li, J. A. (2007). *The kids are OK: Divorce and children's behavioural problems* (RAND Labor and Population Working Paper No. WR-489). Santa Monica, CA: RAND.

Liang, P. H., & Chen, H. F. (2009). Early childhood teachers' use of e-communication notebook. In T. Bastiaens et al. (Eds.), *Proceedings of World Conference on E-Learning in Corporate, Government, Healthcare, and Higher Education 2009* (pp. 3355–3360).

Lingley, S. (2016). How children experience trauma, what parents can do to support them and when it's time to get professional help. Retrieved from https://medicalxpress.com/news/2016-05-children-trauma-parents-professional.html.

Little, L., Sillence, E., Taylor, A., & Sellen, A. (Eds.). (2009). The family and communication technologies. *International Journal of Human Computer Studies, 67*(2), 125–127.

Little Bear, L. (2000). Worldview—Jagged worldviews colliding. Reclaiming Indigenous voice and vision. Retrieved from http://www.learnalberta.ca/content/aswt/documents/fnmi_worldviews/jagged_worldviews_colliding.pdf.

Little Bear, L. (2005). Leroy Little Bear. Retrieved from http://silverbuffalo.org/NAA-LittleBear.html.

Little Bear, L. (2017). Leroy Little Bear (Indspire). Retrieved from https://indspire.ca/laureate/leroy-little-bear-2/.

Livingston, G. (2014). Fewer than half of U.S. kids today live in a "traditional" family. Pew Research Center. Retrieved from http://www.pewresearch.org/fact-tank/2014/12/22/less-than-half-of-u-s-kids-today-live-in-a-traditional-family/.

Lombard, A. (1994). *Success begins at home: The past, present and future of the home instruction program for preschool youngsters* (2nd ed.). Guilford, CT: Dushkin.

Lombardi, J. (2017, February 28). Stepping up efforts to build communities where young children and families can thrive [Blog post]. Retrieved from https://www.cssp.org/media-center/blog/stepping-up-efforts-to-build-communities-where-young-children-and-families-can-thrive.

London, J. (1997). *A koala for Katie.* Toronto: General Publishing.

Long, D. (2011). *The "education" of young fathers: Understanding and addressing their barriers to high school completion.* Edmonton: Terra.

Lopez, M. E. (2010). Valuing families as partners. Retrieved from http://www.hfrp.org/family-involvement/publications-resources?topic=5.

Luong, M. (2008). Life after teenage motherhood. *Perspectives,* May, 5–13. Retrieved from http://www.statcan.gc.ca/pub/75-001-x/2008105/pdf/10577-eng.pdf.

Luxton, M. (2011). *Changing families, new understandings.* Contemporary Family Trends. Retrieved from http://vanier-institute.ca/wp-content/uploads/2015/12/CFT_2011-06-00_EN.pdf.

Macdonald, N. (2015, September 23). Wab Kinew: "Confronting the truth makes you stronger." *Macleans.* Retrieved from http://www.macleans.ca/news/canada/wab-kinew-confronting-the-truth-makes-you-stronger/.

MacNaull, S. (2016). Supporting dads: Paternity leave and benefits in Canada. Retrieved from http://vanierinstitute.ca/supporting-dads-paternity-leave-benefits-canada.

Magnuson, K. (2013). Reducing the effects of poverty through early childhood interventions. Institute for Research on Poverty. *Fast Focus, 17*(August), 16. Retrieved from https://www.irp.wisc.edu/publications/fastfocus/pdfs/FF17-2013.pdf.

Maher, M. (2012). Teacher education with Indigenous ways of knowing, being and doing as a key pillar. *AlterNative: An International Journal of Indigenous Scholarship, 8*(3), 343–356.

Makovichuk, L., Hewes, J., Lirette, P., & Thomas, N. (2014). Play, participation, and possibilities: An early learning and child care curriculum framework for Alberta. Retrieved from http://www.childcareframework.com.

Malaguzzi, L. (1994). Your image of the child: Where teaching begins. *Child Care Information Exchange, 3,* 52–61.

Malvik, C. (2013, July 9). 6 IT management skills you've already mastered as a mom [Blog post]. Retrieved from http://www.rasmussen.edu/degrees/technology/blog/6-it-management-skills-youve-mastered-as-a-mom/.

Mandell, N., & Duffy, A. (Eds.). (2010). *Canadian families: Diversity, conflict and change.* Toronto: Nelson.

Manitoba Trauma Information Centre. (2017). Residential schools. Retrieved from http://trauma-informed.ca/trauma-and-first-nations-people/residential-schools/.

Marshall, K. (2006). Converging gender roles. *Perspectives on Labour and Income, 7*(7). Retrieved from https://www.statcan.gc.ca/pub/75-001-x/10706/9268-eng.htm.

Marshall, K. (2008, June). Fathers' use of paid parental leave. *Perspectives.* Retrieved from http://www.statcan.gc.ca/pub/75-001-x/2008106/pdf/10639-eng.pdf.

Martel, L. (2017). Recent changes in demographic trends in Canada. Ottawa, ON: Statistics Canada. Retrieved from http://www.statcan.gc.ca/pub/75-006-x/2015001/article/14240-eng.htm.

Masten, A. S., & Coatsworth, J. D. (1998). The development of competence in favorable and unfavorable environments: Lessons from research on successful children. *American Psychologist, 53*(2), 205–220.

Masten, A. S., & Gewirtz, A. H. (2006). Resilience in development: The importance of early childhood. In R. E. Tremblay, R. E. Barr, & D. V. Peters (Eds.), *Encyclopedia on early childhood development* (pp. 1–6). Retrieved from https://conservancy.umn.edu/bitstream/handle/11299/53904/resilience?sequence=1.

Masurel, C., & Denton, K. M. (2001). *Two homes*. Somerville, MA: Candlewick Press.

Mathieu, F. (2017, April 19). Signs and symptoms of compassion fatigue and vicarious trauma [Blog post]. Retrieved from https://www.tendacademy.ca/signs-and-symptoms-of-compassion-fatigue-and-vicarious-trauma/.

McBride, S. L. (1999). Family-centered practices. *Young Children, 54*(3), 62–69.

McCoy-Roth, M., Mackintosh, B., & Murphey, D. (2012). When the bough breaks: The effects of homelessness on young children. *Child Trends: Early Childhood Highlights, 3*(1). Retrieved from https://www.childtrends.org/wp-content/uploads/2012/02/2012-08EffectHomelessness-Children.pdf.

McCullough, M. (2017, March 21). Women, poverty, and a basic income guarantee. *Journey Magazine*. Retrieved from https://journeymagazineptbo.com/2017/03/21/women-poverty-and-a-basic-income-guarantee/.

McDaniel, S. A., & Tepperman, L. (2007). *Close relations: An introduction to the sociology of families* (3rd ed.). Toronto: Pearson Prentice-Hall.

McDaniel, S. A., & Tepperman, L. (2010). *Close relations: An introduction to the sociology of families* (4th ed.). Toronto: Pearson Education.

McDaniel, S. A., & Tepperman, L. (2014*). Close relations: An introduction to the sociology of families* (5th ed.). Toronto: Pearson.

McGill Smith, P. (2003). You are not alone: For parents when they learn their child has a disability. *NICHCY News Digest, 20*, 2–6.

McGuire, S., & Shanahan, L. (2010). Sibling experiences in diverse family contexts. *Child Development Perspectives, 4*(2), 72–79.

McIntyre, L. L., & Phaneuf, L. K. (2008). A three-tier model of parent education in early childhood: Applying a problem-solving model. *Topics in Early Childhood Special Education, 27*(4), 214–222.

McKay, A. (2013). Trends in Canadian national and provincial/territorial teen pregnancy rates: 2001–2010. *The Canadian Journal of Human Sexuality, 21*(3&4). Retrieved from http://www.sieccan.org/pdf/TeenPregancy.pdf.

McKay, B., & McKay, K. (2013, October 9). Creating a positive family culture: the importance of establishing family traditions [Blog post]. Retrieved from http://www.artofmanliness.com/2013/10/09/creating-a-positive-family-culture-the-importance-of-establishing-family-traditions/.

McLaughlin, C. (2015). Emerging leaders in ECE and child care. *Interaction, 29*(1). Retrieved from http://www.cccf-fcsge.ca/wp-content/uploads/InterVol291_spring15.pdf.

McWilliam, R. (2010). *Working with families of young children with special needs*. New York: Guilford Press.

Mellor, S. (1995). How do only children differ from other children? In R. L. DelCampo & D. S. DelCampo (Eds.), *Taking sides: Clashing views on controversial issues of childhood and society*. Guilford, CT: Dushkin Publishing Group.

Mendez, N. (2009). Lesbian families. In S. Loue (Ed.), *Sexualities and identities of minority women* (pp. 91–104). New York: Springer. Retrieved from https://link.springer.com/content/pdf/bfm%3A978-0-387-75657-8%2F1.pdf.

Mental Health Commission of Canada. (2013). Making the case for investing in mental health in Canada. Retrieved from https://cmha.ca/media/fast-facts-about-mental-illness/.

Menzies, C. R. (2017). Canada First Nations families. *Marriage and family encyclopedia*. Retrieved from http://family.jrank.org/pages/199/Canada-First-Nations-Families.html.

Métis Family Services. (2017). Métis history. Retrieved from http://www.metisfamilyservices.ca/metis-culture/metis-history.

Métis Nation. (2017). Who are the Métis. Retrieved from http://www.metisnation.ca/index.php/who-are-the-metis/.

Miguez, R., Santos, J. M., & Anido-Rifón, L. E. (2009). Using Web 2.0 technologies in early childhood education. *Proc. of TELearn*, 6–8.

Milevsky, A. (2015, June 10). Only child "syndrome": How do siblings, or a lack of them, affect your personality? *The Independent*. Retrieved from http://www.independent.co.uk/life-style/health-and-families/features/only-child-syndrome-how-do-siblings-or-a-lack-of-them-affect-your-personality-10309792.html.

Milkie, M., Raley, S. B., & Bianchi, S. M. (2009). Taking on the second shift: Time allocations and time pressures of U.S. parents with preschoolers. *Social Forces, 88*(2), 487–517.

Ministry of Indian Affairs and Northern Development. (2000). National Aboriginal Day. Retrieved from http://publications.gc.ca/collections/Collection/R32-179-2000E.pdf.

Mitchell, L., Bateman, A., Ouko, A., Gerrity, R., Lees, J., Matata, K., . . . Xiao, W. (2015). Teaching and learning in culturally diverse early childhood settings. Hamilton, New Zealand: Wilf Malcolm Institute of Educational Research. Retrieved from http://www.waikato.ac.nz/__data/assets/pdf_file/0008/257246/Teachers-and-Learning-for-website_2015-03-05pm.compressed.pdf.

Mo, J. (2010). Stress and resiliency in children living in families impacted by addiction. Retrieved from http://www.norlien.org.

Mollborn, S., & Lovegrove, P. (2011). How teenage fathers matter for children: Evidence from the ECLS-B. *Journal of Family Issues, 31*(5).

Moorhead, J. (2013a, August 16). The biggest problem for parents of a child with special needs? Other people. *The Guardian.* Retrieved from https://www.theguardian.com/lifeandstyle/2013/aug/16/children-disabilities-special-needs-mumsnet-campaign.

Moorhead, J. (2013b, September 17). Breaking the cycle of abuse. *The Guardian.* Retrieved from https://www.theguardian.com/society/2013/sep/17/breaking-the-cycle-of-abuse.

Morrissette, M. (2008). *Choosing single motherhood: The thinking woman's guide.* New York: Houghton Miffin Harcourt.

Munroe, E. A., Lunney Borden, L., Murray Orr, A., Toney, D., & Meader, J. (2013). Decolonizing Aboriginal education in the 21st century. *McGill Journal of Education, 47*(2), 317–338.

Murphy, J. (2015). Canada's Indigenous people raise voices as youth activism surges. *The Guardian.* Retrieved from https://www.theguardian.com/world/2015/oct/18/canada-indigenous-youth-activists-first-nations.

Murray, C. I., Toth, K., & Clinkinbeard, S. S. (2005). Death, dying and grief in families. In P. C. McKendry & S. J. Price (Eds.), *Families and change: Coping with stressful events and transitions* (3rd ed.). Thousand Oaks, CA: Sage.

Mussell, B. (2008). Cultural pathways for decolonization. Retrieved from http://www.heretohelp.bc.ca/visions/aboriginal-people-vol5/cultural-pathways-for-decolonization.

Mytton, J., Ingram, J., Manns, S., & Thomas, J. (2014). Facilitators and barriers to engagement in parenting programs: A qualitative systematic review. *Health Education & Behavior, 41*(2), 127–137.

Najman, J. M., Clavarino, A., McGee, T. R., Bor, W., Williams, G. M., & Hayatbakhsh, M. R. (2010). Timing and chronicity of family poverty and development of unhealthy behaviors in children: A longitudinal study. *Journal of Adolescent Health, 46*(6), 538–544.

Nalls, M., Mullis, R. L., Cornille, T. A., Mullis, A. K., & Jeter, N. (2009). How can we reach reluctant parents in childcare programmes? *Early Child Development and Care, 180*(8), 1053–1064.

National Child Traumatic Stress Network. (2017). National Child Traumatic Stress Network empirically supported treatments and promising practices. Retrieved from http://www.nctsn.org/resources/topics/treatments-that-work/promising-practices.

National Institute on Alcohol Abuse and Alcoholism. (1990). Children of alcoholics: Are they different? Retrieved from http://pubs.niaaa.nih.gov/publications/aa09.htm.

National Scientific Council on the Developing Child. (2004). *Young children develop in an environment of relationships* (Working Paper No. 1). Retrieved from http://www.developingchild.harvard.edu.

National Scientific Council on the Developing Child. (2007). The science of early childhood development: Closing the gap between what we know and what we do. Retrieved from http://www.developingchild.harvard.edu.

National Scientific Council on the Developing Child. (2010a). *Early experiences can alter gene expression and affect long-term development* (Working Paper No. 10). Retrieved from http://www.developingchild.harvard.edu.

National Scientific Council on the Developing Child. (2010b). *Persistent fear and anxiety can affect young children's learning and development* (Working Paper No. 9). Retrieved from http://www.developingchild.harvard.edu.

National Scientific Council on the Developing Child. (2014). *Excessive stress disrupts the architecture of the developing brain* (Working Paper No. 3) (Updated ed.). Retrieved from http://www.developingchild.harvard.edu.

Native Languages of the Americas. (2016). Piikani Nation culture and history. Retrieved from http://www.native-languages.org/piikani_culture.htm.

Nayyar, S. (2006). Focus on the 100 best-comeback moms. Retrieved from http://www.workingmother.com.

Neegan, E. (2005). Excuse me? Who are the first peoples of Canada? A historical analysis of Aboriginal education in Canada then and now. *International Journal of Inclusive Education, 9*(1), 3–15.

NoBullying.com. (2015). Why do parents abuse their children? The cause and effect. Retrieved from https://nobullying.com/why-do-parents-abuse-their-children/.

Norris, J. (2004). *First Peoples' Heritage, Language, & Culture Council: Annual report.* Retrieved from http://www.fin.gov.bc.ca/ocg/pa/03_04/SupE/pdf/FirstPeoplesHeritageLanguage_CultureCouncil2004.pdf.

Nuttall, D. (1993). Letters I never sent to my daughter's third grade teacher. *Young Children, 48*(6), 6.

O'Campo, P., Caughy, M. O., & Nettles, S. M. (2010). Partner abuse or violence, parenting and neighborhood influences on children's behavioral problems. *Social Science and Medicine, 70*(9), 1404–1415.

Office of Family Science Education, Research and Policy. (2017). Office of family science. Retrieved from http://parenteducation.unt.edu/.

O'Grady, C. (2015, March 27). Childhood abuse victims don't always grow up to be abusers. *ARS Technica.* Retrieved from https://arstechnica.com/science/2015/03/childhood-abuse-victims-dont-always-grow-up-to-be-abusers/.

Ogrodnik, I. (2013, June 26). By the numbers: 2013 Alberta floods. *Global News.* Retrieved from https://globalnews.ca/news/673236/by-the-numbers-2013-alberta-floods/.

Olivet, J. (2015, November). *Addressing children's mental health: A solution to family homelessness.* Presentation at the

Child and Family Homelessness Initiative Summit, Toronto.

Olson, D. H., McCubbin, H. I., Barnes, H. L., Larsen, A. S., Muxen, M. J., & Wilson, M. A. (1983). *Families: What makes them work*. Newbury Park, CA: Sage.

Ontario Coalition for Better Child Care. (2017). Building bridges. Retrieved from http://www.childcareontario.org/building_bridges.

Ontario Council of Agencies Serving Immigrants. (n.d.). Positive Spaces Initiative. Retrieved from http://www.positivespaces.ca/find-resources.

Ontario Human Rights Commission. (2017). Indigenous spiritual practices. Retrieved from http://www.ohrc.on.ca/en/policy-preventing-discrimination-based-creed/11-indigenous-spiritual-practices.

Ontario Ministry of the Status of Women. (2015). Statistics: domestic violence. Retrieved from http://www.women.gov.on.ca/owd/english/ending-violence/domestic_violence.shtml.

Pacini-Ketchabaw, V., & Taylor, A. (2015). *Unsettling the colonial places and spaces of early childhood education*. New York: Routledge.

Palusci, V., Crum, P., Bliss, R., & Bavolek, S. J. (2008). Changes in parenting attitudes and knowledge among inmates and other at-risk populations after a family nurturing program. *Children and Youth Services Review, 30*(1), 79–89.

Parents Protect! (n.d.). Quick facts. Retrieved from https://www.parentsprotect.co.uk/quick_facts.htm.

Parke, M. (2006). *Are married parents really better for children? What research says about the effects of family structure on child well-being* (Brief). n.p.: Centre for Law and Social Policy. Retrieved from https://www.clasp.org/sites/default/files/public/resources-and-publications/states/0086.pdf.

Parker, K., & Livingston, G. (2016). 6 facts about American fathers. Retrieved from http://www.pewresearch.org/fact-tank/2016/06/16/fathers-day-facts/.

Pascal, C. (2009). With our best future in mind—Implementing early learning in Ontario. Retrieved from http://afchildrensservices.ca/files/8513/8264/0348/OEYC_Position_Paper.pdf.

Patterson, C. J., Sutfin, E. L., & Fulcher, M. (2004). Division of labor among lesbian and heterosexual parenting couples: Correlates of specialized versus shared patterns. *Journal of Adult Development, 11*(3).

Pearson, C. (2015, July 9). Americans have a better attitudes towards working mothers now than ever before. *Huffington Post*. Retrieved from http://www.huffington-post.ca/entry/acceptance-of-working-mothers-at-all-time-high_us_559d82c9e4b05b1d028f9b6b.

Pearson, J., & Kordich Hall, D. (2006). *RIRO resiliency guidebook*. Toronto: Child and Family Partnership.

Pelo, A., & Davidson, F. (2003). Partnership-building strategies. In C. Copple (Ed.), *A world of difference: Readings on teaching young children in a diverse society*. Washington, DC: National Association for the Education of Young Children.

Penzo, J. A. (2008). Understanding parental grief as a response to mental illness: Implications for practice. *Journal of Family Social Work, 11*(3), 323–338.

Perry, B. (2010). Effects of maltreatment on the developing child: Relational poverty and vulnerability to abuse and neglect. Retrieved from http://www.norlien.org.

Peter, T. (2009). Exploring taboos: Comparing male- and female-perpetrated child sexual abuse. *Journal of Interpersonal Violence, 24*, 1111–1128.

Pew Research Center. (2017). Gay marriage around the world. Retrieved from http://www.pewforum.org/2017/08/08/gay-marriage-around-the-world-2013/#allow.

Pickhardt, C. (2011, December 19). The impact of divorce on young children and adolescents. *Psychology Today*. Retrieved from https://www.psychologytoday.com/blog/surviving-your-childs-adolescence/201112/the-impact-divorce-young-children-and-adolescents.

Planitz, J. M., & Feeny, J. A. (2009). Are stepsiblings bad, stepmothers wicked, and stepfathers evil?: An assessment of Australian stepfamily stereotypes. *Journal of Family Studies, 15*, 82–97.

Poling, D. A., & Hupp, J. M. (2008). Death sentences: A content analysis of children's death literature. *Journal of Genetic Psychology, 169*(2), 165–176.

Polizzi, N. (2017). The art of smudging—A shamanic cleansing ritual. Retrieved from http://www.thesacredscience.com/the-art-of-smudging/.

Poon, J., Zeman, J., Miller-Slough, R., Sanders, W., & Crespo, L. (2016). "Good enough" parental responsiveness to children's sadness: Links to psychosocial functioning. *Journal of Applied Developmental Psychology, 48*, 69–78.

Popkin, M. (2007). *Taming the spirited child: Strategies for parenting challenging children without breaking their spirits*. New York: Fireside.

Portrie, T., & Hill, N. R. (2005). Blended families, a critical review of the current research. *The Family Journal: Counselling and Therapy for Couples and Families, 13*(4), 445–451.

Potter, D. (2010). Psychosocial well-being and the relationship between divorce and children's academic achievement. *Journal of Marriage and Family, 72*, 933–946.

Powell, D. R. (1989). *Families and early childhood programs*. Washington, DC: National Association for the Education of Young Children.

Prigerson, H. G., & Maciejewski, P. K. (2008). Grief and acceptance as opposite sides of the same coin: Setting a research agenda to study peaceful acceptance of loss. *The British Journal of Psychiatry, 193*(6), 435–437. doi:10.1192/bjp.bp.108.053157

Pruett, K., & Pruett, M. (2009). *Partnership parenting: How men and women parent differently—Why it helps your kids and can strengthen your marriage.* Cambridge, MA: de Capro Press.

Public Health Agency of Canada. (2010). *Canadian Incidence study of reported child abuse and neglect.* Ottawa: Author.

Rankin, J., & Ornstein, A. (2009). A commentary on mandatory reporting legislation in the United States, Canada, and Australia: A cross-jurisdictional review of key features, differences, and issues. *Child Maltreatment, 14,* 121–123.

Rauch, P. K., Muriel, A. C., & Cassem, N. H. (2002). Parents with cancer: Who's looking out for the children? *Journal of Clinical Oncology, 20*(21), 4399–4402.

Ravena, Z. R., & Hoffman, J. (2012). Canadian fathers: Demographic and socioeconomic profiles from census and national surveys. In
J. Ball & K. J. Daly (Eds.), *Family involvement in Canada: Diversity, renewal and transformation* (pp. 26–50). Toronto: UBC Press.

Ray, A. (2015). The parent trap: Marketing to parents. Retrieved from https://www.artinstitutes.edu/about/blog/the-parent-trap-marketing-to-parents.

Reaching IN . . . Reaching OUT. (2017). About resilience. Retrieved from http://www.reachinginreachingout.com/aboutresilience.htm.

Rector, N., Bourdeau, D., Kitchen, K., & Joseph-Massiah, L. (2005). *Anxiety disorders—An information guide.* Toronto: Centre for Addiction and Mental Health. Retrieved from http://www.camh.ca/en/hospital/health_information/a_z_mental_health_and_addiction_information/anxiety_disorders/Documents/anxiety_guide_en.pdf.

Reedy, C., & McGrath, W. H. (2010). Can you hear me now? Staff–parent communication in child care centres. *Early Child Development and Care, 180*(3), 347–357.

Religious diversity in Canada: Secularism, multiculturalism, pluralism, with Dr. Peter Beyer. (2014). Retrieved from http://www.ucalgary.ca/events/calendar/religious-diversity-canada-secularism-multiculturalism-pluralism-dr-peter-beyer.

Remarriage and stepfamilies: The impact on children. (2012). Retrieved from http://www.researchomatic.com/Remarriage-And-Stepfamilies-The-Impact-On-Children-110946.html.

Remennick, L. (2007). "Being a woman is different here": Changing perceptions of femininity and gender relations among former Soviet women living in Greater Boston. *Women's Studies International Forum, 30*(1), 326–341.

Report card on child and family poverty in Canada. (2009). Retrieved from http://www.campaign2000.ca.

Resilience Research Centre. (2017). Resources. Retrieved from http://www.resilienceproject.org/.

Resiliency Initiatives. (2011). Embracing a strength-based perspective and practice in education. Retrieved from http://www.ayscbc.org/Strengths-Based%20School%20Culture%20and%20Practice.pdf.

Reviving the culture through naming ceremony. (2008). *Windspeaker, 26*(9). Retrieved from http://www.ammsa.com/node/7283.

Riggs, D., Delfabbro, P. H., & Augoustinos, M. (2008). Negotiating foster families: Identification and desire. *British Journal of Social Work, 39,* 789–806.

Riggs, D., Delfabbro, P. H., & Augoustinos, M. (2010). Foster fathers and carework: Engaging alternate models of parenting. *Fathering, 8*(1), 24–36.

Rios, C. (2015). 7 everyday things poor people worry about that rich people never do. *Everyday Feminism.* Retrieved from https://everydayfeminism.com/2015/05/poor-people-worries/.

Roer-Strier, D. (1999). Coping strategies of immigrant parents: Directions for family therapy. *Family Process, 35,* 363–376.

Roer-Strier, D., Kosner, A., & Shimoni, R. (2017). Grandparenthood in transition: Immigrant grandparents from the former Soviet Union, in Israel and Canada. *Journal of Comparative Family Studies.* Manuscript submitted for publication.

Roer-Strier, D., Strier, R., Este, D., Shimoni, R., & Clarke, D. (2005). Fatherhood and immigration: Challenging the deficit theory. *Child and Family Social Work, 10*(4), 315–329.

Rolland, J. S. (2005). Cancer and the family: An integrative model. *Cancer, 104*(S11), 2584–2595. doi:10.1002/cncr.21489

Rosenthal, C., & Gladstone, J. (2007). Grandparenthood in Canada. Retrieved from http://www.vifamily.ca/library/cft/grandparenthood.html.

Ross, L. E., Steele, L. S., & Epstein, R. (2006). Service use and gaps in services for lesbian and bisexual women during donor insemination, pregnancy, and the postpartum period. *Journal of Obstetrics & Gynaecology Canada, 7,* 505–511.

Royal Canadian Mounted Police. (2012). The effects of family violence on children—Where does it hurt? Retrieved from http://www.rcmp-grc.gc.ca/cp-pc/chi-enf-abu-eng.htm.

Royal Commission on Aboriginal Peoples. (1996). *People to people, nation to nation: Highlights from the report of the Royal Commission on Aboriginal Peoples.* Ottawa: Minister of Supply and Services Canada.

Ruspini, E. (2015). *Diversity in family life: Gender, relationships, and social change.* Bristol, UK: Policy Press, University of Bristol.

Rutter, M., Pickles, A., Murray, R., & Eaves, L. (2001). Testing hypotheses on specific environmental causal effects on behavior. *Psychological Bulletin, 127,* 291–324.

Rutter, V. (2009). Divorce in research vs. divorce in the media. *Sociology Compass, 3*(4), 707–720.

Saffron Centre. (2015). 90% of child sexual abuse victims know their perpetrator. Retrieved from http://saffroncentre.com/90-of-child-sexual-abuse-victims-know-their-perpetrator/.

Sauvé, R. (2010). Canada job trends update: National and provincial labour markets. Retrieved from http://www.peoplepatternsconsulting.com/pub_can_job10.html.

Save the Children. (2016). Child poverty—What drives it and what it means to children across the world. Retrieved from https://resourcecentre.savethechildren.net/sites/default/files/documents/child_poverty_report_4web_0.pdf.

Save the Children. (2017a). Child poverty. Retrieved from http://www.savethechildren.org.uk/about-us/what-we-do/child-poverty.

Save the Children. (2017b). Invisible wounds. Retrieved from https://i.stci.uk/sites/default/files/Invisible%20Wounds%20March%202017.pdf.

Savio Beers, L. A., & Hollo, R. E. (2009). Approaching the adolescent-headed family: A review of teen parenting. *Current Problems in Pediatric and Adolescent Care, 39,* 216–233.

Sawhill, I. (2014, July 15). Are children raised with absent fathers worse off? Retrieved from https://www.brookings.edu/opinions/are-children-raised-with-absent-fathers-worse-off/.

Scaramella, L. V., Neppl, T. K., Ontai, L. L., & Conger, R. D. (2008). Consequences of socioeconomic disadvantage across three generations: Parenting behavior and child externalizing problems. *Journal of Family Psychology, 22,* 725–733.

Schachter, H. (2015, January 15). Can't cope? It's not your fault. *The Globe and Mail.* Retrieved from https://www.theglobeandmail.com/report-on-business/careers/career-advice/life-at-work/cant-cope-its-probably-not-your-fault/article22452100/.

Schaub, M. (2010). Parenting for cognitive development from 1950 to 2000: The institutionalization of mass education and the social construction of parenting in the United States. *Sociology of Education, 83,* 46–66.

Schellenberg, G., & Maheux, H. (2007). *Immigrants' perspectives on their first four years in Canada: Highlights from three waves of the longitudinal survey of immigrants to Canada.* Ottawa: Statistics Canada. Retrieved from http://www.statcan.gc.ca/pub/81-595-m/2010084/e1-eng.htm.

Schmidt, T. (2008). *Standing on my own two feet: A child's affirmation of love in the midst of divorce.* New York: Price Stern Sloan.

Schoppe-Sullivan, S., Brown G. L., Cannon, E. A., Mangelsdorf, S. C., & Sokolowski, M. S. (2008). Maternal gatekeeping, coparenting quality, and fathering behavior in families with infants. *Journal of Family Psychology, 22*(3), 389–398.

Schreiner, M. (2014). Abuse and isolation. Retrieved from https://evolutioncounseling.com/abuse-and-isolation/.

Schwartz, C. (2011). Helping children overcome trauma. *Children's Mental Health Quarterly, 5*(3), 1–16.

Scott, D., & Arney, F. (2010). *Working with vulnerable families: A partnership approach.* New York: Cambridge University Press.

Scully, P., & Howell, J. (2008). Using rituals and traditions to create classroom community for children, teachers, and parents. *Early Childhood Education Journal, 36*(3), 261–266.

Seligman, M. (Ed.). (1991). *The family with a handicapped child.* Boston: Allyn & Bacon.

Seng, A., & Prinz, R. (2008). Parents who abuse: What are they thinking? *Clinical Child and Family Psychology Review, 11*(4), 163–175.

Shechner, T., Slone, M., Meir, Y., & Kalish, Y. (2010). Relations between social support and psychological and parental distress for lesbian, single heterosexual by choice and two-parent heterosexual mothers. *American Journal of Orthopsychiatry, 80*(3), 283–292.

Shimoni, R. (1992a). *Endemic ambiguity: The role of caregivers in relation to parents of children in day care* (Doctoral thesis). University of Calgary.

Shimoni, R. (1992b). Parent involvement in early childhood education and day care. *Sociological Studies of Child Development, 5,* 73–95.

Shimoni, R. (1992c). Rethinking parent involvement in child care. *Child and Youth Care Forum, 21*(2), 105–118.

Shimoni, R., Este, D., & Clarke, D. (2003). Paternal engagement in immigrant and refugee families. *Journal of Comparative Family Studies, 34*(4), 555–568.

Shonk, K. (2017). How to resolve cultural conflict: Overcoming cultural barriers at the negotiation table. Retrieved from https://www.pon.harvard.edu/daily/conflict-resolution/a-cross-cultural-negotiation-example-how-to-overcome-cultural-barriers/.

Shonkoff, J. P., Garner, A. S., Siegel, B. S., Dobbins, M. I., Earls, M. F., McGuinn, L., . . . Wood, D. L. (2012). The lifelong effects of early childhood adversity and toxic stress. *Pediatrics, 129*(1), 232–246.

Siegel, D., Smith, S., & Donaldson, E. (2012). *Openness in adoption: From secrecy and stigma to knowledge and Connections.* New York: Evan B. Donaldson Adoption Institute. Retrieved from https://www.adoptioninstitute.org/wp-content/uploads/2013/12/2012_03_OpennessInAdoption_ExecSum.pdf.

Silverman, P., & Kelly, M. (2009). *A parent's guide to raising grieving children: Rebuilding your family after the death of a loved one.* New York: Oxford University Press.

Sinha, M. (2015). Section 3: Family violence against children and youth. *Juristat.* Retrieved from http://www.statcan.gc.ca/pub/85-002-x/2012001/article/11643/11643-3-eng.htm.

Sirin, S. R., & Rogers-Sirin, L. (2015). *The educational and mental health needs of Syrian refugee children*. Washington, DC: Migration Policy Institute. Retrieved from https://www.researchgate.net/profile/Selcuk_Sirin/publication/287998909_The_Educational_and_Mental_Health_Needs_of_Syrian_Refugee_Children/links/567ccd6c08ae19758384e4bf.pdf.

Skolnick, A. S. (1992). *The intimate environment: Exploring marriage and the family* (5th ed.). New York: HarperCollins.

Smith, J. (2011, July 20). Statistics Canada to stop tracking divorce rates. *Toronto Star*. Retrieved from https://www.thestar.com/news/canada/2011/07/20/statistics_canada_to_stop_tracking_divorce_rates.html.

Smith-Brody, L. (2017).*The fifth trimester: The working mom's guide to style, sanity, and big success after baby*. New York: Doubleday.

Smith-Gilman, S. (2015). Culture matters: The arts, the classroom environment, and a pedagogy of Entewate`Nikonri:Sake: A study in a First Nations preschool. *Canadian Review of Art Education, 42*(2). Retrieved from http://crae.mcgill.ca/article/view/1/3.

Sobon, S. M. (2005). Blended families in three marriage enrichment programs. Retrieved from http://www.mapleleafweb.com/features/general/poverty/consequences.html.

Sociocultural approach. (n.d.) *Psychologist World*. Retrieved from https://www.psychologistworld.com/cognitive/learning/sociocultural-approach-vygotsky-zone-proximal-development.

The Source for Women's Health. (2013). Lone parent rate. Retrieved from http://www.womenshealthdata.ca/category.aspx?catid=124.

Spracklin, P. (2017). The top 10 problems faced by immigrants. Retrieved from https://www.immigroup.com/news/top-10-problems-immigrants.

Stacey, S. (2015). *Pedagogical documentation in early childhood: Sharing children's learning and teachers' thinking*. St. Paul, MN: Redleaf Press.

Statistics Canada. (2005). Greatest difficulties new immigrants faced since arriving in Canada. Retrieved from http://www.statcan.gc.ca/pub/11-008-x/2007000/c-g/4097864-eng.htm.

Statistics Canada. (2006). Women in Canada: A gender-based statistical report. Retrieved from http://www.statcan.gc.ca/pub/89-503-x/89-503-x2010001-eng.htm.

Statistics Canada. (2007a, September 12). 2006 census: Families, marital status, households, and dwelling characteristics. *The Daily*.

Statistics Canada. (2007b). *Snapshot of Canada: Families. Canadian social trends* (Catalogue no. 11–008: 39–40). Ottawa: Statistics Canada.

Statistics Canada. (2008). *Canadian demographics at a glance*. Retrieved from http://www.statcan.gc.ca/pub/91-003-x/91-003-x2007001-eng.pdf.

Statistics Canada. (2009). 2006 Census: Family portrait: Continuity and change in Canadian families and households in 2006: National portrait: Individual. Retrieved from http://www12.statcan.ca/census-recensement/2006/as-sa/97–553/p15-eng.cfm.

Statistics Canada. (2010). Age group of child (12), number of grandparents (3) and sex (3) for the grandchildren living with grandparents with no parent present, in private households of Canada, provinces and territories, 2006 census–20% sample data. Retrieved from http://publications.gc.ca/site/eng/318470/publication.html.

Statistics Canada. (2012). Portrait of families and living arrangements in Canada. Retrieved from http://www12.statcan.gc.ca/census-recensement/2011/as-sa/98-312-x/98-312-x2011001-eng.cfm.

Statistics Canada. (2015a). Lone-parent families. Retrieved from http://www.statcan.gc.ca/pub/75-006-x/2015001/article/14202/parent-eng.htm.

Statistics Canada. (2015b). Section 2: Police-reported family violence against children and youth, 2009. *Family violence in Canada: A statistical profile*. Retrieved from http://www.statcan.gc.ca/pub/85-224-x/2010000/part-partie2-eng.htm.

Statistics Canada. (2016a). 150 years of immigration in Canada. Retrieved from https://www.statcan.gc.ca/pub/11-630-x/11-630-x2016006-eng.htm.

Statistics Canada. (2016b). Aboriginal peoples in Canada: First Nations people, Métis and Inuit. Retrieved from http://www12.statcan.gc.ca/nhs-enm/2011/as-sa/99-011-x/99-011-x2011001-eng.cfm.

Statistics Canada. (2016c). Canadian income survey, 2014. Retrieved from http://www.statcan.gc.ca/daily-quotidien/160708/dq160708b-eng.htm.

Statistics Canada. (2016d). Census family. Retrieved from http://www23.statcan.gc.ca/imdb/p3Var.pl?Function=UnitI&Id=272562.

Stefanac, R. (2015). Do older siblings have too much influence on younger ones? Retrieved from http://www.parentscanada.com/family-life/do-older-siblings-have-too-much-influence-on-younger-ones.

The Step and Blended Family Institute. (2017). Prevailing myths. Retrieved from http://www.stepinstitute.ca/myths.php.

Step-families becoming the new normal in Canada: 2011 census. (2012, September 19). *National Post*. Retrieved from http://nationalpost.com/news/canada/step-families-becoming-the-new-normal-in-canada-2011-census.

Stith, S., Ting Liu, L., Davies, C., Boykin, E. L., Alder, M. C., Harris, J. M., . . . Dees, J. E. M. E. G. (2009). Risk factors in child maltreatment: A meta-analytic review of the literature. *Children and Youth Services Review, 30*(1), 79–89.

Stocks, W. (2011). Risks of child abuse and neglect based on family structure. Retrieved from http://divorceministry4kids.com/2011/risks-of-child-abuse-and-neglect-based-on-family-structure/.

Stosny, S. (2015, June 10). What drives emotional abuse and how to begin to recover. *Psychology Today*. Retrieved from https://www.psychologytoday.com/blog/anger-in-the-age-entitlement/201506/what-drives-emotional-abuse-and-how-begin-recover.

Strohschein, L. (2007). Challenging the presumption of diminished capacity to parent: Does divorce really change parenting practices? *Family Relations, 56*(4), 358–368.

Strow, C. W., & Strow, B. K. (2008). Evidence that the presence of a half-sibling negatively impacts a child's personal development. *American Journal of Economics and Sociology, 67*(2), 177–206.

Sullivan, O., Billari, F., & Altintas, E. (2014). Fathers' changing contributions to child care and domestic work in very low-fertility countries: The effect of education. *Journal of Family Issues, 35*, 1048–1065.

Sullivan, P., Knutson, J. F., & Asford, E. J. (2009). Maltreatment of children and youth with special healthcare needs. *Aggression and Violent Behavior, 14*(1), 13–29.

Swedish Institute. (2017). Quick facts. Retrieved from https://sweden.se/quick-facts/tag/childcare/.

Sweeney, M. M. (2010). Remarriage and stepfamilies: Strategic sites for family scholarship in the 21st century. *Journal of Marriage and Family, 72*(3), 667–684.

Szinovacz, M. E., & Davey, A. (2006). Effects of retirement and grandchild care on depressive symptoms. *International Journal of Aging and Human Development, 62*, 1–20.

Teen pregnancy. (2017). Retrieved from http://www.health-communities.com/teen-pregnancy/children/overview-of-teen-pregnancy.shtml.

Thiele, D., & Whelan, T. (2006). The nature and dimensions of the grandparent role. *Marriage and Family Review, 40*(1), 93–108.

Thomas, A., & Chess, S. (1977). *Temperament and development.* New York: Brunner/Mazel.

Thomson, L., & McArthur, M. (2009). Who's in our family? An application of the theory of family boundary ambiguity to the experiences of former foster carers. *Adoption and Fostering Journal, 33*(1), 68–79.

Thomson, S. (2016, August 30). Justin Trudeau says poverty is sexist. These 5 charts show why he's right. *World Economic Forum*. Retrieved from https://www.weforum.org/agenda/2016/08/justin-trudeau-poverty-is-sexist-charts.

Tornello, S. (2015). Samantha L. Tornello [biography web page]. Retrieved from http://hhd.psu.edu/hdfs/directory/Bio.aspx?id=SamanthaTornello.

Traster, T. (2014, June 10). The elusive, manipulative adopted child. *The Atlantic*. Retrieved from https://www.theatlantic.com/health/archive/2014/06/reactive-attachment-disorder/372259/.

Trawick-Smith, J. (2010). *Early childhood development: A multicultural perspective* (5th ed.). Upper Saddle River, NJ: Pearson.

Truth and Reconciliation Commission of Canada. (2015a). *Honouring the truth, reconciling for the future—Final report.* Retrieved from http://www.trc.ca/websites/trcinstitution/File/2015/Honouring_the_Truth_Reconciling_for_the_Future_July_23_2015.pdf.

Truth and Reconciliation Commission of Canada. (2015b). Residential schools. Retrieved from http://www.trc.ca/websites/trcinstitution/index.php?p=4.

Tucker, C. J., & Updegraff, K. (2009). The relative contributions of parents and siblings to child and adolescent development. *New Directions for Child and Adolescent Development, 126*, 13–28.

Turecki, S., & Tonner, L. (2000). *The difficult child* (2nd ed.). New York: Bantam.

Turnbull, A., & Turnbull, H. R. (1990). *Families, professionals, and exceptionality: A special partnership* (2nd ed.). Columbus, OH: Merrill.

Turrell, J. (2014, October 2). Why parents of autistic children and special needs children turn to entrepreneurship. *Dailyworth*. Retrieved from https://www.dailyworth.com/posts/2973-why-parents-of-autistic-children-and-special-needs-children-turn-to-entrepreneurship.

United Nations. (2009, November 12). Tolerance is not indifference or grudging acceptance, but way of life based on understanding, respect for others, says Secretary-General in message [Press release]. Retrieved from https://www.un.org/press/en/2009/sgsm12605.doc.htm.

United Nations Human Rights Office of the High Commissioner. (2017). Human rights dimension of poverty. Retrieved from http://www.ohchr.org/EN/Issues/Poverty/DimensionOfPoverty/Pages/Index.aspx.

University of Calgary. (2017a). Indigenous ways of knowing and being. Retrieved from http://www.ucalgary.ca/indigenous/research/knowing_being.

University of Calgary. (2017b). Transcultural curriculum in early childhood education. Retrieved from http://werklund.ucalgary.ca/gpe/transcultural-curriculum-in-ece.

University of Toronto and Centre for Addiction and Mental Health. (2017). Welcome to Re:searching for LGBTQ Health! Retrieved from http://lgbtqhealth.ca/.

Unsettling America. (2011). Cultural appreciation or cultural appropriation? Retrieved from https://unsettlingamerica.wordpress.com/2011/09/16/cultural-appreciation-or-cultural-appropriation/.

Updegraff, K. A., Thayer, S. M., Whiteman, S. D., Denning, D. J., & McHale, S. M. (2005). Relational aggression in adolescents' sibling relationships: Links to sibling and parent–adolescent relationship quality. *Family Relations, 54*, 373–385.

U.S. Department of Health & Human Services. (2015). Impact of adoption on adoptive parents: Factsheet for families. Retrieved from https://www.childwelfare.gov/pubpdfs/impactparent.pdf.

U.S. Department of Health & Human Services. (2016). Trends in teen pregnancy and childbearing. Retrieved from https://www.hhs.gov/ash/oah/adolescent-development/reproductive-health-and-teen-pregnancy/teen-pregnancy-and-childbearing/trends/index.html.

U.S. Department of Health & Human Services. (2017). *Child welfare outcomes 2010–2014: Report to Congress.* Retrieved from https://www.acf.hhs.gov/cb/resource/cwo-10-14.

U.S. National Library of Medicine. (n.d.). Native voices: Medicine ways: Traditional healers and healing. Retrieved from https://www.nlm.nih.gov/nativevoices/exhibition/healing-ways/medicine-ways/medicine-wheel.html.

Vanier Institute of the Family. (2010). *Families count: Profiling Canadian families.* Retrieved from http://www.vifamily.ca/node/371.

Vanier Institute of the Family. (2016). Family diversity in Canada 2016. Retrieved from http://vanierinstitute.ca/family-diversity-2016/.

Vanier Institute of the Family. (2017). Definition of family. Retrieved from http://vanierinstitute.ca/definition-family/.

Van Riper, M. (2007). Families of children with Down syndrome: Responding to a change in plans with resilience. *Journal of Pediatric Nursing, 22*(22), 116–128.

Van Velsor, P., & Cox, D. (2000). Use of the collaborative drawing technique in school counseling practicum: An illustration of family systems. *Counselor Education and Supervision, 40*(2), 141–153.

Vézina, M. (2012). *2011 General Social Survey: Overview of families in Canada: Being a parent in a stepfamily: A profile.* Ottawa: Minister of Industry.

Vézina, M. (2015). Being a parent in a stepfamily: A profile. Retrieved from http://www.statcan.gc.ca/pub/89-650-x/89-650-x2012002-eng.htm.

Vuckovic, A. (2008). Inter-cultural communication: A foundation of communicative action. *Multicultural Education & Technology Journal, 2*(1), 47–59.

Walberg, R., & Mrozek, A. (2009, June 1). Private choices, public costs: How failing families cost us all. Retrieved from http://www.imfcanada.org/archive/142/private-choices-public-costs.

Wald, E. (1981). *The remarried family: Challenge and promise.* New York: Family Service Association of America.

Waller, M. (2009). Family man in the other America: New opportunities, motivations, and supports for paternal caregiving. *Annals of the American Academy of Political and Social Science, 624*(1), 156–176.

Wallerstein, J. S. (1991). The long-term effects of divorce on children: A review. *Journal of the American Academy of Child and Adolescent Psychiatry, 30*(3), 349–360.

Wallerstein, J. S. (2005). Growing up in the divorced family. *Clinical Social Work Journal, 33*(4), 401–418.

Walter, T. (2010). Grief and culture: A checklist. *Bereavement Care, 29*(2), 5–9.

Walton, B. F., Goddard, T., Frenette, D., Cooper, L., Paters, N., & Burgess, J. (2009). *Promoting educational success for Mi'kmaq learners on Prince Edward Island.* Charlottetown, PEI: University of Prince Edward Island.

Ward, M. (2006). *The family dynamic: A Canadian perspective* (4th Cdn. ed.). Scarborough, ON: Nelson Education.

Watters, J. A. (2007). *Reproducing Canada's colonial legacy: A critical analysis of Aboriginal issues in Ontario high school curriculum* (Master's thesis). Queen's University, Kingston, Ontario.

Way, P. (2010). That isn't really how it works: Discussing questions of life, death and afterlife with bereaved children and young people. *Bereavement Care, 29*(2), 17–20.

Webb, N., & Doka, K. (2010). *Helping bereaved children: A handbook for practitioners* (3rd ed.). New York: Guilford Press.

Wilcox, B., & Lerman, R. (2014). For richer, for poorer: How family structures economic success in America. Retrieved from https://www.aei.org/publication/for-richer-for-poorer/.

Williams, R. H., & Vashi, G. (2007). Hijab and American Muslim women: Creating autonomous selves. *Sociology of Religion, 68*, 269–287.

Willis, C. A. (2004). Helping children grieve: Implications for directors and teachers. *Child Care Exchange,* September/October, 20–23.

Wilson, D., & Macdonald, D. (2010). *The income gap between Aboriginal Peoples and the rest of Canada.* Ottawa: Canadian Centre for Policy Alternatives. Retrieved from http://www.policyalternatives.ca/sites/default/files/uploads/publications/reports/docs/Aboriginal%20Income%20Gap.pdf.

Wilson, L. (2005). *Partnerships: Families and communities in early childhood development* (3rd ed.). Toronto: Nelson.

Wilson, L. (2010). *Partnerships: Families and communities in early childhood* (4th ed.). Toronto: Nelson.

Wilson, L. (2014). *Partnerships: Families and communities in early childhood* (5th ed.). Toronto: Nelson.

Wolf, L., Fishman, S., & Ellison, D. (1998). Effects of sibling perception of differential parental treatment in sibling dyads with one disabled child. *Journal of the American Academy of Child and Adolescent Psychiatry*, 37(12), 1317–1325.

Woodford, M. (2010). Same-sex marriage and beyond. *Journal of Gay & Lesbian Social Service, 22*(1/2), 1–8.

Woodthorpe, K. (2010). Public dying: Death in the media and Jade Goody. *Sociology Compass, 4*, 283–294.

World Federation for Mental Health. (2012). Depression: A global crisis. Retrieved from http://www.who.int/mental_health/management/depression/wfmh_paper_depression_wmhd_2012.pdf.

Woroniak, M., & Camfield, D. (2013, January 1). First Nations rights: Confronting colonialism in Canada. Centre for Research on Globalization. Retrieved from https://www.globalresearch.ca/first-nations-rights-confronting-colonialism-in-canada/5321197.

Wright, K., & Stegelin, D. (2003). *Building school and community partnerships through parent involvement* (2nd ed.). Upper Saddle River, NJ: Merrill Prentice-Hall.

Yngvesson, B. (2010). *Belonging in an adopted world: Race, identity and transnational adoption.* Chicago: University of Chicago Press.

Youth.gov. (2017). Adverse effects. Retrieved from http://youth.gov/youth-topics/teen-pregnancy-prevention/adverse-effects-teen-pregnancy.

Zajonc, R. B., & Mullally, P. R. (1997). Birth order: Reconciling conflicting effects. *American Psychologist, 52*, 685–690.

Index

National Child Traumatic Stress Network, 54

National Institute on Alcohol Abuse and Alcoholism, 291

National Scientific Council on the Developing Child, 5, 286, 295, 340, 341

Native Languages of the Americas, 147

Nayyar, S., 18

Neegan, E., 146

neglect, 332, 333

neotraditional families, 228

Neppl, T. K., 186

Nettles, S. M., 340, 341

Newcomb-Rekart, K., 230

new family traditions, 234

newsletters, 93–94

Nicholsen, D., 246

Nicholson, J. M., 26

Nishina, A., 29

nontraditional family, 248

Norris, J., 152

Nuttall, D., 126

O

O'Campo, P., 186, 340, 341

O'Connor, T. G., 29, 209

Office of Family Science Education, Research and Policy, 43

Ogilvie, L., 174

O'Grady, B., 256

O'Grady, C., 338

Ogrodnik, I., 46

Olivet, J., 188

Olson, C. D., 226

Olson, D. H., 212

Olson, K., 174

online communication, 96–98

only child syndrome, 30–31

Ontai, L. L., 186

Ontario Coalition for Better Child Care, 308

Ontario Council of Agencies Serving Immigrants, 303, 304

Ontario Human Rights Commission, 157

Ontario Ministry of the Status of Women, 337

open adoption, 251

Ornstein, A., 345

Ouko, A., 170

P

Pacini-Ketchabaw, V., 146, 160

Paliokosta, E., 287, 288, 289

Palusci, V., 338, 339

pansexual, 304

Paquette, D., 25

parent advisory committees, 105

parental influence and control, 69–71

parental subsystem, 268–270

parent boards, 104–105

parent corners, 89–90

parent education, 67–69

Parent Effectiveness Training (PET), 68

parent engagement, 75–76, 79. *See also* parent involvement

  activities, 109

  goals of, 80–81

  need for, 111–114

parenting

  impact of divorce on, 214–215

  transitions in, 43

parent input, 109

parent involvement, 6

  continuity of care ("creating bridges"), 71–73

  defining, 65–66

  empowering parents, 73–74

  family-centred approach, 74–75

  parental influence and control, 69–71

  parent education, 67–69

  parent volunteers, 98–100

  "what and how" of, 80–81

parents

  adoptive, supporting, 254–255

  benefits from parent engagement, 112

  with chronic health conditions, 290

  confidence, 68–69

  emotional availability of, 210

  empowerment, 74

  information sharing, 69

  misconceptions, 121–123

  schedules between educators and, 118–119

  stress on, 269–270

  traditional role of, 17

parent–staff collaboration

  clarification of goals, 80–81

  effective communication, 82–83

  evaluation, 110–111

  input from parents, 109

  making collaboration work, 107–109

  start with the children, 82

  welcoming attitude, 83–85

  working with wider systems, 105

parents with special needs

  addictions, 290–294

  chronic health conditions, 287–290

  early childhood educator, role of, 289–290, 293–294

  effects on children, 286–287

  mental health issues, 294–299

parent–teacher meetings and conferences, 103

Parke, M., 25, 210

Parker, K., 25

Pascal, C., 65

Paters, N., 159

Patras, J., 198, 228

Patterson, C. J., 307

Pearson, C., 21

Pearson, J., 50, 51, 54, 55, 56, 57, 58, 59

pedagogy, 159–161

Pelo, A., 123, 124, 126

Penzo, J. A., 264, 265

permission, 233

Perry, B., 291

Peter, T., 344

Pew Research Center, 306

Phaneuf, L. K., 134, 135

phone calls, 86

physical abuse, 332, 333–334

Pickhardt, C., 207

Pickles, A., 177

Pihl, R. O., 25

Planitz, J. M., 224

Poling, D. A., 324

Polizzi, N., 158

Poon, J., 211

Popkin, M., 31

Portrie, T., 8

Potter, D., 208

poverty

  attitudes toward the poor, 183

  beyond the centre, 105–106

  children, 185, 186–187

  definitions of, 182–183

  early childhood educators, role of, 189–193

  effects of poverty, 186–188

  effects on families and communities, 187

  families and communities, effects no, 187

  homelessness, 187–188, 190, 191–192

  Indigenous people and, 185

  myths, 183–184

  reducing poverty, 188–189

  women and, 185

Powell, D. R., 4, 67

power, 125–127

practice of relationships, 79–80

preconceived ideas, 121–123

preschool children

  death, understanding of, 317–319

  divorce, 213

Prigerson, H. G., 315

Prinz, R., 338

problem solving, 56

Proctor, B. D., 183

protective factors, 51–53, 54

protest, 315

Pruett, K., 24, 25, 212

Public Health Agency of Canada, 287

pyramid model, 7

Q

queer, 304

questioning, 304

R

Raley, S. B., 19

Rankin, J., 345

Rathouz, P. J., 338

Rauch, P. K., 289

Ravena, Z. R., 24

Ray, A., 124

Reaching IN … Reaching OUT (RIRO), 7, 51

Recchia, H. E., 28

Rector, N., 296